Praise for Thomas Powers's

The Killing of Crazy Horse

"Superb. . . . An epic tale. . . . Powers's book reads like a fine historical novel, rich in important detail and fully formed minor characters, filled with felicitous summary of crucial information."
—*St. Louis Post-Dispatch*

"A skillfully written, meticulously researched book that covers far more than the chief's final days and hours." —*Chicago Tribune*

"Masterful. . . . A fascinating portrait of the great and mysterious Sioux war chief and of the pivotal era in our history in which he lived and died. . . . [Powers] is not only an accomplished digger of facts but someone who understands that in matters of war and politics there are very few good—or bad—guys." —*St. Petersburg Times*

"A compelling look into the politics and prejudices that shaped the era. . . . Evocative and evenhanded. . . . A rich and worthwhile read."
—*The Oregonian*

"Packed with hundreds of memorable characters, sharply drawn . . . an incredible mix of life that few books or movies present as well as this book does. . . . This is a masterful book, an epic read. Powers has repaid the Indians he found compelling and mysterious as a kid sixty years ago with this marvelous, well-told tale." —*The Washington Times*

"Sophisticated and unsentimental. . . . [Powers] has crafted a masterful account of the Great Sioux Wars and solved a murder mystery."
—*Tulsa World*

THOMAS POWERS

The Killing of Crazy Horse

Thomas Powers is a Pulitzer Prize–winning journalist and
writer best known for his books on the history of intelligence organizations. Among them are *Intelligence Wars:
American Secret History from Hitler to al-Qaeda*; *Heisenberg's
War: The Secret History of the German Bomb*; and *The Man
Who Kept the Secrets: Richard Helms and the CIA*. *The Killing
of Crazy Horse* won the Los Angeles Times Book Prize for
history; the Western Writers of America Spur Award for
historical nonfiction; and was a finalist for the National
Book Critics Circle Award in the biography category. For
most of the last decade Powers kept a 1984 Volvo at a
nephew's house in Colorado, which he drove on frequent
trips to the northern Plains. He lives in Vermont with his
wife, Candace.

The Killing
of Crazy Horse

The Killing
of
Crazy Horse

THOMAS POWERS

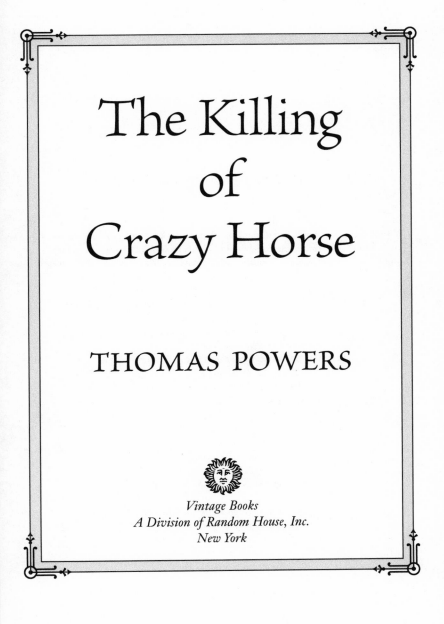

Vintage Books
A Division of Random House, Inc.
New York

FIRST VINTAGE BOOKS EDITION, NOVEMBER 2011

The Library of Congress has cataloged the Knopf edition as follows:
Powers, Thomas.
The killing of Crazy Horse / by Thomas Powers.—1st ed.
p. cm.
Includes bibliographical references and index.
1. Crazy Horse, ca. 1842–1877—Death and burial. 2. Oglala Indians—
Kings and rulers—Biography. I. Title.
E99.O3C7255 2010
978.004'9752440092—dc22
[B] 2010016842

Vintage ISBN: 978-0-375-71430-6

Author photograph © Amanda Gellatly
Book design by M. Kristen Bearse
Maps created by Mapping Specialists

www.vintagebooks.com

Printed in the United States of America
10 9 8 7 6 5 4 3 2

For Halley and Finn,
Toby and Quinn

CONTENTS

Inserts of illustrations follow pages
106 and 314.

MAPS

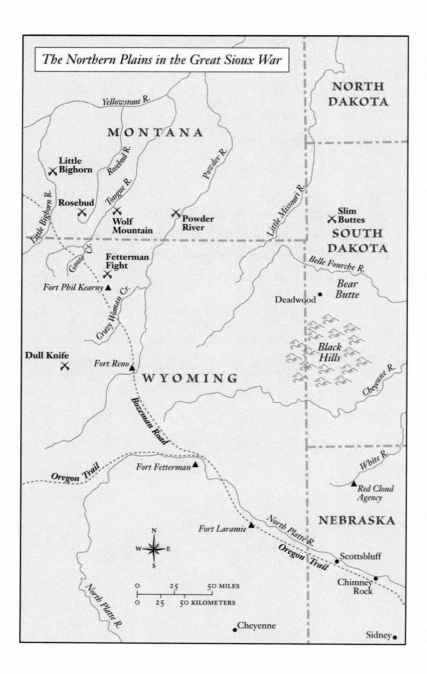

The Northern Plains in the Great Sioux War

INTRODUCTION

"We'll come for you another time."

The half-Sioux interpreter William Garnett, who died a dozen years before I was born, first set me to wondering why Crazy Horse was killed. He made it seem so unnecessary. I read Garnett's account of the killing in a motel at Crow Agency, Montana, not two miles from the spot where Crazy Horse in 1876 led a charge up over the back of a ridge, splitting in two the command of General George Armstrong Custer. Within a very few minutes, Custer and two hundred cavalry soldiers were dead on a hillside overlooking the Little Bighorn River. It was the worst defeat ever inflicted on the United States Army by Plains Indians. A year later Crazy Horse himself was dead of a bayonet wound, stabbed in the small of the back by soldiers trying to place him under arrest.

Dead Indians are a common feature of American history, but the killing of Crazy Horse retains its power to shock. Garnett, twenty-two years old at the time, was not only present on the fatal day but was deeply involved in the unfolding of events. In 1920 he told a retired Army general what happened. A transcript of the conversation was eventually published. That's what I read lying on my back on a bed in Crow Agency's only motel.[1]

It was Garnett's frank and thoughtful tone that first caught my attention. He knew the ins and outs of the whole complex story, but even near the end of his life he had not made up his mind how to think about it. Garnett was present on the evening of September 3, 1877, when General George Crook met with thirteen leading men of the Oglala Sioux to plan the killing of Crazy Horse later that night. A lieutenant who had been working with the Indians promised to give two hundred dollars and his best horse to the man who killed him. The place was a remote military post in northwest Nebraska, a mile and a half from the Oglala agency, as Indian reservations were called at the time. Pushing events was the

Army's fear that Crazy Horse was planning a new war. Then came a report from an Oglala scout named Woman Dress[2] that Crazy Horse was planning to kill Crook. Something about that story aroused doubts in Garnett when he heard it. Crook was a little in doubt himself. He wanted to know if Woman Dress could be trusted. The answer was close enough to yes to propel events forward.

In the event, nothing went according to plan. Killing the chief that night was altered to arresting him the following day, but that plan ran into trouble as well. It was not the Army that finally seized Crazy Horse in the early evening of September 5, 1877, but Crazy Horse who gave himself up to the Army, then walked to the guardhouse holding the hand of the officer of the day. The chief had been promised a chance to explain himself to the commanding officer of the military post, and he trusted the promise until the moment he saw the barred window in the guardhouse door.

In my experience the seed of a book can often be traced back a long way. This one began with a childhood passion for Indians. It was acquired in the usual way, picked up on the playground in the 1940s and '50s when the game of Cowboys and Indians enjoyed a last flowering. Hopalong Cassidy, Roy Rogers, Gene Autry, and the Lone Ranger were predictable staples of kids' television, in my view, but the game itself, played with cap pistols across suburban backyards, invited somebody to take the part of the Indians.

From the beginning I thought cowboys dull, Indians mysterious, compelling, and something that did not fit easily into the game—their road had been a hard one. Kids have quick sympathies, and mine took shape early. My father helped them form with the books he gave me, which went beyond the usual fare. I still own a lot of the books that kept me up late when I was twelve and thirteen: James Willard Schultz's *My Life as an Indian*, Mari Sandoz's *Cheyenne Autumn*, Edgar I. Stewart's *Custer's Luck*. They gave me a lifelong appetite for the particular, and a solid grasp of certain truths. One was the fact that the Indian wars were about land, and specifically about removal of Indians from land that whites wanted. Another was the existence of sorrow and tragedy in history—loss and pain that cannot be redeemed. That was not the way I would have put it at the time, but I got the central idea clearly enough. By the time I was fourteen I understood that the treatment of Indians was something people did not like to describe plainly.

Then I grew up. I quit reading about Indians and was caught up by other sorrows, tragedies, and moral complexities. I became a reporter and moved from one subject to another in a progression that always seemed to make sense. The antiwar movement was the first thing I wrote about seriously. From that I learned something about intelligence organizations, and wanted to know more. Study of that in its turn brought me to the history of nuclear weapons, and eventually I was prompted to wonder why the Germans in World War Two failed to build an atomic bomb of their own. Each of these subjects involved much that was hidden, and each absorbed years of work. That was the personal history I brought to Crow Agency in 1994 when my brother and I decided to spend a couple of days at the Little Bighorn battlefield.

The voice of William Garnett thus found a ready listener. What he said prompted many questions. I hadn't thought about Indians for decades, but Garnett brought me back around. Nothing quite opens up history like an event—the interplay of a large cast pushing a conflict to a moment of decision. It is the event that gives history its narrative backbone. Very often the excavation of an event can reveal the whole of an era, just as an archeologist's trench through a corner of an ancient city can bring back to light a forgotten civilization.

But I confess it was wanting to know why Crazy Horse was killed, not the abstract lessons to be drawn from his fate, that drew me on. It's my working theory that pinning down what happened is always the first step to understanding why it happened. That's where the appetite for the particular comes in, the who, what, and when. Those who watched or took part in Crazy Horse's killing seemed to understand immediately that something troubling had occurred, but the public's interest ended with a week of newspaper stories. No official called at the time for a public accounting, and none was made. Histories of the Great Sioux War have treated the killing as regrettable but forgettable, something between a footnote and an afterthought. The event itself remained obscure, muffled, sketchily recorded. In the histories, William Garnett was typically given a sentence or two, if his role was noted at all.

But in the decades after the killing, witnesses and participants occasionally published a memoir, or spoke to a reporter, or, like Garnett, answered the questions of a researcher. In 1942, Mari Sandoz gathered much of this material into her life of Crazy Horse, which I somehow missed in childhood. I was prompted to read it by William Garnett. Sandoz's book has more art, but not as many facts, as Kingsley Bray's now authoritative biography of the chief.

The sound of Garnett's voice was the small beginning of my own effort to understand why Crazy Horse was killed, but a long time passed before I took the next step. That was to drive out to Fort Robinson, Nebraska, where I spent a week walking the ground, the first of many trips. The killing of Crazy Horse is not abstract at Fort Robinson. The original officers' row remains intact. Huge cottonwoods shade the buildings now, but in the 1870s it was treeless. There, a week before his death, Crazy Horse met with a young Army lieutenant in the large front room of his quarters. It was not his first visit. Generally, he sat in a chair while his friends sat on the floor. In a similar building at the other end of officers' row, General Crook helped to plan the killing of the chief. Across the parade ground to the south a log replica of the old guardhouse has been built on the footprint of the original. You can stand on the spot where Crazy Horse was stabbed by a guard. Sixty feet away is a log replica of the adjutant's office, also erected on its original footprint. You can look at the spot in that room where Crazy Horse lay on the floor for five or six hours until he died. From Fort Robinson, an hour's drive over gravel roads will take you to the Pine Ridge Reservation, a site the Oglala picked for themselves in 1878, and where they have lived ever since. Among them survive people who knew people who knew Crazy Horse, and sometimes a word from them can illuminate an old mystery.

The research materials for this book come principally from books and from manuscripts found in libraries and archives, big ones like the Library of Congress and small ones like the Sheridan County Historical Society in Rushville, Nebraska. But just as important were many encounters with historians long immersed in the history of the western Indian wars, and with descendants of the Oglala of the 1870s. All are identified in the notes or in the acknowledgments at the end of the book. But one struck me with unusual force at the time, and it helps to explain how the people and events of the 1870s gradually became vivid in my mind. The encounter began with a document given to me by Tom Buecker in the Fort Robinson Museum which led eventually to a phone conversation with Allyne Jane Pearce, a descendant of William Garnett's Virginia grandfather. Pearce gave me the name of Joanne Cuny, one of William Garnett's granddaughters, who lives in Rapid City, South Dakota, not far from Pine Ridge. Cuny told me that the family historian was her older brother James, known in the family as Heavy, and she took me to see him.

From Rapid City, Cuny and I drove up to the veterans' hospital in Sturgis, where James Garnett was recovering from an accident in which he had shattered a leg, already broken several times previously in car accidents. From the hospital, James could see Bear Butte, a longtime sacred place of the Sioux and the Cheyenne. It rises some seven hundred feet abruptly from the level plains, tree covered and rocky but from a distance rounded something like the form of a sleeping bear. The Sioux call it Mato Paha and still climb the hill to pray for visions. In the old days some Sioux believed the hill was the center of the world, and was the petrified kidney of a great bear. An old fort near Bear Butte had been turned into the veterans' hospital. James had served in the Navy after dropping out of high school in 1952, and he lived nearby in Rapid City, so it was the natural place for him to recover from his broken leg. The doctors told James Garnett it would be many months before he could walk again.

James related to me a remarkable story about "the Old Man," as everybody in his childhood called William Garnett. James talked about the Old Man in tones of great intimacy and respect. As the Old Man aged he thickened; his back rounded, and his head settled into his torso. The full head of hair turned gray and was slicked to one side. A heavy gray moustache hid his mouth. In early photographs Garnett is watchful, alert to the camera, but in later pictures he seems to have his mind on other things. When James was growing up on the Pine Ridge Reservation in the 1930s and '40s, the Old Man was the subject of much discussion in the household, where old-timers gathered to drink coffee and talk with the Old Man's widow, Fillie, the daughter of an early trapper and trader named Nick Janis. Among Fillie's visitors were men with resonant names like Frank Hairy Chin, grandson of a noted practitioner of bear medicine in the old days. Four days before the fight with Custer on the Little Bighorn, the elder Hairy Chin, with the help of the Black Elk family, had performed a healing ceremony for a man named Rattling Hawk, who had been shot through the hips at the Rosebud. On the day of the Custer fight, Rattling Hawk stood on a hill west of the big village and watched the final moments of the general and his men across the river. Still too weak to fight, Rattling Hawk held a sacred lance of the Tokala (Kit Fox) society and sang a Fox song to encourage the fighters: "Friends, what you are doing I cannot do."[3]

Frank Hairy Chin told James Garnett, and Garnett told me, that his grandmother—the medicine man's wife—"couldn't stand to look at a white man; when a white man came in she would pull a shawl over her head." Frank and Fillie always spoke in Lakota, but that's not the word James used. "She talked nothing but Indian," he said. I often heard that said by people around Pine Ridge.

James told me that another regular visitor to Fillie's kitchen was Dewey Beard, with his second wife, Alice. They used to drop by the Garnett house on the northern boundary of the reservation in the place called Red Water. Red Water was in the Badlands, seventeen miles from the community in Kyle where the band of Little Wound had settled in the early days on the reservation at the end of the Great Sioux War. Red Water Creek was dry most of the year, but after a big rain it fed into the White River not far from a gap in the hills where the "Big Foot trail" came through—the route followed by the Miniconjou in December 1890 when they were hurrying to join their relatives at Pine Ridge during the ghost dance trouble. The U.S. Cavalry was hot on their heels. James Garnett's little brother, Martin, used to prowl along the old trail near the Garnett house. Once he found a rusted four-shot pistol, and another time he found a sword engraved with the name of an Army lieutenant. Very likely the pistol had been dropped by the hurrying Indians, the sword by a cavalry officer chasing them.

In the Garnett household, everybody called Dewey Beard Putila— Beard. He had added the "Dewey" after meeting the hero of the Battle of Manila Bay in Washington. But in the old days Dewey Beard was known as Iron Hail, and he had been in the fight at the Little Bighorn as a young man of twenty. By the time Big Foot came through Red Water in 1890 Iron Hail was a grown man with a wife and an infant daughter. The wife was killed at Wounded Knee, and the daughter died three months later. Iron Hail escaped only by running up a draw, just ahead of the soldiers. He was badly wounded in the right arm and held his right thumb in his teeth as he ran to keep the arm from flinging about.

Henry Young Bear was another regular who joined Dewey Beard at the Garnett house, and so were Eddie Herman, a mixed-blood who often wrote about the old days for the *Rapid City Journal,* and Frank Kills Enemy's mother, who had been at the Little Bighorn.[4]

They used to "skin us kids outside," James said, but the kids hung around, crept back, listened to the old-timers speaking Lakota, remembering the last days on the plains and the first days on the reservation, when the Oglala learned to drive wagons, make fry bread, live in cabins, and call themselves Christians. Many of the old ways were declared illegal, and a special court of "Indian offenses" sentenced men who took part in the sun dance or held a giveaway after the death of a relative. But out on the prairie, away from the agency offices, little changed. In remote places like Red Water the people practiced the old ways in secret. They built sweat lodges down in the creek bottoms and they went up alone into the hills to pray for visions.

What James Garnett remembers of his life till he was twelve or thirteen is the story told by many elderly Lakota on the reservation—living with grandparents, listening to old stories of leading men and remarkable war deeds. Kitchens were the usual scene for these sessions, but sometimes they were held outside around a fire. The older people known as traditionals wore their hair long and sometimes kept tipis and slept in them in the summer. James is a deacon in the Roman Catholic Church, a catechist, and a twelve-step counselor who has worked for many years in the prisons of South Dakota, but he grew up in the world of the traditionals. Every week or two as a child he rode with his family in a wagon into Kyle, to collect rations or visit the store—seventeen miles each way, sitting beside Unci, his grandmother Fillie Garnett. Fillie had been born in Wyoming on Goose Creek in 1856, twenty years before General Crook passed through on his way to and from the Rosebud, where he was beaten in a fair fight by Crazy Horse. In winter before leaving the house at Red Water, Fillie would heat old irons on the stove and then put them in the wagon under the blankets to keep their feet warm. Seventeen miles each way, twice a month or more, while the wheels creaked and the tug chains rattled and the horses snorted and clopped and their harness slapped against their sides.

For fifty years, Fillie's husband William Garnett had been at the very heart of life on the reservation. He knew hundreds of old-timers, the obscure and the celebrated alike. Before he died in 1909, Red Cloud used to ride over to Garnett's house, American Horse was Garnett's friend, and scores of Indians depended on Garnett to help them get pensions for their service as scouts. Occasionally during those years white men hoping to write the history of the Indian wars would come by with questions. Garnett had learned to read and write and he sent many letters to friends from the early days. In conversation he talked freely. Walter Camp, Eli Ricker, and General Hugh Scott all recorded long accounts of Indian war times during talks with Garnett. Much of what is known about Crazy Horse comes from Garnett. He saw Crazy Horse often during the last four months of his life, he carried messages between the chiefs and the Army officers during the last week, and he was present—indeed, came close to being shot—on the fatal day.

Fillie Garnett in James's childhood always walked with a cane, but she was the core of warmth in the household in Kyle, and James says, "She spoiled me rotten." That was the way of grandmothers but it probably had something to do with the actual physical James as well. The old-timers who came to drink coffee said James looked a lot like the Old Man. James's father, Henry Kocer Garnett, was the son of William Garnett's daughter known as Dollie. She was nineteen when Henry was born, and twenty-two when she died three years later, in 1912. There was a streak of bitterness in Henry. Hearing his son compared to the Old Man brought it out. He told his son, "You might look something like him, but you'll never be the man he was."

That bitter note is another thing you sometimes hear from elderly Lakota, especially the men—a regret that the people today don't measure up, themselves included. Henry admired the way the leaders in the old days knew how to take care of the people in big ways and little. "At Christmas they made sure everybody got something," James told me. No longer. "My dad said when those old-timers died they took all that with them."

What the old-timers didn't take was turned upside down when the United States entered the Second World War. One day in 1942, the Garnetts and all their neighbors on Red Water Creek received official notice from the U.S. Army that they had thirty days to pack up and move out; their homes and the surrounding fields and pastures were being requisitioned by the Army Air Force as a bombing range. There was no appeal. Everybody had to go. "They all lost a lot of stuff then," said James.

The Oglala were never rich. Their cabins and houses were small, two or three rooms. But everybody had something wrapped up in a trunk or under the bed from the old days, and those objects—beaded leggings; quilled shirts; the small amulet bags in the shape of turtles or lizards in which every man preserved his umbilical cord—were often lost in the turmoil of packing up and pulling out so the Army could begin to practice bombing runs. Henry had a trunk full of old things that he left behind, thinking it would be safe in the house. After the war it took a long time for the Garnetts to get their land back, more than ten years. When the Army finally let go the house was a wreck, and the trunk was empty.

But by that time the Garnett household had broken up for good. As a boy James spent most of the year at the Holy Rosary Mission in Pine Ridge as a boarding student in the Red Cloud School. He was there when Fillie died in 1946 and the coffee-drinking sessions in the Garnett kitchen came to an end. James didn't go to Unci's funeral; Holy Rosary was too far, there was no way to fetch him back. When James got out of the Navy he returned to high school for a time, then left the mission for good the day before he turned twenty-one on March 3, 1957. The following period James Garnett refers to as "my wild days." It's what James draws on as an alcohol counselor in the prisons—not just the drinking, but the wildness itself, the reckless fury that ends the lives of so many young Indians in car wrecks, in fights with knives or baseball bats, passed out in ditches alongside country roads on sub-zero nights. You would think these young men wanted to die. James Garnett has a big phone bill every month; Indians call him up collect from the county jail in Rapid City and he talks them down over the phone. Succeeding at that he describes as the central work of his life. But it almost didn't happen.

About a year after he left the Red Cloud School, James Garnett was in a car that did not belong to him at a truck stop in Glasgow, Montana, not far from the Canadian border. He was not thinking too clearly. He saw a highway patrol car suddenly pull in, and without hesitating he pulled out. It was pure reflex: run when they're after you. A highway patrolman said, "Kid, you're lucky you're not going back in a pine box. When we got to you, you were already turning blue." When they got to him his car had been crushed by a big tractor trailer that hit him broadside when he roared out of the truck stop onto the highway without looking. Somehow the doctors kept him alive at the local hospital for a week while he was in a coma.

But in James's view it wasn't the doctors who kept him alive. The Old Man spared his life. He knows this because he heard the Old Man say so.

On his sixth night in the hospital, James Garnett woke up when he heard something. It was late, quiet, dark but not pitch black. What James heard first was the tug chains. Immediately he knew it was the old wagon pulling up outside the window of his room on the second floor of the hospital. He heard the tug chains rattling, the creak of the wheels, the harness, the hooves of the horses, and the voices of two people. One of them was Unci. The other was the voice of the Old Man. William Garnett died in 1928, eight years before James was born, but James recognized the Old Man's voice right away, and he could tell that the Old Man was irritated about something. He was grumbling.

In Lakota the Old Man said, "*Ho, iyahna ichuo*"—Well, go in and get him.[5]

Fillie started to get down from the wagon. James heard her. But then the Old Man leaned over and whispered something to Fillie. James heard her stop. She wasn't getting down after all. The Old Man was whispering something in a grumbling, irritated kind of way. James realized Unci was not going to come and get him. Despite his condition, he got out of his hospital bed and went to the window and called out, "*Ah mapeyo!*"—Wait for me! He did not want to be left behind.

Fillie turned around and she said, "*Hiya, dosha ake un kupikteh*"—No, we'll come for you another time.

The Old Man chucked up the horses and they drove off. James saw them clearly—the Old Man with his rounded back and his hat half tilted back, sitting up on the driver's seat with the reins in his hands. Beside him was Fillie wearing a long dress with her hair in nice tight braids down her back. Next day in the Glasgow hospital James came out of his coma and startled his doctors but he himself understood perfectly what had happened: it was not the right time. The Old Man had decided. He told Unci not now, and Unci told James. They would come back for him another time.

The Killing
of Crazy Horse

I

"When we were young, all we thought about was going to war."

IT WAS NEARING MIDDAY on the shortest day of the year in 1866 when Indians attacked a detachment of soldiers sent out from Fort Phil Kearny in northern Wyoming to cut firewood for the post. The weather was mild and clear. A light powdering of recent snow lingered in the shadows of the hills. The Indians could not be seen from the fort itself, but a soldier stationed on a nearby hill signaled the opening of the attack. Through the gates of the fort emerged a relief party of eighty men, cavalry in the lead, infantry hurrying behind. They circled north around some low hills, passing out of sight of the fort. Ahead of the soldiers, retreating back up the slope of a ridge, were ten Sioux and Cheyenne warriors, all practicing the oldest ruse of warfare on the plains. Each man in his own way was hurrying without hurrying, like a quail skittering through the brush away from her nest, trailing a wing, showing herself to hungry fox or coyote. It was the custom of decoys to lure and tantalize—to taunt the soldiers with shouted insults, to show their buttocks, to dismount and check their horses' feet as if they were lame. The decoys would linger back, just at the edge of rifle shot, almost within reach.[1]

This moment had a long history. Fort Phil Kearny was the first of three posts established in the early summer of 1866 to protect whites traveling north to the Montana goldfields along a new road named after the man who had mapped it out a year earlier, John Bozeman. For twenty-five years the Sioux Indians had traded peacefully with whites at Fort Laramie two hundred miles to the south and east, but the Bozeman Road threatened their last and best hunting country. The chiefs spoke plainly; the whites must give up the road or face war. In June, they had been invited to gather at Fort Laramie, where white officials hoped to patch together some kind of agreement for use of the road. A friendly chief of the Brulé Sioux warned an Army officer that talk was futile. "There is a treaty being made at Laramie with the Sioux that are in the country where you are going," Standing Elk told an officer heading north. "The fighting men in that country have not come to Laramie, and you will have to fight them. They will not give you the road unless you whip them."[2]

All that summer Fort Phil Kearny was under virtual siege by the Indians. They prowled the country daily, watching or signaling from the ridges. They often attacked soldiers sent out to cut wood or hay and they killed numerous travelers—thirty-three by the end of August, according to the commander of the fort. At every chance the Indians ran off horses and cattle, threatening the fort with hunger. When the fall buffalo hunting was over, thousands of Sioux and Cheyenne converged on the isolated fort, but they hid themselves, taking care that the soldiers never saw more than a few at a time. During one midday raid on the fort's dwindling cattle herd in November, soldiers on horseback suddenly charged out of the fort in angry disorder, infuriated by the endless attacks. This set the Indians to thinking.

In early December the decoy trick almost succeeded in luring reckless soldiers into an ambush. On December 19, the Indians tried again, but the decoys were too clumsy, or the soldiers too cautious; they turned back when the Indians passed up over the ridge north of the fort. But two days later, encouraged by a promise of success from a "two-souled person" or *winkte*, the Indians organized a second effort on a still larger scale and this time everything was done right. The great mass of warriors hid themselves in the grass and brush on the far side of the long ridge as it sloped down and away from the fort. No overexcited young men dashed out ahead of the others. The horses were held back out of the way. The decoys were convincing. The eighty soldiers never slacked their rush up the ridge after the men they feared were getting away.

In that group of ten warriors retreating back up the ridge, but not too quickly, nor lingering too obviously, were some of the leading men of the Oglala Sioux—Man That Owns a Sword, American Horse, and Crazy Horse.[3] All were respected warriors, men in their late twenties, known for courage in battle. Among that group Crazy Horse did not impress at a casual glance. He was a slender man of middle height. He dressed simply. He wore his hair loose with a few feathers or sometimes the dried skin of a sparrow hawk fixed in his hair. For battle he painted himself with white hail spots. A zigzag line of paint down his horse's shoulder and leg gave it the power of lightning. He had dusted his horse with the powdery earth from a prairie dog mound to protect it from bullets. His usual weapons were a stone war club and a gun. If he ever fired an arrow at a white man it was not recorded.

None of the whites would have recognized Crazy Horse on December 21, 1866. Only a few had met him or knew his name. But Crazy Horse and the others were about to lure eighty soldiers into an ambush where all would die in the second of the three humiliating defeats inflicted on the U.S. Army by the Sioux Indians and their Cheyenne allies. Ten years later Crazy Horse would do it again. But no trickery would be involved in that third and greatest of Indian victories. His friend He Dog, who was in both fights, said Crazy Horse won the battle of the Little Bighorn with a sudden rush in the right spot at the right moment, splitting the enemy force in two—the kind of masterstroke explained only by native genius, in answer to a prayer.

The Sioux Indians of the northern plains had a phrase for the leading men of the band—*wicasa yatapika*, "men that are talked about." From earliest times, whites had called the leader of any Indian community the "chief," and the word matched the reality: in any band, one man was generally respected, listened to, and followed more than any other. But among the Sioux no chief ruled as an autocrat for long; wise chiefs consulted others and were supported in turn by various camp officials, men with authority over decisions about war, hunting, the movements of the band, and the enforcement of decisions and tribal law. For each office the Sioux language provided a distinct term, but all might be called chiefs without doing violence to the meaning, and all were drawn from the *wicasa yatapika*. The talk about those men generally started with some notable deed, and the deed was most often performed in battle.

From an early age the man who would be remembered as Crazy Horse attracted attention, first for his skill as a hunter, then for his courage in war. Many stories are told about the early life of Crazy Horse but few are completely firm. His friend and religious mentor Horn Chips said he was born in the fall on a creek near a sacred hill known as Bear Butte in what is now South Dakota; his friend He Dog said that Crazy Horse and He Dog were born "in the same year and at the same season of the year"— probably 1838, but possibly 1840. The name Crazy Horse belonged to his father before him, an Oglala of the band led by Smoke; when the band split after a killing in 1841 the father remained in the north with Smoke's people. The mother of Crazy Horse was a Miniconjou named Rattle

Blanket Woman who "took a rope and hung herself to a tree" when the boy was about four years old. The reason is unclear; she may have been grieving over the death of a brother of her husband. In 1844–45, the elder Crazy Horse led a war party against the Shoshone Indians to the west, probably seeking revenge for the killing of this brother, whose name may have been He Crow, who may have been a lover of Rattle Blanket Woman, and whose death may have led to her suicide. It is impossible after so many years to be certain about any of it. To a boy of four all of this would have been frightening and vague.

Some facts are a little firmer. The elder Crazy Horse took a second wife said to be a relative of the Brulé chief Spotted Tail, possibly even the chief's sister. All witnesses agree that the boy was called Curly Hair until he was about ten years old, and some say that for a few years afterward he was known as His Horse in Sight.[4]

Of his earliest life we know only what his friend He Dog said: "We grew up together in the same band, played together, courted the girls together, and fought together." Childhood ended early among the Oglala and by the time Crazy Horse was fifteen or sixteen in the mid-1850s his life was increasingly absorbed by episodes of war and violence. The stories that survive follow a familiar pattern: despite great danger horses were stolen, an enemy was killed, or a friend was rescued. On one early raid against the Pawnee when he "was just a very young boy," according to Eagle Elk, Crazy Horse was shot through the arm while rushing an enemy to count coup—that is, to touch him with his hand or a weapon. "From that time he was talked about," said Eagle Elk. Many accounts of Crazy Horse's early fights and raids end with a similar remark—that he was first into the fray, that his name was known, that people talked about him.

"When we were young," said his friend and mentor Horn Chips, "all we thought about was going to war." It was fame they sought; to be talked about brought respect and position. "Crazy Horse wanted to get to the highest station."[5]

When Crazy Horse was about eighteen he lived for a year with the Brulé Sioux, probably with relatives of his father's second wife. The Brulé were bloodily attacked about that time by the American Army, but Crazy Horse's friends in later life did not remark on that. It was his abrupt return to the Oglala which excited curiosity. His friend He Dog asked around to learn what had happened. "I was told he had to come back because he had killed a Winnebago woman," said He Dog.[6] Where the transgression lay is not clear; women were often killed in battle, and He Dog himself later killed a Crow woman, sometime around 1870, although telling about it made him uneasy, as if he were ashamed.[7]

It was at about this time, in the later 1850s, that Crazy Horse acquired the name he was to carry for the rest of his life. His friend Horn Chips said the new name was given to him after his horse ran around wildly—crazily—during a fight with the Shoshones. He Dog offered two stories; one said Crazy Horse got the name when his horse ran down an enemy woman who was hoeing her corn. But it is He Dog's second story that offers the most detail and makes the most sense. About 1855 or 1856 the young man, then still known as His Horse in Sight, took part in a fight with Arapahos, returning with two scalps. For most of the middle decades of the nineteenth century the Arapahos were allies of the Sioux, and of the Oglala in particular, but on one occasion the Oglala chief known as Red Cloud led an attack on a group of Arapahos who were on their way to visit the Prairie Gros Ventres, traditional enemies of the Oglala. This may also have been the occasion when Crazy Horse rescued a leading man of the Miniconjou named Hump, whose horse had been shot. In any event, the young man's feat—two scalps taken from enemies forted up on a rocky hilltop—made the father proud.

It was a custom among the Sioux to celebrate a son's achievement with a feast and the giving away of presents. When a boy killed his first buffalo his father might ask the crier to call out the news throughout the camp, then feed those who came to hear about the feat and perhaps give a horse, or even several horses, to people in need. After the fight with the Arapahos, in which His Horse in Sight twice charged the enemy hiding among the rocks, the father gave the son his own name, Crazy Horse. For the next two decades the father was known by an old nickname, Worm, for which the Lakota word is Waglula.[8]

The meaning of Crazy Horse's name requires some explanation. In Lakota it is Tasunka Witko, and a literal translation would read "His Horse Is Crazy." *Tasunka* is the word the Lakota coined for horse sometime in the early 1700s, a combination of *sunka* (dog) and *tatanka* (big). The word *witko* is as rich with meaning as the English word "swoon." It might be variously translated as "head in a whirl," delirious, thinking in all directions at once, possessed by a vision, in a trance. In the sign language of the plains *witko* was indicated by rotating the hand in a circular motion, but the word's meaning was far from simply "crazy" in the sense of the vernacular English. The meaning of the name Tasunka Witko would be something like this: his horse is imbued with a sacred power drawn from formidable spiritual sources, and specifically from the thunder beings who roil the sky in storms. The operative word is power in the classic Lakota sense—imbued with force and significance. In short, the name of Crazy Horse implied that the bearer was a person of great promise and consequence, and soon his name and his feats were the talk of the plains. Honors followed.

In the late 1860s Crazy Horse and He Dog led a war party west of the Big Horn Mountains to raid the Crow or Shoshone Indians, traditional enemies of the Oglala. On their return to the village they were met by a large group who had come out to greet them, singing praise songs and inviting them back for a feast and the bestowal of an important gift. "The whole tribe," He Dog said, honored the two warriors with a gift of lances decorated with feathers and fur. These were not weapons but emblems of membership in the Kangi Yuha—the Crow Owners society, named after the dried crow skins attached near the base of the spears. "These spears were each three or four hundred years old," said He Dog, "and were given by the older generation to those in the younger generation who had best lived the life of a warrior."[9]

The lances brought honor and a stern duty. Members of the Kangi Yuha accepted a "no-flight" obligation: in battle they must plant the lance in the ground and stand fast until death or a friend released them.

The ten decoys on December 21, 1866, were men honored for their exploits in war. All were respected and widely known, all were committed to driving the white soldiers back down the Bozeman Road. But the man controlling events, the man who came closest to having the power to command, was Red Cloud, who was nearing fifty years of age and had dominated the northern Oglala for twenty-five years. Whites would call the war over the Bozeman Road "Red Cloud's War"; he was the man more than any other who determined when it began, and when it would end. His influence was unmatched during Crazy Horse's life. His hand was often evident in the unfolding of events. He would be standing only a few feet away when Crazy Horse was killed.

Red Cloud was born about 1821, some said on the very night that a meteor streaked across the nighttime sky of the northern plains. "A large roaring star fell," Cloud Shield recorded in his winter count. "It came from the east and shot out sparks of fire along its course." White Cow

Killer described the sound as "a great noise"; The Flame said it made a "hissing."[10]

Oglala were not born equal. The fame of a father or grandfather made a difference, and a chief's son was expected to succeed him—if he measured up to the job. Red Cloud's mother, Walks as She Thinks, was a sister of Smoke, one of the two leading Oglala chiefs. While the boy was still in the womb his father died, possibly of drink, and the name Red Cloud (Mahpiya Luta) was passed to a nephew, then about ten years old, who was like a brother to the half-orphaned boy. But in 1837 on a raid into southern Nebraska the cousin was overwhelmed in battle by the Pawnee. When Cloud Shield returned with news of his death, the whole band clamored for revenge. In later life the chief told the trader Sam Deon that despite his mother's opposition he insisted on joining the war party going out to kill Pawnee to avenge his cousin's death. At that time the sixteen-year-old boy was known as Tall Hollow Horn, but when the people saw him approaching to join the warriors they cried out, "Red Cloud is coming! Red Cloud is coming!" In that moment he assumed the name that had been carried by his cousin, his father, and his grandfather.[11]

It was war that dominated the life of Red Cloud. On several occasions in later life he said that he had counted eighty coups or had been in eighty battles.[12] In about 1840, when Red Cloud was already recognized as a leading warrior of the Oglala, he was shot through with a Pawnee arrow during a raid on a village on the Middle Loup. The arrow penetrated his body up to the feathers, and the iron arrowhead emerged entirely from his back a few inches from his spine. At the shock of the wound Red Cloud lost consciousness; he felt nothing when one of his fellow warriors cut the sinew binding the iron arrowhead in place and then pulled the wooden shaft back through Red Cloud's body. Two months passed before he fully regained his strength, and even then the wound periodically bothered him for the rest of his life.[13] When he told his story to Sam Deon, who had married one of his wife's sisters, Red Cloud's tale was a list of battles. Included was the attack on the Arapaho village where Crazy Horse distinguished himself and won his name. Sometimes Red Cloud went out on raids at the head of a war party, sometimes he went alone. He made a song about his life as a warrior which went,

The coyotes howl over me.
That is what I have been hearing.
And the owls hoot over me.

That is what I have been hearing.
What am I looking for?
My enemies.
I am not afraid.[14]

But Red Cloud's position among the Sioux was not the result of raiding traditional enemies. Nor was it the result of having a large family, although he did, or because he was the son of a noted man, although he was.[15] Red Cloud won his position by killing a leading chief of the Oglala—the climax of a long-festering animosity between the chief named Bull Bear and Red Cloud's uncle, his mother's brother, the chief named Smoke. Crazy Horse was only a few years old when this killing took place, but he would have been present in the camp because his father was a member of Smoke's band. The killing was the signal event in Oglala history before the tribe's confinement to a reservation. Crazy Horse would have grown up hearing stories about this killing; from them he would have learned the harsh truth of the way chiefs were made and deposed.

In the 1830s, Smoke and Bull Bear were each recognized as the leader of about half the Oglala. Both were friendly to the few whites who came to trap and trade. In 1834, Bull Bear brought his people south to trade at the post near the Platte River that would later be called Fort Laramie, and one of his daughters, Bear Robe, married the French trapper Henry Chatillon, whom the Oglala called Yellowhaired Whiteman. Chatillon would later tell the story of Bull Bear and Smoke to the young American writer Francis Parkman. In 1835, following Bull Bear's lead, Smoke also brought his people south to the Laramie plains, and the two bands often camped near each other. The bands had long been known as the Koyas and the Bad Faces (Ite Sica), but they were also known for their chiefs and were called the Bear people or the Smoke people.

What first caused the enmity of the two chiefs is not recorded. By reputation Bull Bear was "fierce and impetuous" and "recognized no will but his own," but the watercolor portrait painted of the chief in 1837 by Alfred Jacob Miller shows a handsome man of serene aspect. Two years later a German doctor and naturalist, wandering Nebraska, encountered a different sort of Bull Bear, and described him as "rather aged, and of a squat, thick figure." It was said that the chief often invited the opinion of his leading men, but in the end he did as he pleased. Smoke seems to have been a more accommodating man, but a line was crossed in 1840 or 1841

when the bands were camped together. The incident was described by
Bull Bear's son-in-law Henry Chatillon to Francis Parkman, who had
come to the Indian country to write a book. In his journal for June 23,
1846, Parkman wrote,

> Bull Bear's connexions were numerous and powerful. Smoke and he once
> quarrelled. Bull Bear ran for his gun and bow, and Smoke withdrew to his
> lodge, Bull Bear challenged him to come out, but Smoke, fearing the
> vengeance of the enemy's relatives in case he should kill him, remained
> quiet, on which Bull Bear shot three of his horses.[16]

The killing of Smoke's horses was a blood offense, and Smoke's refusal
to fight, whatever the motive, was inevitably a source of shame for his relatives, among whom was the twenty-year-old Red Cloud. There were
two ways for dealing with difficult or oppressive chiefs at the time: splitting off to form a new band, or killing the offender. In November 1841,
the humiliation of Smoke was squared in a bloody fray variously described
as an orchestrated murder or a drunken brawl.

That autumn the two bands were camped near each other on a creek
called the Chugwater not far from Fort Laramie. Traders brought some
kegs of whiskey into the camps as a present for the Oglala but the word
"whiskey" does not adequately describe the poisonous swill routinely prepared for the Indian trade by mixing grain alcohol with water, then
adding a measure of tobacco juice, perhaps some molasses, and enough
red pepper to make it burn going down. Whiskey was the backbone of the
fur trade in the 1830s and '40s; once drinking, Indians might pay anything for more. A band on a drunk was ugly and dangerous. When a fight
broke out, one white trader wrote, "it was likely to be serious, for they
knew but two ways to fight—with whips and clubs, and then with the
more deadly weapons."[17] Bloody clashes were routine, killings common.
But the settling of accounts with Bull Bear was something different; for
years it was the news of the plains. Stories multiplied about what happened on Chugwater Creek, and their details refused to line up neatly.
But all accounts agreed on the core event: Bull Bear died, and it was Red
Cloud who killed him.

The Indians called the place Buffalo Falls—Tatanka Hinhpaya. Whites
bringing striped Mexican blankets and silver jewelry came to trade with
the Oglala, but first they opened some of the one-gallon wooden kegs
filled with whiskey brought by the traders. Drinking led to shouting, and

shouting to fighting. It was said later that Bull Bear was angry at a young man of the Smoke people for running off with a girl related to the chief. As the fighting became general, Bull Bear or a friend shot and killed the young man's father, or perhaps another relative. This early casualty might have been Yellow Lodge, the brother—others say brother-in-law—of Red Cloud. A Bad Face warrior named Trunk shouted a taunt: "Where is Red Cloud? Red Cloud, are you going to disgrace your father's name?"

Some said that it had fallen to Red Cloud to avenge Smoke's humiliation, that the brawling was staged to lure Bull Bear from his lodge, that Red Cloud was waiting for the chief when he emerged. Some said Red Cloud killed two people in the battle, others said it was three. When the fighting ended, by one account, eight Indians were dead or dying and another fourteen had been wounded. Chief among the victims was Bull Bear, who had fallen to the ground with a gunshot wound in the leg. Red Cloud rushed up to the injured man. "You are the cause of this," he shouted, according to one story, and shot the chief in the head. A different story says Bull Bear did not die immediately, but lingered for a month, then died of blood poisoning.[18]

The Oglala believed that no crime was worse than killing a relative or a member of the band; they said that the breath of a man guilty of such a killing would develop a bad smell, and all might know of his crime. But revenge killings were different; Red Cloud had killed the man who killed his brother or was in any event responsible—somehow—for an out-of-control battle that led to the death of his brother. The killings therefore canceled each other out, it was said, and for this reason Red Cloud's breath was clean, and people did not turn away from him.

From the killing of Bull Bear in the fall of 1841 Red Cloud was the dominant figure of his generation, a man of such personal authority and commanding force that Indians and whites alike always treated him as a prime mover of events, the man to watch. But it is also apparent that some stigma lingered from his killing of Bull Bear. His leading position was not denied, but it was not entirely recognized, either.

"Red Cloud was never a Short Hair," said Short Bull, a younger brother of He Dog. By this he meant that Red Cloud was never formally recognized as a member of the chiefs' society.[19]

Red Cloud was denied another honor as well. At wide intervals the chiefs' society selected four camp officials called Ongloge Un, or Shirt Wearers, because they were permitted to wear the distinctive shirts traditionally made of two skins from bighorn sheep, often painted blue on the upper half and yellow on the lower. These were decorated across the shoulders and down each arm with dyed porcupine quills woven into bold strips of color, and with scalp locks—each a pinch of human hair, half as thick as a child's little finger, wrapped with pericardium at the top and hanging free for eight or ten inches. The making of such a shirt involved much singing, feasting, and burning of aromatic strands of sweetgrass, whose smoke was believed to be cleansing. An Oglala leader was never recognized with greater public ceremony than when he was named a Shirt Wearer, given a shirt of his own, and instructed in the many and difficult duties of the Ongloge Un.[20]

But despite Red Cloud's record in battle and his long history as a leader of the Oglala, this honor was never given to him. "Those whose prowess and battle accomplishments and characters were undisputed were feasted and honored," said Short Bull. "He Dog and Short Bull were so honored many times while Red Cloud was not, although he was a chief."[21]

Red Cloud was a chief, not a general. He had no power to tell others what to do in the fight at Fort Phil Kearney. Many leading men after long discussion chose the strategy, picked the site for an ambush, and named the decoys. After their early failures, the still-determined Sioux summoned the aid of the spirit world, giving the task to one of the men called a *winkte*—a contraction of the Lakota *winyanktehca,* or "two-souled person," by which was meant a man with womanly qualities. A *winkte* was not a hermaphrodite, as some early writers would have it, but an effeminate man—in fact, a homosexual. *Berdache* was the Cheyenne word.[22]

The Sioux were of two minds about *winkte*s but considered them mysterious (*wakan*), and called on them for certain kinds of magic or sacred power. Sometimes *winkte*s were asked to name children, for which the price was a horse. Sometimes they were asked to read the future. On December 20, 1866, the Sioux, preparing another attack on the soldiers at Fort Phil Kearny, dispatched a *winkte* on a sorrel horse on a symbolic scout for the enemy. He rode with a black cloth over his head, blowing on a sacred whistle made from the wing bone of an eagle as he dashed back and forth over the landscape, then returned to a group of chiefs with his fists clenched and saying, "I have ten men, five in each hand—do you want them?"

The chiefs said no, that was not enough, they had come ready to fight more enemies than that, and they sent the *winkte* out again.

Twice more he dashed off on the sorrel horse, blowing his eagle-bone whistle, but each time the number of enemy he brought back in his fists was not enough. When he came back the fourth time he shouted, "Answer me quickly—I have a hundred or more." At this all the Indians began to shout and yell, and after the battle the next day it was often called the Battle of a Hundred in the Hand.[23]

With this assurance of a big victory, the Sioux and their allies prepared again to lure the soldiers out of the fort. The mass of Indians concealed themselves among the ravines and brush of the long hill—the Cheyenne and Miniconjou on the eastern slope, the Oglala and others on the west. The decoys rode on ahead with a larger group of attackers to threaten the train of woodcutters that left the fort each morning for the hills to the north and west. Among these ten may have been Crazy Horse's two close friends Lone Bear and He Dog who both took part in the battle that followed.

It was late in the morning when the picket on Pilot Hill signaled the fort that Indians were approaching. The gates opened and soldiers sallied forth, not quite a hundred strong. Eighty-one, in fact, was the number of men who rode or marched out at quick time with Captain William Fetterman that morning. As they moved up the valley along the western side of Lodge Trail Ridge the mass of Indian attackers disappeared as they had two days earlier, and the decoys began to pull back toward the north, going up over the ridge and then retreating down the long hill toward the forks of Peno Creek in the valley beyond.

The Indians lying in ambush on the slopes of the long hill pinched the noses of their ponies so they wouldn't whinny. The white cavalry came steadily down the hill, not charging but firing at the retreating decoys while the infantry hurried along behind. By the time the decoys got to the very bottom of the long hill and dashed across Peno Creek all the whites were between the hidden Indians. This was the moment. With a great shout and drumming of horses' hooves, the Indians charged up and out of the brushy ravines and long grass. The soldiers hesitated and then turned back up the hill. By the time the Indians caught up with the infantry they had taken shelter among some rocks partway back up the hill. The cavalry had been in front going down, and they soon overtook the infantry going back up, quickly reaching the top of the hill. There the sheer weight of enemies brought them to a stop and a desperate battle began—a pushing, shoving, club-and-knife sort of fighting which the Sioux called "stirring gravy."[24]

Among the infantry in the rocks were two white civilians armed with

Henry repeating rifles.²⁵ They kept up a hot fire, the brass cartridge shells piling up beside them, and it was some time before the last of the panicked infantry around these two were killed by the Indians. Hunts the Enemy, the brother of Man That Owns a Sword, recorded that he counted a coup when he dashed in among soldiers forted up behind rocks, and it is likely this is where he did it. The battle then surged up the hill toward the cavalry where Fetterman, still mounted, was in command. In the charge on these men American Horse rode his own mount directly into Fetterman. The collision of their horses threw the captain to the ground. In a moment American Horse jumped down, knife in hand, and killed Fetterman before he could regain his feet—a battle honor that would help convince the Oglala chiefs to name him a Shirt Wearer.²⁶

Few Indians were armed with guns on this day. When the guns fell silent it meant the whites had quit fighting, and a noisy, shouting melee followed while a thousand or more Indians swarmed over the field. They finished off soldiers they found still breathing or moving, not leaving it to chance. They tugged off boots, then stabbed iron arrow points between the soldiers' toes. At the same time they began to look for their own dead, care for their wounded, gather up fallen guns, pull cavalry tunics and trousers from bodies, empty pockets of coin and paper money. The coins they would turn into ornaments, the greenbacks were later given as playthings to children back at camp. The fight had lasted perhaps ninety minutes. The Cheyenne White Elk said,

> After all were dead a dog was seen running away, barking, and someone called out: "All are dead but the dog; let him carry the news to the fort." But someone else cried out: "No, do not let even a dog get away"; and a young man shot at it with his arrow and killed it.²⁷

While the Indians were cleaning up the field and the first groups began to move off through the valley of Peno Creek, a second detachment of soldiers appeared on the brow of Lodge Trail Ridge, evidently drawn by the sounds of battle. The Indians shouted and called to the soldiers, inviting them to come and fight, but the soldiers waited beyond rifle shot. With them were five wagons. As the Indians retreated down the long hill and made their way north across open country, shouting and singing their victory, the detachment of soldiers cautiously made their way forward over the rough ground. Soon they reached the first bodies of the men killed with Fetterman and began to load them into the wagons.

Later that night, after the soldiers and wagons had gone back to the fort, a few Indians returned to look for missing friends. The mild day had turned cold. A brief, spitting snow about sundown had stopped. Two of the searchers were the Miniconjou chief known as Hump, or High Backbone, and his friend Crazy Horse. They were looking for a third friend, companion of many war parties, Lone Bear. He was known as unlucky, often wounded in battle. He had been in the thick of the fighting, but when it was over no one knew where he was to be found.

With the end of the snow the sky had cleared again; the moon was full on this longest night of the year, and its brilliance reflected by the scattering of snow made night seem almost day.[28] Lone Bear was not dead when Hump and Crazy Horse found him, but he had been badly wounded, he had lost blood, his arms and legs were frozen. This was one of the moments people talked about in later years. Our only substantial account comes from the enigmatic Frank Grouard, who lived with Crazy Horse's friend He Dog in the early 1870s. Grouard was told, probably by He Dog himself, that the night after the Fetterman fight Hump cried when he and Crazy Horse found their dying friend. There was nothing unusual in that; Indians made no secret of crying, but wept their grief loudly. Grouard added that Lone Bear died in the arms of Crazy Horse. Another account reported only that Lone Bear was shot in the leg, blood poisoning set in, and he died.[29]

Red Cloud's war lasted another year and a half, ending in the spring of 1868 when the chiefs gathered at Fort Laramie to sign a new treaty. Crazy Horse and his friends were not among the thirty-nine Oglala who touched the pen, signaling agreement. This treaty, the last with an Indian tribe to be ratified by the United States Senate, established a "Great Sioux Reservation" incorporating all of South Dakota west of the Missouri River. The government in Washington also recognized the right of the Sioux to ban all whites from a large tract of additional territory, agreed to close the Bozeman Road, and promised that no other lands belonging to the Sioux would be taken without the agreement of three-quarters of all adult males. The government soon regretted this promise. Fort Phil Kearny and the other posts were burned by the Indians as soon as the last soldiers marched out.

In May after signing the treaty the Oglala chiefs went back north sixty or seventy miles to a favored camping site near the headwaters of the Cheyenne River. Nearby were some large blocks of sandstone convenient for the whetting of knives. The people set up their lodges in groups composing a great circle on the flat between two creeks. In the center was the council lodge where the chiefs met to smoke and talk. On special occasions the lodge would be made up of two or three ordinary tipis set up in a row, making a kind of long shelter. Many hundreds of people could gather at such a lodge, some inside, others peering in from the outside. One day in late May or June 1868, a party of men on horseback began to circle around the Oglala camp, stopping first at the tipi of one man, then at the tipi of another, calling them to the council lodge.

As the men on horseback circled the camp, a group of boys were distracted from their play. Wanting to know what was going on they joined the crowd following the men on horseback. One of the boys was a mixed-blood who had just turned thirteen. His mother was Looks at Him, an Oglala of Red Cloud's Ite Sica band. His father was an Army officer, commander for a time at Fort Laramie before he went away. The boy's name was William. Like everyone in the camp, he knew the names of the four men being led to the big council lodge. All had distinguished themselves in the Battle of a Hundred in the Hand—Young Man Afraid of His Horses, Man That Owns a Sword, American Horse, and Crazy Horse. The boy William watched as the chiefs in the lodge solemnly named Crazy Horse and the others as the last Ongloge Un—the last Shirt Wearers of the Oglala tribe. Nine years later William would be present again during the last months of Crazy Horse's life. He would listen while white men and Indians discussed the killing of Crazy Horse. He would be standing only a few feet away when Crazy Horse was stabbed. Again and again over the next fifty years he would describe what had happened. It seemed one had only to ask.

2

"I have always kept the oaths I made then, but Crazy Horse did not."

HALF-BREED, LIKE THE term "mulatto" in the slave-owning South, was a hard word to shake in the western frontier world of the 1850s when Billy Garnett was born in a Sioux lodge near Fort Laramie. Shortened to "breed" it could be a fighting word; softened to "mixed-blood" or "half-blood" it was almost a courtesy. But whatever the word, Billy Garnett was it, born smack in the middle of two peoples destined to fight, half Indian and half white. The white half came from his father, First Lieutenant Richard B. Garnett, a West Point graduate from an established Virginia family who arrived to serve with a company of infantry at Fort Laramie in 1852. In the lieutenant's view this was not a plum assignment. A letter written to a Washington friend, Miss Pattie Brumley, describes the frontier post as "my doom." The letter is studded with italics, quotation marks, and loops of arch wordplay. After a season in the nation's capital the change was "so violent and sudden" that he was left feeling like someone "who has fallen from some *dizzy height* and is just slowly recovering his consciousness." He misses his Washington friends "*fearfully.*" If he is to be "kept long in the 'wilds,' what will prevent me from turning an 'outside barbarian?' And there will be no 'Parthenia' I fear, to humanize and restore me to my former condition."[1]

Garnett was right; no "Parthenia" came to his rescue, then or later. He never married.

But at Fort Laramie Garnett managed to occupy himself. Not long after he arrived in June he took command of the post when his company captain went on leave. Like many Army officers in isolated posts on the western frontier, Garnett found a bed partner among the Indians drawn by the easier life where whites lived. Their lodges were set up along the creeks running into the Laramie River near the post, their ponies grazed on the flats, their children, half- and full-blood alike, played noisily in the shadow of the fort. Soon after Fort Laramie had been established as a fur trading post in 1834 a band of Oglala Sioux under Bull Bear had been coaxed south from their old winter camping grounds near Bear Butte with promises of good trade. The next year the rest of the Oglala came and gradually the post and the surrounding Laramie plains, well known for their abundant game, grass, and water, became a center of Teton Sioux life. By the time Lieutenant Garnett arrived on the scene Indians had been living in sight of Fort Laramie for nearly twenty years. These Indians even had a name—Wagluhe, translated as "Loafers"—and were considered a distinct band among the Oglala.

The whites at Fort Laramie lived surrounded by Indians—not only the Wagluhe established more or less permanently around the fort, but the bands of northern Oglala and Brulé Sioux who came and went with the seasonal flow of trade, and the numerous mixed-blood children of Sioux women and their French-speaking husbands who had come west as trappers and traders. In the 1850s many of these men worked at the military post, cut hay or wood on contract for the Army, or operated trading posts along the overland trail nearby. When a man took a Sioux wife he was soon surrounded by the lodges of his wife's numerous relatives—enough of them, sometimes, to make a small village.

Whites traveling past Fort Laramie on the overland trail were of two minds about Indians. Some were disgusted, like the Reverend P. V. Crawford, who wrote in his journal in 1851 that "the Indians seated themselves on the ground and commenced to pick lice from each other's heads and crack them between their teeth as though they were precious morsels. There was more filth than I expect to see among human beings." Others found the Sioux and their Cheyenne allies to be tall, clean limbed, and attractive. Addison Crane, passing by the fort just about the time Lieutenant Garnett was arriving in the summer of 1852, noted that "the Indians which I saw at the fort impressed me very favorably. They are a well-formed race—tidy and neat in their dress, and of pleasing expression of countenance." Lodisa Frizzell, passing by Fort Laramie the same summer, said the Sioux were "the best looking Indians I ever saw . . . tall, strongly made, firm features, light copper color, cleanly in appearance."[2]

It was from this shifting community of Indians that the thirty-five-year-old lieutenant chose the woman who became the mother of William Garnett. In the summer of 1854, when Garnett was conceived, Looks at Him was fifteen years old. Her relatives must have been numerous as her

father, Fool Elk (Hehaka Gnaskiyan), had seven wives. In the eyes of the
Sioux a man and a woman living together were husband and wife. Lieutenant Garnett was the second husband of Looks at Him; she had already
been married to the French trader and trapper John Boye, who was the
father of her first child, a girl called Sally.[3]

Billy Garnett was born the following spring in the bottomland along
the Laramie River about twenty miles west of the fort, near the point
where Sybille Creek empties into the river. When filling out official
forms in later life Garnett always wrote that the date of his birth was April
25, 1855, so it is probable that someone made note of it. His father had
departed by that time, transferred to New York City for a tour of recruiting duty, before moving on to Fort Pierre on the Missouri River. Billy
never saw his father and did not know his name until he was fully grown,
but some connection between the two survived, if only in the choice of
the boy's given name: William had been the name of both his grandfather
and his uncle, Richard's twin brother, who died the summer Billy was
born during a yellow fever epidemic in Norfolk, Virginia.

Billy's young mother may be glimpsed, indirectly, in a photo of a group
of Indian women taken at Fort Laramie in 1868 by the noted Civil War
photographer Alexander Gardner. They are dressed in their best—long,
full dresses of trade cloth, decorated with the ivory eyeteeth of elk, highly
prized by Plains Indian women. Several are sitting on the ground in the
manner Sioux women considered fitting, on one thigh, with legs and feet
tucked in modestly to the side. Their braids hang in front, over the
breast, signifying that they are married. But something about this photo a
modern observer might find odd: the women, with one exception, direct
their eyes away and down. At first look you might think they were angry
or offended, but it is not so. To look directly at a man, or any stranger, was
considered unseemly by the Sioux. But one of the Indian women gazes
directly at the photographer—not brazenly, but openly and with interest.
We may imagine that Billy's mother, Looks at Him, was like her son, in
the middle—modest in the traditional way, but also frank and comfortable with the way whites behaved.[4]

In its first years the trading post at the junction of the Laramie and North
Platte rivers had several names: Fort William, then Fort John, finally Fort
Laramie after a half-mythical French Canadian fur trapper believed to
have been killed in the area in 1821. The Sioux Indians came to buy guns,

powder and ball, trade cloth and blankets, beads and vermillion, iron pots and steel knives, mirrors and sewing needles, and a growing list of other necessaries, among which often was whiskey. In return they traded furs and skins, especially the hides of winter-killed buffalo tanned with the hair left on and softened to an almost felt-like texture. Shipped east by the scores of thousands these buffalo robes warmed laps in horse-drawn sleighs throughout New England and the upper Midwest. Not long after the post was established it began to appear on the maps of the overland route west from the Missouri River to Oregon. When gold was discovered in California in January 1848, the trapper and explorer Kit Carson carried news of the discovery east. In the summer of 1849, anticipating a flood of travelers and fearing conflict with the Indians, the United States government purchased Fort Laramie from the American Fur Company for use as a military post.

Throughout Billy Garnett's early childhood a large Indian and mixed-blood community lived peacefully on the Laramie plains near the fort, which was lively with the coming and going of soldiers, Indians, trappers, and travelers—especially in June when the wagon trains reached a mid-summer peak. Laramie was the halfway point for travelers hurrying to get over the mountains to California and Oregon before the snow began to fly. By mid-July traffic began to fall off. In the early years, when the gold fever was at its height, Army officers counted as many as fifty thousand travelers passing by the fort. Numbers were down by the time Billy was born, and the decline continued year by year until the completion of the Union Pacific Railroad ended it for good in 1869. But during the 1850s and early '60s Fort Laramie was the great meeting ground of Indians and whites on the western frontier. The noted saddlemaker John Collins, on a first trip west in April 1864 and later Fort Laramie's licensed trader, confessed himself "greatly surprised at the number of well-dressed squaws about the post. The half-breed children showed the 'early settlement of the country by whites.' "[5]

Everything changed in November 1864 when a village of southern Cheyenne and Arapahos was attacked by an undisciplined force of civilian militia from the newly established community, soon to be city, of Denver, Colorado. Some two hundred Indians were killed, most of them women and children. The Sioux were infuriated by this unprovoked attack on their friends and allies, which was followed the next spring by open war across the central and northern plains. Fort Laramie was not spared the bitterness between white and Indian. Twice the summer he was ten years old, Billy Garnett was present when the soldiers hanged Indians at the fort; in both cases the victims were accused of raping white women. Billy knew the first man, a Cheyenne named Big Crow who was camped near the fort while his two sons were attending school. The charge against him was lodged by a married woman whose husband had been killed at the time she was captured. Ransomed by friends and on her way home, she passed through Fort Laramie. There she saw Big Crow in camp with some soldiers, and she accused him of "leading on" the Indians who had killed her husband and raped her.

Of this event Billy remembered two things: the fact that Big Crow had never been out with the hostile Indians and had been living at the fort right along; and the manner of his execution. On April 23, 1865, as a crowd watched, soldiers led Big Crow from the guardhouse, wrapped him in chains, and hanged him from a newly erected scaffold just outside the fort. Billy was watching from the crowd when a squad of soldiers fired two volleys into the body of the writhing man.

A month later it happened again. The commander of Fort Laramie, Colonel Thomas Moonlight, erected a second scaffold near the first and hanged two members of the Tapisleca, the Spleen band of the Oglala, Two Face and Black Foot, blamed for mistreatment of a white woman actually captured by the Cheyenne. In fact, as Moonlight was informed, Two Face and Black Foot had purchased the woman from the offending Cheyenne and themselves brought her to the fort. It made no difference. Moonlight brushed aside objections from the post trader, who knew the facts. "You think there will be a massacre," Moonlight said. "Let me tell you there will be two Indians who do not take part in it. Goodday, sir." The two Oglala went to the scaffold singing brave songs. Moonlight ordered that the bodies be left hanging by their chains "as an example to all Indians of like character." Many months passed before the bodies rotted and fell to the ground.[6]

With tensions rising along the overland trail, the longtime trapper and trader James Bordeaux, a leading figure among the Missouri French, moved his family to the fort from his unprotected trading post on the North Platte east of Laramie. But even after "all the mixed-blood families camped at Laramie, it was not always gloomy," Bordeaux's daughter Susan later told a writing friend. She was only two years younger than Billy Garnett, but their mothers came from different Sioux bands.

We got rations regularly. The soldiers would all chip in and get up a dance. There were many fiddlers among the half-breeds and soldiers. There were quite a number of half-breed girls, all dressed up in bright calico with ribbons in their hair and on their waists, that fly around in a quadrille as well as anybody, stepping to the music in their moccasined feet . . . Stick candy and ginger snaps were passed around. We were just as happy and enjoyed it just as much as if we were dancing in marble halls with chandeliers.[7]

Wedged into Fort Laramie was a schoolroom, along with the sutler's store; the blacksmith and carpenter shops; the parade ground and stables; the officers' quarters, called Bedlam, and the enlisted men's barracks; "suds row," where enlisted men's wives did laundry; the hospital; the adjutant's office; and the guardhouse, where enlisted men with loaded weapons wore a path in the hard-packed ground of the post, pacing out a tour of guard duty by day and by night. In that school was a teacher— "not a Catholic," according to Billy Garnett[8]—and seated there to be taught in 1866 or 1867 was a class of Indian and mixed-blood children. Billy at eleven or twelve was among them, left by his mother at the fort to get some schooling. Likely he was staying with relatives. Later he could both read and write, but he did not learn how at Fort Laramie. He stuck at that school for only two days and then lit out, making his own way nearly seventy miles down the North Platte River, all the way to Scott's Bluff, where his mother was living with her third husband.

Among the Sioux, the children and the buffalo-skin lodge belonged to the woman; men might move on, but the family remained. After Lieutenant Richard Garnett moved away in the late 1850s, Looks at Him and her two children returned for a time to her first husband, father of Sally, John Boye—or Bouyer, as it came to be spelled. In later life, Billy told a writer that "Bouyer bought my mother back"—probably from her father, Fool Elk. But that arrangement did not last long either; sometime during the 1860s Bouyer was killed by Indians, and Looks at Him was soon attached to a new white man knocking about the Laramie area, John Hunter.

At various times Billy Garnett referred to several brothers and sisters with differing last names. One of them was called "Puss Garner," according to John Bratt, an Englishman who came to America in the early 1860s and made his way overland to the Fort Laramie area. Puss Garner was probably one and the same as Sally Boyer, Billy's older half sister. In 1867, Bratt, then twenty-five, took a clerk's job at a road ranch attached to Fort Mitchell, a small Army post just west of Scott's Bluff and about seventy miles down the North Platte River from Fort Laramie. The term "ranch" at that time meant a stopping place along a main-traveled road where food, supplies, and a night's lodging might be obtained. One of the owners of the ranch was John Hunter, a trader, freighter, convicted seller of whiskey to Indians, and general all-around exploiter of frontier opportunity who lived near the ranch buildings in a skin lodge with Looks at Him. Nearby in her own lodge lived Looks at Him's aged mother, Gli Naziwin (Comes and Stands Woman or Antelope Woman)—seventy plus, in Bratt's view.[9]

"Billy was then about 12 years old and a manly little boy," Bratt wrote.[10] Another white man working around Fort Mitchell that summer said Billy liked to hang around the soldiers cutting hay for the fort, and that he was "a very talkative boy."[11] Bratt described Billy's sister Puss as "a beautiful half-breed." He noted that she was ardently courted by two men working in the vicinity: Bob Mason, who soon departed for Texas to buy cattle although he was "very much in love with her and promised to come back some day and make her his squaw wife"; and John Duval, who was disqualified, in the view of Antelope Woman, by the fact that he was a Negro. It is clear Bratt was a little sweet on Puss himself. He describes her appearance on one gala evening, when the stage had pulled in at the ranch and the place was lively with "officers, soldiers, stage drivers and tenders, Indians and half-breeds, bullwhackers and mule skinners." Puss had often hung around the store with her little sisters and brothers, but on this night she was

> rigged up in all her finery and looked very pretty. Her coal-black eyes looked like bright diamonds. She wore a beaded buckskin jacket, short skirt, leggins and moccasins, with a new red blanket thrown around her shoulders. Her long black hair was plainted in one long braid which hung down her back . . . Her features were regular, her teeth white and even. She stood between her mother and Grandmother Antelope.[12]

What's remarkable about this simple description is the fact that Bratt is describing a young Sioux woman without quite knowing it—the single braid down the back is a sign she was of marriageable age but unmarried; the "buckskin jacket" would be more accurately called a yoke, a kind of cape of deer or antelope skin, often heavily beaded or quilled in a wide band across the chest and shoulders. This, with the skirt and the leggings, was the entirely traditional dress of a girl on a dance night. We may imagine that this young woman was close to the age, and probably looked very much like, the fifteen-year-old girl who had caught the eye of Lieutenant Richard Garnett. But despite the fact Bratt called her "Garner" she was not the daughter of the officer.

For a time John Hunter and Bratt were involved, in part as allies, in a complex struggle for ownership and control of the ranch, which survived on the Army's sufferance. It is clear that Hunter was an equally hard man to live or deal with. "John was cross-eyed, but could shoot straight," Bratt wrote.

> He could also drink bad whiskey, play poker, swear, and was treacherous and cold-blooded as an Indian, yet with all this he had a winning, persuasive way about him that usually succeeded in taking the last dollar from the soldiers, and sometimes the officers, the stage-tenders, freighters, bullwhackers and mule-skinners.[13]

About the time the lovestruck courtiers were lining up outside Looks at Him's lodge, Hunter triggered a fight with the Army when he persuaded his partner, Jack Sibson, to sell whiskey to a couple of soldiers from the fort. An hour later a sergeant arrived with a telegram from the commander at Fort Laramie ordering Sibson to vacate the premises. While Hunter was trying to work this maneuver to his advantage things deteriorated at home. The twelve-year-old Billy Garnett came to see Bratt one day to say that Hunter was "mean to his mother, brothers and sisters, his grandmother and himself; that he often whipped them with a quirt; that he had done this last night and that he [Billy] would not put up with it another minute."[14] Billy asked if he might borrow a gun and some ammunition. Bratt gave him two revolvers and fifty cartridges.

Some hours later, about three-quarters drunk, Hunter came rapping on the window and kicking on the ranch door, demanding that Bratt deliver up his Indian wife and family. He was certain all were hiding within. Bratt had no idea where Billy had taken his mother and the rest. He said so, and the next morning watched Hunter mount his favorite horse, cast about to pick up his family's tracks, and then disappear up the trail. Hunter found them soon enough, staying some miles along in the direction of Fort Laramie at the ranch of another old plainsman with an Indian wife, Antoine Reynal. What Hunter said is unknown, but the meeting did not go well. Perhaps Looks at Him was not ready to forgive the quirting, or perhaps Billy blocked the door with his two revolvers. In any event Hunter came back alone. Eventually the dispute was solved in the Indian way: Hunter distributed presents to his offended family and relatives and, after promises he would behave better in the future, the quarrel was patched up and they resumed living together.

In the fall of 1867, John Bratt gave up his clerk's job at the road ranch near Fort Mitchell and headed off for Pine Bluffs to join an outfit cutting railroad ties for the Union Pacific Railroad line. He left in mid-September, riding a thoroughbred mare that had belonged to Bob Mason, the man who swore he would return from Texas to marry Puss Garner. About the same time John Hunter sold out his interest in the ranch and bought another near Fort Laramie, an infamous place of entertainment formally called the Six Mile Ranch for its distance from the fort, but known as the Hog Ranch by the soldiers who frequented the women there. The place was described a few years later by one of General Crook's aides-de-camp, Lieutenant John Gregory Bourke, who recorded in his diary that on mild afternoons he and another of Crook's staff, Lieutenant Walter S. Schuyler, would go riding,

> taking the best road from the post . . . [past] a nest of ranches . . . tenanted by as hardened and depraved a set of wretches as could be found on the face of the globe. Each of these establishments was equipped with a rum-mill of the worst kind and contained from three to half a dozen Cyprians, virgins whose lamps were always burning brightly in expectancy of the upcoming bridegroom, and who lured to destruction the soldiers of the garrison. In all my experience, I have never seen a lower, more beastly set of people of both sexes.[15]

In the decade between 1867 and 1877 eight people were murdered at the Six Mile Ranch, including two owners. The first of them was Billy Garnett's stepfather, John Hunter. The occasion of the quarrel was again whiskey. In August 1868, Hunter had been summoned to the office of the post commander and banned from entering the military reservation "on any pretence whatever." Some fast talk got the ban lifted, but that fall Hunter told one lie too many when he was caught selling whiskey to some Army teamsters at the post. When the Army came to protest, Hunter said the guilty party was another freighter and trader named Bud Thompson. In October, angry at the lie, Thompson killed Hunter.[16] With his death Looks at Him, now in her middle twenties, was once again cast adrift without a protector. It was common among Indian families in times of hardship to separate for a time; children might go to live with grandparents or an aunt. After the killing of Hunter, Looks at Him sent her son Billy off with two of her brothers. We know that Billy had been on his own once before, in the spring of 1867 at Fort Laramie when he was left behind to attend school. It was probably late that same year when he left his mother and his brothers and sisters again. He spent that winter and all the following year living with the Sioux on the plains near the Black Hills, sometimes with the band of Red Cloud, sometimes with others.[17]

It was near the headwaters of the Cheyenne River in the summer of 1868 that Billy had been playing in the Oglala camp with some Indian boys when they noticed the men on horseback. Passing around the camp, the men gathered up four famous warriors and took them to the big council lodge in the center of the camp circle. There the four men were seated on buffalo robes in the center of the shaded area within the lodge. At one end of the lodge the elder chiefs sat. In front of the chiefs were the leading warriors of the tribe. Along either side were younger men. Watching from just beyond the inner circle were the wives of many of the councilors, waiting to serve a traditional feast of buffalo and dog stew. Next came the mass of men and women of all ages who made up the camp, singing and calling out. Beyond them, on the very edges of the crowd, was a throng of children, Billy Garnett among them, peeping and peering and craning their necks to see.

When it was time for the chiefs to speak the crowd fell silent. The four men seated on the robes had been selected by the Hanskaska, the chiefs' society. All were famed as fighters, and all were veterans of the Bozeman War: Man That Owns a Sword, American Horse, Young Man Afraid of His Horses, and Crazy Horse. At least three, perhaps all four, had been selected as decoys in the Battle of One Hundred Slain. According to He Dog, the northern Oglala, successors to the Smoke people, had divided twice in recent years, first into bands led by Man Afraid of His Horses (the Payabya or Payabyapi, or Below) and by Red Cloud (the Ite Sica, or Bad Faces). Later, the first group divided again, into a northern half led by He Dog, Big Road, Holy Bald Eagle, and Red Cloud, and a southern half, which on this occasion, in the summer of 1868, had gathered to appoint the four Ongloge Un to lead the band. When the candidates were all present the chiefs proceeded to instruct them in what was required of Ongloge Un, the Shirt Wearers. He Dog said these instructions were given by Smoke, son of the old chief who had died in 1864; the young Smoke was also a man of influence and the father of five sons, including three who became prominent: No Neck, Charging Bear, and Woman Dress. Garnett later recalled,

> The speaker told them that they had been selected . . . to govern the people in camp and on the march, to see that order was preserved, that violence was not committed; that all families and persons had their rights, and that none imposed on the others . . . To maintain peace and justice . . . they first counselled and advised, then commanded, and if their authority was not then respected, they resorted to blows, and if these failed to secure obedience . . . they killed the offenders without further parley, as was their legal right.

These rules were well known and understood by all the tribe, but in addition there were some instructions that were secret in nature. He Dog, who was made a Shirt Wearer a few years later, alluded to these instructions:

> When we were made chiefs, we were bound by very strict rules as to what we should do and what not to do, which were very hard for us to follow. I have never spoken to any but a very few persons of what they made us promise then. I have always kept the oaths I made then, but Crazy Horse did not.[18]

Among the difficult instructions were rules requiring chiefs to put aside envious or dismissive thoughts of other band leaders; to confront enemies without fear, believing it is better to leave your body naked where it falls, stripped for battle, than to die old and rot inside a wrapping of buffalo hide on a scaffold; to "look after the poor, especially the widows and orphans"; to be bighearted, think of the good of the people, and not give in to anger, even if your own relatives are lying bloody on the ground in front of you; and, perhaps most difficult of all, to practice restraint, stay away from other men's women, and subdue sexual jealousy or possessiveness, even though—as Oglala elders put it to scholars years later—"Many dogs go to your tipi to urinate."[19]

Also present on this occasion was Black Shield, later called Calico (Mnihuhan), then about twenty-five years old. Calico was a nephew of Two Face, one of the men Billy Garnett saw hanged at Fort Laramie in 1865. Calico himself had been lucky to escape hanging in the incident, which helped spark the Bozeman War. According to Calico, after the instructions had been given the chiefs presented to each man a special shirt made from the skin of the bighorn sheep. As the candidates stood there in the center of the people, Calico said,

Four men were then called who had led war-parties that had returned after striking an effective blow at the enemy without a man or a horse being wounded; four others, also, who had counted first honors in battle. The first four sewed the hair on the newly made shirts; then the other four sewed the feathers on: the first feather on the right shoulder of each shirt, the second on the left, the third on the right elbow, the fourth on the left.[20]

Shortly after this ceremony, the Oglala separated, going different ways. According to He Dog, many of the Oglala determined to remain in the north with the northern Cheyenne and some of the Arapahos, to go on living as they liked and to defend the Powder and Tongue river country, the last good buffalo country of the Sioux. Among this group, Crazy Horse, Little Hawk, Holy Bald Eagle, and Big Road were the leading men. They intended to keep away from the whites.

A second group, probably more than half of the Oglala, went south to the country around Fort Laramie with chiefs who had signed the treaty, including American Horse, Young Man Afraid of His Horses, and Man That Owns a Sword—three of the four new Shirt Wearers. Red Cloud was the leading man in this second group, which now intended to live close to the whites. By the end of 1868, or early the next year, Billy Garnett followed the Red Cloud people south with his uncles and was soon living again in the lodge of his mother, close to Fort Laramie.

3

"It is better to die young."

CRAZY HORSE, THE NEWLY selected Shirt Wearer, was a man of middle height and light frame. His skin and his hair were both light by Sioux standards, and for a time he was even called the Light Haired Boy. Susan Bordeaux, daughter of the well-known trader, was struck by his hazel eyes when she saw him once in the mid-1870s. His manner was also strange. Among a people devoted to oratory and accustomed to endless public debate and discussion, Crazy Horse was a man of few words and those plain. In 1870 Red Cloud told a roomful of high officials in Washington, "When we first had this land we were strong, now we are melting like snow on the hillside while you are growing like spring grass." Crazy Horse never said anything like that. When the views of his band were sought in council somebody else usually spoke for him—sometimes his uncle Little Hawk, or other leading men of his band such as Iron Hawk, Big Road, He Dog, and Iron Crow. According to his friend He Dog, "He was a very quiet man except when there was fighting."[1]

Fighting was the important thing in his life, but he did not glory in war. Most Sioux scalped enemies and brought the bloody trophies home proudly, dangling from the end of a long pole, singing war songs as they rode into camp with blackened faces. But Crazy Horse as a grown man did not take scalps, nor did he tie up his horse's tail before battle with fur, feathers, or colored cloth as other warriors did. In the summer of 1868, at the time Crazy Horse was made a Shirt Wearer, the young Billy Garnett heard him describe a vision or a dream in which a man appeared to him with instruction on how to conduct himself. In the story as Crazy Horse told it he was one day near a lake in the Rosebud country, between the Powder and the Tongue, south of the Yellowstone:

A man on horseback came out of the lake and talked with him. He told Crazy Horse not to wear a war bonnet [and] not to tie up his horse's tail [a custom of the Sioux on going into battle]. This man from the lake told him that a horse needed his tail for use; when he jumped a stream he used his tail . . . and as Crazy Horse remarked in telling this, he needs his tail in summer time to brush flies. So Crazy Horse never tied his horse's tail, never wore a war bonnet. It is said he did not paint his face like other Indians. The man from the lake told him he would never be killed by a bullet, but his death would come by being held and stabbed.[2]

Crazy Horse was a plain man, avoiding the personal display cultivated by so many other Sioux. He Dog's brother Short Bull said his only ornament was a shell necklace. Few Oglala had earned more war honors. When Sioux warriors counted a coup in battle by touching or killing an enemy they won the right to wear an eagle feather; noted warriors had full bonnets of eagle feathers, sometimes with single or double trails extending to the ground. It is not known how many coups were counted by Crazy Horse, although his father once said that his son had killed thirty-seven people. But Crazy Horse never wore more than one or two feathers—sometimes the tail feathers of a spotted eagle. In battle, he sometimes attached to his hair the dried skin of a male sparrow hawk or kestrel. With the feathers he customarily placed in his hair one or two blades of grass—slough grass, according to his brother-in-law Iron Horse.[3]

Lieutenant William Philo Clark, chief of scouts for General Crook and one of the few white men ever to speak with Crazy Horse, was a careful observer of the Oglala and noted that they liked to carry intimately on their person things that smelled good, especially

> sweet smelling roots, herbs and grasses, and frequently [they] have tiny sacks filled with something of the kind tied to the hair or fastened to a string around the neck. It is simply wonderful how many sweet-smelling grasses they will find in a country where a white man would fail to find any.[4]

Perhaps more important than the good smell was the power conferred by the grass itself. Crazy Horse once explained to Flying Hawk, a man he called cousin, why he wore grass in his hair:

> I was sitting on a hill or rise, and something touched me on the head; I felt for it and found it was a bit of grass. I took it to look at. There was a trail nearby and I followed it. It led to water. I went into the water. There the trail ended and I sat down in the water. I was nearly out of breath. I started to rise out of the water, and when I came out I was born by my mother. When I was born I could know and see and understand for a time, but after-

wards went back to it as a baby. Then I grew up naturally—at the age of
seven I began to learn, and when twelve began to fight enemies. That was
the reason I always refused to wear any war-dress; only a bit of grass in the
hair; that was why I always was successful in battles.[5]

The Sioux were a sociable, gregarious people, living five to ten or
more in a single lodge. In the vastness of their territory, which later
brought deep loneliness to silent whites on isolated ranches, the Sioux
managed to live in a perpetual crowd, calling everyone brother or cousin,
uncle or aunt. For much of the year they traveled in small bands of three
to six or eight lodges called *tiyospaye*. Periodically they gathered in huge,
sprawling villages for big hunts and ceremonies. Visiting was an integral
part of life. Children might stop at any lodge and expect to be fed.
Women rarely seemed to have gone off on their own, men only to hunt or
fast and pray. But Crazy Horse was noted for the time he spent alone—
not just in lonely, high places seeking visions or guidance, like other
Sioux, but on long solitary hunts, or on war trips into enemy country
alone to steal horses, and sometimes going off by himself simply to think.

Early marriage was common among the Sioux; women became mothers at fifteen or sixteen, and men typically married and lived in their own
lodge by the time they were twenty. But Crazy Horse was late to marry,
past thirty before he took a woman to live with him, according to his
friends. The year was 1870, during a time of constant warfare with neigh-
boring tribes. About ten days after a bloody battle with the Crow near the
river called Peji Sla Wakpa (Greasy Grass), Crazy Horse and a few
friends, including Little Shield, one of He Dog's numerous brothers, set
off on yet another war expedition, intending to steal horses in the Crow
country.

But Crazy Horse did not go alone; he took with him another man's
wife, known as Ptea Sapa Win, or Black Buffalo Woman. Everything
about this affair defies easy explanation. Black Buffalo Woman was a
niece of Red Cloud. She had been married long enough to be the mother
of three children. She left them with different friends or relatives when
she departed with Crazy Horse. Her husband, No Water, was a figure of
significance, younger brother of Holy Bald Eagle and Holy Buffalo,
chiefs of the Hoka Yuta, the Badger Eaters band of Oglala.[6] These men,
important among the Oglala but little known by whites, were often
referred to as "the Twins"—Black Twin and White Twin. Black Twin was
a cousin of Conquering Bear, a chief killed in the first big battle with

whites in 1854. Red Cloud repeatedly sought Black Twin's agreement before signing the 1868 treaty. Black Buffalo Woman thus belonged to a leading family among the Oglala, and taking her was bound to make many enemies.

But equally important, taking No Water's wife violated the instructions Crazy Horse had received when he was made a Shirt Wearer. At that time he and the others had been enjoined to think first of their responsibilities to the people, and to rise above all ordinary or personal concerns, especially those involving women. The simplest explanation for Crazy Horse's act would be love or physical passion. But it is likely that pure bravado and rivalry had something to do with it as well. Aggression was surely no small part of the character of any man who went to war as often as Crazy Horse, and it would be hard to think of a challenge more naked than riding off with another man's wife—especially a wife connected by blood to the leading men of the tribe. "An Indian becomes great by such exploits as stealing other men's wives," Francis Parkman noted in 1846, while spending the summer with the Oglala. "It is a great proof of bravery . . . [But] if the husband claims a present, and it is given, the merit of the thing is gone."[7]

By "present" Parkman means a payment, in effect a fine, the price generally being determined by elders of the tribe and usually set at one or more horses. Disputes between band or tribe members were usually settled by negotiation of this kind. But No Water did not seek the help of elders when his wife ran away with Crazy Horse.

No Water had been away. On his return he found his lodge empty, his children left with relatives. "Crazy Horse had been paying open attention to the woman for a long time," He Dog said, "and it didn't take No Water very long to guess where she had gone." He gathered a group of warrior friends and set off in pursuit riding a fast mule. Along the way he stopped off at the lodge of another of He Dog's brothers, Bad Heart Bull, who was known to have a revolver. No Water said he would like to take the revolver on a hunt, and Bad Heart Bull loaned him the gun.[8]

On the second night after taking Black Buffalo Woman, Crazy Horse and a small party of friends, including Little Shield, set up camp along the shore of the Powder River. That night the chief was sitting in a lodge with Little Shield when without warning the entrance flap was thrown back. No Water rushed in and said, "My friend, I have come!" Crazy Horse jumped to his feet and reached for his knife. No Water brought up the borrowed revolver, aimed directly into Crazy Horse's face, and fired. Crazy Horse fell forward senseless into the fire.

No Water turned back out of the lodge and told his waiting friends that he had killed Crazy Horse. The group rushed off, leaving No Water's mule behind. After they stopped to camp they built a sweat lodge, and No Water, with the aid of steam, sage, sweetgrass, prayer, and song, purified himself of Crazy Horse's murder. Later, No Water went to speak with his brother Black Twin, who said, "Come and stay with me, and if they want to fight us we will fight." For a time things remained tense.

The Oglala chief Yellow Bear meanwhile returned the fatal revolver to the lodge of Bad Heart Bull and reported the chief's killing by No Water. News of the affair spread quickly and widely. A report that Crazy Horse had been shot even reached his cousin Eagle Elk in the far-off Shoshone country, where he was a member of a war party.

But Crazy Horse was not killed. His friends pulled his body from the fire and then took him to the lodge of one of his uncles, Spotted Crow. There it was discovered that the wound was not as bad as it looked, painful but not fatal. The bullet from the borrowed revolver had entered Crazy Horse's face near his left nostril. It followed the line of teeth shattering his upper jaw, and emerged just under the back of his skull. "It took some months for him to get over it," according to Eagle Elk.[9] The angry friends of Crazy Horse wanted revenge, but while the chief recovered tempers cooled and intermediaries negotiated a bloodless resolution of the dispute.

"By good luck," said He Dog, "there were three parties to the quarrel instead of two."

The brothers He Dog, Little Shield, and Bad Heart Bull, from whom No Water had borrowed the revolver, were all opposed to further bloodshed. Three uncles of Crazy Horse—Spotted Crow, Ashes, and Bull Head—were for peace too. Gradually a deal was agreed. On the night of the shooting, Black Buffalo Woman had escaped under the back edge of the lodge. With the understanding that she would not be punished, several men brought her to the lodge of Bad Heart Bull, who was Black Buffalo Woman's first cousin. Bad Heart Bull in turn obtained No Water's agreement to accept her back in peace. After the return of his wife, No Water made a payment to Crazy Horse for shooting him. The price was substantial—three horses, including a roan and a bay, both noted for their quality. With that the affair was officially over—but of course it was not over. Some months later near the Yellowstone, No Water approached a group of Oglala who were butchering buffalo they had just killed. Seeing Crazy Horse in the group, No Water jumped on a buckskin horse tethered nearby and headed off at speed. Crazy Horse chased him right into the river waters before pulling up his horse and letting No Water escape across the Yellowstone.

After that it was clear that no camp would be big enough for both men, so No Water left his brother's band in the north and took his family to the new Red Cloud Agency on the Platte River near Fort Laramie. From that time forward No Water lived with the Wagluhe close to the whites and was rarely seen by the Hoka Yuta and other northern Indians. But news traveled freely back and forth, and sometime later word reached the Oglala camps that Black Buffalo Woman had given birth to a fourth child, a daughter. Many people noted that the child was light-haired, like Crazy Horse, and they believed this girl was his daughter.

The consequences of this affair continued to ripple outward. The friends of No Water said magic must have been used to seduce Black Buffalo Woman. Black Twin and others threatened to kill the medicine man Horn Chips, longtime friend of Crazy Horse, accusing him of making a love charm that bewitched No Water's wife. Horn Chips denied it but took no chances; like No Water he, too, moved south to the agency on the Platte River and kept away from the Badger band in the north. Finally the elders of the tribe, known as Short Hairs, took official note of Crazy Horse's behavior. Stealing other men's wives might be a pastime for Sioux men but it was forbidden to chiefs, and as a result Crazy Horse was stripped of his authority. He ceased to be a Shirt Wearer and the shirt itself was returned to the Short Hairs, who had the power to appoint a new Shirt Wearer to take Crazy Horse's place. But this was never done. No more Shirt Wearers were appointed by the Oglala.

Going to war was the meat of life for Oglala men when young; talking about it was a principal pastime for the remainder of their lives thereafter. As late as 1931 the Yale-educated anthropologist Scudder Mekeel at Pine Ridge, in South Dakota, found He Dog, his brother Short Bull, Left Heron, and others always ready to reminisce about war. "For hours on end," he wrote,

> a group of old men will sit in a semicircle under a shade and discuss old times and the deeds of men now dead, while from mouth to mouth passes

the inevitable red stone pipe filled with "red willow" tobacco . . . If you ask an old woman whether she would like the old times again, she will inevitably say "yes," but will add, "if we could be free from attack by the enemy."[10]

But attack by the enemy was the inevitable result of ceaseless warring by the Sioux against the Crow, the Shoshones, and the Pawnee, who retaliated in kind. It had not always been so. Two things brought perpetual war into the lives of the Plains Indians: horses, acquired as early as 1700, and the guns that soon followed. Peoples who once crept about the periphery of the plains trying to kill the occasional buffalo and growing corn in the river bottoms were suddenly empowered to go where they pleased and kill buffalo in hundreds. Their populations boomed. Feeding them required vast hunting grounds. The ceaseless raiding for horses pushed enemy peoples back out of the good hunting country. Some weaker tribes abandoned the plains altogether. "We stole the hunting grounds of the Crow because they were the best," the Cheyenne chief Black Horse told an Army officer in July 1866. "We wanted more room. We fight the Crow because they will not take half and give us peace with the other half."[11]

The radical changes wrought by horses and guns were roughly a century old when Crazy Horse was born, but they made war the great fact of Oglala life. Every family had lost people in war—men and boys far from home, women attacked while they fetched water or wood, sometimes entire *tiyospaye* that had the bad luck to run into a big war party when they were hunting or moving camp. When the men came back from raids successful with scalps or horses they stopped first to blacken their faces for joy with the soot of burnt grass and then approached the village singing. But if they had failed, and if men had died, they came back quietly, slipping into the camp. And sometimes a war party simply disappeared. Something might be learned of their fate after a year or two, but very often nothing was ever learned.

The old men who sat around discussing these matters while they smoked told an anthropologist on a visit to Pine Ridge, Clark Wissler, in 1902, that in the life of the Sioux there were "four great trials" that tested the quality of a man. Most difficult, they told him, was "to be left wifeless with a small child in winter." And after that: "To be shot in the leg in midwinter and to struggle home with the blood frozen in legging and moccasin . . . To be without food in winter for many days . . . To go on the warpath, be set upon by superior numbers, driven back and wounded." But there was still one more thing, the old men told Wissler, that surpassed all others in pain: "the loss of a young son. That the Indians say is the acme of woe."[12]

With its dangers and difficulties war remained the challenge that Sioux men struggled to meet. Grant Short Bull—by the 1890s, like all of the Sioux, he had added a Christian name—explained to Scudder Mekeel what a man might properly list in his lifelong record of war honors (called "coups," using the French word). Most praiseworthy, in Short Bull's view, was to have served as a *blota hunka* or war leader, sometimes called *canumpa yuha* or "owns the pipe," because a war leader always carried a pipe as the symbol of his authority. Other war honors, in descending order of praiseworthiness, were to be among the first four to strike an enemy, especially if he was alive and armed; to kill an enemy; to seize and carry off a horse that had been ridden by the enemy in battle; to steal a favorite horse tethered right in the middle of an enemy camp near its owner's lodge; to receive a wound in battle; to rescue a friend; and so on. For Mekeel, Short Bull listed a dozen deeds of significance; he rated the taking of a scalp as the least of these, while others thought it belonged higher.

Going to war was not undertaken lightly. A man might go out alone first to pray and seek guidance before embarking on a war raid. He might ask a *wicasa wakan*,[13] a medicine man, for help in weighing his prospects for success, or for an interpretation of a dream. Prayer was an aid to men in war, but it was not enough. Magic was also needed; protection was offered by small bags filled with special herbs, stones, or animal parts called *wotawe*. Even a shield required magic to be fully effective. To make shields of great power a man must himself share in the mysterious power called *wakan*. In later years, some elderly Oglala said that a man was permitted to make *wakan* shields for only four years; others said they could only make four in a lifetime. The shield itself was typically made of rawhide from the neck of the male buffalo, stretched, dried, and smoked until it was hard. Occasionally the hide for a shield was not taken from the neck but from the groin of a buffalo; left open in the center was the hole once filled by the bull's penis. A shield fashioned in this manner was thought to embody the power and strength of the buffalo itself.[14] Such shields were proof against arrows fired from a distance and, held at an angle, might even deflect a musket ball fired with a weak load.

But the real power of the shield came from its magical properties.

These derived from objects attached to the shield or designs drawn on it such as dragonflies for their darting flight, or wavy and zigzag lines to represent lightning bolts, or rough drawings of bears, horses, or thunderbirds—all figures of power. Animal parts attached to the shield lent some of their power to the bearer; a dried hawk conferred speed and sharpness of eyesight, eagle feathers gave power, bear claws conveyed the ferocity of the grizzly. Shields were also believed to have the power to attract arrows, pulling them toward the shield itself and thus protecting the owner.[15] Men believed that the shield's power was not only passive, as a blocking agent, but was active as well, and could strike fear and confusion in an enemy. Other elements were added to a shield for beauty or sound: red trade cloth, ermine tails, tufts of buffalo wool, the rattling dewclaws of buffalo, elk, or a black-tailed deer. The design for a shield, or for any war equipment, would be chosen by the maker in a sacred way, with much singing and praying. Often elements of the design came in a dream, or the animals represented were powerful tokens for the man who intended to use the shield in battle. If a shield struck terror in an enemy, all the better, but its central purpose was simpler—to wrap the owner within a field of protective power, securing him from physical harm. For such a shield a man was expected to pay a horse.

The decoration of shields and shirts, sacred songs and prayers, what a man wore in his hair, the way he painted his face and horse—all protected a man going into battle. Power was what protected. Power came from the unseen world, which men visited in dreams. It was through dreams that men were told how to protect themselves. The spiritual history of Crazy Horse began with the classic quest for a vision—days spent alone in a high place without food or water. For an early site, according to one account, he chose Hill Hard to Get Around, the Lakota name for Scott's Bluff on the south bank of the North Platte River.[16] There he dreamt or saw in a vision horses and thunder beings, who told him how to prepare for war. Other instruction came from the man who rode up out of the lake, and from his friend Horn Chips. Every detail of Crazy Horse's preparation for war had sacred significance, and in each instance they were believed to have talismanic power as well, to contribute to his success and safety. Dangers were many. So much attention to survival and protection is silent testimony to fear.

For in truth, sometimes magic failed. A sacred shield or shirt was trusted to fend off arrows and bullets, except when its power had been defeated by some infraction of sacred rules. Women in particular could dispel magic power by their touch or even their presence, especially when they were menstruating; even "the odor of their flow" was enough to render *wakan* objects powerless.[17] But in truth there were hundreds of ways to ruin the power of magic: by forgetting to use a certain formula in prayer, or dreaming of the wrong animal, or ignoring the nighttime hooting of an owl, or eating the wrong food, or failing to carry a special stone in a particular way. To give themselves courage some men chewed the root of the calamus, then spread the mix on their skin. But that, too, was magic, and when magic failed only true courage remained. The great fact of life in Plains Indian warfare was that men were wounded and killed all the time; to run the risks anyway required acceptance of the danger, which meant acceptance of the probability of injury or death in battle. Elderly Sioux often expressed regret that they had not been killed in battle when young. "It is better to die young on the battlefield than to live to carry a cane," one of them said in 1902.[18]

The embracing of death was a basic feature of the Sioux warrior code. The oldest of the men's military societies—the Miwatani—ritualized courage by presenting certain men with a headdress of owl feathers, a rattle made of the dewclaws of deer or buffalo, and a broad sash with a hole at one end. For battle, the sash wearers would paint their bodies red, would add a black arc from one cheekbone up around the forehead and down to the other cheekbone, and would drive a stake into the ground through the hole in the end of the sash. Once staked, they were obligated to fight where they stood until they were killed or a friend pulled the stake to free them. The founder of the Miwatani was said to have received the details of its organization in a dream. Later he led a war party close to the enemy and then, alone, "galloped down to a small flat, shouted defiance at the enemy, dismounted, and staked himself down. Then he called out to the war party, 'If you get home alive, tell the people what happened. It is better to die naked on the prairie than be wrapped up on a scaffold.' "[19]

Like other warrior peoples Sioux men found something appealing about dying young in battle. It was not a death wish exactly, but a kind of death sentimentalism. The Sioux prayed for success and safety, but they scorned fear. They expected that sooner or later their luck would run out, the charms fail, the enemy prove too strong. To ride to war anyway required a kind of fatalism. In 1846, while traveling with the Oglala, Francis Parkman was told about "that species of desperation in which an Indian upon whom fortune frowns resolves to throw away his body, rushing desperately upon any danger that offers." The idea was not to kill himself, but to risk all in hope of changing his luck. "If he comes off successful," Parkman noted, "he gains great honor."[20] Crazy Horse and his war comrades told each other that they were not only looking for horses and glory; they were daring fate—they were "looking for death."[21]

While Crazy Horse was recovering from his shooting by No Water, according to He Dog, his younger brother Little Hawk failed to return from a war party which had gone south of the Platte River. The character and death of this brother are sparsely recorded, but it is evident the two were close. Facing two Shoshones in battle once, Crazy Horse jumped down from his exhausted pony and turned it loose. "Take care of yourself," he told Little Hawk. "I'll do the fancy stunt." But Little Hawk did not want to leave his brother and turned his own horse loose as well. What made the stunt fancy is unexplained, but the result was one dead Shoshone, one fled from the scene, and the brothers riding off to safety on the horse of the dead man.[22]

He Dog says Little Hawk liked fast horses and fancy dress, was rash in battle, and died when he took one risk too many. The circumstances are vague. He Dog says the brother was killed south of the Platte; Flying Hawk says it happened in the region of Utah, and Eagle Elk implies as much in reporting that Little Hawk was killed "when we were fighting the Utes," which could have meant Utah but probably meant Colorado. The Ute country in Colorado might be described, a little loosely, as south of the Platte.[23] The news of Little Hawk's killing came as Crazy Horse was still recovering from No Water's pistol shot, but when he was well enough to travel, sometime in the spring of 1870, he went south to find and care for his brother's body. With him Crazy Horse brought Little Hawk's best horse, and when he had found and prepared his brother's body he shot the horse at the place so it might help him on his way to the spirit world. Then, according to both Flying Hawk and Eagle Elk, he proceeded to take revenge on the first victims who came his way.

Certain important words in Lakota have a wide range of related meanings. Two of these are *waste* (pronounced "wash-tay") and *sica* ("she-cha"), whose primary meanings are good and bad. But *waste* can mean a great many things; women named Wastewin were good women, pretty women, or faithful, resourceful, steadfast, caring, loving, dependable, even-tempered women. Food could be *waste*, as could be omens, or weather, or the resolution of a problem, or the terms of a treaty, or a heart. Having a good heart meant to be happy, or full of confidence about the future, or reconciled after a quarrel. A bad heart—*cante sica*—could mean many things as well, but among Indians and whites on the frontier all knew that a man with a bad heart was potentially dangerous, especially when his heart was bad after a loss. There are many stories of the chaotic settling of a grievance against life or fate carried out by a man suffering the inner hurt of irreparable loss—an overwhelming desire to strike out, injure, or kill to relieve an aching or bad heart. Justice played little part in relieving a bad heart; any victim would do.

One such story was recorded by the painter George Catlin, who spent six weeks among the Sioux along the upper Missouri in 1832. There he painted a portrait of an impressive young chief of the Miniconjou named Lone Horn. About three years later Catlin was told that the chief was dead. As Catlin heard the story, Lone Horn had been in some manner responsible for the death of his only son. In his rage and grief he mounted a favorite horse, armed himself for war, and raced out of the village proclaiming that he would kill the first thing he met, "man or beast, friend or foe," as the Sioux agent of the time reported to Catlin. On the prairie, Catlin was told, Lone Horn met an old buffalo bull of the kind hardest to frighten or kill. The chief wounded it with arrows, then charged it on horseback. In the struggle Lone Horn was dismounted, but he continued to attack the bull with his knife. Sometime later Indians from his village, alerted by the return of his wounded horse, tracked it back to the spot on the prairie where the bull and Lone Horn both lay dead. The bull had been repeatedly stabbed—a hundred times, they said. Lone Horn had been gored and trampled. Of Lone Horn's reason for this mad combat Catlin said only that "so great was the anguish of his mind at times, that he became frantic and insane"—a succinct definition of what the Sioux meant by a bad heart.[24]

Flying Hawk and Eagle Elk both say that Crazy Horse took his revenge against white people, without offering much in the way of detail. Eagle Elk said that Crazy Horse had taken his revenge while on the way home, twice encountering soldiers along the way. Each time he attacked the soldiers and killed two of them. "Those are the things that aroused the people," Eagle Elk commented, meaning that they fed the legend that was growing around Crazy Horse. Flying Hawk said Crazy Horse went alone to the place where his brother had been killed and remained there for nine days, camped at a hidden spot in the woods. "Every morning he got up and would stand and look," Flying Hawk said. "When he saw some enemy he shot him, until he had killed enough to satisfy him, then went back home."

The date of the killing of Little Hawk is unusually firm, since it happened while Crazy Horse was recovering from the wound inflicted by No Water. According to He Dog, the chief went south to find his brother's body "when Red Cloud went to Washington later in the same year," a trip that extended from April through June of 1870. Crazy Horse was seeking revenge against whites that spring, which probably explains an otherwise puzzling report in mid-April by the Fort Laramie chaplain, Alpha Wright, who described an unprovoked attack on a man named Harris as he had been riding toward the Platte to hunt ducks:

> [W]hen about half a mile from the garrison, as he entered a ravine, an Indian, on a fleet pony confronted him. Though [the Indian] rode past him swiftly, not being able to check his pony, he shot [Harris] just above the ankle joint, inflicting a wound that will cause him to lose his limb. But for the speed at which the Indian was riding [Harris] would doubtless have been killed for their aim is deadly. The Indian was an Oglala chief, by the name of Crazy Horse, a great warrior, belonging to a village now on Rawhide Creek, comprising about 200 warriors, who are now on the warpath.[25]

This newspaper story marks the first known appearance of the name of Crazy Horse in print. But there was no war. When Crazy Horse had killed enough, Flying Hawk said, he stopped.

Crazy Horse was brave, not reckless, said his friend He Dog. "[He] always led his men himself when they went into battle and he kept well in front of them." But it was not war honors he sought. Crazy Horse stuck close to his rifle; his goal was to kill the enemy; even in the heat of battle he would jump from his horse to steady his aim before firing. "He wanted to be sure that he hit what he aimed at," He Dog said. "That is the kind of fighter he was. He didn't like to start a battle unless he had it all planned out in his head and knew he was going to win. He always used good judgement and played safe. His brother and High Backbone [a close friend] were reckless. That is why they got killed."[26]

But Crazy Horse could be goaded into rash acts. On the occasion when High Backbone was killed Crazy Horse was pulled first one way and then another. It came during a time of almost ceaseless warring against white and Indian enemies alike. The fall of 1870 seems a likely date. He Dog and Crazy Horse were in a large war party of sixteen men going into the Shoshone country; some said it was a revenge raid, but it may have been nothing more than a routine effort to steal horses. Included in the party was High Backbone (sometimes called Hump), a Miniconjou Sioux and a close friend of He Dog and Crazy Horse of the sort they called brother. They were all about the same age and were rivals of the friendly kind. Also in the party were the brothers Charging Raven and Painted Horse, along with Good Weasel, Bald Face Horse, and Red Feather, who was probably the youngest in the group. They were nearing a Shoshone village and had just passed a creek. Two factors made Crazy Horse hesitate. One was the weather. "It was in the fall," said He Dog. "There was a drizzly rain turning into snow. Crazy Horse said, 'I wonder if we can make it back to Cone Creek. I doubt if our horses can stand a fight in this slush. They sink in over their ankles.' "[27]

But something else made him hesitate as well. On their way the war party had passed one of the sacred places where men over many years had stopped to draw on a smooth rock face.[28] On it were painted many figures of men and animals. The Oglala believed that a man could foretell the future if he knew how to interpret these markings, which seemed to change with the light and the weather. The war party had stopped at the site, made an offering, and spent the night. But the next morning Crazy Horse concluded that the omens did not predict success for his friends. Men on war parties were always reading the world around them for any sign their medicine was weak or their luck had turned bad. Sometimes a war leader would carry a dried bird or animal, and at night in camp would set it on the ground in front of the place where he slept, watching it closely. "If it moved or turned over," Clark Wissler was told, "it was a sign of bad luck and the warparty usually turned back."[29] A wise man paid attention to these omens.

But High Backbone was scornful of his friend's hesitations. "The last time you called off a fight here," he said to Crazy Horse. "When we got back to camp they laughed at us. You and I have our good name to think about. If you don't care about it you can go back. But I'm going to stay here and fight."

"It is a bad place for a fight and a bad day for it," said Crazy Horse.

"What did we come for?" asked High Backbone. "That's what we came for. Are you afraid?"

"Yes, we're looking for death," said Crazy Horse. "Let's go."

The fight went badly. They reached the Shoshone village in what is now the Wind River Reservation, approached at dawn, and fired into a lodge. In a moment many warriors swarmed out to oppose them, and they had to run for it. Good Weasel and High Backbone were cut off together; Good Weasel broke through a tightening circle of enemies, but High Backbone was set afoot when his horse was shot from under him. He braced to fight his enemies hand to hand. Bald Face Horse and Charging Raven saw him go down. Both were wounded later while fleeing but made it safely into some hills, where they found a spring as night fell. During the night the others joined them at the spring; Bald Face Horse died there. The last to come in was Crazy Horse. Red Feather said, "Four days later Crazy Horse and I went back to find High Backbone and bury him. We didn't find anything but the skull and a few bones. High Backbone had been eaten by coyotes already. There weren't any Shoshones around. When the Shoshones found out whom they had killed, they beat it."

News of this event soon spread across the plains. High Backbone was a famous warrior, and his close friendship with Crazy Horse was well known. Many years later the noted Shoshone chief Washakie claimed on an elk robe decorated with drawings of his exploits that he had been the killer of a "big Sioux War chief" who was "Crazy Horse's brother"—perhaps a reference to the death of High Backbone.[30]

The story of High Backbone's death was soon heard by Frank Grouard, a strange figure who was a white renegade one minute and an Army scout the next. Grouard had been captured on the plains about 1870, when he was just nineteen years old. When the Sioux found him he was wearing a heavy coat and lifted his arms in surrender; they thought he looked like a bear and named him Yugata—the Grabber—Lakota vernacular for bear. After several years living with the Sioux, Grouard was invited by an uncle of Crazy Horse to join the Oglala camp. There he found a place in the lodge of He Dog, where he remained until the summer of 1875. Very probably He Dog himself told Grouard the story about High Backbone, also known as Hump. He described the attack on the Shoshone village and the running battle which ended for High Backbone at Bad Water Creek when his horse was shot from under him and he was trapped alone on the prairie. Years later Grouard recounted the story to a white journalist: "Here Hump was killed, and the Sioux said that Crazy Horse was beside himself with grief and rage. From that hour, said his nearest friends, Crazy Horse sought death."[31]

4

"Crazy Horse was as fine an Indian as he ever knew."

MUCH HAD HAPPENED TO William Garnett since he had watched the making of the Shirt Wearers in the Powder River country in 1868. At the end of a year in the wild with the Indians he had returned to the Fort Laramie area, where his mother had set up her lodge with Red Cloud's Oglala. The site of their new agency was a compromise. The government in Washington wanted the Oglala to move to the Missouri, where feeding them would be cheaper and easier, but Red Cloud refused. In the early 1870s, tired of arguing, the Bureau of Indian Affairs built a new agency for the Oglala on the north bank of the North Platte River about thirty miles downstream from Fort Laramie. Officially it was known as the Red Cloud Agency; informally it was called the Sod Agency for the buildings constructed of slabs of prairie sod stacked like bricks. Garnett lived on the agency for a time with his mother and then took a job with Baptiste Pourier, known as Big Bat to distinguish him from his close friend Baptiste ("Little Bat") Garnier, a mixed-blood guide and hunter. Billy Garnett was only sixteen or seventeen when he went to work for Pourier, mainly as a wrangler, caring for horses.

Baptiste Pourier was a "Missouri Frenchman," one of the many French-speaking whites from the river towns of St. Charles and St. Louis, who opened up the northern plains and Rocky Mountains as trappers and traders in the first half of the nineteenth century. As a youth of sixteen, Pourier sought and won a job from another St. Charles native, John Richard, who had established himself in the Fort Laramie region in the 1830s. When Pourier went west with Richard in 1857, he was joining one of the leading families in Sioux country, a sprawling network of brothers and their Sioux wives and mixed-blood children. Over the next dozen years Pourier became an intimate member of the Richard clan and in 1868 he married Richard's daughter, Josephine, a girl of sixteen who wore the traditional tight braids of the Sioux.

Many whites in the Fort Laramie region were married to Sioux, but Richard's connections among the Oglala were unusually deep. The mother of the clan was Richard's wife Mary Gardiner, born in 1827, the mixed-blood daughter of the white trader William Gardiner and the Oglala White Thunder Woman. Mary Richard was already the mother of two sons who later became noted men among the Oglala—Rocky Bear (Inyan Mato), who took his father's name, and Black Tiger. The father of the boys had been killed in battle, some said by the Pawnee. White Thunder Woman was a sister of the Oglala chief Smoke, and of Walks as She Thinks, the mother of Red Cloud, which meant that her daughter Mary was connected by blood or marriage to half the leading men of the northern Oglala—a network of uncles, brothers, cousins, and nephews who all fought the whites in the Bozeman War. After the Fort Laramie Treaty of 1868 Richard's Sioux relatives split, some remaining in the north living a traditional life while others settled along the Platte with Red Cloud, Man Afraid of His Horses, American Horse, and other chiefs who had touched the pen. It was there that Billy Garnett's mother, Looks at Him, set up her lodge in Red Cloud's camp.

When the elder John Richard married the mixed-blood Mary Gardiner about 1841, she had lived part of her life with the Oglala, following her mother's death when she was still a small child, and part with her white father in St. Charles on the Missouri, where she went to school. Mary's six children with the elder John Richard included four sons known as "those wild Reshaw boys"—John, Junior; Louis; Peter; and Charles—and two daughters—Josephine and Rose. Baptiste Pourier was especially close to John Richard the younger, roughly his own age, who grew into a tall and slender man whom the Indians called Wasicun Tamaheca (Lean White Man) or Tamaheca for short.[1]

After reaching the Fort Laramie region with the elder Richard in 1857, Pourier spent his first winter trading with the Oglala alongside the younger Richard, who had learned Lakota at his mother's knee. Later, Pourier and the younger Richard also traded with the Crow along the upper Yellowstone, and both men became fluent in both languages. Over the next dozen years, Pourier freighted goods to the military and the gold camps, helped to put up the first buildings along Cherry Creek in eastern Colorado, the site that would become the city of Denver; and engaged in the usual range of frontier business speculations with horses, cattle, and military contracts, working sometimes for the Richards or others, and sometimes for himself. Increasingly, Pourier hired out to travelers and then the military as a scout and guide, finally taking on a full-time job as interpreter and scout at Fort Laramie about 1869.

When Billy Garnett went to work for Pourier he was casting his lot with the white half of the mixed-blood community, the men who conducted their working lives in English, hiring out to the military, trading with the Indians, buying and selling, dressing white. But things did not go well for young Garnett in his new job. Not long after he signed on, "two blooded mares" were stolen from the herd in Garnett's care. By "blooded," Baptiste Pourier meant horses of Arabian or thoroughbred stock, "American horses" in the vernacular of the plains. These were not your average Indian ponies worth one buffalo robe or ten dollars. Likely it was Garnett who identified the thief who drove them off. In any event Pourier believed it was Crazy Horse who took his horses.

"Crazy Horse was as fine an Indian as he ever knew," Pourier said in later years, and he supported his opinion with the story of how he recovered his stolen horses. Pourier spoke Sioux, he was not afraid to enter the Sioux camps, and he went out to Crazy Horse's lodge to retrieve his horses. He approached the chief directly and asked for their return.

> Crazy Horse told his wife to get them, but she did not want to do it—did not want to give them up—but he ordered her again to get them, saying they belonged to Bat, and she delivered them. Bat says he was the only Indian who would have given them up.[2]

In relating this tale Pourier said he made no argument for return of the horses, but only "asked for them." It is likely that in the lodge when Pourier came was not only the chief's wife but his only child. By the time of the horse theft in the early 1870s, Crazy Horse had finally taken a wife. Her name was Black Shawl Woman (Tasina Sapawin). Like Crazy Horse, she was in her early thirties, and she was the older sister of Red Feather, a noted warrior from his teens who had been on the raid in 1870 when Crazy Horse's friend High Backbone was killed by the Shoshones. Crazy Horse and Black Shawl had one child, a girl known as They Are Afraid of Her. It is likely that Baptiste Pourier was one of only two white men ever to see the daughter of Crazy Horse. From this moment forward Pourier would be deeply involved in the unfolding conflict which ended with the chief's killing; at the fatal moment, Pourier would be standing only a few feet away.

———

Pourier got his horses back, but Garnett lost his job. He soon found another with Pourier's close friend, the younger John Richard, and his partners, Jules Ecoffey and Adolph Cuny. Among many other enterprises the three men were running an eating and drinking establishment near Fort Laramie for travelers and off-duty soldiers known as the Three Mile Ranch. There a man could get his horse fed and watered, buy a can of beans, eat an elk-steak dinner, play a game of cards or billiards, and drink a glass of whiskey, or two or three.

Billy Garnett had not been working long at the Three Mile Ranch when the younger John Richard on May 17, 1872, asked Cuny if he might borrow the boy for the day. He said he wanted to fetch some horses down at the Sod Agency. But Richard was dressed for an outing, not for work, and he was wearing a fine white straw hat with a wide black band, probably a Panama. Garnett thought it must have cost four or five dollars. Richard planned to stop off first at the fort with some friends—Louis Shangreau and Pete Janis, the son and nephew, respectively, of two long-time Laramie-region traders, Antoine Janis and his brother Nicholas, both "Missouri Frenchmen" from St. Charles. Richard, Shangreau, and Janis all were in their twenties, all had Oglala mothers, and all were armed on this day. Richard and Shangreau carried Winchester repeating rifles, in addition to revolvers. Pete Janis, as usual, was armed with two revolvers with ivory grips; the Indians called him "White-handled Six-Shooters."[3]

John Richard Jr. stood out as something different and notable in the community of Fort Laramie mixed-bloods. He had a bold and impulsive character, a habit of getting into serious trouble, and a gift for getting out of it by exploiting circumstances and connections. Two years earlier, in September 1869, Richard had shot and killed a soldier sitting outside the sutler's store at Fort Fetterman. The commander of the fort, in reporting the incident, described it as "an act of bravado," and others added that Richard had been drunk at the time.[4] After the killing, Richard wasted little time in making his escape north, where he spent a winter in exile with his Oglala relatives beyond the reach of civil and military authorities. Despite the damning circumstances of the murder and his flight, he engineered a pardon as reward for his success in organizing a trip to Washington in June 1870 by Red Cloud and other chiefs to meet with the Great Father—President Ulysses S. Grant—who was at this time committed to a "peace policy" of negotiating with Indians rather than fighting them. A wide range of military officers and other officials wrote on Richard's behalf, urging his pardon for a string of reasons: he had helped the Army during the Bozeman War; there had been a history of bad blood between Richard and the dead soldier; and Richard, outside the law, living with the Oglala, might stir up war. The result was an order from the attorney general of the United States to authorities in the Wyoming Territory: *nolle prosequi;* do not prosecute. Richard returned to Fort Laramie at the end of June 1870 a free man.

It was not quite two years later, in May 1872, that Richard asked Billy Garnett to accompany him down to the Sod Agency to fetch horses. When the four men reached a crossing place on the Platte near Fort Laramie, Richard divided the party in two. He told Garnett to take the buggy waiting on the far side of the river—he pointed out the rig with its two gray horses—and drive down the north bank of the river until he reached the camp of Yellow Bear, a few miles short of the agency. Richard would meet him there with Louis Shangreau and Pete Janis after descending the river by boat. Garnett noted that a case of whiskey was in the boat, but did not worry, as Richard had quit drinking some time previously.

It took Garnett a good part of the day to make the journey driving the grays. Once or twice he was close enough to the river to see Richard and his friends in the boat; they were shooting birds. About midday, Garnett stopped in an Arapaho village where an old man and his wife fed him a lunch of fry bread, bacon, and coffee. Perhaps an hour later, four or five miles on, he passed the large village of Man Afraid of His Horses. Still farther along, around four in the afternoon, Garnett reached Yellow Bear's camp and sat down to wait for Richard and his friends to arrive in the boat. They appeared a couple of hours later, about half an hour before dark. At that point Garnett learned it was not horses John Richard had come looking for, but women.

Even by frontier standards, Richard at twenty-eight was a much-married man. In 1864, he had married Louise, the mixed-blood daughter of a Brulé woman and Joe Merrivale, a Mexican. A few years later Richard parted from Louise in the Indian way—he simply moved out—and married a sister of Yellow Bear, the chief of the Spleen (Tapisleca) band, also in the Indian way. When Richard took off for the north after killing the corporal at Fort Fetterman in September 1869, he took this Oglala woman with him, and that winter, somewhere in the Tongue and Powder river country, he married her sister as well.

The marrying of sisters was common among the Sioux and other plains tribes, and it was not unusual for men or women to marry many times, coming together and parting with little formality. The Oglala man Chase in Winter, a childhood friend of Billy Garnett, spelled out the rules to a pension examiner many years later:

> When we don't want to live together any more, the man goes by himself and the squaw goes by herself and we tell people we are not living together and in our custom that is similar to a divorce and each has the right to again take a husband or a wife. The only tribal custom is that each, the man and the woman, tell people they are separated.[5]

Marriages were sometimes long, sometimes short. Fast Thunder, who called Crazy Horse cousin, had married Cane Woman (Sagyewin) on the Belle Fourche River in 1866 when he was in his mid-twenties. They remained together until his death in 1914. But after the Bozeman War ended Fast Thunder moved with Red Cloud down to the Sod Agency and there, in 1872, feeling the need of another wife, he married Eagle Feather Woman—for two months. Largely forgotten now, Fast Thunder was a noted figure in the 1870s; he would be with Crazy Horse when he was mortally wounded, and he would help lower the chief's body to the ground. Fast Thunder's two-month marriage was by no means unusual. He Dog's brother Short Bull was once married to Good Enemy Woman (Toka Waste Win) for twelve days.[6] When a man parted from his wife it was said that he "threw her away." After his pardon, Richard threw away the two sisters of Yellow Bear in order to marry a fourth wife, fifteen-year-old Emily Janis, the fiery daughter and oldest child of Nick Janis. This made her a first cousin of Richard's friend Pete Janis.

But now, in May 1872, a year had passed since Richard had married Emily at Fort Fetterman, and for some reason Yellow Bear's sisters were back on his mind—especially the younger one. Garnett heard later that it was Pete who suggested they fetch the woman.[7]

As soon as Richard pulled his boat into shore late in the day, Billy Garnett noted that his gait was unsteady and some of the whiskey was gone. Richard told him to hitch the horses back up and drive the buggy to Yellow Bear's lodge, as he was planning to fetch the chief's sister and take her away with him. Garnett immediately sensed trouble. He reminded Richard that he had thrown the Oglala woman away and had replaced her with a fine-looking half-blood. Let well enough alone, he suggested; get in the buggy, let's be on our way. But Pete interrupted, told Billy to get the horses, and started with Richard down to Yellow Bear's lodge. When

Garnett caught up with them a few minutes later with the team and buggy, he found Richard just entering the lodge with the chief. Richard had his Winchester resting on one arm, holding it comfortably to his chest. Garnett remained outside, watching Indians one by one bend to enter through the opening to the lodge, a graceful sideways swooping motion. A dozen entered, then twenty, then forty. None of this looked good to Garnett, who felt increasingly apprehensive. Soon Pete Janis came out to say he couldn't budge Richard; Billy should go in and talk to him and bring him back out. Garnett did not want to enter the crowded lodge; he said he'd already done his best to reason with Richard, adding that it was Pete who had interrupted his efforts and ordered him to get the horses. But Pete pressed and Garnett quit arguing and entered the lodge.

Even thirty-five years later, Garnett remembered in detail the scene inside Yellow Bear's lodge. It was crowded with men sitting or standing. Smoke and light came from a small fire in the center. Things were tense. Above Yellow Bear's head hung a clutch of stuff from one of the lodge-poles—a smoking apparatus, a couple of knives, and a revolver. Yellow Bear's eyes wandered across the hanging revolver, but he was sitting on some rolled-up bedding, leaning against a tripod backrest, the very picture of a man at his ease in his own lodge. The gun was out of reach. Richard was seated partway around the inside of the lodge, chatting with the chief, his Winchester rifle casually across his lap. His hand played with the gun absentmindedly. His thumb touched the hammer.

Richard was in a mood both expansive and erratic, boasting of exploits in the Indian way, then turning sharp and needling the chief. He said he had come to fetch that youngest wife of his. That would be fine, said Yellow Bear. The woman belonged to him. But she was away, down at the agency where a scalp dance was being held to celebrate the return of a war party from a raid into the Ponca country, bringing a scalp. Other Indians in the lodge confirmed what Yellow Bear had said; they had been at the agency and had seen the woman there. Richard's conversation wandered away, then returned. He claimed the woman was right here in Yellow Bear's camp. The chief assured him not.

Richard's finger was now touching the trigger of his rifle. Garnett was sitting a few places away next to the Oglala known as Slow Bear. With a knife, Slow Bear was cutting the inner bark from red willow branches to make kinnikinnick, the mixture of bark and tobacco that Indians liked to smoke. This was a slow, almost thoughtful process, sliding the broad blade of a butcher knife under a sliver of the delicate inner bark, using a thumb to secure it, then peeling back the curly strand.

Nearby was the chief's brother, a broad-chested man known as Yellow Horse. The lodge was shoulder to shoulder with warriors. Garnett believed he was too far from the entrance to bolt out in case of trouble. He had no knife to cut through the wall of the lodge. For two hours he remained trapped in the dim light of the lodge while Richard sparred verbally with Yellow Bear.

Garnett sensed the Indians all turning on Richard, telling him no, Yellow Bear's sister was not in the camp. All were listening intently, all were thinking about Richard's rifle, all were waiting for some line to be crossed. A hundred times Garnett wished he were out of there.

But something was seething inside Richard. Surrounded by forty Indians, with no chance in the world of escape if they turned on him, he continued to goad and taunt the chief. If he could not have the woman, perhaps he should reclaim the horses he had given the chief. They were tied up right outside the lodge. Perhaps he should kill these horses, Richard said. Yellow Bear, all sweet reason, told Richard they were his horses—he could kill them. But he added reasonably that not all the horses tethered outside had been given to him by Richard—some were the foals of Richard's horses. These of course belonged to the chief. And the chief had other horses of his own. These Richard could not take away or kill. Garnett found himself hoping that killing a horse would be enough. Stabbing or shooting horses in the heat of anger was a common Indian way of settling scores. Perhaps shooting a horse or two would rid Richard of his demons and they could go on their way.

By the end of two hours everyone in the lodge knew lives were hanging in the balance. When the hammer of a Winchester is pulled back there is an audible click. Garnett heard it. Richard's hand was on the gun. He rose. He took a step toward the entrance as if the talking were done now. No one would have blocked his departure. But then in an instant he swung back, the gun came up, and Richard fired almost point-blank into the chest of Yellow Bear, who fell back dead. Instantly, the whole lodge exploded with men lunging to their feet, grabbing at Richard and his rifle. The broad-chested Yellow Horse seized Richard from behind and held him up off the ground. Somehow, Richard got his hand on his revolver. Indians held his arm up in the air. Shot after shot ripped up through the gathered lodgepoles and hide cover at the peak of the lodge. Slow Bear and others stabbed Richard repeatedly. Their big, flat-bladed butcher knives left inch-wide wounds. When Yellow Horse dropped Richard he fell dead or dying to the ground. Slow Bear fired a bullet into his head.

The lodge was filled with struggling men, shouts, gun smoke, flying blood flecks. Garnett surged for the entrance and in a tangle of bodies fell through the opening into the night air. Pete Janis had already disappeared. Garnett found himself fleeing through the dark with Louis Shangreau—stuck with him, really; Shangreau was slow and lumbering. When Garnett wanted to cross the river, Shangreau said he could not swim and pleaded with the boy not to leave him. So they took off north through the sand hills along the north bank of the river, making a wide detour to escape the bands of Indians who were charging on their ponies back and forth along the shore, looking for the two mixed-bloods so they could kill them. When the fugitives at last reached the Sod Agency, Garnett begged the clerk for someplace to sleep. The following day Richard's wife of a year, the fifteen-year-old Emily Janis, rode back to Yellow Bear's camp full of rage and fury. She attacked the chief's body with an ax and then set it afire.

Early the same day Billy Garnett was tugged back to consciousness by his former boss, Baptiste Pourier, pulling at his foot. Pourier was Richard's brother-in-law, but the connection went deeper. The two men had known each other since they were fourteen, had lived together with the Indians in their winter camps, were in business together, and were as close as men can be. By Garnett's own account, both men wept open tears as Garnett described the crazy slow progression of events which led to Richard killing Yellow Bear, a man "whose name was a sweet sound to all Indians because of his mild and just character, his peaceable disposition, his exemplary behavior, and his love for all members of his race."[8] Why Richard threw his life away was impossible to explain. Whiskey was part of the reason, but something in Richard himself was the real source of trouble.

Garnett also came close to death that day, and he knew it. For the better part of a week he refused to leave the agency buildings, not even to visit his mother's lodge, which was pitched just outside the agency stockade. He worried the Spleen band Indians would kill him on sight. But the Indians, fearing trouble, had packed up and hurried a hundred miles north to a favorite hunting country along the White River. Garnett, reassured, went back to work for Baptiste Pourier, but he long remembered every detail of the killing of John Richard. It wasn't solely his own close shave that stuck with him; it was being trapped for two hours in smelling distance of a man looking to die.

Soon after the Oglala moved to the Sod Agency, government officials began a new campaign to move them to a site on the Missouri River. Convenience of supply was one motive; moving the Indians away from the Union Pacific Railroad was another. But Red Cloud refused to go. He said the game had all been hunted out along the Missouri, whites came selling whiskey there, white horse thieves were waiting to steal Indian ponies there. In 1873, exhausted by Red Cloud's stubborn refusals, the government compromised again, and agreed to move the Oglala agency about eighty miles northeast to the headwaters of the White River, site of a trading post since the 1830s and a favored winter camping ground of the Oglala and Brulé Sioux. Officials thought the new site was in the Dakota Territory; by the time they learned it was in Nebraska it was too late—yet another set of agency buildings was already under construction. Spotted Tail and the Brulé also moved to the same area. That August a new agent arrived to take charge of the Oglala, J. J. Saville, a medical doctor recommended by the Episcopal Church in keeping with the president's "peace policy." One of Saville's early acts was to hire Billy Garnett, recently turned eighteen, as an interpreter for the new Red Cloud Agency.

Even after the Oglala moved away from the Platte River, life was dangerous for whites in the north. Red Cloud and the other treaty chiefs had little control over band members once they left the agency, and none over the Indians who had refused to touch the pen. There was a steady coming and going between the new agencies on the White River and the "unceded territory" that the Treaty of 1868 recognized as the legitimate hunting grounds of the northern Indians. White officials guessed that as many as twenty-five men and their families daily traveled north or south on what was sometimes called "the Red Cloud Trail"—a heavily trodden road which made a beeline north from the agencies.[9] In the spring, the traffic northbound to the hunting grounds was heavy; in the fall it was reversed. Nothing about this traffic violated the treaty, but officials did not like it. White ranchers and freighters blamed every missing horse on the "coddled" agency Indians, who went out raiding when the grass was good, it was said, and then returned to the agency to eat government rations all winter. The fact that Indian ponies were just as often run off by white horse thieves rarely found notice in local newspapers like the *Cheyenne Leader,* which wasted no opportunity to trumpet its conviction that the Indians needed a good whipping before peace would come to the plains. It was not just horse stealing that fed anger. The bodies of whites (and Indians) were often found in lonely spots, killed without apparent reason. No theme emerges from the scattered reports of violence except the violence itself. Outside the agencies and the military posts it was not peace that reigned but a kind of Hobbesian anarchy in which every man's hand was raised against his neighbor.

These killings fed the tension on the plains. When a white cattleman named Levi Powell failed to return from a routine check on his herd in the early spring of 1872 the news spread quickly. Powell had come up from Texas with a herd of cattle the previous fall. When he was delayed by bad weather north of Cheyenne, he decided to winter over on the river near Fort Laramie before continuing on to Montana. The winter passed without incident until March 5, when Powell disappeared; nineteen days later his body was discovered along the North Platte River. He had been shot twice through the head—either bullet would have killed him—and his horse, gun, hat, coat, and boots had all been taken. Indians were immediately suspected. Red Cloud stoutly denied that the killers came from his agency, but white officials thought he was lying and resented his lordly manner in rejecting responsibility. It smacked of defiance, which they hated above all things. To punish the Oglala, white officials banned the sale of ammunition by the agency trader, a new tool of coercion provided by the Treaty of 1868.

In the old days traders came and went freely on the plains, setting up store in the Indian camps and selling them anything that the Indians had furs or dressed buffalo robes enough to buy. But once the treaty was signed Washington prohibited independent traders from the reservation, and told those with official appointments what they could buy and sell. In the spring of 1872, just as the Indians were preparing to go on the spring buffalo hunt, they found it impossible to obtain cartridges or powder and ball. The northern Indians had always argued that signing the treaty would end their freedom; banning the sale of ammunition confronted the Indians with their growing dependence. Hope of ending the ban was one of Red Cloud's goals when he made a second trip east with a large group of chiefs in May 1872. In Washington, the murder of Levi Powell was repeatedly cited as the reason for the ban, and it was not until the chief promised to help find and deliver the killers that officials agreed that the sale of ammunition for hunting might at last resume.

But Red Cloud was probably right when he denied that his own young men were responsible. Years later evidence appeared that Powell was killed when he chanced upon a group of Sioux in a sweat lodge on a creek bank. A boy tending the fire outside shouted a warning as Powell rode up. Seven Oglala emerged to confront the white man. Among them, the story goes, were Crazy Horse and his friend Little Big Man. The two men had long been close. "In the Sixties," Billy Garnett said, "Crazy Horse and Little Big Man were harassing on the Platte. They carried on a lively business in horse stealing and the killing of white people."[10] Powell did not know who faced him in March 1872, and was evidently slow to sense the danger of the moment. With one hand he held a Henry repeating rifle over the pommel of his saddle while he soothed the neck of his horse with the other. The Indians spoke to him. He tried to make reply but did not take fright or bolt as they approached. One of the Indians reached out to touch Powell's rifle, then gestured as if to inquire whether he might inspect it. Powell relaxed his grip and let the rifle go. It passed around the circle of Indians, from one to another until it reached Little Big Man. According to the story, he raised the rifle to aim in a testing kind of way, then without word or warning leveled the gun at Powell on his horse and killed him with a bullet to the head.[11]

The murder of Powell left a lasting bitterness. Later two more killings of whites by Indians brought soldiers to the Red Cloud Agency and came close to sparking a general war.

Heavy snows made the first winter at the agency on White River a difficult one. Food supplies for the Indians were freighted northeast by oxteam from Cheyenne. A man named Charles Clay had the contract, but for most of the month of January 1874 his teams could not get through; supplies of bacon, flour, coffee, and sugar all ran low and then ran out. The cattle issued twice a month came from grazing areas along the Platte a hundred miles to the south. Every month or six weeks the beef contractors would drive a large herd north, enough for two or three issues at once, but the system faltered under a succession of blizzards. Real hunger came to the Red Cloud and Spotted Tail agencies. Charging Girl, a daughter of Red Cloud, remembered that some of the Indians made the

150-mile round trip to Fort Laramie to get food from relatives living there. Before the weather eased things got so bad that Indians had to kill and eat their ponies, already half starved themselves on their winter diet of cottonwood twigs and bark.[12]

The Oglala's new agent, John Saville, who had hired Billy Garnett, did not much like Indians, calling them "vicious and insolent."[13] The Indians did not think much of him, either. Saville was asked to conduct a census of the Oglala under his control, but the Indians, led by Red Cloud, refused to be counted. About the beginning of 1874, Saville's nephew, a personable young man named Frank Appleton, newly appointed to a position as clerk, arrived on crutches at the agency from Cheyenne, where he had broken his leg in an accident. He told Harry Young and others that he hadn't wanted to come at all but was pressed by his father to take the job. One night in Cheyenne, he said, he had woken from "a dream that something awful was to happen," but he quit worrying when the broken leg seemed to be it.

At the beginning of February his harried uncle put young Frank in charge while he rode forty miles north and east to the Spotted Tail Agency to seek the help of the agent there in asking the military to pro-tect them with a permanent post on the White River. While Saville was gone on the afternoon of February 8, an Oglala on his way north stopped off at the Red Cloud Agency with a bad heart and a desire for revenge. He told agency Indians a brother had been killed by whites down on the Platte and he intended to settle the score by killing a white man before continuing on his journey. The agency interpreter, Joseph Bissonette, tried to talk him down but warned the white staff to take no chances and stay inside the stockade after dark. That night, as usual, Appleton bunked down in the agent's quarters with Harry Young, Mike Dunn, Paddy Sim-mons, and Billy Garnett, then still going by the name of Hunter. Another white employee, Paddy Nolan, had set himself up in a chair to guard the entrance of the stockade, and all felt secure.

But for several days men had been shingling the roof of the agency commissary and someone—very possibly Harry Young, who had done some of the nailing—left a ladder outside the stockade. In the small hours of the night the Sioux with the bad heart climbed the stockade wall using the ladder and went to the building where Appleton and the others slept. He rapped on the window and the door. Appleton was the one to respond, stepping outside to ask what was wanted. When the answer came in Sioux he turned back toward the sleeping room to fetch Billy

Garnett as interpreter. He had taken but a step or two when the Indian raised his rifle, a Winchester, and shot him in the back, just under his left shoulder blade.

The shot and Appleton's cry raised the agency while the Indian disappeared. Mike Dunn set out immediately for the Spotted Tail Agency to warn Saville. Billy Garnett hurried down to Red Cloud's camp, where he told the chief, "Come, they have killed a clerk, they have shot him." Harry Young reported that Red Cloud was joined in the dying man's room by the chiefs Man Afraid of His Horses and Little Wound. When Red Cloud arrived he took Appleton's hand in his own and "with tears trickling down his cheeks, said, 'It is too bad. You are a good man. Bad Indian live up north.' "[14]

It is unlikely that Red Cloud was guessing. He had probably already been told that the killer was a "bad Indian" from one of the northern bands. The shooter was soon identified as the Oglala Kicking Bear, son of Black Fox and full brother of Flying Hawk. All three of these men were noted warriors in the Hunkpatila band of Oglala led by Crazy Horse. Red Cloud's tears may have been prompted by the recent loss of a son, as Harry Young believed, but it is just as likely the chief dreaded what was bound to happen next: the arrival of a military contingent from Fort Laramie. The killing of Appleton made it almost impossible to avoid. Next day, Saville sent a messenger to the fort, ninety miles to the southwest, to warn that an Indian outbreak seemed imminent. If Appleton's murder wasn't enough to raise official fears, another incident near Fort Laramie the following day, February 9, guaranteed a strong reaction: the killing of Lieutenant Levi Robinson and a sergeant surprised by Indians while out on a wood-cutting detail. Over the following days, tension and fear gripped the Red Cloud Agency; some Indians wanted to kill Kicking Bear, others wanted to kill all the whites. The trader J. W. Dear, who made a solid living selling necessaries to the Indians and buying buffalo robes and furs, wrote a friend at Fort Laramie that he was about ready to pull out:

> [I] am still safe, tho living in suspense night and day. Am trying to get all robes, hides, furs etc. out of country, then if worst comes to worst will try to make my escape at night. Have shipped since my return near nine thousand dollars in robes, hides, etc. and hope to heaven they may get through safe . . . I cannot venture out of my room after night. Indians all the time with guns loaded and bows strung. Agent has concentrated every man in stockade with him. Cheyennes held a council yesterday. Told him the Sioux

were constantly coming into their camp saying these houses here would soon be covered with blood . . . What is Agent telegraphing for, troops or what?[15]

The answer was troops, but Colonel John E. Smith, commander at Fort Laramie, needed time to assemble his men. The Army and the Bureau of Indian Affairs both fretted that sending troops to the agencies might precipitate a general Indian war, but their fears were exaggerated. The arrival of troops at the Red Cloud Agency on March 5 was followed by some harsh words and a few shots fired in the general direction of soldiers' tents but nothing worse. By summer's end a proper military camp was under construction under the command of a young veteran of the Civil War, Lieutenant Jesse Lee. The new post was named Camp Robinson after the officer killed in February. Six officers' quarters along the north side of a parade ground were constructed of adobe brick and pine cut in the nearby hills. Barracks for infantry and cavalry went up on the east and west sides of the parade ground. A hospital was added, then a sutler's store. Along the southern border of the parade ground were an adjutant's office and a guardhouse built of stout logs with barred windows and a heavy inner door.

The site of the new post was exceptionally exposed and bleak. Scant brush lined the narrow winding course of the White River, little wider than a creek. No trees sheltered the clutch of buildings, making it exactly the sort of isolated frontier post where the constant wind and dust and sometimes brutal summer heat made officers' wives weep for the memory of home. From the post a road led a mile and a half east to the Red Cloud Agency. Along this road on the last day of his life would come Crazy Horse, who had been promised a good talk with the commander of the military post. Riding beside the chief in an Army ambulance was the man who had built the post, Lieutenant Lee. The two men had known each other for only a day, but Crazy Horse trusted Lee's promise that he would not be harmed and would have a chance to explain everything to the post commander.

5

"A Sandwich Islander appears to exercise great control in the Indian councils."

NO MAN WHO SCOUTED for the U.S. Army during the Great Sioux War excited more argument than Frank Grouard, beginning with the question of what he was. At first it was Grouard's race that was hard to pin down; later it was his allegiance that led to argument. When first seen at the Red Cloud Agency in northwest Nebraska in the late spring or early summer of 1875, Grouard was in his mid-twenties—a good-sized man, perhaps five feet eight or nine inches tall, and weighing two hundred pounds, in the opinion of Billy Garnett. His hair was braided; he wore the long shirt, leggings, and breechcloth of a Sioux, and he was as dark-skinned as any Indian. Grouard always said he was a Sandwich Islander, but many doubted his claim that he was a Kanaka—one of the native people of Hawaii. On the White River in Nebraska, 120 miles from the nearest railroad, Grouard's claim was improbable on its face, and besides, he looked like a mixed-blood. Some said he had a white father and an Oglala or Hunkpapa mother. Others pointed to his broad face, the wisp of mustache, the flat nose and full lips, and said his father was black. At the Red Cloud Agency were people who said they had known Grouard—or at least heard of him—up along the Missouri River. They said a black man named Brazeau or Prazo or Pravost who lived with the Standing Rock Sioux might have been his father. To Luther North, a noted captain of Pawnee scouts, "Frank looked very much like a Negro." But North made no effort to get to know him. "I never cared much for the colored Brethren," he said.[1]

The Red Cloud Agency was well established by the time Grouard arrived. A stockade of pine logs set on end enclosed office buildings, storerooms, stables, living quarters for a small staff of eight or ten, and a trader's store run by the brothers H. C. and J. W. Dear, who had the exclusive right to sell to the Oglala. One of the Dear brothers said he had known Grouard when he was carrying mail for the Army up along the Yellowstone. The agency buildings were on a slight rise with long views over the surrounding prairie. To the north was a row of white clay buttes like a wall, and beyond that a wilderness of grass stretching to Canada. In the distance to the east was Crow Butte, where the Sioux had once trapped a party of Crow horse thieves but lost them when the Crow snuck off during the night. The Sioux were mad about it still.[2] What the U.S. government liked about the agency was its distance from the railroad. It was here at the Red Cloud Agency in the spring or summer of 1875 that Frank Grouard, without occasion of any kind, arrived with his friend, the young Oglala warrior Little Wolf.

Coming and going was little remarked at the agencies at the time. The Indians picked up at pleasure to go hunting, or to visit relatives among the three or four thousand Brulé at the Spotted Tail Agency, forty miles to the north and east. Living with both bands of Sioux was a large floating population of whites married to Indians. Officials spoke of them dismissively as "squawmen," and blamed them for stirring up trouble by advising the chiefs on what treaties actually said, or didn't say. Agents frequently appealed to Washington for permission to expel these whites from the reservations, but the Treaty of 1868 formally recognized them as members of their wives' tribes and permitted them to live on the reservation and to collect rations alongside the full-bloods. There were scores of such men. Many had been trapping, hunting, and trading in the region for decades. They had grown sons and daughters, and among them was no shortage of young men fluent in both English and Lakota, who looked and dressed like freighters or cattle drovers one day and Indians the next.

But Frank Grouard did not quite match the type. He spoke Lakota, but it had been learned at the age of twenty. Most mixed-bloods grew up around military posts like Billy Garnett, but Grouard had lived on the plains with the Indians for six full years—since his late teens, so he said. He spoke with authority and personal knowledge about the leading men among the northern Indians, including Sitting Bull and Crazy Horse. He said he had been back and forth over the whole broad expanse of mountain and prairie between the Missouri River and the Big Horn Mountains, and especially throughout the Powder and Tongue river country south of the Yellowstone, where the Indians made it dangerous for any white man to go. To whites and half-bloods working around the agencies, and later to military officers at Camp Robinson and Fort Laramie, Grouard gave a melodramatic, dime-novel account of his time with the

Indians. He said he had been a captive of Sitting Bull's people, tortured and abused, kept among them against his will for years. But gradually, as Grouard told it, he had gained the Indians' trust, been allowed to go out with the young men on hunting and warring expeditions, and finally had seized an unguarded moment to flee his Indian captors and make his way to civilization. To Indians, this story would have appeared improbable. Indians didn't run prisons; they killed their enemies or let them go. If a white man lived among them for years on end, it was because he had been adopted. But military officers and newspaper correspondents largely accepted Grouard's story at face value.

Parts of the real story emerged over the course of years. Frank Grouard was not a Sandwich Islander, exactly, but he had in fact been born in 1850 in the South Seas, son of a Mormon missionary and a Polynesian woman named Nahina from a small island near Tahiti. When Nahina died, Frank's father gave the boy for raising to another missionary family, Addison and Louisa Pratt. About 1852, the Pratts returned from Hawaii to Utah, where Frank was raised and schooled until he grew restless at fifteen or sixteen and ran away. In her diary, Louisa Pratt described Frank as naturally lazy in the island way. It may have been nothing more than weariness with classroom discipline that prompted his escape, but throughout Grouard's life rumors followed him suggesting something more was involved—trouble with the law, possibly a killing, something about a dead schoolmate. In his "autobiography," a volume of stories ranging from the likely to the preposterous put into print by a hard-drinking Wyoming journalist in the 1890s, Grouard himself said simply that in 1865, he "left school and hired out to a freighter named McCartney in the Big Square at old San Bernardino."[3] His job was "to drive team" to Helena, Montana, site of a gold rush. For the first few days, McCartney's wagon master drove beside the boy, teaching him the art of mule skinning. When the boy got to Montana he stayed there.

For the next several years Grouard lived the knockabout life common on the frontier for young men on their own, working for wages when work offered, joining the militia during an Indian scare, picking up the odd bit of property left lying around, taking a job riding a mail route for the Army, stealing horses from Indians, going back to the mail route. Grouard left the disreputable parts out of his autobiography, but some who knew him at the time made sure the record was complete.[4] In the winter of 1867–68, he appears to have lived with the Prairie Gros Ventres Indians on the upper Missouri, then made off with some of their horses in the spring. Later, he stayed briefly with the Assiniboines and then the Yanktonai Sioux, before resuming his career as a mail carrier.

Just after the turn of the year, on the 2nd of January in 1869 or 1870—it is not clear which—occurred the event which separated Grouard from the common run of wandering, half-literate, out-of-pocket men on the frontier. Hunkered down in a blinding snowstorm, he was heading for Fort Peck, riding one horse and leading another. Against the weather he wore a greatcoat as well as mittens, leggings, and moccasins, all of buffalo hide with the hair on. Suddenly Grouard felt a blow across his back. Till that instant he had believed himself alone. To his biographer, he described a dramatic struggle in the snow immediately following—Grouard dodging and ducking between two scrapping Indians, one trying to shoot him, the other to claim and save him. Losing patience, Grouard's protector finally laid out the shooter with a blow over the head with a heavy bow. Years later, John Colhoff heard a more prosaic version: some northern Sioux out hunting buffalo in the Yellowstone country were told a strange man had been found nearby. They rode over to investigate and found him with his hands raised high. In his buffalo-skin greatcoat he looked like a bear getting ready to fight. They took him to camp to consult with the chief, who was the Hunkpapa holy man Sitting Bull.

Grouard says a debate followed in which two other chiefs—Gall and No Neck—argued for killing the stranger, but Sitting Bull refused, insisting he wanted to adopt the dark-skinned man in the buffalo coat as he had another man captured on the plains, a young Assiniboine later given the name of Sitting Bull's father, Jumping Bull. Grouard once explained that Sitting Bull did not at first understand that he was an English-speaking refugee from the white world; the chief thought he belonged to some Indian tribe far to the west, across the mountains.[5] Sitting Bull prevailed and named his new captive Mato Najin—Standing Bear. The other Sioux knew him more familiarly as Yugata, a word meaning "arms out," as in the act of seizing—thus Grabber.[6]

For two or three years, Grouard remained with Sitting Bull's Hunkpapas, living in the lodge of Sitting Bull's sister, variously known as White Cow or Good Feather, while he learned to speak Lakota and was increasingly accepted as a member of the tribe. These were years of growing tension with the whites, but in his autobiography Grouard skated over that ground. His own account suggests he was a virtual prisoner, closely

watched by members of Sitting Bull's band. Indian accounts said he was
free to come and go, but chose to live and travel with the Hunkpapas.
Either version of events suggests that he must have been present in the
summer of 1872 when Sitting Bull and Crazy Horse had a sharp encounter
with white soldiers.

The Treaty of 1868 barred whites from settling in or even crossing the
"unceded" territory along the Yellowstone, but the Army and government officials brushed aside that clause without bothering to argue the
matter. In the winter of 1871–72, the management of a new transconti-
nental railroad, the Northern Pacific, arranged for detachments of cavalry to accompany surveying crews the following summer as they made
their way along the Yellowstone, mapping out a right of way. One of the
first to tell whites that a new railroad meant war was the Sans Arc chief
Spotted Eagle, who brought his band into Fort Sully that spring to sell
buffalo robes. Spotted Eagle was a man of consequence; a year earlier he
had been among the leaders of a Sioux war party that discovered and
killed all but one of a band of thirty Crow in the Black Hills, a feat
recorded in many winter counts. At Fort Sully he spoke frankly to General David S. Stanley, who paraphrased the chief's words for the commissioner of Indian affairs:

> He stated that neither himself, or any Sioux openly authorized to speak for
> his people had ever given their consent to this and that they never would
> give this consent, or listen to any proposition to that effect. He then said
> that he would fight the railroad people as long as he lived, would tear up the
> road, and kill its builders.[7]

Fort Sully was the military post attached to the Cheyenne River
Agency, named for the confluence of that river with the Missouri. The
agency was the official home of the Sans Arcs and the Miniconjou Sioux.
The mother of Crazy Horse, Rattle Blanket Woman, had been a Miniconjou, and Crazy Horse had many friends in the band. If Crazy Horse
set foot on only one agency, as He Dog said, and if He Dog was right
when he said that it happened "the time that they were laying out the railroad across the country," then it seems likely that it occurred when Spotted Eagle brought his 150 lodges to Fort Sully in April 1872 to sell
buffalo robes. "He got into trouble about it," He Dog added, probably
referring to a fight in August near the winding waterway the Sioux called
Arrow Creek.[8]

A large war expedition of Sioux and Cheyenne was camped near the spot where Arrow Creek, coming up from the south, emptied into the Yellowstone River. It was Crow the Sioux and Cheyenne had organized to fight, not whites, but they promptly changed plans when they discovered a large party of five hundred soldiers and civilians camped in a wood on the north bank of the Yellowstone. When news of the soldier camp was brought in by scouts, Sitting Bull wanted to ignore them. It was said he had agreed with Crazy Horse on a cautious policy for dealing with whites—leave them alone unless they started shooting first.[9] But the young men were strongly tempted by the cattle, horses, and mules with the soldiers, and despite strict orders from the *akicita*—the camp police— to stay away from the whites, some of these young men in the hours before dawn slipped up close to the soldiers in hope of stealing animals.

The men crept into the woods and were making their way cautiously forward when a pistol shot woke the night and brought one of the raiders down. Gunfire immediately erupted generally; the wounded Indian, a Hunkpapa named Plenty Lice, was killed with a second shot, and his body was dragged into the white camp. After an hour of noisy confusion fighting died down shortly after dawn. As the sun rose a long line of Sioux and Cheyenne warriors gathered on bluffs overlooking the woody thicket a few hundred yards distant where the whites and their animals were well concealed. The guns of the Indians, including many Winchester and Henry repeating rifles, could not quite reach the soldiers. The .45/.70 caliber Springfield trapdoor rifles of the soldiers, however, brought the Indian lines comfortably within range.

This classic frontier battle—much shooting, few casualties—contin- ued another few hours longer without meaningful military result. For much of the time Sioux fighters took turns making dare rides—racing in close to the soldier lines to demonstrate their bravery. Several were wounded, and at least two of them later died, including a brother of the Brulé chief Spotted Tail named Hawk Dog. Also mortally wounded was a nephew of the Miniconjou chief Lame Deer.[10] But the fight was princi- pally remembered, by the Indians at least, for two extraordinary displays of daring and physical bravery.

This was not a battle Sitting Bull or Crazy Horse had wanted, but their authority had been brought into question by the young men who ignored the agreed policy and attacked the soldiers. The whites, too, in effect challenged the Hunkpapa and Oglala chiefs after the sun came up when the soldiers brazenly dragged the body of Plenty Lice over to a campfire and threw it into the flames. The white soldiers were many and well placed; direct attack would be futile, but to do nothing would further sap the authority of the chiefs. Now Sitting Bull demonstrated why he had been chosen a leader of all the northern Sioux.

It was still well before eight in the morning. Followed by friends— White Bull, Gets the Best of Them, and two Cheyenne whose names have been lost—the chief started down the face of the bluffs toward the white soldiers, calmly walking until he reached the flat and found a comfortable spot several hundred yards from the woods where the soldiers had taken cover. He sat down. The others sat also. Sitting Bull opened his pipe bag and began the slow and methodical process of preparing a pipe, cutting the tobacco and then tamping it down with a small stick into the bowl of the pipe. It was important to take your time. When the pipe was ready the right way was to light it with an ember, then with slow recital of many prayers offer the pipe to Grandmother Earth—Unci—and Grandfather Sky—Tunkashila—and the four directions. Only then would the pipe be handed around to the left for each man to take a puff or two until the bowl was empty.

That was the right way. Whether Sitting Bull stuck rigorously to protocol was recorded by none of the Indians who smoked with him that day. But according to White Bull, they smoked until the pipe was empty while the soldiers fired at them without cease. The seated Indians could hear bullets zipping through the air. The ground was kicked up by bullets nearby and one of the Cheyenne was cut by a bullet in the shoulder. The .45/.70 cartridge of the trapdoor Springfield makes a big sound—a cracking boom. The thunder of the guns from the woods must have been terrifying. "Our hearts beat rapidly," said White Bull, "and we smoked as fast as we could."

A moment came when White Bull was overcome with tension; he shut his eyes and dropped his head onto his knees, waiting for the inevitable. But eventually the bowl was smoked down. Sitting Bull cleaned it with his stick, emptied the ashes, put the pipe back in his bag, and then got up and without hurry walked back up the bluffs out of range of the soldier guns.

That done, Sitting Bull wanted to call off the fight—already one man had been killed and others had been wounded. But now Crazy Horse wanted a chance to show why he too had been chosen a leader of the northern Sioux. Again White Bull was called to take part, and the two commenced yet another dare ride—wheeling in a circle on their horses at a dead run, veering close in toward the soldier line, and then pulling away as the booming of the guns followed them across the field.

As usual, Crazy Horse had his face painted all over with white spots, and wore his hair hanging loose. He wore a white buckskin shirt and leggins, but no feathers. That was the way he always dressed for battle, White Bull said; and White Bull was a close friend of Crazy Horse. That day Crazy Horse carried only a lance—nothing else.[11]

In battle, a dare ride had a practical purpose: to draw the fire of the enemy and empty his guns. But this was a pure dare ride—a taunting demonstration of courage and indifference to danger. The soldiers were spread along a curving line of a half mile or more, hidden among the trees that lined a looping, water-filled slough, a sluggish branch of the Yellowstone that veered out in an inverted U from the main channel before it rounded back to the river. Crazy Horse's ride at a dead run took him within two hundred yards of the soldiers; it is probable that a hundred or more shots were fired as he raced by, White Bull hurrying just behind him. Whites hidden in the trees later related that "one young warrior rode slowly back and forth for probably twenty times, all the time taunting the soldiers with language and gesture." White Bull thought a hundred shots were fired; the white witness said "a thousand shots must have been fired at him, but he went through unscratched."

At the far end of a run, White Bull said, Crazy Horse turned back for another pass, but this time, as White Bull remembered it, the booming of the soldier guns came all at once in a single volley. One or more of the heavy 405-grain bullets slammed into Crazy Horse's mount; it fell stone dead to the ground. But the chief was unhurt, and he jumped up and ran for the Indian lines, untouched by the bullets whistling after him. White Bull completed the ride breathless but unscathed.[12]

That ended the fight at Arrow Creek. The Indians departed, taking their wounded with them, fifteen or twenty in all. When the soldiers emerged from the woods they counted fourteen dead Indian ponies. One had belonged to Crazy Horse, another to Spotted Eagle, who had also been slightly wounded in the fight. Later in the summer Spotted Eagle sent a message into Fort Sully, where he had talked with General Stanley in the spring; he asked the interpreter there to tell the whites that he would fight them "wherever and whenever he met them."[13]

Frank Grouard makes no mention of this early fight on the Yellowstone, which he must have witnessed, but confesses he was present the following year at a very similar encounter when the Northern Pacific Railroad made a second attempt to survey a route along the river. One of the officers with the soldier party (but not in command) was the man known by the Indians as Pehin Hanska, often shortened to Pahaska— Long Hair. This man with the golden curls was notorious among the southern Cheyenne for a dawn attack on a sleeping village that left scores of dead in the snow along the Washita River in November 1868. When Lieutenant Colonel George Armstrong Custer, famed among whites for his cavalry exploits during the Civil War and a master of self-promotion, was transferred with the 7th Cavalry to Fort Abraham Lincoln on the upper Missouri, his reputation as an Indian killer accompanied him and was soon common knowledge among the northern tribes. While the Indians were moving in for a fight with the soldiers on August 4, 1873, Grouard, watching from a hillside, heard the Army band playing a lively tune. He would hear it often again later—"Garry Owen," the regimental march of Custer's 7th Cavalry.

"That was the first fight I ever saw between the Indians and troops," Grouard told his biographer. He said he took no part, only watched, but got into trouble anyhow when he went down to the river and knelt down for a drink of water. At the jangling of horse furniture he snapped his head up to see cavalry charging straight at him across the river; Grouard's riding mule bolted, and as the guns started popping he ran on foot for a thicket of trees. Grouard remained hidden until the shooting stopped.[14]

But it was not Custer and his soldiers that most threatened Grouard in mid-August 1873. It was the chief who had saved him, Sitting Bull, furious at what he considered a personal betrayal. That spring Grouard and Sitting Bull had quarreled so bitterly that in Grouard's view "there was only one thing for me to do; I had either to kill Sitting Bull or be killed."[15] This quarrel was common knowledge among the northern Indians, but its origins, as always with Grouard, are not easily sorted out. The trouble began when the trader at Fort Peck asked Grouard to help him open trade with Sitting Bull's band. At almost the same moment, Grouard agreed to guide a detachment of troops up the Milk River to apprehend a group of whiskey-selling Red River Metis—mixed-bloods from Canada who had in effect established their own tribe, which the Sioux called the Slota. These people sometimes fought against the Sioux, but at other times sold them arms and ammunition in addition to whiskey. Grouard brought Sitting Bull to Fort Peck so the chief might tell the trader no, but when it was time to head back for camp, Grouard told Sitting Bull to go on alone, since he was going north to steal horses. Of the expedition against the Metis, Grouard made no mention.

When Grouard returned from the Army's raid he brought with him three Metis horses—pay for acting as guide—and gave one each to Sitting Bull and his mother and sister, saying he had stolen them from Indian enemies. But ten days later, some Santee Sioux who knew the true story told Sitting Bull all about it, and he was furious. It was not just the lie that angered him; more important was Grouard's treachery, as Sitting Bull saw it, in secretly agreeing to guide for the *wasicu*, the Lakota word for whites. The two men had once been close. In the summer of 1872, white officials visiting Fort Peck had noted that the chief "has in his company a Sandwich Islander, called Frank, who appears to exercise great control in the Indian councils and who excells the Indians in their bitter hatred to the whites."[16] The quarrel over Grouard's lie poisoned the relationship. From that moment forward, in Grouard's view, his only choice was kill or be killed.

After the fight with Long Hair on the Yellowstone, Grouard was approached by Little Hawk, an uncle of Crazy Horse who had heard about the quarrel with Sitting Bull. To Little Hawk, it sounded like a bad situation; he urged Yugata to join the Hunkpatila band led by his nephew, and that same day the Grabber met Crazy Horse himself.

> Crazy horse had somewhat peculiar features. He had sandy hair and was of a very light complexion. He didn't have the high cheekbones that the Indians generally have and didn't talk much. He was a young-looking Indian—appeared much younger than his age. There were a few powder marks on one side of his face.[17]

Grouard accepted Little Hawk's invitation and found a place in the lodge of a young warrior who had only just married and set up his own household—the lifelong friend and fighting companion of Crazy Horse named He Dog. With this move into He Dog's lodge in the late summer of 1873, Frank Grouard was joining one of the inner circles of Oglala life. *Mitakuye oyasin*, the Oglala liked to say—We are all related—a social fact which brought political as well as personal obligations, and which made political conflicts among the Oglala hard to distinguish from family quarrels. The immediate circle entered by Grouard was He Dog's *tiyospaye*, who were sometimes called the Sorebacks (Cankahuran) after a gray horse afflicted with a saddle gall which refused to heal. As children, He

Dog and his brothers and sisters all rode this horse, which was known for its speed and endurance despite the sore that gave the band its name.

He Dog's father was called by several names—Black Stone, Lone Man or Only Man, and Walking Light[18]—and he had numerous children with his two wives, at least one and possibly both of whom were sisters of Red Cloud. In the early 1840s, when Black Stone was starting his family, he was a chief of the Bad Faces along with Fast Whirlwind and Red Cloud's uncle Smoke. Later, this group split. After 1868 Red Cloud led many of the people south to draw rations at an agency while He Dog and Crazy Horse remained up in the Powder River country. When Frank Grouard moved in with He Dog he was not simply choosing a bed of convenience, but casting his lot with the northern Indians who were determined to have nothing to do with the whites.[19]

The Oglala, and more generally the Sioux, were a fluid social organism; born into one band, men or women might marry and move into another. Brulé one year, they might consider themselves Oglala the next. But over the years between 1850, let us say, and 1900, the Oglala attached themselves to a remarkably stable handful of leading men—Red Cloud, Man Afraid of His Horses father and son, Little Wound, and American Horse were all friendly to the *wasicu* after 1868. A similar group, rarely changing, sided with Crazy Horse, Big Road, Little Hawk, He Dog, and the Twins in trying to keep their distance from whites. Members of these two principal factions of the Oglala almost never switched sides. But it happened once, in the summer of 1877, when many of the supporters of Crazy Horse, for reasons they found hard to explain later, pulled away from him and sided with the *wasicu*. They regretted the switch almost immediately. Within six or eight weeks of the killing of Crazy Horse, his old friends and supporters, with one exception, had all renounced their moment of wavering. If these men had not turned aside it is likely Crazy Horse would not have been killed, and almost certainly not killed in the way that he was, alone in a crowd of rivals and enemies. He Dog was torn by this convulsion; at first a member of Red Cloud's band, he went his own way in 1868 to side with Crazy Horse, then abandoned his friend in the summer of 1877, and finally rejoined Crazy Horse's friends and fled with them to Canada after the death of the chief. This confused indecision was so rare among the Oglala that it is shocking.

Frank Grouard was deeply involved in these events. He rarely spoke about the killing of the chief, and never explained his own actions or motives. He was probably married to an Oglala woman for a time but formed no lasting attachment to any member of the tribe. But Grouard entered more deeply into Crazy Horse's orbit, over a longer period of time, than any other man who was not an Indian.

By the time Frank Grouard joined the Hunkpatila band Crazy Horse had married Black Shawl Woman and their daughter, They Are Afraid of Her, had been born. Red Feather said the marriage occurred "six years before he was killed"—that would have been 1871—and that the girl died when she was "about three." Others say she was two. Grouard, who was living with He Dog at this time, reported that the daughter was four. In any event, it was probably in the summer of 1873 or 1874 that the girl died. Crazy Horse had gone out on a war party against the Crow while the village was camped between the Little Bighorn and the Rosebud. By the time Crazy Horse caught up with his band again after the raid, it had moved seventy miles east. It was then he learned that his daughter had fallen ill and died during his absence. Sudden death was not uncommon; Indians in general and their children in particular were susceptible to a host of fevers and diseases brought by the white men, from cholera and smallpox to mumps and measles. The body of They Are Afraid of Her had been washed and wrapped in the customary manner and placed on a scaffold.[20]

Grief for the dead among the Sioux was unrestrained. Men and women grieving for someone especially close might cut their hair short, slash their legs, arms, or chest with a knife, pierce their flesh with wooden skewers, cut off the end of a finger with a knife or hatchet, go about bloody and filthy and crying loudly for days—generally four days. As in other cultures, grieving was sometimes spontaneous, sometimes obligatory. The Oglala Black Elk describes the grief he displayed for a cousin killed by the Crow. "It was hard work crying all day," he said. "This is the way I had to cry: '*Hownh, hownh*—My cousin, he thought lots of me and I thought lots of him.' I did not feel like crying, but I had to do it all day."[21]

Sometimes at the end of the four days of first grief an elaborate, year-long ceremony was undertaken called "ghost keeping." The body would be left behind in the usual manner, on a scaffold or in a tree, but a lock of the dead one's hair would be carried from camp to camp. This lock of hair was called "the white ghost" and was treated as almost a living person. The lock might be carried in a leather bag, or housed in a separate lodge; it would be talked to and prayed over. At the end of a year the lock of hair would be buried or perhaps burned and the surviving family would hold a giveaway—presenting blankets, beaded clothing, and even horses to friends, relatives, and the needy. The places where bodies were left were not avoided, but talked about and visited from time to time. There was no single or right way to grieve for the dead, but every expression of grief began with tears—weeping loud and long. A newspaper correspondent who spent weeks in the field with Shoshone scouts in 1876 described their grief when a boy left to watch over horses was killed in a sudden attack:

> During the night a melancholy wailing arose from the Snake [another name for the Shoshone] camp down by the creek. They were waking the young warrior killed by the Cheyennes . . . I never heard anything equal to the despairing cadence of that wail, so savage and so dismal . . . the Snake Indians . . . had deferred the burial of their comrade until sunrise. All the relatives appeared in black paint . . . I had been led to believe that Indians never yielded to the weakness of tears, but I can assure my readers that the experience of that morning convinced me of my error."[22]

What we know of Crazy Horse's grief comes from Frank Grouard, who reports that on returning from his war party the chief immediately determined to visit the scaffold holding his daughter's body, two days' ride away. At the chief's invitation, Grouard reports, he went along. When they reached the site Grouard began to set up camp while Crazy Horse climbed up onto the scaffold beside his daughter's body. There he remained for three days and nights—"mourning." Grouard describes it no further. During that time Crazy Horse did not eat or drink. On the morning of the fourth day he woke Grouard at first light and said he was done now and it was time to leave. The mourning had quieted him; Crazy Horse's face was expressionless throughout the long ride home. The dead daughter was his first child. He never had another.[23]

As Frank Grouard was making his way toward the Red Cloud Agency in the spring of 1875, the agency's young interpreter, twenty-year-old William Garnett, was fired and almost immediately rehired by J. J. Saville, who had been having a hard time maintaining control of the willful and unpredictable Indians. Garnett was a guileless young man, which got him into trouble; but he was quick-witted as well, and that got him out of it. The handful of regular agency employees—among them Mike Dunne,

Paddy Simmons, a teamster known as Dutch Joe, Harry Young, and various others—were joined for meals at a common table by transients passing through, such as officials from the Bureau of Indian Affairs, the cowboys who arrived periodically with cattle from Texas, the driver of the regular stage from Cheyenne, mail carriers, and the like. To the table talk one evening at supper Billy Garnett contributed some out-of-school stories he had heard while translating for Saville. An informer in the group repeated what he heard to the agent, and Saville promptly fired the young mixed-blood for his lack of discretion. Garnett was unwilling to accept his dismissal as final. Before departing, he shared a final dinner at the agency mess, and there he mentioned some of the things that he planned to tell General John E. Smith when he got to Fort Laramie. Beef was the subject, and waste was the theme.

The biggest single expense at the Red Cloud Agency was the monthly issue of more than a thousand beeves on the hoof to feed the Indians. Indeed, the great western cattle business found its origin in providing beef for the Army and the growing number of agencies in the territories (and later states) of Nebraska, Wyoming, and Dakota. Fortunes were made on the wild Texas cattle driven north to feed soldiers and Indians, not just by the ranchers who bought cheap in Texas and sold dear at the agencies, but by corrupt agency officials, sometimes including the agents themselves, who stood to gain when they issued a voucher for every scrawny animal as a thousand-pound steer. It was not just traderships that were bought and sold by "the Indian ring." Agencies, too, were political plums and worth money. Within a few years of appointment, an energetic man might retire comfortably. In addition to the skim on just about everything issued to Indians, from coffee to bacon and blankets, agents routinely employed members of their own families—wives, sons, brothers, and nephews. But at the heart of the frequent scandals and official investigations very often was the beef issue—not just full payment for underweight animals, but the provision of beef to imaginary Indians. How many cattle were required was a hit-or-miss kind of calculation. In theory the Indians were issued beef based on a head count, but nobody really knew how many lived at the agency. One newspaper writer in April 1875 claimed that an astonishing 14,200 Indians depended on the 350 beef cattle issued to them three times a month.[24] On issue day at the Red Cloud Agency the Indians, mainly Oglala Sioux with some Arapahos and Cheyenne, would come in from their camps dotted along the winding trickle of the White River. Every ten days during the early 1870s, about

350 animals were issued by Ben Tibbetts, who was carried on the books as
a butcher but in fact held a job closer to chief herdsman. He butchered no
animals; that was left to the Indians. On issue day he would call out the
names of the men with families, then release one or more beeves from the
corral so the Indians could run them down on horseback just as if they
were killing buffalo. It was quite a sight. The artist DeCost Smith
described one typical beef issue a few years later, where a warrior on a
trained buffalo horse waited till a steer had almost reached the spot where
he wanted to drop it, and then

> he would start his horse at a run, and when nearly side by side with the ani-
> mal he would lean forward, holding his gun at arm's length in his left hand,
> and with the muzzle within a foot or two of his mark deliver a shot back of
> the ear. The effect was instantaneous . . . I could not help thinking what a
> few such men . . . could have done to a body of cavalry in disorganized
> retreat.[25]

The beef issue at Red Cloud was part of the tour given every visitor,
and they all returned with stories of the festival atmosphere, the dramatic
slaughter and quick work done by Indian women with their butchering
knives; of the children and young men with blood running down their
necks as they chewed into livers or kidneys plucked steaming from the
freshly killed beeves; of the intestines, carelessly washed of their grassy
contents, chewed on by infants and old people alike. What few visitors
noticed, however, was the extraordinary waste. Garnett said he would be
sure to tell General Smith of the dead and dying animals scattered over
the landscape after every issue—"the choice parts taken and the remainder left to rot. There was too much issued and the Indians could not use
all of it."[26]

What this waste revealed was the embarrassing fact that there was
more meat than Indians. The fourteen thousand souls officially reported
were in fact not nearly so many. An accurate count was something the
agent should have known, and could have known by conducting a simple
census. But Red Cloud wanted no census, and Saville was afraid to conduct one. The over-counted Indians and wasted beef were not the only
subjects which might interest General Smith, Garnett observed at dinner.
The following day he was summoned by Saville, questioned severely,
informed that the agency beef issue was no concern of Smith's, and then
rehired on the spot—with a raise in salary from forty to fifty dollars a
month. This was good pay for a mixed-blood, twenty-year-old interpreter; privates in the Army received only thirteen dollars a month.

When white men and Sioux conversed it was always through an inter-preter; no white officials learned Lakota, and few of the Sioux knew more than a handful of words in English. The first generation of interpreters were mainly white trappers and traders who came to the Fort Laramie region in the 1820s and '30s, married Sioux women, and remained to raise families. These men all spoke Lakota, but the Lakota they spoke was often crude and unreliable, a kind of kitchen Lakota, suitable around the house or for trading but inadequate for negotiating treaties. Red Cloud was not the only Sioux chief who insisted he had never agreed to some point claimed later by officials; the interpreter had said nothing like that to him. In 1875 to a reporter from the *New York Herald*, the chief com-plained specifically of the Reverend Samuel D. Hinman and of Todd Randall, who "had to be corrected several times in his very loose transla-tions."[27] Even Nick Janis, who married a Sioux in 1849 and lived among them until his death in 1902, sometimes required help from his son-in-law Billy Garnett when he got stuck in the denser thickets of Lakota.[28] Garnett was an interpreter of the second generation, which meant that Lakota was his mother tongue, learned as a child. His English was fluent, but he did not learn to read and write until after his mid-twenties.[29]

The conduct even of ordinary business at the Red Cloud Agency could be challenging for an interpreter. Red Cloud and the other chiefs were always unhappy about something. All depended on the agent for material goods, for permission to hunt south of the Platte, for any change in the amount or kind or quality of rations they were issued. A white man who lived among the Oglala for years once remarked, "The Indians have a fac-ulty for consuming the time of a man who will incline his ear to listen."[30] There were other second-generation Lakota speakers at the Red Cloud and Spotted Tail agencies, among them three men all named Louis: the first was John Richard's younger brother; then Louis Shangreau, son of Jules Shangreau and an Oglala woman related to Red Cloud; and finally Louis Bordeaux, son of James Bordeaux and a Brulé woman, sister of Swift Bear. But none of the other second-generation Lakota speakers could match the fluency acquired by Garnett over years of translating for Indians and white officials alike.

Yet it was the Sandwich Islander Frank Grouard who seemed the Indian. Billy Garnett was handsome in the classic Indian way—high cheekbones, finely molded mouth and chin. But he dressed white. On an ordinary working day he wore boots, not moccasins; a felt hat, a bandana around the neck, trousers, a work shirt buttoned at the wrists and neck in the cowboy way. In 1877, when he was twenty-two, he was photographed sitting next to his friend and sometime employer Baptiste Pourier. Garnett's hair was short and neatly parted and combed. He wore a three-piece suit, white shirt, tie. Pourier was in a coarse wool coat and stovepipe pants. Bigger, heavier, and older, with his full handlebar moustache and thick curly red hair, Pourier looks ready to enter a saloon, while Garnett might have stepped from a lawyer's office. Seeing Garnett and Grouard side by side, knowing nothing else about the two men, officials instinctively would have turned to Grouard, fresh from the plains in his sinew-sewn buckskin garb, to ask what the Indians were thinking and saying.

6

"Gold from the grass roots down."

THE INTERPRETER BILLY GARNETT was always among the first to know when the government in Washington wanted something, and beginning in the summer of 1874, Washington wanted the Black Hills of Dakota. Standing in the way were the Sioux Indians, who had been granted title to the hills by the Treaty of 1868. It was done casually. Few whites had ever seen the hills and some officials thought they were in Wyoming, outside of the reservation. But this indifference disappeared in a moment with a torrent of newspaper headlines in August reporting the discovery of gold.

Looking for gold had not been General George Armstrong Custer's avowed purpose when he led an expedition of eight hundred men to the Black Hills in the summer of 1874. Custer said only that the government wanted to see the country and make a map. It was not Custer who wanted the map but General Philip Henry Sheridan, commander of the Division of the Missouri, which encompassed the whole of the plains and the mountain West. Very likely Sheridan's desire for a map had been prompted by the official report of a previous expedition which had approached the hills under Lieutenant G. K. Warren in September 1857. The Hunkpapa Sioux chief Bear Ribs, with a large party out hunting buffalo, met Warren's group on its approach to the hills and warned them away. He told Warren he thought the whites had an eye on the hills, wanted to build roads there, and were looking for the right place to establish a military post—all shrewd guesses. Bear Ribs said the Sioux had no more land to sell; he told Warren, "These Black Hills must be left wholly to [us]." In Warren's report submitted later that year, he confirmed the suspicions of Bear Ribs:

> There are so many inevitable causes at work to produce a war with the Dakotas before many years, that I consider the greatest fruits of the explo-

rations I have conducted to be the knowledge of the proper routes by which to invade their country and conquer them. The Black Hills is the great point in their territory at which to strike all the Teton Dakotas . . . Here they can assemble their largest force, and here I believe they would make a stand.[1]

Warren then sketched in the outline of a military campaign, and urged that it be pressed hard till the Indians "are effectually humbled and made to feel the full power and force of the Government." Such a campaign would require first of all a map.

The Black Hills were named for the pines that covered their slopes. From the plains to the east the hills first appeared as a kind of wavy black line on the horizon, then on closer approach as a formidable wall, so steep and abrupt that an entrance along a creek running east was known as Buffalo Gap. Through it buffalo passed into the hills for the winter, returning the same way in the spring. According to the winter counts the first Lakota to see the hills was Standing Buffalo (Tatanka Najin), who returned from a journey into the hills about the year 1775–76, bringing a bough from an unusual kind of pine tree.[2] As the Sioux in subsequent decades made their way across the plains between the Missouri River and the Black Hills, other tribes gave way—the Kiowa moving south, the Crow north and west, the Shoshones west. The Sioux did not live there but instead visited occasionally, typically when they needed to cut the tall, slender pines that were ideal for use as lodgepoles.

There was something a little forbidding and frightening about the hills. Storms were severe and lightning was frequent, something feared by all Plains Indians. The Oglala Fast Thunder, who called Crazy Horse cousin, had been named for such storms. He told his children and his grandchildren that once, hunting with a friend in the hills, they were chased by a buffalo—probably a magic or sacred buffalo. Just as they were about to be gored or trampled, "a short little man with long hair came" and took them to a safe place—a kind of cave, a tight secret place in the rocks. Fast Thunder called it "a spirit hole"—they could feel and hear a moaning wind breathing in and out through the hole. They were frightened. The little man urged them to take refuge—"Just squeeze in, but don't come any further." Fast Thunder's friend was crying with fear. "Don't be scared," said Fast Thunder—"pray!" In they went and were saved from the magic buffalo. Later, when they got home and told the people what happened, the wind hole became famous as a place of powerful spirits.[3]

In the summer of 1874 one of General Custer's Sioux scouts—a Yanktonai known as Goose (Maga), then in his late thirties—told the whites about a similar spirit cave as the big expedition made its way south and west toward the Black Hills.[4] Custer had marched out of Fort Abraham Lincoln on July 1, well supported by scouts—about forty Arickarees led by Bloody Knife and Bear's Ears, along with thirty Santee and a few other Sioux, including the man named Goose. But among these seventy-five scouts only Goose had previously been to the Black Hills. It was Custer's habit every evening on the trail to gather his officers and chief scouts to discuss the next day's march. One evening in early July he spread out a military map prepared in 1859 by Captain William F. Raynolds when he passed by the northern fringe of the hills on his way to the Yellowstone. At first, Goose did not grasp what the large paper was. Custer pointed out some prominent features: the Missouri and Heart rivers, and Fort Lincoln, which they had just left. After a moment Goose turned the map around until it was comfortable to his eye, and then began to tell the interpreter, Louis Agard, how they had come and where they would be going on the next day. But this, he said, pointing to the Cannonball River, was not right; he took a pencil, corrected the river's course, and added some tributaries. Then he came to the marking for Slim Buttes—off by fifty miles. He grunted dismissal at this gross error and pushed the map aside. Custer conceded Goose might be right. "That map," he said, "was made before anybody ever went there, and the men didn't know anything about it except what the Indians told them."

Goose replied, "The Indians were white Indians, I guess. You can make another map when you go there with me."

"Yes, that is what we are going for," said Custer. "I will give you a map if you would like one."

Goose pointed to his head. "My map is here," he said with pride.[5]

During their first ten days of travel across the plains, Goose told Custer a story much like Fast Thunder's, about a spirit cave and an old man with a long white beard, "without beginning of days or end of years," who lived in the cave and occasionally emerged. The cave was in the side of a butte north of the Black Hills which the Sioux called "the place where the man was killed by the cow," meaning a buffalo cow. On the walls of the cave, he said, were sacred writings and drawings; people went there to pray and to make sacrifices. Sometimes northern Indians going south to hunt left offerings in the hope of success in the chase.[6] Goose called the cave by the Lakota word *wasun*, which whites understood to mean either "hole in the ground" or "spirit cave."[7] A hole it was, but not just any hole.

About midday on July 11, Goose pointed out the butte in the distance and then led Custer and a party of officers and scouts a final ten miles across open prairie until they came to some wooded slopes. Some of the other scouts—Bloody Knife, Bear's Ears, Cold Hand—rushed up one ravine after another looking for the cave until Goose halted, wordless, and pointed down toward a dark recess. Custer and the others rushed up excitedly but were disappointed. What they saw wasn't a cave exactly but a kind of narrow crevice reaching back a few hundred feet into the mountain. There were drawings on the walls of the crevice and numerous small objects left among the rocks: beads, arrows and arrowheads, a knife, a gold ring with the initials "A.L." It was the report of drawings and writings which had excited the whites in Goose's account. Perhaps they were expecting something like Egyptian hieroglyphics. What they found was classic Indian rock art. It struck the newspaper correspondent William Curtis as being

> like the tracery of school children on the walls of a country school house. There were pictures of deer, elk, and antelopes, bears and wolves, ponies and dogs . . . About eight feet high on one of the walls was the impression of a child's foot, half an inch deep in the stone, and as perfect as if it had been molded by a skillful sculptor. Near it were a couple of hands in the same style . . . There were other marks quite as singular . . . but nothing that could be attributed to anything more than average human skill.

Curtis was not alone in his disappointment. Another correspondent, James B. Power, writing in the *St. Paul Daily Pioneer,* found the drawings "all rather rude in design and execution." The whites were much more interested in a skull found nearby with what appeared to be a bullet hole in the forehead. The surgeons accompanying the expedition, Doctors S. J. Allen and J. W. Williams, concluded that it was the skull of a white man.[8] A lively debate followed about the circumstances of the victim's death—doubtless a pioneer or soldier, some said, brought here by Indians to be tortured. Others said no; Indians tortured their victims by burning them. Soon they were making jokes.

Goose said nothing. In his view, the drawings and markings on the walls of the cave were *wakan*—mysterious and powerful—but the whites only shrugged. "He stood at the entrance a few moments," wrote Curtis, "and looked at them silently, then turned away and never came near the place again."

The members of the party all picked up souvenirs from the offerings left by the Indians and then wandered back down the hillside. Custer took the rusty remains of a flintlock pistol, the wood long since rotted away. He abandoned his plan to devote a whole day to exploring the cave and decided instead to press on. But in Custer's mind Goose had proved himself all the same: he told them where the cave was and then he led them directly to it.

Among the scouts Goose was something of an anomaly—older than the rest, long separated from his own people. There was talk of some rift or crime; the newspaper correspondents with Custer were unsure of the details. Something at any rate had persuaded Goose to join the Hunkpapas at the Standing Rock Agency near Fort Yates. His exile from the Yanktonai gave him something in common with Bloody Knife and Bear's Ears, who had both at different times left their own people to live with traditional enemies. Bloody Knife, whose father was Hunkpapa, had gone to live with his mother's people in the mid-1850s, the Arickarees, commonly called the Rees. Bear's Ears, fleeing humiliation in love, spent seven years with the Sioux before returning to the Rees.[9] Both men had fresh reason to be bitter enemies of the Sioux; in mid-June, shortly before Custer's expedition set out for the Black Hills, a Sioux war party from Standing Rock had attacked the Ree village at Berthold on the upper Missouri, killing a Mandan and five Rees. Among the dead were a son of Bloody Knife and a brother of Bear's Ears.[10]

But these recent losses only suggest the depth of enmity felt by Rees generally for the Sioux, who had attacked them relentlessly since the 1780s, until a surviving remnant was confined to a single village of earthmound houses on the Missouri. The Rees on the expedition with Custer had come seeking war; when signs of a small Sioux band were discovered in the Black Hills on July 26, they excitedly stripped for battle, painted themselves and their horses, and began to sing their war songs.

"General Custer caught Bloody Knife's eye," Curtis wrote, "and gave him a significant nod."

But a significant nod was not enough. "In fact," wrote James Power, "it was with the greatest difficulty that they could be restrained from an attack on the village at once, and [they] gave every indication of being in a bad humor with the general . . . 'Do not dare to fire a shot unless the Sioux attack you,' was General Custer's reply to their mutterings."[11]

Soon a wisp of smoke suggested a camp ahead; Custer sent Bloody

Knife and twenty-five Rees to reconnoiter with explicit orders to avoid a fight. The Rees restrained themselves, found and reported a small camp of five lodges, and waited for Custer to come up with his interpreter, Louis Agard.

There had been much talk in the newspapers that Custer's expedition was violating the Treaty of 1868 and would trigger a big fight. Vague reports suggested that thousands of warriors were waiting in the hills to attack him, and it was generally believed by everyone riding with the general, soldiers and civilians alike, that a fight was more likely than not. But what Bloody Knife found was only a small group of Oglala, twenty-seven in all, hunting and cutting lodgepoles in the Black Hills before going back to the Red Cloud Agency a hundred miles to the south. They had no idea soldiers were near. Aris Donaldson, observing with binoculars, described a scene of peaceful serenity:

> I must confess that the encampment looks beautiful, as we saw it through our glasses. The white buckskins newly tanned, that covered the lodge poles, were as white as an officer's tent before it comes in contact with storm or sunshine. The squaws seated on the ground cutting up deer meat, others eating and some beading moccasins, the young Indians lying around in every attitude enjoying their freedom and the sunshine, and the dogs, lying in the shade of a teepee, were happy.

The approach of Custer's interpreter, followed by some of the scouts, sent the Indians running. The only man in the camp when Custer arrived was Slow Bull, "a tall, slim fellow, with sharp features and piercing gray eyes." One of his two wives was a daughter of Red Cloud.[12] Curtis and the others agreed that Slow Bull resembled to an amazing degree a Democratic politician of the day named Dan Voorhees.

Slow Bull had heard nothing about the expedition. Over a pipe, Custer said he had been sent by the Great Father not to fight, but to look around while making a map of the Sioux country. Slow Bull offered to help and called out to the women and children, who cautiously emerged from their hiding places in the brush. He sent one of them after the other men out hunting and soon they appeared, too—Long Arm, Long Bear, Young Wolf, and the chief of the band, One Stab, "an old man with a dilapidated felt hat which would have branded him as a pauper anywhere, a breech-clout and colored cotton agency shirt," according to Samuel Barrows, one of the reporters. Curtis agreed that One Stab was old, "at least 70, I should think." Soon the other men appeared. All gathered to talk with Custer in Slow Bull's lodge, where Red Cloud's daughter gave them cool springwater to drink. "A not uncomely squaw she was," wrote Barrows, who later became a minister, "with a broad full face and a straight nose, a little hooked at the end, long black hair braided into a pair of 'tails,' dark bright eyes, and a fine set of teeth, which just then were composedly chewing the gum of the pine tree."[13]

The conversation which followed was friendly in a stiff and cautious way. All the realities of frontier life were in play. Custer was intruding on Sioux land, not the other way around, and he came with nearly a thousand men, a hundred wagons, a rifled cannon, and three Gatling guns. A Gatling was a primitive form of machine gun, clumsy but lethal, with multiple barrels that fired rapidly with the turn of a hand-driven crank. Through his interpreter Custer said he came in peace, but he wanted Slow Bull and the other men to act as guides, and he expected them to snap to.

Just beneath the polite talk were suspicion and fear—by the Sioux of attack by Custer's Rees, by the whites that the Indians would run off. None of the whites knew anything about the Indians. Two years earlier the "pauper" One Stab and Slow Bull had both gone with a delegation led by Red Cloud to Washington, where they met President Grant and were photographed by Alexander Gardner. In addition, One Stab, more generally known as Stabber, was a noted chief and a leading man at both of the agencies on the White River in Nebraska. The American Horse and Cloud Shield winter counts both record the death of a probable grandfather about 1783 and it was likely Stabber's father who met Lewis and Clark on their overland journey in 1804.[14] Born before 1810 (if Curtis's guess at his age was right), Stabber met Francis Parkman near Fort Laramie in August 1846, but irritated the young traveler by telling him, "as vaguely and as unconnectedly as a child,"[15] of an American victory over "the Spaniards" in the Mexican war. Parkman was usually astute and sympathetic, but on this occasion he failed to note what was remarkable: Stabber brought his news from the Santa Fe Trail along the Arkansas River, hundreds of miles to the south, and he was reporting the outcome of an opening battle of the war with Mexico before officials at Fort Laramie knew anything about it. Twenty years later, at Fort Phil Kearny in January 1868, now a chief in his own right, Stabber addressed white officials negotiating an end to the Bozeman Trail War:

> Send word to the Great Father to take away his warriors with the snow, and he will please us ... We are talking today on our own grounds. God Almighty made this ground, and ... he made it for us. Look about you, see

how he has stocked it with game . . . Your homes are in the east, and you have beef cattle to eat. Why then, do you come here to bother us . . . If you will go away to your homes and leave us, then we will be at peace; but if you stay, we will fight. We do not go to your homes; then why come to ours?[16]

In the Black Hills in 1874, Stabber, an old man half naked (as the whites saw it) in his shirt and breechcloth, did his best to placate Custer, proceeding through the litany of assurances often cited by Indians upon meeting whites in force.

[I]f you want me to send one of my young men today I can do it, I can show you the way clear up this creek here; and then you can go yourselves. I do not want to have any trouble with the white man; I have always been with the white man; I never stayed with the hostiles . . . When I meet a big chief like you I always tell him the best I can. My children were all much scared today because the Rees came; they would not have been afraid of the whites.[17]

Later that day the Oglala men all came to Custer's camp, where they were given sugar, coffee, bacon, and hardtack. But midway through the visit Slow Bull slipped away and did not return. Custer wanted the Oglala as scouts and announced he would send a detail of a dozen men back with the others "to protect their camp."[18] But Stabber and the Oglala named Long Bear[19] mounted and started off before the guard detail was ready to move. Custer immediately dispatched Goose and one of the Santee, a man named Red Bird, to overtake the three men and bring them back. On reaching the Oglala, Red Bird grabbed the bridle of Long Bear's horse, insisting he return to Custer's camp. The Oglala seized the Santee's gun, saying, "I may as well be killed today as tomorrow."[20]

They wrestled for the gun; the Santee fell or jumped to the ground and the young Oglala took off at a run. The Santee had time for one shot, but Long Bear disappeared into the trees.

Stabber was not so quick and was forcibly returned to the soldiers' camp, where Custer was now angry. He accused Stabber of being a liar after learning that the rest of the Oglala broke camp and disappeared while the chief and his men were eating hardtack and drinking coffee with Custer. All pretense of peace was now abandoned and Bloody Knife was sent off with a body of scouts to find the fleeing Indians. Five hours later they were heard returning, howling with anger and disappointment at coming back empty-handed, with neither men nor scalps.

Wrote Barrows,

> The next day our scouts while out hunting discovered the saddle, blankets, and equipments of the Indian at whom our Santee had shot. He had evidently thrown them off to lighten his pony. The saddle and blanket were covered with blood . . . The ball had probably entered the man's thigh and passed out in front of the saddle, inflicting possibly only a flesh wound.[21]

It was possible, but not likely. The heavy lead bullet of the 1873 caliber Springfield trapdoor carbine which the scouts carried was flattish on the nose and big enough to leave a wound you could plug with a corn cob. Chances are that Long Bear was lucky to live. But he did; two years later he was drawing pay as a scout for the U.S. Army.

The fleeing Oglala hurried south to the agencies with alarmed reports of their encounter with Custer's expedition in the Black Hills. During the first week of August word reached Fort Laramie from the Red Cloud and Spotted Tail agencies that "large numbers of Indians coming in from the north . . . say that Stabber . . . and several others were killed by Custer's men."[22] The reports were wrong. It appears that no one was killed. Stabber was held prisoner for three days to serve as guide, then released by Custer's order to rejoin his people. What really hurt and lingered was not the casualty count, but the sense of violation. Whites, accustomed to putting a price on things, never understood the intensity of Sioux feeling for the Black Hills. Lieutenant G. K. Warren had been right in 1857: the Sioux would fight before they would give up the Black Hills.

The prospect of a big fight with the Sioux did not trouble Custer. On the way back across the plains to Fort Abraham Lincoln, when the expedition reached the Little Missouri River, they discovered "the abandoned camp of an immense village of Indians," according to Luther North, who rode most days alongside the young Yale student George Bird Grinnell. North had shown up Custer once or twice in shooting matches with Grinnell as witness. "I don't think he liked it very well," North wrote later. The night they reached the Little Missouri a small group was conversing in front of the general's tent. "It was perhaps just as well that they [the Indians] were gone before we got there," said North to the company—"there were a lot of them."

Custer dismissed the remark. "I could whip all the Indians in the northwest with the Seventh Cavalry," he said.[23]

———

Custer was irritated by his unsatisfactory encounter with the Sioux, and naturally insisted it wasn't his fault: "[T]he Indians have their own bad faith as the sole ground for the collision," he wrote in his official report.[24] The expedition pressed on. The going was not easy. In later years Goose described the trek to a young mixed-blood woman, Josephine Waggoner:

> The road was very difficult to travel over . . . As I talked with Goose about this trip, he told me that many times the expedition had to stop to make a road up and down impassable gulches, ditches and river banks, sometimes letting the wagons down steep banks with chains hitched to mules . . . The scouts had to do a lot of hard riding, back and forth to pick out the best places for the wagons to follow . . . but Goose had been in the hills before and he knew where the travois trails led into the heart of the hills.[25]

What was the goal of all this effort? The young paleontologist George Grinnell was looking for fossils, the geologist N. H. Winchell was looking for interesting rock formations, the engineer and topologist Captain William H. Ludlow was making the map of which Custer spoke so frequently, the botanist Aris B. Donaldson was cataloging plants (fifty-two along Cold Spring Creek alone), the correspondents were hoping for a story, and everybody was seeking game, which abounded. What gave this extended ride in the park a place in American history was the desire for gold, subject of speculation and rumors for years.

"I was talking to an old miner the other day about the probabilities of finding gold here," Curtis wrote wistfully in the *Inter-Ocean* in late July, "and he thinks they are small."

All knew it was a possibility; all felt it was fading away. Custer, some said at his own expense, had recruited two miners to accompany the expedition, old hands named Horatio Ross and William McKay. Both men, Curtis wrote, "have been worth fortunes as many times as they have toes." They got lucky again on the morning of August 2 when they washed out traces of gold in the gravel bed of French Creek.

Goose was a witness. He had watched the whites shrug off the mysteries of the spirit hole. That bored them. Now he saw the reaction of the whites to the discovery of gold—a few yellow specks at the bottom of a pan of water and gravel:

> One very hot day a lot of the soldiers went in the creek to cool off. Goose said he was repicketing his horse. Just then, the soldiers started yelling. Some of them threw up their hats. Some laughed. Some were crying. Oth-

ers were running in circles. Others were jumping up and down. There was the greatest confusion he ever saw. One man had something in his hand. As fast as this man showed what he had to the others they went just as crazy as the others. Goose could not understand for a long time that these men had discovered gold.[26]

Curtis soon added details about the first strike:

[T]he two persevering men . . . came into camp with a little yellow dust wrapped carefully up in the leaf of an old account book. It was examined with the microscope; was tried with all the tests that the imagination of fifteen hundred excited campaigners could suggest, and it stood every one. It was washed with acid, mixed with mercury, cut, chewed and tasted, till everybody was convinced and went to bed dreaming of the wealth of Croesus. At daybreak there was a crowd around the "diggins" . . . And those were few who didn't get a "showing"—a few yellow particles clinging to a globule of mercury.[27]

Reports varied as to the richness of the find; some said it was ten cents to the pan, some fifteen, some even more. But it was Curtis who coined the phrase that swept the country when it appeared under a one-word headline—GOLD!—in the *Inter-Ocean* on August 27: "From the grass roots down," he wrote, "it was 'pay dirt.' "

An aide-de-camp sent on the expedition by General Sheridan was also struck by the phrase; Ross and McKay must have used it. From Bear Butte on Saturday, August 15, Major George Forsyth wrote Sheridan, "The two miners we have with us tell me . . . that, in their opinion, when the eastern hills are rightly prospected, gold will be found there in abundance. I am inclined to think so, for the very roots of the grass would pan 5 cents to the pan in our camp near Harney's Peak."[28]

Times were hard in the United States; the Panic of 1873 had triggered a depression which lingered. "Gold from the grass roots down"—wealth to be picked up as easily as a coin in the street—a way out for desperate men: it was clear where this was going. Before year's end prospectors, speculators, dreamers, and the merely out-of-work were hurrying their way in thousands to Fort Pierre east of the Black Hills on the Missouri River; to Sidney, Nebraska, directly south of the hills on the Union Pacific Railroad line; and to Cheyenne, Wyoming, called by its boosters "the magic city," which was the most direct jumping-off place for the new goldfields.

One awkward fact stood in the way of a full-scale gold rush. The Fort

Laramie treaty had given the Black Hills to the Sioux in perpetuity, and all whites were barred from entry. For a year after Custer's expedition the military tried, vigorously at first, to block whites from the hills or to expel those who had slipped through. But then a different approach was conceived: to buy the hills from the Sioux, or, failing that, to rewrite the Treaty of 1868, compelling the Indians to sign whether they wanted to or not. Red Cloud and Spotted Tail were summoned to Washington in May 1875 to hear the president's views. The *Cheyenne Daily Leader,* which expected boom times as soon as the hills were opened to whites, stated the matter plainly:

> If they decide in conformance with the suggestions of the president, all will be well. They will be voted good Indians and will be voted appropriations to buy food and clothing for years to come . . . But there is no more foolishness to be tolerated in red men. They might as well . . . agree to sell out and go south. If they will not do this, then look out for lively times with the Indians . . . Of the result all may feel sanguine. The Indians will have to accept the president's terms.[29]

"I do not like General Custer and all his men going into the Black Hills," Red Cloud said within days of the first newspaper headlines. He was a careful, thoughtful kind of man. The invasion of the Black Hills remained on his mind all that fall. He did not like or trust the Oglala agent, J. J. Saville, so he told the commander at Fort Laramie privately that he wanted to visit Washington to talk about the hills. The commander was already finding difficulty in keeping whites out of the area. He passed on Red Cloud's request with his endorsement, and Washington, with its own agenda taking form, soon responded with an invitation. When Saville gave Washington's invitation to Red Cloud it was Billy Garnett, about to turn twenty, who did the interpreting.[30]

Red Cloud, always conscious of the danger of getting out in front of his people, now told Saville he wanted a big group of chiefs to go, perhaps as many as fifty, and urged that even Black Twin (Holy Bald Eagle) and Crazy Horse be included. General Sheridan in Chicago had never heard the name of either man. Red Cloud sent couriers to the north and Saville soon wrote Washington that both chiefs were promising to come, although neither one, he believed, had ever been to an agency or attended a council with whites. As spring approached Crazy Horse and Black Twin did not say no, but they did not show up, either, and the delegation left in

May without them. With the chiefs went a large contingent of inter-preters—not just the men working for the agents, Billy Garnett, Leon Palladay, and Louis Bordeaux, but also several men whom Red Cloud and Spotted Tail wanted as interpreters, Louis Richard, Nick Janis, and Todd Randall.

The problem facing President Grant's administration was brutally simple at the core: how to extinguish, in the preferred word of officials, Sioux title to the Black Hills before white miners simply flooded into the gold country, treaty be damned, and sparked a general Indian war. But the government had a political flank it needed to watch. An alert audience in the east of clerics, "friends of the Indian," and former abolitionists, ready to take up a new cause, closely scrutinized the Indian Department. The government tried at first to buy or lease the hills, but from whom? This was never quite thought through. The 1868 treaty granted possession of the hills to "the Sioux," but that included the northern bands who had never signed the treaty, never lived at an agency, never took government rations or annuities. These northerners insisted nobody else had the right to sell their claim to the hills. And what about the price? The Indians all understood why the whites were eager to buy the hills—gold had been found there. Those willing to sell wanted to get a lot for the hills, without really knowing what "a lot" might be.

But the difficulty with the deepest roots was Washington's ambivalence about the true nature of a sale or a lease. An owner, if he is really the owner, is free to say no, or to ask a price no buyer will meet. This freedom the government was not actually willing to concede to the Sioux. Grant was not sentimental about Indian rights. He did not recognize any Sioux right to hold on to the Black Hills. He had made up his mind, and to the Indians he made his views plain. As soon as they reached Washington they were informed that the government wished to remove them to Indian territory. The southern Cheyenne had already been forced to set-tle there, and the Sioux understood this would mean complete loss of freedom and their hunting way of life. It was Grant, personally, who uttered the fatal "or else" looming behind the government's offer to buy the hills. In the White House on May 26 he told the Indians that Wash-ington had not promised to feed them forever. If the Indians refused to sell the hills, if white gold seekers poured into the area, if fighting fol-lowed, then inevitably the government would stop delivering beef to the agencies. Grant and the chiefs both knew that meant the Indians would starve. The threat in his words was unmistakable: sell the hills or starve.

"I want you to think of what I have said," Grant concluded. "I don't want you to say anything today. I want you to talk among yourselves . . . This is all I want to say to you."[31]

But the Indians refused to be bullied into signing a treaty. The chiefs dug in their heels and would not even discuss selling the Black Hills until they had a chance to talk to the people left at home. Back they went in mid-June. Congress, meanwhile, created a commission to press for sale of the hills and appointed Iowa Senator William Allison to run it.[32] A legal sale would require agreement by three-quarters of Sioux men, including those who lived in the north. Hoping to strike a deal within the rules, the Allison commission in the summer of 1875 sent out a delegation to invite the northern Indians to a grand council on the White River in September. Led by Young Man Afraid of His Horses, the delegation of about seventy-five Oglala and Brulé men left the agencies in July, following the well-established road north to the Buffalo Gap and through the hills to the hunting grounds along the Powder and Tongue rivers. With the delegation went two interpreters, evidently as official observers in order to report after their return to the Allison commission. One of the two was the mixed-blood son of old John Richard, Louis Richard, a man called nephew by Red Cloud. With him was a man new to the whites but well known to the northern Indians—the long-haired, dark-skinned, Sioux-speaking, still-buckskin-clad, just-arrived-from-nowhere Sandwich Islander, Frank Grouard.

7

"We don't want any white men here."

IT WAS ALONG THE Tongue River that Louis Richard and Frank Grouard encountered the big camp of the Indians whom the military, depending on the mood of the day, had begun to cite interchangeably as "Northern Indians," "non-agency Indians," or "hostiles."[1] The military thought that gathered in one place they might number as many as five hundred warriors, not more. A better guess in midsummer 1875, as Richard and Grouard reported in August, would have been nineteen hundred lodges with eight or nine thousand people and two thousand fighting men.[2] A big midsummer village like this one would not maintain the same population for two days running; some of the people might linger in a favored spot for weeks, all might depart in a day. Half at least would expect to spend the winter at an agency. It was the task of Young Man Afraid of His Horses to persuade some of them—with luck all—to follow him back down the travois road to the Red Cloud Agency, where the Allison commission hoped to convince three of every four adult males to touch the pen and agree to sell the Black Hills.

The leading men of the northern bands were all in the camp on the Tongue River—Sitting Bull and Black Moon of the Hunkpapas, Lone Horn of the Miniconjou, Crazy Horse and Black Twin of the Oglala, and a great many others besides. They had come together for the annual sun dance, held when the sage was in bloom. When Young Man Afraid and his delegation arrived the northern Indians were preparing a war expedition. Chances are good they were planning a raid on the Ute, who had stolen many Sioux horses that winter, or on the Crow, who were under constant pressure by the Sioux in those years. No year passed without Sioux war parties going out in midsummer to fight the Crow.

As gifts, Young Man Afraid's delegation brought fifty Indian ponies and tobacco, the traditional gesture of peaceful intent, but they found the northern Indians in an angry mood. Some evidently resented the invitation from the *wasicu* and wanted to send Young Man Afraid's delegation back south with a good soldiering or worse. Years later, Grouard told his biographer that he had gone directly to the lodge of Crazy Horse to tell him the whites wanted to talk to him down along the White River. The chief told Grouard tersely, "I don't want to go." He said he would rather fight than make a treaty. But he added that others were free to go if they liked; he would not try to stop them. Next Grouard went to see Sitting Bull, who volunteered little while he tried to get Grouard to say much. The two men had not met since their angry break the previous year, and Sitting Bull now felt betrayed anew by Grouard's arrival bearing messages from the white soldiers. While Grouard was making his rounds, Waglula, the father of Crazy Horse, went out through the camp to cry the news, urging people to listen to what the visitors had come to say.[3]

The following day a large council gathered to consider the request to travel three hundred miles south to the Red Cloud Agency. Treaty meetings always involved big feeds at U.S. government expense, and sometimes presents were given out as well, but the northern Indians were not tempted. According to Grouard, who has left the only detailed account of the discussion, as many as a hundred Indians had something to say. There was nothing casual about a gathering of the Sioux in council to discuss an important matter. In 1857 the Sioux had all met near Bear Butte, where they decided on a common policy of fighting to keep whites out of the northern hunting grounds.[4] Red Cloud was always cautious about breaking ranks with the other Oglala chiefs; before signing the Treaty of 1868 he met in council frequently with Old Man Afraid, Black Twin, Lone Horn, and others to be sure they were ready to end the war. Councils were large public affairs where every leading man was entitled to a place in the circle and the rest of the tribe gathered around to listen.

Before the talking could begin there would be an elaborate pipe ceremony. To smoke together was a gesture of harmony, the tobacco itself represented a kind of gift or sacrifice, and the rising of the smoke in the air was thought to carry the words spoken in council to the spirit being above. The bowl of the pipe was traditionally in the shape of an inverted capital T, carved from a soft red stone quarried in Minnesota. A pipe's wooden stem, as much as three feet in length, was usually made of ash with the pith burned out in latter years with a hot wire. The flattish stem was often carved with a bas-relief figure of a turtle and the head of a buffalo, deer, mountain sheep, or elk. Wrapped around the stem might be porcupine quillwork, horse-hair dangles, bits of fur, and owl, hawk, or eagle feathers. A slender wooden tamper, painted and decorated, would be used to pack the bowl before lighting the tobacco with a hot coal. Pipes were one of the few objects which both Sioux men and women participated in making. The carving was done by men, the beading or quillwork by women. Every step in preparing the pipe for smoking was accompanied by prayers asking for guidance, for pity from the spirit being, for a blue day in which to accomplish the business at hand. The pipe stem would be directed first to the ground—that is, to Grandmother Earth, Unci—then to the four directions, and finally to the spirit being above, addressed as Tunkasila.

The last step in preparing for the council was to smoke the pipe, starting with the man in charge of its preparation, who then passed it to his left. When it came around the far side to the end of the circle it was not simply handed on to the man in charge, but sent back around the circle the way it had come. Even the very act of drawing a puff on the pipe was formal and measured. An Army wife who witnessed a circle of Oglala smoking at a council in Nebraska in February 1875 found it strangely fastidious: "They didn't seem to take the mouthpiece in their mouths . . . only to hold it to their lips with a kind of kissing sound as they puffed." Two or three puffs were enough; then the pipe was handed on.[5] In keeping with the drawn-out ceremony the language that followed was sober and measured. In this way a people quick to fight established a mood of deliberation and restraint, and ensured that important decisions would be supported by consensus.

The chiefs invited Louis Richard to tell them why he had come. Richard explained the desire of the whites to buy the Black Hills, translating as he spoke from a letter that had been given to him. Big Breast spoke first and put the Oglala case in its stark form: "All those that are in favor of selling their land from their children, let them go." Sitting Bull was flatly opposed. "I want you to go and tell the Great Father that I do not want to sell or lease any land to the governement," he said, "—not even as much as this."

He reached down to pick up a pinch of dirt, holding it for all to see.

At this point one of the Indians in the crowd angrily snatched away the letter Richard had been translating, crumpled it up, and threw it in the fire. Just as quickly another Indian pulled it out and said, "Don't do things hastily. We want to consider them. Don't destroy anything like that." He smoothed out the paper and handed it back to Richard. If anyone argued in favor of selling the Black Hills, there is no record of it. Little Hawk, speaking as he often did for his silent nephew Crazy Horse, joined the majority in refusing to leave the Tongue River hunting grounds: "My friends," he said, "the other tribes have concluded not to go in, and I will have to say the same thing."[6]

But it was not just determination to hold the Black Hills that kept the northern Indians from going south to meet with Senator Allison. He Dog's brother Short Bull explained that "it was late and they had to shoot for tipis"—meaning that it was midsummer, the buffalo had shed all the previous winter's fur, and their tanned hides were ideal for making lodge covers, an annual task. That took precedence. According to Short Bull it was generally agreed that "they would come in to the agency the following spring."[7]

It is apparent that feelings on the matter ran the full spectrum: some of the Indians were implacably hostile to talks with the whites, while others said not now, but maybe later. And some, for varying reasons, were ready to go back with Young Man Afraid. Over the next three days those who desired to go crossed from the northern to the southern bank of the Tongue to camp with the delegation from the south. Grouard said that hotheads in Crazy Horse's camp wanted to attack them but the chief intervened. In his view, visitors entering the camp in peace should be given food, water, and a chance to smoke. One by one, addressing each by name, Crazy Horse told those preparing to fight, "My friends, whoever attempts to murder these people will have to fight me, too."[8]

Things blew over; Young Man Afraid led his delegation back to the agencies on the White River in early August. He reported that some northern Indians had promised to follow in time for the meeting with the commissioners; how many, in what mood, he could not say. But the broad answer delivered by Young Man Afraid and the interpreters to the white officials—not just the members of the Allison commission but also the Army's new commander in chief (since March) of the Department of the Platte, General George Crook—was not promising. Who could find a whisper of hope for a deal in the proud, even lordly words of Sitting Bull, as quoted by the interpreter Louis Richard?

> Are you the great god that made me, or was it the Great God that made me who sent you? If he asked me to come see him, I will go, but the big chief of the white men must come see me. I will not go to the reservation. I have no land to sell. There is plenty of game here for us. We have enough ammunition. We don't want any white men here.[9]

We don't want any white men here.

Keeping their distance from whites was the bedrock of northern policy. They fought to keep whites out of the Powder River country in the Bozeman War, they never signed the Treaty of 1868, never lived at an agency, never took government rations or annuities. Their dislike of whites was visceral, and in many ways mirrored white dislike of Indians. A leading man among the northern Indians, the Sans Arc chief High Bear, born about 1840, much later attempted to explain the origin and nature of this hostility:

> When the tribe first mingled with the whites, the braves [that is, the *akicita* or camp police, also called soldiers] would not sanction it because they did not wish to eat the white man's food and the white man would eat all their buffalo. If the braves discovered anyone going among the white people they would intercept him and kill him and his horse. They were afraid that the smell of coffee and bacon (foreign smells) would scare the buffalo and make them stay away. However, they would allow the white traders to come in and bring merchandise but would not buy foods that created a peculiar smell. They did not want the *wakpamni*, the government issue, and did not want the white people coming in.[10]

Nothing strange is sensed more quickly than a difference in smell. It is one of the first things people note about each other. White women, especially, were offended and even frightened by the smell of Indians. "They are so dreadfully dirty," Caroline Frey Winne wrote home from Sidney, Nebraska, in March 1875. Winne was stationed with her husband, Charles, an Army surgeon, at the Sidney Barracks on the Union Pacific Railroad line. Indians hunting south of the Platte frequently camped for a time near Sidney in the hope of trade. Winne recoiled when she encountered them in the streets. Indians filled her with terror—not fear of rape or murder, exactly, but of *them*—their painted faces, the animal skins in which they wrapped themselves, what they ate, their words like grunts, "their nasty little papooses," their relentless begging, their desire to touch, their frank curiosity about *her*.

> It was not pleasant to say the least to look up and find your windows darkened by "Lo" and his brethren and wives and children, their dirty painted faces pressed close to the glass. They are poor miserable creatures. It would be a great *mercy* to them if they would all freeze to death as *many* of them have this winter.[11]

This aside is breathtakingly coldhearted. It is also surprising. Winne was educated, devoted to her family back home, tried to keep current with the civilized world by subscribing to the *New York Tribune* and *Scribner's Monthly*, complaining that "reading matter is scarce here." She disliked the town of Sidney—"nothing but whiskey and vice and wickedness"— and keenly missed the gentle Sundays of her early life. "I haven't been inside a church or heard a sermon since I left home," she wrote her brother. And yet she allowed herself to wish on paper that the Indians would *all die*, an expression almost of panic. "They are the most horrible looking creatures I ever saw," she wrote. To call them creatures was to deny they were human. One afternoon, she reported,

> Charlie and I . . . saw six of them coming out of Captain Hawley's quarters . . . I stood my ground . . . in mortal fear that they would all want to shake hands but they passed by. One was a chief, Red Fly. He nodded and said, "How be you, Doctor?" They are dreadful beggars.

The Oglala chief Red Fly had shaken hands with President Grant in Washington during Red Cloud's first trip in 1870. A few days after the chance encounter with Red Fly, Charlie Winne met Two Lance, a leading man in Little Wound's band of Cut-off Oglala, noted for his strength. In 1872, a member of a group of Brulé Sioux hunting in Kansas with Grand Duke Alexis of Russia, Two Lance had driven an arrow entirely through a buffalo at the request of Spotted Tail. The grand duke kept the arrow as a souvenir. Caroline Winne did not know these things about the chiefs she met in Sidney. To her, "the chiefs look no better than the others,"[12] and the others were nasty, dirty, and foul-smelling.

It was smell that seemed to bother whites most. Many found the smell of Indians strong, sharp, clinging, rank. They blamed it on ignorance of soap, or on the Indians' practice of greasing themselves with animal oils. Early travelers reported that Indians used the entrails of raccoons or polecats (meaning skunks) for this purpose. Lydia Waters, who crossed the plains in 1855, said Indians "took the greatest comfort lying in the sun rubbing themselves with these greasy insides." It was true; Indians did use animal oils—bear fat to make their hair glisten, other oils and fats to heal scratches and rashes, or to repel insects, or to protect against magic. The Sioux believed, for example, that gophers were dangerous animals and could shoot their stiff, bristly whiskers into the necks of people who got too close. If left untreated, the throat would grow hoarse and raw; the cure at that stage was to take the fat of a dead badger and rub it over the skin.[13] Arapaho women treated their hair at night with the oil that melted in a marrow bone left upright close to the fire; they braided the hair tightly before sleep, then shook it out in the morning for the "wavy appearance."[14] White women did not understand these things, or care. The Army wife Francis Roe came west full of romantic notions about Indians; she thought they would all be noble red men like the Seneca chief Red Jacket once met by Roe's grandmother. The romance did not last. Indians, she wrote home in a letter, were "simply . . . painted, dirty and nauseous-smelling savages."[15]

It was commonly believed that horses, dogs, and old frontiersmen could smell the approach of Indians. The Army scout Baptiste Pourier not only believed it but demonstrated it. In May 1876, scouting for a column of cavalry heading north into the Powder River country, Pourier reported to Colonel Frederick Van Vliet that there were Indians ahead. The colonel asked how he knew. The scout replied, "Colonel, I smell them." Charles St. George Stanley, who was present as an artist and newspaper correspondent for *Frank Leslie's Illustrated Weekly*, later recorded,

> Everybody engaged in a regular old-fashioned sniff . . . everybody came to the conclusion that something did smell; it might have been a dead buffalo off on the prarie or it might have been a pair of dirty socks in someone's saddle bags, but our guide averred it was "Injun . . . nothing could smell like that but an Injun" . . . The wind was blowing directly in our faces and it certainly was laden with an odor resembling a mixture of smoked beef, muskrat and polecat.

Three miles further along they crossed a fresh trail left by a traveling group of Indians, one lodge and about fifteen people in all. St. George Stanley was writing for laughs in a manner typical for the time, but at the same time he was convinced. "It seems incredible but it was an actual fact that we had smelled a small party of these smoky creatures three miles away."[16] William Hooker, a driver of oxteams in the Fort Laramie country, said bullwhackers could all spot the odor of an Indian camp as they approached—"a smoky, burnt-leathery smell is the only way I can describe it."[17]

With the word "smoke" Stanley and Hooker approached the explanation. General Crook's aide, Lieutenant William Philo Clark, a naturalist by temperament, tried to pinpoint just what the smell *was*:

> Most Indians have a personal exhalation, a sort of characteristic halo of atmosphere, entirely unlike that which marks a negro, but in its way just as

strong, though less offensive, and which a government mule will trem-
blingly detect at a great distance. It is a pungent, musty odor, something like
that of combined smoke and grease.[18]

Others identified the smoke more exactly as the smoke from tipi fires, so
dense it was used to cure leather by hanging hides up near the smoke
hole. White doctors later speculated that it was smoke-filled tipis that
caused the blindness frequent among Indians as they aged. Ever present
as well were the smell of sweetgrass and sagebrush smoke, both used to
cleanse and purify. Others thought the smoky odor of Indians came from
kinnikinnick—the mixture of red willow bark, fragrant herbs and roots,
and the strong twist tobacco used in Indian pipes. "The smoke . . . made
a sweet and pleasant odor," wrote Captain J. Lee Humfreville, who
attended many meetings with Indians at Fort Laramie in 1868. "The
Indian's person and all his belongings were completely saturated with it,
and it lasted a long time. Horses, and particularly mules, whose sense of
smell is very acute, would scent an Indian by this odor at a long distance."[19]

Whites believed the characteristic Indian smell endured over time as
well as distance. In the spring of 1877, under circumstances to be related
later, Crazy Horse personally handed a ledger book containing eight
drawings to a high-spirited young reporter for the *Cheyenne Ledger* who
had been invited into his lodge. With Billy Garnett as interpreter, the
chief told the reporter, George P. Wallihan, that the drawings illustrated
war exploits in the career of a "famous warrior," but he declined to confirm that the warrior was himself. Through a long career Wallihan held
on to the small ledger book, only three and a half by eight inches. Forty
years later he typed up a brief account of the gift of the ledger book while
living in Pomona, California. He must have leaned over to give the book
a good sniff, because he concluded his account by remarking, "It still carries the Indian odor which was with it when I got it and does not yield to
fumigation." Nothing lingers like the smell of smoke. There is evidence
to suggest that what whites smelled when they smelled Indians was the
smell of smoke—of pipes, of smudges and tipi fires, of leather clothing
which had cured for days or weeks above a smoky fire.[20]

The point here is not smells sweet or sour, but difference—the unfa-
miliar that separated white and Indian. Difference worked both ways.
Some Sioux on first encounter did not like the smell of bacon or coffee.
Hardest to tolerate for the ten-year-old Brulé Sioux Ota Kte (Kills

Plenty), son of Standing Bear, was the smell of cattle, first encountered at the Spotted Tail Agency.

> One day we boys heard some of the men talking about going to the agency. They said the government had sent some spotted buffalo for the Indians. This was the name the Indians gave to the cows, there being no word in the Sioux tongue for the white men's cattle . . . So we got on our ponies and rode over to the agency with some of the men. What a terrible odor met us! It was awful! We had to hold our noses. Then I asked my father what was the matter around there, as the stench was more than I could stand. He told me it was the odor of the spotted buffalo. Then I asked him if we were going to be obliged to eat those terrible animals. "The white people eat them," was his reply.
>
> Now we had several white people around us, but they were all bald-headed. I began to wonder if they got that way from eating those vile-smelling cattle. I then recalled that buzzards were bald-headed, and they lived on carrion, and I began to feel sorry for the white people who had to live on such stuff.[21]

For the northern Indians who wanted nothing to do with whites visceral differences like smell were only the beginning. Still more important was resentment of white treatment of Indian women. White trappers and hunters in the early years often married Indian women, remained in the Indian country to raise their families, learned to speak the language, were counted as friends and relatives by the families of their wives. Spotted Tail and Red Cloud were both close to whites who had married their sisters, daughters, or nieces. In negotiating treaties with white officials the chiefs always insisted that white men with Indian wives along with their children should be treated as full-blood Sioux. But many whites beat or abused Indian women, exploited them sexually after capture in battle, and sometimes bought them for cheap trinkets and liquor and later cast them aside. Trouble often followed. In June 1867, at about the time he loaned the young Billy Garnett a revolver so he could protect his mother, the freighter and sometime storekeeper John Bratt woke one night to hear a drunken ranch hand beating an Indian girl he had just purchased for two ponies. "When I went to get my horse the next morning I came across the poor girl," Bratt wrote. "Her face was swollen and covered with blood, and one eye was swollen shut from his heavy blows." Later that day relatives of the girl returned, burned one of the ranch buildings, and carried off the woman beater, who was not seen again.[22]

White writers of the period were curiously transparent about the attractions of Indian women. Older women were dismissed as hags and harridans but many whites said frankly enough that the younger were appealing, or not bad looking, or pretty in their way. "A not uncomely squaw she was," the reporter Samuel Barrows had said of a daughter of Red Cloud encountered in the Black Hills. Whites rated the tribes by looks and accessibility. Cheyenne women were commonly believed to be unapproachable, Sioux women a bit easier, although the *Chicago Times* correspondent John F. Finerty reported in 1876 that "the girls of that race seldom yield to the seducer."[23] But with the Crow and Arapahos, by common report, it was liberty hall. "The Arapahoes do not hesitate to make merchandise of their women," wrote a correspondent for the *Chicago Tribune* in 1875, "and that, too, for almost anything, from a pup to a blanket."[24] Lieutenant Henry Lemly wrote that Friday, a well-known scout and leading man of the Arapahos, "was a pander of the vilest description," whose knowledge of English helped him keep busy at Camp Robinson and the Red Cloud Agency, where the Arapahos lived with the Oglala until the fall of 1877.[25] In fact, such arrangements were transactions, with willing buyers and willing sellers on either side. Even General Sheridan, when a lieutenant in the Rogue River country of Oregon, lived for a time with an Indian girl named Frances who taught him to speak Chinook.[26]

It was different in wartime, when whites simply took women as a spoil of war. After the Battle of Blue Water Creek in 1855 General William Harney drove a large number of captured Brulé Sioux from Little Thunder's band from central Nebraska to Fort Laramie in Wyoming. Among them, according to the mixed-blood writer Josephine Waggoner, were seventy women who were shared out among the soldiers. "The best-looking women were taken by the officers and there were many war orphans or fatherless half-breed children born among the captive women," Waggoner wrote. One of these exploited women was an aunt of Standing Bear taken by Harney himself, who fathered a girl. A grandson of Iron Shell, a Brulé chief who took part in the battle, said later, "Some of the Indian women got caught . . . After awhile they were released from the white people and they all came back pregnant. Some of the squaw women disappeared."[27]

No man was safe on the plains, and no Indian woman was safe in her village. In November 1868 the 7th Cavalry under General Custer—his rank was lieutenant colonel, but everyone, and especially his wife Libbie, called him General—led an expedition west of the Indian Territory looking for Cheyenne Indians. His orders from General Phil Sheridan were simple and unambiguous: "to destroy their villages and ponies; to kill or hang all warriors, and bring back all women and children."[28]

All was beyond Custer, but he did well enough in a dawn attack on a large village camped on the Washita River, a traditional wintering ground for Indians on the southern plains. In the battle which followed, lasting a couple of hours after a wild ten minutes for the initial charge, Custer's men killed 103 Cheyenne warriors, including their chiefs Black Kettle and Little Rock; captured fifty-three women and children; and killed more than eight hundred Cheyenne ponies. The ponies' throats were cut to save ammunition. Some of the men who witnessed the slaughter remembered the blood and shrieks of the horses for the rest of their lives. Among the captured women some refused treatment for their wounds, fearing they would be killed. Later, after reaching Custer's base at Camp Supply on the Canadian River in Oklahoma, they learned that Custer and his men had something different in mind. Raphael Romero, a Mexican who had learned the Cheyenne language while living in their camps, brought the youngest and prettiest of the captive women at night to visit the tents of the officers, who called the interpreter "Romeo." Cheyenne in later years reported that one of these women was the daughter of a chief killed on the Washita. Mo-nah-se-tah caught the eye of General Custer, they said, and eventually gave birth to his daughter.[29] Quite possibly this is true. It is certainly true that he told Sheridan he planned to take Mo-nah-se-tah and two other captive women with him when he went after the rest of the Cheyenne the following spring. When Custer and a few men, out in front, caught up with the Indians on Sweetwater Creek in mid-March 1869, Mo-nah-se-tah was with the main body of troops. There, according to Custer's own account, he told the chiefs it was surrender or else.

The southern Cheyenne remembered this encounter in a somewhat different light, as the solemn moment in which the white soldier they (like the Sioux) had begun to call Hi-es-tzie—Cheyenne for Long Hair—told the chiefs Medicine Arrow and Little Robe that agreement meant he would fight the Cheyenne no more. "I will never harm the Cheyennes again. I will never point my gun at a Cheyenne again."[30] This pledge or promise, as the Cheyenne remembered it, was delivered in council after a formal ritual of smoking together. All were seated on the ground in Medicine Arrow's lodge. On Custer's left was Medicine Arrow, on his right the medicine man preparing the pipe. Custer was wearing the high, brilliantly polished boots he favored. He lay his white hat on the ground beside him. His long hair, a fine, silky gold, fell back over his shoulders. It is unlikely Custer knew that Medicine Arrow was called so after his position as keeper of the sacred arrows given to the Cheyenne people by the spirit being on Bear Butte many years earlier, or that the arrows had been in Medicine Arrow's keeping since the killing of the previous keeper, Gray Thunder, about 1838. The Cheyenne name of Medicine Arrow was actually Stone Forehead, but it is unlikely Custer knew that, either. Nor did the general know that Medicine Arrow had invited him to sit directly beneath the sacred arrows, which were suspended high in the lodge from a forked stick.[31] On these arrows the Cheyenne believed their power and well-being depended; smoking in the proper way in the presence of these arrows guaranteed the words spoken.

Custer described the smoking in Medicine Arrow's lodge at length:

> From another buckskin pouch which hung at his girdle he [the man in charge of the pipe] drew forth a handful of *kinnikinnick*, and placed it on a cloth spread on the ground before him; to this he added, in various amounts, dried leaves and herbs, with which he seemed well supplied. After thoroughly mixing these ingredients, he proceeded with solemn ceremony to fill the pipe with the mixture, muttering at times certain incantations, by which no doubt it was intended to neutralize any power or proclivity for harm I may have been supposed to possess . . . My interest perceptibly increased when the medicine man, who was sitting close to me, extended his left hand and grasped my right, pressing it strongly against his body over the region of his heart, at the same time and with complete devoutness of manner engaging in what seemed to me a petition or prayer . . . Finally releasing my hand, the medicine man lighted a match, and applying it to the pipe made signs for me to smoke.[32]

According to George Bent, a mixed-blood who lived his entire life with the Cheyenne, it was Medicine Arrow who actually held the pipe while Custer smoked, saying to him in Cheyenne, "If you are acting treachery toward us, sometime you and your whole command will be killed."[33] But Mo-nah-se-tah and Custer's interpreter, Raphael Romero, were both absent, and the general had no idea what was being said. The ritual and prayers were all mumbo jumbo to him. Custer was not a smoker; he worried mainly, as he drew puff after puff, that the kinnikinnick would make him sick.

For the Cheyenne there was nothing perfunctory about this ceremony. In a dawn attack at the Washita Custer had already killed a hundred Cheyenne; Medicine Arrow and the other chiefs feared he might do it again and invoked the power of the sacred arrows, of prayers and spells, and of the specially prepared tobacco to guarantee Custer's promise of peace. The unusual ritual was described many years later by Magpie, a young man present during the ceremony. When the pipe was filled in the lodge where the sacred arrows were kept it was handed to Custer to smoke, as Magpie remembered it—not just the usual puff or two, but the entire bowlful of tobacco. Custer guessed it took him a quarter of an hour. When the general was done, and after the other chiefs had smoked as well, Medicine Arrow with his tobacco stick broke up the tobacco ashes in the bowl and then sprinkled them on Custer's boots. In the Cheyenne view that made the promise sacred and binding. Magpie related that the sprinkling of the ashes "made the peace pipe stronger . . . [it] meant that if he went contrary to the pipe again he would be destroyed like ashes." This was the significance of Medicine Arrow's words, which meant nothing to Custer.[34]

In the end many of the Indians followed Custer back to Camp Supply on the north fork of the Canadian River in the Oklahoma panhandle while some, including Magpie, went north to live with their relatives in the Tongue and Powder river country. By midsummer, Custer's 7th Cavalry returned to its then-permanent post at Fort Hays in Kansas, where the women and children captured on the Washita were imprisoned in a stockade. With Custer and the 7th came Mo-nah-se-tah, close to term with a baby daughter born that summer. Of that child Custer may or may not have been the father, but he and his wife Libbie both speak openly of the Cheyenne girl in memoirs, and stress her youth and beauty. It is hard not to feel that Custer was hiding Mo-nah-se-tah in plain sight, and that Libbie sensed some strong current of sexual connection between the two.

In his memoir, *My Life on the Plains*, Custer remarked that Mo-nah-se-tah "preferred to live in the cavalry camp, where she was allowed to roam without the restraint of a guard."[35] His brother Tom, a captain in the 7th, grew familiar enough with the girl to give her a nickname: Sallie-Ann. Libbie conceded that the girl had "the beauty of youth, whose dimples and curves and rounded outlines are always charming." But she disliked the looks of Indian women—"high cheekbones and square jaw being the prevailing type"[36]—and she was never quite free of the fear that Sallie-Ann carried a knife concealed in the folds of her dress and in a moment of anger might kill her or the general. Custer left little doubt how the girl struck him. He called her

> an exceedingly comely squaw, possessing a bright, cheery face, a countenance beaming with intelligence, and a disposition more inclined to be merry than one usually finds among the Indians. She was probably rather under than over twenty years of age. Added to bright, laughing eyes, a set of pearly teeth, and a rich complexion, her well-shaped head was crowned with a luxuriant growth of the most beautiful silken tresses, rivalling in color the blackness of the raven and extending, when allowed to fall loosely over her shoulders, to below her waist.[37]

Maybe Custer shared his soldier's cot with Mo-nah-se-tah. Maybe not. But about the sexual convenience supplied by the other Cheyenne women captured on the Washita there is no doubt. From Fort Hays in May, while Libbie Custer was trying to decide just how she felt about Indian girls, Captain Myles Keogh, a company commander in the 7th Regiment, wrote to his brother back in Ireland,

> We have knocked the Indians up a cocked hat, yet they are still on the warpath. We have here about 90 squaws—from our last fight—some of them are very pretty. I have one that is quite intelligent. It is usual for officers to have two or three lounging around.[38]

What's missing almost entirely from the record is how Cheyenne men felt about it. Very probably their feelings mirrored those of the Sioux, who considered sexual jealousy a weakness, and insisted that chiefs rise above it. The northern Sioux had contempt for the Wagluhe who idled around Fort Laramie. "They were accused of trading their daughters to the white men for loaves of light bread," reported Josephine Waggoner. "The hostiles who did not want to mix their blood with the whites made the accusation."[39] The agency Sioux on the White River shared the feeling, and seventeen of them signed a letter to President Grant in March 1876 protesting plans for replacing civilian agents with military officers, something the Army had long been seeking to do. The Indians had plenty of experience by that time of living next door to white men. Spotted Tail and other leading men of the Brulé—Swift Bear, Looking Horse, Crow Dog, Standing Bear, No Flesh, and White Thunder among them—told the interpreter Louis Bordeaux and the Reverend William J. Cleveland what to write to the Great Father:

> Soldiers generally are obnoxious to our young men and their dislike for us is
> so evident as always to provoke ill-feeling . . . They corrupt our women and
> introduce . . . the vice of drinking, gambling, etc. . . . They have through
> their trader introduced whiskey among the people here which . . . has
> already resulted in one murder and much other domestic trouble.[40]

The whites called the northern Indians "hostile," but proud or standoffish would have been more accurate terms. The hunting grounds south of
the Yellowstone River were *their* country. In 1857, Bear's Rib had told
Lieutenant G. K. Warren on the edge of the Black Hills that the Sioux
had no land to sell. The chief had heard that the Yanktonai Sioux on the
Missouri were preparing to sell their own land, and he asked Warren to
tell the Yanktonai they were free to do as they liked, but they must not
expect to move west to join the Oglala and the Hunkpapas; they would
not be welcome. Other chiefs of the Hunkpapas felt Bear's Rib had
become too close to the whites. They told him to stop frequenting the
forts on the Missouri, to stop accepting annuities or eating white food. In
the summer of 1862 they concluded that his ears were closed to them, and
they killed him "to open his ears."[41]

Sitting Bull and Crazy Horse were the two principal men of the northern Indians. Both wanted nothing to do with whites or agencies. But Sitting Bull was the talker, and what he says is probably good evidence of
what Crazy Horse thought and felt. The attitude of the Hunkpapa chief
toward whites had a long history and came from the gut. He explained
himself once to General Nelson Miles in council:

> Sitting Bull said that Almighty God had made him an Indian and not an
> agency Indian and he did not intend to be one. He said there never was a
> white man who did not hate the Indians and there never was an Indian who
> did not hate the white race.[42]

In 1867, at Fort Union on the upper Missouri, Sitting Bull told the
trader Charles Larpenteur he had no respect for the agency Indians. "I
don't want to have anything to do with people who make one carry water
on the shoulders and haul manure." Better, he said, to "have my skin
pierced with bullet holes" than starve like the agency Indians, "getting as
poor as snakes." He urged them to leave the agencies, move out into the
buffalo country and live on meat, and when they needed a horse, to steal
one from the whites at some fort.

"Look at me," he told the Indians who lived on free government food, "see if I am poor, or my people either. The whites may get me at last, as you say, but I will have good times till then. You are fools to make yourselves slaves to a piece of fat bacon, some hardtack, and a little sugar and coffee."[43]

In 1875 the message Sitting Bull sent south with Louis Richard to the Allison commission put it plain: *"We don't want any white men here."*

8

"The wild devils of the north."

AMONG THE INDIANS APPROACHING the agencies along the White River in August 1875 was a short, muscular warrior who had been living in the north with Crazy Horse's Hunkpatila band of Oglala, a man of two names. Indians seem to have known him generally as Charging Bear (Mato Watakpe) but in Army and newspaper reports he was mostly called Little Big Man (Wicasa Tanka Ciqala), sometimes altered to Little Bad Man, possibly in error, or perhaps in the same sarcastic spirit that prompted a *Chicago Tribune* reporter to refer to Spotted Tail as "Variegated Caudal."[1] A white rancher who met the short, muscular Oglala at a sun dance in 1881 remarked that, "while owning a scant five feet in height, [he] had the breadth and depth of chest, and length and power of arms of a giant."[2] Little Big Man came to the White River country with two hundred lodges of northern Indians, not out of respect for Young Man Afraid, who brought the invitation, or to meet and talk in council with the Allison commission, but to ensure that no sale of the Black Hills took place.

Of all the Indians who played an important role in the Sioux war or the events leading to the killing of Crazy Horse none left fewer traces than Little Big Man. About the others there are often stories, the text of remarks in council, detailed genealogies, sometimes drawings depicting hunting or war exploits, even the transcripts of interviews or written accounts of ceremonies and religious beliefs. Little Big Man's passage through events is central and vivid but brief. He was said to have killed the white rancher Levi Powell with his own rifle in March 1872, but the name of Little Big Man did not enter the written record until a year later, in the annual report of the agent for the Oglala, J. W. Daniels, who placed him second among the leaders of hostiles who had been attacking whites along the Platte—Crazy Horse, Little Big Man, and Little Hawk.[3] This report made slight impression. Two years later military officers, including

General Sheridan, thought they were hearing about Crazy Horse for the first time. About Little Big Man's origins it is reported that he was one of twins born about 1840 to Yellow Thunder, an important Oglala chief met by Francis Parkman in 1846, and Her Holy Breath. His twin sister, Tocha Cesli, married a white man at Fort Laramie about 1860. A brother, variously known as Poor Bear or Fishgut (Howatezi), scouted for the Army in the mid-1860s, but was later accused of numerous thefts and killings, including the murder of two pregnant white women on the Sweetwater in July 1873. Army officers at Camp Robinson knew this brother as Sioux Jim and called for his arrest on sight.[4]

As the Indians gathered along the White River near the Red Cloud Agency in September 1875, Little Big Man soon attracted attention for his threats to block a sale of the Black Hills. This friend of Crazy Horse was not alone in his determination to hold on to the hills. Early in the summer the Tokala or Kit Fox society, a men's group that performed the policing duties of the *akicita*, formally vowed to enforce the consensus of the chiefs. No sale would be permitted until the commission agreed to the central demand of the Indians. Any man who broke ranks and touched the pen would be killed—a threat all knew was serious. This core demand had been prompted by President Grant's threatening remark in Washington that the rations given to the Indians could be taken away at any moment. That was not the way the Sioux had understood the Treaty of 1868. It was the whites who wanted the Indians to live at an agency. How could they do this unless food was provided for them? Without government rations they must roam and hunt or starve.

The author of the Indians' countermove was Red Dog, a longtime chief reported to have scars on his body from eighteen wounds received in battle, and father of two noted warriors, Fills the Pipe and Kills a Hundred. Originally a Hunkpapa, Red Dog had married into the Oyuhpe band of the Oglala and lived with them thereafter. In 1870 he had gone to Washington with Red Cloud on his first trip; some people said it was Red Dog who persuaded Red Cloud to move the agency to White River. In July, he had gone to the agencies on the Missouri with Slow Bull, a son-in-law of Red Cloud, to urge the Hunkpapas and Miniconjou to meet with the commissioners, and he was often asked to speak for Red Cloud in council.[5] At a meeting that summer it was Red Dog who summed up in a phrase what would become the chiefs' position:

> Chief Red Dog got up and told them that if they did not sell the Hills, the whites would take them from them without paying for them. Red Dog told

them to let the Hills go into the hands of the Great Father . . . till some of our children could read and write; that these would figure the value of the Black Hills with the Great Father and sell to the government . . . and let it pay the Indians to the seventh generation.[6]

The commissioners—Senator Allison and seven others—had planned to hold the council on the Missouri River, perhaps at Fort Sully, but that hope was soon scrapped. Red Cloud and Spotted Tail and their followers flatly refused to go east for the meeting. The first commissioners to reach the White River country came in July and then lingered for the next two months waiting for the Indians to arrive, to agree on a place to meet, and to decide on a day to begin talking. At the end of August the full commission boarded a train in Omaha for Cheyenne, then traveled north by Army ambulance to meet in council, in the words of the *Chicago Tribune* reporter James Howard, "with the dusky deadbeats now fattening upon the bounty of the government."[7] Howard, who sometimes signed his stories as "Phocion" after the Athenian statesman, believed that mixed-blood interpreters were inflating Indian hopes for the price gold-hungry whites would pay for the Black Hills. This made him angry. In his view no special payment was necessary at all. He believed that the "Sherman treaty" of 1868 needed a modest revision only—subtract the Black Hills from the great Sioux reservation in return for continued rations, and announce, not negotiate, the amendment. But the *Tribune*'s man on the ground feared that the "obstinacy" of the "hungry cormorants" might make it impossible for the commission to write a new treaty at all. In that event, he warned, the northern Indians, disappointed in their dream of a "Big Bonanza treaty," might turn to fighting.

Not all Army officers feared this outcome, Howard reported.

General Crook is of the opinion that the Sioux desire just that sort of performance; and furthermore, that a good sound drubbing is the only thing that will make the insolent fellows keep their proper station. In the spring, not less than 30,000 miners will go into the hills, whether a treaty is made or not . . . then it would be "nip and tuck" between the miners and savages, and the miners would hold their own, and the Hills too.[8]

"Good sound drubbing" was Phocion's variation on a frontier theme. Whites more generally said the Indians needed a "whipping," by which they meant the sort of crushing and bloody military defeat required to break the Indians' fighting spirit for good and all. Variations of the word "whipping" appear repeatedly in letters, memoirs, news stories, and official military dispatches. The word is used so often it seems clear that what frontier military officers meant by "whipping" was, in fact, whipping. Rare was the soldier who had not been whipped in his youth. General Sheridan described the beatings he received as an Ohio schoolboy on the third page of his *Personal Memoirs*. The school was run by "an old-time Irish 'master' " who practiced the biblical dictum that "to spare the rod was to spoil the child." If some schoolboy offended the order of his classroom, Patrick McNally would "apply the switch to the whole school" until the guilty party was delivered up. The lesson stuck. In the late 1850s, following McNally's lead, Sheridan hung nine Cascade Indians for its "salutary effect" on the tribe, caring little for the facts in each individual case. One of the nine had saved the lives of whites with a timely warning that very morning, but he dangled from a cottonwood tree with the others. Sheridan was ready to do the same to warring Cheyenne in Texas in the late 1860s, urging in an official paper that the Indians "be soundly whipped, and the ringleaders in the present trouble hung, their ponies killed, and such destruction of their property as will make them very poor."[9]

Ulysses Grant's childhood was also shadowed by a schoolmaster "with his long beech switch always in his hand. It was not always the same one either. Switches were brought in bundles from a beech wood near the schoolhouse . . . [and] often a whole bundle would be used up in a single day." Grant insisted he "never had any hard feelings." It was the custom of the time, he said. But how else to explain the freshness of Grant's feelings fifty years later, if they were not hard? Captain Anson Mills, who served under Crook, remembered teachers from the same mold in the log schoolhouse he attended in Indiana from the age of six. "These schoolmasters were almost invariably Irish, and governed entirely by fear, punishing cruelly," Mills wrote. "Of course the children became stupid, uninterested, and learned slowly."[10]

Stupid, uninterested, and slow is the way to describe a broken spirit, and that is what Phocion hoped the Army might impose on the prideful Sioux. Howard's low opinion of Indians in general was common on the frontier; he placed them in "the class known as cumberers of the earth . . . [who] should be cut down." Did he have extermination in mind? Many whites certainly did, and said so. Howard probably shared their view without imagining the details, but in his dispatches to the *Tribune* he tempered his scorn for the "scalp-lifters," urging only that they be treated firmly as recalcitrant children with heavy recourse to the beech switch.

But forcing the Indians to mind was not so easy. The commissioners reached the Red Cloud Agency on September 4 but failed to bring the chiefs to bay for three weeks. First came a protracted dispute over a site for the talks. Spotted Tail had interpreted an earlier remark by one of the commissioners, the Reverend Samuel D. Hinman, as a promise to hold the council on Chadron Creek, about thirty miles east of the agency. Red Cloud declined to ride so far. Spotted Tail insisted. The commission asked the two chiefs and some close associates[11] to resolve the matter. They failed. Finally, after much palaver and delay, Senator Allison ruled that the meeting would be held six or eight miles east of the Red Cloud Agency on the bank of a creek known as Little White Clay, at a spot marked by a lone cottonwood tree.

One date was set for the general council, then another. By mid-September as many as fifteen or twenty thousand Indians had arrived, and their camps stretched forty miles along the White River. The grassy hills back from the river were covered with vast herds of Indian ponies—as many as fifty to a lodge, scores of thousands in all, serving as a kind of ticking clock. The commission had arranged for contractors to drive several thousand cattle to the agency to feed the Indians, but the grass could not long sustain so many ponies, and the Indians from the Missouri River were particularly anxious to head back across the prairies before the onset of winter—which in that part of the world could arrive with a blizzard more or less at any moment after the first week of September.

As the weeks went by the Indians debated endlessly among themselves. James Howard and the other reporters sent dispatches recording the steady escalation in the price the Sioux thought would be right for the Black Hills. Sometimes it was expressed in dollars—six million, thirty million, seventy million, a hundred million. As the asking price went up white officials insisted that the value of the hills was going down; it was said that a second expedition under Professor Walter P. Jenney of the New York School of Mines had failed to confirm Custer's reports of gold from the grass roots down. By the time the Indians and the commissioners were at last ready to sit down and talk they were in the midst of a small city. The old-time traders like Nick Janis and James Bordeaux who had lived for decades with the Indians said they had never seen a greater number gathered in one place—not at Fort Laramie when the treaty was signed in 1868, not even on Horse Creek in 1851, when Indians came from all the tribes on the northern plains for the *wakpamni*—the great distribution. In 1875, some said twenty thousand Indians were camped along the White River, some thought more.

To fill newspaper columns before the negotiations began Howard offered his readers a diet of wild Indians, beginning with Indian women, always an object of fascination for white men with a pen.

> Many of the warriors brought their favorite squaws with them, who, being favorites, of course had a monopoly of all the fine store clothes. They presented . . . an appearance quite romantic and fascinating, showing an independence of the use of soap that would scarcely be allowed in a belle of [Chicago's] Prairie Avenue. Some of these dusky Cleopatras wore [buffalo] robes worth from two to five horses . . . Some of the warriors claimed as many as four wives, but the majority content themselves with two—one for work, and the other as a sort of personal servant and mistress.[12]

Howard's ethnographic fieldwork next took in the dances held by the Indians inside the stockade of the Red Cloud Agency. "Some old women, above 80, kept up the noise and stiff-legged jump for hours," Howard reported. But what really caught his attention was a war dance in which, he wrote, "many of the warriors appeared almost naked." Painted in "hideous" fashion, they sang of their victories and shook the scalps they had ripped from enemies. In the great crowd of Indians peacefully camped along the riverbanks Howard singled out Little Big Man's group, the wild Indians from the north who went armed at all times. "You can scarcely approach one," Howard wrote in the *Chicago Tribune*, "save in the company of a more civilized Indian; and then you always find the wild individual nervously fingering a navy revolver or repeating rifle."[13] Naked warriors, scalps, nervous men with guns—all contributed to the frisson of danger Howard described for his readers. "Another noble red man," Howard reported, "sports a necklace made of the nails and ends of fingers of whites killed. Nice, ain't it?"

If that wasn't enough to prove the Indians savage, Howard offered up the example of Little Big Man, who had once, he says, killed six Crow in a single day—three women and three children. In the great camp surrounding the agency, furthermore, the chief "goes whistling about"—but not with the usual whistle strung around the neck of Sioux warriors, made from the wing bone of an eagle and blown in war to frighten enemies, and by sun dancers as they beg for pity from the spirit being. Little Big Man's whistle, Howard tells us soberly, "was made out of one of the bones of the forearm of a white woman killed in 1868." Even that is not horror enough. Another warrior, the *Tribune* informed its readers, wore a "highly-ornamented robe . . . the fringe of which was composed entirely of white women's hair, wavy, soft, and silken black, brown and auburn in its shades." These trophies came from "the massacre of some emigrant families"; the women had been "outraged and killed," and their children "abandoned to death by exposure."[14]

Did Howard really believe what he was writing? Was any of it true? In a single paragraph, the *Tribune*'s correspondent has concentrated all the classic horror stories of the frontier, and all had been true somewhere, sometime, somehow. Very likely Howard did see a necklace of human fingers. A year later soldiers would find the necklace when they attacked an Indian camp—Indian fingers, it would turn out, but fingers all the same. It is the race of these trophies that gives the game away: white fingers, the silken locks of white women, the forearm bone of a white woman, emigrant women "outraged." It seems clear that all this horror was fed to Howard for a reason, and was preliminary to a land grab from the Indians.[15]

But no land grab occurred. The Indians proved maddeningly elusive. Even after they agreed on a place to meet, and a time to meet, and the subject to meet about, they would never quite pin down what they were willing to sell or what they wanted to be paid for it. The opening session on Monday, September 20, achieved little. Red Cloud, still unhappy about the site, refused to attend, and in the middle of Allison's opening speech Red Dog interrupted to say, "It will take seven days for us to study in our minds about this, and we will now hold a council among ourselves."[16]

Red Dog was as good as his word; the Indians took a week to decide what to tell the impatient commissioners, who had a hard time understanding what the problem was. All should have become clear on September 23, when a struggle between Sioux factions at one dicey moment threatened to bring open violence. But the moment passed, and Allison continued to press. On Sunday the 26th he told twenty of the principal chiefs they must come prepared to negotiate on the following day. They did. Some three hundred chiefs and leading men assembled by the lone tree on the bank of Little White Clay Creek early Monday afternoon. The commissioners were shaded from the sun by a tent fly. The cavalry was out in force to ensure the peace. Red Cloud told the commissioners he wanted one of his own people—he pointed out a mixed-blood among the Indians—to write down all that was said, and then added that he had selected Red Dog to speak for the Oglala. The heart of his remarks was paraphrased in the *Chicago Tribune:*

> Red Dog said six generations of Indians had been fed by the government. His people now want guarantees of food and clothing seven generations more. He said the Indians were ready to make a treaty. He wanted pay for the gold already taken out of the Black Hills and wanted to sell only such portion of the Black Hills as gold had been discovered in, and, for relinquishing their right therein, he wanted a light wagon, a span of horses, six work cattle, a gun and ammunition for each head of an Indian family. He also insisted that the southern boundary of the Indian reservation be changed to the middle of the North Platte River . . . He also wanted back pay for what had been taken out of the Black Hills. He again repeated that he would only dispose of that portion of the Black Hills where gold was found. He meant he would not dispose of the Big Horn, Powder River country as suggested by the Commissioners. He said he didn't want any other roads running through the Black Hills or through the reservation except the one the thieves travelled by. He meant General Custer's trail from Bismarck.[17]

Later a military officer asked Red Cloud what was meant by "seven generations." The chief pointed to his son, Wicasa Wanka (Above Man),[18] a boy of fifteen, and said, "My son is the first generation."[19]

The chiefs all had a point of view, and each wanted to get his requests on the table. Red Dog was followed by Little Bear, a Miniconjou, who unfolded a similar list of demands for better or at least different treatment on the reservations: new agent and interpreters; Catholic priests, not Protestants, to run a school; a duplicate list of annuity goods so the Indians could be sure they were receiving everything intended for them. He added that "when the white men had a good thing they got rich on it. His people wanted to get rich out of the Black Hills."

After Little Bear, Spotted Tail told the commissioners that troops stationed at the agencies would be better used keeping whites out of the Black Hills. Also, he wanted it understood that whites married to Indians were considered family and must be allowed to live with their relatives at the agencies. Spotted Bear of the Cheyenne River Agency on the Missouri suggested that the value of the Black Hills was about $70 million—bad news for the commissioners, who had a much smaller number in mind. Over subsequent days the commission spelled out its offer: $6 million for the hills outright, or $400,000 annually to lease the hills for an open-ended period, plus a side offer of $50,000 a year for the Big Horn country (where many whites also expected to find gold).

The Indians did not say yes and they did not say no. Their final best offer was unrolled by Red Cloud himself on the last day of discussions, September 29, in a stately address almost biblical in tone:

> For seven generations to come I want our Great Father to give us Texan steers for our meat. I want the Government to issue for me hereafter, flour and coffee, and sugar and tea, and bacon, the very best kind, and cracked corn and beans, and rice and dried apples, and saleratus and tobacco, and soap and salt, and pepper, for the old people. I want a wagon, a light wagon with a span of horses, and six yoke of working cattle for my people. I want a sow and a boar, and a cow and bull, and a sheep and ram, and a hen and cock, for each family. I am an Indian, but you try to make a white man out of me. I want some white men's houses at this agency to be built for the Indians. I have been into white people's houses and I have seen nice black bedsteads and chairs, and I want that kind of furniture given to my people . . . I want the Great Father to furnish me a saw-mill which I may call my own. I want a mower and a scythe for my people. Maybe you white people think I ask too much from the government, but I think those hills extend clear to the sky—maybe they go above the sky, and that is the reason I ask for so much."[20]

There it was, exactly what Allison had been asking for—what the Indians wanted. From the senator's point of view they wanted the moon. There was no give and take, nothing like a negotiation. Things had gone completely wrong. Newspaper writers like Howard thought the problem was the mixed-bloods—they had convinced the chiefs the Black Hills were made of gold and the whites would pay accordingly. Spotted Tail came a good deal closer to the nub in a private meeting with the commission on its last night at the Red Cloud Agency. The two sides should try again with a smaller group—just two chiefs from each tribe—at another meeting in Washington with the Great Father. "Then when we are away from our young men, who do not know anything, we can look these things all over in the right light, and make a good, strong treaty, and preserve peace forever."[21]

The man was a realist, but so was Senator Allison. He had concluded that buying the hills was impossible. The next day, Thursday, September 30, the commission packed up and headed for home.

While the commission was making its way to the railroad, a full day to the south, General Custer in New York City in an expansive mood explained to a local reporter how they had gotten it all wrong. The problem began with the commissioners themselves, he said.

> [They] were not sufficiently well acquainted with the Indian character . . . [the first mistake was] in letting the Indians have so much of their own way. Indians are like children that get spoiled if they are petted, and had the Commisioners been firm and backed up by strength, they would have [succeeded] . . . It is the result of holding the council right in the heart of the Indian country, where the chiefs had the squaw men to advise them. Each of these men were anxious to make the payment as large as possible . . . They should have held the council at some spot remote from the Indian agencies . . . The fact of the matter is they [the Indians] are too much pampered and require a little different treatment. An equitable and just arrangement should be made, and after a certain show of strength, in order to convince them that business is meant, there will be no difficulty.[22]

"A certain show of strength"—that was to be Custer's job.

The failure of the Allison commission was momentous. It is true that the Indians wanted a lot for the Black Hills, and that the commission hoped to pay little, but it was not Indian overreaching or white parsimony that ran the effort aground. To find the true cause we must go back to the abortive second meeting of the council on September 23, when divisions among the Indians almost led to fighting. James Howard, who shared the eagerness for an agreement felt by the *Tribune*'s readers, had reported that "the temper of the Indians never was better," but this was not true. By the time the chiefs and their men began to gather by the lone tree—Spotted Tail and his Brulé riding in first, followed by Red Cloud and the Oglala, then the rest—a foreboding of violence hung over the meeting. Runners were reported to have come in from the camps in the Powder and Tongue river company, where the hearts of the Indians were said to be very bad. It was known that Little Big Man had visited Spotted Tail in his lodge the previous night and the two men had quarreled. Spotted Tail was for a sale at the right price; for Little Big Man no sum would be enough. Behind this quarrel were the threats already made by Little Big Man to kill a commissioner, and by the Tokala warrior society to kill any chief who touched the pen before the central demand had been met. Anticipating trouble, Red Cloud and Old Man Afraid had appointed the *akicita itancan* (chief of police), Drum Carrier, also called Sitting Bull, to organize a force of about a hundred men to keep order. Young Man Afraid was placed near the lone tree where he could keep an eye on things and signal Drum Carrier in a moment of need.

Prior to the meeting came a grand pass in review by the Indians, who never missed an opportunity for gorgeous drama. First were the chiefs in their feathered bonnets and scalp shirts, many carrying lances or coup sticks wrapped in fur or dangling feathers, followed by men on their war horses, painted and decorated. Among the reporters probably none knew how to read the distinctive dress, painting, and paraphernalia—the meaning of a horse's tail, for example, tied up in red trade cloth in the mode for war, or the difference between stone-headed clubs and tomahawks— some for public occasions only, and some for killing. The *New York Times* reporter summed it up as "a splendid sight." Almost all the Indians were armed; only a few Yanktonai from the Missouri arrived without their guns. Some of the Indians dismounted and seated themselves in a great three-quarter circle with its two horns stopping well short of the commissioners' tent fly. This gap in the line troubled some of the old hands watching. They knew Indians liked to be close to the talking, unless they feared fighting. Then they kept their distance, and they were keeping their distance now.

Many other warriors arriving on horseback said they preferred to remain mounted. The commission didn't like this but was in no position to issue orders, hence many Indians sat on their horses in a mass surrounding the meeting ground. Each man held his rifle—mostly breech-loading carbines of a late model, reporters noted—in his right hand, upright, with the rifle butt resting on his right thigh. An Indian crier in a loud voice announced the beginning of the meeting, at which time a hundred or more chiefs lined up behind Spotted Tail to shake hands one by one with the commissioners. When the greetings were concluded Red Cloud, in his middle fifties, entered the circle accompanied by Little Wound. Red Cloud paused. Spotted Tail and his friend Two Strike approached him. All four sat down and began to talk privately. Almost immediately they were joined by other chiefs, including Man That Owns a Sword (brother of Hunts the Enemy) and Old Man Afraid of His Horses, the oldest at about seventy-five of the important chiefs.

The council was never formally called into session. None of the chiefs addressed the commissioners, but while they talked Little Big Man was much in evidence. At the outset during the grand pass in review, "the dreaded chief of the north . . . arrived in a perfect state of nudity," wrote the *Times* reporter. He may have meant Little Big Man wore only moccasins and a breechcloth, but it is possible he was actually naked. Showing buttocks and genitals to an enemy was a signal of contempt. Little Big Man was mounted on a spirited gray war horse, followed by a band of "evil-looking warriors" fifty or more in number. It was his custom to paint in red the wounds he had received in battle. The reporter noted that he was "thickly painted," his hair wild and loose—a small, compact, tightly muscled man full of threat and danger. He and his men remained on their horses and were constantly moving, guns in hand—sometimes passing behind the commissioners' tent and the hundred cavalry troops under Captains Teddy Egan and Anson Mills keeping watch nearby; sometimes disappearing into the brush along the river, then pushing their way back through the throng of Indian onlookers.

Red Dog, speaking with the chiefs, had remarked that "it did not look good for both whites and Indians to come into council armed." American Horse stressed the same point, saying it made whites nervous to be surrounded by armed men. It was better to remove the guns and carry them outside the great circle, he said. Now arose Bull Eagle, a Miniconjou with a history of anger toward the whites. In the Fetterman fight ten years earlier, Bull Eagle had been shot in the thigh and seriously injured. "He lay on the prairie . . . bleeding freely and groaning—but like a wounded bear, to show that he still had a strong heart."[23]

In 1872, while a brother was fighting the whites on the Yellowstone, Bull Eagle had disrupted a meeting at the Cheyenne River Agency between chiefs there and the Reverend Samuel D. Hinman, who was now sitting under the tent fly with the rest of the Allison commission. At Cheyenne River, Bull Eagle had snatched paper from the hands of a white man keeping notes and tore it up, "saying that all white men are liars, and ought to leave the Indian's country and never come to it again."[24] Now he took issue with American Horse, said it was the whites who first brought armed men to the council—he meant the hundred troops under Egan and Mills—and the whites must live with the result. American Horse denounced Bull Eagle as a fool and threatened him with a beating if he did not shut up. Bull Eagle stormed off and a few minutes later was seen talking with Little Big Man. Almost immediately Little Big Man began moving his men—now grown to several hundred—toward the flank of the dismounted cavalry under Egan and Mills. More men joined the Indians every moment.

"In a few minutes," the *Tribune* reported, "the [cavalry] force was heavily covered by Winchesters, Sharps and Remington rifles at not more than ten to fifteen paces."

The troops now "stood to horses," carbines in hand. In the view of the *Tribune*, "A single shot fired today would have made indiscriminate slaughter."

Watching this rapid unfolding of events the commissioners grew concerned, then nervous, at last alarmed; urgently they messaged Red Cloud and Spotted Tail to take things in hand. Young Man Afraid, nearby, signaled to Drum Carrier to end the trouble.

And now occurred something extraordinary, alarming at the moment and more troubling the more it was thought of later. The great circle of Indians had been only three-quarters complete; none found a place directly in front of or near the commissioners, and observers wondered about this strange gap in the line, opening a lane to the cavalry. At this moment of rising tension, when Little Big Man and his group were crowding in on the troops, most of the mixed-bloods and some of the interpreters who had been watching near the commissioners' tent began to get up and move away—not in a rush, but not quite casually, either, saying nothing. The reporters, military officers, and commissioners all noted it. That was the moment when it seemed the ball was about to begin. The reporters listed the evidence later: the gap in the circle, Little Big Man and his warriors crowding close, the sudden disappearance of the mixed-bloods, who must have received warning, the fact that "an unusually large number of shells for breach-loaders were sold yesterday by the traders," the existence of a still-larger band of warriors "armed *cap à pie*" (head to foot) and hidden in a spot ideal for blocking any relief from the garrison at Camp Robinson, seven miles distant.

> All the cavalry-men were to be shot down at the first fire, the horses stampeded, and then the commission were to get particular Jerusalem from that vacant space in front, which was held by Little Big Man and his crowd . . . A thousand facts known here all point to a corroboration of a plan for a massacre of the whole outfit by the young men under the lead of the wild devils of the north.[25]

The "danger was very great," said the *Times;* but disaster was "happily averted," wrote the *Tribune* reporter, by the "coolness and good judgement" of Young Man Afraid of His Horses. Drum Carrier and his men rode directly into Little Big Man's group, crowding them back. It was fight or give way. The confrontation was between factions of Sioux; the whites were almost an afterthought. Red Cloud and Spotted Tail commanded the allegiance of many hundreds of fighting men on the field. It was no secret which way this was going—the *akicita* had quirts out and bows in their hands ready for beating, with all-out battle not far behind. Little Big Man and the wild devils of the north gave way; the cavalry troops held their fire; the commissioners kept their seats. The moment of danger passed. "Meanwhile the Young Man was smoking his pipe as contentedly as though in his own tepee," noted the admiring reporter of the *Tribune*.

The council did not end at that moment, but it never got any closer to reaching agreement. Little Big Man appears no more in the proceedings. When he departed for the north is unknown but he had made his point: selling the Black Hills meant fighting, and the chiefs who touched the pen would be first on the list for killing. Of course nothing was said about this by the chiefs. Only Spotted Tail came close when he remarked that the young men "did not know anything." But the endless list of Indian demands for the hills finessed the danger: they never rejected the commission by saying no, they never angered the wild devils of the north by saying yes.

In any negotiation between equals that would have been that, but the parties were not equals. Red Dog was right when he told the chiefs they were in a tight spot: if they did not sell the Black Hills, "the whites would take them . . . without paying for them." Allison saw it the same way, but argued that one further step would be necessary. "We do not believe," he wrote in the report issued in mid-November, "their temper or their spirit can be changed until they are made to feel the power as well as the magnanimity of the government . . . They never can be civilized except by the mild exercise, at least, of force in the beginning."

Allison's report would contain many thousands of additional words about civilizing and improving the Indians but official Washington did not wait to receive or read it. On the 3rd of November, while Allison was still scribbling, President Grant met in the White House with the men he expected to solve the Sioux problem: Secretary of War William Belknap; the new secretary of the interior, Zachariah Chandler; General of the Army William Tecumseh Sherman; the commander of armies in the West, General Philip Henry Sheridan; and the new commander of the

Department of the Platte, General George Crook. The president's new policy, never announced or acknowledged, had three points: the Army would withdraw from the Black Hills and let gold seekers go where they liked; the northern Indians would be ordered to report to an agency before the end of January; those who refused would be attacked by the Army as hostiles.[26] Sheridan and Crook, traveling back west together by train after the meeting, discussed plans for a campaign against the hostiles while winter kept them still trapped in their lodges.

Ulysses Grant, grown weary of the endless frustrations of his peace policy, had made up his mind: no more wild Indians roaming the plains.

9

"This whole business was exceedingly distasteful to me."

ON HIS RETURN FROM the north the Sioux-speaking scout Frank Grouard was paid in cash for his trip to the hostiles in the summer of 1875. This was the first money he had earned in five years—"or handled," he said later, hoping to dispel rumors that he had robbed the mails on the upper Missouri. For some weeks after returning to the Red Cloud Agency he kept his hair long in the Indian way and continued to wear buckskin shirt, leggings, and breechcloth—"regular Indian costume." For a time Grouard sought no job but lingered about the agency with his scouting money, "getting familiar with the English language again."

Over the years Grouard gave differing accounts of his reasons for leaving the Indians. One was that he had married a Sioux girl and "a misunderstanding with his wife's relatives made the village too hot for him."[1] At the agency that fall another woman caught his eye, a mixed-blood named Sally, the older half-sister of Billy Garnett. Grouard married the girl according to Indian custom, by simply moving in with her, and it was probably about this time, late one day in the middle of October 1875, that he stepped back across the line and rejoined the white world. From his friend the agency trader J. W. Dear he bought a suit of clothes, and he took a chair while a barber cut his hair. It chanced that on the same night a white man, Bill Rowland, killed a Cheyenne on the agency, infuriating the tribe and alarming officials that a serious outbreak of fighting might follow. Whites were warned to stay out of sight in their quarters but Grouard, short hair notwithstanding, agreed to go among the angry Indians to help quiet them. Soon thereafter he joined Rowland on the agency employment roll as a "laborer" at seventy-five dollars a month, but like Rowland his real job was to serve as an interpreter and to handle Indians. By the turn of the year Frank Grouard was married, had resumed dressing like a white man, and had found a profession—serving as a guide, scout, and interpreter until the Indian wars came to an end.[2]

That winter Grouard learned from white friends that the military was planning a big expedition; General Crook, commander of the Department of the Platte, would be seeking scouts to lead the soldiers north against the hostiles. At dusk one afternoon in February, learning that Crook would soon be at Fort Laramie and told he needed to move quick if he wanted a job, Grouard set off on horseback from the Red Cloud Agency, rode ninety miles through the night, and reached the fort about eight o'clock the following morning.

He arrived to find the bustle and turmoil of a major expedition preparing to take the field. Wagons were loading with supplies, companies of cavalry and infantry were following the North Platte River north to the jumping-off point at Fort Fetterman, and a host of men claiming frontier experience had arrived seeking jobs as scouts. Crook would hire thirty of them before the end of the day on February 25. It was here that Grouard first met Baptiste Pourier, known as Big Bat, and renewed his acquaintance with Bat's brother-in-law Louis Richard, who was just as deeply schooled in the Sioux language and frontier ways. But despite the long experience and deep knowledge of these men it was Frank Grouard who won General Crook's confidence and became his favored guide.

That confidence was not won overnight. Crook's aide-de-camp, Lieutenant John Gregory Bourke, reported in his diary that on February 25 the general "was busy all day . . . in examining guides and scouts and studying maps of the country in which we are to operate."[3] Very little was known at the time of the vast country between the Missouri River and the old Bozeman Road and thence north to the Yellowstone. No map could lead Crook to the hostile camps; for that he needed a man who had been there. Years later, Grouard described his first meeting with the general:

> I had an interview with General Crook. He asked me if I was acquainted with the country, and I told him I was. Wanted to know if there was any possible show of jumping Indians there in the wintertime. I told him if he worked it right, there might be . . . He said if I would furnish my own horse, he would give me $150, but I didn't have a horse and told him that he would have to furnish the horse. So he said he would give me $125 a month. He said that he expected to start out the first of March.[4]

Crook knew what he wanted: a crack at the hostiles in their winter camp. Grouard promised to give it to him. But Crook did not trust Grouard entirely at first. Many of the Indians at the Red Cloud Agency had known Grouard in the north; some believed he lived with the Indians because at heart he was an Indian, and said he had taken part in the fighting with soldiers on the Yellowstone in 1873. It was said that Grouard helped the Indians kill mail riders and steal mail, that he read the officers' letters to Sitting Bull so he might know their plans. Some whiff of this suspicion reached General Crook. He took no chances. About the time his expedition pushed off from Fort Fetterman in a snowstorm on March 1, the general spoke privately to the Bats, Pourier and Garnier. "General. Crook told them to watch Grouard and if he betrayed his companions to shoot him."[5]

George Crook brought with him a great reputation as an Indian fighter when he set out against the Sioux in March 1876. He had fought Indians in California as a young lieutenant fresh out of West Point in the 1850s, and he had fought Apache in Arizona in the 1870s. He carried an arrowhead in his leg from a Pitt River Indian but his reputation was unscarred; he had won all his battles and campaigns against Indians and had firm opinions about how Indian fighting ought to be done. Later he had risen high in the Union Army during the Civil War. The trick had been to get a command. As a captain in the regular army in the first summer of the war he was taken to meet President Lincoln in Washington—"the most ungainly man I had ever seen, particularly his legs and feet," Crook recalled.[6] From the president Crook learned that state governors, not the adjutant general of the Army, would be giving out the best appointments, and he soon accepted an offer to become colonel in command of Ohio's 36th Voluntary Infantry Regiment, then stationed in Summersville, West Virginia.

When Crook joined his new regiment in September he found a little-trained rabble of Ohio farm boys fresh from the plow—"rare as a piece of beefsteak," in his words. Many still had no uniforms and the summer clothes they had brought from home were in rags. Many had no boots or shoes of any kind and went barefoot. They did not know the manual of arms or how to march and did not think they needed to know. The officers were not much better; they could read, but had no knowledge of things military. Crook went to work to turn his regiment into a disciplined fighting force while attempting to deal with the immediate challenge posed by irregular Confederate forces—the "bushwhackers" who infested the forested valleys of West Virginia, shooting passers-by from ambush and in general conducting themselves more like bandits than an army.

The men of the 36th Ohio were not alert to the danger; they were careless about posting guards or challenging suspicious persons. "Being fresh from the Indian country where I had more or less experience with that kind of warfare," Crook wrote, "I set to work organizing for the task."[7]

Half the job was acquiring intelligence—detailed knowledge of the mesh of country roads, isolated farms, and tiny hamlets and the men who lived there. Some were plain country folk, while others were rebel partisans waiting for a chance to shoot nodding pickets or careless travelers and maybe pocket something of value at the same time. The other half of the job required a certain kind of character which Crook had—a combination of realism, resolution, and hardness of spirit.

This hardness of spirit was partly learned, partly born in the man. The colonel's commanding volunteer regiments at the outset of the Civil War were all appointed by their governors, as Crook had been, but most at heart were political men, gregarious and widely acquainted, which Crook was not. Like the enlisted men in his regiment he was an Ohio farm boy, raised on hard physical labor. He liked to hunt but got little opportunity. The ninth of ten children, son of a prosperous farmer with 340 acres along the Miami River, he was sent to school in Dayton, where a classmate, James Greer, remembered him as "a farmer's boy, slow to learn, but what he did learn was surely his. He was older, somewhat, than his comrades, and was good-natured, stolid, and was like a big Newfoundland dog among a lot of puppies. He would never permit . . . bullying of smaller boys."[8]

For boys like Crook the United States Military Academy at West Point offered a free practical education in engineering and surveying along with the chance for a career in the Army. Crook at nineteen apparently had no wish for either when his father was approached by a political friend, Congressman Robert P. Schenck, in 1847, asking if any of his boys might want an appointment. The father was as deliberate as the son: "After studying awhile he said he didn't know but what he had." The young Crook submitted to an interview. It is clear that Schenck was not bowled over.

The boy was exceedingly non-communicative. He hadn't a stupid look, but was quiet to reticence. He didn't seem to have the slightest interest or anxiety about my proposal. I explained to him the requirements . . . and finally asked him, "Do you think you can conquer all that?" His monosyllabic reply was, "I'll try."[9]

Hadn't a stupid look seems faint praise at best. Noncommunicative—watchful, silent, contained—Crook remained for life. But Schenck had an appointment to give and Crook got it. Four years later he graduated thirty-eighth in a class of forty-three but with a clean nose. West Point is stickling about rules; every infraction is punished and recorded. But Crook's record is short and dull: fined for breaking dishes in the mess, absent from drill, confined to quarters for submitting work that was not his own. Likely it was a friend's. The Point didn't think it mattered much. At West Point, Crook made only a faint impression. On the first day of December 1852 he arrived in San Francisco, reported for duty as brevet second lieutenant with Company F, 4th Infantry. He was immediately assigned as a file closer at the funeral of a fellow officer, dead of drink at the age of fifty-one. Crook "was very abstemious," a military aide wrote many years later; "in no case was he ever known to drink to excess. He did not use tobacco in any form . . . to all forms of gambling he was bitterly opposed."[10]

Perhaps the abhorrence of drink came early in Ohio, perhaps he learned it in California. There the ranking officer at the funeral gathered the dead man's fellows around his corpse and said, "Well fellows, Old Miller is dead and he can't drink, so let us all take a drink." Crook was horrified by the whole bunch of them. "Not a day passed but what these officers were drunk at least once, and mostly until the wee hours of the morning. I never had seen such gambling and carousing before or since."[11]

Crook soon found an escape from this chaos—the field. He was stationed at Fort Jones in a mining district of California north of Sacramento, near the town of Yreka. The officers' mess in those days was run and paid for by the officers themselves. California prices were painfully high; Crook's share threatened to consume his entire monthly pay of sixty-three dollars.

He took to hunting. "For over a year we never had any meat on our table except game." When he was not on duty he was out with rifle or shotgun in all weather, in every kind of country, alone or with a local Indian as guide and companion. Crook had always loved hunting, rarely got the chance as a boy in Ohio, and now roamed the mountains and rivers all about the post. Crook was so successful that a fellow officer was soon selling meat to the miners in Yreka; the mess operated at a profit and even declared cash dividends. But it was the country and the hunting that enthralled him. The forests were virgin, the rivers were filled with fish, deer abounded. It was the discovery of America all over again—rich, empty, and free for the taking. In California, Crook confirmed a lifelong passion for hunting; in the field his solitary, reflective character restored itself. The numbers of birds and game he shot, the fish he caught, are astonishing. In the late summer of 1854 he was camped with his unit surrounded by mountains on the Deschutes River:

> I upon one occasion took a couple of the soldiers and went up to the summit on a hunt. It was one of the grandest and most picturesque countries I had ever seen. The summit must have been from twenty to forty miles in breadth, covered with lakes and parks scattered amongst a heavy growth of pine and spruce timber . . . In some lakes were runs of magnificent trout, which could be had in the greatest quantities just for the catching. In one lake I killed two loons and shot at a beaver. In another, while walking close to its edge, I heard snorting in the tule which bordered on the shore for half a dozen yards, sounding like hogs rooting. Finally I discovered them to be otter. I shot one that measured five feet three inches from tip to tip. Half a dozen others swam out into the clear water at the report of my gun, cocking their eyes up at me, seemed quite tame. I could have killed several others, but had no use for them, the one being all I could carry.[12]

Late one afternoon as Crook was setting up camp near one of these pristine lakes far from any other human being, or so he thought, the young lieutenant was startled to see a fellow officer emerge from the dusk—not just any fellow officer, but his West Point classmate Lieutenant Philip Henry Sheridan, a boy from Ohio like himself. They had begun together in the class of 1852 but Sheridan, an Irish Catholic of plain origin, was prickly and combative. In his third year, infuriated by a peremptory order from one of the old-family Virginians who ruled social life at West Point, Sheridan attacked his fellow cadet with his fists. Sheridan was small—five feet six inches on Army records but perhaps shorter still. In a surviving photograph of Sheridan between his two great Ohio friends at the Point—George Crook on his right, John Nugen on his left—Sheridan in the middle seems diminutive. At West Point, a much-bigger cadet sergeant from Virginia was giving Sheridan the worst of it when an officer stopped the fight. Physically attacking a cadet who ranked him was no modest slip; Sheridan was lucky to escape with only a year's suspension. He graduated in 1853, a year late, thirty-fourth in a class of fifty-two. Fresh out of West Point, Crook and Sheridan did not seem bound for glory, but they were friends, Crook was delighted to see

him in the mountains of California, and they stayed up late "talking over
what we had seen, etc." What they had seen at that point was miners who
earned more than Army officers, bleak frontier posts run by drunken
despots, and a lot of Indians distinguished for poverty, misery, and a
sneaking way of war.

Crook was divided in his opinion of Indians. The first ones he ever
encountered were the Wiyot on Humboldt Bay in northern California—
"they are filthy, odiferous, treacherous, pitiless, cruel and lazy," he wrote
later. But Crook had an even lower opinion of the whites who stole from
the Indians, killed them on a whim, and raped their women. "Such a thing
as a white man being punished for outraging an Indian was unheard
of . . . It is hard to believe now the wrongs these Indians had to suffer in
those days." Throughout the 1850s, he traveled all over California to deal
with one tribe after another as white abuse led to Indian outbreaks.
Between fights he hired Indians as hunting guides. Around campfires in
the evening he listened to their grievances, stories, and beliefs about
things supernatural. "Most of their little legends I have forgotten, and in
fact," he confessed, "I fear I was not a very good listener."

But his *Autobiography* contradicts him. He has a great deal to say about
the culture and religion of California Indians. His goal, he wrote, was to
understand "all these little 'bed rock' secrets, especially those of a sacred
character," in order to better control the Indians. Maybe so, but a reader
of the *Autobiography* gets the strong impression that Crook was in fact
intensely interested by the Indians. Suffering once with an infection in his
arm his fears were aroused when "a squaw came into my room one day,
and wanted to know to whom I was going to give my things when I died."
She seemed to know something Crook didn't. At that moment he realized
the infection might well kill him, and he "finally took my own case in
hand," treating the injury daily with calomel and jalap for the month it
took to heal.[13]

One of the tribes he got to know well was the Ala-a-gnas, who lived
along the banks of the Klamath River, subsisting on fish, acorns, wild
grains and roots, "and occasionally a little venison." The Indians talked to
Crook by the hour about God and the devil. They confessed to him they
had never personally seen the devil but had sometimes heard him nearby,
and they knew of people who had seen him. From various reports they
knew the devil to have "long claws, hooked bill, long tail, and was covered

all over with pitch." A man caught unaware by the devil in the brush would be snatched away and never seen again. "It was regarded as an insult to express any doubt as to the truth of these stories."

Crook was a practical sort of fellow. He thought life was contrary and it didn't take evil spirits to explain trouble and difficulty. But the Indians took an entirely different view. They described the world as broadly and uniformly alive with power to help men or hinder them; a rock could be more than a rock, a tree more than a tree, and a gust of wind or a bolt of lightning might spare a man, or seek him out. All these powers could be controlled by witches.

> These *Al-a-gnas* . . . were particularly superstitious . . . Nothing that occurred, it made no difference how insignificant, but what they had some reason to account for it that was satisfactory to themselves. For instance, if they went out hunting and failed to see game, or if they saw some and failed to kill it, or if it rained while they were out, or if they lost something, and a thousand and one things like that, they would declare that some person had bewitched them, and generally they would tell you the person that did the mischief. I used to try to reason with them that the deer were not where they hunted, but they would answer that they saw so many deer there before, and they were there now, but someone had turned them into brush or rocks, and nothing could shake their belief.[14]

God, Crook was told once, had visited the Indians long ago, coming with his son from the east. God's name was Wa-peck-a-maw[15] and he did many good things for the Indians, but the son was trouble, unruly in behavior and "bad after women." Fed up with the son at last, the Indians killed the boy, but the father was too clever for them. Wa-peck-a-maw escaped down the coast and turned himself into a tree, thereby eluding the Indians. A crow refused to help the god escape from the tree and was turned black as a punishment, but a woodpecker worked so hard to free him that Wa-peck-a-maw gave him a brilliant red head as reward. When white prospectors first appeared in the Indian country the Al-a-gnas welcomed them as relations of Wa-peck-a-maw and rubbed their skin to see if the white would rub off. But soon rapes and killings by whites angered the Indians, and they determined to kill them all as their ancestors had killed Wa-peck-a-maw's son. Listening to these stories made Indian fighting difficult for Crook. He knew how severely the Indians were abused by whites. But "when they had been pushed beyond endurance and would go on the warpath," the military officer's duty was to fight them, and this Crook did.

In the summer of 1857, following a handful of indecisive expeditions, Crook found himself in a serious Indian campaign, pursuing Indians who had attacked whites living in the Pitt River valley, about a hundred miles east of Yreka. The challenge was to find the Indians. One day out scouting on horseback Crook spotted the track of a woman; other tracks soon joined it, and all were running. His command was several miles back, but Crook spurred his horse into a gallop—"The chase had now become so exciting that I thought but little of the danger." Sighting a man he shot him once, then shot him a second time, killing him with his pistol. At that moment Indians appeared all around him "with frightful yells, letting fly a shower of arrows at me." Crook spurred his horse for safety and barely escaped his pursuers. When he returned to the site with his command the Indians had fled, leaving only an old woman grieving beside the body of the man Crook had killed with his pistol. "This was my first Indian," he writes. The woman told them nothing.

A few days later—on June 10, 1857—Crook killed his second Indian. His men were with him but again he rushed ahead of his command to reach a camp of Indians down a steep bluff along a riverbank below. The alarmed Indians scattered; some plunged into the water and started to swim for the far shore. Crook proceeded pell-mell down a faint trail in hope of getting close enough for a shot. "I saw a buck swimming with his bow and arrows and wolf robe held above his head," Crook recalled. "I aimed at the edge of the water. At the crack of the rifle he sank, and the robe and the weapons floated down the stream."

Crook was reloading his rifle when a shower of arrows came at him. One plunged into his right thigh. He grabbed the shaft and tugged; the shaft slipped away from the arrowhead and came out with two inches of blood smearing the wood. The Indians commenced to yell when they saw Crook was wounded and from their hiding places across the river chased him back up the trail with more arrows. Luck spared him a second wound, but by the time he had pulled and scrambled his way back to the top he was sinking into shock, "deathly sick" and pouring sweat. "Excruciating pain" wracked his hip on the horseback journey back to camp, and by the time he arrived "my groin was all green."

At this point in the narrative of his life, Crook digresses to explain what sort of poison the Indians might have smeared on the arrow that wounded him. Taking the liver of a freshly killed deer, he writes, the Indi-

ans would attach it to a long stick with a string, then taunt a coiled rattlesnake with the dangling liver, provoking the snake to strike again and
again, until the liver was well saturated and dripping venom. The final
step was to run an arrow shaft through the liver, smearing it thoroughly.
"Under the most favorable circumstances this poison would retain its
strength about one month," Crook writes, "but during moist weather it
would not last over a few days." Weak or strong, the poison failed to kill
him. Two weeks later he was back on his horse chasing Indians who had
run off some cattle. But for the rest of his life Crook carried that arrowhead in his hip.[16]

He did not let up on the Indians but pursued them relentlessly all summer through the mountains to their camps. In relating the campaign
Crook eases back on the detail of his own kills, simply noting the bag—"I
killed one, and the soldiers the other." But sometimes the details were too
interesting to omit. In an attack on a camp at first light he notes that he
killed two Indians early in the fight. It was the second that interested him.

> He was half-bending and half squatting, with his breast toward me, jumping
> first to one aside, and then to the other, evidently trying to draw my fire,
> keeping an arrow pointed at me all this time . . . He was singing his death
> song. I took a rest on my knee, and, moving my rifle from one side to the
> other, following his movements, I got a good aim, when I pulled the trigger,
> and broke his back. In this condition, while lying on the ground, he shot five
> arrows into the soldier's mule . . . before I could kill him with my pistol.[17]

A moment later Crook killed a third Indian. From that point on the
count grows hazy. The campaign continued into the fall but after awhile
there were no more battles; the Indians grew too cautious, like spooked
game, and try as he might Crook surprised no more sleeping villages. But
at the same time the Indians quit attacking white settlements in the area
and when they asked for peace in September, Crook agreed to end the
war. The Indians then moved camp close to the soldiers "and seemed to
feel perfectly at home." Crook renewed his education in Indian ways, taking careful note of "their cunning in all their little ways of capturing a
livelihood." He describes their skill in digging pits as animal traps, from
which the Pitt River Indians took their name. What particularly struck
him, however, was their method of tracking down yellow jackets—not for
honey, of course, which yellow jackets do not make, but for the larvae of
their young. An Indian would take a single plume of duck down, the
frailest sort of white fuzz attached to a tiny quill. To this he would tie a

tiny bit of meat. Yellow jackets love meat. One would seize the meat and start for the hive but the duck down offered just drag enough through the air to slow the yellow jacket and allow an Indian to follow it to its nest. A smoky fire would then deal with the yellow jackets and leave the larvae for the Indians' dinner. Crook remembered it all thirty years later, and records in tones of evident admiration their many techniques for making the wilderness "pay tribute to them. Game, fish, nuts, roots, grass seed, grasshoppers, crickets, water fowl and their eggs, the larvae of hornets, yellow jackets etc."[18]

The many similar passages in Crook's unfinished autobiography are evidence he spent a lot of time listening to Indians, but at the same time he did not hesitate to kill them in battle, and he is not shy about recording a hunter's pride in the rigors of the chase, outwitting his quarry, or making a difficult shot. When his blood was up he forgot danger and plunged on till he had made his kill. But it took a fight to get his blood up. Absent the heat of battle, killing itself made Crook uneasy. Indians were masters of escape and evasion, and fighting them was mostly hard slogging followed by brief, violent encounters. But not always. Sometimes Crook's blood was cold when killing was required.

In the late summer of 1858, Crook was ordered north to the Washington Territory to join an expedition against Yakima Indians. The commander of the expedition was Major Robert S. Garnett, who had been commandant of cadets at West Point during Crook's last two years. Crook much admired Garnett. "He was strict but just, and those who did their duty well were certain to be rewarded, while those who failed . . . were made to feel it."[19] Garnett, recently married and the father of a six-month-old son, was a first cousin of another officer, Captain Richard B. Garnett, and was thus—although it is unlikely he knew it—a first cousin once removed of the mixed-blood toddler Billy Garnett, then three. To Crook, of course, Garnett was just another professional soldier from Virginia.

Major Garnett's task was to chastise some Yakima Indians who had whipped an Army unit the previous year, and to track down another smaller group who had killed a party of prospectors that spring. These Indian raiders were considered to be murderers, and Garnett's orders were to kill them in battle or execute them after capture. In the course of the expedition Crook was sent ahead up the Wenatchee River with his company to seize some of the killers reported to be living with a band of friendly Yakima. "Game was scarce," Crook notes, "except sage hens and a few sharp-tailed grouse."

At the end of two days' hard going, Crook and his men suddenly encountered a young Yakima standing beside the trail, leaning on his old muzzle-loading rifle. Questioned by the Indian guides, the young man divulged that the killers sought by Crook were in camp a few miles ahead where the young man's father, Skimarwaw, was chief. This set Crook's mind to working. When his company was close to attacking distance of the camp he took the young man to one side and presented him with a careful argument:

> I . . . explained to him what we had come for, the great risk they ran in harboring those men, that in a fight we would have to kill many of our friends, which we were anxious not to do, that they would lose all their stock and many of their families, camp equipage, etc. etc. I suggested that he go to the village and tell his father privately what I had told him, and also to have his father come with him to see me.[20]

These suggestions were accepted and the following day as arranged Skimarwaw brought his whole band into Crook's camp, where the unsuspecting killers were quietly pointed out to the white soldiers and then, on Crook's signal, were seized by the soldiers who had sidled up to each of the accused men. Once they were tied up and powerless Crook "told them the object of my mission, and that I intended shooting them before I left. I wanted them to make any final preparations they wished, and a reasonable time would be given them, etc. etc." The five accused men were now condemned men. While they began alternately to make excuses and to pray, twenty soldiers were detailed for the firing squad. To ease their conscience, five guns were loaded with powder only; no man need be sure he had fired a fatal round. No such evasion would be available to the officer who gave the command to fire, however, and Crook did not want to do it. "This whole business was exceedingly distasteful to me," he wrote, "and as my 2nd Lieutenant [T. E.] Turner rather enjoyed that kind of thing, I detailed him to execute them."[21]

Fighting Indians in the far West as a young officer developed in George Crook the hardness of spirit which he displayed in the first summer of the Civil War. He drilled and trained his men from the farms of Ohio, detailed his most apt officers to learn the countryside, and ordered them

after the bushwhackers. "Very soon they commenced . . . bringing them
in as prisoners." Crook sent the captured men across the border into
Ohio, where they were briefly held at Camp Chase and then turned loose
by the officers there. Soon they were back in the region of Summersville,
"fat, saucy, with good clothes . . . in a defiant manner, as much as to say,
'Well, what are you going to do about it?' "

Crook bristled at a challenge; he detested behavior he called "insolent"
or "impudent." We may recall the schoolmate who said the young Crook
would not abide a bully. In California his orders from Major Garnett had
been clear: execute any of the Yakima killers who might be captured. He
does not cite his orders in West Virginia and on this point probably did
not have any—at any rate, not explicit orders put down in writing. But
Crook was in command and his task was to clear the country of bushwhackers:

> In a short time no more of these prisoners were brought in. By this time
> every bushwhacker in the country was known, and when an officer returned
> from a scout he would report that they had caught so-and-so, but in bring-
> ing him in he slipped off a log while crossing a stream and broke his neck, or
> that he was killed by an accidental discharge of one of the men's guns, and
> many like reports. But they never brought back any more prisoners.[22]

The progress of General Crook as he set forth in March 1876 to attack
the "hostiles" in their winter camps was recorded by his personal Boswell,
an aide-de-camp who maintained a voluminous diary, Lieutenant (later
Captain) John Gregory Bourke. What Bourke knew of Indian fighting
had been learned during four years in Arizona with Crook, and he
embarked on the campaigns of this fateful year with opinions equally
acerbic of the Sioux and the government alike. "We are now," he wrote in
Cheyenne's Inter-Ocean Hotel in mid-February, freshly arrived from
Omaha, "on the eve of the bitterest Indian war the Government has ever
been called upon to wage: a war with a tribe that has waxed fat and insolent on government bounty, and has been armed and equipped with the
most improved weapons by the connivance or carelessness of the Indian
agents."[23] In one diary entry after another he expressed confidence that
victory over "the haughty Sioux"—"the castigation so long merited"—
"may be accepted as a foregone conclusion."[24] Bourke was a few months
short of his thirtieth birthday; he had fought as an enlisted man during
the Civil War, gone on to West Point, from which he graduated in 1869,

and chased Apache all over Arizona in Crook's company between 1871 and 1875, when the general was transferred to command of the Department of the Platte. Bourke knew nothing of the Sioux but much of Crook, and with the loyalty required of an aide-de-camp he asserted that the general was up to any challenge. In mid-March on the road north Bourke described his commander at length:

> The General in size is about six feet even, weight one hundred and seventy pounds, built very spare and straight, limbs straight, long and sinewy; complexion, nervo-sanguine; hair, light-brown; cheeks, ruddy without being florid; features, delicately and firmly chiseled, eyes blue-gray; nose, a pronounced Roman, and quite large; mouth, mildly chiseled, but showing with the chin much resolution and tenacity of purpose. His general expression is placid, kind and good-humored. Unaffected and very accessible in his general demeanor there is a latent "noli mi tangere" [don't-touch-me] look of dignity about him repelling undue familiarity. His powers of endurance are extraordinary and his fortitude remarkable. A graceful rider, a noted hunter, and a dead shot, skilled in all the secrets of wood-craft and Indian warfare, having the prestige of complete success in every campaign hitherto undertaken, he is by all odds the worst foe the Sioux have ever yet had to meet.[25]

About the Sioux soon to be whipped by General Crook, Bourke knew almost nothing—barely their names. At Fort Fetterman, shortly before jumping off, Crook had learned from the Arapaho chief Black Coal that "Sitting Bull and the Minneconjous" were camped beside the Powder River about one hundred miles north of Fetterman. Sitting Bull was a Hunkpapa; various bands of the Miniconjou were led by Lame Deer, Hump, and Touch the Clouds since the death of Lone Horn a few months previous. This sort of elementary knowledge would be picked up by Bourke over time, but it hadn't happened yet.

Of the causes of the war Bourke also appeared to know nothing. The hotels and saloons of Cheyenne were chockablock with whites eager to push into the Black Hills, but between gold and the war against the Sioux Bourke seems to have drawn no connection—none, at any rate, he was willing to write down for posterity in his diary. Two weeks later, on the eve of the first battle in what came to be known as the Great Sioux War, writing with numbed fingers and the stub of a pencil because his inkwell had frozen, Bourke tried to explain what it was all about:

> Our government has been so vacillating in its deportment towards these Indians . . . that the Sioux, proverbially insolent, have grown bolder and

more haughty, imagining our people subsidiary to them. I speak now of those on the reservations. The sentiments entertained by chiefs like Sitting Bull of the North, Crazy Horse and Little Big Man, who have never gone on a reserve, and refused all offers of peace, scorned all concessions and particularly adhered to a career of spoliation and murder, would not be exaggerated by any flight of rhetoric.[26]

Insolent, bold, haughty, scornful—to Bourke these affronts seemed cause enough for war.

At Fort Laramie during the 1868 treaty council all but one of these women averted their eyes from the camera in the manner considered seemly by the Lakota. Only the woman on the right, the wife of a man named Grey Eyes, gazed openly at the photographer, Alexander Gardner.

After the 1868 treaty the Oglalas split, half going south to live on the Red Cloud Agency in Nebraska (shown here in 1876), while the other half remained in the north with chiefs like Crazy Horse, He Dog, and Black Twin, who wanted nothing to do with whites.

The mixed-blood interpreter William Garnett (right) dressed neatly for his photograph seated beside his friend and sometime employer, Baptiste Pourier, a scout for the military at Fort Laramie. The photo is a tintype and the image is therefore reversed. The photographer may have been D. S. Mitchell, who visited the Red Cloud Agency in 1877, the year Garnett turned twenty-two.

William Garnett, son of a Confederate general, spent his life among the Sioux. He is shown here about 1905. Standing behind him are his wife, Fillie, daughter of the well-known trader Nick Janis, and four of Garnett's children.

Red Cloud dominated the Oglala for more than sixty years after killing chief Bull Bear in 1841. This portrait was probably taken in October 1876, when photographer S. J. Morrow visited the Red Cloud Agency at the time General Crook, angered by Red Cloud's defiance, tried to depose him.

Spotted Tail with wife and daughter, photographed by S. J. Morrow in October 1876, when General Crook proclaimed him chief of the White River Sioux. Spotted Tail was a dogged defender of his people, but he stopped fighting the whites for good about 1865.

General George Crook began an autobiography in the 1880s but abandoned the manuscript after a brief, guarded account of the battle of the Rosebud, where most of his officers thought he had been whipped by Crazy Horse. He is pictured here near the end of his career, about the time he was appointed commander of the Military Division of the Missouri.

Lieutenant William Philo Clark, General Crook's chief of scouts, was confident he could "work" Indians to do the Army's bidding. He was photographed by D. S. Mitchell standing beside Little Hawk, uncle of Crazy Horse, at the Red Cloud Agency in 1877.

General Crook's favorite scout, Frank
Grouard, lived with Crazy Horse's band
for several years before showing up at
the Red Cloud Agency in 1875. He is
pictured here in 1891 at the Pine Ridge
Agency in South Dakota, shortly
after the battle of Wounded Knee.

Woman Dress, a nephew of Red Cloud
enlisted as a scout by Lieutenant Clark,
was the source of a report that Crazy
Horse was planning to murder General
Crook in council. As a reward he was
retained as a scout when most others
were dismissed in 1878.

He Dog, a lifelong friend of Crazy Horse, said they were "born in the same year and at the same season of the year. We grew up together in the same band, played together, courted the girls together, and fought together." But during the last weeks of Crazy Horse's life He Dog sided with Red Cloud.

American Horse joined Crazy Horse as a Shirt Wearer of the Oglala in 1868, but sided with Red Cloud thereafter. He was standing near Crazy Horse when the chief was fatally stabbed and helped to carry him into the adjutant's office.

George Sword (front, right) with Two Bears appeared in a play, *May Cody, or Lost and Won*, when it premiered in New York City on September 3, 1877, one day before the Army attempted to arrest Crazy Horse in his camp on the White River. Sword is shown here with Buffalo Bill Cody (center) and three other members of Cody's theatrical troupe.

When the Army came to arrest him, Crazy Horse fled with his ailing wife from the Red Cloud Agency to Camp Sheridan (shown here in October 1877). That night, promised by Lieutenant Jesse Lee that no harm would come to him, Crazy Horse agreed to return to Camp Robinson the following day.

The body of Crazy Horse was taken by his father and mother to the Spotted Tail Agency, where it was wrapped in a red blanket and placed in a low tree overlooking the military post. A day or two later, Lieutenant Jesse Lee arranged to surround the traditional scaffold with a board fence to protect the body from wolves.

Little Big Man in Washington in September 1877. His right hand covers the wound on his left wrist received two weeks earlier in the struggle with Crazy Horse. Most of the northern Indians fled back to the Powder River country in October 1877 but Little Big Man, hoping to become an important chief, stayed behind.

10

"I knew this village by the horses."

IN THE FALL OF 1875, the chiefs and the white soldiers sitting under the shade of the tent canvas near the lone tree on Little White Clay Creek had been watched as they talked day after day by the twelve-year-old Oglala boy known as Black Elk, son and grandson of men of the same name. The boy asked his father what the talk was about, and the elder Black Elk told him the whites wanted the Black Hills for themselves. The father was partially crippled; his leg had been crushed by a falling horse in the Fetterman fight nine years earlier and he never walked right afterward. He said that Red Dog, the chief who spoke for Red Cloud at the council, warned the Indians that "if they did not lease the Black Hills to the grandfather at Washington, the Black Hills would be just like snow held in the hand and melting away. In other words, they were going to take the Black Hills away from us anyway."

After the talking was over and the commissioners went away, Black Elk's family and some others packed up their new lodges made of canvas duck and left the Red Cloud Agency for the north. "We wanted to join Crazy Horse's band on the Tongue River," Black Elk recalled later. Crazy Horse was much talked about and closely observed. On the way north Black Elk's band found that the buffalo were plenty along the Powder River and camped for ten days with a group of Wagluhe from the agency. But when this group of Wagluhe learned that the others were going north to join the war chief they broke away and hurried back south, fearing trouble.

The elder Black Elk called the father of Crazy Horse cousin, so the boy naturally called the chief cousin as well and was anxious to see him. Two years earlier, when Black Elk was ten, he had helped the well-known medicine man Horn Chips build a sweat lodge in the Black Hills, where the band had gone to cut lodgepoles. Black Elk believed that it was Horn

Chips who gave Crazy Horse his power in battle, and that the transaction perhaps took place right there, that summer, in that sweat lodge. But when the band finally reached the big Oglala camp along the Tongue River after a journey of several weeks the boy was disappointed to learn that Crazy Horse was not there. "He must have been on a warpath against the Crow," he concluded. Black Elk's mother, White Cow Sees, pitched their lodge on the upper reaches of the Tongue near the lodge of an uncle, Iron Crow. The camp was just downstream of the mouth of a stream coming in from the east called Hanging Woman Creek.[1]

The Tongue River was in the heart of what had once been the Crow country. The Sioux had pushed them west, but the Crow resisted, and the big camps of Sioux along the Tongue and Powder were always half expecting a raid by Crow horse thieves. Fighting between the Sioux and the Crow at this time was constant, and about the time Black Elk's family moved close to Iron Crow, a war party set out from the camp for the winter villages of the Crow further west. The eight men who left on this raid, as it happened, were all Wagluhe from the Red Cloud Agency who had come north with their chief, Blue Horse, to camp with the Oglala for a time. Not long after the war party set out under its leader, Young Iron (Maza Cinkala), some Oglala scouts came into camp with a warning that Crow were in the area. By this time winter had set in; it was late January. Camp was rarely moved and the horses were thin. Everyone was urged to keep a close eye on their horses. That night guards were posted about the camp. The best horses were tethered close to lodges. Others were closed into corrals made of thick brush. With dark the camp gradually settled down and the boy Black Elk was soon asleep, but others remained awake.

After the excitement was all over young Black Elk learned what happened, but at the fatal moment he was asleep. Not asleep was a man named Crow Nose or Crow Head (Kangi Pa), whose lodge was on one side of the gate of a large corral filled with horses, not far from Black Elk's lodge. On the other side of the gate was the lodge of the son-in-law of Crow Nose, a man named Yellow Shirt. Staying with Crow Nose this night was the Wagluhe chief Blue Horse, who went to sleep leaving Crow Nose to peep occasionally at the corral through a small flap in the tipi wall. Crow Nose had an uneasy feeling the enemy were coming for his horses, but hours passed without incident.

Finally he told his wife to keep watch while he went to sleep. Soon, peeping through the flap, Crow Nose's wife saw a figure in the corral among the horses, leading one toward the gate. "Old Man, you'd better get up," she said, "I see a man there among the horses."

Taking his gun Crow Nose slipped out of the lodge and crept close to the corral where the horse thief was quietly lowering the bars of the gate. The horse hopped over the last bar, and the thief jumped up onto his back, and just at that moment Crow Nose shot him point-blank.

The boy Black Elk woke instantly at the sound of the gun. In a moment there was more shooting followed by shouts and cries and the sound of people running. The remainder of the night was all excitement as the whole village, Black Elk too, gathered to look at the Crow, killed just as he thought he was getting away. The killing of any enemy justifies four coups—one for the killer, the others for those who strike the body. Crow Nose had called for his son-in-law to count first coup on the Crow, and others followed. Soon the whole village was striking the dead man's body with sticks and leaving them in a pile on the ground. A fire was built; people began a kill dance right there and kept it up for the rest of the night. When morning came the village crier walked around loudly calling that it was time to move, the new site would be on Kills Himself Creek to the south. In the bustle of striking the lodges and packing horses Crow Nose, still exulting, painted his face black, put on his war clothes and his necklace of bear claws, mounted the horse the Crow had tried to steal, and rode about the camp. The black paint made the women shout in joy and Crow Nose sang in triumph of his great deed:

> Yellow Shirt, come forth, I have got him.
> All you have to do is coup him.

But this triumph over the horse thief almost immediately soured. The crier was back again a day or two later, calling out, "Yeah-hey! The Loafers who went to the war party, it has been reported that they have been slain." The women in the village all "sent up the tremolo," said Black Elk, referring to the high-pitched, ululating cry of grief and dismay. The news had been brought by Young Iron after two days' hard journey through the snow.

The first to see Young Iron, coming wrapped against the cold in his blanket with his gun, was He Dog's brother Short Bull, out looking for horses in the morning chill. It was not the custom of the Sioux to blurt out important news. Short Bull invited Young Iron to smoke, and they did. Then he told Short Bull what had happened. The group had camped. Young Iron said that early one morning he had gone out to scout, staying away all day. When he returned he gave a wolf howl to alert the others but heard no sound in response. This worried him. He crept close. All he saw was a lifeless arm in the snow, still in its coat. At that he departed for home, resting only one night along the way.

Later a party went back and found the seven dead men lying in the snow with blood in several places nearby suggesting some of the Crow, too, had been killed or wounded. It seemed clear what had happened—the party of Crow horse stealers, fleeing the Oglala camp after one of them had been killed by Crow Nose, stumbled on the young Wagluhe in their camp. Surprise and numbers overwhelmed the Sioux. The nephew of Short Bull known as Amos Bad Heart Bull later drew a picture of the discovery. In a small circle were six bodies piled almost on top of each other; a seventh lay a little way off. A water bag was still hanging from its tripod. None of the dead was missing an arm; probably one of the bodies had been partially covered in snow with only an arm exposed. That was the story as Young Iron told it, but not all of the Oglala believed him. Young Iron had been the leader; he was supposed to protect his men or die with them. Some said that Young Iron, sensing trouble, must have run, leaving the others. But He Dog and Short Bull accepted his story, and nothing was ever proved against the survivor.

The killing of the seven Wagluhe found its way into the winter counts, with all the other killings large and small that punctuated the life of the Oglala. The killing of the Crow horse thief was the big subject of talk in the Sioux camps that winter, not the expeditions being mounted against them by the white soldiers to the south. It is not clear if any of the northern Indians knew in late January that they were facing an ultimatum—return to the agencies in the next week or two or face war. It is certain the twelve-year-old Black Elk didn't know it. What made the biggest impression on him was what he saw when he ran toward the excitement the night Crow Nose killed the horse thief.

When the boy got to the scene he was jolted with horror—people in their frenzy of anger and triumph had already been at work on the horse thief's body with knives and hatchets. The Crow's arms and legs had been hacked off; his skull was bloody and wet where the scalp had been torn away. By the light of the fire the people sang and danced. Black Elk watched as the dead man's torso was propped up. Men ran up with bows and arrows and with guns, filling the body with arrows, shooting the dead man to pieces. Before the camp broke next day the dismembered limbs of the Crow were tied to bushes and trees in triumph and in warning.[2]

For two weeks in March 1876, Crook's column, nine hundred men strong, marched north through fair weather and foul, roughly following the course of the abandoned Bozeman Road. On the very first night some Sioux came boldly into the camp, shot a beef herder, and then stampeded the forty-five cattle intended to feed Crook's men. Chase gained nothing. When the Indians realized a detachment of cavalry was following fast behind they cut loose from the cattle and disappeared. Nor did Crook get his cattle back; the cavalry couldn't turn them and abandoned the herd to disappear into the prairie. The wounded beef herder, shot through the lung, was placed in a wagon, where he suffered but eventually recovered. The column kept up its steady pace of twenty or more miles a day. Afternoons when the sun was out could be mild, in the low fifties. Nights were often bitter, falling to ten or more degrees below zero. On really cold nights the mercury was said to congeal in the thermometer; officers and men speculated that it had dropped to twenty, thirty, even forty below.

Crook wanted Indians and there was sign of them everywhere. Along the way the scouts often crossed Indian trails—the broad scuffings left by travois poles and the unshod ponies of the Indians, plus a few shod horses stolen from whites. The trails of large camps were always littered with debris—bits of clothing, discarded hides, worn-out moccasins, kettles with a hole in the bottom, broken knives. Once two Indians on horseback were sighted a long way off—"young bucks," Bourke wrote, although they rode away when the column was still a thousand yards away. A day later a white trail of smoke rose from a high hill ahead of the column, a "signal smoke," in the opinion of the scouts. The flashing of mirrors was occasionally seen. On the fourth night out another group of Indians was discovered trying to enter the camp; a lively skirmish broke out in the dark. One soldier was shot through the cheek. All reflected next day how badly things might have gone if the Indians had succeeded in stampeding the horses and mules, sending them every which way through the camp.

Crook let all these incidents go by; in his view harebrained chasing after Indians would only break down the horses. What he wanted was one clear shot at a camp of Indians who weren't expecting him. The general believed he had been watched from the moment the column crossed the North Platte River near Fetterman; he assumed Indian scouts were carrying word north of his approach, but he pressed the column hard, still hoping for surprise.[3]

The principal drag on the column was the wagon train, loaded down with a hundred tons of forage and grain for the cavalry horses. While camped on Crazy Woman Creek on the evening of March 6, Crook met first with his officers and then with his scouts. To speed his progress he had decided to divide the column. The wagons with the great bulk of supplies would stay behind on the site of old Fort Reno, abandoned in 1868. The rest of the men with rations for fifteen days would be free to travel with a fast-moving packtrain of mules. The idea was to cut directly across the Badlands separating Crazy Woman from the Clear Fork of the Powder River to the north, leaving the Indians to wonder where he had gone. What Crook wanted to know from the scouts was whether it could be done. Frank Grouard says that on this occasion he had "about the first talk I had with General Crook after he hired me." A number of the scouts in Crook's expedition had been through the Powder River country—Louis Richard; the Shangreau brothers, John and Louis; the Bats, Big and Little; Speed Stagner; and others. But Grouard never hesitated to put himself at the center of the story:

> There were none of the scouts able to take him through. He wanted to make the trip after night had set in. He asked me if I could take him through. I told him that I could. He asked me what the distance was, but I could not tell him the distance because I didn't know anything about miles. I told him I could tell him what time he could get there—that if he would start after dark, he could get there at daylight on a good fast walk.

Arrangements were completed in camp during the following day while Bourke wrote copiously in his diary. At dark around seven o'clock they set out, helped by level ground at first, a brilliantly clear night, and a three-quarters moon. Grouard may not have known how many miles they had to travel—thirty-five, as it happened—but he was right about how long it would take. After ten hours of steady going, with the ground about midway growing increasingly rough and mountainous, they came abruptly upon the banks of Clear Creek. Grouard said much of the trip was made in the dark in a heavy snow. At daylight, when "you could not see fifty yards ahead of you on account of the snow," Crook rode up to ask Grouard how far it remained to the creek. "Not more than two or three hundred yards," Grouard said he answered. He knew by the lay of the land. And in a moment they were there.

Here we encounter the Grouard known as slippery with the truth, inflating his success as scout. Crook in his memoir said it didn't begin to snow until they had made camp at daylight and rolled into their blankets and buffalo robes. Bourke, who recorded the night march at the time, described the brilliant moonlit landscape they traversed under "Cynthia's silvery beams," then the cold awakening on the Clear Fork after three hours' sleep with plunging temperatures and a "bitter, pelting storm of snow."[4] As a witness Grouard is a tricky customer, but the reader should not jump to conclusions.

The column now continued cross-country to the Tongue. Crook sent all the scouts ahead down the Tongue to the Yellowstone, looking for trace of Indians.

> The command [Grouard says] was to go as far as Otter Creek and wait there until our return. General Crook asked me how he would know the creek when he got to it. I told him there were three pine trees in a row right in the forks, all by themselves . . . He asked me if I knew every rock and tree in the country, and I told him I came pretty near it. He was surprised at my knowledge of the country. The other scouts could travel along the road, but after they got a little distance from the highway, they didn't know a thing about the country.

But no Indians. The scouts found evidence of many camps down along the Tongue, all abandoned. They ranged west as far as the Rosebud, but found nothing there. Crook with the main column continued more slowly on down the Tongue, living on hardtack, coffee, and frozen bacon with the occasional tough and stringy bit of meat from an old buffalo bull, brought in by the scouts. Crook in the advance fired on one old bull and badly wounded him in the shoulder, but he escaped. At another point in the march Crook did better when a covey of pin-tailed grouse suddenly broke across his path. The general killed six with seven shots. According to his Boswell, "all but one were shot in the neck or head."

But no Indians. The officers began to fear a failure; rations were running low and they would soon have to turn back. And yet signs of Indians were everywhere. In one abandoned camp of sixty lodges the scouts found a dead puppy tied to a tree; it had been strangled—the right way to kill dog for a stew—but left behind. Bourke speculated that the Indians must have learned of Crook's advance and pulled out in a hurry. On the morning of March 13 near the point where Hanging Woman Creek joined the Tongue, the scouts came in with a stray mule, a sure sign, they said, of Indians nearby. The column passed several burial trees with wrapped bodies tied into the branches. There were many places where lodges had been pitched. Bourke noted the forked-stick frames used by Indian women for drying meat, still standing. Huge stacks of firewood were piled here and there. Big cottonwood trees had been felled so the ponies might browse on the upper branches. In the little villages strung out along the river, Bourke noticed the brush corrals for enclosing horses at night, some big enough for scores, even hundreds of animals. In another camp discovered on March 14, Bourke examined some Indian drawings. "On the soft inner bark of the cottonwood trees," he wrote in pencil—this time his bottle of ink had not only frozen but burst the previous night—"rude, obscene pictures have been scrawled by the young Indians in a number of places. In execution they are as feeble as in design they are disgusting." That day, Bourke recorded, the scouts brought in something unique:

> A human arm, belonging to an Indian, and still in a fair state of preservation, was picked up in the abandoned Indian village today. It has been amputated at the elbow-joint, two of the fingers had been shot off and five buckshot wounds were in it.

Grouard and the other scouts had been returning from one of their scourings of the countryside. Unlike Bourke, Grouard understood what he was seeing:

> We found where they had killed a Crow Indian, quartered him, and hung him up. It was on Tongue River, just below the mouth of Hanging Woman. His arms, legs, head and everything were hung up in different places where the village had been, and it had occurred before the command started. I heard the Indians had killed a man there in camp. He was stealing horses. It must have been done a month before. There is nothing left of a horsethief after the Indians catch him.

Grouard was convinced the Indians would be found on the Powder River, not the Tongue, as the trails all seemed to be going east. It was now that he felt he made an enduring enemy of some of the other scouts, especially Louis Richard, who argued that the Indians had moved west over to the Little Bighorn. But Crook had come around to Grouard's side by now; he trusted him, and about midnight on the night of March 15–16 he sent the scout east up the valley of Hanging Woman Creek in the direction of the headwaters of Otter Creek, which marked the divide between the valleys of the Tongue and the Powder.[5] Dismounting near a high overlook early next morning, Grouard spotted two Indians far up the creek, apparently tracking an animal. For several hours he watched the Indians closely with a telescope as they went slowly about their business until suddenly they appeared to be looking at him. Grouard was sure he was hidden, but through his glass they seemed to be staring directly at him. Looking back he saw what was holding their attention—to his rear the rest of Crook's scouts were coming over the hills. Recruiting several of them, Grouard went after the Indians, who had turned tail. He wanted to be sure they hadn't seen the command. When Crook and the main column came up late in the day Grouard told him they had found Indians at last. All that remained was to track the two hunters back to their camp, which Grouard expected to find just where he had said it would be—on the Powder. Crook divided his command one more time, detailing Colonel Joseph J. Reynolds of the 3rd Cavalry to go on ahead with about three hundred men and attack any Indians to which Grouard might lead him. With the soldiers went Lieutenant Bourke and Robert Strahorn, a reporter whose dispatches appeared in the *Chicago Tribune*, the Denver *Rocky Mountain News*, and other newspapers.

If there was to be any hope of surprising the Indians at dawn, a night march was necessary, but the going was brutal—bitter cold, icy rocks, a constant wind with frequent snow squalls that made even the ground almost invisible. Grouard dismounted and followed the trail of the two hunters on foot. Frequent ravines had to be crossed carefully, lest horses break a leg or fall and crush a rider. At one point they passed an eerie scene, heavy black smoke issuing directly from a crevice in the ground, exhaust from a burning coal seam deep below. Grouard typically suggests that he was the man of the hour, doing all the hard trailing with just a companion or two to keep him company, but Strahorn, riding at the head of the column with Bourke, confirms that the feat was impressive:

> I had, during the night, an excellent opportunity of witnessing the truly remarkable achievement of Frank Grouard, our principal guide and trailer. His knowledge of the country had been noteworthy ever since the opening of the campaign, but the duty he was now called upon to perform was of just the nature that would have bewildered almost anyone in broad daylight . . . Over rugged bluffs and narrow valleys, through gloomy defiles and down breakneck declivities, plunged the indomitable Frank; now down on his hands and knees in the deep snow, scrutinizing the faint footprints, then losing the trail for an instant, darting to and fro until it was found, and again following it up with the keenness of a hound.[6]

The other scouts—"his valuable assistants," in Strahorn's phrase—did their part, but it was Grouard who led the way, pushing on so rapidly that the trailing column of troops frequently sent word up the line, begging the scouts to halt, so the column stringing out along the trail might be closed up.

The snow stopped in the small hours of the morning; the temperature plunged as the night sky cleared. While the command halted, struggled to remain awake, and battled frostbite, Grouard went on ahead. Then, in the very first light of dawn, Grouard saw before him rising in a long roll a dense fog coming up from the waters of the Powder River. Grouard could hear the bells on Indian ponies, faint in the morning quiet. He sent his companion, Buckskin Jack Russell, back to alert Colonel Reynolds to bring up the command. Grouard made his way forward, came within a mile of the village below, and eventually got close enough to hear the camp crier calling out that scouts sent out by the chiefs had found no soldiers. "I could hear it as plain as could be."

Now, surely, Grouard steps over the bounds of possibility. He says he pointed out the village to Reynolds when he arrived, and the colonel responded, "What am I going to do?"

"Fight them Indians," said Grouard.

"How will I place my command?"

It seems hard to credit: Grouard says first he found the Indians, and then he told Reynolds how to plan his attack. But this amazing claim is half confirmed by Reynolds, who wrote in an official report, "After getting an imperfect view of the village and questioning Frank Grouard as to the best mode of approaching it, I immediately made disposition for attack."[7]

Before the attack began, Grouard says, he went down the mountain to the flat by the river where the horses were grazing. He walked across the flat through the horses. They did not spook, but let him pass quietly. He recognized some of these horses; he had seen them when he was living in He Dog's lodge with the Hunkpatila Oglala. "I knew this village by the horses. Knew every horse there was there."

The sun was well up now; the cavalry was poised to come sweeping down on the village. Troops in a ravine nearby were waiting for the shooting to begin.

> When I got within twenty yards of the camp, I yelled to Crazy Horse. I recalled what he had told me during my endeavors to secure the Black Hills Treaty—that he would rather fight than make a treaty—and told him that now was the time to come out and get all the fighting he wanted, as the troops were all around his camp![8]

11

"He is no good and should be killed."

AS THE INDIANS REMEMBERED it, the first warning came from an old man who had gone out early, maybe to check on his horses, maybe to pray. "The soldiers are right here!" he shouted. "The soldiers are right here!"[1]

But he shouted in Cheyenne, not in Lakota. Some Oglala were also camped there on the Powder River—eight lodges belonging to He Dog, his brother Little Shield, and other relatives—but most of the people were Cheyenne, with their chiefs Old Bear, Little Wolf, and Two Moon. Moments later came the warning cry of a boy who had been out with the horses a few hundred yards to the south of the village. Then a woman emerging from her lodge and seeing the soldiers began to yell. The sun was well up; people were dressed and about their business, and as soon as the warnings were shouted and the horses of the cavalry could be heard everybody began yelling and running. After that came the sound of gun-fire—the revolvers of the cavalry as they charged across the flat to run off the Indian ponies, some firing of carbines from the bluffs to the west, the rattle and pop of Indian guns in response.

Many of the warriors were gone from camp—ten had been sent out the night before to check on a report that soldiers were near. According to He Dog another group of men were on a war expedition in the north.[2] The camp was not expecting an attack. Only a day or two earlier some Sioux had arrived from the south, among them a man named Crawler, bringing a message from the Red Cloud Agency: "It is spring; we are waiting for you."[3]

The first shots and cries ended the peace of the morning. While the women were snatching up the smaller children and running for the river, He Dog took a position in a clump of trees at the south end of the village, facing the charge of the cavalry. He had a revolver, two rifles, a bow, and a quiver full of arrows. He immediately opened fire on the attacking force and inevitably it shied to one side. As the cavalry closed on the village, horses went down, then some soldiers—ten were killed or wounded in all, many right there at the edge of the Indian camp. The cavalry dismounted, holstered their revolvers, and began to fire their carbines as they moved in among the lodges. But the attack had come too late and too slow. The Indians all escaped across the river or into the hills to the north, even Old Bear, leading his wife on a horse. After the women and children had been hurried to safety the Cheyenne warrior Wooden Leg turned back to fight and found himself with two friends, Bear Walks on a Ridge and young Two Moons, son of the chief. Before them was a soldier, somehow cut off from the rest of his unit.

> Two Moons had a repeating rifle . . . he stood it up on end in front of him and passed his hands up and down the barrel, not touching it, while making medicine. Then he said, "My medicine is good. Watch me kill that soldier." He fired but his bullet missed. Bear Walks on a Ridge then fired . . . [and] hit the soldier in the back of the head. We rushed upon the man and beat and stabbed him to death. Another Cheyenne joined us to help in the killing. He took the soldier's rifle. I stripped off the blue coat and kept it. Two Moons and Bear Walks on a Ridge took whatever else he had and they wanted.[4]

By nine thirty in the morning the initial fighting had died down. The soldiers were in possession of the camp and most of the Indian ponies. Despite the heavy firing from many directions only one Indian had been left behind dead, a man named Whirlwind. He had been caught in the open on the shoulder of the hills to the west. No one knew exactly how he was killed or when. Where his body was found later was high enough to give him a good view over the camp to the east, so maybe he was one of those restless men who are always up early to watch the sun rise.[5]

The village was on a flat curled into a bend of the Carli Wakpa Tanka—in Lakota, the Big Powder River. All around the camp from the north to the west and south was a kind of bench or shoulder, backed by a rising tier of hills. Scrambling down that shoulder to reach the village on foot was not easy, on horseback impossible. So the village was both hemmed in and protected all around its western edge. The cavalry had attacked after making its way down through a narrow defile to the southern end of the flat. In a ravine on the southwest were soldiers on foot, also firing into the village. But on the shoulder to the west and above it in the hills to the north there was no enemy—the way was entirely open—and this fact allowed all the Indians to escape in the first minutes of the attack save only the one man killed and an old woman who had been shot in the thigh. From the rocks and hills above the village the Indians watched while the soldiers rounded up the ponies and began to set fire to their lodges and all their possessions, including all that remained of their winter's supply of food. Everything went into the flames—robes and quilled clothing and rawhide boxes filled with *wasna*, the mix of dried meat and animal fat, which burst into flame and sent thick clouds of smoke boiling up into the sky. From time to time cartridges or a canister of gunpowder exploded. Soon after, to the Indians' surprise, the entire force of white soldiers mounted up and departed upriver toward the south, driving the Indian ponies as they went.

That night, reinforced by the Indians who had been off scouting, the Cheyenne and their Oglala allies sent a party in pursuit of the soldiers in hope of recapturing the pony herd. Passing through the burned village they found one lodge still standing; in it was the old woman who had been shot during the fight. "We talked about this matter," Wooden Leg remembered, "all agreeing that the act showed the soldiers had good hearts." Also at the edge of the burned village were the abandoned bodies of four dead white soldiers, a most surprising fact. Indians did all in their power to rescue their own dead from the field and whites normally did likewise, but not this time.

This lapse of battlefield discipline was followed by another of greater moment for the Indians left poor by the burning of their possessions. As night fell twenty or thirty warriors followed the white soldiers to their camp upriver. While the soldiers slept the Indians crept up on the pony herd. "I see my horse," one man might whisper. "There is mine," another would add. Luck was with them; for some reason guards were few so the Indians spooked the horses and drove off some of them. Shots were fired. When one bunch had been driven to safety the Indians came back for another. The night was punctuated with shooting and excitement as they gradually reclaimed the larger part of their horses and then headed back north to the hills where the women and children were sheltering from the cold.

Early the next day the village began to move north down the Powder in search of their relatives, guided by He Dog and his brother Little Shield. On the fourth day, after crossing the Little Powder, they found the Hunkpatila village of Crazy Horse. The Oglala were almost as short of food as the northern Cheyenne, so the two camps decided to join and march together to the north and east until they found the village of Sitting Bull. It took two days. There two large council lodges were set up to shelter the people who had lost everything. Hunkpapa women came with gifts of clothing, robes, and blankets. Horses were given to the men who had none. "I can never forget the generosity of Sitting Bull's Hunkpapa Sioux," said Wooden Leg.[6]

The impoverished Cheyenne and Sioux from the Powder River told Sitting Bull that the soldiers had been led to their camp by Yugata, the Grabber. Some had seen him and some had heard him shouting in Lakota, calling on Crazy Horse to come out and fight. The Hunkpapa chief was angry with Grouard and himself alike. "One time that man should have been killed and I kept him, and now he has joined the soldiers," the chief said. "He is no good and should be killed." His nephew White Bull later remarked, "Grouard was the only white man who ever fooled Sitting Bull, and he fooled the whole tribe."[7]

When the Cheyenne and the Oglala all joined Sitting Bull the camp grew large—probably three hundred lodges or more, as many as fifteen hundred to two thousand people. Soon came a large band of Miniconjou under Lame Deer, then more Cheyenne under Lame White Man arrived, followed by a steady accretion of other groups, large and small, as winter softened into spring. The chiefs and leading men were in constant discussion. They knew by this time that the white men had threatened war if the Indians did not come into an agency. Most said they would rather fight than submit. He Dog said later that before the attack they had been planning to work their way south to the Red Cloud Agency, keeping their promise of the previous summer to Young Man Afraid of His Horses. Now his band wanted nothing to do with the whites. Every few days the growing camp in the north moved to find clean ground, grass for the ponies, and meat for the people. For a time, feeling safer as the camp grew with fresh arrivals from the agencies, the combined Sioux and Cheyenne moved north up the ladder of creeks which ran into the Powder River from the east, then crossed the river and headed west by easy stages toward the Rosebud and the Little Bighorn, following the grass and the buffalo as spring came to the northern plains.

Heading down through broken country the day after the fight, Crook and his men blundered into a band of Indians driving a large herd of ponies. In Crook's view those Indians should have been dead or running. It was his first hint that things had not gone well the previous day. Crook himself snapped off a quick shot at a man in a warbonnet and knocked him off his horse, but other Indians lifted the wounded man from the ground and carried him off. After they met up Crook told Bourke about his freehand shot. Bourke in turn told the general about the fight, which was officially described henceforth as the first victory in the war against the Sioux and as a painful blow against one of the "worst" of the chiefs, Crazy Horse. Crook and Bourke both insisted as long as they lived that it was Crazy Horse who had been attacked on the Powder River. But Bourke wrote in his diary, and probably told Crook on seeing him, "that when our men were leaving the village on one side, the Sioux were entering on the other."[8] That told the story of the fight on the Powder River.

From Bourke, Reynolds, Grouard, and others Crook soon gathered an account that raised troubling questions. Why had the Indians all managed to escape when the soldiers had the advantage of surprise? Why had Colonel Reynolds burned all the dried meat found in the Indian village when the soldiers were short of food themselves? Why had all the ammunition found in the village been destroyed when the soldiers were short of ammunition? Why had the Indian blankets and buffalo robes been burned when scores of soldiers were suffering frostbite from the bitter cold? Why had Reynolds hastily abandoned the village when the soldiers were in firm control? Why had the bodies of dead soldiers been left behind in Reynolds's precipitous retreat, and with them, it was said— Bourke didn't see it, but he believed it—"one poor wretch, shot in arm and thigh, [who] fell alive into the hands of the enemy and was scalped before the eyes of a comrade"?[9] And finally, why had Reynolds left the Indian ponies unguarded the first night, thus allowing most of them to be recaptured?

But Crook was a realist. Surprise was gone, food and ammunition were low, there were wounded to think of, so he turned around and led his command back up the Powder River to rejoin his wagons at old Fort Reno. Next day, continuing south, Crook told Grouard to ride with him in the ambulance on the trip back to Fort Fetterman. For two days Grouard had been telling Crook "about everything that occurred at the Crazy Horse battle . . . I didn't spare them a bit in the world," Grouard recollected. "I told him just how the whole thing had been run." Now, in the ambulance going south, Crook told Grouard a few things.

He spoke of the stories that had been told against me by the scouts, the bad reputation they had been giving me . . . Reshaw [Louis Richard] had been trying to put up a job on me from the time I had started out by myself on Tongue River. He had circulated stories around amongst the officers and told the general I was in communication with the Indians every night, that I was fixing up a plot with them to have the command massacred . . . General Crook told me that all the officers believed it except himself.[10]

The way Grouard added it up, the most suspicious of all was Colonel Reynolds, who feared Grouard had led him into a trap. The colonel panicked and fled, in Grouard's view. Bourke in the privacy of his diary had a simpler explanation: "incompetency" and "imbecility."[11] The *Rocky Mountain News* reporter Robert Strahorn came closest to saying outright what most believed—that Reynolds had botched the affair, destroying supplies he should have saved and allowing the Indians to recapture their ponies.

Was a botch the same as a defeat? This Crook did not want to concede. The answer came down to numbers. By official count, Reynolds's command suffered four dead and four wounded. Strahorn hedged on his estimate of Indian casualties, quoting soldiers who "state it all the way from thirty to fifty."

Bourke in his diary was shy on the question as well. Despite the absence of actual bodies, he scribbled the night after the fight, "we had excellent reasons for believing we had killed and wounded many in the enemy's ranks."[12] In the first published reports of the fight, Strahorn's "thirty to fifty" and Bourke's "many" were bandied freely, but the dispiriting truth spread in military circles soon enough. Caroline Frey Winne, wife of the Army surgeon stationed at the Sidney Barracks, wrote scornfully to her brother a month after the fight, "Come to get down to the facts of Crook's expedition, the one hundred Indians killed amounted to just four killed, so some of the Indians who have come into the agencies report . . . we fail to see the success. 'But 'twas a famous victory.' "[13]

What Crook thought he kept at first to himself. Bourke recorded that the general was "annoyed and chagrined,"[14] but a week's brooding convinced him that Reynolds's failures were inexcusable. At Fort Fetterman, on his way back from the winter campaign, Crook drew up formal charges and specifications against Reynolds preparatory to a general court-martial to affix responsibility. Reynolds protested bitterly to no effect.

With charges filed, and prodded by an impatient General Sheridan, Crook began to organize a second expedition to go after the hostiles. A few weeks later, in May, it was all unfolding just as it had the first time—

gathering of officers and men at Fort Fetterman, perched high on the south bank overlooking the North Platte River. From the fort it was quite a drop down into the river valley below, well greened up by now. The view north from bluff's edge was unobstructed—an endless rolling emptiness of grass and sage disappearing into the sky. For two weeks men, wagons, and animals were ferried across the river to a tent city where Crook, in the last days of May, took command of a new expedition of twelve hundred men and made ready to follow Frank Grouard and the Bats north against the hostiles.

George Crook was in charge of his own show, but he was answering to Sheridan at his headquarters in Chicago. The two men had gone into the Civil War as little-known officers of modest rank, friends from their days at West Point, eager for command. But from the very outset luck seemed to favor the odd small man with the red face, long arms, and big head. Both men were offered regiments by state governors—the 2nd Michigan Cavalry to Sheridan, the 36th Ohio Infantry to Crook. But Sheridan managed to succeed with General Henry Halleck, the Union Army's chief of staff, where Crook had failed with President Lincoln. Halleck stretched the rules to let Sheridan serve as an officer in the regular army, while Crook was a volunteer. A colonel was a colonel, but only till the war was over, at which moment the volunteers would revert to their prewar rank.

So it went. Within days, lucky Phil Sheridan was jumped to command of a brigade to fill the vacancy of a general moving up. Three weeks later, when his eight hundred men were attacked by a Confederate force of five thousand at Booneville, Mississippi, Sheridan extracted an astonishing victory by sending two companies down a little-known woods road to attack the Confederates in the rear just as he assaulted them in front. The rebels panicked and fled. Five fellow officers, all brigadier generals, promptly wired Halleck: "Brigadiers scarce; good ones scarcer . . . The undersigned respectfully beg that you will obtain the promotion of Sheridan. He is worth his weight in gold."[15]

A general's star soon came Sheridan's way. In Mississippi, too, he acquired a black gelding with three white stockings which stood five feet eight inches at the shoulder, a gift from one of his officers. Sheridan named the horse after the Mississippi town where he got him: Rienzi.[16] It was a big horse for a small man. President Lincoln himself once remarked that Sheridan was "a brown, chunky little chap, with a long body, short legs, not enough neck to hang him, and such long arms that if his ankles itch he can skratch them without stooping."[17] Soldiers joked that Sheridan, at five foot four (or five, or six, according to the witness), had to climb up his saber to mount the big Morgan. Sheridan may have been small—by the last year of the war his men were calling him "Little Phil"—but there was a great deal of fight in him. When fortune offered him an opportunity he generally improved it, and in 1864 General Ulysses Grant brought him east to command Union forces in the Shenandoah Valley. Among the generals under Sheridan was his friend from Ohio, West Point, and the Indian wars in California, George Crook, in command of a force with the imposing title of the Army of West Virginia. In reality it was little more than two divisions stretched thin.

Sheridan had risen fast, Crook not so fast. If Sheridan was lucky, you could say Crook was unlucky. He got off to a slow start, no fault of his own, under Major General John C. Frémont, known as "the Pathfinder" for his early explorations of overland routes to California. Frémont ran for president but lost, and then proved a failure at war. The men under him, including Crook, got little chance to show their merits. In one early fight Crook was wounded in the foot by a "spent ball," which soon hurt like blazes, worse even than the poisoned arrows of the California Indians. After Frémont resigned his command, Crook and his 36th Ohio were attached to Major General John Pope's headquarters in time to witness the Union disaster at Second Bull Run in August 1862; after the battle Crook rounded up stragglers—"my first introduction to a demoralized army." Nightfall ended the rout and a drizzling rain next day gave the Union forces time to move out.

Crook's Civil War followed the classic pattern—an endless ordeal of marching and counter-marching, bad food and foul weather, opportunities lost and campaigns that sputtered out, all of it punctuated with bloody fights small and large. Sometimes these fights were very large, with thousands of men killed, wounded, or reported missing. Crook was at South Mountain on the fourteenth day of September 1862 and at Antietam on the sixteenth. From Virginia he was transferred to Tennessee for a year's list of places and dates, including Chickamauga, where armies broke or held, then returned to Virginia and the Shenandoah early in 1864.

Crook rose, but not fast. It was the custom to reward officers in the regular army with brevet ranks for valor or performance. Besides the honor, the practical consequence was the fact that a brevet rank could trump regular rank when command on the field was in question. But that rarely happened. The honor was the main thing. Crook got his share of brevets, and he was promoted general of volunteers, and he was eventually placed in command of the grandly named Army of West Virginia. But in a long war which catapulted all sorts of unexpected men to national prominence, glory in the newspapers, and excited talk in Washington, the steady, dependable, laconic George Crook never approached center stage. He was not outwardly a warm or effusive man, but the officers under him, and the men under them, generally trusted and liked him. One who learned to value Crook was Colonel Rutherford B. Hayes, commander of the 23rd Ohio Infantry at the Battle of Cloyd's Mountain in May 1864. On the morning of the battle Crook surveyed the rebel position with a field glass and remarked, "They may whip us, but I guess not."[18] A battery of Confederate artillery entrenched on a hill threatened Crook's men. To put it out of action required a charge across a muddy stream and an open field three hundred yards wide. It was soon littered with the bodies of dead and wounded Union officers and men, but the battery was taken and the field won. "It being the vital point," Hayes wrote to an uncle of the desperate run across the open field, "General Crook charged with us in person . . . Altogether, this is our finest experience in the war, and General Crook is the best general we have served under."[19]

Crook in his clipped way had guessed right; it was the Confederates who got whipped. His men rarely heard him go beyond a few flat words of that sort. But there was something reassuring in his watchful way. "We all feel great confidence in his skill and good judgement," Hayes wrote his mother. Calm on the outside, Crook was imagined by his men to be calm all the way through, but it was not entirely so.

Hurt pride was Crook's secret vice. He felt others got the credit for things he achieved. "It has been ever thus through my life," he wrote of an early incident in California when a newly arrived officer took credit for something Crook had done. "I have had to do the rough work for others afterwards to get the benefits from it."[20] After Sheridan took command in the Shenandoah in July 1864, Crook perhaps felt his star might shine a little more. Sheridan was a friend; he knew the sort of man Crook was and wouldn't need reminding. They often met in the evening to talk about the California days.

But credit for military success proved harder to share than memories of early Army days, and in the course of the Shenandoah campaign small injuries to Crook's self-regard gradually accumulated, opening a gap

between the two men which steadily widened. First came fights at Opequon Creek near the town of Winchester and at Fisher's Hill, two of the
three climactic battles that ended southern control of the Shenandoah.
No arena of conflict had changed hands more often during the war. By
one count the town of Winchester had been won and lost seventy times
when Sheridan set his sights on it again in mid-September 1864. Grant
listened to his plan and told him, "Go in."[21]

The battle eventually called Third Winchester was one of the stupen-
dous fights so common during the war, with almost ten thousand men
killed, wounded, or missing on both sides in the course of the day. Crook's
part in the fight was small but critical and brilliantly executed. In mid-
battle he departed from the letter of his orders when he saw an opportunity to flank Jubal Early's men, breaking their line and capturing over a
thousand Confederate soldiers. By day's end Early was in full retreat up
the valley turnpike to Fisher's Hill nearly twenty miles to the south.
Crook and Sheridan shared a moment of strange intimacy on entering the
town of Winchester, where they were met in the street by three highly
excited and effusive girls, exulting over the victory. They spoke so openly
and loudly of their pleasure in the Union victory that Crook, who knew
them well, tried to quiet them with a reminder, as Sheridan recorded in
his memoirs, "that the valley had hitherto been a race-course—one day in
the possession of friends and the next of enemies—and warned [them] of
the dangers they were incurring by such demonstrations." Something of
Crook's plain, steady character is revealed in this frank warning to the
girls that the Union's brilliant victory, owing so much to his own role,
might be followed as quickly by a reversal.[22]

But even as these two men savored the day's victory a seed of anger
was sprouting in Crook's heart; the thousand Confederates his men
had captured had been led from the field—"gobbled up"—by the late-
arriving Union cavalry, who got the credit for their capture. "I complained of this to Sheridan," Crook recorded, "who asked me to say
nothing about it in my report, but that he saw the whole affair, and would
give me credit for it."[23]

Two days later at Fisher's Hill the story was repeated almost verbatim.
In Sheridan's quarters on September 21, the night before the battle,
Sheridan at first wanted to attack Early's right, which was anchored on a
bluff—the actual Fisher's Hill—overlooking the Shenandoah River. A
different approach was suggested by one of Crook's division commanders, Colonel Hayes. Better, he said, to send Crook's two divisions

around to Early's left, up over a timbered mountain. Early had placed his weakest units there, a clear sign he was convinced no attack would come that way. Sheridan at length agreed, and prepared the rest of his army to make a great to-do next day along Early's front, convincing the Confederates that the attack would come head on. Hayes did the talking, but one of the officers present, Captain Henry A. Du Pont, later wrote that everybody understood the plan to move secretly up over the mountain was really Crook's idea.

Conceiving it was the easy part; much harder was the exhausting uphill march the following day, starting before dawn and continuing until four o'clock in the afternoon, with Crook on foot leading the way. He believed that an officer of infantry should walk with his men, not ride. They made the climb in two long parallel lines, with flags lowered and keeping silence. When the time came to attack, Crook had only to order a left flank, march! and his divisions were instantly facing down the timbered hillside toward the unsuspecting Confederates, who were still expecting an attack from the opposite direction. As soon as Crook's men started down the hill a great roar came up from all of their throats at once. This must have been one of the signal moments of Crook's life—a perfectly executed maneuver, an unsuspecting enemy, the soft fruit of victory ready to fall into his lap. In his autobiography he wrote,

> Unless you heard my fellows yell once, you can form no conception of it. It beggars all description. The enemy fired a few shots afterward, but soon the yell was enough for them. The most of them never stopped to see the fellows the yell came from, but dug out. By the time we reached the open bottom there weren't any two men of any organization there.[24]

The collapse of Early's left was soon followed by the breaking of his whole army, one division after another peeling away, as the panic spread across the southern line from left to right. Soon Early was retreating pellmell up the valley turnpike, heading south. Sheridan was hoping for the ultimate in military success—the capture of an entire army—but the cavalry divisions he had sent on ahead to block the turnpike and trap Early's army, and the infantry he had sent in pursuit, pressing Early from behind, both quit as darkness came and went into bivouac. Sheridan was infuriated by this "backing and filling"; what he wanted, he roared in a message, was "resolution and actual fighting, with necessary casualties."[25] But of course the moment was lost. Early had received a sound whipping, but his army was intact. At day's end Sheridan was thinking of the failure, Crook of the triumph. He had conceived the plan and marched his men for twelve hours to get into position. His attack had rolled up the enemy. But the newspaper reports did not single out Crook for praise; recognition of his merit would have to wait on Sheridan's official report, just as it did for the battle at Winchester.

But it was a third incident not quite a month later that poisoned the friendship of Crook and Sheridan for good and all. Over the intervening weeks Sheridan and his army chased Early right up the Shenandoah Valley, until the northern transport began to show signs of strain. Better, Sheridan thought, to call a halt and move back down the valley, destroying barns and carrying off the year's harvest. Grant could not argue. This had been his idea—to "eat out Virginia clean and clear as far as they go, so that crows flying over it for the remainder of the season will have to carry their own provender with them."[26] Sheridan did the job thoroughly. By mid-October he was back down the valley near the town of Middletown and the point where Cedar Creek flowed into the Shenandoah, just north of Fisher's Hill. Early's army had of course followed them back down, his cavalry nipping at Union heels. Sheridan was meanwhile summoned to Washington for a meeting on endgame strategy. Grant, Sheridan, and Halleck, general of the Army, all had different ideas about what to do next. But Sheridan went uneasily; an intercepted message suggested Early might have been reinforced. Sheridan thought the message a ruse but wasn't sure. He spent half a day in the capital, then hurried back to Winchester, where he spent the night of October 18, about fifteen miles north of the point where his army had deployed in a line blocking the valley turnpike. Holding the left of the line was Crook with his two divisions.

Now Crook learned about flanking marches from the receiving end. On the ground at the time there was only one clear warning of what was to come. Crook's officer of the day, hearing noise in the dark beyond the pickets standing guard, went out to investigate. He did not return. It is not clear when Crook learned of this fact, which should have stirred him to action. But he recorded early signs of trouble aplenty in his memoirs, beginning with Sheridan's removal of the cavalry pickets from Crook's front. These pickets were an early-warning system; without them Crook's divisions were exposed. Crook also notes that his divisions were deployed more than a mile from the rest of the army. This meant they were further exposed. Finally, Crook informs us that his divisions had been whittled away by losses in battle and by the removal of men detailed for guard duty and the like elsewhere. He was down "to less than three thousand men." He was simultaneously exposed and weakened.

The reader of Crook's memoir, noting the many excuses for the general laid out in advance by Crook the author, is amply warned of the gathering catastrophe, which arrived on the morning of October 19. "Just at the peep of day," Crook writes, his men in their tents and trenches were suddenly assaulted by four Confederate infantry divisions which had made their way undetected over a narrow mountain path—much as Crook had done at Fisher's Hill. Surprise was complete. Crook's men broke. The rest of Sheridan's army panicked as well and soon the whole Union force was retreating in the direction of Middletown in total disarray. At a stroke, in effect using Crook's own plan, Early was about to regain everything he had lost, and it was Crook, whose men broke first, who had opened the way. By late morning Sheridan's army was desperately reforming itself west of the town of Middletown. "Our new line was getting stronger all the time by stragglers joining from the rear," Crook recorded.[27] It was as close as he could bring himself to claiming that the situation was under control. Of course, it was not.

Sheridan meanwhile had been woken at about six o'clock in the morning by an officer reporting the sound of artillery to the south. Desultory firing was not uncommon, so he did not immediately rise. He lay and worried. Then he got up, asked again about the artillery, ordered breakfast, ordered the horses to be saddled, worried about the message he had concluded was a ruse.

Sheridan thus stirred himself with increasing urgency until he mounted at about nine a.m. and with three staff officers and a cavalry escort headed south on the road to Cedar Creek, listening all the while. At one point he dismounted and put his ear to the ground. Now he stopped trying to reassure himself. The sound of the cannons was steady, it was louder, and it was coming his way. Just south of Kernstown, he came to the first signs of disorder and confusion among troops and wagons along the road, soon followed by the panicked chaos of an army in full retreat.

At first, Sheridan thought of trying to establish a new defensive line at Winchester, but then the fighting spirit boiled up in him, he remembered his victories, he told himself the men would fight if he rode to lead them, and that is what he did. Sometimes he was on the road, sometimes he took to the fields alongside to get round the wagons and men. He took his hat off because the soldiers liked that. The cheers buoyed him along and the officers riding with him noted that his jaw was set, his eyes were fiery.

"About-face, boys!" he shouted to the soldiers streaming down the pike away from Cedar Creek. "We are going back to our camps! We are going to get a twist on those fellows! We are going to lick them out of their boots!"[28]

Twelve or fifteen miles up the valley pike Sheridan charged on his big black horse, Rienzi. When he got to Middletown he found his army in the process of reforming, just as Crook would write later. From about ten thirty until about four in the afternoon Sheridan reformed and reorganized his army, waiting until he thought it was ready, and then he attacked back up the road to Cedar Creek. "Go after them!" Sheridan yelled when the Confederates took to their heels. "We've got the god-damnedest twist on them you ever saw." He drove Early's divisions first from their captured positions and then, whipped and thoroughly beaten, all the way back to Fisher's Hill, where the Confederates spent a night before continuing on south.

While Early was facing the reality of defeat that evening at Fisher's Hill, Sheridan took a seat beside Crook at a campfire on Cedar Creek. Crook's worst day was Sheridan's greatest. But by Crook's account Sheridan said to him a remarkable thing about his ride from Winchester and the turning of the tide of battle. Sheridan was no sentimentalist, but it is hard to see his words as anything but salve on the wound of a friend. "Crook," he said, "I am going to get much more credit for this than I deserve, for, had I been here in the morning the same thing would have taken place, and had I not returned today, the same thing would have taken place."[29]

More credit than he deserved? It had been another bloody day—5,600 men lost by Sheridan, half as many by Early—but the casualties did not reveal the import of the event. Cedar Creek was one of the great and decisive Union victories of the Civil War; it turned defeat into resounding triumph in the space of a day, pushed Early right out of the valley, and sealed the reelection victory of President Lincoln three weeks later. Sheridan had the kind of warlike spirit that inspired men on the battlefield; at Cedar Creek they felt better as soon as they saw him. He deserved plenty of credit, but what he got was astounding, the kind of thing that lifts a man from ordinary mortal to legend. It happened this way. On Monday morning, November 3, in Cincinnati, Ohio, the actor

James Murdoch was preparing a selection of patriotic verse he had promised to read at a local theater that night. His friend Buck—Murdoch's nickname for the painter and occasional poet Thomas Buchanan Read—was with Murdoch when Read's brother-in-law arrived with a copy of the latest *Harper's Weekly*. In it was Thomas Nast's drawing of Sheridan on Rienzi, dashing from Winchester to Cedar Creek. "Buck," said the actor, "there's a poem in that picture."

Read went to work. By noon he had written something. That night, just eight days before the election, Murdoch rose to read a dramatic poem celebrating "Sheridan's Ride." It was the kind of thing an actor could boom out over the footlights, and the poem went on to sweep the country.

> Up from the South at break of day,
> Bringing to Winchester fresh dismay,
> The affrighted air with a shudder bore,
> The terrible grumble and rumble and roar,
> Telling the battle was on once more,
> And Sheridan twenty miles away.[30]

On it went for sixty-three lines. That poem would be a staple of patriotic gatherings for years to come. No general of the Civil War ever enjoyed a more intoxicating whirlwind of fame than Sheridan at thirty-three, and he got it lavishly and right away. Crook's failure of the morning at Cedar Creek had been reversed by day's end, but that was about the best that could be said of his performance. For his solid achievements at Winchester and Fisher's Hill in September, Crook still awaited the recognition and credit promised by Sheridan. These never came—quite the contrary. In May 1876, as he prepared to cross the North Platte in pursuit of the hostile Sioux, he carried in his heart a tender place fed by resentment of Sheridan. His onetime friend had waited until the war was over to write up his long-promised report. When Crook read it in February 1866, he was stunned by Sheridan's cleverly worded implication that turning the Confederate left at Winchester had been his own idea—not Crook's. When Sheridan wrote of Fisher's Hill he did it again, sliding over Crook's role in his report, then flatly claiming the plan as his own in his memoirs.[31] There is no evidence that Crook protested to Sheridan himself when he saw these bald grabs for credit and glory. Probably he said nothing. Grown men are not supposed to cry at being overlooked. But in Crook's heart bitterness grew.

12

"Crook was bristling for a fight."

GEORGE CROOK LEARNED a stern lesson during the Civil War: men get credit for what appears in the newspapers. No correspondents had been attached to his command in the Shenandoah; when Sheridan took credit for victory at Winchester and Fisher's Hill there was no public record to contradict him. The brooding Crook did not intend to make that mistake again. On his summer campaign in 1876, the Big Horn and Yellowstone Expedition, the general arranged to bring a full complement of the writing fraternity: Robert Strahorn of the *Chicago Tribune*, who had charged on the Cheyenne village on the Powder River in March; T. C. McMillan of the *Chicago Inter-Ocean*, despite a persistent cough that suggested tuberculosis; Joseph Wasson, part owner of the *Owyhee Avalanche* in Idaho, who had accompanied Crook on previous Indian-fighting campaigns; John F. Finerty of the *Chicago Times*, game for any adventure; and Reuben Davenport of the *New York Herald*, youngest of the reporters at twenty-four.

There was evidently something awkward and risible about Davenport. The other correspondents, the scouts, and some of the military officers joked about him, thought him the greenest of the greenhorns, and occasionally fed him tall tales about frontier life and Indian ways, several of which made their way into print. But Davenport in fact knew his way around. The previous year he had traveled with Professor Walter Jenney in the Black Hills, then ridden a hundred miles cross-country to cover the government's effort to buy the hills from the Sioux at the grand council near the Red Cloud Agency. With Louis Bordeaux as interpreter Davenport interviewed Spotted Tail and in his story even attempted to reproduce some of the chief's replies in the original Lakota.

Davenport's interest in Indians was unusual. The rest of the correspondents focused their stories on the military men or the scouts, especially Frank Grouard. As the summer progressed Finerty of the *Chicago Times* expressed a particularly low opinion of Indians. He says he got it sitting around campfires, listening to Army officers talk about frontier life. Finerty was just thirty, had been born in Ireland, fought with a regiment of New York volunteers during the Civil War, and had worked for Chicago papers for the previous eight years. His first big assignment on moving to the *Times* was to join Crook for the summer campaign in 1876. The instructions of his paper's editor, W. F. Storey, were terse: "Spare no expense and use the wires freely, whenever practicable."[1]

In mid-May, Finerty took the train from Omaha to Cheyenne, and it was probably there that he saw his first Indians. By October, he had completed his education. As a writer Finerty liked to string adjectives, and he rolled them out by the yard for the red men, whom he found "mysterious, untameable, barbaric, unreasonable, childish, superstitious, treacherous, thievish, [and] murderous." The women he described as "squatty, yellow, ugly and greasy looking." Summing up, he found the Sioux nation to be "greedy, greasy, gassy, lazy, and knavish."[2]

But name-calling aside, Finerty grasped from the beginning that as fighters the Sioux were not to be despised. His first night on the trail, dining on "plain military fare" in an officer's tent, he listened attentively to Captain Elijah Wells, a veteran of the Battle of Cedar Creek. Too bad, Wells joked, that Finerty and McMillan had cut their hair short—"it would be a pity to cheat the Sioux out of our scalps." Crook might know the Indians of the far West and of Arizona, remarked Wells, but the Sioux and Cheyenne were a different order of being. "The Indians were in stronger force than most people imagined," the captain said. "General Crook . . . hardly estimated at its real strength the powerful array of the savages."

As Finerty and Captain Wells made their way north from Cheyenne, Crook was also on his way to join the summer campaign after a flying visit to Camp Robinson and the Red Cloud Agency. Wells was right. Crook was overconfident. At the outset of his summer campaign, he was sure he knew what made the Indians tick, and he fully expected to get the better of them. For one thing, he believed the Sioux and Cheyenne were few; in Washington some said the northern Indians would be hard pressed to gather five hundred warriors at one time. Crook intended to press the hostiles relentlessly, just as he had in Arizona, where he made his reputation as an Indian fighter and won his general's star. He believed it was his Apache scouts that had given him the edge. The hostiles held whites generally in contempt, soldiers included, but they feared their brother Apache, who knew their tricks, their hideouts, and their secret trails leading from one desert spring to the next. Chasing the Apache with their own had worked in Arizona, Crook felt, and it would work in his campaign against the Sioux and the Cheyenne. On his way to the Red Cloud Agency in mid-May, "rolling over the endless plains" in an Army ambulance with his aide, Lieutenant Bourke, the general predicted that the Sioux and Cheyenne would prove an easier foe than the Apache. The Plains Indians were comparatively rich, he observed, and, having more to lose than the impoverished Apache, would be less willing to risk it in war. Sitting Bull and his people had too many horses and too much property and valued it too highly. In Crook's view they couldn't long withstand the kind of punishment the Apache had endured. Bourke thought this made sense.[3]

But when the general got to the agency the reception was cool. It was a job just getting the Indians to sit down to talk. When they did, Red Cloud and Spotted Tail were dismissive of Crook's fight on the Powder River, beginning with the fact that the soldiers didn't know the camp was Cheyenne. Crook might go on insisting till the end of his life that it was the village of Crazy Horse his men had charged in March, but the chiefs knew better, just as they knew the fight was no victory for the whites. The botched affair was the talk of the plains. Spotted Tail rubbed it in with one of Crook's officers: "If you don't do better than you did the last time you had better put on squaw's clothes and stay at home." Red Cloud was as little impressed, telling Crook to his face that "an expedition went out and whipped some Cheyennes and now we have trouble and here is the man"—meaning the general himself—"who made all this trouble."

Who ordered this expedition, Red Cloud asked, the president or the secretary of the interior?

Crook said it was both.

Then both had made a mistake, Red Cloud said. "This is a peaceful house." The chiefs could talk to the northern Indians, there was no need for all this trouble. Red Cloud was not tempted by Crook's promise that his warriors could have all the ponies captured in the north. "I don't want to go anywhere," the chief said with finality. The longer the talk went on, the clearer the answer: it was no. The chiefs did not want their young men to go out with Crook as scouts.

Crook and Bourke were convinced that the chiefs "had been tampered with."[4] They suspected it was the doing of the new agent at the Red

Cloud Agency, James Hastings. After inquiry Frank Grouard confirmed their suspicions; he said he had learned from Three Bears and Sitting Bull the Oglala that it was not Hastings himself who had urged the chiefs to say no. The message had come indirectly, from the agent's clerk, a man named McCavanaugh, put into Lakota by the interpreter Billy Garnett. Talks at an end, Crook left the agency the same day, May 16, for the beginning of the campaign. Fort Fetterman was 120 miles straight west, Fort Laramie about midway. The general had plenty of time to think. He was in a sour mood.

In later years, Crook described in his unfinished autobiography the spirit of the Indians he had been sent to whip. "These Indians . . . were insolent . . . and declined to be restrained in their freedom in the slightest particular," he wrote. He called them "refractory" and "hostile." At the Black Hills conference in 1875, Crook wrote, "every white man found himself surrounded by these Indians, stripped to the buff, painted, ready for action . . . [They] looked as if they would want no better fun than to kill everybody there, just to see them kick."

After the Powder River "affair"—Crook would not call it a victory, nor a defeat, nor even a battle—"the Indians became more defiant than ever."[5] This was the sort of language he had used about the bushwhackers who challenged him at the beginning of the Civil War. Nothing stirred Crook's pugnacity more than disrespect, insolence, defiance, haughty demeanor, or a resistant spirit. Someone had told the general—probably the Sioux at Red Cloud—that Crazy Horse was expecting Crook, and would begin to fight him "as soon as he touched the waters of the Tongue."[6] That kind of dare left the general itching for a fight.

It was not just Crook and his soldiers, reporters in tow, who were making their way by stages to the North Platte and the vast unconquered Sioux country beyond. Shadowing them to the east, up along the Black Hills and then west to the Powder and Tongue river country, traveled a constant stream of Sioux and Cheyenne, bound for the buffalo herds in the north and the sun dance to be held in June—the yearly occasion for the gathering of the bands. Early in the year James Hastings insisted in a letter to Washington that "the Indians here are perfectly quiet . . . the recent newspaper reports that an Indian outbreak was imminent are entirely groundless."[7] But Captain William Jordan, commander of the military post at Camp Robinson only a mile and a half away from the agent's office, did not trust Hastings to know what was going on, or to tell him if he did. Jordan got a different version of events from his twenty-five-year-old brother Charles, a clerk in the agency, who had married a niece of Red Cloud, Julia Walks First. All the previous fall Indians had been traveling freely between the agency and the northern camps exactly as they pleased. When the Army began to move onto a war footing about the turn of the year, Captain Jordan quietly called in Billy Garnett and hired him to keep track of the agency Indians—"when certain ones arrived [or] . . . when a certain Indian withdrew to the north and how many lodges went with him."[8] As spring came, Hastings continued to deny that his charges were disappearing, but he also protested often to the Indian office in Washington about one of the things driving them: hunger. Promised beef cattle failed to arrive, supplies were low. Hastings warned Washington that unless provisions came soon the Indians "will be reduced to a starving condition." Making the problem worse was an influx of Indians from the north; they had been ordered to come in, and many did—more than a thousand of them by the end of February. In the last week of April the Oglala chiefs Pawnee Killer and Red Cloud separately came to Captain Jordan "begging for the first time since I have been here [1874] for something to eat for their families . . . If the beef does not arrive soon, I think the Indians will be compelled to . . . join the hostiles to keep from starving."[9]

It seems elementary—if Washington wanted the Indians to settle at the agencies, Washington would have to feed them. But distances were great, contractors were venal, the weather often blocked travel, Congress was slow to appropriate funds and quick to cut them. Hunger remained a fact of life at the agencies for sixty years,[10] but in 1876 Indians had an alternative—the road north—and they took it. Hastings complained constantly of the supply situation, but minimized the exodus it caused. "From the best information I can get," he wrote in early June, "not more than 400 Cheyennes and 400 Sioux have left the agency, including women and children. They belong to that part of my people who have been in the habit of going north every summer."[11]

The truth was very different; at least two thousand had departed, perhaps more. In the last days of May, Captain Teddy Egan, scouting with a company of the 2nd Cavalry north of the agencies, encountered a large band of Oglala—he guessed it at six hundred to eight hundred fighting men—threatening a wagon train corralled for defense near Sage Creek. Egan did not know it, but the band was led by the Oyukhpe Oglala chief Big Road, and among the Indians was a son-in-law of Red Cloud, probably Slow Bull, as well as the chief's son Wicasa Wanka (Above Man). Called Jack by the whites, the boy was about eighteen years old and armed with a fancy Winchester, ornamented in silver, which had been given to his father in Washington the previous year by the commissioner of Indian affairs.[12] Others in the band going north were Little Big Man and Black Elk with his twelve-year-old son of the same name. No big fight occurred; the soldiers, the Indians, and the wagon train all went separate ways. But when Egan got to the Red Cloud Agency he found it nearly deserted; he was told a thousand men had gone north from Red Cloud with their families, as well as another hundred or more from the Spotted Tail Agency.[13]

Much the same was happening at the agencies on the Missouri River. In previous years the agents and the military had always given the same explanation for this annual migration: "grass fever." When spring came the ponies got fat on the new grass and the Indians, restive after the confinement of winter, grew anxious for the open road and a hunt. The year 1876 was the pattern as before. No great alarm was sounded about the Indians going north in May and June, but soon—before eight weeks were out—the military and the agents would count again, carefully this time. They would find that by mid-June thousands of Sioux had departed for the buffalo country along the skein of rivers running north into the Yellowstone—the Bighorn and Little Bighorn, the Tongue, the Powder, and the Rosebud.

Crook's doubts about the scout Frank Grouard had been put to rest on the winter campaign to the Powder River in March. Over the following months the Sandwich Islander made himself so useful he was commonly described as first among Crook's scouts. In an early dispatch Robert Strahorn wrote that the general "would rather lose a third of his command, it is said, than be deprived of Frank Grouard."[14] There was no mystery about it; Crook was looking for Indians, and Grouard found them.

Before crossing the North Platte, Crook sent Grouard with a few men ahead to check on the trail. The patrol was followed closely by Sioux, nearly ambushed on the Dry Fork of the Powder, then chased all the way back to Fort Fetterman. "I have always considered that trip as close a call as I ever had," Grouard told his biographer.[15]

Soon after Crook's column was on the road Grouard was sent ahead again when some Crow scouts failed to show up as promised. This time he traveled with Louis Richard and Big Bat Pourier, who was called Left

Hand by the Crow and spoke their language. They were two weeks on the trail, survived numerous close brushes with the hostiles, and finally met up with the Crow on the bank of the Bighorn River. Much talk was required before several Crow chiefs agreed to sign on as scouts and raised a company of about 170 to follow Grouard and Big Bat to the soldier camp on Goose Creek. There on the night of June 14 the crier, known as Old Crow, made a rousing speech by the light of the campfire, translated sentence by sentence by the scouts. "Crook was bristling for a fight," said *Chicago Times* reporter John Finerty. The Crow were bristling too. First the chief listed the many outrages committed by the Sioux, then stipulated how they would get even:

> Our war is with the Sioux . . . We want back our lands. We want their women for our slaves—to work for us as our women have had to work for them. We want their horses for our young men, and their mules for our squaws. The Sioux have trampled upon our hearts. We shall spit upon their scalps. The great white chief sees that my young men have come to fight. No Sioux shall see their backs.[16]

Next morning about daybreak the officers heard "an old Crow Warrior," loud and agitated, riding through the camp—at times bellowing pugnaciously, at others pleading, or lifting up his hands and face and praying, even weeping. "Great tears rolled down his cheeks," remembered Crook's aide-de-camp, Azor Nickerson. The warrior was dressed for war—"stripped almost naked," said Bourke—and carrying his rifle, swinging it in the air. The sight was enthralling and mysterious. The old hands explained that the warrior was preparing for battle, pleading to the Great Spirit for aid in killing his enemies—the Indians called it "crying for scalps."[17] The Crow chiefs told Crook that the Sioux "are numerous as grass," and said the hostile village would be found on the Yellowstone. Grouard, when Crook asked him, thought the Rosebud a better bet. By this time Crook took Grouard's word as gospel. The general put his infantry on mules so they could travel faster, left his wagons and the bulk of supplies behind on Goose Creek, and on June 16 marched north toward the Rosebud, hoping to surprise the Sioux in their village.

By this time Lieutenant Bourke had begun to know a few things about the Sioux. Much of it he picked up from Frank Grouard, who was running a kind of campfire seminar in Sioux politics, religion, and social organization. The letters, diaries, and memoirs of military officers who traveled with him often cite things Grouard told them about the Indians. Bourke's curiosity had begun to quicken; his diary account of the frustrating failure to sign up scouts at the agencies was frequently interrupted to describe something interesting about the Indians—the way they painted a streak of vermillion or red ochre down the part in a man's hair, the decoration of a plain wool blanket with a beaded strip across the middle, the fact that a pipe's bowl was slightly elongated below the draw hole so the bitter tobacco juices might collect there instead of traveling down the stem. "Each Indian takes three or four whiffs," Bourke noted, "and then passes the pipe along to his neighbor on the left." One day during the summer campaign Grouard told Bourke how the Indians made a shield using the skin from a buffalo bull's neck, which might be an inch thick. The women would cover the untanned hide with earth, then build a fire over it. The slow heat cured the rawhide to a hardness that could "turn a lance point and repel arrows."[18] Knowing the enemy is a basic rule of war, but Bourke wasn't interested solely in what would help the general win; he wanted to know who the Sioux *were*.

Sometimes Grouard told the soldiers what they wanted to hear, and one of the things they always wanted to hear was how many Indians had been killed in battle with the whites—the bigger the number, the better they liked it, especially when the whites had been beaten. Only a couple of days out on the summer campaign, Grouard showed Bourke and two newspaper writers—Joseph Wasson and the all-ears Reuben Davenport—around the "desolate solitude" of old Fort Reno, one of the Bozeman Road posts abandoned by the Army eight years earlier. "A lonesome spot," Bourke called the post cemetery with its weathered headboards. Strange, bleak feelings warred in the lieutenant's heart. Just up the road, Fetterman and his eighty men had been "surrounded by thousands of Indians and after a desperate fight . . . slaughtered to a man." In fact, Grouard told his companions, the brave little force had been attacked by eight thousand Indians—Grouard said he had it from the Indians themselves. And the brave eighty, he added, had killed and wounded 185 of their attackers. The first number was preposterous, the second seriously exaggerated, but they made Bourke feel better.[19]

On another occasion Bourke and a fellow officer, Schuyler, spent a whole afternoon listening to Grouard explain the political organization of the Sioux. Few whites knew much about this at the time—there were chiefs and subchiefs and warriors and that was all they knew. But Grouard started to explain about the secret men's societies like the Cante Tinza (Brave Hearts), the Tokala (Kit Fox), and the "Owl Feathers, " a nickname for the Miwatani, who decorated their headdresses with the feathers of owls. Bourke's notes refer also to the concept of "dreamers." There came a time in the life of young men when they went out alone into the wilderness "crying for a vision" (*hanbleceya*). Fasting and praying for many days, usually four, they were sometimes visited by an animal spirit—a bear, a wolf, an owl, even a bighorn sheep. Woman Dress, a grandson of Smoke, son of Black Twin, and nephew of No Water, was visited in a dream on the morning of his second or third day fasting on a hilltop. "Looking up," Woman Dress related, "he saw before him a mountain sheep with its curling horns and large yellow eyes. The sheep remained an instant, then vanished and in its stead was its skull."[20] Thereafter, he said, the sheep gave him unique protection and powers.

Bear, wolf, or owl dreamers used special prayers, performed certain ceremonies, sometimes associated in small, informal groups. Bear dreamers were healers; owl dreamers could foretell death; horse dreamers could call on the power of the sky beings. Grouard told the officers about the society lodges, often maintained and guarded by a man who served also as village herald. The Sioux understood the concept of an oath, Grouard said; returning scouts, called "wolves," were particularly enjoined to report truthfully what they had learned about an enemy village or a buffalo herd. In front of the village elders—the chiefs known as *wakiconza* (deciders)—the scouts held "in each hand a piece of dried buffalo manure," and only then reported what they had seen.

Like the Sioux, Grouard was drawn to mystery, but he was sensitive to the skepticism of Bourke and Schuyler. He told them about a Hunkpapa medicine man named Yellow Grass in Sitting Bull's band who claimed the Great Spirit for father and said he had been born in the sky, not on the earth. "A very bold-faced impostor," Grouard called him.

This Yellow Grass claimed the ability to make ammunition through magic power. He would swallow a cartridge, allow the process of digestion to work awhile, then unveil "box after box, each holding its cool thousand of bright metallic cartridges."[21] Grouard explained the trick: Yellow Grass purchased the boxes of ammunition in the ordinary way from the mixed-blood Metis traders in the north, then hid them in his camp, and at the right moment sent the women of the village to find them. "All scoffing was silenced and the impostor's influence waxed apace," said Grouard.

But some mysteries the scout did not try to explain. Speaking to Schuyler once, Grouard said the Sioux believed the sky was dominated by thunder beings who made the weather. Hailstorms were the result of sky battles between spirits riding white horses and black horses—real horses, the Sioux insisted, huge in size. Grouard said the Sioux knew the sky horses were real because they sometimes found their huge bones in the fossil beds along the Niobrara and the White River where it runs north through the Badlands.[22] The crashing of thunder in a storm was the sound of the sky horses' feet as they charged across the heavens; their spirit riders cast lightning to the earth. When a man was killed by lightning it meant that he had ignored the commandments of a vision.

"They represent lightning on their war ponies with paint," Schuyler wrote. "They believe they fight after the plan of the spirits."[23]

Schuyler was a practical fellow, a rising star in the frontier army, scion of a famous New York family, brother of a well-known American diplomat posted in Russia. What Grouard said interested the young officer, but Schuyler was not frightened by painted horses.

13

"I give you these because they have no ears."

IN EARLY SUMMER, IT was the habit of the buffalo to move westerly up the Yellowstone, crossing from one north-flowing river valley to the next, drawing the Indians in their wake. By June the big village of Sioux and Cheyenne was camped on the Rosebud, where it was growing almost daily with new arrivals from the agencies. The chiefs had been urging the young men to let the whites alone, but trouble seemed inevitable. Scouts had reported a big force of white soldiers to the west, near the point where the Bighorn River emptied into the Yellowstone. Indians arriving from the agencies on the Missouri said soldiers were coming that way, too. On June 9 some northern Cheyenne hoping to steal horses from the whites happened across a big Army camp on the headwaters of the Tongue—General Crook's Big Horn and Yellowstone Expedition, in fact, but the Indians, led by a Cheyenne in his late twenties named Little Hawk, did not know that. An effort to run off the soldier horses failed and the Cheyenne, perhaps a dozen men in all, showed themselves on a bluff across the river, overlooking the camp. For no good reason they began to fire into the camp. Soldiers scrambled for cover and an officer's favorite horse was wounded in the leg. The skirmish ended when the soldiers charged the Indians on the bluff and sent them running. Crook thought "a hundred or so" Indians had fired into the camp. The *Chicago Times* reporter John Finerty put their number at fifty. Bourke believed they were Sioux sent by Crazy Horse to make good on his threat to attack as soon as Crook's men "touched the waters of the Tongue." The Cheyenne gave up their horse-stealing raid to carry the news back to the big camp on the Rosebud, about forty miles distant.[1]

The chiefs in the big camp all knew by mid-June that white soldiers were converging on them from three directions, but they were encouraged by their own numbers, steadily growing as young men from the agencies came in, and by a sense that the sky beings favored their cause. This good news had been delivered to Sitting Bull, best known among the Sioux as a spiritual leader, not a war leader. Twice that spring he had experienced powerful visions foretelling the future. The first came in the third week of May when the chief had climbed to a hilltop to pray. Later, speaking to a gathering of leading men back in the camp, he described what had happened. On the hilltop he had prepared himself, then prayed, and after a time fell asleep. In a dream he saw a cloud of dust propelled by wind as if charging into a skyscape wall of billowing clouds that looked, in Sitting Bull's dream, something like a village of tipis camped before a range of mountains. From the east the cloud of dust came and thunder crashed when it collided with the sky village of clouds. Sitting Bull explained to the others that the dust cloud was a force of white soldiers, the sky village was their own big camp, and the storm meant a big fight was coming. If the Sioux and the Cheyenne kept watch and remained alert, the chief said, they would win a big victory.[2]

A week later Sitting Bull prayed again and this time vowed to sacrifice his flesh during the sun dance. The village was camped on the Rosebud. It was early June, two or three days before the Cheyenne Little Hawk discovered Crook's camp at the headwaters of the Tongue. The dance on these days was conducted by the Hunkpapa, but of course all the bands in the big village gathered to watch. A sun dance is not a one-day affair; preparations begin weeks, even months in advance. The climax starts with the choosing of a center pole, made from a straight cottonwood tree. This year it was Crazy Horse's friend Good Weasel who cut down the tree and oversaw its removal to the dance ground. It is on the fourth day that the sacrifice occurs.

In the past Sitting Bull had danced in the classic way, tied to the sun dance pole in the center of the dance ground by rawhide straps pulling on wooden skewers inserted beneath the flesh and muscle of his chest. This time he had something different in mind. First the chief purified himself with a sweat in the lodge, then he seated himself on the ground, smoked in the sacred way, and finally leaned back against the dance pole. He was now assisted by his adopted brother, an Assiniboine captured in battle when a boy about 1857. At the time some of the warriors had wanted to kill the boy, but Sitting Bull had spared him, just as he would do later when some of the chiefs wanted to kill Frank Grouard. The adopted brother was sometimes called Stays Back, sometimes Kills Plenty, sometimes Little Assiniboine, and sometimes Jumping Bull—the name of Sitting Bull's father. Now in the sun dance, Jumping Bull, using an awl and a knife, began to cut out bits of Sitting Bull's flesh. With the awl he pricked a bit of skin and lifted it up. With the knife he cut off a piece about the size of a grain of wheat. He took fifty flesh offerings from one arm, then fifty from the other.

The purpose of this ordeal was not to show bravery, but to offer a blood sacrifice to the unseen powers of the world, to make a gift. Sacrifice was a token of gratitude to Wakan Tanka, the Great Spirit; a pinch of tobacco before smoking, a bit of food before eating, a splash of water on the ground before drinking were routinely sacrificed to acknowledge the greater gift of life. A small sacrifice was appropriate to a small request. A hundred pieces of flesh opening a hundred streams of blood was a big sacrifice. In this way Sitting Bull was praying for the lives of his people, who were threatened by the columns of soldiers invading their country.

As the blood began to flow Sitting Bull cried out in prayer. When the cutting was done he got up and danced around the pole for many hours until at last, exhausted, he fell unconscious to the ground. His helpers revived him with cold water. When his eyes opened the chief told his uncle Black Moon, one of his helpers in the sun dance, what he had seen. Black Moon then repeated his words in a big voice to the whole crowd gathered around.

Sitting Bull had seen a great many white soldiers in the sky—as many as locusts during a plague—but the soldiers were upside down and they were falling into the Indian camp. A voice in his dream told the chief there would be a big fight and the Indians would win. "I give you these," the voice said, "because they have no ears"—that is, all the soldiers would die.[3] This dream made a powerful impression on all who heard it described.

A few days after Sitting Bull's vision, the Cheyenne Little Hawk with some friends went out again on a scout to the south, hoping to steal horses from the white soldiers. The first night they stopped in the Wolf Mountains. The next day about noon on the Rosebud they killed a buffalo bull and stopped to roast some meat. No sooner was it cooking than some buffalo cows appeared over a hill. These were much better for eating, so Little Hawk and a few others rode to see if they might kill one. Then Crooked Nose, who was tending the fire, signaled that he saw some men in the distance. Little Hawk thought they were probably Sioux, and he decided to sneak up on them; it was a joke he had in mind, but he proceeded like a man taking the necessary precautions on the plains. He rode up a ravine, got off his horse, carefully made his way to the crest of the hill. His friends followed him.

On the plains, every man who hoped to live would take care to see without being seen. Little Hawk raised his head slowly—it is movement that the eye picks up first—then lowered his head again. In a low voice—a very low voice—he told his friends there were soldiers over that hill—"it seemed as if the whole earth were black with soldiers"—and they were *right there.* The whole party crept away, mounted their horses, rode down into the brush along the Rosebud, and took off for the big camp a day's ride to the north and west. That first section of their escape was rough—Little Hawk said later that "he left a good many locks of his hair in the brush."[4]

When Little Hawk and his friends reached the camp with their news after a hard ride the people became greatly excited. Some of the women were frightened and even began to strike their tipis; many of the young men wanted to prepare for war and ride out at once, but the chiefs—Sitting Bull and Crazy Horse and others meeting in council—at first said no. The camp criers—*eyapaha*—went out to announce the chiefs' decision: "Young men, leave the soldiers alone unless they attack us."[5]

But the young men refused to accept these directions. That night they began to slip out of their respective camps and head south, more of them all the time until at least five hundred were on their way to attack the soldiers. At that point the chiefs realized they could not avoid a fight, and Sitting Bull and Crazy Horse also prepared for war, then headed south across country toward the Rosebud, where the soldiers had been seen. Sitting Bull was still recovering from swollen eyes and arms, the result of staring at the sun and sacrificing the hundred bits of flesh. He was in no condition to fight and in any event was beyond the age when a man customarily went to war. For Crazy Horse it was different. He did not sacrifice his flesh in the sun dance in this or any other year. He had been chosen war leader of the big camp and he rode out toward the Rosebud with many of his close friends from other fights—among them were He Dog and his brothers, Bad Heart Bull, Short Bull, and Little Shield. Others named were Black Deer, Good Weasel, who had been in the fight where High Backbone had been killed, and Kicking Bear, the man with the bad heart who had killed Frank Appleton at the Red Cloud Agency.

Not since the Bozeman War had the Sioux gone out in such numbers to attack soldiers, and they went prepared, dressed in their war clothes, with faces and horses painted in the right way, wearing the protective amulets called *wotawe*, singing their sacred songs. Some Indians said the warriors did not number more than 750 in all; others said maybe a thousand. Only a few had the best new guns—Henry or Winchester repeating rifles. Others had the one-shot military guns using cartridges, the kind Crazy Horse called "open and shoot," or old trade guns, much repaired. The Cheyenne Wooden Leg said he brought his six-shooter. Perhaps two-thirds of the Indians had firearms of one kind or another. But it was not numbers or weapons alone that made the Sioux strong, in their view; it was the protection that comes from the favor of Wakan Tanka and the power acquired in dreams or visions.[6]

June was the month of gathering, feasting, and dancing—not only the sun dance but others as well, some for fun, like the night dance that brought the young men and women together, and dances of the men's societies to pray for help and strength. Just before the fight on the Rosebud, according to He Dog, the cult dreamers had conducted some of their most powerful dances, elaborate ceremonies invoking the special power of the black-tailed deer, the elk, and the bear.[7] All are sources of power, and the religion of the Sioux was an intellectual discipline for understanding and partaking in that power.

Sioux religion is a complex body of thought that defies neat description, but at its heart is a sense of the world as fluid and interconnected, controlled by an animating power that inhabits the Four Winds. This power is sometimes called *Taku Skanskan*—"that which stirs" or "something that moves"[8]—a godlike spirit or entity that shares its power with every creature and thing. These in turn can grant favor or withhold it. On the spirit level, accessible principally in visions or dreams, all creatures and things speak a common language. What they say is sometimes transparent, sometimes obscure. The men whites call medicine men the Sioux call *wicasa wakan*, or men sharing in holy or sacred power, as opposed to *pejuta wicasa*, who are herbal doctors. The sacred medicine men can query or intercede with Wakan Tanka, and can interpret the instructions received in visions or dreams, thereby helping men to control the power given to them by the animal or natural world. These powers reside not only in the world of the spirit but in things themselves—the speed of the hawk, for example, in the body of a hawk; the power of the eagle in an eagle's talon; the ferocity of the bear in a bear's tooth or claw; the elk's power to attract females with his bugling call in the horn or ivory tooth or dewclaws of the elk. These physical things, properly prepared, share their inherent power with the man who carries them on his person or ties them to his shield or lance. It is the same with the representation of things: the image of a dragonfly gives a man some element or aspect of the quickness of the dragonfly; the zigzag lightning streak down the leg of a horse gives it the trampling power of thunder, making it fearful to enemies; a drawing of a bear or even of its claws can convey the actual power and ferocity of the bear.[9]

When Sitting Bull's twenty-six-year-old nephew White Bull joined the Indians riding toward the Rosebud it was not only his "open and shoot" carbine that he carried to make him strong. In two other ways he was prepared as well. First he dressed for battle in the finest clothes he owned or could borrow. He wore leggings of woolen trade cloth in dark blue, a favorite color of the Sioux. Beaded strips ran down each leg, with blue triangles on a white background. The beading of his moccasins matched his leggings. Over his regular loincloth he wore a long breechcloth of red flannel reaching to his ankles front and back. To complete his array he borrowed from his brother-in-law Bad Lake a single trail warbonnet with alternating groups of seven white eagle feathers and then four red feathers indicating the many wounds which Bad Lake had received in battle. White Bull donned all this splendid garb, he said, because it made him feel brave and helped him fight well. Besides, if he was killed in battle he did not want men to sneer at his body lying on the ground, and say, "This was a poor man . . . See how shabby he lies there."

But more important was White Bull's *wotawe*—his war charm—which hung on a thong across his chest from right shoulder to left side. Under his left arm supported by the thong was a hoop of rawhide, and attached to the hoop were the tail of a buffalo, the first and strongest of the creatures that lived on the surface of the earth; then a feather from an eagle, first among the creatures that fly in the air; and finally four small leather pouches, each containing different kinds of earth with magical properties. His horse, a roan, was painted with lightning streaks in red down his legs, from the horse's ears in front and from the hip in back, right down to the hoof. In the mane and tail of the roan White Bull had tied golden eagle feathers. In White Bull's view the warbonnet and the feathers on his horse made the two of them handsome; the *wotawe* under his arm and the painted lightning streaks down the horse's legs made them strong.[10]

Crazy Horse too went into battle with the aid of a *wotawe*, prepared for him by a friend and mentor, the medicine man Ptehe Woptuha, whose name in Lakota meant something like the crushed residue of a pulverized buffalo horn. Whites called him Horn Chips, or just Chips.[11] It is said that Horn Chips was three or four years older than Crazy Horse, that his father and mother died when he was still a boy, and that after he went to live with a grandmother the cruelty of village children made him so unhappy he determined to kill himself. But on his way to the spot where he planned to end his life, Horn Chips was stopped by the voice of Wakan Tanka telling him no, he had another destiny—to become a great man. The voice told him "to go to a high mountain, dig a hole four feet deep, cover it with boughs, and stay there four days with no food or drink."[12] Horn Chips did as the voice directed and was rewarded with a dream in which a snake came to him with instructions. Later, he also dreamed of eagles, thunder beings, and rock, all sources of great power.

It was Horn Chips who had interpreted for Crazy Horse the meaning of his vision many years earlier, which the twelve-year-old Billy Garnett had heard Crazy Horse describe. In the vision he had seen a man emerging from the lake on a horse. Horn Chips had prepared protective charms for Crazy Horse. He directed that Crazy Horse should wear only one feather, plucked from the center of the tail of a war eagle. From an eagle's wing bone Horn Chips made for him a whistle to blow as he rode into battle. About the year 1862 or 1863, according to Red Feather, Horn Chips prepared for Crazy Horse the most powerful of all his protections. It was made from a rock, drilled through the center, which Crazy Horse was to wear on a thong under his left arm. Another tiny stone he wore behind his left ear. Such stones were known as *tunkan wasicun*—spirit rocks; they possessed magical properties given by their nature, their shape, their source, or the songs sung over them.[13]

Chips was a stone dreamer; he went about with painted stones in a medicine bag. With the aid of these stones, which could fly through the air, Chips could find lost things, horses, or people. According to Ota Kte (Kills Plenty), the stones "could be heard striking the teepee and after we moved into houses I have heard them dropping down the chimney and have seen them lying about on the floor where they had fallen."[14] It was commonly believed by the Oglala that Crazy Horse was protected by the *wotawe* Horn Chips had given him. With their aid, he could hide from bullets in battle, or bullets were knocked away by the power that dwelt in his stone.

But that was not all. It was said that Horn Chips conferred power on Crazy Horse in many other ways. On his body the chief carried a medicine bundle or war sack. There are several descriptions of the sack itself and what it contained, some provided by those who knew him, others by a later generation for whom Crazy Horse had already become a mythic figure. Some say the chief's bundle was wrapped in deerskin, suspended on a braided thong. Bundles typically were made of the skin of a small animal like a badger, weasel, or otter. They might be decorated with beads or quills. The sacred objects within would be carefully wrapped in trade cloth, or tied in small pouches of leather or muslin. A medicine bundle of this type was prepared for the white medical doctor James Walker in the 1890s by the Brulé medicine man Short Bull,[15] who called it a *sicun*.

> Short Bull chose the material, which consisted of a soft-tanned fawn skin as the container, the tusk of a bear, the claw of an eagle, the rattle of a rattlesnake, a wisp of human hair, and a wisp of sweetgrass. The holy men consecrated the container by each invoking the potency of his *sicun* to make the container sacred. Then I was required to smear a little of my blood on each of the things to be enclosed in the container. When this was done I was required to hold them all in my hands while the holy men placed their hands on my head and implored the gods to give me their aid when I should need it. Then the articles were carefully enclosed in the container and it was folded about them and bound with cords made of sinew, each holy man tying a knot in the cords, muttering his special formula while doing so.

The medicine bundle given to Crazy Horse by Horn Chips would have been prepared in a similar way. A grandson of James Bordeaux the trader, Peter Bordeaux, who was born two years after the chief's death, said that this medicine bundle contained the dry seed of the wild aster, mixed with the dried heart and brain of an eagle. A son of Fire Thunder reported that Crazy Horse "had on his person a little medicine bag. Just before each battle he would chew a small portion of this medicine and rub it on his body."[16] Chips himself said that eagle claws were part of the medicine bundle, and that he further instructed Crazy Horse to make "a zigzag streak with red earth from the top of his forehead, downwards and to one side of his nose at the base, to the point of the chin. This was done with one finger." He added that the chief "striped his horse with a mould from the earth."[17] Many of these details were included in an account by Eagle Elk, who described what he had watched Crazy Horse do as he readied himself to go into battle:

> He always wore a strand of braided buckskin—at the lower end was something like medicine tied up in the buckskin. He had an eagle wing whistle tied on. He had it with him all the time. Just before the start of a battle when

they were ready to go into it, he got off his pony and got a little dirt from a molehill and put it between the ears of his horse and then on the hips of the horse and then he took some and got in front of the horse and throws it over toward the tail, and then he got around behind the horse and threw some toward his head. Then he went up to the horse and brushed it off and rubbed it on. Then he rubbed a little on his hand and over his head. Then he took a spotted eagle feather and put it upside down on the back of his head instead of standing up, as most did . . . Chips was the one who directed Crazy Horse to do these things so he would not be hurt.[18]

The dirt from the molehill had the power to make his horse invisible from the front and the rear, and to hide from enemies both the chief himself and the weapon in his hand. Thus Crazy Horse rode to war protected and strengthened by magic, secret knowledge, the power of animal guardians, the favor of gods and spirits. Many stories survive of the ways in which he used sacred power. It is evident he believed they kept him from harm and helped him defeat his enemies. But he was not the only one to benefit from the favor of the spirit beings. When he came onto the battlefield, his friends said, everybody felt stronger. Crazy Horse had dreamed of horses, which were thunder beings. As a thunder dreamer he enjoyed power that went beyond the ordinary calculation of weapons, numbers, or clever plans.

Some of his friends were also thunder dreamers, including Kicking Bear, a man Crazy Horse called cousin. In the summer of 1902, when the wars were long over, Kicking Bear told the anthropologist Clark Wissler what thunder dreamers could do. Their power came from Wakinyan, the sky bird whose beating wings were heard by men as the sound of thunder. Inyan, the rock, was the first of all things. Inyan created Wakinyan as companion, the second of all things. To dream of Wakinyan could complicate a man's life almost beyond imagining, requiring him to behave as a *heyoka*—a contrary, who laughed when he was sad, plunged his hand into boiling water, went naked when it was cold. But there was a second kind of thunder dreamer and these also had very great power—so great that they could control the weather. By this it was not meant only that they could provide a blue day for a ceremonial event, or make it rain during a dry season. Their power was much greater and more explicit. Kicking Bear described this power to Wissler. Surprised once in the open by an approaching storm, Kicking Bear said, he did not hide as the Sioux usually did. They were frightened by lightning and for good reason; lightning often killed men and horses trapped in the open, sometimes many horses at once when they were all pressed together, tails to the storm. On this occasion, Kicking Bear related, he took a pipe and climbed a hill directly in the path of the storm as if inviting the sky beings to strike. He lit his pipe in the sacred way and offered a prayer to the Great Spirit and with the power granted him . . . *he split the storm.* By this Kicking Bear intended no figure of speech. He meant that the roiling clouds and black sky and flashes of lightning divided in two and passed on either side of him—split down the middle by Kicking Bear's power. "He says that anyone can do this if they are worthy," reported Wissler.[19]

That is what rode south toward the Rosebud on the night of June 16–17, 1876: thunder dreamers, storm splitters, men who could turn aside bullets, men on horses that flew like hawks or darted like dragonflies. They came with power as real as a whirlwind, as if the whole natural world—the bears and the buffalo, the storm clouds and the lightning—were moving in tandem with the Indians, protecting them and making them strong. Frank Grouard had tried to explain the power of the Indians, but it is doubtful that Crook's officers understood what he was telling them. The whites all thought they were a match for any rabble of ignorant savages.

14

"I found it a more serious engagement than I thought."

GEORGE CROOK WAS A slow and careful thinker. He kept things to himself while he made up his mind. On the trail he liked to be alone, which meant riding ahead, which meant he would be the first to know if hostiles were lying in wait. "He was frequently warned of the risk he ran," the correspondent John Finerty wrote, "but paid no attention to the advice."[1]

Riding out in front of the column, thinking, hunting when opportunity afforded—this was the pattern of Crook's day. The enlisted men on the expedition imagined that he spoke only to the officers, while the officers complained that the general had time only for his scouts and Indian guides. During the week that Crook's force spent cooling its heels on Goose Creek in June the reporters and officers were all trying to plumb what was going on in his mind.

> Nobody knows but General Crook [one of his officers wrote] and he won't tell. The general doesn't make any confidants. If an officer asks him a question, he doesn't "sit on" him, as we call snubbing out here . . . but generally simply says, "I don't know" . . . he has a faculty for silence that is absolutely astonishing . . . Grant is loquacious when compared with him . . . It is generally believed that we are waiting for the arrival of either the Shoshones or the Crow.[2]

The writer's guess was a good one. Did Crook himself know what he would do next, or was he still waiting for a plan to form? No one knew. "Crook makes up his mind at the last moment," an officer wrote in his diary, "and then acts at once."[3] Luther North, a commander of Pawnee scouts on a later expedition with Crook, complained of the uncertainty. "We never knew when we were to move camp," he wrote.[4] But that was the man's way; others had to hustle to keep up. Once the Crow and the Shoshones had arrived Crook pointed his men north, hoping to surprise the Sioux in their village on the Rosebud.

The first day's march took them thirty-five miles to the headwaters of the Rosebud, where the Crow irritated Crook by ignoring his order to build no fires. They built big ones exactly as they pleased to roast some buffalo they had shot along the way. Crook was angered further when the Crow refused to scout ahead after dark, but he kept these feelings to himself. While the Crow feasted, Frank Grouard and a couple of others went out, returning later to say they had found the remains of a campfire in a gulch—probably a sign that the column had been sighted and the hostiles warned. Crook concluded he still had but one choice: push on and hope to surprise the Indians in their village. That night John Finerty slept next to Captain Alexander Sutorious, who remarked, "We will have a fight tomorrow, mark my words—I feel it in the air."[5]

The column was off again by first light on June 17, following the Rosebud downstream. At about eight o'clock Crook ordered a halt on the banks of the stream. Bridles were removed so horses and mules could graze. For half an hour the men lounged while the rear of the column closed up and the scouts crossed the Rosebud and probed beyond the hills and bluffs to the north, looking for hostiles. With the sun well up the June morning grew hot. Crook sat down by a spring to play a few hands of cards with Lieutenant Bourke and others.[6]

The Rosebud was called a river but here, sixty miles from the Yellowstone, it was little more than a winding stream. The spot where Crook ordered a halt was an east-west stretch of a few miles through a narrow valley with bluffs to the north and south until the valley suddenly narrowed into a tight canyon as it veered sharply north. In that direction, Crook believed, was the hostile village. Above the steeps of the bluffs the ground rose away more gradually; swales between gave the high ground a look like the fingers of a hand. In a few spots rocks broke through the surface, offering cover to riflemen. A horse could carry a man pretty much anywhere, panting and scrambling up the steeps, at speed along the fingerlike ridges or down across the swales between them.

About eight thirty came the sound of shots. Captain Sutorious thought the scouts were probably after buffalo again, but moments later the first Crow raced into camp shouting, "Sioux! Sioux!"

Men jumped to their feet and grabbed for horses. The first scouts were almost immediately followed by thirty more. Behind them to the north across the Rosebud the ridgeline came alive as Sioux and Cheyenne horsemen rode into view and began to fire into the men scrambling below. What happened in the next few minutes established the course of the fight that unfolded over the following six or seven hours. The view from Crook's place near the stream was poor. His first order was to deploy infantry in a skirmish line north of the streambed to meet whatever came. Then he ordered Captain Anson Mills with his men to seize and hold a line of commanding bluffs on the right while he himself, mounted on a black horse, rode north to the top of a low hill to get a sense of the landscape and form a plan of battle. Only one or two men rode with him. This was classic Crook—by himself, silent, figuring out what to do before issuing orders.

But while Crook was thinking the matter through, the battle was rapidly taking shape without him. Mills was already heading for the bluffs on the right. In the same moments three additional movements determined all that followed. Captain George Randall, in command of the Indian scouts, charged the hostiles on the bluffs to the northwest and in a brief, hot fight drove them back. Frank Grouard said later that "if it had not been for the Crow, the Sioux would have killed half of our command."[7] At about the same time Major Andrew Evans, a West Point classmate of Crook who had been active all through the Civil War, dispatched two companies of cavalry under Captain Frederick Van Vliet to occupy heights south of the stream. These men reached the summit just ahead of an attacking force of Sioux, who did not contest the terrain. Finally a cavalry force under Lieutenant Colonel William B. Royall made its way through the skirmish line of infantry to relieve the Crow scouts and drive the hostiles back from the bluffs northwest of the streambed. As the Indians pulled away Royall pressed after them, driving all the way up one of the fingerlike ridges to a high plain two miles or more from the valley floor.

These opening movements roughly account for the situation Crook found when he returned to the mass of his men along the stream: Mills secure in control of bluffs to the north and east above the narrowing canyon where the Rosebud turned north; Van Vliet secure in control of heights to the south; Colonel Royall with a substantial force pushed far out to the northwest in continuing contact with the hostiles. With the infantry under his immediate command Crook now moved north up one of the ridges just west of Mills, halting on a broad open flat where rocks in a few spots gave cover.

These opening stages of the fighting had occupied about two hours. Crook believed that the Indians had attacked because their village was nearby, right up that narrow canyon out of sight to his right. To go after the village Crook needed to concentrate his men, but Royall had his hands full out on the far ridgeline. At about ten thirty in the morning Crook issued a terse order to Captains Thomas Burrowes and Andrew Burt: "Stop those Indians and occupy that ridge."[8] He meant the Indians attacking Royall's men half a mile to the west. After they finally succeeded in this maneuver at about twelve thirty in the afternoon Crook ordered Mills to proceed up the Rosebud canyon and attack the village when he got to it; he sent Captain Henry E. Noyes with five troops of cavalry to follow and join Mills; and he ordered Colonel Royall to rejoin the main force. Perhaps Crook thought Royall had only to turn his men around and ride back; in the event it took another two hours and involved intense fighting. At several points during the struggle Royall feared that one or another of his companies would be cut off by the Indians and annihilated.

Unfolding throughout the day was a classic cavalry battle of lathered horses and clouds of dust with a rising and falling rattle of gunfire. Crook's men carried 100,000 rounds and shot off a quarter of the whole; much of the rest was scattered and lost on the ground as they moved from place to place. The Indians yelled without ceasing. Their whooping, Finerty noted, "has a sort of wolfish bark to it." He was astonished by the scores of Indian ponies lying dead on the field—heaps of them—but, "strange to relate," curiously few bodies of Indians. In the give and take of the fighting there were many close calls and daring rescues. Bourke at one point helped the bugler Elmer Snow from the field after a shot had broken both of his arms. Captain Guy V. Henry with Royall's force was shot through both cheeks and overrun by the Sioux after he fell to the ground, but Crow and Shoshone scouts managed his rescue.[9] Horses ran away with soldiers. Frank Grouard succeeded in slowing one just enough for the soldier to throw himself to the ground at the last minute. Another disappeared with its rider into a mass of Indians. Crook was desperate to concentrate his men and seethed inwardly at the delay.

Who was commanding this furious assault on Crook and his thousand men? Crook had no idea. If any of the scouts recognized Crazy Horse they did not say so. Finerty felt sure he had spotted Crazy Horse signaling commands with a mirror during the battle, but that was only later, when he came to write about the fight. But the Indian accounts all agree; it was Crazy Horse who was leading this fight, and his warriors were in command of the ebb and flow of battle over a period of five or six hours. Most of the whites had been through the shock of mass battles during the late war, when half a thousand men might die in a day in a fight hardly big enough to be given a name. But here at the Rosebud they were probed and assaulted by a fluid and shifting enemy in a manner that astounded them all.

Indians on both sides did not make things any easier. There were moments when the soldiers had to stop shooting because they could not tell which Indians in the fray were friendly scouts, which hostiles. Some Crow early in the fight spotted Red Cloud's son Jack just as his horse fell dead from a bullet. The young man did not stop to take the horse's bridle—a warrior custom to show he was not afraid—but jumped up and began to run away. The Crow rode up alongside of him, whipped him with their pony quirts, and snatched away his warbonnet and his father's fancy gun. The fact they did not kill him was eloquent expression of contempt.[10]

All seemed confusion. Finerty, riding with Mills on his first charge up the bluffs, wasn't even sure if the cavalry firing their revolvers had managed to kill or wound any Indians. "All passed like a flash of lightning, or a dream," he recorded.

The Indians confronted them from the rocks on top of the bluffs until the soldiers approached within fifty paces—close enough for the shooting to become almost point-blank. Then the hostiles scattered. The soldiers let out "a mad cheer." The breathless Finerty exulted that the Sioux were "unable to face the impetuous line of the superior race." Away the Indians flew "with what white men would consider undignified speed."[11] Bourke was also irritated when the hostiles broke. "The cowardly whelps would not give us a show at close quarters," he wrote in his diary the following day.[12]

Much the same happened to Crook in the center as he made his way with the main body of the force uphill from the river, rising from one crest to another. But after each scattering retreat of the hostiles, Finerty noted, "the Sioux became bold and impudent again. They rode up and down rapidly, sometimes wheeling in circles, slapping an indelicate portion of their persons at us and beckoning us to come on."

Crook did come on, from one crest to the next, but gained nothing. "The Sioux . . . took to their heels every time we came within fifty or sixty yards of them," Bourke wrote. "We followed them seven miles, chasing them from position to position."[13]

So it went. For all the charging and shooting Crook could not bring the fight to a climax. At one point in the early afternoon his horse was shot from under him; when the horse went down the general was tossed over the horse's head to land hard on the ground.[14] That was as close as Crook got to closing with the Indians.

Royall meanwhile seemed unable to withdraw from his extended position. The aid given by Burt and Burrowes was not enough. Royall had to fight every step of the way back, in constant danger of being overwhelmed. An hour passed, then a second. Of the whites killed in the fighting on this day, almost all died with Royall while he was trying to carry out Crook's order to rejoin the main body. By early afternoon concentrating his forces was the whole of the general's plan; once done he planned to go up the Rosebud canyon to support Mills on his way to attack the Indian village.

It never happened. Mills pressed on alone, eager to strike a blow, but many of his men grew nervous as they felt the canyon walls closing in. Above them on both sides were numerous spots where hidden enemies might open fire. Bourke and Finerty rode with Mills. Grouard was leading the way, thinking the hostile village was somewhere ahead, around the next twist or turn. "Some of the more thoughtful officers had their misgivings," Finerty wrote.

After proceeding several miles into the narrowing canyon Grouard came to a kind of opening of the canyon wall to the west, steep enough to require a panting climb but open enough for the force to make its way out toward the plain. Here he cocked an ear to the left while the men tightened saddle girths, sure they would find a battle just ahead. To Mills, Grouard said, "I hear firing in that direction, sir." That direction was out and around to the ridges where Royall was trying to fight his way free of the Indians. Before Mills could answer that it didn't matter, he had his orders, the men around him all turned to the sound of approaching horses. It was Crook's dust-whitened aide-de-camp Azor Nickerson, arriving with a change in orders. He had ridden through the canyon with only one man for companion.

"Royall is hard pressed and must be relieved," Nickerson said. "Henry is badly wounded and Vroom's troop [with Royall] is all cut up. The General orders that you and Noyes defile by your left flank out of this canyon, and fall on the rear of the Indians who are pressing Royall."[15]

Here something interesting emerges. Mills and others said later that they had reached the Indian village—they even *had* the village. They could not understand why they were being pulled back with the village and success in sight. But there was no village, not there nor around the next bend. It was twenty miles away, across the divide, where the streams fed west and north into the Little Bighorn.

Mills did as ordered. Leading their horses his men ascended the broken hillside to the west, not really much of a climb, and as they emerged from the canyon the sound of firing became clear. Mills gave the order to mount; the force moved quickly until it reached the plateau and open ground and saw Royall's men facing a growing mass of Sioux threatening to attack. "We dashed forward at a wild gallop," wrote Finerty, "cheering as we went." In a moment the Battle of the Rosebud was over. "The cunning savages did not wait for us." They scattered, and this time—it was midafternoon—they kept on going. The rule of thumb when an enemy breaks is to chase him down, but Crook ordered no pursuit.

Mills was puzzled at the way the fight petered out. Then he saw the explanation in the general's face. "I never saw a man more dejected." But he wanted an answer in words. "Why did you recall me?" he asked. "I had the village and could have held it."[16]

To this question Crook might have answered truthfully either of two things. The first was that he needed Mills—Royall was in danger of being overrun. Men who had been in the thick of it told Mills immediately after the fight that the Indians "had swung around and overwhelmed them, charging bodily and rapidly through the soldiers, knocking them from their horses with lances and knives, dismounting and killing them, cutting the arms off several at the elbows in the midst of the fight and carrying them away."[17]

And there was a second reason Crook had recalled Mills. He had concluded that it wasn't safe to follow him into the canyon. First to give him pause were the doctors, who refused to stay with the wounded unless a big guard was left behind to defend them. Crook did not have men enough. Then the Crow scouts said there were too many Indians. Baptiste Pourier was acting as interpreter for the Crow, and later described the moment:

> When the Crow scouts came to the Rosebud canyon they refused to go into it . . . White Face was spokesman. He told the General they wanted to go back. The General asked them what for. He said they did not want to get killed, as they all would be if they went into the canyon . . . The General said that he wanted to get to the Sioux village and fight them there. White Face answered and said that the force you have been fighting is only a little

war party; if you go to the village you will find as many Indians as the grass . . . you will all be killed, and the knowing Indian rubbed the palms of his hands together in imitation of grinding stones, which is the Indian sign for complete destruction.[18]

To Mills, Crook said none of this. "Well, Colonel, I found it a more serious engagement than I thought," he replied. "I knew I could not keep my promise to support you with the remainder of the force."[19]

Brought back together at last, Crook's men retraced their way down the hills to the stretch along the stream where they had stopped to water and graze their animals in the morning. There were wounded to care for, dead to bury. After dark ten bodies were put into a common grave on the banks of the streambed. A big fire was built on the spot and fed through the night. It was not uncommon for Crook to eat his dinner and drink his coffee without speaking. What he did is all we know of what he thought. "General Crook decided that evening to retire on his base of supplies," Finerty wrote. That meant turning around to rejoin the freight wagons he had left on Goose Creek. It made sense; his men were short of everything, and the wounded could not be left or sent back alone. Of the Battle of the Rosebud, then, it might fairly be said that Crook came, he fought, he withdrew—not the sort of thing to bring men to their feet for "three cheers and a tiger," ending with the growl customary at the time.

But officers and men were not ready to leave it at that; they wanted to know who won the fight. In the absence of fiery words from the general his men worked out a verdict on their own. The first step was to count casualties. Finerty, Bourke, and others were convinced that most of the Indian dead had been carried off by their friends. Many pools of drying blood suggested the toll was heavy. But actually on the field were found thirteen dead hostiles, the bodies of perhaps 150 Indian ponies, and, Finerty noted, "a few old blankets and war bonnets." Bourke in his diary recorded loss among the soldiers as ten killed outright, another four wounded so seriously they were expected to die, and perhaps forty more with injuries of more or less severity. The casualty count would suggest a draw, but Bourke wouldn't have it. "This engagement gives us the morale over the boastful Dakotas," he puffed in his diary, but it was curious language to describe a victory. He quoted Colonel Royall as authority that they had been fighting fifteen hundred hostiles, "maybe more."[20]

Bourke was working himself up to a claim that they had given the Indians what for.

But Mills with his questions got the drift of things soon enough. Once men and horses had been looked after, he wrote later, "The officers then mingled and talked over the fight." Foremost was the horrifying account of Royall's close call with disaster; Indians passed right through his lines—it was the way they hunted buffalo, riding in close. As bad in a different way was the discovery by the streambed after the fighting of the dead body of a Shoshone boy, left to guard horses. He had been horribly mutilated—scalped from the nape of the neck right up over the top of his head, "leaving his skull ghastly and white," in Bourke's words. The boy had been painting his face for war, one cheek done and one still to do when he was shot through the back. But it wasn't the sorrow of the loss that made the soldiers stop to reflect: the Sioux who killed the boy had ridden entirely around the command to do it—the soldiers had been surrounded—and none of them had known it. "We then all realized," Mills said in 1917 to a veterans' group, "that while we were lucky not to have been entirely vanquished, we had been most humiliatingly defeated."[21] One of his officers, Lieutenant Daniel C. Pearson, who brought up the rear and was last to leave the canyon, was equally blunt: "No conclusion," he wrote, "was so apparent as our defeat."[22]

Very early the next morning Crook's force pulled out of camp. The dead Shoshone boy was buried by his friends and relatives, their faces painted black. "The tears of the young men and of the squaws rolled down their cheeks," Finerty wrote. Where the big fire had burned down over the common grave, men on horses rode forward and back over the ashes to hide the site. On the way out of camp some Crow scouts chanced on the body of a Sioux. "They said life was not yet extinct and the Sioux was moving when they came up," Bourke wrote. "He was not moving much when they left."

Finerty was there with his friend, Lieutenant Adolphus Von Leuttwitz, and watched what happened:

> The Crow set to work at once to dismember him. One scalped the remains. Another cut off the ears of the corpse and put them in his wallet. Von Leuttwitz and I remonstrated, but the savages only laughed at us. After cutting off toes, fingers, and nose, they proceeded to indecent mutilation, and this we could not stand. We protested vigorously, and the Captain [Sutorious], seeing that something singular was in progress, rode up with a squad of men and put an end to the butchery. One big, yellow brute of a Crow, as we rode

off, took a portion of the dead warrior's person out of his pouch, waved it in the air, and shouted something in broken English which had reference to the grief Sioux squaws must feel when the news of the unfortunate brave's fate would reach them. And then the whole group of savages broke into a mocking chorus of laughter . . . I lost all respect for the Crow after that episode.[23]

Next day, rejoined with the supply wagons he had left on Goose Creek, Crook wrote his first dispatch for General Sheridan in Chicago and sent it south to Fort Fetterman with a courier, Ben Arnold, a scout in his early thirties who had been hired by Captain George Randall when the campaign was organizing back at Fort Laramie in the spring. The newspaper correspondents all sent stories at the same time, each describing in greatest detail the part of the battle they had witnessed personally: Finerty of the *Chicago Times* and T. C. McMillan of the *Chicago Inter-Ocean* had ridden deep into the canyon with Captain Mills; Robert Strahorn of the *Chicago Tribune* had remained in the center with Crook; Reuben Davenport wrote a long and detailed dispatch about the daylong fight of the men under Colonel Royall.

Arnold later said he was paid $250 for making the hazardous, 190-mile trip back to Fetterman. That was probably his Army pay; very likely he got something extra from one or more of the newspapermen as well. It was their dispatches he filed with the fort's telegrapher as soon as he arrived, then waited two and a half hours "before I turned the government dispatches in," as he related to his stepdaughter, Josephine Waggoner. "I did as I was told to do; there my duty ended," he said. Told by whom? Elsewhere in his account of the summer campaign Arnold refers to a "Captain Davenport." The only Davenport on the expedition was the correspondent of the *New York Herald*, who evidently secured an advantage over his rivals—a small matter in most cases, but not in this one, and not to Crook.[24]

Crook's account of the fighting was brief, ending with a casualty report: nine dead and twenty wounded. "I expect to find those Indians in rough places all the time," he added, "and so have ordered five additional companies of Infantry and shall not probably make any extended movement till they arrive."[25] He was as good as his word. Except to move camp a few miles every two or three days to find new grazing and firewood, the Big Horn and Yellowstone Expedition did not budge for six weeks.

15

"I am in constant dread of an attack."

WITH LITTLE TO DO while General Crook waited for reinforcements, the officers and men of the Big Horn and Yellowstone Expedition frequently left camp to go fishing. A week and a day after the fight at the Rosebud—it was Sunday, June 25—Captain Anson Mills and two soldiers rode up into the foothills near the camp in search of a stream. From a high point, Mills reported on his return, they had seen "a dense smoke" far off to the north and west across the plains. "All agreed," Finerty wrote, "that it must be a prairie fire or something of the kind."

What struck Bourke was not the smoke but the one hundred fish Mills and his companions brought back to camp. "Rapids and deep pools of icy cold water, shaded by a heavy growth of willow trees, give a home to multitudes of mountain trout," Bourke recorded in his diary. The diarist was fascinated and enchanted by this bounty—day after day he recorded in his diary the number of trout caught by this officer or that. Lieutenant Henry Lemly caught twenty in one go, and Major Henry Noyes twice as many. Crook, always competitive when it came to hunting or fishing, went angling with the rest, hoping to achieve on his own what Mills and his men had done together. "General Crook has caught seventy in one day," Bourke wrote, "and expresses his determination to make the number an even hundred." Bourke variously identified the fish as mountain trout or "pan trout" and called them "very toothsome"; Lemly said they were "salmon or rainbow trout." Over a period of weeks, Bourke estimated, Crook's command caught an average of four hundred fish a day— perhaps fifteen or twenty thousand in all before the expedition resumed its hunt for Indians.[1]

But it wasn't just fishing that occupied the general's time. At the beginning of July, Bourke went with him on a four-day hunt into the Big Horn Mountains rising abruptly to the west of the camp, which they called

Cloud Peak after the tallest mountain in the range. There the mountain sheep and the occasional black-tailed deer offered a welcome change from the meat of buffalo and elk, shot in numbers down on the plains. "Mountain sheep mutton is very juicy and tender," Bourke wrote. He liked to roast steaks two at a time on a sharp stick, angled toward the fire with bacon slices between the pieces of meat. He called the sheep's heart when boiled a "*bonne-bouche.*" Finerty was along on the hunt, and noted that "dozens of American eagles rose majestically from the rocks and soared proudly above us, screaming with all their might." The tracks of game were everywhere; the trees and undergrowth "assumed a tropical richness." He grew almost giddy describing the "ethereal beauty" of the lakes in the valleys looking "like pieces of the blue sky which had fallen from the heavens." To his companion Anson Mills he said, "Bring along your Italy." Mills was just as charmed. The next day the whole party marched back down out of the canyon to celebrate "the centennial fourth" with the rest of the command. "We had nothing but coffee wherewith to drink to the memory of George Washington," Finerty wrote, "but we had a banquet on elk, deer and mountain sheep killed by Crook and his officers."[2]

While his officers feasted Crook brooded. Waiting for him in camp that afternoon had been a telegram from General Sheridan, brought in from Fort Fetterman a day or two previous by Ben Arnold, who had already headed back south. Sheridan's instructions were brief: "Hit them again and hit them hard." It seems Finerty was watching nearby.

> Crook smiled grimly when he read the telegram, and remarked, "I wish Sheridan would come out here himself and show us how to do it. It is rather difficult to surround three Indians with one soldier."[3]

Crook had about twelve hundred men in his command. Did he think he had been fighting 3,600 Sioux at the Rosebud—more than twice the number estimated by Royall on the day of the fight? Was Crook making excuses? Bourke reassured himself no excuses were needed. On July 6 he wrote, "The absence of hostile demonstrations since our fight of June 17th speaks very plainly of the severe handling the Sioux received that day."[4] Sitting around camp unmolested, catching trout, feasting on elk and mountain sheep—all were proof they had whipped the Indians, in Bourke's view. This pleasant dream continued another four days.

———

The cable from Sheridan had been delivered with other mail and official dispatches to Crook's camp by Ben Arnold, one of several couriers who made the trip between Fort Fetterman and Goose Creek every week or so. Arnold had come west to the Fort Laramie area with a unit of Ohio cavalry during the Civil War, then remained as a freighter and scout. It was his friend Nick Janis who had urged him to sign on with the expedition at Fort Laramie—as a courier, Arnold insisted to Captain Randall, not as a scout. "I didn't want to fight," he told his stepdaughter. Early in July, Arnold found himself back at Fort Fetterman worn out by the hell-for-leather, three-day ride and so sick with a bug that "I couldn't even keep water on my stomach."[5]

While Arnold languished in bed at the fort, too ill to work or travel, Major Alexander Chambers of the 4th Infantry oversaw the packing of supplies for General Crook, then set out early on the morning of July 4 with a wagon train and six companies of infantry, bound for Goose Creek. Arnold, still weak, elected to stay behind. Leaving the fort with Chambers were two officers of the 14th Infantry, Lieutenant Frederic S. Calhoun, who had joined the regiment a year earlier, and Captain Thomas F. Tobey, accompanied by his dog, Walloper, a heavy-shouldered scrapper who sometimes walked, sometimes rode in the feed box of one of the wagons. Tobey in his mid-thirties was the man of greater accomplishment. He had graduated from Brown University in 1859 and Harvard Law in 1861, then fought all the way through the war, including the Battle of Fredericksburg, where he was wounded, and the Siege of Vicksburg. Malaria forced his resignation from the Army in 1864 as a major; need of a job brought him back a year later as a second lieutenant.

Calhoun had served in 1864 only as a "one hundred day volunteer" before mustering out and returning home to Cincinnati, where his father, a distant relation of the president of the Confederacy, was a prosperous merchant. Peace did not favor Calhoun, and he hoped to follow his brother James into the cavalry. In the summer of 1873 he rode along with his brother's regiment guarding the survey crew laying out a route for the Northern Pacific Railway up the valley of the Yellowstone River. The following spring officers in his brother's regiment signed a joint letter to the secretary of war, the Honorable William H. Belknap, urging Calhoun's commission as a second lieutenant. Fourteen names followed, including those of Calhoun's brother James, Lieutenant Donald McIntosh, Captain Myles Moylan, Captain George W. Yates, and Brevet Major General George Armstrong Custer. It wasn't just a brother that Fred hoped to join, but the family of the 7th Cavalry; James had married Custer's sister, Margaret. An examining board quizzed Calhoun on simple arithmetic, U.S. history, and other subjects and declared him satisfactory, but the Army evidently felt there were enough Custer relatives in the 7th and appointed Fred to the 14th Infantry in the Department of the Platte, a sore disappointment to the new lieutenant.[6] He was still in his twenties, a trifle blank before the camera but fresh-faced with a dimpled chin and a fringe of blond mustache. Heading north in the first week of July 1876, Calhoun and Tobey rode, messed, and slept together as the wagons creaked and bumped along the old Bozeman Road, abandoned eight years earlier.

Late on the night of July 6, two days after the wagon train had pulled out, the telegrapher at Fort Fetterman received a cable addressed to Crook from Sheridan reporting the bare outlines of a military disaster on the Little Bighorn River in the Montana Territory—General Custer dead with hundreds of officers and men. The telegrapher found Ben Arnold's bed about midnight, roused him from sleep with the news, and handed him the dispatches from Sheridan. "I got right up," Arnold later told Josephine Waggoner, "mounted my horse and within half an hour after I was awakened . . . I was on my way with the message to General Crook." Riding with Arnold was the mixed-blood Louis Richard, freshly arrived from the Red Cloud Agency. On the trail the two men averaged fifty miles or more a day. Midday on Saturday, near old Fort Reno, Arnold and Richard overtook Colonel Chambers and the wagon train of supplies headed for Goose Creek. In a moment news of the disaster on the Little Bighorn was conveyed. Lieutenant Tobey recorded the moment in his diary:

> On the road Louis Richard, with some half-breed scouts from Laramie, overtook us and gave us the news of poor Custer's affair. Calhoun, of course, is very much distressed. I have not been specially anxious, hitherto, to be personally engaged in a fight with the Sioux but I do want a chance at them now. The tone of the men seems good. I think this news makes them eager for a fight.[7]

Arnold and Richard did not linger, but hurried on and rode into Crook's camp on Goose Creek with their grim news as daylight was breaking on Monday morning, July 10. The air was dark with the smoke of a prairie fire set by the Indians during the night. Smoke towered high into the darkened sky and fine ash settled everywhere, making it difficult to breathe. The general himself was off in the mountains hunting but was expected back at any time.

Custer's fate was of course the sensation of the day but Bourke, worried how the Rosebud fight would reflect on Crook's reputation, turned his attention first to the dispatch from Major William Jordan, in command at Camp Robinson, where Indians coming in from the north reported that the Rosebud fight had been "hotly contested." That irritated Bourke. But he was pleased to read that the Indian camps were loud with mourning, a sign (he hoped) that many had been killed. Louis Richard said that "all the young bucks" had gone north from Red Cloud; only half of the families carried on the agency books had showed up on issue day. For Bourke, that explained the Indian hordes confronted by Crook on the Rosebud. The lieutenant was beside himself with indignation at the excuses civilian agents made for their red wards. "The damnable frauds perpetrated at that sink of iniquity daily call to Heaven for redress," he wrote. Only after a full venting of these angers did Bourke shift his attention to Sheridan's report of "the terrible disaster lately befallen Custer's command."[8]

What Sheridan knew came from early press reports and the hurried dispatches from General Alfred Terry's command. Plans for the campaign had called for three independent forces to converge on the hostiles in the Powder and Tongue river country—Terry's command including Custer's 7th Cavalry approaching from the east, Colonel John Gibbon with seven companies of infantry from the west, and General Crook with his twelve hundred men from the south. Crook, of course, was out of the game. After the fight on June 17, he had pulled his men back to Goose Creek and gone to ground. On the morning of June 25—the day Anson Mills, out fishing, had wondered about the smoke of distant fires off to the north—Custer and his men had come upon a huge Indian village and attacked it. All we know of what Sheridan told Crook about this fight is what Bourke recorded in his diary. Custer split his command, Bourke wrote, taking five companies to attack the north end of the camp while Major Marcus A. Reno attacked the other end. What happened next was sketched in briskly:

> Terry and Gibbon, pressing forward upon hearing the noise of battle, found Reno with his command entrenched on a hill near the village which was in flames. Swarms of Indians surrounded the devoted remainder of the Seventh, but were kept back until the arrival of our reinforcements, when they took to flight. Terry, moving forward, found the ground covered with dead ponies, saddles, burnt and burning lodges and charred corpses. He soon dis-

covered the bodies of Custer and eleven of his officers and more than three hundred dead soldiers, but no wounded. In one pile, two hundred and seventy-one of our dead were found and buried in one grave. Terry, after burying the dead and destroying the remains of the village, fell back to the mouth of the Big Horn to refit.[9]

The numbers by themselves suggest the magnitude of the event. Even during the incomparably bloody Civil War no substantial force on either side had ever been wiped out to the last man. "The shock was so great," Bourke summed up later, "that men and officers could hardly speak when the tale slowly circulated from lip to lip."[10] Every man had learned the worst by the time Crook reached camp late in the day. His good humor was swept away by news of the disaster. The glow of the successful hunt— fourteen elk, three or four thousand pounds of meat—faded as Crook realized what Crazy Horse had done. Reports from Terry soon arrived with further details of the Custer fight. All made one thing overridingly clear, as Bourke wrote in his diary: "Custer, moving up the Rosebud, had struck the same village fought by us on the 17th."[11] What did that do to Crook's claim he had whipped the Indians who killed Custer only a week later?

All eyes were on Lieutenant Calhoun when the wagon train of supplies rolled into the camp on Goose Creek on July 13; his brother James was one of the officers of the 7th whose bodies were found naked and muti- lated at the Little Bighorn. There was already heated talk of Reno's fail- ure to come to Custer's aid in mid-battle. Ride to the sound of the guns was a soldier's first commandment. Reno's men all heard the firing down the river. It grew heavy, then died away. Reno made a tentative move, then pulled back to his hilltop. About Reno even the word cowardice was being used. What, then, was the word for Crook, who had hastened away from the inconclusive affair at the Rosebud for hunting and fishing on Goose Creek?

For weeks thereafter Crook did not budge. The additional companies of infantry brought in by Lieutenant Calhoun and the others were not enough, nor were the two-hundred-some Shoshone scouts who soon arrived with Chief Washakie. Sheridan was anxious for Crook to stir him- self and strike a blow against the hostiles; he reassured Crook that he would soon be reinforced by a column of the 5th Cavalry under Colonel

Wesley Merritt, but Crook took that to mean he was to stay put till Merritt arrived. While he waited he brooded, and what he brooded about was the infamous betrayal of the correspondent for the *New York Herald*, Reuben Davenport. It was Davenport's dispatch that Ben Arnold had arranged to send out a few hours previous to Crook's own. It beat the competition by a day, appearing in the *Herald* on July 6. Copies soon reached Crook in the field. Davenport's account of the fighting that nearly swallowed up Royall's men looked nothing like a victory. Crook's conduct of the battle appeared confused; he sent Royall out, then ordered him back, but never marched to the colonel's aid himself. Captains Andrew Burt and Thomas Burrowes were given the job of relieving the Indian pressure so Royall could retreat, but it was a drawn-out affair. Davenport himself reached safety only with the help of covering fire from Burrowes's men. He described a misshapen battle. Royall's men did all the fighting and suffered all the casualties. The rest did a lot of riding about but achieved nothing. "Colonel Royall was circumscribed by orders in every one of his movements," Davenport wrote, "and the disaster attending the retreat would have been much greater had it not been so skillfully directed by him."

The *Herald*'s man did not criticize Crook openly, and he closed with the remark that "the northern Sioux . . . have been severely crippled." But Davenport was describing no victory. The Crow and Shoshones departed the day after the fight for home, and Crook, "dreading to march forward through so rough a country after the desertion of his scouts," turned back toward Goose Creek. Dread is not a soldierly quality. Crook did not hide his fury; we may imagine his resentment at hearing his decisions explained by dread. Nothing was said to Davenport, but nothing needed to be said. All knew what the *Herald* had printed. "Mr. Davenport," Bourke noted, "has been prowling about the camp like a whipped cur."[12]

At Goose Creek, hostile Indians were now pressing close almost daily, trying to steal horses, shooting into camp, firing the grass. There was nothing Crook could do about it. To send men chasing out after the Indians would only put them at risk. Some weeks earlier he had told Ben Arnold it would be folly to chase Indians about the countryside— "We are foreigners, you might say, and this is their country. They know every nook and corner."[13] As weeks passed, Crook felt the growing impatience of Sheridan, who was himself vigorously urged to take action by General Sherman. Crook's state of mind—excitable, confused, frightened of failure—emerges in a rambling dispatch from the field to Sheridan on July 23.

> I find myself immeasureably embarrassed by the delay of Merritt's column, as the extremely hot weather of the last few days has so completely parched the grass, excepting that on the mountain tops, that it burns like tinder . . . On Powder, Tongue and Rosebud rivers, the whole country is on fire and filled with smoke. I am in constant dread of an attack; in their last, they set fire to the grass, but as much of it was still green, we extinguished it without difficulty; but should it be fired now, I don't see how we could stay in the country. I am at a loss what to do: I can prevent their attack by assuming the aggressive, but . . . I could do little beyond scattering them.[14]

So Davenport was not wrong; Crook's decisions were driven by dread. Bitterly he complained to Sheridan about the "most villainous falsehoods" published by Davenport in the *Herald*. "A correct account" of the battle had been sent to the *New York Tribune*, Crook insisted, but evidently "it was suppressed in the telegraph office at Fetterman." Crook felt the turning of opinion against him. He did not mention but surely knew that at Goose Creek the enlisted men had begun to call him "Rosebud George."[15] It was not a term of affection.

But the waiting, if not the brooding, ended at last with the arrival of Colonel Merritt and the 5th Cavalry in early August. Sheridan was expecting Crook to join General Terry on the Yellowstone, then strike the Indians "a hard blow" if they could find them. Crook's fighting spirit stirred. He determined to travel light, hoping "to make his column as mobile, if possible, as a column of Indians," Bourke wrote in his diary. Once again, on August 5, excess baggage was moved to the wagons and left behind. "It was ten weeks before we saw those wagons again," remembered Captain Charles King, who had arrived with Merritt.[16] A train of 360 pack mules would carry fifteen days' rations, most of the ammunition (250 rounds per man), whatever else did not fit in saddlebags or rucksacks. Nothing was permitted beyond weapons, blanket, personal tin cup, frying pan, and spoon; half of a shelter tent, an overcoat, and the clothes on a man's back. Crook did not except himself. Some weeks later, the general was found one morning sitting naked on a riverbank, waiting for the underclothes he had just washed to dry.[17]

On the march north to meet Terry on the Yellowstone, Crook and his staff passed through the Rosebud valley. A huge Indian village had camped there following the fight six weeks earlier. Bourke noted there was "no grazing for our horses." The valley had been "picked clean as a bone" by the vast numbers of Indian ponies, "not less than ten thousand," in the view of Frank Grouard. Scouts rode up the canyon where Crook had sent Mills to attack the illusory Indian village. "A trap had been set," the scouts reported back. "Across the canyon at its narrowest, deepest and most precipitous part, they had constructed an abattis of fallen timber, to prevent our escape to the north." If Mills had not turned back, Bourke wrote, Crazy Horse and his hostiles would have "slaughtered our battalion to the last man."[18] It was an ever-plainer fact that the Indians who wiped out Custer had almost done the same to Crook.

Many survivors of the Custer fight were with General Terry when Crook's command joined them at the mouth of the Powder River on the Yellowstone in mid-August. For ten days among the officers talk was the principal business of the day. Not far beneath the usual joking and fooling ran a deep current of apprehension about the Sioux. Bourke in his soldierly way tried to brush this aside. Of Major Reno's performance at the Little Bighorn he wrote, "He saw enough at that fight to scare him for the rest of his life. He will never make a bold move for ten years to come."[19] Bourke read the man correctly; Reno had indeed been chastened—but why not? He had left sixty-five of his men dead on the field.

One night around the fire two officers of the 7th—Captains Thomas Weir and Thomas McDougal—described to some of Crook's men the moment on June 27 when they had ridden out from Reno's hilltop to look for Custer's command. For two or three miles there was nothing. Then the bodies began. "The first thought that seemed to strike every man of us," said McDougal, "and the first words spoken were, 'How white they look!' "[20] The thought must have struck all of Crook's men: stripped to the buff, they would have looked the same.

Before Crook separated from Terry on the Yellowstone in the last week of August he gained one officer and lost a few. The man he gained was a lieutenant in the 2nd Cavalry, William Philo Clark, unmarried and not quite thirty, who had freshly arrived from Fort Ellis on the upper Yellowstone in command of a mackinaw, one of the large, shallow-draft, freight-carrying open boats that were steered by rudder and carried downriver by the current alone. At the mouth of the Powder, Lieutenant Clark had

unloaded recruits and a Gatling gun for General Terry, who then sec-
onded Clark to Crook as an aide-de-camp—exactly why is unknown.
Clark, from the small town of Deer River in upstate New York, had
served mainly on the western frontier since graduating from West Point
in 1868. Bourke and another of Crook's officers, Colonel Thaddeus Stanton, first met Clark in a crowded sutler's tent where officers and men alike
were buying "canned fruits and fresh vegetables, eggs and beer at fabulous prices." Clark, dressed in a "suit of Indian-tanned buckskin" and carrying a hunting knife that weighed as much as a hatchet, invited Crook's
men for lunch in his tent, where he served them bacon, bread, canned
peaches, and whiskey. Bourke believed they would have called it "rot-gut"
or "hellfire" if not for the bottle's handsome label. They found Clark a
man of broad curiosity and considerable charm; Captain King said Clark
was soon recognized as "unquestionably the show-figure" of Crook's
staff.[21]

At the same time, a number of Crook's officers and men were placed
on the steamboat *Carroll* and sent down the Yellowstone headed for
Omaha, disabled by wounds at the Rosebud or broken down by the campaign. One lieutenant had accidentally shot off a finger with his pistol.
Another had broken his arm. Two men were "insane," and about twenty
were ill or recovering from injuries. In command of the invalids was Captain Thomas Burrowes, one of those uncelebrated frontier military officers who passes in and out of the history of the Sioux wars. At the
Rosebud, Burrowes had ridden to the aid of Colonel Royall, plunging
into the thickest part of the fight. He survived the battle without injury,
but old wounds from the Civil War made it impossible for him to go on.
In the Battle of Jonesboro, Georgia, on September 1, 1864, Burrowes had
been shot twice. One musket ball shattered his right arm and a second
punctured his chest and lung near the heart. For weeks he was expected to
die, then to lose his right arm, but he recovered and returned to service.
But over time scarring in the chest cavity resulted in an enlarged heart,
which impeded blood flow. Increasingly, Burrowes was quickly exhausted
by even mild exertion. On the Yellowstone, following two months of hard
travel and fighting, Burrowes was diagnosed with hypertrophy of the
heart, and a military surgeon ordered him to retire from the campaign.
He left Crook's command on the *Carroll* a physically broken man.[22]

In the last week of August, Crook felt ready to resume the war. His
wounded were off his hands, his men had replenished their rations, and
his scouts, Frank Grouard and Baptiste Pourier, had returned from a

reconnaissance to report that the hostile camp, still largely intact, was moving east and south. The two generals in their discussions had devised a simple plan. Terry would remain on the Yellowstone and prevent the Indians from crossing and escaping to the north; "Crook was to stick to the trail and follow it wheresoever it might lead him."[23] Bourke felt Crook was the man for the job. He had observed the two generals daily since August 10, and noted in his diary,

> Of the two men, Terry would be the more pleasing companion, Crook the stauncher friend. In Terry's face I sometimes thought I detected faint traces of indecision, vacillation and weakness; but in Crook's countenance there is not the slightest trace of anything but stubbornness, stolidity, rugged resolution and bull-dog tenacity.[24]

A week of sometimes violent rain and thunderstorms had turned the country muddy. "Morning cold and foggy," Bourke noted as Crook's command moved out on August 26, determined to overtake the hostiles and strike a hard blow. Over the next ten days the rain was nearly continuous; between downpours it was cloudy and cold. For awhile the scouts said the trail of the Indians was growing fresher, but by September 5 it was clear the big camp had broken up at last and Crook's men were chasing a phantom. Paused on the Heart River and down to half rations, Crook explained his thinking to the correspondent John Finerty, who listened in disbelief. More or less straight east was Fort Abraham Lincoln, about 160 miles distant—five days of riding, by Crook's calculation. Seven days' riding and two hundred miles south was Deadwood and the Black Hills, swarming with miners who talked a brave game but knew nothing of fighting Indians. Common sense pointed east; Crook was determined to go south. "It must be done," he said. "The miners must be protected, and we must punish the Sioux on our way to the south, or leave this campaign entirely unfinished."

In tranquility twenty years later Finerty wrote:

> I looked at him in some amazement, and could not help saying, "You will march 200 miles in the wilderness, with used-up horses and tired infantry on two and one-half days' half rations!"
>
> "I know it looks hard," was the reply, "but we've got to do it, and it shall be done ... All will be glad of the movement after the march has been made. If necessary," he added, "we can eat our horses."[25]

16

"General Crook ought to be hung."

WHILE CROOK'S MEN MADE their wet way east, half drowned and half starved, what remained of the big camp of the Indians somehow, mysteriously, kept always a day or two ahead. Crook was convinced, and insisted in dispatches to Terry and Sheridan, that he was closing on the Indians, but his scouts, Frank Grouard and Baptiste Pourier, could not seem to find and keep hold of their trail. The Indians, for their part, generally knew Crook was about but they treated his army as they might have treated a grizzly sow with cubs down in the brush by a river— unpredictable and dangerous, but easily avoided. In one mood the Indians might go in and kill the bear; in another they might ride well around. Crook was in deadly earnest, but the Indians seem to have had enough of fighting the whites for awhile. They kept out of Crook's way.

The scattering of the big camp had begun soon after the fight the Indians were already calling "Pehin Hanska Kasota." Pehin Hanska—Long Hair—was the Indians' name for Custer. During the actual fight few, perhaps none, of the Indians knew who they were fighting, but within a few days word spread that it was Custer they had killed. For those wiped out in battle the Indians used the sign of two hands rubbing together; it meant both killed and swept away, "rubbed out"—*kasota*.[1] Immediately after the fight some of the Indians hurried away to the agencies, hoping to escape blame for the killing of so many soldiers, but for most of the Indians life went on as before.

Summer was the time for hunting and for raiding. One of the first war parties to leave camp after the Custer fight was led by Crazy Horse, who went north with two hundred men to steal the horses of the Assiniboines. Back from that foray by late July he spent only a few days in camp before setting out again, heading south this time with a smaller group for the

Black Hills. Crazy Horse himself would have cited no special sense of mission for this constant raiding. It was simply what a Sioux warrior did, as a farmer might rise every morning to hoe his corn.

The northern plains were alive that summer with white miners and freighters crossing from the Missouri to the Black Hills, with Indians hunting and raiding, and with soldiers criss-crossing the plains trying to catch up with the Indians. Heading for the Black Hills to steal horses in early August were Sitting Bull's nephew White Bull and his friend Iron Claw, just the two of them, thinking a small group might be missed or ignored by the soldiers. One night they were camped on the headwaters of the Hinhan Wakpa (Owl River)[2] when a party of a dozen Indians tried to run off their horses. After a moment of excited confusion they all recognized each other; it was Crazy Horse and his friends, on their way back from their own raid into the hills.

Once that was sorted out the two parties camped together for the night. In addition to Crazy Horse himself and four Cheyenne the group of ten included Black Fox, Short Bull, Looking Horse, Low Dog, and Dog Goes—all (save the last) well-known Oglala fighting men close to Crazy Horse.[3] That night Crazy Horse and his friends danced in the traditional way to celebrate success in war. After the singing was over White Bull made his bed beside the bed of Crazy Horse; before sleep they talked about the Custer fight. White Bull does not record what was said, but the fight was the talk of the plains that summer, and the Indians all seemed to understand that the big killing had settled nothing. More trouble was bound to come. In the morning White Bull and his friend continued south to the hills while Crazy Horse headed back for the big camp, then moving east from the Powder River. This encounter on the Hinhan Wakpa took place about the middle of the second week of August, when Crook and Terry were conferring on the Yellowstone.

Over the following weeks the big camp seems to have separated gradually into at least three or four large groups as it made its way east toward Beaver Creek, then on to the Little Missouri. There Sitting Bull and his Hunkpapas left the others to head north for Killdeer Mountain, while two or three other groups, including the Oglala under Crazy Horse and the Miniconjou under Red Horse, Roman Nose, and Iron Plume (a man of many alternate names), went south up the Little Missouri on a course pointed toward Deadwood in the Black Hills. Once Crook understood that the Indians were breaking up he slowed his progress to think. Bourke recorded,

The reason of our short march was that the trail began to split, showing that the hostiles knew we were in pursuit and were employing every artifice to bewilder us. Louis Richard and Frank Grouard both think they mean to draw us over to the broken country . . . where they can scatter like quail and reunite in our rear, or on our flank, at pleasure. Our scouts went out examining the trail with the utmost care: indications are becoming plain that we are close to a considerable band of the enemy, perhaps a strong rearguard, watching our progress.[4]

The scouts were seeing through a glass darkly. The Indians were indeed splitting up, and they did know Crook was following their trail, but they weren't laying plans for an elaborate trap, and they were no longer even acting in concert. One large group (of which the Miniconjou Eagle Shield was a member) headed east, planning to surrender at Fort Sully, where the Cheyenne River joined the Missouri. But when Crook went south instead this band turned around and headed back toward the Powder. A second group (of which Swollen Face was a member) went into camp near the Little Missouri and prepared to fight, only to watch in some puzzlement as a fast-moving detachment of Crook's men hurried on past them only nine miles away. This group may have included Crazy Horse and his Oglala. A third group of forty-eight lodges led by Red Horse and Iron Plume (of the many names) continued on south about two jumps ahead of Crook's column. Red Horse says his band was going straight south "to give ourselves up" at the agencies near Camp Robinson in northwest Nebraska, and it may have been true—or not.[5] Unsure of Crook's location or line of march, the Red Horse group went into camp along a tributary of the Moreau River called Mashtinca Putin (Rabbit Lip), a creek bed near the sandstone outcroppings known as Slim Buttes. From this spot some of the men went out raiding while others went hunting, leaving a handful of warriors and the women and children behind.

Crook, meanwhile, having turned south at the headwaters of the Heart River, led his column of two thousand toward the Black Hills. "Frank Grouard says he knows nothing of the country this side of the Little Missouri," Bourke wrote in his diary. The day of the turn broke with a "cold, drizzling rain"; after nightfall it turned into a downpour. At first light on September 6 the march south resumed in a "cold, chilling mist and rain." The next day the rain was heavier. "We often stood up at nights," one enlisted man remembered, "for to lay down we had to do so in mud and water."[6] So it continued—rain, cold, great difficulty making fire enough to boil a pot of water for coffee; very little bacon, six flat biscuits of hardtack per man per day, soaking clothes, sleeping on wet ground, and then on the third day the first slabs of half-cooked horsemeat. Some of the men pronounced it quite palatable, but the majority called it tough, repellent in flavor, with little to keep a man going.

By the third day it was apparent that the accumulating hardships were no joke. Horses were giving out and men were straggling, sure signs of trouble for any military force making its way through enemy country. "Footsore, lame and weary," Bourke called the column stringing out along the trail; at day's end late arrivals made their way into camp an hour behind the first, "leading tired horses." Clothing was all but rotting on their bodies. Cracked boots could not be replaced or repaired. Blisters had no time to heal. The rain turned the gravelly soil into a porridge-like mud or gumbo that clung so heavily to feet and hooves it had to be scraped off every few hundred yards. Cavalrymen leading their horses brought up the rear of the march; from time to time a carbine or a pistol shot announced the dispatch of a horse that could go no further. The official reason for shooting the horses was to stop the Indians from getting them, but the real reason was to eat them. Whenever a horse went down men fell out to skin the carcass and slice off steaks to eat later in camp— steaks, they joked, that had "a horse or a mule shoe at one end of them." It did not amuse the soldiers to know that the mule packers with the column were eating better than the military; unlike Crook, they had taken care to bring what they needed. Weighing these realities, Crook on September 7 ordered a detachment under Captain Anson Mills of 150 men on the best horses to hasten south to Deadwood to buy up emergency food supplies, then hurry back to relieve the main column. Riding out with Mills late in the day were the newspaper writers Robert Strahorn and Reuben Davenport, the latter doubtless hoping to escape the cold shoulder prompted by his dismissive stories in the *New York Herald*. John Finerty wanted to join them but his horse had played out. Mills departed in the late afternoon in a "cold, penetrating rain."

Next day Crook's men—more than eighteen hundred of them—shared the meat of three or four antelope shot by the scouts, barely enough for two bites per man. Passing a thicket of plum bushes in the afternoon, Lieutenant Walter S. Schuyler wrote to his father, "the whole staff, including the General, stampeded down into [the] plum patch, going down on our hands and knees to pick up the ripe fruit that the wind had shaken off."[7] Some of the men when they had a chance roasted and ate the plump parts of the cactus called Indian fig. It was filling but caused diarrhea.

It was on this day—September 8—that the eating of horses became general. One of the men on the march remembered that "there was not fat enough on a dozen horses to season the gruel for a grasshopper."[8] The remaining bacon was just enough to grease the frying pans. That night sitting with his officers Crook passed around a pint flask of whiskey he'd brought along to celebrate his forty-eighth birthday. The general and a dozen men each took a mouthful. Some of the officers had hardtack crackers to eat with their whiskey; the rest went without. "Take it for all in all," wrote Bourke, "it was decidedly the 'thinnest' birthday celebration I have ever attended."[9]

The men in Crook's command, Bourke fails to add, were in no mood to be toasting the general on his birthday. With little to eat, soaked day after day in a cold rain, in clothes they had been wearing for a month, walking beside faltering horses, with mud to sleep on and nothing to hope from the morrow but more of the same, the men of Crook's Big Horn and Yellowstone Expedition were about as worn down and played out as it was possible for a body of soldiers to be. Those who made "the horsemeat march" never forgot it, and never forgave Crook for marching off into the wilderness without plan or rations. One of the officers, Captain Samuel S. Sumner, gave his opinion unvarnished in a letter to his friend Charles King in 1918:

> The fact is, King, I always recall that campaign with more or less disgust. We suffered so much needless hardship, and the cavalry was practically used up by a vicious system of marching. Merritt complained bitterly at the time, while Carr simply laughed at the whole campaign as a joke in Indian warfare.[10]

Carr made a joke of what infuriated ordinary soldiers. Two days before the fight at Slim Buttes, Merritt told Carr that he'd heard the muttered resentment of an orderly in the headquarters tent—"General Crook ought to be hung."[11]

While Crook was sharing his whiskey with his officers, many miles to the south Mills was preparing to attack an Indian camp discovered that afternoon by Frank Grouard, who had spotted the pony herd. The place was one of the favored camping grounds of the Sioux—good grass along a pleasant, winding stream, some sandstone bluffs nearby that offered protection and gave the place its Sioux name, Paha Zipzipela, Slim Buttes.

Grouard told Mills he feared the village was too large to attack safely. But Mills, unlike Crook, did not think much of the scout. "[He] knew the ways of the Indians," Mills conceded, but was a slippery, evasive character, "not to be relied upon. I always regarded him as a coward and a big liar."[12]

Mills chose an odd moment to label Grouard a coward. That night he sent the scout to pin down the location of the village for a dawn attack, the sort of creeping about in the dark that might strike fear into any man. Grouard not only went but returned leading two stolen horses—a paint and a black stallion, picked out of the village herd. That worried Mills. "I at once suspected he was getting himself in shape to get away should we get into a hot fight."[13]

Mills concealed his men that night in a ravine where they huddled to escape the steady rain. A bite or two of bacon or hardtack was all they had to eat. How many Indian warriors might be found in the village no one knew. The drenched soldiers each carried only fifty rounds of ammunition. A hundred and fifty worn-out men on broken-down horses were not exactly a shock force, but Mills was determined to attack. He argued that surprise would give them the advantage. His second in command, Lieutenant John W. Bubb, wanted to send word back to Crook, but Mills refused. He divided the command into three columns. They would approach the village in the dark. When there was light enough for a man to see the sight of his carbine they would charge. The center column of twenty-five men on horseback under Lieutenant Frederick Schwatka would stampede the Indian ponies. It was just what Custer had done at the Washita in 1868, and what Reynolds had done at the Powder River the previous March—a textbook dawn attack sending the Indians in all directions, or so it was hoped. There was no more to Mills's plan than that.

About three a.m. the men began to move. By five they had closed on the camp and Schwatka was getting his column into position. The smoke from the dying fires of the Indian camp hung low with the rain and mist. But before any decision could be made or order given the pony herd picked up some alien sound or scent on the night air and snapped alive—grazing quietly in the valley one moment, then tensing the next, heads and ears up, nostrils flaring, bursting as one into an instant dead run for the Indian camp whinnying loudly.

Mills had warned Schwatka to be ready, and the lieutenant spurred up; the center column of twenty-five mounted men chased right into the village after the horses, revolvers out and firing right and left as Indians rushed out of the lodges. Figures fell on both sides dead or wounded. In a matter of moments the Indians were gone, across the stream and up into the rocks and bluffs south of the village. Some moments of relative calm followed as the day brightened; then a desultory fire opened from the Indians in the rocks on one side, and the soldiers on the other. For a time the village itself was no-man's-land. Indians on horseback could be seen riding about between the hills and bluffs. The sun was well up by the time the soldiers all made their way into the village. They soon discovered that one small group of Indians had taken cover in a winding ravine. The occasional shot from the ravine reminded everybody to keep an eye out in that direction. It did not seem a problem at first. Meanwhile the hungry soldiers had begun to prowl around, emerging from the abandoned lodges with dried meat, dried plums and berries, even a little coffee, sugar, and flour which had been carried away from the agencies—and something else. A private held up a cavalry guidon—one of the swallow-tail flags lost on the Little Bighorn by Custer's men. From other lodges came more looted items: McClellan Army saddles, bits of cavalry uniform, paper money, a sergeant's notebook already filled with colored drawings by some Indian, creating a kind of diary of his summer of war. Particularly noted were the leather gauntlets once worn by Captain Myles W. Keogh of the 7th Cavalry. All the officers knew Keogh. Marked neatly with his name, the gauntlets had been wrapped up with the guidon in a parfleche, one of the painted-rawhide wallets in which the Plains Indians kept precious things.

As soon as Mills had the site of the village secure (save the ravine where the Indians were holed up) he dispatched two men on the best remaining horses to summon Crook on the double. As the morning wore on the shooting subsided but Mills continued to worry. Indians were seen in the rocks and bluffs, more all the time after the women and children had been led to safety. Every little while a detachment of cavalry would rush some point where the Indians were pressing too close. It wasn't fighting exactly, but it wasn't quiet, either. The Indians shouted out to the soldiers. Grouard said they were taunting the whites, claiming big villages were nearby, warriors were on the way to rub out the soldiers. Grouard allowed that this was possible. The trail they had been following over the last week had been left by a lot more Indians than Mills had just chased into the bluffs. Thus matters stood for a number of hours until Crook and an advance guard of about 250 men rode up in the late morning.

The ride had been steady and hard. Baptiste Pourier and John Finerty rode side by side, talking as they had been doing for weeks past. Pencil and notebook in his pocket, ready to hand, even on horseback, Finerty peppered Pourier with constant questions. If an answer excited Finerty's interest, he would pull out his notebook, saying, "Wait a minute, Bat, while I make a note of that." Even hurrying to battle Finerty kept the questions coming, then stanched the flow of Bat's commentary while he made a note of this, that, or the other.[14]

The country was rough, the horses of Crook's men tired and unsteady. Bourke and King both later commented on the using up of the horses by exhausted men riding over hard ground. The Irish-born Captain James Kennington, a veteran of the Civil War, where he was wounded at the Battle of Fredericksburg, rode at the head of Company B of the 14th Infantry. Worried about Mills and his small force, Crook pressed the men quickly. Only a few miles short of Slim Buttes, coming down the gravelly slope of a steep ravine, Kennington's tired horse suddenly stumbled and Kennington lurched forward with great force, crushing his testicles against the pommel of his saddle. Ten years later he told an Army retirement board, "It hurt me underneath here"—placing his hand beneath his groin. At the time the pain was so intense that he fainted. While the rest of the command hurried on Kennington was laid on the ground. When he regained consciousness the pain seemed to have gone away. He remounted and continued on to the battlefield site at Slim Buttes, arriving after Crook was already busying himself taking command. Kennington would be tormented by this injury for the rest of his life.[15]

Crook's first task was to assure himself the command was secure. He then turned his attention to the deep ravine where the Indians had taken cover. He ordered his new aide-de-camp, Lieutenant Clark, to drive out the Indians with a body of volunteers. As Clark's group rushed up firing from several directions at once, other soldiers drifted over to watch the action, and maybe take a shot or two themselves. Bourke observed from the edge of the ravine as soldiers pressed in with shouts and curses and were met by heavy fire. One man was shot in the ankle joint, another was hit in the leg by a bullet, "carrying away the whole calf." Down in the ravine itself Bourke saw "a pile . . . of squaws, and little papooses, covered with dirt and blood and screaming in a perfect agony of terror . . . Just in front, three or four dead bodies lay stretched, weltering in their own gore."

On the other side of the ravine scouts had crawled close—among them Baptiste Pourier, Frank Grouard, and a scout variously known as Charley or Jim White, also called Buffalo Chips. Not far from Pourier was John

Finerty, trying to see what was going on. Pourier shouted, "Keep down, Finerty, or you'll get your damned head shot off." But Finerty could not resist; as he lifted his head to peer into the ravine a bullet smacked into the earth next to him, driving grit into his hair and ear. Seeing this, Pourier shouted, "Make a note of that, Finerty!"[16]

The *Chicago Tribune* reporter wasn't the only one trying to get a good look. Charley White was sticking his head up as well. Some accounts of this moment report that the Indians were hiding in "a cave," but it seems to have been little more than a hard-to-see, hard-to-reach spot at the bottom of a gravelly ravine, hollowed out by the Indians with fingers and knives. It was an awkward spot to approach, invisible until a man peered over the lip of the ravine. Clark's group of volunteers reeled back under the Indian fire. Charley White was lying near the lip beside Finerty and the other scouts, perfectly safe so long as he kept down. But White was determined to get off a shot. He told Baptiste Pourier he was going to get himself a scalp. Rifle in hand he raised himself up to take aim and in the same instant was hit in the chest. "My God!" he shouted. "I am shot." With that he tumbled dead into the ravine.

In that same instant Pourier, peeping over the hill, saw the Indian who had shot White, reaching for the dead man's revolver. "Before I could say anything," remembered Frank Grouard, "Bat jumped into the cave where the Indians were and about five seconds afterward jumped out with an Indian's scalp in his hand, telling me he had scalped one of the redskins alive, which I found out to be true."[17] Another witness to this astonishing moment was Valentine McGillycuddy, a surveyor with medical training who was attached to Crook's command as a contract surgeon. "I well remember him," he wrote later of Pourier—"that bright red hair and beard of his standing on end, he dancing on the hill, swinging the scalp around his head, and howling."[18]

With that, shooting stopped. The scouts began to shout down to the Indians in the ravine, urging them to come out peaceably; nothing would happen, they had the promise of Wicahpi Yamni (Three Stars). "*Waste yelo!*" shouted Pourier—"It's all right." Soon, a few women and children appeared around a bend in the ravine and made their way downhill to the spot where Crook waited. The coaxing and reassurance went on for some time. One of the women returned to the Indians in the ravine, then brought out a young man of perhaps twenty named Charging Bear. More talking followed. Finally Baptiste Pourier, unarmed, went back into the ravine with Charging Bear, hoping to talk the headman into surrendering. The anticipation at this moment was "almost painful in its intensity," wrote Bourke; "for the first time, almost in the history of Indian warfare, hostile savages were about to lay down their arms in the open field."[19]

Back in the ravine Pourier found an older man, sitting with his rifle in a kind of hollow which "he had scooped out with a butcher knife"—the cave of so many accounts. The correspondent Robert Strahorn later claimed that it was Pourier himself who had shot and wounded the man earlier in the fight.[20] After some moments the red-haired Pourier reappeared helping the older man from one side; on the other he was supported by Charging Bear, his brother. Soon the rest of the Indians emerged from the ravine, at least twenty in all. Later still the dead were hauled forth, horribly mutilated by the heavy rifle fire of the soldiers.

As the older man approached it was not immediately apparent that he had been wounded. He walked erect and uttered no sound. Then Finerty saw that he had been shot in the stomach. His hand across his midriff was holding back his intestines, which were bulging forward and partly visible. A woman approached and tied her shawl around his middle, securing the wound. Frank Grouard, watching with the rest, says he shook the bloody hand of the silent chief as he made his way down the hill to a small campfire, where he sat down with the women and children. The wounded man was the many-named Iron Plume, also known as Black Shield, also known as Iron Shield, also known as American Horse.[21]

McGillycuddy and another doctor, Bennet Clements, attempted to sew up the man's wound while he bit grimly on a wooden stick; he had refused a hypodermic of morphine. "As the surgeons work, and the sweat of agony breaks out upon his forehead," King remembered, "he bites deep into the wood, but never groans nor shrinks."[22] But the wound was too severe. One of the doctors said to Baptiste Pourier, "Tell him he will die before next morning." Despite his wound the Indian spoke freely. He said that there were other Indian villages nearby, including the camp of Crazy Horse and his friends He Dog and Kicking Bear. Three hundred lodges was a number mentioned. By this time all the Army officers could do the math: three hundred lodges would house a thousand men of fighting age, maybe more.

For the rest of the day the soldiers methodically looted the village. Food came first—the dried meat and fruits. A brisk trade in captured Indian ponies persisted through the afternoon as footsore cavalrymen sought to replace the horses that had died. Then attention was diverted to material goods. The frontier military was always quick to snatch up Indian "relics" or "curios," to sell or to send home as souvenirs. Even before the Indians had been rooted out of the ravine great piles of stuff were accumulated. The officers and men were invited to take what they wanted, and many of them loaded up. In a report to an Ohio newspaper one of the officers wrote that the village was "filled with soldiers wandering about, muddy, tattered, lean and gaunt, rather sleepily lounging around looking over the plunder, scattering over prized paint and porcupine quills, nosing about robes and *parfleches*."[23] The rifle used that day by Iron Plume was taken by the scout and frontier poet Jack Crawford. Captain Anson Mills carried off a dozen items including a pipe, pouches, and a horned headdress. He considered taking but on reflection left behind a ten-year-old girl whose mother had been killed.

Among the items most eagerly sought were relics of the 7th Cavalry at the Little Bighorn. A locket containing the portrait of Captain Keogh was given to an officer who claimed he was a relative. A cavalry sergeant took a Spencer rifle, which he sold a few days later for two loaves of bread.[24] Many bitter remarks followed the discovery of two "passes"— notes attesting to the trustworthy character of this Indian or that, issued by missionaries, agents, military officers, or traders to help "good" Indians pass safely through the countryside. One, dated in January, had been written in broken English by the half-literate François Boucher, a son-in-law of Spotted Tail rumored to have been selling ammunition to the Indians. The bearer was Stabber, the chief who had been briefly detained by Custer in the Black Hills in 1874. In January Boucher had reported Stabber's promise to return from a visit to relatives in the north after ninety days "without disturbing any white man."[25]

As the day wore on Crook made no attempt to mount an expedition to go out against the nearby village cited by Iron Plume, but he deployed his men around the battlefield in anticipation of attack. Indians were seen among the rocks, and signal mirrors occasionally flashed. Late in the afternoon some officers and men gathered by the bodies of two dead soldiers wrapped in white, to read a brief service before they were committed to the earth. The service was in midsentence when gunfire from the rocks south of the creek bed commenced the second fight of the day. Soon the firing was general and continuous—"a rattling of small arms," wrote Captain King, "the sharp, vicious 'ping' of the carbine and the deep 'bang' of the longer-ranged rifle . . . Just as we expected, Crazy Horse has come to the rescue, with all his available warriors. It is just half-past four o'clock by General Carr's watch."[26]

Some guessed as many as eight hundred warriors were taking position in the rocks and bluffs. Crook sent units to drive them off and an hour's shifting fight took place as the Indians fell back before the soldiers, then pressed forward against some other point. Blue gunpowder smoke hung heavy in the air and gradually obscured the field. Some later called it a "pretty" fight—for the light at the end of the day, the flashing of guns in the smoky air, the magnificence of the scenery with its soaring sandstone buttes like "Norman castles," in the words of John Finerty. Prettiest of all, few were killed on either side, although the whites after it was over eagerly counted pools of blood and riderless ponies as proof positive of warriors dispatched.

At the Rosebud, Finerty was the only man who claimed to have seen Crazy Horse himself taking part in the battle. Now at Slim Buttes, late in the day, he was sure that he saw him again. For two hours or more an Indian on a white horse was everywhere evident, charging close and then veering away with such persistence he "seemed to possess the power of ubiquity." The Indians all appeared to draw courage from this man—"doubtless Crazy Horse himself," in Finerty's view. Perhaps it was true. He Dog and Red Feather said that Crazy Horse could turn a battle by himself; "when he came on the field of battle he made everybody brave."[27]

There may have been one other man with his eye on Crazy Horse at the Battle of Slim Buttes—General Crook himself, who told the scout Charles Tackett "that on one occasion he had shot deliberately at Crazy Horse more than twenty times without effect."[28]

If it happened at all it must have happened at Slim Buttes, where Crook was right in the middle of things. The general always traveled with expensive sporting arms, and had a hunter's respect for the kind of free-hand shooting that could bring down an animal on the run. Perhaps he had his eye on the same man Finerty was watching—the warrior on the white horse. Perhaps he took a shot at this dashing figure, then another, and a third . . . With a man like Crook the first shot would have been a casual try of luck; the twentieth would have been grimly determined, with teeth clenched, hands steadied by murderous will.

With night, the Battle of Slim Buttes drifted to an end. The burial service interrupted earlier was completed; interred with the dead private was the leg of an officer, amputated after an Indian bullet tore off his kneecap. Fires were built and captured Indian ponies killed for their meat—"grass-fed, sweet and succulent," noted Captain King. "Better eating than beef," said his friend Lieutenant Schuyler, in a letter home to his father, "though one does not like to see them killed."[29]

During the night, Finerty recalled, Iron Plume "fell back suddenly and expired without uttering a groan."[30] When the command pulled out the next morning, many of them riding Indian ponies and carrying Indian plunder, the body of Iron Plume was left behind as a sign of respect. The chief's wife and several other women and children were left as well, but not Charging Bear. He rode south with the soldiers. Crook set the village ablaze, then moved his men out "through the same overhanging pall of dripping mist," noted King. The misery of the day reflected the mood of the general. "They had to go. There wasn't a hardtack north of Deadwood."

King was one of the officers who stayed behind with two companies of cavalry as a rearguard. As the last of Crook's men disappeared to the south, the rearguard came under brisk fire from the surrounding ravines. It was soon obvious Crazy Horse had returned in force. Indians pressed them every step of the way, King wrote—"the slopes swarming with dusky horsemen, dashing towards us, whooping yelling, firing and retiring, always at speed, except where some practised marksman springs from his pony and prone upon the ground draws bead at our chief."[31]

Perhaps it was King, not Finerty or Crook, who had the fortune to see Crazy Horse in battle; the chief's friend He Dog said he often dismounted to take aim—he didn't like to waste his shots.

None of the soldiers was killed in the retreat but no one doubted the fighting was serious, nor doubted it was a retreat. None of the white chroniclers of this campaign was blunt enough to note that Crook was hastening away from a second field of battle that summer. "Men are weary and hungry," an officer noted; "one can see looking at the infantry line that the men stagger and are weak."[32] What had these bearded scarecrows achieved in their months of marching and fighting? "Nothing but disaster," summed up one private in a letter home to a Kansas newspaper.[33]

The flight south spoke for itself. "Discipline had become strained," noted Lieutenant Daniel C. Pearson of the command as it neared the Black Hills. "A condition akin to mutiny was smoldering."[34] The men of the Big Horn and Yellowstone Expedition delivered a collective judgment with new verses added to a popular dancehall tune "The Regular Army O."

But it was out upon the Yellowstone we had the damndest time,
Faix, we made the trip wid Rosebud George, six months without a dime.

Some 1,800 miles we went through hunger, mud and rain,
Wid backs all bare and rations rare, no chance for grass or grain.

"Etc. Etc.," added Charles King.[35]

Rosebud George himself was obsessed with the newspapers. They had
been abusing him all summer. Generals Sheridan and Sherman were privately disgusted by Crook's failure at the Rosebud but tried to buck him
up. "Do not be the least bit discouraged by newspaper attacks," said
Sheridan in a letter two days after Slim Buttes. "You have done as well as
could be expected and I will faithfully support and supply you."[36]

But Crook was a brooding man by nature. He knew Sheridan and
Sherman had a low opinion of his campaign, and he knew the newspapers
wanted his blood. He took his case after Slim Buttes to Cuthbert Mills, a
reporter for the *New York Times*. Crook gave Mills a short course in
Indian fighting: travel light and fast, give the Indians no respite, hit them
in winter, crush the bands one by one. He told Mills he was going to track
down the Indians with Indians. "Some people say it is wrong to use the
people of a tribe against itself," said Crook. "'*P'shaw!* If I can kill one rattlesnake by making another bite him, I shall do it."[37]

He had one rattlesnake in particular in mind. "Our next objective
point is Crazy Horse," Crook told Mills. "He should be followed up and
struck as soon as possible. There should be no stopping for this or that
thing. The Indians cannot stand a continuous campaign."

But Cuthbert Mills was not charmed. In a story summing up the campaign he stated plainly that Crook abandoned the field at Slim Buttes for
one reason only: "the command was in too crippled and broken down a
condition from starvation and overmarching" to go on fighting.[38] Crook's
officers carried a similar verdict back with them after the Big Horn and
Yellowstone Expedition disbanded at Camp Robinson in October. One
of them was Captain George M. Randall, a good friend of the Army
surgeon Charles Winne stationed with his wife at the Sidney Barracks in
Nebraska. Randall had been in charge of the several hundred Indian
scouts who fought beside Crook at the Rosebud and then promptly
pulled out for home. Maybe the campaign had achieved something, Randall felt, but it was too little, and at too great cost. Caroline Winne
summed up Randall's remarks in a letter home to her father. "Crook has
discovered that he has a different people to deal with in these Northern
Sioux," she wrote. "He acknowledges now that he had no idea when he
started in this war that he had such a warlike nation to deal with."[39]

17

"You won't get anything to eat! You won't get anything to eat!"

WITH THE SNAP OF fall in the air many of the Sioux and Cheyenne began returning to their agencies. The route of the Oglala was south along the Red Cloud Trail, crossing a notional boundary marking the end of Indian country at Hat Creek. From that point the trail passed south over grass-lands broken by a fine tracery of dry creek beds until white clay buttes rose in the distance to announce the site of the Red Cloud Agency. A journalist following the trail in July 1876 remarked that he was expecting something "about as broad and as much travelled as Fifth Avenue." It was nothing of the kind: "they showed me a little path about a foot wide; I have seen more respectable cowpaths." All the same, he added, "probably twenty-five or thirty warriors go over it each day."[1]

North in spring, south as winter approached had been the pattern for a decade, but this year the Indians were wary on their return, slipping into the agencies quietly. In mid-July, the civilian agents had all been replaced by military officers. There was talk of arresting Indians coming in from the north, and rumor said even the year-round agency Indians were to be stripped of their firearms and ponies. The big killing of white soldiers on the Little Bighorn had angered the military and the government as never before. Whites seemed ready to discard the old distinction between "friendlies" and "hostiles" and treat all Indians as enemies. Dark threats were in the air: forced removal of the Oglala and Brulé two hundred miles east to the Missouri, or perhaps even to the Indian Territory, never a home for the Sioux.

Billy Garnett found himself at the center of these fears and alarms. He was variously carried on the agency books as a laborer, watchman, guide, and interpreter at fifty dollars a month, but he was considerably more than that—the bearer of messages and commands, a handler of Indians in moments of tension, a sometime spy for the commander of the military post. Billy remained a boy in appearance, slender and smooth-skinned, but in April he turned twenty-one and in June he became a father, of a boy he named Charles. The mother was Zuzella Janis, sister of the fifteen-year-old Emily who had set fire to the body of Yellow Bear.[2]

For the previous three years Garnett had worked for what was called the Indian Department, but suddenly in July 1876 he found himself with two masters: the agency on one day, the Army on the next. The tenor of things to come was set early in September when a delegation of officials from Washington arrived at Red Cloud to revisit the question of the Black Hills. The opening remarks of Bishop Henry Whipple were anodyne in the usual manner—"[the] Great Father does not wish to throw a blanket over your eyes, and to ask you to do anything without first looking at it."[3]

But Garnett translating for the Oglala quickly realized things were going to be very different this time. The commissioner chosen to drive the talks was the former attorney general, A. S. Gaylord, and he was blunt: President Grant wanted the chiefs to sign a new piece of paper giving up the Black Hills and the so-called unceded territories—the last of the Sioux hunting grounds in the Tongue and Powder river country. In addition, the Oglala and the Brulé would be compelled to leave their agencies along the White River. The rumors were true; it was the Great Father's wish that they go to the Indian Territory, and he wanted them to send a delegation of chiefs to inspect that country. If they agreed to these demands, Gaylord said, the people would continue to receive their regular beef issue and other rations.

This stark choice was delivered to the Oglala at the Red Cloud Agency on September 7. It swept aside everything that had been promised in the Treaty of 1868, most importantly the provision which said no further surrender of Sioux lands would be legally valid unless agreed to in writing by three-fourths of all adult Sioux men. The Indians requested a week to talk things over, then delayed in the customary way, perhaps hoping the commissioners would go away. They did not. A second meeting finally convened at the agency on September 19, but things did not go well. Spotted Tail had been the first of the chiefs to stop fighting the whites in the mid-1860s, but his tongue remained sharp. He did not want to give up the Black Hills, and he did not want to take his band to the Indian Territory. "The white man wants another treaty," he told the commissioners. "Why does not the Great Father put his red children on wheels, so that he can move them as he will?"[4]

Nor did Red Dog and Young Man Afraid of His Horses want to give away the Black Hills. "This is the country where I was born and I want to remain here," said Young Man Afraid.

Whipple and Gaylord began to press the chiefs to sign a document immediately—right there and then. They promised only one concession: if the Sioux did not like the Indian Territory the government would allow them to settle on the Missouri River. The commissioners were insistent, the chiefs restless and unhappy. Red Cloud did not want to move to the Missouri. "There are bad men and whiskey there. I do not want to go."[5]

At this point the Oglala chief Sitting Bull made his way to the center of the council, shouting his displeasure. He was carrying his great gunstock war club with its three knife blades, sign of his office as a chief of *akicita*. Sitting Bull was considered a friend of the whites; fifteen months earlier, in the spring of 1875, Grant in Washington had given him a Winchester rifle engraved with his name, "for bravery and friendship." But his mood had changed. "The dose in this treaty infuriated him," said Billy Garnett later.

The Oglala knew nothing of the Indian Territory, they had never lived on the Missouri, they wanted to remain in their own country. Sitting Bull denounced this new request from the government as "all foolishness." He said they could sign nothing away, too many of the Indians were still north hunting. He began ordering the Indians to leave the agency stockade.

Now one of the chiefs close to the whites—White Bird, who had succeeded as chief of the Spleen band after John Richard's murder of Yellow Bear in 1872—began to taunt Sitting Bull: what about his reputation as a friend of the white man? Had that all gone by the way? All knew where White Bird stood. In June he had helped American Horse kill a man named *Howatezi* (Fish Guts) by the Indians and Sioux Jim by the whites, who called him a renegade. This Sioux Jim was a brother of Little Big Man. White Bird was taunting Sitting Bull—was he switching sides? Was he going north?[6]

But Sitting Bull was not to be talked down; with his club reversed—knives turned away—he struck White Bird a heavy blow, all the while shouting to the other Oglala, "Get out! Get out!"[7]

That was the end of the day's talking. The Indians got up and departed, perhaps relieved. The commissioners made no objection. That night, or a day or two later, Sitting Bull left the agency and headed north. His sons were hunting on the Yellowstone that summer, and he had loaned his engraved Winchester to a friend who had also gone north. Sitting Bull went after the friend to retrieve his gun, and to see his sons, so he said, and very likely to absent himself from what he knew would happen the following day.

On September 20 at the agency the commissioners insisted the chiefs sign. Many of the chiefs who had chosen peace in 1868 were present, including Red Cloud and Young Man Afraid of His Horses.[8] None wanted to sell the Black Hills or give up the hunting territories along the Powder and Tongue rivers, and none believed that is what they agreed to do. The official report of the commissioners identified the Reverend Samuel Hinman as interpreter for the Oglala, but in fact Billy Garnett did the interpreting that day. When the Indians objected to some provision of the new treaty, Garnett duly translated the Reverend Hinman's promise that it would be changed. It was Hinman, also, who described the new western boundary of the Great Sioux Reservation as proceeding from the Niobrara River north to this stream and to that—along the 103rd meridian. The whole of the Black Hills are west of the 103rd meridian. There is no word in Lakota for meridian. Garnett repeated Hinman's words, but none of the chiefs understood that signing this new treaty meant giving up the Black Hills.[9] What they understood was Gaylord's naked threat that the beef issue would halt if they did not sign.

According to Bishop Whipple, Gaylord made promises as well as threats to the chiefs. After the Little Bighorn there had been much talk of disarming and dismounting the Indians, and before leaving Washington, Gaylord had requested Grant's instruction on the point. Grant was reassuring: "Tell the Indians that as long as they remain at peace they shall be protected in their property."[10] Whipple reported that Gaylord read Grant's words to the commissioners out of his notebook, and that Grant's promise was repeated to the chiefs on September 20: if the chiefs signed they would keep their guns and they would keep their ponies.

But what the Indians heard most clearly was Gaylord's threat to end their food ration if they did not sign. The Indians felt cornered and bullied. The previous day Long Soldier had protested the new agreement so vehemently that he was threatened with arrest by the soldiers at Camp Robinson; now, when the signing began, Long Soldier touched the pen and then stalked away, pulling off his shirt and shouting to the Indians gathered near the chiefs' circle, "Even these clothes do not belong to me, everything will belong to the whiteman, it is now a good time for the Lakotas to learn that and say, yes, yes, yes to the whiteman from this day forward."[11]

Another angry signer was Fire Thunder, a noted chief and warrior who had played a leading role in fights with the whites at Horse Creek in 1865, on the Bozeman Trail when Fetterman was rubbed out in 1866, and in the wagon box fight in 1867. He signed the treaty in 1868 and he signed again in 1876, but as he approached the table to touch the pen, remembering the opening words of Bishop Whipple on September 7, Fire Thunder raised his blanket up over his head, covering his eyes, and touched the pen blindfolded. Also bitter in protest was Standing Elk, who told the white military officers at Fort Laramie in 1866 that he had come in with all his people because he had no choice: "The white soldier has killed all the buffalo . . . none are left for us to kill." In the same spirit he signed the treaty in 1868. In 1876 when he touched the pen he bitterly reproached the implacable Gaylord:

> Your words are like a man knocking me in the head with a stick. What you have spoken has put great fear upon us. Whatever we do, wherever we go, we are expected to say yes! yes! yes! yes!—and when we don't agree at once to what you ask of us in council, you always say, You won't get anything to eat! You won't get anything to eat![12]

In the end the commissioners got what they wanted—agreement by the Oglalas and Brulés to give up the Black Hills forever.

The day after Gaylord promised the chiefs they could keep their guns and their ponies if they signed the new agreement, Crook and Colonel Ranald Mackenzie met with General Sheridan at Fort Laramie to plan the seizure of their guns and their ponies. Crook had been brooding. Of Red Cloud over the summer of defeat the general later wrote, "I can accuse him of no overt act of hostility." But open conflict was not what angered Crook most. Worse was sullen defiance, resistance, the challenge implicit in silent refusal.

> In every way in which he could [he] manifested his sympathy for the Indians on the war path, sent them supplies of ammunition, aided and assisted them with information in regard to our movements, he showed himself to be an alert, ill disposed and dangerous rascal. When enough testimony had accu-

mulated . . . I determined to lose not a moment in stripping him of every
vestige of authority.[13]

Sheridan and Sherman wanted to seize the guns and horses of all the
Sioux—hostile, friendly, or in between. Crook balked at all; he refused to
dismount Spotted Tail's Brulé, who had been loyal to the whites throughout. But he wanted to break the spirit of Red Cloud, and he believed that
setting him afoot would do it. At Fort Laramie on September 21 a simple
plan was devised. Red Cloud and Red Leaf were camped with their bands
on Chadron Creek, about twenty miles east of the agency and the military
post at Camp Robinson. The officers agreed that Mackenzie would order
the chiefs to return with their people, and force them back with soldiers if
the chiefs refused. In early October, Mackenzie sent Billy Garnett to
deliver the colonel's order to the chiefs. Garnett rode over to Red Cloud's
lodge on Chadron Creek and there he also found Red Dog, the man who
often spoke in council on the chief's behalf. For some reason Red Cloud
did not take Mackenzie's threat seriously. He ignored the order to bring
in his people and he dismissed the threat to cut off rations and use soldiers
to force the Indians to return.

Red Dog told Garnett it was all right, the soldiers could have the
agency if they wanted it, the Indians would be content with a building
owned by their friend, the trader Joseph Bissonette, called Grey Hat
(Wapahahota) by the Indians. Red Dog asked Garnett to tell Mackenzie
to ship their rations out to Bissonette's house and to bring the herd of
beef for the next issue when they came. The chiefs asked Garnett to
return when it was issue day to help things go right.[14]

But of course no rations and no beef were sent to Chadron Creek. Garnett was dispatched again to tell the chiefs that Colonel Mackenzie would
send soldiers if the Indians did not come in. They did not budge. A few
days later, on the night of October 19, 1876, Garnett was sent off with
orders to the road ranch maintained by the trader Hank Clifford near the
Red Cloud Agency. As he approached Clifford's ranch, Garnett found
Major Frank North and his brother Luther camped on Snake Creek with
a detachment of about forty Pawnee scouts, bitter hereditary enemies
of the Sioux. The Norths were to meet up with Mackenzie that night to
surround the resistant chiefs, Garnett said. All set out in the dark and
rode at a steady trot for about five hours, reaching the Oglala villages on
Chadron Creek just as daylight was breaking.

When a boy looking after horses called the alarm, soldiers and scouts charged in among the lodges. First into the village was Garnett, shouting to the Indians not to run and not to fight—the soldiers would not harm them if they did not fight. Things almost went awry some moments later when an Indian leveled a revolver at the commander of the soldiers, but Garnett and the Brulé chief Swift Bear stopped him before he could fire. Quickly the Indians were disarmed and the ponies rounded up and started southwest with the North brothers. From Camp Robinson that night the Norths drove more than seven hundred ponies straight on through to Fort Laramie, where most were later sold for about five dollars each. On Crook's order about seventy-five of the ponies were retained by the Norths and their Pawnee scouts. For themselves, the North brothers chose a dark bay and a gray, said to be the two fastest in the whole Sioux tribe. The day of the seizure the great majority of the Indians followed the Norths and their horses back to Camp Robinson on foot; only the elderly and some of the women and children were permitted to ride, and on arrival at the agency even these horses were taken away. Red Cloud and his leading men were required to walk. Crook was determined to humble the chief while all the people were watching.[15]

The population of the Red Cloud Agency in October 1876 was variously estimated at about four thousand. Perhaps half of them had been with Red Cloud at Chadron Creek. A fair guess would say that about two thousand Oglala walked the twenty-some miles back to the agency, where their straggling arrival was witnessed by a party of whites from the military post who had gone out for an afternoon climb into the hills overlooking the White River valley:

> At three o'clock p.m. Monday we saw one of the most magnificent sights ever witnessed on the plains. After experiencing four days of heavy winds and clouds and some rain, with no small degree of nervous anxiety, we ascended a mountain or butte some five hundred feet above the plain of the agency which stands about a mile off, when the sun broke out from its hiding place . . . brilliant and warm, opening up . . . as far as the eye could see, with a good field glass . . . the moving Sioux could be seen, wending their way in towards the agency from every point of the compass, most of them disarmed, dispirited and compelled to come . . . The vast hoards of squaws, children, ponies and dogs, will not get half in tonight, and already the shadows of evening begin to shut out from view this last, grand demonstration of the power of the Sioux nation. This is the first march on their downward course . . . At ten o'clock today [Tuesday] the captured and disarmed bands arrived at the agency, resembling vast droves of Texas cattle crossing the praries. A grand Indian council was held today and the long tried and

trusted Spotted Tail was duly installed chief of the Dakota Sioux . . . Red
Cloud was put in prison [on arrival Monday], but again breathes the free
air.[16]

It was Crook's idea to depose Red Cloud as chief of the Oglala, and it
was apparently Swift Bear who convinced the general to elevate Spotted
Tail in his place.[17] On Crook's instruction a big crowd gathered in front
of an agency warehouse on October 21. Spotted Tail and a stolid Red
Cloud stood front and center while Crook acted the part of kingmaker,
and declared Spotted Tail to be "head chief of all the bands of the Sioux
nation." The frontier photographer Stanley J. Morrow was visiting the
agency and took a stereoscopic photograph of the gathering. It must have
been chilly that day. Indians and whites all seem to be wearing wool coats
and caps. About twenty feet to the general's right can be seen Billy Garnett, looking slender and young. Next to him is Frank Grouard.

Crook prided himself on knowing Indians, but his attempt to depose
Red Cloud was eccentric, revealing a dim understanding of what it was
that made a chief. It was not power and it was not the law, but rather force
of personality. The camp marshals or police, the *akicita*, could demand
the obedience of any man, including a chief. Those who defied the *akicita*
could be punished by a beating, the destruction of a lodge, or the killing
of horses. In extreme cases the offender himself might even be killed. In
the 1860s Red Cloud once defied the orders of the *akicita* to break camp
and was lashed across the face with a quirt—not lightly, or only once,
but "repeatedly and severely," according to the Oglala Hunts the Enemy.
Red Cloud may have been chief, but he was in the wrong. "He quietly
submitted."[18]

Red Cloud once said he had been a chief since he was nine years old. In
1870, following his first trip to Washington, he appeared at Cooper
Union in New York City and declared to a packed lecture hall, "Look at
me! I am poor, naked, but I am chief of a nation." It was Red Cloud who
summoned the white traders to camp with the Ite Sica Oglala every winter. Many stories survive of his war exploits, and he told whites that he
had been in more than eighty battles. The Bozeman War did not end
until Red Cloud touched the pen.[19]

A chief's power was in some degree *wakan*—mysterious, great. In the
early 1860s, the mother of a young Oglala came to Red Cloud to ask for a
new name for her son, who had just returned from a raiding party with
war honors. Until that time the son was known as Clam, a name given to

him previously by Sitting Bear, the father of American Horse. The woman promised to pay a horse for the new name. Red Cloud gave the horse to someone needy and said to the woman,

> Once I dreamed that I visited a certain group of stars and after I got there I found the inhabitants to be bears. Hence I will name him Afraid of Bear. He is the bear and the enemy will all be afraid of him. In after years his name will be well-known on account of his killing of many enemies.[20]

A man who had traveled to the stars was not likely to be overawed by a general wearing a pith helmet or riding a mule, as George Crook often did, and he was not likely to believe that Crook could take away what no man had the power to give. None of the Oglala or Spotted Tail's Brulé paid any attention to the general's attempt to humble the Oglala chief and bring him down a peg or two.

It was probably on that day, October 21, that Stanley Morrow also took a stereograph of Red Cloud sitting outside a log building, possibly the guardhouse at Camp Robinson. Red Cloud is wearing a long black coat and holds a black hat in his hand. He is an imposing man with a face of planes and creases that might have been designed by an architect.[21] On the order of General Crook, he had just spent a night in the guardhouse, but nothing of that can be seen in his face. Crook had not made Red Cloud a chief, and he could not unmake him.

18

"When spring comes,
we are going to kill them like dogs."

BUT IT WAS CRAZY Horse who was the ultimate target of George Crook's plans. No sooner was the Big Horn and Yellowstone Expedition formally dissolved at Camp Robinson on October 24 than the general began preparations for a renewed winter campaign back into the Tongue and Powder river country. This time he was determined to go after the hold-out chief with Oglala and Brulé scouts—the men who knew him best. Helping the Army officers sign them up were Frank Grouard, Baptiste Pourier, and Billy Garnett as interpreters. Eventually hundreds of scouts took part in the campaign, including a group of Shoshones from western Wyoming, some Arapahos under Sharp Nose, a large contingent of Pawnee commanded by the North brothers, and as many as 150 Sioux from the agencies on the White River.

But only two of these scouts were Spotted Tail's Brulé. The failure was blamed mainly on the civilian agent E. A. Howard, who told Garnett on the 28th that in his view "it was not right for the Indians to fight against each other." After a day of futile effort at the Spotted Tail Agency, Grouard and Pourier gave up in disgust and returned to Camp Robinson, but Garnett stayed on and eventually managed to enlist seven men from the camps along Beaver Creek.[1] One of them was the Oglala Fast Thunder, who had chosen to live with the Brulé, and who had been to Washington with the other Sioux chiefs in 1875. It was not the pay, the horse, or the gun provided by the Army that Fast Thunder wanted, but a home in the north. He and other scouts believed they would more easily win an agency in the Powder and Tongue river country if they helped Three Stars bring in the northern Indians. When Billy Garnett returned to Camp Robinson he, too, was enlisted as a scout and interpreter in Company B, with a rise in pay to $85 a month.[2]

As the scouts prepared to leave for Fort Laramie and the renewed campaign, Crook arranged to send a spy north to locate the winter camp of Crazy Horse. The man chosen for this mission was Sitting Bear (Mato Iyotanke), who had joined American Horse in June to find Sioux Jim for the soldiers, and finished him off with a bullet in the head. A man of about thirty, son of the Oglala Ohitika (Brave) and Coarse Voice Woman, Sitting Bear had enlisted as one of the "Red Top" scouts at Fort Laramie in the mid-1860s, had been to Washington with Red Cloud in 1870, and was now, like Billy Garnett, a scout in Company B. Also sent north about the same time as Sitting Bear were two other spies, Lone Bear and Iron Bear, who were given a related mission—to travel with the Crazy Horse camp until Crook's force was almost upon them, and then to slip away to tell the general where the Indians planned to go after the impending fight.[3]

These two spy missions were probably arranged by General Crook's newest aide-de-camp, Lieutenant William Philo Clark, who had joined Crook's summer expedition on the Yellowstone in August and distinguished himself at Slim Buttes in September. It is difficult to say which came first—instructions from Crook to manage the Indian scouts, or Clark's natural inclination to take on the job. Soon after his arrival at Camp Robinson, Clark began to learn sign talking. This was no casual effort; eventually he became a leading authority on the subject, collecting signs from Indians all over the plains. In the beginning his tutor was William Rowland, an old plainsman in his sixties who interpreted for the northern Cheyenne at the Red Cloud Agency, where Rowland lived with his Cheyenne wife of many years.[4] Soon Clark was conversing freely in signs with chiefs and leading men, including Red Cloud, himself a noted sign talker with his own peculiar style. Most signers made generous use of a big circle of space, moving their hands emphatically within a circle thirty inches in diameter. But Red Cloud was restrained; his gestures were tight and small in a circle no more than a foot across.[5]

From signing with Red Cloud, Clark progressed into deeper conversation, speaking frankly of his own life and inviting the chief to do the same. At the core of Clark's approach was a discussion of sons—of himself as the son of a prosperous upstate New York farmer, anxious for the lieutenant's rise in the world; and of Wanka Wicasa (Above Man), the only son of Red Cloud, known to whites as Jack. Fathers wanted their sons to succeed, Clark said. His own father, William, back home in Deer River, New York, helped the young man win appointment to West Point, and after his commission settled enough money on him to triple his Army salary of $125 a month. That, Clark said, was why he could spend his own money to help the Indians.

Later the father worried that military service on the frontier was too dangerous. "He wanted me to resign, but I liked the service so well that I would not quit it." Clark spoke frankly about Red Cloud's son, who had been humiliated at the Rosebud when the Crow seized the rifle given to Red Cloud in Washington. It was natural for fathers to worry about sons. "This is one reason I have not married," he told Red Cloud. "I do not wish to leave any orphans, for a man in my place is liable to be killed at any time."[6] Clark once made a similar observation to another man: being single, he said, allowed him to rise more freely in his profession. Clark illustrated his point "by the index finger of my right hand, raising it slowly and showing that nothing pulled it down." The man he was speaking to signed "that this was wrong, a mistake. He had two wives, and they formed a support on each side of the index, and helped to raise it."[7]

From spending time with the Indians, Clark soon gravitated to handling scouts generally. He grew confident of his ability to "work" Indians by playing them off one against the other. By mid-October Crook had appointed Clark his new chief of scouts, and sent him off to check on Frank Grouard, who had fallen ill at Fort Laramie. Crook wanted Grouard on the winter campaign, and the scout promised Clark he would meet the general at Fort Fetterman when he was well enough to travel.[8] It was Clark, again, on November 4, who stuck his head into Frank North's tent at Laramie and said, "Well, Major, are you going on the expedition? The general has already gone."[9]

North was nonplussed. This was his introduction to Crook's habit of sitting and thinking until he was ready to move, and trusting others to note when he got up and went. Thereafter the Norths kept track of Crook and moved their Pawnee scouts when he moved.

The following day, on November 5, the general signed Special Order Number 1 of the newly named Powder River Expedition, identifying the various units and their commanders. Clark's job was defined only as "Special Duty," but in fact Crook placed him in command of the Indian scouts from the White River agencies, a job he held for the following year. Clark was a bright and eager young officer, a man everybody seemed to like. He listened to the Indians, took extensive notes on their customs and ways, made sure he knew what they wanted, and respected them in a way unusual among military officers. His interest in the Indians was genuine and deep, but his purpose was to control them—"working them," in his phrase—by playing one off another to achieve the government's aims.[10] But at the very outset Clark ran into trouble keeping the peace between North's Pawnee and the Oglala from the Red Cloud Agency.

While the expedition was forming at Fort Fetterman, Clark distributed arms to the scouts and made sure that all had horses. One of his headmen, already becoming an intimate of the young lieutenant, was Three Bears, a sergeant of scouts in Company B, who for several years past had been an ally of white officials at the Red Cloud Agency. The horse of Three Bears had given out on the trip up to Fetterman, so Clark took him down to the horse herd to pick out a replacement. Most of these surplus horses had been seized from Red Cloud's people, and it is likely Three Bears knew exactly what he was doing when he selected the big bay famous among the Oglala for its speed. Some of North's Pawnee saw Three Bears and the lieutenant start off with the bay and protested. Clark agreed to discuss the matter with Frank North, but when they met up a few moments later North told Clark nothing doing: "This horse belongs to me."

Clark said he was following Crook's instructions to pick out horses for his scouts and Three Bears wanted the bay.

"Well, he can't have him," said North.

After further words both stated they would ask Crook to settle the dispute.

Clark and Three Bears left directly for the fort, where Crook was attending to business in the sutler's store, but the North brothers were delayed a moment while Luther hunted up his gray. When they finally got going their route to the fort took them past the Oglala camp, and there the Norths found a group of Sioux with Three Bears at the center, apparently relating his grievance about the horse.

Pawnee and Sioux had been blood enemies for as long as they had possessed horses to steal from each other, about 180 years.[11] It wasn't just Indians who were serious about horses; whites treated stealing one as a hanging offense, and the penalty was routinely imposed. Now Crook's new chief of scouts had managed to bring the Oglala and the Norths to the point of bloodshed over a horse. Luther North later described how the brothers handled this delicate moment.

> The road passed within thirty or forty feet of [the Oglala], and as we got near them Three Bears quit talking, and they all stood looking at us. Frank touched his horse with the spur, and as he was highspirited he commenced

to dance. Frank began to sing the Pawnee war song and I joined in with him, and we danced our horses and sang our song past them. No one spoke a word, nor did any of them make a move, and we rode on to the fort, where Frank found [Lieutenant] Clark, and asked him to go with him to see the general.[12]

According to Luther North, Crook blamed Clark for the ruckus, saying he should have asked before taking, but more likely the general issued soothing words in both directions. The upshot was that Clark's Oglala got plenty of horses but North's Pawnee kept first pick of the best ones.

But the quarrel had been a near thing, it got Crook to thinking, and it contributed to a series of full-scale councils with all the Indians as the expedition left Fort Fetterman in mid-November and started north in hope of finding the camp of Crazy Horse. At these councils Crook and the Oglala both described what they desired at the end of the war. Crook wanted peace on the plains, not just between Indians and whites but between all the tribes; and the Oglala wanted a home in the north. The first two conversations were held on November 8, when the Indian scouts arrived at Fort Fetterman, and on the 13th, the night before the expedition crossed the North Platte and took the road north. There was much talk of horses at these first two councils—how to divide the horses taken from Red Cloud's people, who would get the horses captured from the northern Indians. The Oglala chief Fast Thunder carried the discussion one step further on the 13th, putting into words what all the Sioux were thinking. He reminded the general that in Washington the previous spring President Grant had asked the Sioux to protect the horses of white people as they would their own; if any were stolen Grant hoped the Sioux would help the whites to get them back. Fast Thunder had promised to do so, and he had done as he promised.

> The Indians that stay at the agency have never done any harm to the white man and I think it very wrong to take away their horses. I wish you to tell the Great Father not to take away any more of the horses from these Indians. The reason I am going out to fight the Northern hostiles is that the country up there was given us by the Great Father and I want to get it back . . . I want you to tell the Great Father to give us back the country where we were living . . . The young men want this. We are your friends now and we don't want you to take our homes away any more.[13]

After a week's thinking, Crook addressed all these matters again on the morning of Sunday, November 19, when the expedition was camped at

Antelope Springs near the site of old Fort Reno. It was Crook's third stop at the site in the year 1876, each time as he was riding north with the hope of bringing Crazy Horse to bay. Lieutenant Bourke noted in his diary that eight tribes listened to Crook's words: Sioux, Cheyenne, Arapahos, Shoshones, and Pawnee, with a sprinkling of Nez Percé, Ute, and Bannock.

"We don't want to kill the Indians," said the general in opening the conference, speaking of the northern Cheyenne and the Oglala with Crazy Horse. "We only want to make them behave themselves." By that he meant that the government wanted them to abandon their wandering life, come in to the agency, and "live like the whites."

Crook had many further words of practical advice about scouting, saving ammunition, not abandoning a fight in order to round up horses, not killing the women and children, etc. But the part of his talk which all remembered came at the end, when he said that warring among the plains tribes must come to an end. Bourke recorded some of his words:

> I want you now all to be friends together, just like the soldiers are. You must remain friends and stick to this thing right through until it is ended . . . Now we have met here as friends. We must give up old grudges, shake hands and be good friends together. That's all I've got to say: I want you all to act together.[14]

As transcribed by Bourke, Crook's words have the perfunctory tone of preacher's boilerplate. But Billy Garnett translated the general's words into Lakota and he remembered them vividly when he described them thirty years later. When Crook told the Indians that he wanted them all to be friends, Garnett recalled, "they did so with great rejoicing and handshaking and some of the Indians made presents to other Indians, giving even horses in some cases." These gestures were not hollow or empty, Garnett insisted, but marked a dramatic change in the way the tribesmen dealt with each other from that moment forward. The Sioux and the Pawnee had been nervous and standoffish during the first week of the march north from Fetterman, but after Crook's words "there was the fullest freedom and warmest friendship and most cordial intercourse." It was not a sham, Garnett insisted. Judge Ricker noted Garnett's evident sincerity: "He never saw, before or since, such manifestation of good will and genuine happiness."[15]

The explosion of good feeling began with Three Bears and Leading Chief (Li-heris-oo-la-shar), a longtime Pawnee scout, who was dressed in a military tunic but was painted in the Pawnee way—cheeks and jaw yellow, forehead dark brown, eyelids and ears a brilliant red with red streaks down the part in his hair and the line of his nose. Leading Chief was the right-hand man of Frank North. Addressing himself to Leading Chief, Three Bears said,

> When I want to have a friend, I give him horses and shake hands with him. This is the first man who shook hands with me. I'll give him a horse. It's a poor one, but I'll give it anyhow. It's the best I've got.[16]

But the Sioux did not forget why they had agreed to come. They told Crook they did not like the agreement wrung out of the chiefs by President Grant's peace commissioners. They told the general the chiefs who met with the commissioners had no right to give away what was not theirs, meaning the Black Hills and the unceded territories where the buffalo could still be found. The scouts did not want to move to a strange country. They had joined the expedition "for the purpose of getting an agency in their own country." These explicit words Bourke failed to record, but Garnett remembered what Crook promised clearly enough.

> He told them that his business was to get the Indians who were out. If [the scouts] would be loyal to his purpose and aid him all they could, when the object was gained he would exert his influence to get them settled down in the country of their choice, with an agency as they wanted.

There was nothing ambiguous about it. The Sioux wanted an agency in the Powder and Tongue river country, and Crook promised to help them get it.

Standing among the crowd of officers during the council with the Indians was Colonel Richard Irving Dodge, a veteran of the Civil War who had seen much service on the plains in the decade since. Dodge was typical of many educated whites of the time: he was interested in the Indians, admired their horsemanship and scouting skills, and even referred to the chief Pawnee scout as "my old friend Frank White," while confessing he could never pronounce or remember Frank's Indian name, Li-heris-oo-la-shar.

Like other military officers, Dodge was not indifferent to Indian women, describing one Cheyenne as "a very handsome girl, for an

Indian." But he was from South Carolina; it was impossible for him to ignore a man's race, he believed whites were naturally superior, and he was generally repelled by the Indians physically. The Shoshones he described as "almost all very ugly" and the Pawnee "next in general ugliness." The Arapahos he liked better because they were "very copper colored" and lighter than other Indians "except the Sioux, who have some admixture of white blood." For Dodge, white blood was important; in his view, it was white blood that explained why the Sioux mixed-bloods were "rather handsome and intelligent looking men." Among the mixed-bloods he noted the young fellow who had been interpreting Crook's words to the Sioux, "the son of my old friend Dick Garnett of Virginia."[17]

Billy Garnett had witnessed a great deal of violence in his short life, but the Powder River Expedition was his first experience of war. His father had died in war. No one seems to have asked Garnett when he learned of his father's death, or how it felt for a mixed-blood scout to be the son of a famous general killed in battle. But it was about this time that Garnett dropped his stepfather's name, Hunter, and began to use his own. It is likely that one of the Army officers told him whatever he knew about the death of his father, killed at Gettysburg during Pickett's charge on July 3, 1863.

Garnett rode into battle because he could not walk; a few days previously, a horse had kicked him in the knee. About twenty-five paces downslope from the Union lines Garnett's luck ran out. Soldiers said he was killed twice in the same moment—by a minié ball in the head and by a cannon load of grapeshot at point-blank range. The shot tore him in half and ripped open the right shoulder of his horse, who bolted away spewing blood from a severed artery that soon killed him. Garnett's body fell to the ground, where it disappeared into the general mass of Confederate dead and was never identified. But killed at Gettysburg is likely all that Billy Garnett knew of the fate of his father when Colonel Richard Irving Dodge listened to him putting Crook's words into Lakota at Antelope Springs.[18]

The day after Crook's council with the Indians he sent out a small group of ten scouts—five Sioux and five Arapahos—to push out ahead in hope of finding the village of Crazy Horse. In charge of the group were two sergeants, Sharp Nose and the Oglala Red Shirt. None wore any part of a military uniform, but dressed solely as Indians. On the night of November 20 they camped and began to prepare dinner when one of the scouts, Kills a Hundred,[19] noted a young Indian wrapped in a blanket just beyond the light of the fire and near the horses. "Come up!" one of the scouts called to the man in the shadows; "the meal is on!"

He did come, he took a place by their fire, and he began to eat. The young man's name was Many Beaver Dam; he was Cheyenne and a member of a small band of a few lodges making its way to join the main Cheyenne village in the Big Horn Mountains along one of the feeder streams of the Powder River. The northern Cheyenne were not a numerous people; just about all of them were in that village, and the number was probably less than a thousand. Many Beaver Dam talked freely, mentioning that he had followed the ten scouts for quite awhile that day until he noted that some of them were Sioux and decided it would be safe to approach.

At about this point Red Shirt and Sharp Nose leveled guns at him and told him he was their prisoner. The following day they brought him back to Crook's camp, where he repeated everything he had already said and added a good deal more, including the fact that Crazy Horse was again camped on the Rosebud near the site of last summer's battle. He added that his friends knew Crook's men were heading their way, and had doubtless ridden to warn Crazy Horse. Next morning Crook dispatched a courier back to Fort Fetterman with a cable to Sheridan saying he was going after Crazy Horse.[20]

But as Crook was preparing to pull out on the morning of the 23rd, an Indian waving a white flag from the crest of a nearby hill caught the attention of Frank Grouard. This was the Oglala Sitting Bear, who came in and reported to Crook all that he had learned in Crazy Horse's camp. There had been a falling out between Crazy Horse and Sitting Bull, who was thinking of giving up the war after a small, inconclusive fight with General Nelson Miles up north.

"Crazy Horse was quite indignant at the news," Colonel Dodge summarized in his diary, "and said that if all the other chiefs made peace he would do so also, as he had no notion of encountering the whole force of the whites alone."[21]

Sitting Bear confirmed that the tiny village of Many Beaver Dam had in fact hurried off to warn Crazy Horse of Crook's approach. The Sioux scouts, hearing these things, then formed a new plan for operations and proposed it to Crook—first attack the Cheyenne village in the Big Horn Mountains, closer by a hundred miles, then go after the Oglala under

Crazy Horse, "thus destroying the hostiles in detail." Garnett said later he knew "that this was planned by the Sioux, because he interpreted for the Sioux when they went to Crook with it."[22]

Crook adopted the plan as his own. That evening he dispatched eight scouts to locate the Cheyenne village and the next morning sent a big force under Colonel Mackenzie to follow the scouts, who doubled back about midday with report of the village's location. The soldiers pressed on into the night. Leading the force was the Arapaho Sharp Nose, with Lieutenant Clark and Billy Garnett on his heels the whole way. Garnett later remembered,

> The weather was clear and cold, no light save from the stars and it was therefore pretty dark; there was snow on the mountains and spots of ice along the line of march, all remaining from former snows, but there was no fresh snow to leave a trail but there were places where they would cross crusted snow . . . all the time going deeper and deeper into the mountains while ascending in elevation. Here in this valley [the Red Fork of the Powder River] some ears a little quicker to catch sound than others heard the first faint notes of drums in the village echoing in the night air among the hills.[23]

The sound of the drums was heard by the soldiers as they entered the first of two valleys. At its far end was a saddle of higher ground which then fell away into the second and broader valley where the Indian village was strung along the south bank of the creek. The first light of morning was touching the sky; smoke and haze lay over the ground. With the camp in sight, Mackenzie sent the scouts forward to run off the Indian ponies, telling them not to shoot unless the Cheyenne shot first. The colonel apparently hoped they might take the village without killing anyone. But the scouts had their own ideas and were vying to see who would get into the village first. Mackenzie saw one of them pushing out ahead of the soldiers.

"Who is that man down there?" he demanded.

Told it was the Wazhazha scout, Scraper, Mackenzie sent Baptiste Pourier and Billy Garnett to fetch him back, but when Garnett caught up with Scraper the Wazhazha, tying on his feathered warbonnet, said it was no use, he had made up his mind: "I never allow anybody to think before me in a case of this kind . . . I'm a-going."[24]

At that moment the Oglala Fast Thunder rode up and joined Scraper. The two Indians, joined by Garnett and Pourier, now set off for the village on their fast horses. It was rough going over fallen timber and rocky ground, and some minutes passed before a lone Indian guarding the horses scattered about the valley spotted the four men, fired a shot at them with his revolver, and then bolted back for the village. "He fired first!" Garnett yelled. "Now fire!" The rest of the four began to shoot, and the ball had begun.[25]

In the gray morning light columns of scouts and of cavalry streamed up the valley on both sides of the Red Fork, scattering the Cheyenne pony herd as they went. From the lodges came shouts, confused cries, and the barking of dogs. Panicked knots of Indians were running in all directions for the surrounding hills. The new chief of scouts, Lieutenant William Philo Clark, was in the front ranks of a large group pressing directly for the village when his companion, Three Bears, suddenly bolted ahead of the others—he had lost control of his horse. What happened next, Clark wrote later, was about the bravest thing he ever witnessed:

> Feather-on-the-Head, another scout, seeing the trouble his friend was in, dashed after him, urging his own fast pony forward with vigorous strokes of the whip, at the same time throwing himself from side to side of his pony to avoid the shots of his enemies. Thus he followed Three Bears through the bushes and across the stream, down among the tepees, and into the very centre of the village, where Three Bears' horse had fallen dead, shot through the neck. His rider had scarcely touched the ground when Feather-on-the-Head, sweeping past, took him behind himself and bore him safely away.[26]

The scouts in the village were soon joined by soldiers. All of them began piling up loot to carry off—buffalo robes, blankets, quill and beadwork. Lodges were pulled down and stacked for burning. Loose horses were rounded up. Firing continued all the while and at moments heated up into a serious fight near one part of the village or another. Several Cheyenne in the hills to the north exposed themselves and deliberately drew fire to give the women and children time to escape. Baptiste Pourier, Frank Grouard, and Billy Garnett, among others, fired repeatedly at two men carrying buffalo heads and waving them in the air.[27] Grouard was lying half concealed, loading his trapdoor carbine with one shell after another, taking careful aim. The news correspondent Jerry Roche, lying nearby, said, "What are you firing at, Frank?"

The distracted Grouard answered Roche in Lakota, then laughed—Roche of course knew no Lakota. He pointed at one of the dancing men on a hill almost half a mile away, across the valley. Despite Grouard's steady shooting the dancing man escaped unharmed. Near Pourier was Billy Garnett, also taking careful shots at the enemy. He shot the horse out from under one man, then shot the man himself as he got to his feet— the first man he had ever killed in battle. Garnett shouted his success to Pourier, sure there was no mistake; he had watched his bullet smack the man down.

But a moment later Grouard was just as certain he had killed the same man, who was now on foot. It was a Cheyenne Grouard knew from the Red Cloud Agency, the chief known as Little Wolf. Grouard said later that he aimed carefully, then waited for the chief to show himself. In a moment the Cheyenne jumped up. "With the report of my rifle," Grouard recalled, "Little Wolf fell to the ground and lay motionless." Later in the day, he said, he walked by the man's dead body. It was Little Wolf all right.[28]

The fighting went on for hours, sometimes flaring up, then tapering off. When Clark made his way back through the village he reported to Mackenzie, who wrote up a dispatch seeking help from Crook, then asked Garnett to send it back by courier. Garnett gave the task to the scouts Red Shirt and Charging Bear, who made the twenty-six-mile ride over rough and frozen ground. Crook set out immediately with the infantry and completed the grueling return journey in twelve hours, but still arrived too late. The fighting was over.

As the day drew to an end the Cheyenne speaker Bill Rowland called out to the men on the other side, urging them to surrender. Most of the Cheyenne voices were still full of fight. They said there was another big Sioux village nearby; they were sending for help and soon the whites would be in trouble.

"You have killed and hurt a heap of our people," one of the Cheyenne shouted to Rowland. "You may as well stay now and kill the rest of us."

But Dull Knife was of a different mind; two of his sons had been killed in the fighting. He told Rowland he was ready to give up but the other chiefs would not listen to him. To the Indian scouts, Dull Knife called out, "Go home—you have no business here. We can whip the white soldiers alone but can't fight you too."[29]

Soon after this exchange darkness settled on the field. The destruction of the village begun in the morning continued throughout the day and into the night. Many observers commented on the immense variety and store of property that went up in flames—not just the ordinary tools and clothing of daily life but also thousands of pounds of dried meat prepared for winter and very nearly the whole cultural patrimony of the tribe. Bags filled with buffalo fat made the fires roar. Sometimes exploding in the flames were boxes of cartridges and at one moment even a whole barrel of gunpowder. Many relics of the Custer fight also turned up—a soldier's hat, officers' tunics, a pillow case made from a 7th Cavalry flag, horse tack, soldiers' notebooks taken from bodies on the Little Bighorn. Several of these notebooks had been used by the Cheyenne for drawings of war and hunting exploits.

Some grisly discoveries helped to explain the drumming and singing heard by the soldiers before the fight began. Billy Garnett, Lieutenant Bourke, Jerry Roche, and others reported that some saddles found in the village were recognized by Shoshone scouts as those of friends. Fresh scalps were hanging from lodgepoles. With discovery of the saddles and the scalps the Shoshone scouts began to cry openly as they moved about the village. Baptiste Pourier in going through lodges also found two necklaces made of human fingers; one was buried that night, the other given to Lieutenant Bourke. Finally a buckskin bag was opened. Within were the right hands of a dozen Indian children, all members of a band of thirty Shoshones out hunting which had been surprised and rubbed out by the Cheyenne only a few days earlier. The bag was given to the Shoshones. Bourke later recorded,

> There was little sleep for our people during that cold, frosty night. Half crazed with grief, the Shoshones gave full range to their sorrow in their weeping and singing, weirdly monotonous but deeply impressive . . . Letting their hair hang down over face and shoulders, they danced and wailed until daylight.[30]

In midafternoon the soldiers had been fighting in their shirtsleeves, but with the coming of night the temperature plunged. Fires were built to warm the wounded. Killed outright had been one lieutenant and five troopers. Bourke thought the Indian dead numbered at least thirty, perhaps more. The Pawnee had taken twelve scalps, he wrote, the Shoshones three or four. Frank Grouard later claimed one. None of the 150 Sioux scouts who took part in the fight claimed a scalp, a probable sign that they were willing enough to run off Cheyenne horses but balked at killing former allies. Billy Garnett had been one of those counting the dead Cheyenne, making his way through the destroyed village, where the bodies of horses littered the ground and thick smoke from burning lodges filled the air. Garnett's personal count was seventeen dead, one of them a woman. Another was a dead son of Dull Knife, killed early in the fight by Luther North.

With Garnett at that moment was Louis Shangreau, the mixed-blood called Louis Hanska—Tall Louis—by the Indians, who had run for his life with Garnett the night of the killing in Yellow Bear's lodge. Together they approached the body of Dull Knife's son, someone Garnett had often seen at the old Sod Agency on the North Platte in the early 1870s. Garnett was not quite sure which of Dull Knife's two eldest sons lay dead before him, but he remembered the moment vividly.

> [He] was lying across the stream southwest of the village on . . . his back as if he had dropped asleep, undisturbed and at peace with all the world. He was a young man of noble mien and handsome face. He wore a blanket of fine cloth in two colors—one-half red, the other blue. This was doubled and suspended from his waist . . . Garnett says his hair was light, tinged with golden hue, unusually long, and the most beautiful he ever saw on an Indian.[31]

Hung by a leather thong around the dead man's body was a standard cavalry trooper's trapdoor carbine, the gun he had been leveling at Luther North when North shot and killed him. Garnett and Shangreau had both been working for whites for years but now, suddenly, Garnett wanted to do an Indian thing. He suggested to Shangreau that they count coup on the fallen enemy, and they did, jumping down from their horses in classic fashion and striking the dead man with their horse quirts.

Shangreau went a step further, taking plunder from the body. He pulled loose the dead man's gun and then slipped his moccasins off his feet. These moccasins, Garnett remembered, were beaded and finely worked. Garnett took nothing from the field, but a couple of days later, when Mackenzie was distributing the captured Cheyenne horses among the scouts, he asked the colonel if he might have two that he said the Indians would not want. "Mackenzie told him to get them and he did." These were American horses, and both had been taken from Custer's men at the Little Bighorn.[32] So Garnett returned from this expedition with classic Sioux war honors: he had killed one man and counted coup on another, and he rode home leading captured horses.

Crook's plan immediately after the fight on the Red Fork was the same again—push after the village of Crazy Horse, somewhere up along the Tongue. The weather did not cooperate; temperatures plunging below zero and snow the first night pinned Crook's men where they were, and over the following days it was hard going to the Belle Fourche River, where they camped as winter deepened. On the Belle Fourche, Crook seemed to run out of steam. Several weeks went by as he waited for news and ruminated alone how to proceed. In mid-December his Sioux scouts came up with a new idea and proposed it to him in a council a few days before Christmas. About twenty Indians and military officers filed into a large tent where Fast Thunder from the Spotted Tail Agency and Keeps the Battle from the Red Cloud Agency laid out a simple plan, repeating each other and speaking at length: winter had set in, the horses were already in poor condition, better if they all returned to Camp Robinson and tried suasion instead of war. As remembered by William Garnett, the two scouts described the alternative strategy as follows:

> If the command should go back now the Indians would undertake by all the influences in their power to get the hostile Indians to return to the agency this winter and the coming spring; that they would persuade the Indians on other Agencies who had members of their tribes out with Crazy Horse and Sitting Bull to send embassies to the camps of these chiefs to induce them to return to their homes on the reservations; and if possible, they would convince the chiefs themselves that it was a vain hope to stay out and perhaps could bring them in.[33]

The other Indians often interrupted Fast Thunder and Keeps the Battle. At every interruption, General Crook would lean over to Garnett to ask what he was saying. Garnett assured him they were only trying to make sure nothing was left out. All had been exhaustively discussed beforehand. The central point was spelled out by one of the two scouts— probably Fast Thunder, who had already stressed it in an earlier council:

> The Indians proposed to use as an argument with the hostiles when they should go out to see them, that they were working for a home agency with General Crook assisting them to obtain it. This was another reminder to the general that they were relying on him and that they were doing their part in the agreement they had with him; and this is one more instance showing that they did not intend he should forget his obligations.

Crook talked over this approach with his staff, then summoned the Indians back to a second meeting, where he appropriated the scouts' proposal as his own. "Most of you have friends or relatives out with Crazy Horse and the Northern Cheyennes," Crook told them. "You had better advise your friends to come in . . . They will have easy terms if they come in now, but when spring comes, we are going to . . . kill them like dogs wherever we find them."[34]

Generals Sheridan in Chicago and Sherman at Army headquarters were both still breathing fire, eager for Crook to crush the hostiles in midwinter. But Crook had now made a decision for talk, not war. This he kept to himself for the time being. To Sheridan he merely wrote that the hostiles were running in all directions, his own horses and mules were played out, and no fresh ones were to be had.

"Will start back for Fetterman in the morning," he said.[35]

19

"All the people here are in rags."

SOME OGLALA WITH FIELD glasses were first to spot the approaching Cheyenne. The whole village turned out to meet the travelers, and with a glance realized these people had lost everything. The Cheyenne told a story of hardship and suffering. When the fight had ended and dark fell it began to snow and turned bitterly cold, they related. Most of the people were on foot; few had blankets or buffalo robes. That first night eleven small children froze to death. Three more died the following night. Many other members of the band had been killed in the battle itself. The keeper of the Sacred Buffalo Hat, who had waved it during the battle to protect the people, had managed to escape with this important item, but most of the people got away with little more than the clothes on their bodies and the weapons in their hands. Few lodges had been saved and most of the horses were gone. Only the very young and the very old traveled on horseback, while the rest walked on ragged moccasins or no moccasins at all, using scraps of hide to bind their feet.

Their journey north in search of the village of Crazy Horse took as long as two weeks over rough country with no game. For the first ten days they ate only meat from butchered ponies. At last, early in the second week of December, the Cheyenne met a party of their own people, returning from a horse-stealing raid. These men had been traveling with the band of Crazy Horse since the fight on the Little Bighorn, and now they led the Cheyenne refugees across country to the place where Crazy Horse was camped on Beaver Creek east of the Tongue.

The Cheyenne had been attacked and their village burned twice in a single year. This time the whole of the northern Cheyenne people had been reduced to complete poverty. The Oglala shared what they had. "We helped the Cheyennes the best we could," said Short Bull, brother of He Dog. "We hadn't much ourselves."[1]

The Cheyenne also told of a troubling new change in the war. While the people were traveling north after the fight a small band of warriors went back to see if they might recover some of their horses. In fact they found quite a few—about eighty. These were the horses the old people rode. But while they were nosing about several warriors one night slipped up close to the soldiers' camp, making their way through the bushes to the very edge of the firelight where they could hear the soldiers and the scouts talking. They were shocked to hear people talking Cheyenne there—not just William Rowland, the interpreter, but some of their own kinsmen. They had hired on as scouts to help bring in the northern Indians, and they were sitting by the fire with the soldiers.[2]

For several months after the arrival of the Cheyenne, Crazy Horse was in a quandary what to do. His pride and warrior instinct pulled him one way, but realism suggested another. Meat was not the problem. There were plenty of buffalo in the Tongue country; Crazy Horse's camp made two big surrounds in January, enough to load down horses with meat and hides. General Crook—Three Stars—was no threat for the moment; he had marched his men back to the forts in the south, and sent all the scouts back to their agencies on the White River. But Crook might return and General Nelson Miles with another army was close by, camped for the winter in hastily built barracks near the place where the Tongue flowed into the Yellowstone. No man was bolder than Crazy Horse when fighting was the thing to do, but now, in the winter after the fight called Pehin Hanska Kasota, it was increasingly apparent that the people did not want to fight anymore.

Crazy Horse was not the only chief camped for the winter along the creeks east of the Tongue. Among the scattered villages was the camp of his friends Lame Deer and Spotted Elk, chiefs of the Miniconjou. Living in Lame Deer's camp was his brother Touch the Clouds (Mahpiya Iyapato), a noted Miniconjou warrior who left his agency in September when the soldiers began seizing the guns and the horses of the Indians. Even among the Sioux, a tall people, Touch the Clouds was distinguished for his height. Some whites guessed he was as much as six feet seven inches tall.[3] He was related to Crazy Horse, whose mother, Rattle Blanket Woman, is said to have been a sister of Lone Horn, father of Touch the Clouds. But he did not want to fight the whites, and many of the people felt the way he did. Crazy Horse was not ready to give up the fight, but his people were tired. He did not know what to do, and this indecision, which he described to a friend as a kind of weakness of spirit, would deepen over the course of many months as Crazy Horse would try to find a different way to lead his people.

From the hills above the Sioux camps near the Tongue it was possible to see the Army post beside the Yellowstone in the far distance. The soldiers were so conveniently close—not thirty miles away—and the Army herds were so poorly guarded, that the Indians ran off the big American horses with ease. But after the fourth time some of the chiefs decided this was a mistake; they did not want to fight the soldiers anymore and thought relations could be improved if they took the horses back. So a group of fifteen leading men made arrangement to ride down to the Army post with the stolen horses to give them back.

It is clear that peacemaking was the goal behind this friendly gesture. Talk was general in the camps that some of the chiefs were "going in"—a phrase used to indicate a pacific mood, a readiness to talk.[4] It was said later that Crazy Horse, He Dog, and others favored talking to General Miles to discuss ending the war. The chiefs wanted to know if their horses and guns would be taken? Would they have an agency in their own country? Would those who had killed Long Hair be hanged or imprisoned? All these questions remained open. But there were practical motives as well. One of those making the trip was Sitting Bull. He had recovered the fancy rifle given to him in Washington and stayed on with the northern Indians to argue for ending the war. He told the Indians he could perhaps talk General Miles into giving them some food. Another chief in the group was Spotted Elk, who arranged to pack the stolen horses with robes and furs. "We thought it would be a good opportunity to trade," he said.[5]

On Saturday, December 16, the group started down from the hills— perhaps fifteen or twenty men leading the stolen horses loaded down with hides. Some went ahead and some held back, waiting to see how things went. Riding in front were Sitting Bull and four or five other men.[6] Two of the men had attached white flags to their lances. Sitting Bull had left his fancy rifle with one of the men who lingered to the rear. On their way down the west bank of the Tongue the Indians met a group of soldiers out cutting wood; they explained their mission and continued downriver. As they approached the soldiers' camp they passed the lodges of some Crow scouts who had arrived three weeks earlier. But the Sioux did not hesitate as a dozen of these traditional enemies approached; the meaning of a white flag was recognized on the plains as everywhere else.

Many excuses were offered for what happened next. Sometime earlier that fall Crazy Horse had been on a raid into the Crow country. Horses were taken and people killed. It was said that the killer of a Crow woman on this raid had been Crazy Horse himself, and that one of the Miniconjou, Gets Fat with Beef, was riding this woman's horse; and it was said that the husband of this woman, riding out to meet the peace talkers, recognized his wife's horse and, overcome with anger, shot and killed Gets Fat with Beef. Whatever the reason, the Crow set upon the peace talkers and killed some right there, pulling them from their horses, and some after chasing them down a mile or two. Spotted Elk and the party that had lingered behind with the stolen horses turned and fled. The man who had been holding the fancy rifle dropped it when he was shot and a Crow seized it. For perhaps a day the Crow had possession of both of the fancy rifles given to the Oglala in Washington in June 1875—the gun of Sitting Bull the Good, and the gun of Red Cloud taken from the hands of the chief's sixteen-year-old son at the Rosebud.

But the Crow didn't hold on to that second gun for long. It was promptly confiscated by Miles. The general had been hoping to end the Great Sioux War right there on the Tongue by convincing not only the Miniconjou but the Oglala with Crazy Horse to stop the fighting. He was furious at the treachery of the Crow, threatened them with hanging, and took their horses and weapons. Two days later the whole contingent of Crow scouts fled across the Yellowstone and went back to their own country—"frightened as well as shamed," according to their white interpreter, Thomas Leforge. Miles sent a gift to the Sioux of twelve Crow horses with a written explanation and apology "for such brutal and cowardly acts," but the anger was too great to brush aside. "Crazy Horse thought the soldiers had helped the Crow to do this," said Black Elk later, "so they were mighty sore over this."[7]

"Mighty sore" does not quite capture it. Not long after the killing of the peace talkers two men arrived from the Cheyenne River Agency, Fool Bear and Important Man, sent by the military officers to persuade the Miniconjou to come in. If Crazy Horse and He Dog had been thinking about peace the impulse had passed. Fool Bear and Important Man found the northern Indians angry and full of fight. They met with the chiefs in council and told them what was in store for any Indians who came in to the Cheyenne River Agency. They said the soldiers had instructed them "to tell the truth and keep nothing hid, so that they [the northern Indians] would not be disappointed should they come in." Surrender would be required; their guns and horses would be taken from them. "The Sans Arcs and Minneconjou were disposed to listen to a little kind talk from us," the emissaries reported back to the agency in January. "But the Cheyennes and Ogallalas would not listen, but abused us very much." They rejected the talk of "disarming and dismounting . . . They declared they never would submit to it as long as they lived."[8]

Fool Bear and Important Man reported a most extraordinary reason for the readiness to fight of the northern Indians. Among them was a medicine man, formerly known as Yellow Grass, who had the power to make ammunition. This man said he was the son of Wakan Tanka; he had been born in the sky, then slid down to earth on a rainbow. Recently he had taken on a new name and a new identity and was now known as Long Hair because he was "in constant communion with the spirit of General Custer." Fool Bear, Important Man, and another Miniconjou named Eagle Shield all witnessed Long Hair make ammunition by swallowing a cartridge, then hunting about until he found a whole store of cartridges—not handfuls but wooden boxes, each holding a thousand rounds. Fool Bear and Important Man watched him make eight boxes. "We saw the ammunition with our own eyes," they reported. "[Long Hair] told us to tell you this." The men in Crazy Horse's camp all had cartridge belts, Fool Bear and Important Man said; some had almost a hundred rounds, others not so many, but Long Hair said he would go on making more for another seven months.[9]

Thus supplied, Crazy Horse and the rest for the moment rejected talk of surrender. But Fool Bear and Important Man lingered in the northern camp to talk with the relatives of five Miniconjou who had surrendered to Miles as hostages in October. The emissaries from the Cheyenne River Agency spoke with the families of these men "to induce them to come in" as they had promised, but their arguments were interrupted by the arrival of Crazy Horse,

> who said we would never be allowed to take anyone from that camp. If any left they would be followed and killed. Even after Crazy Horse had said this to us, we did not stop doing all we could to induce those people to come in here. We succeeded in fixing upon a certain night and all those who were coming in were to pack up and come with us in the dark, after the camp was all quiet.[10]

"Followed and killed" was a serious threat, but it was not an illegal threat. Chiefs in wartime had the power to issue orders that must be obeyed; defiance might result in the destruction of lodges, the killing of horses, and even the killing of men—the punishment called "soldiering." Despite Crazy Horse's warning to kill any who attempted to desert, Fool Bear and Important Man went ahead with their plan, and arranged to flee with about thirty or forty Miniconjou whose relatives had gone into the Cheyenne River Agency as hostages in October.

The Crazy Horse camp must have been alive with whispers and rumors. One of those planning to leave, the Miniconjou White Eagle, was on the verge of departure with his people when "Crazy Horse, with about a hundred of his soldiers, surrounded my camp . . . entered our lodges, and took our guns."[11] Angry at this treatment, White Eagle started out of camp anyway, whereupon the *akicita* shot two of his horses. Fool Bear and Important Man did a little better. Their group quietly slipped out on the appointed night and took off east toward the Missouri. They covered so much ground they began to think they had got away,

> when all at once Crazy Horse appeared with a good many warriors, who shot all our horses, took our arms and knives, and all our plunder and then told us, if we wanted to go to the whites to go on, but the snow was so deep we could not travel without horses, and we had to return to the hostile camp.

Little Big Man was one of the group led by Crazy Horse to stop these deserters. The report of Fool Bear and Important Man is plain and direct. It leaves out the fear and drama of the moment—forty or more horses shot dead in the snow, a like number of people told to go on if they liked across the barren plains of winter, without food, blankets, or shelter. In this moment we see Crazy Horse for the only time in the remorseless role of a war leader trying to maintain discipline, ready to abandon his Miniconjou relatives to die on the prairie. But as soon as we see this harsh and resolute side it begins to ebb. The very next day in camp Fool Bear and Important Man openly called on all those who wanted to leave to gather around them. Again the *akicita* threatened death to any who left, but then told the two emissaries they might go. Fool Bear and Important Man rode away alone but halted about fifty miles off, then crept back to the Crazy Horse people and stole away first two lodges, then two more— eighteen people in all. The *akicita* did nothing.

But there was still fight in Crazy Horse himself. While Fool Bear and Important Man were persuading their friends to sneak off in the last days of December, some young men from Crazy Horse's camp rode down the Tongue to the soldier fort and ran off a herd of more than a hundred beeves. As the raiders drove the animals back up the river several companies of soldiers guided by white scouts chased after them. General Miles soon followed with additional troops, and the makings of a big fight unfolded. For several days the soldiers made their way up the valley of the Tongue, crossing and recrossing the river, sometimes huddled in buffalo-hide greatcoats against temperatures that fell to twenty or more degrees below zero, then slogging through slush left by mild days of rain. Signs of Indian camps were frequent—cottonwood boughs stripped of their bark by the Indian ponies, the carcasses of oxen killed and eaten, the rough shelters of sticks, bark, and pine boughs put up by the impoverished Cheyenne when they first arrived. The hope of surprising a big Indian camp drew Miles on.

The weeklong chase ended on January 7 when the soldiers reached Hanging Woman Creek, sometimes called Suicide Creek. There the scout Luther Kelly, known as Yellowstone, captured a party of seven or eight Cheyenne, women and children, making their way up the valley after a buffalo hunt. Other Cheyenne following just behind saw the capture and hurried on with the news to the big camp. One of the Cheyenne women was a sister of Wooden Leg, who immediately joined a mixed group of Cheyenne and Oglala that raced off to attack the soldiers and attempt to free the captives. That first sustained exchange of gunfire brought the situation to a head, and the following day Miles and his four hundred men deployed across an open valley while the Sioux and Cheyenne occupied the heights around them, shouting taunts. "You have had your last breakfast!" they cried. Yellowstone Kelly shouted back, calling the Sioux women and challenging them to fight.[12]

A daylong battle followed of dashing thrusts and retreats that resembled the fight on the Rosebud with Crook—five hours of fire and maneuver with small result. The Indians appeared to have plenty of ammunition and kept up a steady fire, a lot of it from repeating Winchesters, but the white casualties were few: two killed outright, and a third who died of his wounds a few days later. The whites as usual claimed a big toll of Indians killed, arguing that every smear of blood in the snow was another dead warrior. Eagle Shield, a Miniconjou who took part in the fighting, said he was aware of only two Indians killed; one was a man he knew—Runs the

Bear—and the other was a Cheyenne whose name he could not recall. Others identified the dead Cheyenne as Big Crow, a medicine man who deliberately attracted fire by striding in the open on top of a butte that commanded the field, pausing to shoot at the soldiers below. Eventually he fell wounded, was dragged from the field by some Sioux, and then was left to die, covered by a buffalo robe.

Shortly after Big Crow was hit Miles sent a detachment to charge up the butte and clear the top. That pretty much ended the fighting for the day. "Crazy Horse led the fight," said Eagle Shield. Short Bull said that Crazy Horse had a horse shot from under him in the fight, and at the end of the day was one of a small group of four men who kept up a cautioning fire against the soldiers while the rest of the Indians left the field.[13] In a sense Crazy Horse achieved what he had against Crook in June—sending the white soldiers back the way they had come. Miles pulled out two days later, crossing and recrossing the Tongue all the way back down the valley to his winter quarters.

But Crook's withdrawal in June had contributed to an event of consequence: the defeat of Custer a week later. The battle named after Wolf Mountain was followed only by winter and more winter. The day of heavy fighting exhausted the Indians' half-starved horses. The ammunition they shot up could not be easily replaced. Their own journey further up the Tongue took them away from the buffalo herds that had been feeding them all winter. "About this time there was a bad famine," remembered Black Elk, who had watched the fight with other boys. "Finally we got to the mouth of Rosebud Creek."[14]

In mid-January, only a week after the fight at Wolf Mountain, the chiefs in the northern camp decided to send couriers south to the camp of Spotted Tail to ask for tobacco—testing the ground for peace. Crazy Horse did not oppose this effort; he did not know what else to do. The message the chiefs gave to Charging Horse and Makes Them Stand Up was simple and direct: "They all desire to make peace and the best terms obtainable."[15]

General Nelson Miles had failed in his attempt to end the war with Crazy Horse. Now it was General Crook's turn. In early February, Sheridan instructed Crook to prepare a new campaign to deliver yet heavier blows. "The hostiles now out must be whipped until they surrender unconditionally and we must go at it again as soon as the weather will permit."[16]

One part of Crook's mind embraced this approach. He hated "the tone" of Indians who stood their ground against whites; it angered him to find the Sioux "sore, sullen and extremely insubordinate."[17] But in December his Indian scouts had convinced him to abandon his midwinter campaign and let the Indians seek out Crazy Horse in the wilderness and convince him to surrender. Crook pressed ahead with this plan, giving the job to his aide, Lieutenant Clark. Beginning in February, Clark organized three separate groups of Sioux peace talkers to go north with Crook's message, assuring Crazy Horse that surrender did not mean death or prison. First to set out was a group of fifteen Oglala led by the younger brother of the Shirt Wearer Man That Owns a Sword, the Oglala known as Hunts the Enemy.[18] With them they carried packages of tobacco, some wrapped in blue cloth and some in red, one package for each of the chiefs in Crazy Horse's band. A gift of tobacco was the traditional way of proposing peace. If the chiefs opened the packages and shared the tobacco with their leading men there would be peace; and if the tobacco were rejected, fighting would continue.

Travel was hard and game was scarce. About four nights out the group ran into Charging Horse and Makes Them Stand Up, the two men who had been dispatched by the northern camp to learn the state of affairs at the agency.[19] The two parties exchanged news and separated, the smaller going south, the larger north. A few nights later, while Hunts the Enemy and the others were sleeping, some Indians ran off with all their horses. Four of the group chased the thieves, learned they were Cheyenne, and managed to recover some of the stolen horses, but not all. Many in the party felt luck was against them and they should turn back, but Hunts the Enemy persuaded them to go on. When they reached the Powder River doubts flared again, and this time the majority said enough. Only four— Running Hawk, Crow Fire, Long Whirlwind, and Hunts the Enemy— refused to give up. Their food ran out, they found no game, and for three days they had nothing to eat. Again some wanted to turn back but Hunts the Enemy urged them to press on. After ten or twelve days of hard travel the four travelers came at last to one of the streams that fed the Tongue, east of the Big Horn Mountains, which the Oglala called the Rocky Mountains. By this stream, called Otter Creek, the people with Crazy Horse were camped.

So Hunts the Enemy and his three friends approached, and all the people stopped to gaze at them coming, and then an uproar went up, and the men jumped on their mounts and rushed over to surround them, with weapons standing out, but they did not do any violence to them. They took them to their camp, and on the second day, the great mass of wild Dakotas and the Cheyennes swelling their number, all gathered in a great council, and Hunts the Enemy and Running Hawk attended. The other two did not join, being frightened. So an Indian warrior from the great council stood forth saying, "Now, then, Hunts the Enemy, speak then, whatever you came hither for." So Hunts the Enemy spoke.[20]

Hunts the Enemy was well known to the people in Crazy Horse's camp. He had fought in the Bozeman War and had led many war parties against Indian enemies as a *blota hunka*. He once showed a white man the four scars he had received in battle—three from the Crow, one from the whites. He had been a bear dreamer and a *wicasa pejuta*—a healer with the use of herbs. He had also been a *wakiconze*, one of the village officers who decided when and where to camp. In later life he said, "The scars on my body show that I have danced the Sun Dance, and no Lakota will dispute my word."[21] But Hunts the Enemy was falling away from Lakota ways; by his own later account he came to believe that Wakan Tanka was not as powerful as the white man's god. He had been impressed by the words of General Crook at the big council with all the scouts in November before the attack on the Cheyenne at the Red Fork. To the assembly of Crazy Horse's people he said,

> I was sent by a soldier named Three Stars, who said, "The Great Father wants no more wars in this day and age, and all fighting is to cease throughout the land, and no matter who they are, all shall be in peace. So all my friends there will now come together to dwell in peace, and they, like the peaceful Indians here, shall abide in friendship." And he said, "When my friends return, there shall be nothing untoward done to them," he said.[22]

That was the heart of Crook's offer: if you surrender, the fighting will end and no man will be punished. Hunts the Enemy told the northern Indians that the whites wanted to move the Oglala agency away from the White River to the Indian Territory or the Missouri. At the agencies the leading men were all arguing for a new site in their own country. In the spring, it was said, the chiefs would go to Washington to make their case; Hunts the Enemy told Crazy Horse that he would be invited to make the trip as well. Crazy Horse thus well understood that giving up horses and guns would be only the first step, to be followed by a trip to

Washington and a campaign to secure an agency in the Indians' own country.[23]

The man chosen to reply to Hunts the Enemy for the Oglala in the north was Iron Hawk, a noted warrior who had been in the fighting at the Rosebud and at the Little Bighorn. In the Custer fight, although badly wounded himself, he killed a soldier running up a dry creek bed.[24] Iron Hawk was in his forties—an "old man" in the view of Red Feather, Crazy Horse's brother-in-law. In 1875 Iron Hawk had been "way up north in Montana" when word arrived from the agencies that the whites wanted to buy the Black Hills. He was against it then and he was against it now; he would not listen to any proposal for selling the hills. So it was a longtime opponent of giving in to the whites whom the Oglala asked to reply to Hunts the Enemy, but they cautioned Iron Hawk first. "Speak as we said to speak only," they said.[25]

The words used by Iron Hawk had already been the subject of much debate in Crazy Horse's band. There was nothing unusual in asking Iron Hawk to make the reply. Red Cloud often let another man speak for him, and Crazy Horse almost always kept silent himself. But Crazy Horse was the leading man of the two thousand northern Indians who had been wintering in the Tongue and Powder river country. What Iron Hawk said was what Crazy Horse and the rest had decided.

The message which Hunts the Enemy brought from Crook was what the northern Indians had wanted to hear. The answer delivered by Iron Hawk was what "we said to speak only"—the collective decision of all the leading men. This speech, which signaled the end of the Great Sioux War, is preserved in two versions. Hunts the Enemy recorded the fuller of the two:

Now then, Hunts the Enemy, carefully harken as you sit. This land is mine. The great spirit raised me like this, and I live in accordance with it. But Friend, the white man from the sunrise advances, stealing my land as he comes, and by now the land is small, therefore I do not permit him on my territory but he works himself in, and when he sees me he shoots at me, so I shoot back, and I kill some of them. And when I contemplate what I have done I am sad. Alas, I am whipping the relatives of these men, I think, and I bring sorrow on myself.

And now you say someone who is said to be a leader thinks he wants peace. Very well, he shall have it. There shall be a great big peace! I am the very one who, when someone tries to outdo me in being agreeable, always win.

So I shall move camp and approach. But I am burdened down with much meat. I am heavy. There is much snow. All the rivers lie across the road, and they are deep. I must travel slowly. So, Hunts the Enemy, before I arrive, you shall come to me again, or else send your men to me.[26]

Red Feather, the brother of the wife of Crazy Horse, was also present on this occasion, and in 1930 he summarized the words of Iron Hawk: "You see all the people here are in rags, they all need clothing, we might as well go in."[27]

In the end talking did what fighting could not—convinced the Indians the whites were too many. Crazy Horse did not drive this decision to end the war, but he also did not resist it. Between mid-February and the first week in May a swelling number of Indians came in to the agencies from the northern country, all bearing news. From their numerous and by no means consistent reports emerges a rough history of Crazy Horse's last weeks as a traditional Lakota free to roam as he liked.

The first substantial group to arrive, about forty people in all, reached Camp Robinson in late February led by the Cheyenne chief Little Wolf. His appearance must have startled Billy Garnett and Frank Grouard; both thought they had shot and killed him in the fight on the Red Fork. Little Wolf explained that they had indeed shot him—at least five or six times!—but the wounds were all superficial.[28] Little Wolf's Cheyenne, who had started south sometime in January, were the last of the northern Indians to report threats by the *akicita* in the village of Crazy Horse.[29] Little Wolf told the soldiers that the northern Indians "want more fighting," but that was not the message brought by Charging Horse and Makes Them Stand Up, who arrived at Camp Sheridan and the Spotted Tail Agency on February 9 seeking news of the terms of surrender. At about the same time Red Sack, married to the sister of Crazy Horse, arrived at Camp Robinson to say the northern chiefs had "sent him in to the agency to ascertain how matters were and to return and let them know as soon as possible."[30] Red Sack was followed by members of the group that went out with Hunts the Enemy—Few Tails, Running Hawk, and Tall Man. A Brulé Sioux named Good Breast arrived at the Spotted Tail Agency on March 9 bearing a note from Spotted Tail's son-in-law, the trader François Boucher, reporting, "We getting all the Sioux to come in . . . slow and sure."[31]

But it was Crazy Horse himself the generals wanted safely under control. In a letter to his father from Camp Sheridan, Lieutenant Fred Schwatka remarked in February that Crazy Horse "is the only chief of importance."[32] As the northern Sioux came in—the Oglala to the Red Cloud Agency, the Miniconjou and Sans Arcs to Spotted Tail—they mostly said Crazy Horse was coming along behind them with his village. But some said not. It seems clear there had been at least two large councils in the north, the first when Hunts the Enemy met with Iron Hawk in mid-February, the second when a group under Spotted Tail met with about a hundred lodges of Miniconjou and Sans Arcs near the mouth of the Little Powder River in mid-March. After this second council Boucher penned another note to Major Horace Neide at the Spotted Tail Agency and sent it south by courier.

> We on our way back home from the mouth of Little Powder River, we could not go any further on account of deep snow and deep water, also no grub. We sent courier all over the country with tobacco . . . the Oglala moving to Bear Lodge Butte with the calculation of stopping there and all the men going to our agency to trade their robes and furs, they heavy load with meat and robe. Crazy Horse send news that Sitting Bull came over last winter try to get the Oglala to move across the Missouri he did not succes he went cross the Missouri himself with his Band. We sent a courier to notify Crazy Horse to move right straight to the agency not stop at Bear Butte Lodge. We moving back with very near 200 lodges Mineconou different bands. We got a big camp no grub and starving . . . No game horses very poor.[33]

In their meeting with Spotted Tail the chiefs in the Miniconjou and Sans Arc camp—Touch the Clouds, Roman Nose, Red Bear, and Fast Bull—promised to follow the Brulé south to the agency. The father of Crazy Horse was also there and told Spotted Tail "that Crazy Horse, though not here, makes peace the same as if he were here, and shakes hands through his father the same as if he himself did it."[34] As a gesture of peace the elder man gave a horse to Joseph Merrivale, an old plainsman married to a Brulé woman of Spotted Tail's band.

Two weeks later, in mid-April, Touch the Clouds, Roman Nose, High Bear, and about a thousand northern Indians arrived at the Spotted Tail Agency and formally surrendered to General Crook, who gave the arrivals a long speech full of fatherly advice. On an impulse he promised that when all the hostiles had come in the agency Indians might be allowed to go north again with soldiers as escort for a big buffalo hunt up along the Tongue. "This announcement was loudly greeted with a chorus of enthusiastic '*Hous!*' " reported Lieutenant Jesse Lee, who was about to take over as acting agent for the Spotted Tail Indians.[35]

Coming south more slowly were the people belonging to the village of Crazy Horse. Periods of mild weather were followed by intense storms. By chance the route south taken by the Indians was paralleled by a party of whites which included the Camp Robinson contract surgeon, Valentine McGillycuddy, and his wife, Fanny, who remarked on the weather in her diary. The party set out on the eastern slope of the Black Hills on March 2, "but in about half an hour the wind came up and such a snow storm I never wish to be caught out in," she wrote. "Oh terrible, terrible." A month later, still on the road, "A fearful snow storm came upon us in the night and raged all day. Some of the weak horses died . . . a fall of 15 inches of snow—covering up all trace of the road. Some of the drifts are four and five feet deep."[36] The Indian ponies were in poor condition, heavily loaded with meat and hides from two big surrounds of buffalo in the north, slowed by the swollen, ice-clogged rivers.

But it was probably not winter alone which explained the slow progress of Crazy Horse. The reassuring words of Hunts the Enemy, Spotted Tail, Red Cloud, and others could not disguise the implications of their move south—something Crazy Horse and the others had vowed never to do. He Dog for one was not quite sure why they were going at all. "When we started in," he said later, "I thought we were coming to visit and to see whether we would receive an annuity, not to surrender."[37]

Crazy Horse was also in continuing perplexity. Lone Bear arrived to report that Crazy Horse was not with the rest of the northern Indians in March; he was out in the hills hunting with a small group. The medicine man Horn Chips, who had gone north with the Brulé from the Spotted Tail Agency, reported that Crazy Horse had returned south with him as far as the Powder River. There the chief separated from the band and went off by himself with about ten lodges, perhaps seventy or eighty people. After a time Crazy Horse left the larger group and camped with only one other lodge. Soon any companion was too many.

Sometime in March or April the family of the elder Black Elk, traveling south to the agency, came upon Crazy Horse camped on a creek with no one for company but his wife, Black Shawl Woman. Lakota often went out alone to pray for guidance and help in a time of trouble. What the solitary Crazy Horse was thinking during this period is suggested by scattered bits of evidence. After listening to arguments for surrender he told friends like He Dog and Red Feather that he did not want to go in to the agency but would do what the others wanted to do. He took none of the tobacco brought out by Hunts the Enemy but sent it around to the chiefs of the scattered bands. He told the emissaries who brought the tobacco that his people were free to "decide what they would do; that if he told them to stay they would do so, even if they were to die, but he would let them say."[38]

Crazy Horse took seriously the promise he had been given of an agency in the north. Before leaving Beaver Creek east of the Tongue he planted a stake in the ground to mark the place where he wished to have his agency.[39] And finally, he told the elder Black Elk, a man he called uncle, why he had gone off apart from the rest of the people as the northern Indians were all making their way south. The chief's words were related by the elder Black Elk to the younger, who took the name Nicholas in the 1880s. Nick Black Elk in turn repeated the words of Crazy Horse to the white poet and historian John Neihardt in 1931. The words were translated from Lakota into English by Black Elk's son, Ben, and transcribed by Neihardt's daughters, Enid and Hilda. By this tortuous route the words of Crazy Horse have reached us. In their Delphic ambiguity they say little and much, nothing and everything. Said the younger Black Elk:

On the road to Fort Robinson we found Crazy Horse all alone on a creek with just his wife. He was a queer man. He had been queer all of this winter. Crazy Horse said to my father, "Uncle, you might have noticed me, how I act, but it is for the good of my people that I am out alone. Out there I am making plans—nothing but good plans—for the good of my people. I don't care where the people go. They can go where they wish." (There were things that he had to figure out and he was wanting the spirits to guide him. He would then go back to his people to tell them what he had learned.) "This country is ours, therefore I am doing this," said Crazy Horse.[40]

20

"I want this peace to last forever."

GENERAL SHERIDAN AT HIS headquarters in Chicago was leaving nothing to chance. He wanted to force an end to the Sioux war and didn't quite trust the good news from General Crook, who reported that Crazy Horse was close to surrender. Welcome if true, in Sheridan's view, but he pressed Crook to prepare a spring campaign against the Indians all the same. At the military posts and in the Indian camps nobody was sure which would happen first—the surrender of the Oglala chief with the last of the hostiles, or the outfitting of another expeditionary force to take the field against the holdouts. Western newspapers reported the progress of both developments, stirring the wives of military officers with dread and uncertainty. "There are rumors of another Indian expedition in the spring," Caroline Frey Winne wrote her brother from the Sidney Barracks in late February, "but nobody knows anything."[1]

At Fort Leavenworth in Kansas where she had been spending the winter, the uncertainty weighed heavily on the spirits of Alice Baldwin, prey to extreme emotional swings under the best of circumstances. Her husband, Lieutenant Frank Baldwin, had distinguished himself in the battle with Crazy Horse at Wolf Mountain, leading the charge up the butte which drove off the Indians and allowed General Miles to claim a victory. An account of his exploit in the *St. Louis Globe-Democrat* a week before Christmas filled her with pride—"I seemed to tread on air for a day," she wrote. But the pride didn't last long. "What a pity," she reflected miserably, "[that] Frank has made himself famous . . . [because] he has not a wife worthy of him."

Self-pity filled her letters, a despondent cry from the heart of a woman pushed to the snapping point by the constants of frontier military life: boredom, loneliness, and fear. From Fort Leavenworth, as winter drew to a close, Alice started north by steamboat to join her husband at Miles's headquarters. "I have been looking at the illustrations in *Harper's Weekly* of the cantonment on the Tongue River," she wrote Frank. Shown in woodcuts were structures little better than huts, half buried in snow. "It looked dismal enough," she commented. Dread of life in the wilderness was joined by fear.

> I read in a late paper that Crazy Horse threatened to wipe out everyone on the Yellowstone and that active preparation was being made by them for war . . . [a friend] told me tonight that those Indians surrendering and giving up their ponies was merely a blind. That probably they were reserving their best horses etc. etc. Oh this eternal, inevitable "spring campaign" I am tired of. And apparently as far from being ended as ever. Look at past experiences. Facts can't be denied. You and all the others know, no matter how badly they may be whipped and punished—they keep out and with renewed vigor when spring comes and the grass has grown . . . If I could only know you would be safe and not get killed.[2]

Alice Baldwin feared a renewed war, a husband dead on the prairie like so many with Custer the year before, an impoverished widowhood. Lieutenant Fred Calhoun at Camp Robinson was following the news as well, but it was anger, not fear, that tormented him. He had been brooding all winter about the killing of his brother Jim, whose body had been left in a shallow grave on the hills east of the Little Bighorn. Only a week or two after the fight, Captain Myles Moylan, an officer of the 7th married to Calhoun's sister Charlotte, had written to say, "I was present when Jim was buried and recognized him at a glance." Fred had the consolation at least of knowing where his brother lay; many of the dead had been too badly mutilated or decomposed for identification.[3]

That fall after the end of the Big Horn and Yellowstone Expedition, Calhoun spent his days in the office at the Red Cloud Agency, where his commander, Captain Thomas Tobey, was serving as the acting agent for the Oglala. One of Calhoun's duties was to take a census of the Indians, recording their names, bands, and other information in a ledger book. Later that winter Calhoun helped Lieutenant Clark recruit Brulé Sioux to serve as scouts. In April, when fifteen hundred northern Indians came in to surrender at the Spotted Tail Agency, several of them turned in small items taken from the dead at the Little Bighorn. Among them was a pocket watch, soon identified as one owned by Fred's brother James. Fred mailed the watch with a letter to the sorrowing widow, Margaret.

Thus continually reminded of his brother's death, Fred Calhoun brooded. As spring approached, he learned that an Army detail would be sent out in the coming summer to retrieve the bodies of officers from the Little Bighorn. Fred wanted to go, and he wrote seeking help from an old Cincinnati friend, Charles Turner, a close supporter of President Rutherford B. Hayes. Fred told his friend that the Custer family was "anxious" for him to go and of course he "wanted to be present when my brother's remains are to be removed." Behind these mild hopes anger seethed. Scouts coming in from Crazy Horse's band said the chief would surrender with two hundred lodges of his people in a week's time—early May, he wrote.

> This ends the Indian war for the present. Of course it does not permanently end it for history will repeat itself and in a year or two they will all go out again. It is a very unsatisfactory ending for me, as I wanted to see them completely crushed, if not exterminated. Of course, the massacre of the entire Indian race would not repay my loss of last summer, but the only way to insure lasting peace with them is to give them a good sound whipping, and these northern Indians have never yet been whipped.[4]

Anger at the Indians was not limited to those in the field. Sheridan and Sherman wanted to hurt and humble them as well. Over the previous decade both had spoken often of "exterminating" the Indians if they did not submit, but the word was used casually, almost as a way of letting off steam. The humiliating defeat of Custer added a sharp new edge to their anger. In the first week of May, Sheridan wrote Sherman to suggest that surrender of the Indians might now "permit us to take up the question of punishing the leaders . . . Have you any views on the subject?" Sherman did. As Sheridan's query crossed his desk on its way through official channels Sherman scribbled a stark sentence on the document: "If some of the worst Indians could be executed I doubt not the result would be good—but that is impossible after surrender under conditions." He sounds almost wistful. But in the end he and the rest of official Washington went back to the old plan: transfer of the Sioux to new agencies on the Missouri River. "Better to remove all to a safe place and then reduce them to a helpless condition," Sherman wrote.[5]

There was one trouble with this plan: the Indians did not want to move, and the military officers at the agencies believed the Indians would refuse to go. In mid-April the influential chiefs of three Oglala bands— American Horse, Yellow Bear, and Young Man Afraid of His Horses—

told Colonel Mackenzie that if they had to leave Nebraska they wanted a new agency on the Tongue River.[6] Lieutenants Clark and Jesse Lee at the Spotted Tail Agency had been telling Crook the same thing: the Indians didn't want to go to the Missouri. Crook was under no illusions about Indian feeling on the matter. The previous fall, on the expedition that attacked the Cheyenne on the Red Fork of the Powder River, Crook had promised the scouts he would try to get what they wanted: a home in the north. But he spoke with care. Crook promised to help, to tell the president what the Sioux wanted, to argue in their behalf, but added that such matters were not up to him alone. "They must be decided in Washington."

A promise was as sacred as a threat, in Crook's view; neither should be made lightly. He explained his philosophy of dealing with Indians to Jesse Lee in late February when the lieutenant arrived to take over the Spotted Tail Agency. "He told me, for one thing, not to promise anything that I could not carry out," Lee said later, "and whenever I did promise anything to always keep my word."[7]

Crook's promise to help the Sioux find a home in the north was tested many times over the spring and summer of 1877, beginning with a telegram from Sheridan on April 22 saying that Sherman and the commissioner of Indian affairs were prepared and determined to move the Indians to the Missouri in June. "I want your opinion on this proposition," Sheridan wrote, "and would like to have it as soon as possible."[8] Crook felt this matter was too important for a letter; he delivered his response in person a week later, arguing against the move. It was the proposed relocation that brought Crook to Chicago, but during an interview with a reporter for the *Chicago Post*, held in the Grand Pacific Hotel, the general concealed the purpose of his trip, stressing instead that it was time to put the Sioux to work. "They did absolutely nothing but loaf about," the *Post* reported. "General Crook saw no reason why the Indians could not make their own living . . . 'Give him a piece of land,' said General Crook, 'show him how to cultivate it, and he will be anxious to hold on to what he has and to better himself.' "

Not a word about moving the Indians out of Nebraska. Crook took his thoughts on that to Washington, where he had a long conference on May 5 with the secretary of the interior, Carl Schurz, and the commissioner of Indian affairs, John Q. Smith. The newspapers led their stories next day with the general's tough talk: "[T]he Indians should be compelled to work for their grub." Those who read to the end learned, almost as an afterthought, that "the Indians will not be removed until next autumn."[9] Crook had kept his promise and done what he could.

Crazy Horse shook the hand of a white official for the first time on the first or second day of May 1877. The honor went to a young Army officer sent out with food for the hostiles, Second Lieutenant J. Wesley Rosenquest.[10] The place was a flat along the bank of Hat Creek, one of the many winding and frequently dry creek beds that crisscrossed the grasslands where the state of Nebraska met the territories of Dakota and Wyoming. The stage road from Fort Laramie to the Black Hills crossed Hat Creek about forty miles from Camp Robinson, and it was near that spot that Crazy Horse met the soldiers. Watching the historic handshake was Billy Garnett, just turned twenty-two, who had ridden out with the ten wagons of provisions to serve as interpreter. Also along were some drovers with a hundred agency beeves and a body of about fifty Indian scouts led by American Horse, who was by this time one of the Oglala chiefs most trusted by the U.S. military.

As the Crazy Horse band approached, American Horse led his scouts out in front of the whites and bade them sit upon the grass. Rosenquest was baffled by this maneuver, but Garnett knew what the chief had in mind. It was the custom of Indians coming to make peace to give a present to the men they first met, and accordingly some of Crazy Horse's men moved ahead of the others, leading horses, and gave one to each of the scouts sitting in line. They did not overlook American Horse or Rosenquest, who was surprised to be handed the lead string of a pony. Then Crazy Horse stepped forward to shake the hand of the lieutenant, followed by "all the chiefs," according to Garnett.[11]

From Hat Creek over the following days Crazy Horse and the small military escort under Rosenquest made their way to Soldier Creek, which fed into the White River near the parade ground at Camp Robinson. The progress of the Indians was reported by daily telegrams sent on the newly completed line between the post and Fort Laramie. Solemn and deliberate ceremony marked the day on which Crazy Horse gave up his old life, along with his horses and guns, to make his home at the agency. It was only now, as they approached Camp Robinson, that He Dog realized they were not coming in to trade or to receive annuities or to visit with relatives; they were coming in to surrender. But they did not use the word "surrender." Crazy Horse told his relative Little Killer that he had been "captured." From Fort Robinson he would be going on to Washington. "The white people . . . wanted our guns and horses—the things we fought with," said Little Killer later. "Crazy Horse said, 'All right, let them have them.' "[12]

When the northern Indians were about seven miles from the agency they were met by Red Cloud with a large group of Indians and white soldiers including Lieutenant Clark. This was no casual encounter. According to Clark, it had all been spelled out in advance by Crazy Horse, who had stipulated how "making peace"—not surrender—should be conducted. As Clark approached he was met first by Crazy Horse seated on a spotted pony with "about ten of his headmen," formed in a line. Behind them in a second line were the rest of the fighting men, also on horseback, several hundred in all. And behind the fighting men were the women and children. Taken all together they numbered one short of nine hundred.[13]

Many of the Indians and whites who took part left accounts of what was said and done.[14] All accounts agree that for the Oglala, Crazy Horse and He Dog played the leading role. Each laid a blanket on the ground, Crazy Horse making a place for Red Cloud to sit, He Dog a place for Clark. According to Billy Garnett, who was seated near Clark, one of the Indians told Crazy Horse, "Shake hands with him with your left hand for that is the side your heart lays." Explaining further, the Indian added, "The right hand does all manner of wickedness."

Crazy Horse shook hands with Lieutenant Clark, saying, "I want to shake hands while seated, because that means our peace shall last." He said, "*Kola* [friend], I want this peace to last forever."

Garnett then interpreted as the lieutenant gave an opening prayer. He Dog in turn prepared a pipe in the proper way, offering it up toward the sky and speaking the proper words. "Now if you are in earnest," he said to the lieutenant, "I want you to take a puff of this pipe of peace." Clark puffed on the pipe and then, according to He Dog, he "blew some of the smoke out of his mouth, and rubbed the smoke on his body, his clothes, to show he meant what he said."[15] After that, He Dog said, "I gave him my war clothes, my gun and my horse in token that I would fight no more."[16] Crazy Horse in turn made similar gifts to Red Cloud, saying, "I want the children . . . to be protected, and the women, and for that I am giving you this horse and blanket which is trimmed with porcupine work."[17]

To Clark, Crazy Horse said, "I have been a man of war and have always protected my country against invaders. Now I am for peace. I will look at the ground and fight no more. I will settle down and attend to my own business."[18] According to He Dog's brother, Short Bull, Crazy Horse also said one more thing, describing to Clark the place where he wanted his people to live. The chief said his first choice would have been Goose Creek, where General Crook had camped for so long after the Rosebud fight. But if he couldn't take his people to Goose Creek, he knew of another good country where there was plenty of grass for horses and for game. It was near the Tongue River. Crazy Horse said, "There is a creek over there they call Beaver Creek; there is a great big flat west of the headwaters of Beaver Creek; I want my agency put right in the middle of that flat."[19]

With those words said and those gifts bestowed the whole company made their way to the Red Cloud Agency. Crook was away in the east but his aide John Bourke, standing with other military officers at the post, watched the mass of Indians approach at about two o'clock, calling it "one of the most impressive spectacles I ever witnessed." For sheer gorgeous splendor there was nothing like a great crowd of Indians all dressed in their finest, sitting on their ponies, singing their songs. They made a column "not much under two miles in length," Bourke estimated. He and others all noticed that Little Hawk was wearing around his neck a silver peace medal. At first opportunity Bourke determined that the medal had been struck during the term of President James Monroe and given to Little Hawk's father at a peace conference on the North Platte in 1817. But Bourke and others also noted that the ponies were thin, and the lodges in tatters. Something else struck Bourke's eye. The bustle of an Indian camp on the move usually included packs of dogs running and yipping, but on this day only the occasional furtive dog was seen. Most of the dog tribe, Bourke guessed, had been eaten.[20]

The Indians may have insisted that they were "making peace," but the military at Camp Robinson wasted no time in taking away their guns and horses—the first step in reducing them to a "helpless condition," in Sherman's words. During the talk and handshaking at Hat Creek, American Horse and his scouts had taken careful note of the men with guns. As soon as the lodges were up, Lieutenant Clark called for the guns to be brought forward and a pile began to gather in front of him. The range was wide, according to one military officer, starting with "muzzle-loaders of every pattern, from the small-bore Kentucky squirrel-rifle to a terrible weapon approaching the blunderbuss style."[21]

The antique weapons belonged mainly to old men and boys. It was the warriors in their prime who laid down a "Colt's improved army revolver" or breech-loading carbine taken from the dead at the Little Bighorn. Others were armed with large-caliber Sharps sporting guns, mostly seized, the officers guessed, from whites killed in the Black Hills. Crazy Horse and his uncle Little Hawk between them surrendered five late-model Winchester repeating rifles. Other chiefs came forward and, in Bourke's words, "laid sticks down upon the ground, saying, '*Kola*, this is my gun, this little one is a pistol; send to my lodge and get them.' " In each case, Bourke said, when Billy Garnett and Frank Grouard went around with military officers to the man's lodge the guns were found, just as described.[22]

But when the pile in front of Lieutenant Clark was declared complete by Crazy Horse there weren't enough guns, in the officer's view—only seventy-five or so. The scouts with American Horse said they had counted another thirty or forty which were missing. "Lieutenant Clark at once told him that was too thin," Bourke recalled.

With Grouard, Garnett, and a small detachment of soldiers, Clark went around to the lodges and collected another forty weapons, piling them into a wagon. One of the officers at the same time took a census of the 899 Indians who had ridden into the agency that day. This was the last significant body of hostile Sioux south of Canada, where Sitting Bull and his people had taken refuge. It was hard to see how so few had caused so much consternation—217 fighting men ("adult males" in the census) armed with bows and arrows and 117 firearms, by final count.[23] The toll of so much fighting over the previous year was apparent; the men were heavily outnumbered by the women, 312 in all, some listed in the census as "widows" who were heads of families. The whole band had ridden into the agency with about seventeen hundred horses and mules, quite a few branded "U.S." All were seized and given to the scouts who had signed up with Crook since the previous fall, according to Garnett.

But almost as soon as the northern Indians were gunless and on foot, the military changed its mind. Only a week after the surrender, Clark told Billy Garnett he planned to give Crazy Horse and about twenty of his men a chance to enlist as United States Army scouts. Not only would they get their horses back, but they would be issued Sharps carbines and Colt revolvers. Garnett believed this was foolish and overtrusting; he was sure that General Crook would be against the idea. The other scouts had signed up with Crook's promise they would be treated as leading men. Now the Crazy Horse Indians were to be made equals, given guns, and paid just like the Indians who had actually gone to war at Crook's side.

Garnett was ten years younger than Clark and he was a mixed-blood, held in low esteem by most whites. But he spoke his mind and he "kicked to Clark," he said later, denouncing the plan to make scouts of Crazy Horse and his men. But Clark "in the goodness of his heart" was determined to go through with his plan. Making them scouts, he believed, would "convince the late hostiles of his confidence in them." So Garnett rode out to Crazy Horse's camp several miles down the White River with Clark's offer, and "they jumped at the chance." That same day they returned with Garnett to the post and touched the pen. Crazy Horse and several others were given rank as sergeants. Among the twenty who signed up with him were Little Hawk, He Dog, Big Road, Looking Horse, and Little Big Man—all considered dangerous hostiles only a week earlier.[24]

"I cannot decide these things for myself."

NEWSPAPER CORRESPONDENTS WERE quick to make their way to north-west Nebraska to describe the surrender of the Indian who had killed Custer. The Union Pacific Railroad made the first leg of the journey an easy matter of a day or two; the last leg from Cheyenne, Wyoming, or Sidney, Nebraska, was a grueling, daylong ride on horseback or in a jolting stagecoach to Camp Robinson and the agency. Among the early arrivals were "Alter Ego"—Robert Strahorn of the *Chicago Tribune* and Denver's *Rocky Mountain News;* John W. Ford, the longtime telegraph operator at Fort Laramie who had been recruited by the *Chicago Times* to cover the story; and George P. Wallihan, a lively young reporter for the *Cheyenne Leader.* Strahorn had spent the winter in Cheyenne finishing up a book with which he hoped to make a fortune, a guide to the already-booming gold towns in the Black Hills. Reporters were meagerly paid and Strahorn was engaged to be married, so he needed the money. But he interrupted his writing to make his way to Camp Robinson to cover the story of the day.

Strahorn, who had traveled with General Crook all the previous season, was first on the ground at the Red Cloud Agency, present for a big feast held by Little Wound less than a week after the making of peace. Crook had not yet returned from Washington, but Strahorn joined Lieutenant Clark on a red blanket placed on the ground in front of a hundred men gathered at Little Wound's invitation, including Crazy Horse. Two large tipis had been joined to make a single immense structure, and within it the Indians arranged themselves in four concentric circles. At one point, Strahorn wrote, "an old Indian, ragged, wrinkled and fairly tottering in his weakness," was led into the circle by a young warrior who said the man should be clothed and fed. Little Wound immediately pulled off his own blanket and handed it to the mendicant. Crazy Horse, "stolid and relentless," as described by Strahorn, bettered the single blanket with clothes and a pony.

But what really held Strahorn's attention was the preparation for the feast, and it appears Clark shared his attitude. While the chiefs discussed large matters of policy—"a carnival of oratory," in Strahorn's phrase— candidates for the cooking pot were dispatched by two Indians with a rawhide lariat. Crazy Horse's village was short of dogs; Little Wound had plenty. The lariat was looped around a dog's neck—chubby, half-grown puppies were favored for eating—and then pulled taut, back and forth, strangling the victim. Butchering followed. Strahorn and Clark watched carefully.

> About a dozen of the largest of their pets were slaughtered [Strahorn wrote]. A large number of pots were on hand . . . All the heads were thrown in one, all the legs in another, the tails in another, and so on. These were placed upon the fire in the midst of the circles of debaters now assembled.

A moment of truth now approached. One of the rites of passage for whites on the plains was the first encounter with dog meat. Everyone knew it was a favorite of the Indians, and everybody who spent time with Indians was sooner or later invited to sample dog stew. Eventually the oratory ended, and a "prayer heralded the feast." Strahorn and Clark were seated in the center, the only whites in the group, all eyes upon them as the main course was handed out. Clark was planning to sign up Crazy Horse and twenty of his leading men as scouts the following day, and could not hesitate now. Strahorn confessed that he, too, was "forced to eat with the savages." But he elected to describe his experience in the third person:

> The latter gentleman [meaning himself] says he narrowly escaped being handed a tail by turning his head at the right moment. Dog's ribs, however, he sampled thoroughly and pronounces them . . . [not] quite as good as mule meat, but somewhat superior in flavor to that of wild cats.[1]

This was an informed comparison. For weeks with General Crook the previous fall Strahorn had joined the rest of the expedition in eating so much horse- and muleflesh during the long trek from the Tongue that soldiers began calling it "the horsemeat march." Strahorn did not linger at Red Cloud after the feast. Three days later he was back in Cheyenne, writing up his recent adventure. What is striking is the tone of the piece—good-humored, warmed by the bonhomie of palling around with Army officers surrounded by wild Indians, a little skittish about acknowledging his fascination with the strangeness of "the savages." His colleague John Finerty had confessed he "detested the race." Not Strahorn. He had watched a hundred leading men of the Sioux debate peace with the whites. He had shared a meal of dog with Crazy Horse and had even discussed with him the great battles of the previous summer. It was the whites who got whipped in those battles, not the Indians. White readers across the country were hungry for every word about the warriors who killed Custer. But no correspondent of the time would say flatly that he admired or respected Indians. Strahorn remained on the safe side of the racial divide by making gentle fun of the whole show, writing to amuse. With other writers the edge was sharper, the stance less conflicted.

George P. Wallihan, still in his mid-twenties, had already been chased out of one town (Denver) and had enemies in plenty in another (Cheyenne) when he headed for the Red Cloud Agency in the middle of May 1877. His career to date had been typical for the times. With his father and ten brothers and sisters he had come west to Denver from the small town of Footville, Wisconsin, about 1870. George's father, Samuel, a medical doctor, found a position as a small-town postmaster but also did some doctoring at Indian agencies. George was soon hanging around the offices of the *Rocky Mountain News* in Denver, aspiring to become a newspaperman. He didn't have a job, exactly, but the editors gave him odd small tasks including the fetching of the daily mail. Eager to see his work in print, and needing money, Wallihan in February 1873 wrote for the *Chicago Times* an anonymous and "sensational" account of scandal and malfeasance which the *Times* published under the one-line head "Denver Deviltries." Outraged citizens wrote angrily to Chicago demanding to know who had written this work of "venom and maliciousness." The young Wallihan was soon suspected. "George has been a little too reckless with the pen," a newspaper remarked, adding that the youthful reporter had been "kindly advised to leave for 'greener fields and pastures new.'" Wallihan escaped to the *Cheyenne Leader*, where he never passed up an opportunity to abuse rival newspapermen, or make fun of the "Crazy Horstiles," or warn readers against the hardship and dangers of the road to the Black Hills which began in Sidney, Nebraska.[2]

Wallihan's style was to take nothing too seriously. He signed his pieces for the *Leader* as "Rapherty" and was generally making fun of somebody, often himself. In late April 1876, when General Custer was preparing for his march west to the Little Bighorn, the *Cheyenne Leader* reported, "Rapherty finds that his meager salary ($20 per hour) will not support a dog and cane, and therefore offers for sale cheap a broken-legged rat-and-tan. Josephus must speak quick if he wants that dorg." On the 5th of July, one day before the nation learned of Custer's disastrous fight, the readers in "the magic city" (Cheyenne) were informed that "a national salute was fired by the Rapherty boy at sunrise on the fourth, said boy sitting up all night in order to awake at the proper hour."

The following spring, with the Indians on the run, traffic north to the booming gold towns of the Black Hills doubled and redoubled. The *Leader* sent Wallihan to cover the story, and on April 16, he departed on the newly established Cheyenne and Black Hills Stage Line with eight companions, including J. M. Studebaker, a principal of the wagon-making firm of Studebaker Brothers. In his first dispatch Wallihan wrote that "John Featherstun . . . [who] joined us at Fort Laramie, and your correspondent, both armed to the teeth, ride 'on top' and keep vigilant watch over the outfit."[3] On the 24th Wallihan and company passed the Hat Creek station, five or six days before the stage route was crossed by Crazy Horse and his people on their way to surrender at Camp Robinson.

The Black Hills frenzy had reached new intensity after discovery of gold along Whitewood Creek—forty cents' worth of gold to the pan, was the early report. In a shantytown at the headwaters of the creek there were fifty miners by January 1876 making an average of ten dollars a day—a royal sum for a working man in the wake of the Panic of 1873. When Wallihan arrived in Deadwood on April 27, 1877, the population had boomed to five thousand and the city fathers were arguing bitterly whether they were in Wyoming or Dakota territory. The city editor of the *Cheyenne Leader* promptly sided with Wyoming in the dispute, dashing off an assault on "the gassy carcass of that king of blowhards" who dared suggest that Dakota, not Wyoming, was the home of the fabulous diggings.

But Wallihan saved his real passion for the raw excitement of Deadwood itself, where even the newsboys on the crowded streets selling copies of the *Deadwood City Times* and the *Black Hills Pioneer* carried gold scales to weigh out ten cents' worth of dust for the paper. "Dust is the currency of the country," Wallihan wrote. "The four banking houses here each buy from one to ten thousand dollars in gold dust per day." There was hammering and sawing as long as the light held—"carpenters, all busy as bees . . . [are] paid from four to six dollars a day"—and the saloons were open all night.[4]

Soon the *Cheyenne Leader* felt it had printed enough on the new El Dorado; now it wanted Indian stories, and Wallihan headed south to the Red Cloud Agency. What elated Wallihan—the noise and crowds and muddy wagons jamming Deadwood's main street, the bustle of the Grand Central Hotel, the gold dust tossed down on saloon bars to pay for whiskey—frightened the Hunkpapa Army scout Goose, who had watched the miner Horatio Nelson Ross shout himself hoarse on finding the first dime's worth of gold in French Creek in 1874. "For a few days," Goose remembered of Ross, "he could not be heard above a whisper."

To Goose only three years later, Deadwood seemed tense and dangerous. Formally enlisted as a U.S. Army scout a few months after the close of Custer's expedition, Goose was sometimes asked to carry Army dispatches from Fort Rice across the prairie to the Black Hills and Deadwood. On the plains he kept his distance from the huge wagon trains heading for the goldfields, sometimes four teams abreast. Even dressed in a scout's regulation military uniform Goose did not feel safe. "He was an Indian," he told Josephine Waggoner toward the end of his life, "and all Indians looked alike to the emigrants. They would just as soon shoot at a scout no matter what kind of clothes he had on."

But at Deadwood, Goose had no choice; to deliver his dispatches he had to enter the town. Everything had changed; the hills were teeming with white men, the game had disappeared, whole mountainsides had been stripped of their trees, and mud ran down into the valleys with every rain. But one thing had not changed since 1874: when Goose returned to Deadwood he found the whites still in the grip of unrestrained gold fever. "Every man he met was tense with excitement; everybody moved with hasty strides; the noise was confusing to him. Gun shots could be heard at all times, it seemed dangerous to sleep in a town like Deadwood."[5]

Crazy Horse rubbed Colonel Ranald Mackenzie the wrong way. Mackenzie was waiting to be replaced as commander at Camp Robinson, grumbling to his officers about the chief's "proud and almost contemptuous behavior" in the camp. The colonel considered Crazy Horse the most culpable of "Custer's brutal butchers" and made no secret of the fact that he would like to bring the chief down a peg or two—quickly accomplished, in his view, with "a dose of the Camp Robinson guard house, and the exercise afforded by attending upon the post water wagon."[6] Mackenzie's desire, thinly veiled, was to break and crush the chief.

"Stolid" and "silent" were words often used about Crazy Horse, but no one else called him contemptuous. That suggests Mackenzie felt personally slighted. The cause may have been a small incident not long after the chief's arrival, when Mackenzie summoned the leading men at the agency to a council. Crazy Horse sent word that he was ill and could not attend. To his brother-in-law Red Feather, the chief described the illness as "his tiredness." The word suggests sorrow or depression, not illness. But his absence irritated the colonel, who wanted to squeeze the Indians one more time for any rifles or pistols still held back. Mackenzie sent the chiefs away with an angry command to "go out and find those guns at once."

"Sick as he was," wrote a correspondent of the *Denver Daily Tribune*, probably one of Mackenzie's officers, "Crazy Horse went from tipi to tipi, consuming nearly the entire night, coaxing and commanding by turns, that if any guns could be found they must be turned in before daylight."[7]

News that the chief was sick spread through the agency. It was one of the first things George Wallihan learned after his arrival on May 15. Some said the chief had hovered for a time near death. Wallihan was unimpressed. The doctor's son made an instant diagnosis: "His illness was caused by over-eating and the sudden change from buffalo straight, and but little of that, to wheat bread, coffee, sugar, and strawberries and cream, which are furnished at this place of plenty, and it nearly killed him."[8]

Sick in body or spirit, Crazy Horse for the moment was the principal tourist attraction in northwest Nebraska, and the *Leader* wanted a Crazy Horse story. Wallihan had little interest in Indians. His father that summer took the trouble to write to Secretary of the Interior Carl Schurz to complain of the "bad faith and outright dishonesty . . . the swindling and robbery" of the Indian agents in charge of the Ute, but the doctor's son was unmoved by their plight. He did not like Indians. On first arriving at Red Cloud he wrote with disgust of the "wrinkled and frightful looking squaws" and their daughters, "the buxom Sioux lasses [who] lead a life of shame with young bucks and degraded white men," and of the "lazy bucks who follow one about begging for candy, canned fruit and crackers." Wallihan declared openly, "The more I see of Indians and Indian customs, the more I despise and detest the original inhabitants of this great continent."[9]

But Crazy Horse was the story of the day, and Wallihan soon arranged with the post trader, J. W. Dear, and Crook's chief scout, Frank Grouard, to pay a visit to the leading Oglala "in their various suburban residences located near the agency." Wallihan's party included two women—one of whom, "by the way, is unmarried." Her name was Ella. Wallihan noted that the chief was "still suffering" from his illness and left others to carry the burden of the conversation. Grouard introduced the party, and one by one, women with the rest, they shook hands with their hosts: "Maniacal Equine" and "Little Big Man, the blowhard, and several other chiefs of lesser note."[10] Introductions over, "all sat down to smoke," reported Wallihan. "The pipe was handed from mouth to mouth, the ladies taking their puff in order." The chief, noted for "keeping his mouth shut," was described by Wallihan as "quite ungracious" and "sullen." It was already common belief on the plains that Crazy Horse was the war leader who had defeated Custer, but it appears Wallihan asked nothing about that. He reserved his pen for describing the next visit on the agenda.

Red Cloud may have been deposed by General Crook seven months earlier, but Wallihan noted that he was "still acknowledged leader of all the reds." When the party of whites entered Red Cloud's lodge a favorite daughter was seated by his side. Wallihan's friend Ella asked the chief if she might take the place of honor, at which, Wallihan reports, "I saw a blush suffuse the bashful old fellow's phiz." At a word the daughter moved aside. While the pipe was passed and during the conversation that followed the chief flirted with "the fair white stranger . . . He smiled and joked with her, poked her in the ribs." This was the era of *Daisy Miller*, Henry James's novel about a new type of brash American girl who ignored convention, horrified their mothers, and dazzled men. It was evidently a Daisy Miller who smoked and joked with the chief. "She enjoyed the affair hugely," Wallihan reports, "until late in the evening." When she began to fidget, fuss, and scratch, Wallihan gently told her that she "might have 'taken on a small cargo of live insects' "—lice or fleas—while sitting with the chiefs.

This is Wallihan's sort of story: he satisfies the reader's curiosity about the wild Indians who had achieved the inconceivable—wiping out to the last man a strong force under the dashing Custer, a national hero of the late war. But Wallihan shaped his whole account to the sly conclusion that the Indians were lousy. The chief's real character and achievement

Wallihan seems to have ignored. He called Crazy Horse ungracious but failed to mention two gifts presented by the chief to his guests. To Ella, whom Wallihan married soon afterward, the chief gave the pipe which had passed around the circle, and to the young reporter he presented a ledger book containing eighteen drawings.[11]

The book is small—about three and a half by eight inches, the sort of book commonly used at military and trading posts for keeping accounts or taking inventory. Beginning in the 1860s, Plains Indians coveted these books as a source of drawing paper, using the blank pages to depict their war and hunting exploits, and sometimes drawing right over a page of sums or the names listed in a company roster. The cover of the Wallihan ledger book is marbleized board. A number of pages have been cut out, probably pages with writing on them. On the remaining pages are ten drawings of Plains Indians carrying weapons, stealing horses, charging enemies. Two depict battles with the Pawnee. In one a Sioux kills a Pawnee woman with a lance. A second shows a warrior charging with a cavalry saber in his left hand. Perhaps this was Man That Owns a Sword, appointed as one of the last Shirt Wearers of the Oglala at the side of Crazy Horse in 1868.

The drawings were made almost entirely with black and colored pencils; only a few strokes were done with pen and ink. Crazy Horse gave the book to Wallihan the day he visited the chiefs at the Red Cloud Agency in their "various suburban residences." With the help of Frank Grouard as interpreter, Crazy Horse explained his gift to the young reporter; the chief said that "it pictured the life of a famous warrior, but would not say that it was himself." If Wallihan thanked the chief he did not record the fact. Later, examining the book after the visit, Wallihan wrinkled his nose and noted that its pages gave off a strong whiff of "Indian odor." He tried to remove the smell but found that it "does not yield to fumigation." Forty years later, as he typed up a brief account of the gift, Wallihan drew the book to his nose and sniffed again. To Wallihan the odor was unmistakable: the smell of Indian.[12]

Wallihan met and talked with Crazy Horse only once, but he saw him a second time a few days later at a grand council called by General Crook, freshly arrived from Fort Laramie with two aides-de-camp and the telegraph operator turned reporter, John W. Ford of the *Chicago Times*. Crook had come to settle outstanding matters with the Indians. Chief among these was the location of their new agency. Most of the Cheyenne would be leaving in a few days for the Indian Territory, but the Sioux had flatly rejected that proposal, and were no keener on moving east to the Missouri. Nevertheless, Crook was confident he would sort things out with the Sioux. "I have made a thorough study of their character and proclivities," he told Wallihan in an interview before the council.

> The Sioux are by far the most tractable Indians I have ever dealt with . . . I find them easy to manage when the proper method is pursued, and I anticipate no further trouble with them. They must be talked to frequently, as they are like children, and need constant care and guidance.[13]

Crook enjoyed his big councils with the leading chiefs of the Oglala and the Brulé, and a huge crowd gathered on Friday, May 25, 1877, for the grand council on a flat near the Red Cloud Agency. "Old Spot," as Wallihan called the chief of the Brulé, had arrived the previous evening with his leading men. They spent the night in the village of Crazy Horse, then rode in all together the following morning. About midday Lieutenant Clark paraded his three companies of mounted scouts, led by their sergeants, Crazy Horse, Red Cloud, and White Thunder. Later the sergeants and other chiefs on their horses approached Crook, dismounted, and stepped forward. Conspicuous among them was Little Big Man, who liked to appear on grand occasions dressed only in moccasins and breechcloth, with his battle scars marked in red paint.

Before the talking came handshaking. The chiefs were received by General Crook and Colonel Mackenzie.[14] When Crazy Horse came forward to take the general's hand he did something remarkable and unusual: he knelt before him on the ground. Why he did this is unknown. When Sioux scouts came in to report on important matters like the location of enemies or buffalo they promised to speak the truth and sometimes knelt; perhaps it was in this spirit that Crazy Horse knelt before Crook.

"His example was followed by most of the others," Wallihan reported at the time. Four months later, describing this moment again, Wallihan tacked on a new detail: after the handshake Crazy Horse "rose and slunk away like a whipped cur." The reporter's intent to insult and diminish is so clear that we might dismiss the claim outright if it were not confirmed by Colonel Luther P. Bradley, who told his mother in a letter that Crazy Horse "kneeled at Gen. Crook's feet in token of submission." John Ford reported no kneeling, remarking only that "[a]ll the Indians, in speaking today, squatted on the ground in their peculiar Indian fashion."[15]

The council was an all-afternoon affair of numerous speeches with the long preambles and frequent oratorical flourishes favored by the Sioux. No one surpassed Red Cloud's mastery of the Sioux high style. "Three Stars, listen!" he boomed out. "I am going to talk to you . . . Look at me! I have been a white man the last six months. Look at all the men standing around! They have all got children . . . My friend, help me! I want your help!"

What followed in this and similar speeches, according to Crook's aide Lieutenant Walter S. Schuyler, was "the usual complaining of broken promises on the part of Commissioners and the customary begging for money on account of roads through the reservation." But the real thrust of discussion was quite different: the speakers all wanted a home in their own country, somewhere in the north along the Powder or the Tongue. Crazy Horse spoke first but briefly:

> General, you sent us tobacco . . . From the time I received it, I kept coming in and toward the post . . . While coming this way, I picked out a place and put a stick in the ground for a place to live hereafter, where there is plenty of game. All of these relations of mine who are here, were with me when I picked out this place. I would like to have them go back with me and stay there with me. This is all I have to say.[16]

"I don't want to move," said Little Wound. "I almost cried when we moved before."

"Bear Butte is a country to look ahead to," said Young Man Afraid of His Horses. "Over there in that country there is plenty of game. We can raise our children there."

"I want a place somewhere in my own country, north, where we can get some game, where we can run around and see my people hunt buffalo," said High Bear. "We want a large agency so we can be free."

"We want to move north," said No Water.

After many similar speeches all making the same point, Red Dog, who frequently acted as spokesman for Red Cloud, interrupted. "I want you Indians to hold on," he said. "We want the man to give an answer before anything more is said to him. Too much talk confuses white men."

The man was General Crook.

> My friends [said the general] I have had councils with your young men who first went out with me, and they had asked me for help. I told them that I would help them if they helped me . . . we will go to Washington and there I will help you . . .

You asked for a reservation in the upper country. This is taken down and will be sent to Washington. I cannot decide these things for myself. They must be decided in Washington. The commissioner promised he would let some of you go and talk to him at Washington . . . I will try and be in Washington myself, so I can hear both sides.[17]

When the talking was done, Iron Hawk of Crazy Horse's band blessed the feast that had been prepared. By the estimate of Billy Garnett, he spoke for ten straight minutes. Then the customary delicacy was handed around: dog. This time Clark quailed; he paid an Indian a dollar to eat his portion and offered to do the same for Crook.

"I can eat anything the Indians can eat," the general said. He proved it. "Nice," he commented.

The Indians were watching the white officers and Garnett was watching the Indians. He noted that they were surprised to see Clark refuse what the general accepted. Next day, Schuyler cabled headquarters in Omaha to say all had gone well. "Everything was said in a very submissive manner," he explained.[18]

During his first weeks at the Red Cloud Agency it was evident that Crazy Horse had determined on peace. He had one overriding goal: to secure an agency in the north. To achieve this goal he expected to go to Washington with the other chiefs. He intended to live like the whites. He enlisted as a scout in the Army and accepted the rank of sergeant. He met on several occasions with newspaper correspondents. He gave presents to his white visitors. But whites often did not know what to make of him.

Crook's aide John Bourke was one of the first to meet Crazy Horse after his arrival, and his description of their brief exchange is filled with tension and contradiction. On the very day of the chief's arrival Bourke went to see him in the company of Frank Grouard, who had arranged to take Crazy Horse to dinner. They found the chief sitting in front of his lodge while two women busied themselves roasting coffee and preparing food. Someone had told Bourke that Crazy Horse at the Little Bighorn had killed one of Custer's men with a stone war club while the soldier struggled to control his horse. This fact appears to have colored the impression of the chief which formed in Bourke's mind.

Frank is the only one whom Crazy Horse seems at all glad to see [he wrote in his diary]. To the rest of the world he is sullen and gloomy. His face is quiet, rather morose, dogged, tenacious, and resolute. His expression is rather melancholic . . . Crazy Horse remained seated on the ground, but when Frank called his name, *Tsunka Witco*, he looked up and gave me a hearty grasp of the hand. He looks quite young, not over thirty years old, is lithe and sinewy and has a wound in his face.[19]

Spare as Bourke's account is, it still conveys two things about the chief: the brooding power and authority of his person, and his willingness to lean forward, reach out, speak a greeting, and shake a white man's hand. Bourke did not come away fearing that war would soon be renewed.

A few days after Bourke's only meeting with the chief, Billy Garnett invited Crazy Horse, Little Big Man, and several others to join him for dinner in the small, three-room house where Garnett was living with his second wife, Emma Mills. By custom the Sioux in their lodges sat on the ground and ate with their fingers, sometimes aided by a knife, but in Garnett's house Crazy Horse and the others sat in chairs at table before a setting of plate, mug, knife, and fork. The agency chiefs often ate with military officers and other whites. A journalist passing through at this time noted that Spotted Tail "understands perfectly the use of the four-pronged fork and napkin." Crazy Horse told Garnett that he, too, "would begin to learn the use of the fork at the table." He did not say he wanted to do it. "He said he had got to do it," Garnett recalled.[20]

Crazy Horse also asked Garnett about the trip to Washington—not the purpose of it, but the practical logistics of it. How would they travel? Where did they stay when they got there? What did they eat and drink? Garnett had been to Washington two years earlier with the big delegation led by Red Cloud, so he knew the answers to these questions and could describe the boardinghouse where the Indians put up and the kind of rooms where they met with the president. Perhaps he added a few warnings against the trouble and temptations that came an Indian's way in Washington. Whiskey was the big one.

Use of the fork was soon followed by use of the chair. Crazy Horse seemed to pick up quickly the fact that in crowded meetings the man who sat in the chair was in charge of the room. The chief clerk at the agency that summer, Charles P. Jordan, remarked that when Crazy Horse came to see the agent, James Irwin, "he was always accompanied by a body-guard of men," as many as six or eight in all. Crazy Horse did little talking, but he sat in a chair. The men with him sat on the floor, three or four on each side.

Crazy Horse was notoriously a man of few words; people thought of him as a warrior, not a maker of treaties or a settler of disputes. But in the early summer of 1877 he was thinking and acting in a political way, discussing agency matters with Irwin, meeting regularly with Clark, whom Crook had placed in charge of the Indians. The traveling correspondent who noted Spotted Tail's mastery of the four-pronged fork was invited by Clark to join him in a meeting with Indians one morning in early June. Under discussion was a growing problem at the agency: the frequent theft of Indian horses and cattle by white men who drove them north for sale in the Black Hills. Whose job it was to chase down these horse thieves was unclear. The state of Nebraska would not do it, the military was not supposed to do it, and the Indians were not permitted to do it. In the event, a compromise was reached: the Army aided by Indian scouts trailed the thieves until they caught up with them, then called in the civilian or federal authorities. Dealing with horse thieves was a political, not a military, question, and the status of Crazy Horse in the discussion was plainly visible. Clark had called a large group of chiefs to his rooms at the western end of the row of officers' quarters at Camp Robinson.

> Lieutenant Clark, sitting on the rim of an office chair, with his feet on the seat, high enough to see and be seen, [was] talking with the Indians in the sign language that is universal to all Indians. Sitting near him in a chair was Crazy Horse. Squatting on the floor and passing around the pipe were Black Coal, Yellow Bear, Swift Bear, Little Wound, American Horse, Young Man Afraid of his Horses, and perhaps 25 others of lesser note.[21]

The man who made sure to take a chair in long meetings with Clark did not neglect the other whites who had a measure of control over his fate. The morning after the big council with Crook, Crazy Horse was on hand at nine o'clock to greet Colonel Luther Bradley when he arrived at Camp Robinson on the stage to take command of the post from Mackenzie. All the leading chiefs were present, but Bradley in a letter mentioned only one. "I had an introduction to Crazy Horse and a hand shake," he wrote to his wife, Ione. "He is a young, slender and mild-mannered fellow but he is evidently the leader of his band."[22]

Something like a policy was forming in the mind of the leader of the Hunkpatila. Crook had promised the northern Indians they could go north to hunt during the summer, and Crazy Horse was determined to do so. In mid-June, during one of his frequent meetings with Lieutenant Clark, Crazy Horse reminded him of Crook's promise and said he wanted to go out in about a month's time—around the second week in July. The proposed trip to Washington was also much discussed. Clark's strategy for "working" the Indians included soft assurances that Crook had a high regard for the chief, that a successful move to the new agency would bring new authority and status to Crazy Horse, that all could be arranged with the president in Washington.

The rumor in the Indian camps was that Crazy Horse was to be the new head chief of the Sioux, and it is possible that Clark said as much in so many words. But more probably it was presented as an if-then proposition: if the chief went to Washington, and if he reached agreement on a new location for the Oglala agency, and if he took his people there in the fall, *then*, surely, General Crook would recognize him as the leading man of the Sioux. These flattering promises, intended to make the chief pliable, seem to have worried him instead. He told White Rabbit, a member of his band who had come in to the agency with the rest in May, that he knew "the talk that he was to be made chief over all was causing intense jealousy."[23]

What Crazy Horse wanted was simple and clear: to take his people on a buffalo hunt in the north, and to establish an agency on Beaver Creek in the Tongue River country. After that he would go to Washington with the other chiefs. General Crook had promised the hunt and he had promised to help with the location of the agency. There seemed to be no room for misunderstanding. The chief discussed what he wanted with his friends Short Bull and He Dog. "He said to me, 'First, I want them to place my agency on Beaver Creek west of the Black Hills,' " He Dog remembered, " 'Then I will go to Washington—for your benefit, for my benefit, and for the benefit of all of us. And that is the only reason why I will go there.' " But in Short Bull's view this simple desire planted the seed of trouble.

> Crazy Horse wanted to have the agency established first, and then he would go to Washington. The officers wanted him to go to Washington first. The difference of whether Crazy Horse should go to Washington before or after the site of the agency was settled upon brought on all the trouble, little by little.[24]

But for the moment things ran smoothly. Crazy Horse spoke often with Clark, called Wapostan Ska (White Hat) by the Indians, and twice he sent scouts from his band north to look for the last band still loose on the prairie—several hundred Miniconjou whose chief, Lame Deer, a cousin of Crazy Horse, had been killed in a scrap with General Miles in early May. The scouts found trails but no Indians, and said they might be heading east toward the agencies on the Missouri. The military officers all believed the Sioux war was over for good. Bradley, the new commander at Camp Robinson, was painting buildings and planting trees to brighten the place up. The wife of Lieutenant Jesse Lee, Lucy, was running a school for Indian children at the Spotted Tail Agency, where many northern Indians had settled, including Crazy Horse's friend Touch the Clouds. On visits to the agency, Crazy Horse sometimes stopped in at George Jewett's store, where one of the part-time clerks was the mixed-blood scout Charles Tackett, who had married the twenty-year-old Susan Bordeaux, a niece of the Brulé chief Swift Bear. On a visit to the store Susan's mother-in-law, a Brulé Sioux, once pointed out Crazy Horse to the girl.

> He was a very handsome man [she remembered] . . . He was not so dark; he had hazel eyes, nice, long light-brown hair. His braids were wrapped in fur. He was partly wrapped in a broad-cloth blanket; his leggins were also navy-blue broadcloth, his moccasins were beaded. He was above the medium height and was slender.[25]

In mid-June, Tackett was called away from storekeeping to go out with a military detachment looking for the killers of a mail carrier whose body had been found about twenty miles north of Camp Sheridan on the road to Deadwood. The soldiers were commanded by Lieutenant Frederick Schwatka and Tackett's job was to interpret for the scouts, Fast Thunder, Good Voice, and the recently surrendered High Bear. It was not Indians but white horse thieves who had killed the mail carrier, a young man from New Jersey, Gilbert Fosdick, who had come west hoping to make his fortune in the goldfields. Lieutenant Schwatka delivered the killer to the authorities at Camp Sheridan, but within a day or two orders were received to release him for lack of evidence.

Some days later, Clark arrived at Camp Sheridan with Billy Garnett to sign up scouts for new ninety-day tours of duty. Along with a hundred others, High Bear, Good Voice, and Fast Thunder agreed to serve through September, and made their marks on the enlistment papers. Clark had learned to trust Fast Thunder, and he was promoted to sergeant. Schwatka, meanwhile, had been told that a big sun dance was planned for the end of the month in Crazy Horse's village. He wanted to go, and after some palaver Spotted Tail and Swift Bear told him it had been arranged.[26]

22

"It made his heart heavy and sad to think of these things."

CRAZY HORSE MAY HAVE vowed to use a fork and learned to sit in a chair, but he did not abandon Oglala ways and in June 1877 his village presided over one of the largest sun dances ever held by the Sioux. A sun dance was not a casual affair. Preparations properly began when snow was still on the ground. One or more medicine men would begin to instruct those who would take part—men who sought the help of Tunkasila, or wished to give thanks for some special favor. Fast Thunder had danced when his only sister survived a serious illness. Red Fox danced after the war party on which he first killed an enemy. Black Wolf danced when the women and children escaped from soldiers by safely crossing the Platte River in 1865. The medicine man Sorrel Horse, who impressed John Bourke with his feats of magic, danced with heavy buffalo skulls attached to the skin of his arms and shoulders—he showed Bourke the scars. Hunts the Enemy cited his own sun dance scars as proof his word could be trusted. Preparation for the sun dance might involve prayer, fasting, the ceremony of the sweat bath, committing no violent acts, or forgoing sexual relations. Left Heron said that only a *wicasa waste*—a good man—could preside over the sun dance.

"A good man is one who had no bad thoughts or desires," he explained, "who is not cruel to animals and treats them as human beings. A person like this would be chosen to paint his hands red in the Sun Dance." Only a man with his hands painted red could touch or raise the sun dance pole, bless the dancers, or pierce their flesh. Every sun dance was a little different, according to the understanding of the man in charge, and of course the Sioux calendar allowed for setting no invariable date. Instead, the dance was held when the time was right, and the time was right, all agreed,

When the buffalo are fat
When new sprouts of sage are a span long

When chokecherries are ripening
When the moon is rising as the Sun is going down.[1]

June was usually the month chosen, but not always. In 1877, the four-day celebration of the sun dance held by the village of Crazy Horse began on the 26th of June. The dates are clear, but many other details about this sun dance are difficult to pin down. The *Cheyenne Leader* reported that the sun dance was run by Kill Eagle, a Blackfoot Sioux who had been at the Little Bighorn and soon after provided whites with one of the first Indian accounts of the battle. Many years later an Oglala named Dana Long Wolf said that the leader was a man named Fool Heart, with the help of three assistants. Others, whose fathers had witnessed the sun dance, said the man with red hands who pierced the flesh of the dancers was Fast Thunder. It is possible that one, all, or none of these men took part. Similar confusion attaches to the number and identity of those who danced. Colonel Bradley, the new commander at Camp Robinson, said that seven dancers were pierced on the fourth and final day. Lieutenant Schwatka estimated the number at "six to twelve." Lieutenant Clark, who took a close interest in everything the Indians did, reports that in the beginning three men vowed to dance but that ten in all took part on the day of piercing. Clark did not record any of the dancers' names, but many years later a son of Chase in Morning, brother of an Oglala killed at the Little Bighorn, reported the names of five dancers—all identified as blood cousins of Crazy Horse. The dancers named by James Chase in Morning were Eagle Thunder, Walking Eagle, and three well-known brothers who were all close companions of Crazy Horse: Kicking Bear, Black Fox, and Flying Hawk.[2]

The purpose of the sun dancers was to gain power, and their method was to endure pain and shed blood as a sacrifice. It was the blood that would make the deepest impression on Lieutenant Clark. The Oglala Left Heron said the sun dance was given in a vision to a medicine man named Iglukati (Stretches Himself), who conducted the first dance about seventy years after White Buffalo Woman taught the Sioux the proper use of the sacred pipe. Left Heron also noted that Iglukati received his vision about thirty-five years before the Sioux first encountered white men, which the Sioux winter counts generally date as occurring in the late 1700s.[3] If these dates are correct then the sun dance witnessed by Clark, Bradley, and Schwatka was about a hundred years old.

Variants of the plains sun dance were encountered by whites on the upper Missouri in the 1830s, but many decades passed before anthropologists obtained a full description of all the prayers, songs, and beliefs incorporated in the dance. Clark was one of the first educated whites to witness and describe a sun dance, and he may have been the very first to have gone out on the first day of the ceremony to watch the moving of the sun dance pole—a carefully selected cottonwood tree, perhaps seventy-five feet tall, which branched at just the right distance above the ground. Billy Garnett was not surprised to find him on the scene. "He was quick to observe and get into anything brewing," said Garnett of the lieutenant. Clark brought with him not only a lively curiosity but the authority of his position as commander of the three companies of Indian scouts, and as the special representative of General Crook.

Crazy Horse's entire village of about a thousand turned out for the felling and moving of the sun dance pole on June 26. "Spring was radiant in her beauty," Clark recorded, "and the savages decorated themselves and their ponies with crowns and shields of wild clematis and other foliage." Old women howled, chanted, and sang as they crowded in around the designated tree while men distinguished for bravery approached and each took a swing or two at the tree with an ax. These men then handed sticks to the old women, each representing the gift of a pony. Thus blessed, the old women, Clark says, "chanted and danced more vigorously and hideously than before."

Young women beautifully dressed in elk-tooth dresses also struck at the tree, which was actually felled by the headmen in charge of the ceremony. Using ropes, the headmen lifted up the tree and started in the direction of the sun dance ground a few miles away. But they did not go far before they lifted the tree onto the running gear of a wagon. Once unknown, wagons had now become common at the agencies; every leading man wanted the government to give him one. Sitting near Clark was an elderly Oglala who said he did not like to see a wagon used to move the tree. This was not the old way. He explained to the lieutenant that "he was afraid the Great Spirit looking down would see it, and would not like it."

On the first day of the ceremony a kind of sham battle was traditionally staged as the sun dance pole approached the special camp prepared as a site. In 1877, according to Colonel Bradley, this camp was about seven miles north of the Red Cloud Agency on a flat near the White River. There, perhaps 250 lodges of the Crazy Horse people were arranged in a grand circle about a third of a mile in diameter. In the center of that grand

circle was the sun dance arbor itself, a structure made of poles and covered with branches to form a kind of circular gallery big enough to shade
the several thousand people who would gather beneath it. In the center of
the ground surrounded by this gallery, about a hundred feet across, the
sun dance pole would be erected.

But before this happened an effigy of a man was placed on the spot
where the pole was to go—or perhaps just outside the dance ground
on the approach to it; Lieutenant Clark and Billy Garnett, who both
describe what happened next, are not quite clear on the point. On this
occasion, Garnett tells us, the mixed-bloods (including himself) and the
"friendly Indians" were assigned to represent one side in the sham battle, while the warriors in Crazy Horse's village took the other. Perhaps
inevitably, it was not just any generic battle that was reenacted, but the
Custer fight which had taken place almost exactly a year earlier. Clark sat
on a nearby hill and watched as the sham battle commenced. Both sides
on horseback, with shouts and war cries, were to rush on the effigy and
touch it, in effect counting coup, showing their prowess and bravery, and
then engage in a running "fight," lightly touching instead of striking vio-
lently at each other as they would in a genuine battle.

But almost immediately the sham battle veered toward a real one. The
Crazy Horse Indians with their war clubs and bows charged right up to
the mixed-bloods and "friendly Indians" and struck them solid, painful
blows. Anger flared up in Garnett and the others. Pistols were drawn. As
the mounted men charged each other with yells and gunshots, Clark felt
he was watching the battle of a year ago—the same men wheeling about
the flat, led by the same chief, had swept in and overwhelmed Custer and
his soldiers. Garnett felt it too; something real had been unleashed. The
Crazy Horse warriors were "killing" the friendlies as they had killed
Custer. Real killing might have followed if Clark had not rushed down
the hill just as the mixed-bloods, with their pistols drawn, were driving
the Crazy Horse people away from the sun dance ground. Clark's sudden
arrival in the center of things, Garnett recorded, "stopped the firing and
prevented what might have been a serious affair."[4]

Clark remained in the middle of things for the whole of the next three
days, his curiosity intact but his conscience under assault. He was not
ready for what he saw. On the second day he watched the setting of the
sun dance pole and on the third day he was present for the customary
gathering of parents with small children at the foot of the pole. Blood was
the coin of the sun dance. Iglukati had ruled that all should take part.

"Even the children had to have their ears pierced," said Left Heron. Clark saw no sense or beauty in it. Custom said that the parents of the children must not comfort them until the piercing had been accomplished. What the medicine men with their knives did to "these little wretches," Clark wrote, was nothing more than "cutting holes in the ears of the babies."

On the fourth day the shedding of blood reached its climax when the dancers were "mutilated . . . in this horrible worship called a Sun Dance." With the word "horrible" he judges the event before he has described it. Throughout the day Clark busied himself with fieldwork, asked questions, and took notes. One of the Sioux explained to him that the whole of the sun dance ground and its enclosing gallery should be seen as a church. The grass and the sage tied to the pole represented Unci, Grandmother Earth. A cross was drawn at the foot of the pole to represent the sun and the stars. A careful observer might see that every particular of the Sioux view of the world, and of man's relationship to the unseen power called Wakan Tanka, were incorporated into the sun dance. Clark acted the earnest student, but it was "the horrible"—the cutting, the bleeding, and the suffering—that impressed him.

How many whites gathered to watch on the fourth and final day is unknown, but Garnett, Clark, Schwatka, and Bradley were all there, and we may imagine that they sat together. There was only one member of the Christian clergy in that corner of Nebraska: the Reverend William J. Cleveland, who ministered to the Brulé at the Spotted Tail Agency. He may have been present and sitting with the officers. The day was clear, but violent winds from the south had been whipping up the white dust of the bare earth for more than a week—"dust storms that beat anything I ever saw," wrote Bradley in his diary. The winds were so strong on the 29th that some whites gave up plans to attend the dance and never left Camp Robinson at all.[5]

But the Indians were not deterred. All the bands had gathered for the dance and the crowd was immense—Clark thought it reached six thousand. The sun dance pole had been painted with the colors of the four directions: black, red, yellow, and white. The upper branches shimmered with colored strips of cloth, pinches of tobacco tied in bits of cloth, medicine bags, and the tattered remnants of two silhouettes cut from rawhide of a man and a buffalo bull, both with exaggerated sexual organs. The air was filled with singing, chanting, and the high ululating cry of the women.

The shedding of blood began about two o'clock in the afternoon when the leader of the dance and his assistants cut small bits of flesh from the upper arms and shoulders of about twenty-five young men. In addition to the blood which ran freely down their arms the bodies of these young men were painted. "Later," wrote Clark, "the women kinsfolk, wives, sisters and sweethearts came in singing, and had their arms slashed by the medicine man's knife, thus endeavoring to support with their suffering the pain and torture undergone by the men."

Finally it was the turn of the dancers themselves. Each had selected the form of sacrifice he was to make—some to drag buffalo skulls attached to the skin pierced above their shoulder blades, others to be pierced in the chest or back and then tied to the sun dance pole by leather thongs. Schwatka describes the procedure in fullest detail. When the moment came for piercing, the dancers lay on the ground, head nearest to the sun dance pole.

> Each one of the young men presented himself to a medicine man, who took between his thumb and forefinger a fold of the loose skin of the breast, about half-way between the nipple and the collar bone, lifted it as high as possible, and then ran a very narrow-bladed but sharp knife through the skin underneath the hand. In the aperture thus made, and before the knife was withdrawn, a strong skewer of bone, about the size of a carpenter's pencil was inserted. Then the knife blade was taken out, and over the projection of this skewer, backwards and forwards, alternately right and left, was thrown a figure-of-eight noose with a strong thong of dressed skin. This was tied to a long skin rope fastened, at its other extremity, to the top of the sun pole in the center of the arena. Both breasts are similarly punctured, the thongs from each converging and joining the rope which hangs from the pole. The whole object of the devotee is to break loose from these fetters.

Breaking loose meant tearing through the pierced skin. The sliver of bone "about the size of a carpenter's pencil" says much; it was thick enough to withstand great stress, and needed to be, because the whole weight of the body of the dancers would be thrown against this bone piercing the skin of the chest.

When the dancers were ready they were led out to the end of the thongs attaching them to the sun dance pole. Drummers began to beat and the singing rose in intensity. Clenched between the teeth of each dancer was a whistle made from the ulnar bone of the wing of an eagle, and the high *scree* of these whistles was added to the din. With a mirror in his hand the dancer reflected the light of the sun. Then he pulled back against the thong attached to his chest, gently at first, according to Schwatka, "to get him used to the horrible pain." Between whistles he shouts out and cries—"huge drops of perspiration pour down his greasy, painted skin." In Clark's description one can almost hear the dancer's gasp as he threw himself full force back against the thongs, trying but failing to rip through the skin. "One or two were very weak-kneed, heart-sick with fear and fasting," he wrote. "If I ever saw regret, it was on their painted faces."

Colonel Bradley, a different kind of man, said the dancers went at it "with right good will." He found the whole experience "very interesting." Schwatka in contrast continues almost brutally explicit. As a dancer threw himself back, he writes, "every muscle stands out on his body in tortuous ridges, his swaying frame . . . being convulsed with shudders." But tearing the skin does not come easy.

> The wonderful strength and extensibility of the human skin is most forcibly and fearfully displayed in the strong struggles of the quivering victims. I have seen these bloody pieces of bone stretched to such a length from the devotee that his outstretched arms in front of him barely allow his fingers to touch them.

How long does it take a dancer to break free? Schwatka says, "generally in two or three hours." Bradley thought not so long—"from fifteen minutes to an hour and a quarter." It was in Clark that the horror ran deepest. "Horrible torture," he called it. He shrank from describing "this horrible ceremony in detail." But he watched till the end. After one man fainted his friends came forward and ripped him free. In the whole process Clark saw not just courage and endurance but anger tinged with despair. He seems to have sensed a terrible intensity of feeling in the dancers, something born of the moment when they gave up their guns, their ponies, and their freedom. The dance shouted defiance, a readiness, even a longing to die.

At about this time the Cheyenne chief known as Ice, also called White Bull, told Clark it hurt to think of what was happening to his people—"The spoilation of his country, the driving away of all the game, and the crowding out of existence of his people." White Bull said "it made his heart heavy and sad to think of these things." It was probably this same man who described to Clark the agony of making his mark on papers that sold his country: "The clouds pressed down close above me, and the earth seemed to tremble when the first paper was signed."[6]

Like the Cheyenne, the Oglala knew their world was slipping away. In describing the suffering of the Crazy Horse dancers, Clark cites another sun dance he witnessed a few years later among the Ponca in the Indian Territory, where they had been forcibly removed to make room for the Sioux in their old home along the Missouri River. The Ponca, too, were "suffering great sadness at the loss of their country." One man insisted that the incisions be made very deep, so deep he could not break free on his own. He instructed his companions to hitch a pony to his legs and drag him away from the pole by brute force—"Which was done," Clark writes as if slamming his fist on the table. "Another cut off his little finger and ate it."

Clark, Garnett, Schwatka, and Bradley while watching this spectacle all independently thought of the same thing: these were the Indians who had killed Custer—"the very ones," Bradley wrote in his diary. A year and four days had passed since the shock of the greatest defeat ever suffered by whites on the plains. Clark had talked to Crazy Horse about the Custer fight. The lieutenant was under instruction to gather from the Indians an account of the battle. He knew that the chief believed he was protected by his magic—"he could not be killed by a bullet." The chief told him that at the Little Bighorn he "had two ponies shot and killed under him." Watching the dancers, Clark in his imagination saw the chief "in his demon-like way" riding into the confusion of Custer's men to kill them with his club or his gun. Three hundred men had ridden into the Red Cloud Agency with Crazy Horse; all or almost all of them had been at the Little Bighorn. They had not been driven into the agency. The victors of the Little Bighorn thought things over, debated in council, and chose to come in. The Oglala sun dancers were not men who had been crushed, broken, or whipped. They glistened with sweat, courage, pride, and anger.

From the sun dance on June 29, 1877, we may date the beginning of the erosion of Lieutenant Clark's confidence that he knew how to work the Indians.

23

"They were killed like wolves."

THE SUN DANCERS FROM the Crazy Horse band were still preparing to sacrifice their flesh in Nebraska when General George Crook started north for the Big Horn Mountains of Wyoming with his old West Point friend, Civil War rival and now commander, General Philip Sheridan. Keeping them company were a dozen officers, most of whom were friends or aides-de-camp of the two generals. All traveled well equipped, with fly rods and sporting rifles. When a reporter in Cheyenne asked the purpose of the excursion, Sheridan answered simply, "Hunting and fishing."

Numbering a hundred in all, the group was big enough to defend itself, but Crook said there was no danger of Indian attack. Finding the way through the Big Horns, not fighting, was the task of Crook's favorite guides, Frank Grouard and Baptiste Pourier, who also served as interpreters for a contingent of Oglala and Brulé scouts. The latter had all been enlisted by Lieutenant Clark, and several were veterans of the campaign against Crazy Horse. Among them were Charging Bear, captured the previous fall at Slim Buttes, hostile then but trusted now; Lone Bear, who had been sent as a spy to Crazy Horse's camp late the previous fall; and Hunts the Enemy, leader of the first delegation sent out to talk peace with Crazy Horse in January. On this trip with Crook, Hunts the Enemy would take a new name; henceforward he would be known as Man That Owns a Sword, after his dead brother.[1]

The party gathered at Camp Brown in the Wyoming Territory at the end of June, then headed north in a gay mood on the first day of July 1877. Five days out the scouts discovered a herd of buffalo and all gave chase. Lieutenant Bourke with great effort and many shots finally downed an old bull. While he was cutting out the tongue, heart, and some doubtless stringy steaks, three of the Oglala scouts, Sorrel Horse, Sword, and

Charging Bear, passed them on the way back to camp, "their ponies heavily laden with meat and fat" from sixteen buffalo they had killed.

So things went on this leisurely jaunt. The country was lively with game—thousands of buffalo one day, herds of elk and antelope the next, fish teeming in the creeks and rivers. The Oglala scouts all knew the country well; for decades they had passed through it coming and going on their way to steal horses from the Shoshones. To Bourke they pointed out a "medicine rock," one of the big sandstone boulders used by passing Indians to draw figures of "horses, elk, mountain sheep etc.," all full of meaning to other Indians who later paused to study the drawings. Seven years earlier, on his way to the Shoshone country with He Dog and High Backbone, Crazy Horse had hesitated at just such an inscription rock, perhaps even the very one shown to Bourke. The drawings changed according to the light and the weather. In 1870, Crazy Horse felt the omens were bad and wanted to turn back, but High Backbone taunted him: "What did we come for?" Frank Grouard and the Oglala with Crook's party all would have known this story of the war party that ended with the death of High Backbone, but it does not seem that any of them told it to Bourke.[2]

This was the kind of country Crook loved to amble through, keeping an eye out for game and riding so far ahead of the company that he might be alone. The Indians liked it in the same way for the same reasons—time alone and good hunting. The big excursion was accompanied from time to time by white miners, keeping close for protection, but they need not have worried. For the first time in a century there were almost no Sioux roaming through the northern country, perhaps none at all; they had been driven into the reservations, save a few who had gone north to Canada with Sitting Bull, and a remnant of Lame Deer's band, which sent word it would surrender after a final buffalo hunt.

Generals Sheridan and Crook and their party had the whole magnificence to themselves. Bourke faithfully recorded what the excursionists shot or caught in the rivers and streams. As they were riding along the bank of Shell Creek one day, traveling generally north and east in the direction of the Little Bighorn River, a black bear suddenly burst across the trail heading for the water. Frank Grouard broke the bear's back with a rifle shot, then Sheridan shot him twice without apparent effect. It was now Bourke's turn; he missed twice, then hit the bear in the head. They took the skin and paws and abandoned the rest. The meat, Bourke noted in his diary, smelled too strongly of wild onions—the *tsimpsila* which was often the first fresh green thing the Sioux ate after the end of winter. On the day of the big fight at the Little Bighorn the year before many of the women had gone out in the morning to dig for *tsimpsila*. But it was game everybody was after on the journey with Crook and Sheridan. One morning the scouts killed three elk but took away only the hindquarters. The next day they killed twenty-seven elk. "A great waste," Bourke noted. "On this march we have left on the ground four times as much meat as we took for consumption."[3]

The travelers were in no hurry. Plenty of time was devoted to hunting, fishing, climbing in the hills, and lounging about the camp while they waited for another splendid feed laid out by the black cook, Clay—"our Ethiopian chief de cuisine," Bourke called him. One dinner included elk steaks, boiled ham, potatoes, green peas, tomatoes, and corn bread with jelly, the whole accompanied by beer in bottles from Denver and a bottle of red wine brought along by Lieutenant Homer Wheeler, who had passed this way earlier in June, after a trip to the Custer battlefield. On the earlier trip, Wheeler and Colonel Sanford Kellogg had gone up to the battleground on the Little Bighorn to rebury some of the enlisted men who died with Custer. The two officers were now leading Crook and Sheridan back to the battle site to give the generals a chance to walk the ground and gain some sense of what had happened.

Editorialists in the western newspapers referred to the battle in the main as "the Custer Massacre," but military men called it "the Custer fight." A massacre in the strict sense it certainly was not. Custer, after all, had forced the battle by attacking the Indians. Some officers mourned the loss of Custer as a friend; others thought him careless and a fool. It was not simply Custer's defeat but the death of every man in his immediate command that prompted the continuing hunt for an explanation. The obvious question, troubling to every officer in the frontier military, was how an experienced cavalry commander with a score of major victories to his credit in the Civil War, followed by nearly a decade of fighting Indians on the plains, had managed to blunder so completely.

But General Crook took a yet closer interest. He had been roughly handled in the newspapers for his failure at the Rosebud a week before Custer was killed. Crook had sound reasons for his retreat back to Goose Creek, but many now blamed him for leaving Custer to face the hostiles alone. Crook's pride was especially tender on one point: whispered claims that he had been whipped by Crazy Horse at the Rosebud. In addition, many of his officers thought the general at one point during the battle came close to blundering as badly as Custer himself. Some of the Indians thought so too, including the lately surrendered Crazy Horse. He had said so in May to the part-time news correspondent John W. Ford, sent to report on the chief's surrender by the *Chicago Times*.

Ford was one of the many convenient pens, civilians along with military officers, who wrote when chance allowed for leading newspapers of the day in Chicago, New York, Denver, Omaha, and small towns all over the West. Being on the scene was the first requirement. In his early thirties, recently married and a new father, Ford had been working at Fort Laramie as the telegraph operator since April 1874, salaried at $100 per month. Lieutenant Bourke met him at Fort Laramie in February 1876 when he stopped for a night while the officers and ladies of the post were staging a popular play of the day, *Faint Heart Ne'er Won Fair Lady*. Bourke cited Ford for a strong performance, and it appears the telegraphist generally had a dramatic turn.

Later that summer, when the first reports of the fight at the Rosebud were brought into Fort Laramie, Ford hurried them over to the quarters of Captain Andrew Burt, where he read the news to Mrs. Burt and her friend Cynthia Capron. Ford's audience was bigger two weeks later, early in July, when it was his lot to deliver first word of Custer's disaster to the officers of Fort Laramie. It was the custom of the post commander, Colonel Luther Bradley, to meet every morning at about nine with his assembled officers in the adjutant's office. On the morning of Wednesday, July 5, as news of the disaster came in over the wire, Ford sent Bradley a hastily penciled note saying he would bring an important dispatch to the meeting as soon as it had been transcribed. Many years later, in a note to friends, Ford recorded,

> When I reported at the Adjutant's office all were waiting. Some began badgering me about its assumed importance, no one anticipating how alarming and important it was. I gave the written message directly to General Bradley as courtesy required, but he, knowing it was general news, asked me to read it for the benefit of all. I did so as well as I could for I personally knew numbers killed in the fight. As I progressed the silence became oppressive and when concluded was unbroken.

Bradley was the first to speak. He was shocked by what he had heard— the 7th Cavalry Regiment almost annihilated, and Custer himself dead? He put the obvious question to Ford: "There can be no doubt of the authenticity of this report?"

"Not a particle, General," Ford answered. He explained that every post was receiving the same message from the government, and that newspapers were supporting the story in detail. "It is absolutely the truth," he said.

"It was an awful shock to the garrison," Ford wrote later. "The officers were blanched and still, even the soldiers were silent. Women wept from sympathy. It might have been their fate"—their fate, he meant, to receive such news about their own husbands.[4]

Skilled as a telegraph operator and an accepted member of the military family at Fort Laramie, where he would spend eleven years, Ford could write, too. In April 1877, leaving his wife, Celia, and two small children, he departed Fort Laramie to spend several days with Bourke and Crook at the Spotted Tail Agency on assignment for the *Chicago Times* when the big band of Miniconjou under Touch the Clouds came in to surrender. On April 24, when the excitement was over, Ford went on the ninety-mile trip back to Fort Laramie, the very day, as luck determined, that a group from Crazy Horse's band came in to surrender. One of this group was the Oglala Horned Horse, who provided Bourke and Clark with an early account of the Custer fight, remarking that he did not see it all— "There were two young bucks of my band killed in the fight and we had to look after them." Clark later learned that one of the two was a son of Horned Horse, a young man known as White Eagle, killed early in the fight. But Ford had a second chance at the Indians' version of the Custer story a month later, when he returned to the Red Cloud Agency with Crook on May 23.[5]

The next day Clark arranged a meeting with Crazy Horse, who listened and "approved," Ford wrote, while others told the bulk of the story. Ford quotes the chief directly only once. Most of the talking was done by Red Dog, Red Cloud's sometime spokesman, and Horned Horse. But Ford had learned something about newspapering; he insisted from the get-go that this was Crazy Horse's story of the fight, and it got him onto the front page of the *Chicago Times*. "Your correspondent has obtained some very valuable information in regard to the Custer massacre," he wrote, using the word then favored by the western press.

Interpreting for Ford at the meeting was Billy Garnett, described by the reporter as "a man perfectly reliable and thoroughly conversant with the Indian language."[6] What Ford wanted was the Indian version of what happened in "the Custer massacre" and his story publicly established some basic facts of the disaster for the first time, starting with the north-to-south order of the Indian bands camped along the west bank of the Little Bighorn on the morning of Custer's attack.[7]

"The attack was a surprise and totally unlooked for," Ford wrote. The Indians responded with attacks on Custer from two directions. While one force confronted Custer's men as they approached the Indian camp, Ford was told, a second assaulted Custer's men from the rear.[8]

Too many Indians was the core of the problem, as Ford described it. The village consisted of eighteen hundred lodges plus four hundred wickiups, temporary shelters of the kind the young men constructed when out on the warpath without their families. Ford's working of the numbers added up to "a fighting force of over seven thousand Indians"—maybe more. How could Custer and his five companies, about 212 men in all, deal with such a multitude? "They had him at their mercy, and the dreadful massacre ensued," Ford wrote. He was not the only correspondent to stress the vastness of the warrior horde that overwhelmed Custer. Inflating the numbers was a customary way for whites to soften the sting of defeat.

Ford failed to grasp just how everything went wrong, but Horned Horse described for him the terrible intensity of the battle's final moments.

> Horned Horse says the smoke and dust were so great that foe could not be distinguished from friend. The horses were wild with fright and uncontrollable . . . Horned Horse represented this hell of fire and smoke and death by intertwining his fingers and saying, "Just like this, Indians and white men."

As the conversation grew general it touched also on the fight at the Rosebud, a subject of particular interest to General Crook. None of the whites had spotted Crazy Horse in the fight for sure, but Red Dog and Horned Horse reported that he was running the show: "In both the Rosebud fight and the Custer massacre the Indians claim he rode unarmed in the thickness of the fight, invoking the blessing of the great spirit on him—that if he was right he might be victorious, and if wrong that he might be killed."

Rode unarmed? That doesn't sound right. Perhaps Horned Horse sweetened the pill, because he was worried that Crazy Horse would be punished for whipping Crook and killing soldiers. But the chief himself volunteered that his scouts had shadowed Crook's command from the moment it left Goose Creek until it arrived on the Rosebud forty-eight hours later. Crazy Horse's plan, it was said, had been to draw Crook's men into some tight corner where they might be crushed. It is likely the tight corner he had in mind was the canyon of the Rosebud, which Captain Anson Mills at Crook's direction entered with a large force in hope of striking the Indian village. But Crook had changed his mind and sent his aide, Captain Azor Nickerson, to call the detachment back. Mills then made a left-face up out of the canyon, escaping whatever punishment Crazy Horse had waiting for him. Ford gave the credit for this timely decision to Crook, noting with a tip of the hat to his host, "It shows as much generalship to avoid defeat and massacre as to win a battle."

Ford's long report was published in the *Chicago Times* on May 26, only two days after the interview itself; it had been sent through on the just-completed telegraph line to Fort Laramie. Ford thus confirmed what Crook's officers already believed: that sticking to the general's plan for chasing up the canyon of the Rosebud until they reached the village would have meant, in the words of reporter John Finerty, "that all of us would have settled there permanently."[9] The near thing at the Rosebud, the retreat to Goose Creek, the six-week wait for resupply while the hostiles killed Custer and then dispersed at their leisure into the wilderness . . . these were the implicit charges that made Crook wince with injured pride.

On July 20 the generals' excursion reached the valley of the Little Bighorn. Bourke described the following morning as, "Sky perfectly spotless. Weather charming in softness and Italian warmth." Heading north toward the battlefield the party crossed from the east to the west bank of the winding, looping river and made its way a dozen miles downstream through easy bottomland. Bourke loved this rolling grass country and thought the prospectors who had come up from the Black Hills were fools to grub in the earth with picks. "They will never find gold fields richer than those waving in green grass at their feet."[10] He predicted that the country would be flooded with cowboys and cattle "inside of two years."

Paralleling their route across the river "ran a low chain of bluffs and sandstone," tougher going for men on horses than the grassy meadow Bourke was passing through. The bottomland along the west bank of the Little Bighorn was just the sort of place the Sioux liked to camp—plenty of grass for the ponies, abundant water, firewood in the thickets of cottonwoods that fringed the river. "One clump of these was pointed out by our guides as the position assumed by Major Reno when he first attacked the village," Bourke recorded.

Just beyond this point the soldiers began to pass through the camp ground occupied by the Hunkpapas the year before. The ground was still littered with village detritus–"pots, pans, kettles, tipi poles, cups and dishes." On the fatal day Reno had forded the river at an easy crossing, formed his men into line, and then advanced toward the Hunkpapa village until he was checked by a growing swarm of Indians. A mile beyond the point where Reno turned back the excursion came to the ford "where Custer vainly essayed to cross the stream to charge the village near its center." The Sans Arcs and Miniconjou had been camped near this spot, and it was here that the big excursion set up their tents and prepared to explore the ground rising away to the right and the left across the river.

Bourke with Lieutenant Homer Wheeler headed up to the left, following a coulee toward higher ground. A terrific rain- and hailstorm had battered the landscape only a week earlier, flattening the grass and washing out many of the shallow graves. Signs of the battle were plain everywhere: the bones of horses and men, bits of equipment, tattered coats and hats, whole bodies partially emerging from the earth. Bourke spotted government-issue cavalry boots strewn upon the ground. The uppers from ankle to calf had been cut away by Indians scavenging the field. They liked the polished boot leather. The lowers, Bourke noted with horror, revealed "the human feet and bones still sticking in them."

The bodies had been shallowly buried where they lay the year before, then reburied only a month earlier by another detachment under the command of Colonel Michael Sheridan, the general's brother. Many of the graves of the officers and some of the men had been identified by slips of paper wedged into the split end of a stick driven into the ground. It was this placement of the bodies on the field that provided the earliest and to a large degree still the best evidence of the unfolding of the battle. A rough wooden cross marking the grave of Lieutenant J. J. Crittenden of Company L was the first which Bourke noted. A hundred yards further along Captain Myles Keogh was buried with the men of Company I. Bourke made no careful study of what he saw, but in passing over the ground he absorbed a quick sweeping impression that suggested to him how the battle had gone.

The bodies around Keogh were close together, Bourke noted. He concluded that Keogh's men had dismounted and "attempted to make a stand on foot to enable Custer to get away." To the left along an easy rising slope—northward, downriver—was another cluster of bodies on the side of a hill, not far from the top. The top would have been better ground to defend, but the cluster of men did not make it. There Custer died with many of his soldiers. The skeleton of his horse, Vic, lay nearby. Bourke was not immune to souvenir hunting, or the glamour that attached to Custer's name. Vic was well known to the men of the 7th—a handsome sorrel with three white fetlocks. Bourke and Lieutenant Wheeler cut the hooves from Custer's horse, and each carried a pair away with them.[11]

A line of additional graves—"a frightened herd of 30 or 40 poor wretches"—stretched down the hill back toward the river. "They were killed like wolves." Among them, Bourke noted, well down along in the ravine where this final group had evidently been killed, were the graves of Custer's two brothers.[12] As Bourke read the field they had bolted after the death of the commander—"ran like frightened deer for the river." Boston got furthest, Tom not quite so far. The graves were still marked, but the bodies had been exhumed and carried away a month earlier by the party under Colonel Sheridan.

That pattern of graves revealed the shape of the battle as Bourke understood it. Keogh alone of Custer's men, Bourke believed, had time or wit to pick a spot for defense. The final stages of the battle began with a brief stand by Keogh and his men around a buffalo wallow, the bowl-like depression left in the ground where buffalo deviled by insects would roll vigorously on their backs to thicken their fur with dirt. More than once on the plains an outnumbered group of men had stood off attacking Indians from the shelter of a buffalo wallow. But this time the Indians were too many. "This was the only position we found," Lieutenant Wheeler recorded many years later in a memoir, "where it looked as if a defense had been made, for the men had fallen all over the battlefield, here and there."

Bourke noted the same impression at the time. With the exception of the tight bunch around Keogh's buffalo wallow, "the graves are scattered in irregular clumps and at intervals about like those in a slaughter of buffaloes." That was the core of Bourke's impression of the battle—after Keogh the men all died in confusion like buffalo when the hunters rode in among them. "I will close this little sketch," Bourke wrote in his diary, "by saying I don't believe fifty Indians were killed in any way during this action."[13]

The generals' excursion lingered on the battleground for two days. Before departure a detail of men was ordered to rebury the dead where they had fallen. Bourke began to mull on the battle. Too many Indians, he concluded firmly, like John W. Ford of the *Chicago Times*. But still—it might have gone another way. "It would have been better to make the onslaught by charging across the open plain near the locality of Reno's first attack," he wrote. Better, he is saying, if Custer had not divided his men. The whole outfit might have gone to ground and held out "until Terry came to his rescue."

Thus Bourke started down the road taken so often over the next hundred years—a strong, clear, initial impression, followed by a growing cascade of second thoughts and reconsiderations. The scouts meanwhile told them many stories. They pointed out a lonely skeleton on the field and said it belonged to a soldier who bolted on a fast horse at the close of the battle on the hill where Custer died. Indians gave chase but the soldier's horse pulled steadily away, heading upstream in the direction of Reno's men. The Indians pressed the chase for a mile but then pulled up—it would be good, they thought, "that someone might be left alive to tell the tale."

But then something incomprehensible happened. Indians told and retold this story over the next forty years. Bourke was probably the first to write it down. "The soldier must have been crazed with fright," he recorded, "as he was seen to pull out his revolver and blow out his brains."[14]

In the scouts' stories as recorded by Bourke, only one of the Indians was identified by name. That was Crazy Horse. The man they described was not Crazy Horse the weaponless chief calling on the Great Spirit as reported by Ford. This was the warrior chief who killed his enemies. "Crazy Horse killed the first one of Reno's men who entered the village," Bourke wrote in his diary. "He split the man's head with a war club."

General Sheridan came away from the Little Bighorn battlefield convinced that the fault was Custer's. He read the ground pretty much as Bourke did. One fact explained much: Custer had died nearly five miles from the hilltop where Reno and half the regiment had been besieged by the Indians for a day and a half. The men with Custer had been killed in several clusters, with others all over the field. A month after his visit to the Little Bighorn, Sheridan wrote Sherman that if Custer had kept his command together he could have escaped disaster, and might even have beaten the Indians outright.[15] Sheridan's curiosity seems to have halted at the moment when Custer divided his command. He showed little interest in how things went after that, probably because no white had survived with the story, and he doubted an Indian could tell him.

What General Crook thought about Custer's fate is unknown; he kept most of his thoughts to himself, and his judgment on the disaster at the Little Bighorn was one of them.

But unlike Sheridan, Crook thought that the Indians might know the secret of Custer's defeat, and he asked his aide, Lieutenant William Philo Clark, to write up a report of what the Indians had to say about the battle. No officer had spent more time with Indians than Clark since Crook had put him in command of the scouts at the Red Cloud and Spotted Tail agencies the previous November. For nine months he had studied the sign language, had talked and negotiated with the Indians daily, and had assembled the reports of hostiles as they came in. These months of contact, Clark reported that summer, placed him "on excellent dog-eating terms" with Crazy Horse and his leading men.[16] Clark took his task seriously. To keep one jump ahead of any brewing trouble the lieutenant also organized a network of informers—spies, in plain language—to circulate among the camps and let him know what the Indians were saying and planning.

Dragging out the details of the Custer fight was not easy. "The Indians from Crazy Horse down have been extremely reticent," Clark reported. One group of eighteen surrendered hostiles solemnly insisted to a man that they played no part in the fight at the Little Bighorn or in any other battle during the Sioux war.[17] But others, like Horned Horse, were ready to talk, and Clark had the benefit as well of occasional reports in the press, including Indian accounts from Kill Eagle, Red Horse, and a string of hostiles interviewed by Colonel W. H. Wood at the Cheyenne River Agency on the Missouri. From these many sources Clark assembled his report on the Sioux war and submitted it in September. Crook's fights at Powder River, the Rosebud, and Slim Buttes were all discussed, but the core of Clark's narrative addressed the fight on the Little Bighorn.

Much has been learned in the 130 years since the battle, but nothing that has fundamentally changed the bare-bones outline of John Ford in the *Chicago Times*, or the better-detailed account Lieutenant Clark prepared for General Crook. The big question in 1877, just as interesting but less urgent now, was how the Indians managed Custer's crushing defeat. Was Sitting Bull a kind of Red Napoleon, a native genius plotting future assaults from his refuge in Canada? Or was the man to be feared closer to home—the slender, melancholic, slow-to-speak Crazy Horse, who had surrendered his guns and ponies to General Crook?

Since giving up the gun, Crazy Horse had ignored official requests to camp close to the agency, moving instead five or six miles down Little White Clay Creek, where he remained out of sight but much on the mind of Crook and the watchful Lieutenant Clark. The answer to the big question—who beat Custer?—was not self-evident. It required an understanding of the structure of the battle—what happened first, what happened next, until the historian could at last point to the error that proved fatal. The story then and the story now may properly begin with the first stirrings in the Indian camp spread for a mile and more along the west bank of the Little Bighorn River as the sky grew light in the east at the start of a hot and sultry day.

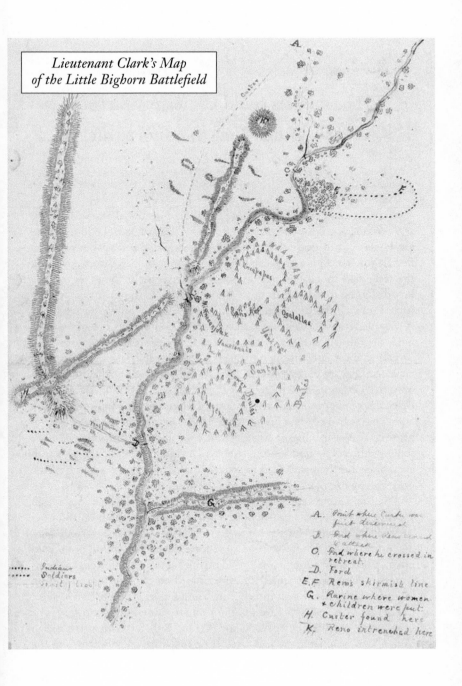

Lieutenant Clark's Map
of the Little Bighorn Battlefield

A. Point where Custer was
   first discovered
B. Ford where Reno crossed
   & attacked
C. Ford where he crossed in
   retreat.
D. Ford.
E.F. Reno's skirmish line
G. Ravine where women
   & children were put
H. Custer found here
K. Reno intrenched here

Indians
Soldiers
Custer [trail]

24

"The soldiers could not go any further, and they knew that they had to die."

SUNDAY, JUNE 25, 1876, began like every day for the Lakota: with horses and cooking fires. It was early when Black Elk's father woke him to take the horses out to graze. "Daybreak," he recalled, meaning the predawn first light when all is a greenish blue-gray. The people in the camps along the river had thousands of horses, so many of them they covered the broad sloping grassland rising to the west thick as the fur on a buffalo's back. From a distance seen through summer heat the hills would ripple as if they were alive. Twenty thousand horses could strip the grass from miles of prairie in a day or two, and the elders in the assembled camps had agreed to meet later in the morning to discuss removal of the village—perhaps today, perhaps tomorrow. In the village itself at this hour were only the best horses, tethered close to their owners' lodges for safety. Black Elk's father was known as a hater of whites; in the Fetterman fight a falling horse had crushed his right leg, and he limped for the remainder of his life. The possibility of a white attack was much on his mind. Before sending him off he told his son, twelve years old, to be careful, to keep an eye always on the camp, and to make sure he had a rope on one of the horses so he might catch it quickly in the event of danger.

The sun was just cracking over the horizon as Black Elk and a cousin led their horses up the nearby hill. Throughout the camp men and boys were taking the good horses out to graze, and they were not the only ones up and about. First light was the time for mothers and grandmothers to poke up last night's cooking fire. Old men went out early to relieve them-selves or pray or just smell the morning. There would have been an immense but quiet stir all through the camps along the Peji Sla Wakpa, Lakota for Greasy Grass River, but nothing to cause alarm or fright. The Hunkpapa woman known as Good White Buffalo Woman (Pte San Waste Win) said later she had often been in camps when war was in the air. "The Sioux that morning had no thought of fighting," she said. "We expected no attack."[1]

Those who saw the assembled camp said they had never seen one larger. There were at least six separate camp circles, perhaps seven, cheek by jowl, with the Cheyenne, by general agreement, at the northern (downriver) end near the broad ford where the Medicine Tail Coulee and Muskrat Creek emptied into the river. At the southern (upstream) end were the Hunkpapas. Between these two along the river's bends and loops were the camps of the Sans Arcs, Brulé, Miniconjou, Santee, and Oglala. Some said the Oglala were the biggest group, the Hunkpapas next, with perhaps seven hundred lodges between them.[2] The other circles might have totaled five to six hundred. That would suggest as many as six to seven thousand people in all, with a third that number being men or boys of fighting age. Further confusing the question of numbers was the constant arrival and departure of people from the agencies—whole bands out to hunt, small groups of young men coming for the sun dance and the war parties sure to follow, a few Arapahos who happened to be passing through, men out alone on the plains tracking lost or stolen horses. The great camp had come together in March or April, even before the plains started to green up, according to He Dog. Indians arriving from the agencies on the Missouri reported that soldiers were coming out to fight, so the various camps made a deliberate point of keeping close together, seeking strength in numbers, moving every few days in the constant pursuit of grass for the ponies and buffalo for the people.[3]

Among the many who rode out early on the 25th were a group of hunters going after buffalo some miles to the east along Tullock's Fork, and several parties heading southeast, traveling independently of each other, and making for the divide that separated the valleys of the Little Bighorn and the Rosebud. One small group, Fast Horn and a friend or two, had reached a spot near the high point of the divide later known as the Crow's Nest, by five thirty in the morning. Also going that way were the Hunkpapa Little Bear with two sons, Wicohan (Deeds) and Hona (Little Voice), looking for lost horses.[4] Ahead of them was a larger group led by a well-known agency man, the Oglala Black Bear, who had come out from the Red Cloud Agency some weeks earlier, also in pursuit of missing horses. Explaining later, Black Bear did not say the horses had been stolen, exactly, just that they had gone north with some Oglala who were hoping to join Crazy Horse. Black Bear did not travel alone, but brought with him half a dozen friends.[5] Having recovered their horses, they set out early on the morning of June 25—probably just about the time Black Elk and his cousin were thinking of returning to the camp for something to eat.

There was constant traffic along the 400-mile route connecting the Red Cloud Agency on the White River with the hunting grounds along the Tongue and the Powder. The first day's journey would take Black Bear and his friends over the divide into the valley of the Rosebud, where the fight with soldiers had taken place a week earlier. Black Bear would have heard the frequent reports of soldiers moving about the plains, but it was probably something of a shock when his party spotted a large company of soldiers moving rapidly along Davis Creek, heading west for the divide the Indians had just crossed. Black Bear said they watched the soldiers from a ridge or rise, concealing themselves in the traditional way of men on the plains. As they watched, five or six hundred soldiers rode by, followed by a packtrain with more than a hundred mules. The hour would have been close to nine thirty in the morning, and the little group of Indians had already come about twenty miles from the big camp.[6] The soldiers were putting up a lot of dust and traveling fast—so fast, as Black Bear told Indians later, that he was sure he had no chance to beat them back to camp to give warning. It was a delicate point. Warning was just what the big camp on the Little Bighorn needed.

Shortly after the passing of the soldiers, Black Bear and his friends were approached by three Cheyenne, who said they had been following these soldiers for several days, all the way from the Powder River. Only an hour or so earlier, they said, some soldiers surprised them as they were preoccupied trying to break open a wooden box of military supplies they had found in the trail. Shots had been fired. The Cheyenne fled. After talking the two groups separated—Black Bear and friends heading for the agency, ten days away, the Cheyenne continuing to track the soldiers.[7]

The big village on the Little Bighorn was thus surrounded by a kind of informal early-warning system—a wide screen of travelers, hunters, women out gathering roots and herbs, and seekers of lost horses making their way hither and yon over a broad expanse of prairie a dozen miles or more from the campsite. There as the morning turned increasingly hot and sultry large numbers of adults and children were swimming in the river. The water would have been cold; the river, Black Elk remembered, was high with the June rise of meltwater from the snowpack in the mountains. Groups of women had gone into the hills to the east or the prairie to the west with sharp sticks to dig for *tsimpsila*. There were many late risers this morning following dances the previous night which ended not long before first light. One very large tent near the center of the village— probably two lodges raised side by side—was filled with the elders called chiefs by the whites, but variously named "short hairs," "silent eaters," or "big bellies" by the Indians. The council lodge was painted yellow. There in the morning the leading men decided to put off moving the camp for another day.[8]

It was approaching midafternoon when the first warnings began to reach the big village. Which came first is hard to establish. Not long after the camp criers had gone out to say there would be no move of camp that day, the Oglala Runs the Enemy was smoking with several leading men in the big council lodge when a report arrived that soldiers were coming. "We could hardly believe that soldiers were so near," he said later. It made no sense. For one thing, whites never attacked in the middle of the day, and the men with Crook were known to have retreated back down to Goose Creek. For several moments more, Runs the Enemy confessed, "We sat there smoking."[9]

But other reports followed quickly. The Hunkpapa White Bull was watching over horses not far from camp when scouts rode down from Ash Creek[10] with the news that soldiers had shot two boys at the forks of the creek two or three miles back.[11] Women who had been out digging turnips across the river to the east "came riding in all out of breath and reported that soldiers were coming," said the Yanktonai chief Thunder Bear. "The country, they said, looked as if filled with smoke, so much dust was there." One woman in their group had been shot and killed by the soldiers during the escape.[12] The Oglala Fast Horn came in to say he had been shot at by soldiers he saw near the high divide on the way over into the Rosebud.[13] But the first warning to bring warriors on the run proba- bly occurred at the Hunkpapa camp a little before three o'clock when horse raiders—Arickarees working for the soldiers, as it turned out— were seen making a dash for horses grazing in a ravine not far from the camp. Within a very few moments shooting could be heard at the south end of camp. With the boom of gunfire the peace of the big camp was quickly replaced by pandemonium: shouts and cries of women and chil- dren, men calling for horses or guns, boys sent to find mothers or sisters, swimmers rushing from the river, men trying to organize resistance, looking to their weapons, painting themselves, or tying up their horses' tails.

As warriors rushed out to confront the Ree horse stealers, people at the southernmost (upstream) end of the Hunkpapa camp were shouting alarm at the sight of a line of approaching soldiers, first glimpsed on horseback a mile or two away.[14] By the time the soldiers were nearing the camp at ten or fifteen minutes past three o'clock Indians had boiled out of the lodges to meet them. Now came the first shots heard back at the council lodge, convincing Runs the Enemy at last to put his pipe aside. Moving Robe Woman, a sister of Deeds then in her early twenties, heard a volley of shots from the soldiers followed by the clatter of bullets hitting the lodgepoles of the camp. "Bullets sounded like hail on tepees and tree tops," said Little Soldier.[15] Already people were beginning to die; the family of Gall (Pizi), two wives and their three children, were shot to death near their lodge at the edge of the camp. Moving Robe Woman was singing a death song for her brother; she had painted her face red, carried a Colt revolver, and intended to kill soldiers in revenge (and did before the day was over). Near her a man running for his horse jerked in mid-stride and fell to the ground dead.

But now the Indians were rushing out in front of the soldiers and shooting back, making show enough to check the attack. The whites dismounted. Every fourth man took the reins of three other horses and led them along with his own into the cover of the trees near the river. The rest of the soldiers deployed in a skirmish line to confront the Indians. It was all happening very quickly. As the Indians came out from the edge of camp to meet the soldiers, the river was to their left, obscured at this point by thick timber and undergrowth. Gall's wives and children died just inside those trees. The soldiers' skirmish line was straight ahead. To the right was the open prairie rising away to the west, and out there, beyond the end of the line of soldiers, there began to accumulate a rapidly growing force of mounted Indians. These warriors on horseback were swinging wide, swooping around the end of the soldiers' line of perhaps a hundred men. Some of the Indians, He Dog and Brave Heart among them,[16] rode still further out, circling a small hill to appear behind the soldiers. By that time the soldiers in the skirmish line were bending back around to face the Indians behind them. In effect the line had halted; it moved no closer to the Hunkpapa camp. Firing was heavy and rapid, but the Indians racing their ponies were hard to hit. Ever-growing numbers of men were rushing out to meet the soldiers while women and children fled the camp, heading downriver. Not more than fifteen or twenty minutes into the fight it was the Indians who were gaining control of the field; now the soldiers were pulling back into the trees that lined the river, recoiling from the men rushing out to meet them, more every moment.

The battle's pattern was already established: moments of intense fighting, rapid movement, close engagement with men falling dead or wounded, followed by a period of sudden relative quiet as the two sides reorganized, took stock, prepared for the next clash. The soldiers disappeared into the trees, and Indians by ones and twos cautiously made their way in after them while others gathered nearby. Shooting fell away but never halted completely. Simultaneously two large movements were unfolding: most of the women and children were moving north down the river, leaving the Hunkpapa camp behind, while a growing stream of men passed them on the way to the fighting—"where the excitement was going on," said Eagle Elk, a friend of Crazy Horse's brother-in-law Red Feather. Crazy Horse himself was approaching the scene of the fighting at about the same time. He was far from first on the scene. He had been swimming in the river with his friend Yellow Nose when they heard shots. Moments later, horseless, he met Red Feather, who was bridling his pony. "Take any horse," said Red Feather as he prepared to dash off, but Crazy Horse hung back to wait for his own mounts. Red Feather saw him again ten or fifteen minutes later, when the Indians had gathered in force near the woods where the soldiers had taken refuge.[17]

It was probably during that quarter hour that Crazy Horse prepared himself for war. In the emergency of the moment many men grabbed their weapons and ran toward the shooting, but not all. War was too dangerous to treat casually; a man wanted to be properly dressed and painted before charging the enemy; without his medicine, and time for a prayer or song, he would be weak. The Cheyenne Brave Bear once described to his friend George Bent how his father helped prepare him for the battle:

> I took my small sack that had my porcupine-tail hairbrush and my paints. I had to put on same paint that my shield was painted with, and had to put it on just as my shield was painted. This was on my face. My father took off my shield [the] blacktail deer tail. This was to [be] tied to my scalp lock. This charm was to turn bullets from me. My father touched my head four times with this tail before tying it on to my scalp lock. This shield my father gave me of course knew all the medicine that belong to it. As I went out . . . my father held my shield towards the sun and said to the shield [and] to the sun to protect me from bullets. Then he put the shield on my right side and told me to go and die in the battle.[18]

Waterman, an Arapaho who took part in the battle, said he took time to paint his face yellow and red and hang a deerskin bag containing a certain root about his neck. His companion Left Hand stuck two feathers through a cross-shaped piece of buffalo hide which he fixed into his hair.[19] Crazy Horse, too, prepared himself before fighting. Nearby in the river, when Crazy Horse heard the first shots, had been the daughter of his friend Standing Bear, just eight years old, who had been learning to swim. The girl, called Fast Eagle Woman, remembered that her father and Crazy Horse told the women there to pack up quickly and move away from the sound of shooting. Her seventeen-year-old brother, also known as Standing Bear, reported that after the first warnings Crazy Horse took time to ready himself for battle, calling on a *wicasa wakan* to invoke the spirits and then taking so much time over his preparations "that many of his warriors became impatient."[20]

Another young Oglala, Spider, noted several details of the chief's preparation. Ten young men who had sworn to follow Crazy Horse "anywhere in battle" were standing nearby. Crazy Horse dusted himself and his companions with a fistful of dry earth gathered up from a hill left by a mole or gopher. Into his hair he wove some long stems of grass—no feathers, according to Spider. Then he opened the medicine bag he carried about his neck, took from it a pinch of stuff, "and burned it as a sacrifice upon a fire of buffalo chips which another warrior had prepared." The wisp of smoke carried his prayer to the heavens. Others reported that Crazy Horse painted his face with hail spots and also dusted his horse with the dry earth. With these preparations completed, according to Spider and the younger Standing Bear, Crazy Horse was ready to fight.[21]

By the time he caught up with Red Feather and his cousin Kicking Bear the warriors were massing near the timber along the river just south of the Hunkpapa camp. It was hard to see the soldiers, but there was a lot of shooting; the bullets clattered through the tree limbs and sent leaves fluttering to the ground. Several Indians had already been killed and others were wounded, including Long Elk, Pretty Bear, and Elk Heart.[22] There was shouting and singing; some women who had stayed behind were calling out the high-pitched, ululating cry called the tremolo. The twelve-year-old Black Elk saw a "very pretty" young woman singing encouragement to the fighters. Iron Hawk said this woman was his aunt, and she was urging on the warriors who were arriving in numbers:

Brothers-in-law, now your friends have come.
Take courage.
Would you see me taken captive?[23]

At just this moment the crowd near the timber cried out, "Crazy Horse is coming!" From the hill to the west where Indians were circling around behind the soldier lines came the charge word: "*Hokahey!*" Many Indians present at the fight near the wood said that Crazy Horse several times raced his pony alone past the soldiers, drawing their fire—an act of daring sometimes called a brave run. Men were blowing their eagle-bone whistles. Red Feather remembered, "Some Indian shouted, 'Give way; let the soldiers out. We can't get at them in there.' Soon the soldiers came out and tried to go to the river." As they bolted out of the woods, Crazy Horse called to the men near him, "Here are some of the soldiers after us again. Do your best, and let us kill them all off today, that they may not trouble us anymore. All ready! Charge!"

Crazy Horse and his followers and all the rest now raced their horses directly into the soldiers. "Right among them we rode," said Thunder Bear, "shooting them down as in a buffalo drive."[24] Wild confusion marked the fighting; the whites were fleeing for their lives, each man fighting off the nearby Indians as he could. Horses were shot and soldiers tumbled to the ground; a few managed to pull up behind friends, but on foot most were quickly killed. "All mixed up," said the Cheyenne Two Moon of the melee; "Sioux, then soldiers, then more Sioux, and all shooting." Crazy Horse and Kicking Bear were right there in the front of the mad race. Kicking Bear's brother, Flying Hawk, said it was hard to know exactly what was happening:

> The dust was thick and we could hardly see. We got right among the soldiers and killed a lot with our bows and arrows and tomahawks. Crazy Horse was ahead of all, and he killed a lot of them with his war club; he pulled them off their horses when they tried to get across the river where the bank was steep. Kicking Bear was right beside him and killed many, too, in the water.[25]

"The air was full of smoke and dust," said Two Moon; "I saw the soldiers fall back and drop into the river-bed like buffalo fleeing." The water was deep and fast from the June rise. "Several of the troops were drowned," said Red Horse.[26] The young Cheyenne Brave Bear, painted and dressed for battle, watched the slaughter at the river crossing.

> The worst of it was [when] the soldiers struck very high banks of the river and all went over. When they struck the water it sounded like cannon going off. This was awful as the bank was awful high. When I rode to the bank the

Indians were shooting the soldiers as they came up out of water. I could see lots of blood in the water.[27]

It was a scene of confusion and horror. At the river, Red Feather and Kicking Bear caught up with two fleeing men dressed in white shirts and blue trousers, but they weren't soldiers. "Those two are Indians," shouted Kicking Bear, *"Palani!"* He used the Lakota word for Arikara/Arickaree; the Rees had been first on the scene, just long enough to round up some Sioux horses and kill several people. Red Feather shot the horse from under one of the fleeing Ree scouts, then jumped down on the Ree struggling to regain his feet. He stabbed him to death with a knife. In almost the same instant Kicking Bear shot the second man twice. Many of the Indians charged right across the river after the soldiers and chased them as they scrambled up the bluffs toward a hill. White Eagle, the son of Horned Horse, was killed in this part of the chase. A soldier stopped just long enough to scalp him—one quick circle cut with a sharp knife, then a yank on a fistful of hair to rip the skin loose.[28]

The whites had the worst of it. More than thirty soldiers were killed in all before they reached the top of the hill and threw themselves down to make a stand. The bodies of soldiers and dead horses were left on the flat by the river below. Among them were a couple of wounded Ree scouts. The Oglala Red Hawk said later that the warriors did not hesitate when they found these men. "The Indians said these Indians wanted to die—that was what they were scouting with the soldiers for; so they killed them and scalped them."[29] Black Elk was there, stripping the dead of clothes and weapons. He rode by a wounded soldier, legs twitching and kicking in his agony. A man rode up to young Black Elk and said,

> "Boy, get off and scalp him." So I got off and began to take my knife. Of course the soldier had short hair so I started to cut it off. Probably it hurt him because he began to grind his teeth. After I did this I took my pistol out and shot him in the forehead.

Black Elk completed his bloody task. He had never taken a scalp before. We may recall his horror on the night when he watched by firelight as the people of his village dismembered the body of a Crow who had been shot and killed while trying to steal horses. Black Elk was slow to see the glory in scalping the white soldier grinding his teeth in pain. He had had enough. "I returned to where my mother was standing on top of the hill with the others." But when his mother saw the scalp she did not hesitate. "My mother gave a shrill tremolo for me."[30] This made Black Elk feel proud.

The crossing of the river by the soldiers brought a second breathing spell in the fight. Some of the Indians chased the soldiers to the top of the hill, but many others, like Black Elk, lingered to pick up guns and ammunition, to pull the clothes off dead soldiers, or to catch runaway horses. In this opening phase of the fight, many Indians saw Crazy Horse charging among the soldiers as they raced their horses for the river, but no one saw him go up the hill or attack the soldiers who were making a stand at the top. Instead, he stopped at the water's edge and promptly turned back with his men toward the center of the great camp. The only Indian to offer an explanation of his abrupt withdrawal was the Hunkpapa Gall, who said that Crazy Horse and Crow King feared a second soldier attack on the camp downriver, and returned at a run to block the danger. Gall said they had seen soldiers heading in that direction along the bluffs across the river. Establishing what they might have seen requires a sense of the chronology of the battle.[31]

The whole fight along the river flat—from the first sighting of soldiers riding toward the Hunkpapa camp (shortly after three o'clock) until the last of them crossed the river and made their way to the top of the hill—lasted about an hour. During that hour a second group of soldiers was visible at least three times on the eastern heights above the river and the Hunkpapa village.[32] The first sighting came only a minute or two after the initial group of soldiers began its mile-and-a-half ride down the valley toward the Hunkpapa camp—about five minutes past three. Ten minutes later, as the first group was dismounting to form a skirmish line, the second group across the river was sighted again, this time on the very hill (now known as Reno Hill) where the first group would take shelter after their mad retreat back across the river. At about half past three the second group could be seen for a third time on a high point above the river not quite halfway between Reno Hill and the Cheyenne village at the downriver end of the big camp. At that moment the first group of soldiers was just completing its retreat into the timber, back away from the massing Indians. It is very likely that the second group got their first clear view of the whole long sprawl of the Indian camp from this high bluff, later called Weir Point, and that may explain the three cheers bellowed out by the men which were heard and later described by White Bull, Brave Wolf, and the Miniconjou chief Hump.

Of course it is entirely possible that the Indians saw the soldiers all three times, and perhaps more often than that. The country was alive with Indians coming and going in all directions on both sides of the river. The Yanktonai White Thunder saw soldiers make one false move toward the river south of the ford by the Cheyenne camp, then turn back on reaching "a steep cut bank which they could not get down."[33] While the soldiers retraced their steps to find a new way to reach the river, White Thunder and some of his friends went east up and over the high ground to the other side, where they were soon joined by many other Indians. In effect, White Thunder said, the second group of soldiers had been surrounded even before the opening of that phase of the battle.

But He Dog said it simplest, "We looked and saw other soldiers coming over the big hill right over east. They kept right on down the river."[34] Downriver meant toward the center of the big camp. Gall at any rate was certain it was fear of a second attack by the soldiers which sent Crazy Horse and his friends racing downriver while many other Indians were still stripping bodies or chasing the first group up onto the bluffs.[35]

From the spot where the soldiers retreated across the river to the next crossing place at the north end of the big camp was about three miles—roughly a twenty-minute ride. Between the two crossing places much of the eastern bank of the river was blocked by steep bluffs coming down almost to the water's edge, but just beyond the Cheyenne camp was an open stretch of several hundred yards which in later years was called Minneconjou Ford. It was here that Indians say the second group of soldiers came closest to the river and to the Indian camp. By most Indian accounts it wasn't very close.

Approaching the ford at an angle from the high ground to the east and south was a dry creek bed at the bottom of a shallow ravine now known as Medicine Tail Coulee. The exact sequence of events and placement of men at the opening of this phase of the battle is difficult to establish, but it seems likely that the first sighting of soldiers at the upper end of Medicine Tail Coulee occurred at about four o'clock, just as the first group of soldiers was making its dash up the bluffs toward Reno Hill, and as Crazy Horse and his followers were turning back from that fight to head downriver. Two Moon was in the Cheyenne camp when he spotted some soldiers as they emerged over an intervening ridge and began to descend toward the river. Also watching was Shave Elk, later known as Thomas Disputed, who said, "There were a few soldiers ahead of the main body."[36]

Gall and three other Indians were watching the same body of soldiers from a high point on the eastern side of the river. Well out in front were two soldiers. Ten years later Gall spoke of them as Custer and his orderly. It may have been Custer, but more probably it was not. This man he called Custer was in no hurry, Gall said. Off to Gall's right, on one of the bluffs upriver, some Indians came into sight as Custer approached. Feather Earring said Indians were just then coming up from the south on that side of the river "in great numbers." When Custer saw them, Gall said,

> his pace became slower and his actions more cautious, and finally he paused altogether to await the coming up of his command. This was the nearest point any of Custer's party ever got to the river . . . Gall is of the opinion that when Custer slowed his pace and finally halted, the latter began to suspect he was in a bad scrape. From that time on Custer acted on the defensive.[37]

Others, including Iron Hawk and Feather Earring, confirmed that Custer and his men got no closer to the river than that—at least several hundred yards back up the coulee. Most of the soldiers were still further back up the hill. Some shots were fired by the soldiers into the Indian camp, which by this time was almost entirely deserted; the women and children had largely made their way still further downriver, some taking refuge in the ravine that marked the course of Onion Creek, some going further down. The few Indians at Minneconjou Ford fired back at the soldiers. The earlier pattern repeated itself. Little stood in the way of the soldiers at first, but within moments more Indians began to arrive and they kept coming—some crossing the river, others riding up along the eastern bank of the river. But there was no battle at or near Minneconjou Ford—"not much shooting there," said He Dog. By the time fifteen or twenty Indians had gathered near the ford the soldiers had already hesitated, then began to ride on up out of Medicine Tail Coulee, moving generally downriver at a billiard-shot angle from their original approach, heading toward high ground, where they were joined by the rest of Custer's command coming across country.[38]

We might pause here to suggest the probable pattern of the fight which followed as described by the Indians.[39] It took about an hour, but to those involved it must have appeared to be unfolding with relentless speed. The battle known ever since as the Custer fight began when the small leading detachment of soldiers, choosing caution, recoiled back from their approach to the river toward higher ground at about fifteen minutes past four in the afternoon. This move may be described as the last freely taken by the soldiers when those nearest the river decided it would be smart to pull back and away. Their exact thinking, of course, cannot be known. But from this moment forward everything the soldiers did was in response to the pressure of Indian attack growing steadily and rapidly in intensity.

The speed with which events succeeded one upon another continues to amaze more than a century later. As described by Indian participants, the fighting followed the contour of the ground and its pace was determined by the distance covered, the time it took for Indians to gather in force, and the comparatively few minutes it took for each successive group of soldiers to be killed or driven back. The path of the battle follows a sweeping arc up out of Medicine Tail Coulee across another swale into a depression known as Deep Coulee. That in turn opens up and out into a rising slope cresting at a ridge (Calhoun Ridge) which rises to a hill (Calhoun Hill), and then proceeds, still rising, on a northwest course past the depression in the ground—Bourke thought it a buffalo wallow—identified as the Keogh site, and thence to a second elevation known as Custer Hill. The high ground from Calhoun Hill to Custer Hill was what men on the plains called "a backbone." From the point where the soldiers recoiled away from the river to the lower end of Calhoun Ridge is about three-quarters of a mile—a hard twenty-minute uphill slog for a man on foot, much quicker for a man on horseback. Shave Elk ran the distance after his horse was shot at the outset of the fight, and he remembered "how tired he became before he got up there." From the bottom of Calhoun Ridge to Calhoun Hill is another uphill climb of about a quarter of a mile.

But it would be a mistake to assume that all of Custer's command advanced in line from one point to another, down the coulee, up the coulee, and so on. Only a small detachment had approached the river and then recoiled away. The greater part of the command, probably including Custer himself, marched across country while the separate detachment had gone down toward the river. By the time this group rejoined the rest of Custer's command the soldiers had occupied a line from Calhoun Hill along the backbone to Custer Hill, a distance of a little over half a mile. This is evidently what He Dog meant to convey when he said Custer's command "kept right on down the river and crossed Medicine Tail coulee and onto [a] little rise. Here Custer's line was scattered all along parallel with river."[40]

Flying Hawk, brother of Kicking Bear and cousin of Crazy Horse, described the move this way: "Custer came down off the second ridge [after crossing Medicine Tail Coulee] and went up onto Calhoun Hill, leaving a detachment there, and he went right on over to Custer Hill and made a stand there."[41]

Another account of the position of Custer's men at the opening of the battle was given by the younger Standing Bear, who described the whole course of the fight in a few lucid sentences:

> Custer . . . made no known attempt to reach the river to cross. He went right up on Calhoun Hill and disposed his forces along the top of the ridge to Custer Hill. The men on Calhoun Hill finally gave way and fell back toward Custer Hill. Keogh made a desperate stand and he and his men were killed. The men fell back along the ridge leading their horses . . . uniting with those left alive on Custer Hill [who] broke and ran on foot down toward the ravine and river.

Keep in mind that sweeping arc; imagine you have stretched your right arm out and then swept it up and around to the left just as if you were signaling to someone the way to go. That was the uphill route of the soldiers as they headed from Medicine Tail Coulee up to the ridge toward Custer Hill. The whole distance would have been about a mile and a half or a little more. A man on foot following the arc without opposition would have reached Custer Hill in about forty minutes, badly winded, at perhaps five minutes before five o'clock in the afternoon. It took longer than that because Custer's men encountered successive attacks along the way. The arc made no twists and turns. Only at the end, when the last of the soldiers ran for the river, was there an abrupt right-angled turn from the route the battle had been following.

Keep in mind, also, the five site names: Calhoun Ridge, Calhoun Hill, the Keogh site, Custer Hill, and the Deep Ravine, where the last of the soldiers were killed. Red Horse said that Custer's command "made five different stands."[42] At each of these sites there was a round of combat which began and ended in a little more or a little less than ten minutes. Think of it as a running fight, as the survivors of each separate clash made their way along the backbone toward Custer at the end. In effect the command collapsed back in on itself. As described by the Indians, this phase of the battle may be said to have begun with the scattering of shots near Minneconjou Ford mentioned by He Dog; to have unfolded in brief, devastating clashes at Calhoun Ridge, Calhoun Hill, and the Keogh site; to

have climaxed in the killing of Custer and his immediate entourage on
Custer Hill; and to have ended with the pursuit and killing of a last thirty
or so soldiers who raced on foot from Custer Hill toward the river down
a deep ravine.

And keep in mind, finally, what was heard by the soldiers preparing
their defenses on Reno Hill just over four miles to the south, and by a few
additional men left behind in the timber when the soldiers made their
mad retreat. Coming upriver was the sound of three episodes of heavy firing from the direction of the Custer fight—one at four twenty-five in the
afternoon, about ten minutes after the soldiers recoiled away from their
approach to Minneconjou Ford; a second about thirty minutes later; and
a final burst about fifteen minutes after that, dying off before five fifteen.
The distances were great but the air was still that day, and the .45/.70 caliber round of the cavalry carbine made a thunderous boom. Twenty or
forty shots all fired at roughly the same moment told any listener there
was a fight going on in earnest. At twenty-five past five o'clock some of
Reno's officers, who had ridden out with their men toward the sound of
shooting, glimpsed from the high ground known as Weir Point a distant
hillside swarming with mounted Indians who seemed to be shooting at
things on the ground. They were not fighting; more likely the Indians
were finishing off the wounded, or just following the Indian custom of
putting an extra bullet or arrow into an enemy's body in a gesture of triumph. Once the firing began it never died away entirely between volleys;
the last scattering shots continued until night fell.

The officers at Weir Point at five twenty-five also saw a general movement of Indians heading their way—a lot of Indians, more Indians than
any of them had ever encountered before. Soon the forward elements of
Reno's command were exchanging fire with the warriors, and the soldiers
then all returned with dispatch to Reno Hill. Those are the parameters by
the clock of the Custer fight—first shots near the Minneconjou Ford
about four fifteen, battle over and Indians heading back upriver to renew
the attack on Reno by five thirty.[43]

As the soldiers made their way from the river toward higher ground at the
beginning of the Custer fight, the country on three sides was rapidly filling with Indians, in effect pushing as well as following the soldiers uphill.
"We chased the soldiers up a long, gradual slope or hill in a direction
away from the river and over the ridge where the battle began in good

earnest," said Shave Elk. By the time the soldiers made a stand on "the ridge"—evidently the backbone connecting Calhoun and Custer hills— the Indians were beginning to fill the coulees to the south and east. "The officers tried their utmost to keep the soldiers together at this point," said Red Hawk of the soldiers on Calhoun Hill, "but the horses were unmanageable; they would rear up and fall backward with their riders; some would get away." Crow King said, "When they saw that they were surrounded they dismounted."[44] This was cavalry tactics by the book. There was no other way to make a stand or maintain a stout defense. A brief period followed of deliberate fighting on foot.

As Indians arrived on the scene they got down from their horses, sought cover, and began to converge on the soldiers. Taking advantage of brush and every little swale or rise in the ground to hide themselves, the Indians made their way cautiously uphill "on hands and knees," said Red Feather. From one moment to the next, the Indians popped up to shoot before dropping back down again. No man on either side could show himself without drawing fire. In battle the Indians often wore their feathers down flat to help in concealment; the soldiers appear to have taken off their hats for the same reason. Hatless soldiers, some dead and some still fighting, were noted by a number of Indians. From their position on Calhoun Hill—not much of a hill, but higher than the ground nearby—the soldiers were making an orderly, concerted defense. When the Indians approached dangerously near, a detachment of soldiers suddenly rose up and charged downhill on foot, driving the Indians down back to the lower end of Calhoun Ridge. Now the soldiers established a regulation skirmish line, each man about five yards from the next, kneeling in order to take "deliberate aim," according to Yellow Nose. Some Indians noted that there was a second skirmish line as well, stretching perhaps a hundred yards away along the backbone toward Custer Hill. It was here in the fighting around Calhoun Hill, many Indians reported later, that the Indians suffered the most fatal casualties—eleven in all, according to Gall. For some minutes the soldiers' steady fire held the Indians at bay—but not for long.[45]

Almost as soon as the skirmish line was thrown out from Calhoun Hill the Indians pressed in again, snaking up to get within shooting distance of the men on Calhoun Ridge while others made their way around to the far (eastern) slope of the hill, where they opened heavy, deadly fire on the horse holders. The breaking of white resistance began with a threat to their horses. Without horses the soldiers could neither charge nor flee.

Loss of the horses meant loss of the saddlebags with all the reserve ammunition, about fifty rounds per man. Fear of losing the horses brought panic. Daniel White Thunder later told a white missionary, "As soon as the soldiers on foot had marched over the ridge, White Thunder and the Indians with him stampeded the horses . . . by waving their blankets and making a terrible noise."[46]

"We killed all the men who were holding the horses," Gall said.

When a horse holder was shot down the frightened horses began to lunge about. "Their horses were so frightened that they pulled the men all around," said the Oglala Low Dog.[47] "They tried to hold on to their horses," said Crow King, "but as we pressed closer they let go their horses." Many of the horses charged away down the hill toward the river, adding to the confusion of battle. Some of the Indians quit fighting to chase after them.

The fighting was intense, bloody, at times hand to hand. Men died by knife and club as well as gunfire. The Cheyenne Brave Bear saw an officer riding a sorrel horse shoot two Indians with his revolver before he was killed himself. Brave Bear managed to seize hold of the horse. At almost the same moment, Yellow Nose wrenched a cavalry guidon from a soldier who had been using it as a weapon. Eagle Elk, in the thick of the fighting at Calhoun Hill, saw many men killed or horribly wounded—one Indian who was "shot through the jaw and was all bloody." The young Standing Bear, climbing up the hill toward the fighting, apparently saw this same man; he had blood in his mouth, was "very dizzy," fell, and then got to his feet again. The Cheyenne Wooden Leg also saw this man, falling, getting to his feet, falling again. "His whole lower jaw was shot away. The sight of him made me sick. I had to vomit," said Wooden Leg.

Eagle Elk saw a Cheyenne whose horse fell and broke both of the man's legs. He saw a horse shot in the head, running in circles. He saw an Indian lying on the ground, almost certainly dead. "He wore a bird on his head, and the bullet went through the bird and his head." He saw his brother's horse, riderless, and feared his brother had been killed.[48]

The hill was swarming with men—Indian and white. As the fighting around Calhoun Hill approached a climax a Cheyenne chief on horseback suddenly charged into the middle of the soldiers. Some called him Crazy Wolf; others knew him as Lame White Man. He fell from his horse, killed by a bullet which passed entirely through his chest, exiting from his back, but in the chaos of the battle he was scalped and his body stabbed by some Sioux, who thought he was one of Custer's Arikara scouts. With the death of Lame White Man, Two Moon became the leading Cheyenne chief in the battle.[49]

The soldiers put up a stout resistance around Calhoun Hill. "At this place the soldiers stood in line and made a very good fight," said Red Hawk.[50] Some of them fired as many as twenty or thirty rounds from a single position, slowing the Indian advance up the hill and inflicting many casualties. But a soldier with a Springfield trapdoor carbine could fire that many bullets in five minutes or less. The soldiers were completely exposed. Many of those in the skirmish line down the ridge died where they knelt; when their line collapsed back up the hill the entire position was rapidly lost and the whole character of the battle suddenly changed. It was at this moment that the Indians won.

In the minutes before the collapse, the soldiers continued to hold a single, roughly continuous line along the half-mile backbone from Calhoun to Custer Hill. Men had been killed and wounded but the force of some 210 remained largely intact. It is likely that the eleven dead and wounded among the Indians cited by Gall were matched by similar numbers among the soldiers. The Indians heavily outnumbered the whites, but nothing like a rout had begun. What changed everything, according to the Indians, was a sudden and unexpected charge up over the backbone by a large force on horseback. The central and controlling part played by Crazy Horse in this assault was witnessed and later reported by many of his friends and relatives, including He Dog, Red Feather, and Flying Hawk.

When the first group of soldiers—Reno's men—were retreating across the river and up the bluffs on the far side, Crazy Horse had headed back toward the center of camp. He had time to reach the mouth of Muskrat Creek and Medicine Tail Coulee at roughly fifteen minutes past four o'clock, just as the small detachment of soldiers watched by Gall had recoiled back away from the river toward higher ground. It was here that He Dog heard the few shots exchanged before the soldiers moved away and the Indians started to climb the hill after them. Flying Hawk, brother of Kicking Bear and friend of Crazy Horse, said he had followed Crazy Horse down the river toward the center of camp. "We came to a ravine," Flying Hawk recalled for a friend. "Then we followed up the gulch to a place in the rear of the soldiers that were making the stand on the hill."

Gall said much the same: "Crazy Horse went to the extreme north end of the camp and then turned to his right and went up another very deep

ravine and by following it, which he did, he came very close to the soldiers on the north side." From his half-protected vantage at the head of a
ravine, Flying Hawk said, Crazy Horse "shot them as fast as he could load
his gun."[51]

This was one style of Sioux fighting. Another was the brave run or the
charge. Typically the change from one to the other was preceded by no
long discussion; a warrior simply took it into his mind that the moment
was right. He might shout out, "I am going!" Or he might yell out the
charge word "*Hokahey!*" or give the war trill or clench an eagle-bone
whistle between his teeth and blow the piercing *scree* sound. Red Feather
said Crazy Horse's moment came at the point in the battle where the two
sides were keeping low and popping up to shoot at each other—a standoff
moment. More Indians were coming all the time; it may be that Crazy
Horse simply felt the moment was ripe to overwhelm the soldiers. The
Arapaho Waterman said the Indians had "moved up the hill and closed in
on the soldiers. There was a great deal of noise and confusion. The air
was heavy with powder smoke, and the Indians were all yelling." Out of
this chaos, said Red Feather, Crazy Horse "came up on horseback," blowing his eagle-bone whistle and riding down between the length of the two
lines of fighters. "Crazy Horse," said Waterman, "was the bravest man I
ever saw. He rode closest to the soldiers, yelling to his warriors. All the
soldiers were shooting at him but he was never hit." Red Feather said the
same: "The soldiers all fired at once, but didn't hit him."[52] It was this
brave run of Crazy Horse, thought Red Feather, that triggered the first of
the two major charges the Indians made on the soldiers.

The excitement of Crazy Horse making his run in front of the soldiers,
the piercing *scree* of his whistle, the crashing of the soldiers' guns coming
all at once suddenly impelled a great mass of Indians up into motion. Red
Feather thought the critical element was the concerted volley at the gal-
loping chief; it would take a few moments for the soldiers to reload. In
that brief moment of imagined safety the Indians rose up and charged.
Here and now, said He Dog in 1910, "is where Crazy Horse charged and
broke through and split up soldiers into two bunches." Ten years later he
told a second interviewer much the same: "There is a sort of gap in the
ridge which Crazy Horse broke through, cutting the line in two." Panic
followed instantly; the men gathered around Calhoun Hill were suddenly
cut off from the rest of the soldiers stretching along the backbone toward
Custer Hill, leaving each bunch alone to face the hordes of Indians on
foot and horseback in among them.

Red Feather had charged with Crazy Horse; his horse was shot from under him.

> He came to an officer who was shot through the stomach who was sitting on the ground, holding a gun in his hand. Red Feather tried to take the gun away, but the officer dropped the gun and grabbed Red Feather [who] was scared to death until someone shot the officer.

Soldiers always tried to keep an enemy at bay, to kill him at a distance. The instinct of Sioux fighters was for exactly the opposite: to charge in and touch the enemy with a quirt, bow, or naked hand while he was still alive. There is no terror in battle to equal physical contact—shouting, hot breath, the grip of a hand from a man close enough to smell. The charge of Crazy Horse brought the Indians right in among the soldiers who were clubbed and stabbed to death. The soldiers recoiled away in the two bunches cited by He Dog.[53]

The soldiers still alive at the southern end of the backbone now made a run for it, grabbing horses if they could, running on foot if they had to. Foolish Elk said,

> All were going toward the high ground at end of ridge. The gray horses went up in a body; then came bay horses and men on foot all mixed together. The men on horses did not stop to fight, but went ahead as fast as they could go. The men on foot, however, were shooting as they passed along.[54]

"Bunches" was the word He Dog had used. There were no more skirmish lines. Men crowded in on each other for safety, too panicked to think clearly. Organized resistance was at an end. Iron Hawk said the Indians followed close behind the fleeing soldiers, "picking up arms and revolvers and ammunition and . . . using these instead of clubs and bows and arrows." Red Hawk said much the same: "By this time the Indians were taking the guns and cartridges of the dead soldiers and putting these to use." There were plenty of guns to take—a carbine and a revolver from each of thirty bodies on Calhoun Ridge and Calhoun Hill, more all the time from the bodies of soldiers killed along the backbone leading toward the Keogh site and Custer Hill. It is likely the guns taken earlier from as many as thirty soldiers killed in the retreat to the river had by this time also reached the fighting along the backbone. Now the boom of the Springfield carbines was coming from Indian and white fighters alike. Now the killing was quick and one-sided.

"We rode among them and pulled them from their horses," said White Bull.

"Everywhere the Sioux went the dust rose like smoke," said Two Moons.

Indians shot into the fleeing men from behind. In the rush of survivors from Calhoun Hill to rejoin the rest of the command, the soldiers fell dead with no more pattern than scattered corn. In the depression or buffalo wallow where the body of Keogh was found were the bodies of perhaps twenty men, all crowded tight in around him. But the Indians describe no real fight there—just a rush without pause right up along the backbone, killing men all the way. "They made no stand here," said Foolish Elk. Keogh and the men who clung to him were evidently overrun in a moment, shot down and killed in the time it takes to write it. While these died others ran; the line of bodies continued along the backbone. "We circled all around them," Two Moons said, "swirling like water round a stone."[55]

Another little group of dead was left on the slope rising up to Custer Hill, ten or more. On the ground stretching from the site of this group to Custer Hill, a distance of about two hundred yards, no bodies were found. The soldiers on the gray and bay horses had dashed ahead, leaving the men on foot to fend for themselves. Perhaps this last group that died on the slope were all that remained of the soldiers on foot. Or it is possible the open stretch of ground with no bodies was the result of organized firing from Custer Hill, holding the Indians at bay while survivors ran up the slope. Whatever the cause, something briefly halted the momentum of the pursuit. The Indian accounts mostly agree that there was some kind of pause in the fighting before the final climax—some moment used for positioning, closing in, creeping up, delivering a hot fire onto the soldiers who were falling all the time, preparing for the second and the last of the charges cited by Red Feather.

But this pause was brief; it offered no time for the soldiers to count survivors. Officers and men were all jumbled up, many wounded. Certain big facts must have been obvious: half of Custer's men were already dead, huge numbers of Indians were pressing in from all sides, the horses were wounded or dead or had run off, there was nothing to hide behind. "When the horses got to the top of the ridge the gray ones and bays became mingled, and the soldiers with them were all in confusion," said Foolish Elk. Then he added what no white soldier lived to tell: "The Indians were so numerous that the soldiers could not go any further, and they knew that they had to die."

Indians on horseback raced around the soldiers; others crept closer to shoot carefully. The whites were in chaos. The shouts and yells and crashing of guns terrified the horses, who became "wild with fright and uncontrollable," said Horned Horse. Red Feather said the plunging of their horses "pulled the men all around, and a great many of their shots went up in the air." The Indians surrounding the soldiers on Custer Hill were now joined by others arriving from every section of the field, from down near the river where they had been chasing horses, from stripping the dead of guns and ammunition along the ridge, from up the river where Reno's men on their hilltop could hear the beginning of the last heavy volley of firing a few minutes past five o'clock. "There were great numbers of us," said Eagle Bear, "some on horseback, others on foot. Back and forth in front of Custer we passed, firing all the time."

Kill Eagle, speaking only a few weeks later, said the firing came in waves; he clapped "the palms of his hands together very fast for several minutes" to demonstrate the intensity of the firing at its height, then clapped slower, then faster, then slower, then stopped.

The soldiers were helpless; in this final stage of the fight they killed or wounded very few Indians. The young Cheyenne Brave Bear said, "I think Custer saw he was caught in bad place and would like to have gotten out of it if he could, but he was hemmed in all around and could do nothing only to die then."[56]

When Custer died is unknown; his body was found in a pile of soldiers near the top of a hill surrounded by other men within a circle of dead horses, one of them his own. It is probable that he fell during the second and final charge by the Indians. In this final charge almost everybody took part. The job did not take long. Low Dog called to his followers, "This is a good day to die: follow me." The Indians raced up together, a solid mass, close enough to whip each other's horses with their quirts so no man would linger behind. Low Dog and Crow King were in the thick of it. "Then every chief rushed his horse on the soldiers, and all our warriors did the same," said Crow King. "There was great hurry and confusion in the fight." This is what Horned Horse had described when he tangled his fingers together—"Just like this, Indians and white men."

In their terror the soldiers threw their guns away, put their hands in the air, and begged mercy, saying, "Sioux, pity us; take us prisoners." But the Sioux took prisoner only women or children, not grown men. Red Horse said the Sioux "did not take a single soldier, but killed all of them;

none were left alive for even a few minutes." Now the mass of whites disintegrated utterly, men died without firing their guns, the surviving horses stampeded away from the noise and struggle, and the young Standing Bear heard Indians shouting, "They are gone!"[57]

Not more than half the soldiers had lived to reach Custer Hill. Now half of that half were dead or dying and the last forty or more of the soldiers on foot with only a few on horseback—Two Moons said five; others said two—dashed away downhill toward the river. One of the mounted men wore buckskins; Indians said he fought with a big knife. "His men were all covered with white dust," said Two Moons.

These soldiers were met by some Indians coming up from the river; among them was the twelve-year-old Black Elk. He noted that the soldiers were moving oddly—"They were making their arms go as though they were running, but they were only walking." He thought they were panicked; more likely these men were wounded, hobbling, lurching, throwing themselves forward in the hope to escape.[58]

All these men were hunted down by the Indians following them downhill, killing them all the way. Some of the whites jumped or clambered down into a deep ravine in the hope of escape. On the steep, far side of the ravine soldiers left claw marks in the gravely banks as they tried to scramble up with their hands. "We were right on top of the soldiers and there was no use in their hiding from us," said the young Standing Bear. The Indians chased them down "with arrows, guns and war clubs," he said. Respects Nothing remarked that some of the clubs were of stone, and some were of the kind known as gunstock clubs, with two or three knife blades protruding from the edge. To be crushed and stabbed to death with such a weapon was the ultimate horror.

Brings Plenty and Iron Hawk killed two men running up a creek bed and figured they were the last. Others said the last man dashed away on a fast horse, pulled steadily ahead of his pursuers as he raced upriver toward Reno Hill, and then inexplicably shot himself in the head with his own revolver. Still another last man, it was reported, was killed by the sons of the noted Santee warrior chief Red Top (Inkpaduta), a leader of the Sioux war of 1862. Two Moon said no, the last was a man with braids on his soldier shirt (i.e., a sergeant) who rode one of the remaining horses faster than the others heading in the final rush for the river. He eluded his pursuers by rounding a hill and then making his way back upriver. But just as Two Moons thought this man might succeed in escaping a Sioux shot and killed him. It is possible this was the same man Flying Hawk said was killed by his friend Crazy Horse—a white soldier who bolted on horse-back in the final moments of the fighting. He seemed to be getting away until Crazy Horse "got him" about half a mile to the east. But the truth is that none of these "last men" was really the last to die. The truly last were the soldiers lying wounded on the field or pretending to be dead.[59]

Very quickly after the fight was over the hill was swarming with Indians: warriors putting a final bullet into soldiers, women and boys who had climbed the long slopes from the village. They joined the warriors who had dismounted to empty the pockets of the dead soldiers and strip them of their clothes. It was a scene of horror. Many of the bodies were mutilated, but in later years Indians did not like to talk about that. They said they had not seen it and did not know who had done it. But the testimony of witnesses was impossible to ignore. Soldiers going over the field in the following days left many detailed descriptions of the mutilations, and drawings made by the Miniconjou Red Horse left no room for doubt. Red Horse gave one of the earliest Indian accounts of the battle, and a few years later he made an extraordinary series of more than forty large drawings of the fighting and of the dead strewn over the field. Many pages were devoted to the dead Indians, each lying in his distinctive dress and headgear. Additional pages showed the dead soldiers, some naked, some half stripped. Each page depicting the white dead, like the battlefield itself, showed many severed arms, hands, legs, heads. These mutilations, like the killing of every soldier, were evidence of the Indians' anger; they believed a man was condemned to have the body he brought with him to the afterlife.[60]

"The young boys between the ages of 11 and 15 years old," said Eagle Bear, "ran from one body to another, shooting arrows and firing rifles into them." Eagle Ring, the eleven-year-old son of Respects Nothing, was one of these. He was on the hill with the women after the fight and watched as women beat the corpses with sticks. "They stripped the dead naked," he said, "but did not mutilate the bodies."

Black Elk was also on the hill. When he and his friends found a soldier with arrows sticking out of him they would grab hold of the shaft and shove it in further. After the men's boots had been pulled or cut off, boys would jam iron arrow points in between the toes of the soldiers to be sure they were dead. Occasionally one of the soldiers was still alive. At any sign of life, said the Arapaho Waterman, "The squaws would become frightened and scatter." But not all ran away. Men named Swift Bear and White Bull, brothers of Crow King, had been killed in the early part of the fight.

When it was over two sisters of the dead men climbed the hill with the rest of the women and children; they "came with axes and knocked the brains out of some wounded soldiers." Moving Robe Woman killed soldiers to avenge the death of her brother, Deeds.

Acts of revenge were integral to the Indians' notion of justice, and they did not forget quickly. The Cheyenne White Necklace, then in her middle fifties and wife of Wolf Chief, had carried in her heart for a dozen years bitter memories of the death of a niece, killed in the massacre at Sand Creek in 1864. "When they found her there, her head was cut off," she said later. Coming up the hill in the first minutes after the fighting had ended, White Necklace came upon the naked body of a soldier lying dead. She had a hand ax in her belt. "I jumped off my horse and did the same to him," she recalled. "I cut off his head!"[61]

In one case, talked about for a hundred years among the Cheyenne, some women on the hill took their revenge on the body of a man they recognized. Most Indians claimed that no one really knew who was the leader of the soldiers until weeks or even months after the battle. He Dog always said he learned that General Custer was at the Little Bighorn two weeks later when some Indians coming out from the Standing Rock Agency said it was Long Hair they had killed on the hill. Others said no, there was talk of Custer on that very first day. The Oglala Little Killer, twenty-four years old at the time of the battle, remembered that Custer's name was sung by warriors during the dancing held in the big camp that night. Nobody knew which body was Custer's, Little Killer said, but they knew he was there. Sixty years later in 1937, he remembered the song.

> Long Hair, Long Hair,
> I was short of guns, and you brought us many.
> Long Hair, Long Hair,
> I was short of horses, and you brought us many.[62]

It is possible that some Indians knew Custer was there while most did not. As late as the 1920s elderly Cheyenne said two southern Cheyenne women on the hill came upon the body of Custer. He had been shot in the head and in the side. The southern Cheyenne Magpie, known to have been at the Little Bighorn, was one of those who repeated this story. Kate Big Head was another. Magpie and Kate Big Head, along with others, said that the two southern Cheyenne women knew Custer from the time of the Battle of the Washita in 1868, and had seen him up close the following spring when he had come to make peace with Stone Forehead and smoked with the chiefs in the lodge of the Arrow Keeper. There Custer had promised never again to fight the Cheyenne, and Stone Forehead, in order to hold him to his promise, had emptied the ashes from the pipe onto Custer's boots while the general, all unknowing, sat directly beneath the sacred arrows hanging from the lodgepoles above.

It was said that these two women were relatives of Mo-nah-se-tah, the Cheyenne girl whose father was killed at the Washita by Custer. Many believed that Mo-nah-se-tah had been Custer's lover for a time. No matter how brief, such a connection was considered to be a marriage according to Indian custom. On the hill at the Little Bighorn, it was told, the two southern Cheyenne women stopped some Sioux men who were going to cut up Custer's body. "He is a relative of ours," they said. The Sioux men went away.

Every Cheyenne woman routinely carried on her person a sewing awl in a leather sheath decorated with beads or porcupine quills. The awl was used daily, for sewing clothing or lodge covers, and perhaps most frequently for keeping moccasins in repair. The moccasin soles were made of the heavy skin from a buffalo's neck; this was the same material used for shields and it was prepared in the same way—not tanned, but dried into rawhide. Pushing an awl through this hide required strength. "The making and keeping in repair of moccasins was a ceaseless task," noted Lieutenant Clark in his notes for a book on the Indian sign language. "The last thing each day for the women was to look over the moccasins and see that each member of the family was supplied for the ensuing day."[63] In the many photos of Plains Indian women taken during the nineteenth and early twentieth century their hands are notable for thickness and strength.

In the early days the awls of the Plains Indians consisted of a five- or six-inch sliver of bone, polished to a fine, slender point at one end for piercing leather, and rounded at the other to fit into the palm of the hand for pushing through tough animal hides. In later times Indian women acquired awls of steel from traders. It will be recalled that Custer's wife, Elizabeth, had once worried that Mo-nah-se-tah would pull out a knife concealed about her person and stab her husband to death. Now the southern Cheyenne women among the bodies on the hill overlooking the river took their awls and pushed them deep into the ears of the man they believed to be Custer. He had not listened to the warning of Stone Forehead, they said. He had broken his promise not to fight the Cheyenne anymore, they said. Now his hearing would be improved, they said.[64]

The morning after the big fight the Indians renewed their attack on the soldiers forted up on the hill, but along about the middle of the afternoon scouts reported that more soldiers were coming up the river. It was decided to break off the fight and move the big camp. For several hours a huge mass of Indians and ponies moved upriver. The dust kicked up by the ponies and the smoke from a prairie fire partially obscured the departing Indians, but soldiers on the hill said later the mass was so dense it was impossible to distinguish one Indian from the next, or a man from a woman, and the whole body was at least a mile wide and a mile and a half or two miles long. While the big camp was moving away a number of Indians pinned down the soldiers on the hill with well-aimed shots. After the people were gone, the last of the fighters took their horses and departed.

The soldiers were watched closely the next day by Indian scouts. One of them was He Dog's younger brother, Short Bull, who was nearby when the soldiers walked over the battlefield, picking things up and burying the dead. The wounded survivors from the first fight were placed on litters which headed downriver to the mouth of the Bighorn. "I was one of the scouts who saw this and reported to Crazy Horse," said Short Bull.[65]

On that day or perhaps the next it was said that Crazy Horse sought out an inscription rock along Ash Creek, which winds up and away from the Little Bighorn toward the divide in the east. He was accompanied by a noted Cheyenne warrior named Braided Locks, who watched as Crazy Horse scratched or etched into the sandstone a petroglyph of his name— a horse, a snake, and jagged streaks of lightning. A wavy line in the air was the sign for snake, and it was also a sign for crazy. The lightning streaks suggested a modified craziness, something closer to a vision or sacred swoon. Braided Locks later told his son, Whistling Elk, that this drawing on the rocks came from a vision:

> Crazy Horse had dreamed the horse was standing on a high pinnacle and he saw the snake above it and streaks of lightning moving over it. He must have had the vision back when he was a young man, and maybe he used it for power all his life afterwards."[66]

Over the summer of 1877 Lieutenant Clark questioned many Indians about the fight at the Little Bighorn. From Crazy Horse himself Clark seems to have learned only that two horses had been shot from under him in the fighting. Clark does not name the other Oglala he asked about the fight, but one of them drew a rough map of the battlefield in pencil on the floor of Clark's quarters at Camp Robinson. Before leaving the Indian attempted to scuff out the map with the sole of his moccasin, but sufficient remained, Clark said, "to allow me to retrace it, which I did and then copied it on paper."

Like every early map, Clark's showed a series of camp circles along the west bank of the Little Bighorn with the Hunkpapas (upriver) in the south and the Cheyenne (downriver) in the north. A dotted line showed Custer's route down toward the river at Minneconjou Ford. A coulee and ridge lead up and away to the hilltop where Custer was found dead. Clark gives a brisk, no-frills account of the fight. His explanation for the disaster is already familiar: too many Indians. "The troops attempted to rally once or twice but were literally overwhelmed with numbers and in a few moments not one was left alive to tell the story."

Lieutenant Clark was writing for the Army. His report was addressed to the adjutant general of the Department of the Platte; Crook read it and forwarded it to Sheridan, who passed it on to Sherman. Clark's conclusion was unadorned.

This fight brought Crazy Horse more prominently before all the Indians than any one else. He rode with the greatest daring up and down in front of Colonel Reno's skirmish line, and as soon as these Indians were driven across the river, he went at once to General Custer's front and there became the leading spirit. Before this he had a great reputation; in it he gained a greater prestige than any other Indian in the camp.

These words left no room for doubt: among the Indians, Crazy Horse was the dangerous man.

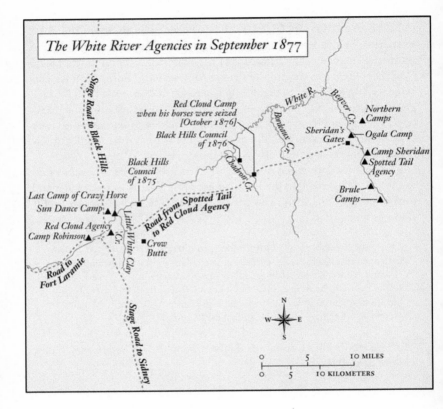

The White River Agencies in September 1877

Stage Road to Black Hills

White R.

Beaver Cr.

Northern Camps

Red Cloud Camp when his horses were seized [October 1876]

Black Hills Council of 1876

Sheridan's Gates

Ogala Camp

Bordeaux Cr.

Camp Sheridan
Spotted Tail Agency

Black Hills Council of 1875

Chadron Cr.

Brule Camps

Last Camp of Crazy Horse
Sun Dance Camp

Road from Spotted Tail to Red Cloud Agency

Little White Clay Cr.

Red Cloud Agency
Camp Robinson

Crow Butte

Road to Fort Laramie

Stage Road to Sidney

N
W   E
S

0   5   10 MILES
0   5   10 KILOMETERS

25

"It is impossible to work him through reasoning or kindness."

GEORGE CROOK CONSIDERED HIMSELF a skilled handler of Indians. Firmness was important, in his view, but honesty and steadiness came first. In March 1877, he took time to explain his approach to the new agent at the Spotted Tail Agency, Lieutenant Jesse Lee. The general, Lee said later,

> personally gave me instructions as to how best to handle Indians. He told me, for one thing, not to promise anything that I could not carry out, and whenever I did promise anything to always keep my word . . . I should take hold with a firm hand and lead them to think and believe that whatever I said they could rely upon.[1]

But Crook ignored his own sound advice and made promises which he could never keep. At the big council in May he promised to take up the matter of Crazy Horse's agency in the north with the Great Father personally, and he spoke of the removal as still very much up in the air. This was not true. Crook was in no doubt about General Sherman's policy for handling the Sioux: "remove all to a safe place and then reduce them to a helpless condition." The safe place the government had in mind for the Oglala and Brulé Sioux was some two hundred miles east at new agencies on the Missouri River, well away from the Union Pacific Railroad along the Platte River and the goldfields in the Black Hills. The decision to move the Indians before winter had already been reached. An act of Congress in mid-April, Crook was told, "provides for their removal to the Missouri River and there is no law which will permit them to remain where they are, or will warrant their removal to any other location."[2]

All that summer the bureaucratic machinery for removal of the Indians was in motion. Two sites were picked on the Missouri, construction began on new buildings, contracts were let for shipment of beef and rations to the new agencies. Of these things Crook told the Indians nothing. After awhile the general's silence in itself became a promise. What he wanted was quiet, and that is what he got. In mid-July, while Crook was walking over the Custer battlefield, the new commander of the military post at Camp Robinson, Colonel Luther P. Bradley, wrote to assure the general that all was well: "We are as quiet here as a Yankee village on a Sunday."

But as an afterthought, a sentence or two later, he remarked, "I think there is a little rivalry between Spotted Tail and Crazy Horse." Bradley thought it was probably Crazy Horse who bristled most. At issue was "who shall have the largest following of the northern Indians."[3] He was referring to the Miniconjou and Sans Arcs who had surrendered with Touch the Clouds in April after spending the winter in the Tongue River country with Crazy Horse. Now these northern Indians were camped nine miles upstream from Camp Sheridan along a creek that fed into the White River. They were drawing their rations at the Spotted Tail Agency, but many of their relatives lived in the Crazy Horse camp some forty miles distant. There was a good deal of movement back and forth between the agencies. Things were unsettled. A little rivalry between the chiefs might be a good thing, or it might not. To keep track of the shifting mood of the Indians Bradley depended on Lieutenant Clark, who did not trust to chance but watched the chiefs with spies. Clark's quarters were at one end of the row of officers' quarters and Bradley's were at the other. To Clark's rooms as it grew dark following taps Indians came all summer long with their reports.

Luther Prentice Bradley was a slow, deliberate man of strong principles. It was the Civil War which made him a soldier. Before the war Bradley had been a stationer and bookseller in Chicago, then in the fall of 1861 joined the 51st Illinois Volunteers two months short of his thirty-eighth birthday, rose to command a brigade, fought from Kennesaw Mountain to Spring Hill, Tennessee. As an officer he was entitled to ride, but he bought and paid for his horses himself. At Stone's River, two horses were shot from under him: Charlie, a seven-year-old bay, purchased a month before enlisting; and John, a smallish, dark brown horse he had owned but a few weeks. His favorite horse was perhaps Salem, sixteen hands high—"a fine old fellow, stout and brave." Salem was shot at Kennesaw Mountain in June 1864.

Bradley recorded the death of his horses as methodically as he did his own wounds. At Chickamauga he was on Salem leading a charge against

Hood's division when he was shot twice within the span of a minute, balls passing through his right hip and shoulder. "The wound in my hip is doing finely," he wrote his mother two weeks later, "and I can already walk pretty well with a crutch and cane. My arm scarcely troubles me at all, though I suppose the ball is still in there." One of Hood's men shot him again at Spring Hill in November 1864, this time in the left shoulder. A doctor reported the arm partly paralyzed in February; three months later it was still almost useless. Bradley resigned shortly after war's end as a brigadier general of volunteers, then a year later rejoined the regular army as a lieutenant colonel. It was a common pattern—old job gone, or bored with civilian life, often both.

Bradley's introduction to Indian fighting was a sobering one; in the spring of 1867 he served on a commission inquiring into the defeat of Captain William Fetterman by the Sioux in the fight they called the Battle of a Hundred in the Hand. The next year, after a period in command of one of the forts along the Bozeman Road, Bradley took leave to get married in Chicago. He was forty-six. Over the following eight years he became the father of two boys and held commands all over the plains. In May 1877, General Crook sent him to replace Colonel Mackenzie at Camp Robinson.

Bradley arrived at the isolated post on Saturday, May 26, after a jolting, all-night stagecoach ride from Sidney, Nebraska, playing whist with fellow officers to kill time. On the first day, he shook hands with Crazy Horse, finding him "a young, slender and mild-mannered fellow." Before bed he wrote to his wife, Ione, telling her "I haven't had time to be lonely yet." For the remainder of the summer and the early fall he wrote Ione faithfully twice a week, usually on Sunday and Wednesday, invariably four pages on a single sheet folded in half.[4]

Bradley had married late and doted on his wife. His letters were generally prosaic and cheerful, ending with sweet words for Ione and the boys. His news was intended to reassure, not alarm. The weather was a regular topic. He told Ione it was hot, it was dusty, and the wind blew from all points of the compass. When he spoke of Indians his tone was light. "If you know of anyone who wants to see Indians—wild or tame ones—send them up here," he wrote Ione at the end of May. "I have all kinds in my charge, and they swarm around us."

Bradley took particular note of one elderly Indian, recently arrived with the band of Crazy Horse, who rode to the post on his pony for a visit. He was too frail to dismount easily, so Bradley came out to chat.

The interpreter on this occasion was probably John B. Provost, a mixed-blood in his early twenties who had recently been hired to interpret for Dr. Valentine McGillycuddy. Provost had grown up among his mother's people, the Oglala, and the year before had married Sunka Wakanwinla (Holy Horse Woman), a seventeen-year-old daughter of the elder Black Elk, who had come in to surrender with Crazy Horse in May.[5]

The old man thanked Bradley for coming out to shake his hand. Bradley asked about a stick he carried. It was about six feet long, "covered with notches, thousands of them."

"It was the history of the world from the beginning, handed down by his fathers," Bradley remarked in his next letter to Ione.

We hear nothing more about the old man or his stick, but there can be little doubt it was a Sioux chronicle called a winter count, a *waniyetu;* the notches represented the names of years which the old man could read to recount the history of the Oglala. Numerous examples survive of winter counts painted onto hide, muslin cloth, or the pages of ledger books. Oglala counts are mostly related to the No Ears count with variants introduced by the different Oglala bands—the Year (or Winter) He Crow Was Killed by the Shoshones (1844–45) recorded by one band might be named by another the Year the Crow Came and Killed Thirty-Eight Oglala. Same year, different band, different name. The history notched onto the six-foot stave by Bradley's visitor would have recorded the specific history of Crazy Horse's Hunkpatila band. If the old man returned to tell Bradley the story, as he promised he would do, there must have been an awkward moment when it came to the last notch. For the members of Crazy Horse's band there can be little doubt what it was: 1876–77 would have been Pehin Hanska Kasota Waniyetu—the Year Long Hair Was Rubbed Out.

But evidently Bradley did not know this. Describing his conversation with the old man brought Bradley to the end of his four pages. "Kiss the dear fellows for me and . . . take a kiss for your dear self too."[6]

Valentine McGillycuddy was the second doctor at Camp Robinson, and as such often got the hardest jobs. In early 1877 he had been sent out with a cavalry detachment into the Black Hills for several months of travel and camping in the subzero temperatures, biting winds, and snow of Dakota winters. In McGillycuddy's absence the senior doctor at Camp Robinson, Curtis E. Munn, treated not only soldiers, including the officers and their wives, but the Indians at the Red Cloud Agency and the hundreds of Cheyenne who made their way in to surrender. Munn had served through the Civil War, but the wounds he saw then were no worse than some of the injuries he treated among the Cheyenne. One man, shot through the kneecap in the fight on the Red Fork of the Powder River five months earlier, had been severely crippled when the muscle and scar tissue contracted—"ankylosed" was the term then as now—so the heel of his right foot touched the upper leg. Surgery—without anesthetic—was the treatment for such a condition. Munn handled the Indians by himself until McGillycuddy, the contract surgeon, returned on April 19 from his months in the Black Hills. Three weeks later McGillycuddy was on call when Crazy Horse and his band surrendered on May 6, a Sunday morning. That afternoon the young doctor, still in his twenties, was summoned to Crazy Horse's lodge to treat the chief's wife, Black Shawl Woman. He diagnosed her illness as consumption—"far advanced"—and said later that in the course of speaking with Crazy Horse "we became good friends."[7]

Sometime that summer, Crazy Horse took a second wife. Some accounts say that his own father had two wives during the latter part of his life, sisters who were related to Spotted Tail. But many open questions attach to Crazy Horse's second wife, beginning with the abruptness of her appearance on the scene in the summer of 1877. The woman in question was Ellen Larrabee, whose last name was spelled half a dozen different ways. She was commonly known as Nellie, the twenty-four or twenty-five-year-old daughter of a French trader from St. Charles on the Missouri River, Joe Larrabee, and a full-blood Cheyenne woman called Shahunwinla (Cheyenne Woman) by the Oglala. Larrabee's four attractive daughters were well known in the area: Zoe married the blacksmith at Camp Robinson, Connie Utterback; Julie married the boss of the agency beef herd, Mike Dunn; and Sally the next year would marry a local rancher, Scotty Philip. Only Ellen married Indians and lived out her life among them. Baptiste Pourier said later that it was Lieutenant Clark who somehow arranged Ellen's marriage to Crazy Horse, thinking that a mixed blood wife would "make him more kindly disposed to the whites." No exchange of horses or long courtship was involved; Ellen simply arrived one day and presented herself to the chief, an event witnessed and later described by a sister of Crazy Horse married to a man named Clown, who had arrived with Crazy Horse's band to surrender in May. Clown's lodge had been set up near the chief's, and his sister was sitting outside one day while Crazy Horse was off on a visit to Wapostan Ska (White Hat), as Clark was called by the Indians.

> I was about to leave for a visit to another lodge, not far away, when I saw this strange woman strolling in my direction. She entered the lodge of my brother and spoke to his wife, who was sewing on a robe . . . When he returned she met him at the door and said, "I am Joe Laravie's daughter so I am part white. I have heard about your great deeds, for my father has told us about you and your victory over Long Hair . . . I pick this day to offer myself to you for your second mate."[8]

Ellen's twelve-year-old half brother, Tom, said later the family knew nothing of her plans. The first sign was her failure to return home one evening. The next day Tom's mother came back from a visit to the Indian camps to tell the family Ellen had married Crazy Horse and was now living in his lodge. None of this was unusual in itself. Among the Indians and the mixed-blood community along the Platte and White rivers men and women from their mid-teens on came together and separated—married or divorced "according to Indian custom," as agency records would say for the next fifty years. It was not uncommon for a woman to tell a pension examiner that she had been married to one man for three days, and to another for fifty years. In the eyes of the Oglala both were marriages. Crazy Horse was married to Black Buffalo Woman for three or four days, to Black Shawl Woman from about 1870 until his death, and to Ellen Larrabee for the last part of the last summer of his life.

But Ellen was something more than simply a third wife. She helped to determine the chief's fate. Just when the marriage took place is unclear. A cousin of Crazy Horse said it was about a month before his death, meaning early August. Ellen's half brother remembered that Ellen's absence from home occurred "a few days after" the arrival of Crazy Horse's band at the agency. That would have been mid-May, about the time Crazy Horse signed on as a sergeant in the Indian scouts with Lieutenant Clark. For something between one and four months, then, Ellen Larrabee lived in the lodge of Crazy Horse.[9]

Camp gossip said she was a woman of strong opinion who did not shy from telling the chief what she thought about the plan to send the chiefs to Washington, or General Crook's promise to help Crazy Horse acquire a new home in the Tongue River country. The only surviving photograph of Ellen in early life shows a slender, attractive young woman sitting on a log in front of a cottonwood tree. Others, taken much later, reveal a still slender, white-haired, stooped woman dressed in Indian finery at festivals and powwows. But all the Larrabee girls were described as handsome in their youth.

Billy Garnett did not like "the Larrabee woman." She was, he said, "not of the best frontier variety," perhaps referring to an off-again, on-again romance with an Oglala variously known as Little Bear, Rascal Boy, or Sioux Bob. Some said that Ellen's father, Joe Larrabee, smiled on Sioux Bob as a son-in-law. Garnett's friend Ghost Bear said later that Sioux Bob "was mixed up with a number of women in his early life." In the summer of 1877, according to Ghost Bear, Sioux Bob was married to "a Cheyenne woman." It is not clear if Ghost Bear meant the half-Cheyenne Ellen Larrabee, or some other woman. In any event, Sioux Bob brought into his lodge a second woman to join the Cheyenne wife: Zuzella Janis, daughter of Antoine Janis and a full-blood Oglala called Mary by whites and Maka Oyate Win (Earth Tribe or Earth Nation) by the Indians.

With Zuzella Janis, Billy Garnett had a long history. They met in the Fort Laramie area when both were about fifteen or sixteen, a year or two after Billy had returned from his time with the Indians in the north. In early 1875, before either turned twenty, Zuzella and Billy Garnett married according to Indian custom, but the relationship lasted only long enough for the birth of Garnett's first son, Charles, in June 1876. In August, Zuzella and Billy separated by Indian custom and a year later both had entered new relationships—Billy with Emma Mills, Zuzella with Sioux Bob. Perhaps Garnett separated from Zuzella with an easy heart, and cared little when she married Sioux Bob. Perhaps not. A year later, after Crazy Horse was killed, Ellen would marry (for three weeks) another man Garnett knew well: Kills a Hundred, who had gone into battle with Garnett on the Red Fork of the Powder River.

How far these entanglements help to explain Garnett's feelings is hard to establish, but it is clear that those feelings were strong. In later life Garnett spoke with unusual asperity about the entrance of Ellen Larrabee into the life of Crazy Horse. He called the woman "insidious and evil." He said she twisted the chief's mind with "her invidious arts." He said, "This woman at once set about to imbue his mind with poisons." Garnett believed Crazy Horse was powerless against Ellen's whispers. The chief ignored the warnings of "a trustworthy advisor." Distrust entered his heart. Plans often discussed and apparently settled, like the trip to Washington, were now called into question. At Garnett's house in early May, Crazy Horse said he must practice with the white man's fork before the

Washington trip, so he would be ready to eat at white men's tables. Now Ellen planted a fatal seed of suspicion. "She told him the trip to Washington was a trick to get him out of the country and keep him, that if he went away he would not be allowed to return."[10]

This poisoning of the chief's mind was not something Garnett witnessed himself. He learned of it bit by bit from gossip in the camps, and from the Indian informants hired by Lieutenant Clark. There was nothing casual about Clark's effort to manage or control the Indians. "Crazy Horse and his people are getting quite sociable," Clark wrote General Crook on August 1, "and I reckon I shall have to be considered one of their tribe soon, as I have been invited down to three feasts." He thought of this process as "working" the Indians by hiring them as scouts, speaking with them frequently, taking their wants seriously, playing to their anxiety or pride, and participating in their amusements, especially horse racing, which was almost a daily affair. Clark had a "running horse," a trained buffalo hunter, sorrel in color, which was much admired for its speed. Many Indians tried to bargain for this horse, but Clark turned them all down. Over the course of the summer, he felt, he had "succeeded in getting on excellent 'dog-eating' terms" with Crazy Horse and his followers.[11]

But Clark did not limit his efforts to being a good fellow, nor take Crazy Horse simply at his word. For control he also depended on a network of watchers who would circulate through the camps with their ears open, perhaps the simplest and oldest system of espionage. Among those trusted by Clark were Few Tails, Iron Bear, the brothers Lone Bear, Little Wolf, and Woman Dress.[12] The first three had been sent north to Crazy Horse's camp during the previous winter, then had slipped back onto the agency with the northern Indians as they came in to surrender. But of all Clark's spies probably the most important and the best connected throughout the agency was Woman Dress, a thirty-year-old grandson of the noted Oglala leader Smoke, a son of Black Twin, and a relative in the complex Indian way (perhaps a nephew, perhaps a cousin) of Red Cloud.

As the son and grandson of chiefs, Woman Dress—Winyan Cuwignake—moved easily in the affairs of the tribe. Once, on the second or third day of a fast on a hilltop, Woman Dress in a dream "heard a rumbling noise. Looking up, he saw before him a mountain sheep with its curling horns and large yellow eyes. The sheep remained an instant, then vanished and in its stead was its skull." The meaning of his dream is elusive, and the mountain sheep was an unusual animal to visit in a dream. Some Oglala said there was no society of sheep dreamers, but others said there was. Woman Dress remembered the visit of the sheep in his dream for the rest of his life, describing it to a white man when he was nearly seventy years old.[13]

Beginning about 1860, when Woman Dress was only fourteen or fifteen years old, he joined one after another the societies known as Sotka Yuha (Bare Lance Owners), Tokala (Kit Fox), Cante Tinza (Brave Hearts), Wiciska (White Marked), and Miwatani (Leading Men). All were men's societies which encouraged responsibility for the tribe or bravery in battle. As a member of a leading family among the Oglala, Woman Dress would be given precedence over men of more obscure background, but admission to these societies was never automatic. The history of Woman Dress suggests he was a man of considerable standing, and he was connected to the whites as well. His wife, Gray Cow, was a first cousin of Josephine Richard, who married Baptiste Pourier in 1869 about the time he signed on as a scout and guide for the soldiers at Fort Laramie. Not long after Pourier married Josephine, Woman Dress was one of a raiding party of young Oglala who ran off all the horses and mules belonging to the couple. But then Woman Dress learned that the victim was Pourier, who had become his relative by marrying a cousin of Red Cloud. He insisted on returning Pourier's animals, ignoring the threats of the other raiders, who said they would kill him. Thereafter, Woman Dress and Pourier were bound together by obligation, blood, and family connection.[14]

Woman Dress and the others had all enlisted as scouts, and Crazy Horse soon discovered, according to Crook's aide-de-camp, Lieutenant John Bourke, that "the Indian soldiers . . . acted as a police force, and exercised a system of espionage." Crazy Horse was himself a sergeant of a company of Indian scouts with twenty of his own men under his control. But there were two other companies of scouts, and all of them reported to Lieutenant Clark. Crazy Horse's camp, Bourke wrote, "was filled with soldiers, in uniform or without, but each and all reporting to the military officials each and every act taking place under their observation. Even his council lodge was no longer safe; all that was said therein was repeated by someone."[15]

On the surface the agency may have been as quiet as a Yankee village on a Sunday, just as Colonel Bradley had described it, but beneath the surface rivalries and resentments were the meat of camp gossip. In early spring, the chiefs had all favored the trip to Washington. Red Cloud and Slow Bear, who had both gone north to convince Crazy Horse to surrender, "told him that he ought to go to Washington and that it would be all right." Crazy Horse told his friend He Dog that he would go. But as spring turned into summer things changed. The chiefs turned against Crazy Horse. Plain jealousy was a big part of it. Red Cloud and Spotted Tail had been great warriors in their day, but now Crazy Horse, the man who rubbed out Pehin Hanska, was the chief looked up to by all the young men. Setting the chiefs against each other was part of Crook's method for controlling them, beginning with his humiliation of Red Cloud the previous October when he publicly appointed Spotted Tail as chief of all the Sioux. Now the general let it be known that he planned to put Crazy Horse still higher. It was common report everywhere. "Crazy Horse was much favored at first by the authorities," it was said. "The rumors were that at first Crazy Horse's demands were granted and . . . he got special favors." The young warrior Little Killer, a man Crazy Horse called cousin, said Red Cloud and Spotted Tail "were jealous of him and afraid that if he went to Washington they would make him chief of all the Indians on the reservation." Crazy Horse told White Rabbit, one of the warriors in the chief's band, that he hesitated to make the trip, "for the talk that he was to be made chief over all was causing intense jealousy."[16]

But the resentment of the chiefs did not stop at jealousy. "Everyone knew that Spotted Tail and Red Cloud were jealous of Crazy Horse and wished him out of the way," said Susan Bordeaux, whose husband Charles Tackett was a scout and interpreter at the Spotted Tail Agency. "Out of the way" was not a neutral term. In the Oglala political world the wish was often father to the deed. Red Cloud became chief when he killed Bull Bear. Spotted Tail confirmed his position as chief when he killed Big Mouth. Word filtered back to Crazy Horse that the other chiefs "conspired to get him out of the way." Some of the bearers of tales were friends, some enemies. "These Indians came to him and told him a lot of stories," said Little Killer, whose brother, Club Man,[17] was married to Crazy Horse's sister. In his work for Lieutenant Clark, Billy Garnett heard many of these stories. The elder Black Elk, bitterly opposed to the whites since he had been crippled in the Battle of a Hundred in the Hand, told the chief "substantially the same silly falsehoods" as Ellen Larrabee. Black Elk's son-in-law, the scout John Provost, "likewise had the chief's ear," said Garnett.

But Provost introduced a darker strain of suspicion. He cited the fate of another captured Indian chief, Captain Jack of the Modoc, who had killed a general named Canby a few years back. Captain Jack and two others had been hung by the soldiers in revenge. What Provost told Crazy Horse, according to Garnett, insinuated that the whites were planning for the killer of Custer what they had done to the killer of Canby. "When once he was conveyed east," Provost told Crazy Horse, "he would be imprisoned, perhaps placed on some island in the sea and indefinitely confined, or otherwise disposed of so that he would never return." Who repeated these conversations to Garnett is unknown. It may have been Provost himself, or Black Elk, but more likely it was one of Clark's spies who had been lingering around the chief's camp. The meaning of "otherwise disposed of" was plain enough, but some of the men who whispered warnings to Crazy Horse were more explicit still. The wife of Slow Bear, known as Carrie by the whites, said later that "another Indian told him they would kill him either at Fort Robinson or in Washington." Asked who told him that, the wife of Slow Bear hesitated, reluctant to name a man once counted among Crazy Horse's closest friends.

"Little Big Man told him that," said Carrie Slow Bear.[18]

Added up, the stories reaching Crazy Horse warned of danger on every side. But at first he did not want to believe the stories that the other chiefs wanted to kill him, and that the soldiers did too. "He merely said that if they wanted his life they could take it without trouble when he was off his guard and his back was turned."[19]

Poverty came quickly to the Indians who surrendered with Crazy Horse at the Red Cloud Agency. The grass all along the White River had been cropped clean by the vast herds of Indian ponies. Four years of hunting by thousands of Indians had killed or driven away the bigger game—buffalo first, the rest soon after. There were no deer and antelope skins for clothing, no buffalo hides for the soles of moccasins. The whites promised, and sometimes delivered, blankets, white men's clothes, and canvas duck for lodges. On ration day at the agency officials handed out the staples—flour (which the Indians were only just beginning to know how to use), coffee, sugar, salt, bacon, and beans. But the larger part of Indian subsistence was provided every ten days when the beef cattle driven up from Texas were distributed on the hoof to heads of families. Agency officials wanted to slaughter the animals and distribute the meat and hides in orderly fashion, but the Indians insisted they be turned loose on the prairie for the young men to chase and shoot. On issue day life seemed briefly familiar.

But the agency was unprepared to feed the number of Indians who had arrived from the north, and officials in Washington did not stir themselves to make up the shortfall. The new agent at Red Cloud, James Irwin, who took over officially on the 1st of July, wrote frequently to Washington that he had run out of this or was about to run out of that. If there was no flour he issued extra beans. If the bacon was moldy he promised more beef. Sometimes he begged supplies from the military at Camp Robinson. Everything was stretched thin. Indians were not strangers to hunger, but now it came in a predictable cycle—three or four days of feasting followed by six or seven days of hunger waiting for the next beef-issue. With little to do but think about the old life it was inevitable that the Oglala spoke often of General Crook's promise that they could go north on a hunt. In the Tongue and Powder river country there was still plenty of grass, and buffalo might be encountered over the brow of any hill—not some clutch of straggling old bulls, but a great spreading herd stretching across the floor of a river valley as far as a man could see.

The buffalo in the north were no dream. It might even be said truthfully that the hunting had not been better for many years. An early agent for the Oglala, Thomas Twiss, had reported in 1859 that the Indians feared the presence of whites was scaring away the buffalo. "The Indians entertain a superstitious belief," he wrote to the commissioner of Indian affairs, "that the buffalo will not return to the same place where they may have scented a white man." For years the Oglala fought to keep whites out of their hunting grounds in the north. Now the Sioux had all left for the agencies but white ranchers and hunters, still cautious, had not yet poured into the country behind them. The first to take advantage of the departure of the Sioux were their old enemies the Crow, who killed a thousand buffalo in June in the valley of the Bighorn River only twenty miles north of the place where Long Hair had been killed the year before. Lieutenant Hugh Scott rode into that country with the first burial party in June. His detachment camped briefly near a white trader at the mouth of the Bighorn, where Scott purchased four of the beautifully tanned buffalo hides called "beaver" or "silk robes." Scott watched the trader at work. From the Crow, he bought four thousand tanned robes "for six cups of brown sugar apiece, holding his big thumb all the time in the cup."[20]

A few weeks later Scott and Captain Frederick Benteen were up along the Dry Fork of the Missouri River, called the Mini Pusa by the Sioux. This was the heart of the hunting grounds once roamed freely by the northern Indians. Old-timers might speak wistfully of the wild bounty in decades past, but Scott marveled at what remained, and never forgot it.

> We were sitting one day on top of a high peak that overlooked the country in every direction for twenty miles on all sides, and everywhere we looked the prairie was full of buffalo. Benteen thought that we could see at least three hundred thousand buffalo in one view. And if we could see that many, there were many thousands more out of sight in the ravines and hollows.[21]

While Scott was gazing out over the last of the great North American buffalo herds, Crazy Horse, three hundred miles to the south, was speaking often with Wapostan Ska, commander of the Indian scouts at Camp Robinson. Lieutenant Clark kept the scouts busy, sending them out in pursuit of white horse thieves or up north to spy out the last of "the hostiles"—a remnant band of a few hundred Miniconjou under Fast Bull that had promised to come in and surrender, but not till they had completed a final buffalo hunt. Following a meeting in Clark's quarters on June 1, a party of five scouts from Crazy Horse's camp was sent north to the Little Powder. The group was under the command of Four Crow, who had surrendered with Crazy Horse in May and was now enlisted as a corporal in Company A of the Indian scouts. Two weeks later the scouts returned with news of an Indian trail, probably left by Fast Bull's band heading east toward the agencies on the Missouri. The same day, June 13, Clark rode out to Crazy Horse's camp at the chief's request—one of the several occasions that summer when he sat down to share a meal with the chief. "The application to go out hunting was renewed," Clark wrote the same day to Lieutenant Walter Schuyler, Crook's aide. "They will want to start in about 25 days and I think nearly all of Crazy Horse's, Yellow Bear's, Young Man's and a few of Little Wound's band will want to go."[22]

That brief list contained much to think about. A recent census at the agency showed that the four bands totaled exactly four hundred lodges, homes to nearly 2,800 people. Just as important was the absence from Clark's list of the Cheyenne and of the bands of Red Cloud, American Horse, and Red Leaf. The latter clutch totaled 270 lodges and about 1,720 people. Also significant was the fact that in mid-June the band of Crazy Horse was nearly twice as big as Red Cloud's, and a chief's following was a sign of his prestige and his power. Clark did not spell out the significance of these numbers in his letter to Schuyler, but Crook, when he saw it on his return from the Custer battlefield, cannot have failed to grasp the potential for trouble. Crook's promise of a buffalo hunt now threatened to send the greatest warrior of the Sioux north to the Powder and Tongue river country with fully half of the Oglala *oyate* (nation). Keeping them in line would be at most a few troops of cavalry as escort. But Crook let things ride, and it was late July before the general's long-standing promise of a buffalo hunt reached the moment of decision, yes or no, go or no go.[23]

When the moment came at the end of July, seventy chiefs and leading men were summoned to a council at the Red Cloud Agency. Among them were Crazy Horse and Little Big Man, apparently as close as ever, along with Red Cloud, Red Leaf, American Horse, and all the others. Lieutenant Clark delivered two messages from General Crook: "that he was about to redeem" his promise of a trip north to hunt buffalo, and that following the hunt a delegation of eighteen leading men would depart about the middle of September for Washington, where the Indians could make their case opposing a move to the Missouri River. After much talk at the council on July 27 a feast was held; Irwin, the new agent at Red Cloud, contributed three beeves, which were butchered on the spot. A few days later Clark wrote Crook to say all had gone well: "Crazy Horse and his people are getting quite sociable, and I reckon I shall have to be considered one of their tribe soon, as I have been invited down to three feasts." Crook in a cable to Sheridan's headquarters passed on the good news, singling out Crazy Horse and Little Big Man as "peaceable and well disposed." On July 28, the day after the council, the general issued an order granting permission to sell arms and ammunition to the Indians who were planning to go on the hunt, and several days after that, probably on August 6, Crook told reporters that a big hunting party from the agencies would soon head for the Big Horn Mountains led by Spotted Tail, "who can be trusted to keep them within bounds."[24]

But that was as far as Crook's promise went. Within a day or two of the news story in the *Cheyenne Leader* all came undone. Hostiles in April, friendlies in August? Crook was the only one who believed it. Report of the ammunition sale raised alarm, especially at the Red Cloud and Spotted Tail agencies, where officials quickly blocked their own traders from selling ammunition to the Indians. At Spotted Tail, Lieutenant Jesse Lee "felt that probably a crisis had come." He repeated later what worried everyone at the time: "If all the Indians, wild and tame . . . went out on a general buffalo hunt with all the wild Indians from Red Cloud, trouble might ensue."

Trouble in fact began immediately. A public outcry from the Black Hills mining towns predicted calamity from turning loose thousands of Indians with guns and fresh supplies of ammunition. Crazy Horse might break to join Sitting Bull in Canada, it was said. A new war could not be ruled out. Clark had been trying to quash rumors all summer that young men from the agencies were slipping off to raid and steal horses. All were accounted for, Clark insisted. Swift Bear, the longtime ally of Spotted Tail, told Lieutenant Lee that the Brulé were as worried as the whites. "The man who planned this hunt needs a heart and a brain," said Swift Bear.

But many of the Brulé chiefs wanted to go on the hunt, too. Lee and Captain Daniel Burke, commander of the military post at Camp Sheridan, making their case to the chiefs for staying put, turned them around with "24 hours of incessant work." Precisely what convinced Crook to reverse himself is not known, but once Spotted Tail decided against the hunt it was hard to go forward. "Spotted Tail talks against the hunt and tells the Indians they had best stay at home," Colonel Bradley told the general in mid-July. Crook withdrew permission for the hunt and ended the ammunition sales.[25]

No white promise was ever disowned more abruptly. The breaking of that promise opened a fissure between Crazy Horse and the military officers he had allowed himself to trust. Bradley briefly imagined that disappointment was the problem, and it might blow over. On August 15 he cabled Crook's headquarters in Omaha to say he expected "no trouble about postponing the hunt," but in fact trouble was rising on all sides. When the hunt was canceled, Crazy Horse changed his mind about the planned trip to Washington. By August 18, Clark had concluded that the chief was beyond control. The only course was to break his power and influence, disarm his men, take away their horses, and disperse the band. "It is impossible to work him through reasoning or kindness," Clark wrote to Crook in Omaha. "Absolute force is the only thing for him."

But Clark remained confident that this new trouble would not interrupt the government's plan to move the Indians to the Missouri. The chief's power and influence, Clark wrote, "could be easily broken at the present time." Absent Crazy Horse, the delegation would go to Washington as planned. Meanwhile, Clark said, he was "keeping a sharp watch, through some of the scouts I can fully trust, on both agencies, and they keep me pretty well posted."[26]

26

"If you go to Washington they are going to kill you."

HE DOG, THE FRIEND of Crazy Horse, said the chief made no secret of what he wanted: a home in the north on Beaver Creek near the Tongue River, right in the middle of the last good hunting country. "First, I want them to place my agency on Beaver Creek," Crazy Horse told He Dog. "Then I will go to Washington." He left no doubt about the place he had in mind; he sent his sister's husband, Club Man, to place a stone marker on the spot.

The chief did not believe he had to fight for his home in the north; it had been promised to him. But then General Crook broke his promise about the buffalo hunt. In almost the same moment Wapostan Ska, the chief of scouts who wore a white hat, told Crazy Horse that Crook wanted him to go to Washington—now.

Crazy Horse said no. He made no threats. "I came here for peace," he said. "No matter if my own relatives pointed a gun at my head and ordered me to change that word, I would not change it." He Dog heard his friend say this many times. But he would not go to Washington until his agency had been placed on Beaver Creek. "You have my horses and my guns," he told the soldiers, according to He Dog. "I have only my tent and my will. You got me to come here and you can keep me here by force if you choose, but you cannot make me go anywhere that I refuse to go."[1]

The stubbornness of the chief at first irritated and eventually angered Lieutenant Clark, but it did not worry him. Clark believed the chief's power "could be easily broken" because over the summer with patient talk and promises of preferment he had steadily peeled away the allegiance of a number of Crazy Horse's leading men. Among them was one of his oldest friends and allies, Little Big Man, who had been a war comrade since the early 1860s. Little Big Man had arrived at the Red Cloud Agency with a reputation as dangerous and untrustworthy. "Small but exceedingly vicious," was the way one of General Crook's aides, Captain Azor Nickerson, described him. John Bourke called him "crafty," and added, "Little Big Man I did not like in those days." He was speaking of the first month or two after Crazy Horse surrendered. "He and I became better friends afterwards," Bourke continued—meaning after Little Big Man broke away from Crazy Horse, and tied his fate to the whites.[2]

By mid-August Little Big Man had shifted his loyalty completely. When Clark wrote Crook to urge the breaking of Crazy Horse he assured the general, "There is no trouble with Little Big Man." Clark's fellow officer Lieutenant Henry R. Lemly later said, "Little Big Man . . . was known to the officers as a paid spy in the employ of the agency." It was evidently ambition that brought the change; it was said that Little Big Man dreamed of becoming a bigger chief than Spotted Tail. But Little Big Man represented the break with Crazy Horse as a quarrel. Horn Chips, the *wicasa wakan* who had fashioned powerful medicine for Crazy Horse, said a woman brought on the trouble. "Crazy Horse," he said, "had forbidden Little Big Man to sleep with one of the squaws. They got into a fight over it and were never friends after that."

"I don't know what it was about," an Army sergeant said of the quarrel in 1904, "but at all events the two were deadly enemies from that time forward."[3] Sometime in May, Little Big Man moved his people and their lodges away from Crazy Horse's camp, some two miles up Little White Clay Creek, closer to Red Cloud and to the agency itself.

The sergeant, William F. Kelly, was stationed at Camp Robinson with Company F, 14th Infantry. In June, friction between Crazy Horse and Little Big Man erupted openly during a regular beef issue as the acting agent, Lieutenant Charles A. Johnson, was counting out animals. The interpreter—probably Billy Garnett—told Johnson that Little Big Man wanted the beeves for his people to be issued separately from those for Crazy Horse. Kelly described the tense moment as Johnson, who was also commander of the sergeant's Company F, realized the difficulty of his position.

"The acting agent was perplexed," said Kelly of his lieutenant. "He realized that whatever he did he was certain to arouse the anger of one or the other of the two men." Johnson asked the interpreter what he should do. "The latter replied that he thought the best plan would be to issue rations as requested by Little Big Man," said Kelly.

So Johnson instructed the chief herder, Ben Tibbetts, to count off the beeves for the people of Little Big Man, whose young men were waiting on horseback with guns and bows and arrows to run the animals as they were released. "Crazy Horse flew into a fury," Kelly said, "refusing to accept his share, and riding back to camp followed by his people."

Clark sent a measured report of this affair to Schuyler, who was passing on news of the agencies to Crook. "Some of the agency bucks here are a little restless," Clark related; "Johnson has had some little trouble with his beef issue." A later report in the *Cheyenne Leader* filled in a detail or two: "Crazy Horse refused to take the annuity goods provided for him, and his band, and did not take them while Lt. Johnson was agent."

On the 1st of July, when James Irwin took over the agency from Johnson, he was told that part of the problem was the matter of *signing* for the receipt of supplies. "Many of them object to signing any paper," Irwin wrote the commissioner of Indian affairs. The Indians had been tricked and bullied into signing away the Black Hills the previous year. They remained angry and suspicious. They could not read, did not know what they were signing, and did not trust the whites to tell them. Demanding that the Indians sign for every beef and bag of flour, Irwin concluded, would only "increase rather than diminish their deep-seated distrust." He asked Washington to abandon the signing requirement. By the end of the month, Crazy Horse had resumed picking up rations for his band.[4]

The warrior Crazy Horse, who disliked speech making and politics, found himself as the summer progressed increasingly isolated. Lieutenant Clark sought his company, but many whites hated him for his victory over Custer. On a visit to the agency, W. R. Felton, the bitter survivor of an episode known as the Metz massacre, reported to the *Cheyenne Leader* that "Crazy Horse . . . is strutting around the agency bigger than a lord." Rumor had it that Indians were paying "extravagant prices" for guns and ammunition; one report said even "an ordinary rifle" was worth four ponies. "A large number of young bucks have gone back north," the *Cheyenne Leader* reported a few days after the big sun dance in Crazy Horse's camp.

No one disliked or distrusted Crazy Horse more than Lieutenant Fred Calhoun, whose brother James had died with Custer. At the end of July, Calhoun left Camp Robinson for Kansas to join the families of other 7th Cavalry officers killed at the Little Bighorn. Scores of relatives were gathering in the town of Leavenworth, near the fort of the same name, where they waited for the military detachment bringing in the bodies of their dead fathers, brothers, husbands, and sons. Calhoun did not believe the Indian war was over. "In a year or two they will all go out again," he had written to a friend in Cincinnati in April. In his view no peace would last until the Indians had received "a good sound whipping." On August 3, he passed by the five caskets in the post chapel, then joined the procession of three hundred carriages to the cemetery for interment. By August 7 he was back at Camp Robinson, a post he detested.[5]

Calhoun's hatred for Crazy Horse was intense but impotent; as a military officer under orders there was nothing he could do but grumble. More dangerous was the malice of the chiefs, who came to envy and resent Crazy Horse. They said and did nothing openly, but were active in a hidden way. At the end of the big council on Friday, July 27, when Lieutenant Clark had read out General Crook's telegram describing the plans for the trip to Washington, the Indians made preparations for the traditional feast. Young Man Afraid of His Horses suggested that all should gather at the lodges of the new men at the agency, Crazy Horse and Little Big Man. At that moment the mood of the Indians was good; they were still expecting to go on the buffalo hunt promised by Crook. James Irwin made the customary gesture and promised to donate coffee, sugar, and three beeves for the feast. Sitting with Irwin at the council was an inspector or "special agent" from the Bureau of Indian Affairs in Washington, a man named Benjamin K. Shopp. These traveling inspectors moved from one agency to another, reporting on administrative matters or checking into claims of theft of supplies or inadequate rations. The two were frequently related. Shopp had come to report on Irwin's progress in taking over control of the Oglala. The special agent noted that on July 27 several of the chiefs got up and left the council when Man Afraid suggested that Crazy Horse should host the feast. This struck Shopp as odd. No one had protested Man Afraid's choice. There were no heated words or angry looks. Then why, Shopp wondered, did Red Cloud, still the biggest of the chiefs at the agency which bore his name, get up with one or two others and leave the room?

It seemed a small thing, but that evening at about ten o'clock, Shopp learned what lay behind the chiefs' abrupt departure. Two Indians arrived at Irwin's door, interrupting his conversation with Shopp, and pressed the agent to send at once for the interpreter. Shopp is our only witness to this conversation; he was new to the agency and did not note the name of the interpreter who arrived. Irwin told the Indians the hour was late; he asked if their trouble could not wait till morning. The Indians insisted the matter was too urgent for delay, and the interpreter was soon putting into English a flood of angry complaint about the attention and favoritism shown to Crazy Horse despite his recent arrival at the agency, his reputation for being difficult and stubborn, his history of hostility toward the whites, and his unpredictability. Irwin's visitors said they spoke not for themselves but for Red Cloud and the chiefs of several other bands. It was apparent to Shopp that all had turned against Crazy Horse in a decisive way. In a report two weeks later, he summarized their angry complaint for the commissioner of Indian affairs:

> Crazy Horse . . . had always been regarded by them as an unreconstructed Indian; he had constantly evinced feelings of unfriendliness towards the others; he was sullen, morose and discontented at times; he seemed to be chafing under restraints; and in their opinion was only waiting for a favorable opportunity to leave the agency and never return . . . The other Indians these men represented had no confidence in him. He was tricky and unfaithful to others, and very selfish as to the personal interests of his own tribe . . . These Indians told Dr. Irwin that they came with no lie—they simply presented a true story.[6]

Thus was planted a seed of growing distrust. Irwin, a month into the job, had expressed no anxious thoughts about Crazy Horse before the late-night visit on July 27, but now he told Shopp "that Crazy Horse and his band were not in a friendly attitude towards the government really, although nominally they were." He said "trouble was to be apprehended" if Crazy Horse was turned loose to go hunting. Later, Shopp talked to the chiefs at the Spotted Tail Agency. "All the Indians here too," he reported to the commissioner on August 15, "entertain the same ideas about the unfriendliness of Crazy Horse, etc." This late-night tale bearing did not cause the trouble that followed, but it marks the first official expression of a swelling chorus of apprehensions about the chief that rapidly turned into a crisis.[7]

The wedge was the trip to Washington. Many of the chief's friends and relatives, including his new wife and the interpreter John Provost, warned that the whites would kill him if he went, but most of his old war comrades favored the trip. Clark had patiently talked them around, visiting them in their lodges in the first ten days of August, or inviting them to his quarters at Camp Robinson. Big Road, Iron Crow, and He Dog, old allies of Crazy Horse, all urged him to go to Washington. The chief was whipsawed by the conflicting advice and whispered warnings. The man driving events seems to have been Red Cloud, who sent his emissaries to warn Irwin that Crazy Horse was restive and could not be trusted. But at the same time, He Dog believed, many of those who warned Crazy Horse against going to Washington were put up to it by Red Cloud.

"That about going to Washington is only a decoy," he was told by one of his uncles, Spotted Crow. "They want to get you away from us and then they will have you in their power." Even Little Big Man, who had moved his camp closer to Red Cloud's, said the whites would kill Crazy Horse if he went, and others said the same. "If you go to Washington," they told him, "they are going to kill you . . . they are going to stuff you in the mouth of a cannon, and kill you."[8]

But whites were not the only danger. Camp gossip said some of the chiefs also wanted to kill Crazy Horse. "One day during that summer," it was said later by friends of Crazy Horse, a group of angry Indians took their "grievances" to his lodge. Only one of the group was named: Little Bear, whom the whites called Sioux Bob. According to Ghost Bear, Sioux Bob had an interest in Ellen Larrabee, the new wife of the chief, and had perhaps even been living with her. Horn Chips said there was an element of sexual tension in the quarrel between Crazy Horse and Little Big Man. What "grievance" brought Little Bear and the others to the lodge of Crazy Horse is not clear, but sexual tension and political jealousy are both common drivers of violence.

The story of Little Bear's angry confrontation with Crazy Horse was related by George Colhoff, who collected information for a winter count from eight Oglala, all close friends of Crazy Horse, including the brothers He Dog, Little Shield, and Short Bull. Colhoff was told that Little Bear and two or three others challenged Crazy Horse "for some grievances that they had against him and shot his horse." Among the Sioux, the shooting or stabbing of a man's horse was the last stage of anger before open fighting began. It will be recalled that Bull Bear in 1841 provoked the plotting that ended his life when he stabbed and killed the horse of Smoke. Now the enemies of Crazy Horse killed the chief's horse in front of his lodge. "But Crazy Horse did not do anything about it," it was said.[9]

There is one additional source of tension and distrust to be considered. At the beginning of the summer, the scout Frank Grouard had been one of the few persons at the Red Cloud Agency who could speak easily with Crazy Horse. "Frank is the only one whom Crazy Horse seems at all glad to see," Lieutenant Bourke wrote in his diary. "To the rest of the world he is sullen and gloomy." For two years, it will be remembered, Grouard had lived in He Dog's lodge as a member of Crazy Horse's band. Grouard said later he had been close to the chief's family, and that Crazy Horse's father had given him a winter count that the old man had painted on deerskin. On the very night he had surrendered, it was Grouard who took Bourke to have dinner with Crazy Horse in the chief's lodge. "We all believed," Bourke recorded, "that if anybody could make Crazy Horse unbosom himself, Frank was the man."[10]

Thus matters stood when Grouard left the agency in late May with the party of scouts sent out to guide Generals Crook and Sheridan up to the Little Bighorn. He was absent until late July, when Clark noted that "since his return," Grouard has "done what he could" to persuade Crazy Horse to listen to the friends who urged him to go to Washington. Clark sensed nothing wrong. But according to Louis Bordeaux, the interpreter at Camp Sheridan, something had changed. Grouard by early August was no longer easy around Crazy Horse. At about that time, the scout later told his biographer, Crazy Horse "told Grouard he was looking for death and believed it would soon come to him." This surprising confidence evidently troubled Grouard; a man looking for death was dangerous. "Grouard became afraid and very fearful of Crazy Horse," Bordeaux reported. The scout told Bordeaux that Crazy Horse had turned against him, and now sought revenge for Grouard's treachery in guiding the soldiers who attacked the village on Powder River. Bordeaux said he knew this was true; Crazy Horse himself had told him so.[11]

But Grouard had another cause for worry, in Bordeaux's view. Crazy Horse told Bordeaux, and perhaps others, that Grouard was not what he seemed. He was no captive in the Indian camps, as he insisted to whites, but a full member of the band who fought alongside the rest. Crazy Horse said Grouard "used to kill mail carriers and bring in the mail and read the letters and tell Crazy Horse where the soldiers were, etc." What Crazy Horse told Bordeaux appeared to confirm other charges against the scout which had been circulating since November 1876 when one of Grouard's former employers, a freighter named George Boyd, had published a long article in the *Bismarck Tribune* claiming the Sandwich Islander had taken part in fights against whites, had secretly warned the Indians of the impending attack at Slim Buttes, and had served as a kind of adviser to Sitting Bull. As Bordeaux described it, Crazy Horse endangered Grouard from two directions at once: by threatening to take revenge for his betrayal of the Indians, and by denouncing him to whites as a renegade. Trapped between this rock and a hard place, Bordeaux said, Grouard concluded that "by stirring up trouble, Crazy Horse might be disposed of in some manner . . . Accordingly, Grouard began to circulate stories to the effect that Crazy Horse was becoming discontented and trying to stir up another war."[12]

The chief who disliked talk was now, in early August, at the center of a whirlpool of conflicting rumor and accusation. The allies of Red Cloud and Frank Grouard were spreading stories of his unreliability, sullen discontent, and growing hostility toward the whites. The chief's young wife and other intimates were telling him that the whites planned to lure him away from the agency so they could kill him. It was common gossip in the camps that Red Cloud and Spotted Tail wanted Crazy Horse out of the way.

The chief, threatened and unsure what to do, was closely watched in this period by spies reporting to Lieutenant Clark, who wrote later that one of them was openly courting a girl who lived near the chief. It was the custom for a young Oglala in love to intercept the woman he hoped to win as she made her way through the camp on some errand. If she did not object he would enfold her in his blanket, pulling it snugly around the two of them, covering head and all, so they might whisper or embrace unmolested. It was not unusual for such a couple to stand in the same spot for hours. In this manner, Clark wrote, his spy planted himself within earshot of the chief's lodge, noting all that was said. By mid-August, Clark understood that Crazy Horse was torn and undecided, urged this way and that. He cautioned other officers to be patient; he said Crazy Horse told him that "he wanted to do right, but wanted plenty of time to consider."

Clark's fellow officer Captain George Randall picked up the same impression in late July on returning to Camp Sheridan from a long scout through the Black Hills in pursuit of white horse thieves. He told Lieutenant Lee and Captain Daniel Burke, commander at Sheridan, that Crazy Horse should be given plenty of leeway. "Crazy Horse was all right, was doing just what they wanted him to do," Randall said. "If they would let him alone and not 'buzz' him so much he would come out all right."[13]

But Clark did not heed his own counsel. The general stir among the Indians, and the difficulty of knowing what was passing through the chief's mind, left him anxious about unanswered questions. Why, for example, had 150 northern Indians left the Spotted Tail Agency to join Crazy Horse on Little White Clay Creek in mid-July? Among them was Black Fox, married to a sister of Touch the Clouds and one of Crazy Horse's closest war comrades. What was the significance, a month later, of a second visit to the Spotted Tail Agency by Crazy Horse's friend and ally Two Lance, who tried to coax back another group of northern Indians?

There was nothing especially threatening about this effort. Transfers were common. Relatives wanted to camp near each other. But a big group breaking north with Crazy Horse would obviously threaten more trouble than a small group. A spy in the northern camp reassured Captain Burke that Two Lance got "a very cool reception." Colonel Bradley at Camp Robinson was told that the Spotted Tail Indians all believed this rebuff of Two Lance would help persuade Crazy Horse to make the trip to Washington. Clark was not so sure. His trust in the chief was eroding.[14]

Everything hung on Crazy Horse's willingness to go to Washington. To pressure him one last time, Colonel Bradley summoned Crazy Horse for a conversation at Camp Robinson on August 15. Bradley was a quiet, reasoning kind of man. He did not threaten Crazy Horse with arrest and punitive detail on the water wagon—bluster typical of Bradley's predecessor, Colonel Ranald Mackenzie. He merely told Crazy Horse and Little Big Man that the Great Father in Washington had written to him and asked for the chiefs to come. "Little Big Man immediately gave his consent to go," said Billy Garnett later, "but Crazy Horse would give no satisfactory reply as to what he would do."

Both Bradley and Lee, the acting agent at Spotted Tail, were probably referring to this conversation when they later described the escalating quarrel, Bradley in a letter to his mother, Lee in a memoir. "Crazy Horse became more uneasy than ever," Bradley related to his mother in early September. "[He] told us he did not intend to stay with us, that he had never agreed to stay at any agency, and that he intended to take his band away."

To the request to go to Washington, Crazy Horse did not merely "give no satisfactory reply" to Bradley's request, according to Lee. He rejected it with a flourish. "He was not hunting for any great father," the chief said, as Lee remembered it. "*His* father was with him, and there was no Great Father between him and the Great Spirit."[15]

But the whites kept the pressure up. On August 17, Crook sent another telegram to Camp Robinson, where Clark gathered all the chiefs in council, including Crazy Horse, to listen to the general's words as Clark read the telegram aloud to all. He did not leave the matter there but urged and implored the chief:

> I explained to him that in addition to the other interests involved, you wished him to come on with the others and work with you . . . That the president wanted him to come and you were anxious to have him go; that it was important and necessary for us all to work earnestly and honestly together in this matter, etc. etc.[16]

We should take Clark at his word, and assume that he meant what he said, and that he believed that talk, and the meeting with the president in Washington, and patient goodwill, could resolve all difficulties. But his patience ended decisively three days later when Crazy Horse returned to the military post to say all he had to say about the trip to Washington. He named several men from his own band whom he wished to go. The other chiefs—Spotted Tail, Red Cloud, Little Wound, and the rest—he wanted "thrown away and only the men he had picked . . . sent on." Crazy Horse said the whites knew where he wanted his agency. He had been saying it all summer: Beaver Creek on Tongue River, the valley where Club Man had placed his stone marker. If the people in Washington wanted to know more, then the men he sent could tell them.

Clark insisted to Crook on August 18 that he had responded to these peremptory conditions "kindly and firmly," then ended with a request for a clear yes or no. "He had been asked if he would work with the president and yourself in this matter and I wanted to know if he would do so."

The chief's reply, as related by Clark: "He had already stated he was not going."

Both pride and frustration crept into Clark's angry response. "Force is the only thing that will work out a good condition in this man's mind," he wrote to Crook. "I am reluctantly forced to this conclusion, because I have claimed and felt all along that any Indian could be 'worked' by other means; but absolute force is the only thing for him."

About a week after this heated encounter, Crazy Horse had a dream. Clark called it "a most remarkable dream," and recorded it in his diary. It seems likely he was told of the dream by one of his spies.

> While walking on the prairie near his camp one day he came across a dead eagle. He went to his tepee and gloomily sat there for many hours afterwards. Being asked by some of his people as to what was the matter, he said

"that he had found his dead body on the prairie near by," and a night or two after this he dreamt that he was on an elevated plateau riding a white pony. He was surrounded by his enemies and big guns (cannons), and he was killed, but not with a bullet. He had always claimed that he bore a charmed life, and could not be killed by a bullet.

The dream is recorded by one other contemporary—Frank Grouard— who added a detail. He said that Crazy Horse was watching the eagle soaring in the sky when "presently it seemed to fold its wings and fall." When Crazy Horse came up to the eagle he saw that its body had been pierced not by a bullet, but by an arrow, and he recognized that the eagle was himself.[17]

27

"We washed the blood from our faces."

GENERAL GEORGE CROOK WAS a man of narrow focus; it was his nature to brood about only one thing at a time, and it was rescuing his reputation, not the troublesome Oglala Crazy Horse, that was on his mind in the forenoon of the last day of August 1877. With his aide-de-camp, Lieutenant John Bourke, Crook left the three-story brick headquarters of the Department of the Platte in Omaha to catch the Western Express—the daily Union Pacific Railroad passenger train bound for San Francisco. Crook's destination was Green River, Wyoming, about 840 miles west. There, under orders from General Sheridan in Chicago, Crook planned to disembark and proceed north overland by stage to Camp Brown in the Wind River country, where Shoshone scouts were waiting to join him on a mad dash another hundred-some miles north to cut off a fleeing band of Nez Percé Indians.

The job of rounding up the Nez Percé had been given initially to General O. O. Howard, an earnest, one-armed, Bible-quoting gentler of Indians for whom Crook felt mainly pity and contempt. After his much-criticized campaigns against Crazy Horse a year earlier Crook was hungry for a success, and he quite looked forward to cleaning up Howard's botch. But Crook's mission was somehow both trivial and desperate at the same time. The Nez Percé were running away to Canada under their chief, who was known as Joseph, and in any event were too few to do much harm along their path. But at this moment the standing army of the United States, cut and cut again since the end of the Civil War, was stretched to the breaking point. A rapidly spreading strike by railway workers in the East was about half contained by the Army, and more soldiers were begged daily by state governors trying to keep the trains running. Sheridan feared that Joseph's defiance of the Army might stir war fever in other restive tribes confined to reservations where there was little to eat and nothing to do. In Sheridan's view it would be impossible for the Army to fight a new Indian war and keep the trains running at the same time. In the days before Crook left Omaha, rumors had spread that Sitting Bull was preparing to cross back into the United States to resume his war. Military officers at Camp Robinson feared that Crazy Horse would join him, and the warnings of rival chiefs at the agencies encouraged that fear.

Crook departed Omaha about noon with his mind fixed on the Nez Percé, but the complications of the moment pursued him down the Union Pacific tracks. At the first stop along his route, in Fremont, Nebraska, the telegraph officer met the train with an urgent cable. In the hour or two the general had been gone a message had arrived in Omaha from Colonel Bradley at Camp Robinson reporting a refusal by Crazy Horse to help in the campaign against the Nez Percé. Worse, the chief and his friend Touch the Clouds said they were going north with their people. "Crazy Horse is behaving badly," said Bradley. "Every influence that kindness could suggest has been exhausted on him." He urged Crook to break his journey for a stop at the Red Cloud Agency. "If anyone can influence the Indian," said Bradley of the general, "he can."

Breaking his trip was not what Crook wanted to do. When the general's train halted during the night at Grand Island, Nebraska, he responded with a cable to Bradley declaring flatly, "I cannot come to Robinson."

But the general had been thinking hard over the previous hours. He was a meticulous planner. He had crafted a strategy while his train rattled its way up the Platte River valley at thirty miles an hour. In his years fighting the Apache in Arizona, Crook had learned one thing above others: the chiefs were the problem. He told Bradley to round up Crazy Horse and his band while Captain Daniel Burke did the same with Touch the Clouds at Spotted Tail. Additional troops already on their way from Fort Laramie would be plenty for the task. "You should so arrange matters," Crook told the colonel, "that they shall arrive during the night and make the round up early in the morning." The great danger was a stampede— a sudden panic and scattering by Indians fearing massacre. "Use the greatest precaution in this matter," said Crook. The colonel should say nothing until the last moment, then ask the head chiefs—Red Cloud and Spotted Tail—to pick their own men to make the arrests. And move quickly, Crook counseled. "Delay is very dangerous in this business."

But Sheridan did not trust Bradley to handle the matter. He had seen the colonel's original telegram and worried that catching Joseph and the Nez Percé was "but a small matter compared with what might happen." He cabled Washington to say he was pulling Crook from the westbound train. "I very much fear that Crazy Horse has been treated too well," Sheridan explained. Waiting for Crook when his train steamed into Sidney, Nebraska, at nine a.m. on the first day of September were new orders he could not ignore. "I think your presence more necessary at Red Cloud Agency," Sheridan wrote, "and wish you to get off at Sidney and go there."

Crook and Bourke left the train as they were bid, obtained an Army ambulance from the post commander at the Sidney Barracks, and set out in the freshness of the morning for the journey to Camp Robinson 120 miles to the north. The country they passed over was mainly level, with an occasional descent into a long gentle swale ten miles or more from the near end to the rise at the other. Silence was Crook's natural state. The day- and nightlong jolting ride over the open plains provided him with plenty of time to brood and plan.[1]

It had been the Nez Percé whom Sheridan and Crook were worrying about in the latter days of August. Sheridan gave Crook authority to enlist an additional thirty Oglala and Brulé scouts for an expedition up into the Yellowstone country, and a day or two later Lieutenant Clark sent word by Indian courier to Touch the Clouds, Red Bear, and High Bear that he wanted them to attend a meeting at the Red Cloud Agency. The telegraph line had not yet reached Camp Sheridan so communications with Camp Robinson were slow; the forty-three-mile trip routinely took Indian couriers six hours or more. Touch the Clouds told Lieutenant Jesse Lee about the summons, and the next day Lee and Captain Burke received official word that the Army wanted to enlist a new company of scouts "to go northwest and fight the Nez Perce." There was no air of urgency bordering on crisis in these developments, but the request was not quite routine, either. Touch the Clouds and the other chiefs left in good time for the meeting, which was held in Clark's office on the morning of Friday, August 31.[2]

While Crook had been preparing to leave Omaha that Friday morning, Billy Garnett on a routine errand was heading down to Camp Robinson along the mile-and-a-half, winding road that connected the post to the Red Cloud Agency buildings. No threat of trouble hung in the air. As he neared the post, Garnett saw Frank Grouard riding up toward him, obviously agitated. "Billy," said Grouard, "go back to Lieutenant Clark's office. It is too hot for me."

"What's the matter?" asked Garnett.

"Crazy Horse is up there with his people," answered Grouard.

When Garnett reached Clark's quarters at the western end of officers' row he found the big front room filled with twenty or more northern Indians, including Crazy Horse and Touch the Clouds. As an interpreter, Garnett often arrived or left in the middle of a conversation without any idea what was being sought or objected to. But on this Friday morning he grasped immediately that the company was thoroughly stirred up. He was pulled into the thick of it with Clark's direction "to ask Crazy Horse if he would not go out with the scouts . . . that the Nez Perces were out and off in the country where he used to roam."

"No," said Crazy Horse. It is likely Clark understood the word "no" on his own. "I told him," Crazy Horse told Garnett, "what I wanted to do. We are going to move. We are going out there to hunt."

Clark objected. "You can't go out there."

Garnett saw that Crazy Horse "was not right"—he was agitated and angry. "If you want to fight Nez Perces, go out and fight them," Crazy Horse said, speaking directly to the lieutenant now. "We don't want to fight. We are going out to hunt."

"You cannot go out there, I tell you," Clark repeated.

Now Crazy Horse turned to his own people. "These people can't fight," he said. "What do they want to go out there for? Let's go home. This is enough of this."[3]

With that, Crazy Horse and his people emptied the room and departed the post—Crazy Horse for his camp six miles down the White River, Touch the Clouds and his friends for the forty-three-mile ride back to the Spotted Tail Agency, where they arrived the following day, the 1st of September. Billy Garnett was left to put together what the argument had been about as best he could.

Clark immediately proceeded to Bradley's quarters to report the fact that mattered most: Crazy Horse and Touch the Clouds had told him "that they are going out with their bands." Bradley, in turn, telegraphed the troubling news to the adjutant general in Omaha, while Clark rounded up Frank Grouard and gave him a written message for Captain Burke at Camp Sheridan. In this message, delivered by Grouard at about the same time Touch the Clouds reached Camp Sheridan the following day, Clark worded the statement of the chiefs more starkly, stating flatly what he had only implied to Bradley: Crazy Horse and Touch the Clouds "were going north on the warpath." Clark went on to ask Burke for help in rounding up the Crazy Horse band so horses and guns could be seized. Burke showed the letter to Jesse Lee. If Clark went ahead with the proposed roundup, Burke said, "Hell would be popping, surely."[4]

Lee was baffled. He liked and respected Clark personally, but something was badly wrong—Clark's note and Grouard's version of events both claimed that Touch the Clouds "had made use of very threatening and hostile language." But to Lee, Touch the Clouds himself, who had arrived at Camp Sheridan at roughly the same moment with Grouard, seemed in no warlike mood. "His manner was so friendly and so entirely unchanged from his accustomed conduct," Lee felt, "that I could hardly believe he had a hostile intent."

Lee knew Touch the Clouds, had talked with him many times over the summer, trusted the chief to speak the truth, and did not believe he could have threatened to go back to war. Only a few days earlier, Touch the Clouds had sent some of his own men out to talk in the remnants of Lame Deer's band, the very last of the "hostiles." None of this squared with the threatening words reported by Clark and Grouard. "There must be some mistake about this matter," Lee told Burke. "Touch Cloud is honest and he could not be up to anything like that. Get all of the head men among the Indians in your house and we will talk it over."[5]

The crowd which gathered that night in the captain's house to council with Burke and Lee was a tightly knit company of Indians and mixed-bloods who had known each other most of their lives and were related by blood, marriage, and band allegiance. Among them was the whole company of available interpreters, not only the visiting Grouard but also the Army's chief interpreter at Camp Sheridan, Louis Bordeaux, and his brother-in-law Charles Tackett, who was married to Bordeaux's sister, Susan; and the Mexican Joe Merrivale. Also present were Spotted Tail and the chief who had been closest to him for twenty years, Swift Bear, brother of Bordeaux's mother and uncle of Tackett's wife. Two other leading men of the Brulé were also present, Two Strike and White Thunder. Completing the group were the man suspected by Lieutenant Clark of plotting war, Touch the Clouds and his friends Red Bear and High Bear, who had all gone to the meeting with Clark that morning. In this crowded room there was only one outsider—Crook's favorite scout, Frank Grouard.

The gathering that night constituted a kind of ad hoc court of inquiry; its purpose was to establish what had been said at the meeting with Clark. In doubt was the veracity of Clark's claims in his letter. Clark had written, and Grouard at Camp Sheridan had confirmed, that Touch the Clouds and Crazy Horse had refused to go after the Nez Percé, but insisted they were going back north to hunt. As Clark read the mood of the chiefs, Touch the Clouds had talked Crazy Horse around to his position and they were itching for a fight. Once begun, the chiefs threatened, fighting would continue until the last man was killed. As Grouard interpreted it, their meaning was unmistakable. "We will go north and fight," Touch the Clouds had said (according to Grouard), "until there is not a white man left."[6]

It was the raw hostility of this threat which struck Lee as all wrong. Both chiefs had been at the meeting with Clark, but in keeping with his custom Crazy Horse had let his friend do most of the talking. Crazy Horse only signaled his assent—"*Hau! Hau!*"—after Touch the Clouds made the long speech. To settle the matter Lee wanted Touch the Clouds to repeat everything he had said to Clark.

Chief interpreter at the meeting in Burke's house was Louis Bordeaux, paid a hundred dollars a month for his work at Camp Sheridan. Bordeaux was a son of the well-known trader James Bordeaux and of the full-blood Brulé woman Huntkalutawin (Red Cormorant Woman), sister of Swift Bear. Not yet thirty years old, Bordeaux was a handsome man in photographs, on the short side but slender in youth, and "a man of very dark complexion." On his upper lip was a sparse mustache. The Teton Lakota dialect of the western Sioux had been his first language. He had grown up in his father's trading posts along the North Platte River. The companions of his youth had been mixed-bloods and Indians. He was married to a Brulé full-blood. For two years he had been a principal interpreter at the big councils between Indians and whites. He had been to Washington with Spotted Tail in 1875, and the chief insisted he come again on the new trip planned by Lieutenant Clark. It was Bordeaux who now put into Lakota the request of the officers to Touch the Clouds—"to repeat what he had said at the council at Red Cloud."[7]

"Why, they had interpreters over there," said a surprised Touch the Clouds. "What do they say?"

But the officers pressed their request, and Touch the Clouds did as he was asked, explaining how the meeting with Clark came about, and what was said. There had been talk of sending the Indian scouts out to fight the Nez Percé but the Sioux did not want to go. Clark called a meeting to press his case, and Touch the Clouds, speaking for himself and the others, told Clark at length why they said no:

> We washed the blood from our faces and came in and surrendered and wanted peace. My heart is on the ground but now there is dust in the air and trouble is threatening. You ask us to put blood on our faces again, but I do not want to do this, neither does Crazy Horse. You enlisted us for peace. Then you gave up the buffalo hunt, to our disappointment, and you put a bit in our mouth and turned us around and proposed to go to Washington, but we did not want to go. This latest plan of yours is hard medicine, but we will go north and the soldiers must go with us. We will surround the Nez Perces and whip them and there will be peace all around.[8]

These were the words put into English by Louis Bordeaux. They had a very different meaning from the words reported by Clark and Grouard. After listening with growing agitation for several moments, Grouard interrupted Bordeaux and "called [him] down, saying he was not correctly interpreting Touch the Clouds."

"Louis, you do not understand the dialect of those Northern Indians," Grouard said.

Bordeaux was furious. He thought Grouard "a very ignorant man in the use of English," and his command of Lakota was worse—"very broken," Bordeaux called it. "Frank," he said, "you cannot teach me my mother tongue."

Now followed "quite a wordy dispute as to the interpretation of what Touch the Clouds said." Touch the Clouds grew angry. "You lie!" he said to Grouard. "You lie! You are the cause of all this trouble."

Touch the Clouds "told Grouard he had misinterpreted him." Grouard protested that Touch the Clouds was saying something different now; he had changed his words. At this point Burke interrupted, saying all the English-Lakota speakers at the agency trusted Bordeaux; all thought him a "brave interpreter"—he reported what a man said, not what others wanted to hear. "Bordeaux could not be impeached," said Burke.[9]

At that Grouard backed off. He would not admit that Bordeaux was right, but when asked if he thought Touch the Clouds planned to go north to fight the whites *now*, Grouard replied, "I don't believe he intends doing so *now*."[10]

By this time Burke and Lee were satisfied that Touch the Clouds was telling the truth; the chief was angry and disappointed but he had no intention of going to war, and he insisted that Crazy Horse felt the same way. Knowing that additional companies of troops from Fort Laramie were already on their way to Red Cloud, and convinced that a roundup of Crazy Horse's band could result in a needless killing, Lee told Burke he would go to Camp Robinson to convince Clark and Bradley that a terrible mistake was about to be made. With his wife Lucy and ten-year-old daughter Maude, Lee set out from Camp Sheridan in an Army ambulance early the following morning, the second day of September.

The Oglala He Dog had been a lifelong friend of Crazy Horse, born in the same year and the same season of the year. They had played together as children, courted the girls together, and went to war together as young men. He Dog's half brother Short Bull said the men in their band "did so much fooling around with girls" that the other bands had begun to call them the Ite Sica—the Bad Faces. He Dog was a nephew of Red Cloud, and the older man was instrumental in having He Dog appointed a chief, one of the Shirt Wearers of the Ite Sica. The Onloge On—the Shirt Wearers—were called the "owners of the tribe"; they made important decisions collectively. He Dog and Crazy Horse were both Shirt Wearers when they turned thirty in 1868, the year the Fort Laramie treaty was signed, but they did not touch the pen. Both remained in the north when Red Cloud, American Horse, and other chiefs led their bands to the agencies. Over the following years, He Dog and Crazy Horse remained war comrades in the north and fought beside each other in the big battles, and in May 1877 they rode south together to surrender at the Red Cloud Agency. A week later both men enlisted as scouts. It was the soldier known as White Hat, Lieutenant Clark, who showed He Dog where to make his mark. In return, He Dog was given a military tunic and a revolver.[11]

He Dog had hated whites since his brother Only Man had been killed ten years earlier during the Bozeman War, and like Crazy Horse he had never stayed at an agency. But at the moment of He Dog's signing it appears that Lieutenant Clark opened a continuing conversation with him. This was a remarkable achievement. Clark worked men with words, listening to what they said, patiently explaining his own views. The Oglala were proud men; Clark seems to have won their allegiance by taking them seriously. The change in He Dog was unmistakable by mid-August, when Clark wrote General Crook to say that he had managed to separate Crazy Horse from some of the leading men who had surrendered with him in May. "There is no trouble," he wrote, "with Little Big

Man, Jumping Shield [also known as Iron Crow] and Big Road." Clark added, "He Dog, also a strong man, has joined Red Cloud." Over the next two weeks Clark managed to widen this gap, leaving Crazy Horse increasingly isolated as he rejected the urging of the other chiefs to do as White Hat wished and go to Washington.[12]

The stream of visitors to Crazy Horse's lodge was constant. They would come, sit, perhaps smoke a pipe, and tell the chief all the reasons why he should do as White Hat wished and go to Washington. "After awhile," He Dog said, "Crazy Horse became so he did not want to go anywhere or talk to anyone." Clark recruited many others to press his case, but did not go himself. "One day," He Dog said later, "I was called in to see White Hat and asked to bring Crazy Horse in for a talk because I was such a friend of his."

He Dog went to see his friend in his lodge, then on Little Cottonwood Creek. He delivered White Hat's invitation, but it was no use. "He would not come," said He Dog. "This made me feel bad, so I moved my people from where Crazy Horse was camping and camped over near the Red Cloud band."

"There was no quarrel," He Dog added. "We just separated."

This is not quite convincing. To feel bad, to have a bad heart, was to admit deep disaffection, and to move his people was a big thing. The people were He Dog's immediate *tiyospaye*, a kind of extended family including his many brothers and a few others, nine separate lodges of fifty or more people. Someone in the group had once owned a gray horse famous for its fast running and endurance. Indians never named horses in the sense that whites do; they called them by some identifying characteristic, referring to the Sorrell, or the Horse with the White Stockings. When the fast gray developed a kidney sore or saddle gall they called it Cankahuhan (Soreback), and eventually He Dog's immediate band was called by that name, too—Cankahuhan, the Sorebacks. Everyone in He Dog's band was related to Red Cloud, and He Dog was his nephew; to move close to Red Cloud might be called a natural thing, but all knew it signaled a break with Crazy Horse. From that moment He Dog was on the side of Red Cloud, on the side of White Hat, on the side of General Crook.[13]

The night after the meeting between Crazy Horse and White Hat, while Crook was heading west on the Union Pacific Railroad, Red Cloud and some of the other chiefs went to the agency for a talk with the agent, James Irwin, who had asked them to come. Irwin was thoroughly stirred up by the talk of the camps; in a letter to Washington he described Crazy

Horse's mood as "silent, sullen, lordly and dictatorial," called him "impudent and defiant," said he objected to everything, and warned the commissioner of Indian affairs that the chief's intransigence "had disturbed and excited the Indians."

In his office Irwin told the chiefs he had "heard some bad talk" and wanted to know if he could help. The chiefs appointed American Horse to respond. He said the leading men had all been meeting daily for more than a week and had "done all we could to quiet Crazy Horse and bring him into a better state of feeling." But Crazy Horse refused to meet with the other chiefs. "We can do nothing with him," American Horse said. The chiefs present—Red Cloud, Little Wound, Young Man Afraid of His Horses, and American Horse—then collectively made Irwin an oddly worded promise "that they would see that Crazy Horse did nothing about the agency that would hurt my feelings."[14]

What did Irwin mean—the Indians would *see* that Crazy Horse did not *hurt his feelings*? What did Irwin think that the chiefs were promising to do?

In Irwin's two, back-to-back letters to Washington, written on the last day of August and the first day of September, it is clear only that Irwin, like Clark, had now turned decisively against Crazy Horse. Where things were headed can be glimpsed in two remarks made by an officer at Crook's headquarters in Omaha. One was uttered in an interview with a reporter for the *Omaha Herald*, and a second was scribbled onto Bradley's telegram of August 31 before it was filed—the telegram reporting Crazy Horse's threat to go north. General Robert Williams, Crook's adjutant general, often briefed the newspapers on what to expect in the Department of the Platte. On the day of Bradley's telegram he told the *Herald*'s reporter that Crazy Horse had taken on the role of "a sort of general 'objector' . . . it was feared he would make them trouble yet . . . he had been moody and ill-natured since his return to Red Cloud, and showed that he was not to be trusted."

That same day Williams penciled a note onto Bradley's telegram. He had not been to Red Cloud himself. What he scribbled must have been the gist of what he had been told by someone else. "Crazy Horse is . . . objecting to everything," he recorded. "General Crook alone can influence him. It is doubtful if Crazy Horse will go to Washington."

But Williams was satisfied that the rest of the chiefs at Red Cloud could be trusted. If Crazy Horse tried to break away to join Sitting Bull and resume the war, he wrote, "the present indications are that other chiefs would endeavor to kill him."[15]

28

"I can have him whenever I want him."

DURING HIS DAYLONG RIDE north to Camp Robinson, Crook had plenty of time to think about the trouble brewing with Crazy Horse. Colonel Bradley thought Crook could still talk the chief around and it is likely that Crook thought so, too. But Crook was not sentimental about such matters; once he determined that a chief could not be worked around to a compliant way of thinking, the general hardened his heart against the man and acted vigorously to get him out of the way. Crook had hoped to make use of Crazy Horse by setting him against the other chiefs, and bringing them down a peg or two. But he did not make the mistake of thinking Crazy Horse harmless, or a man who could be pushed around. Crook paid his adversaries the respect of considering them dangerous. One such had been the Apache chief Eskiminzin, leader of a "saucy, impudent lot of cut-throats . . . [who] would walk through our camp in that defiant, impudent manner, as much as to say, 'I would like to kill you just for the fun of it, just to see you kick.' "

Crook called him Skimmy, kept clear of his men, and wrote in his *Autobiography*, "I must confess I was afraid of them."[1]

Skimmy only looked daggers, but another Apache chief named Ochocama devised an elaborate plan to murder Crook at a council in September 1872. A Hualapai Indian scout delivered timely warning of the plot. As Crook and the chief exchanged greetings in the first moments, Ochocama would begin to roll a cigarette. Then he would light it. His first puff would be signal for another Indian to shoot and kill Crook.

Despite this warning, Crook went ahead with the meeting anyway, perhaps thinking it too good a chance to arrest the Indians he wanted. He made sure the Indians at the meeting were outnumbered by soldiers and mule skinners but he noted that even so a nervous Ochocama started to roll his cigarette. Then events parted from the script. An Indian stabbed a soldier, a shot was fired, and Ochocama's confederate swung his rifle on Crook. The shot that might have killed him went wild when a lieutenant kicked the Indian's rifle aside. A furious hand-to-hand fight ensued; several Indians were killed or wounded while the rest, including Ochocama, succeeded in escaping to the mountains, leaving Crook with a deepened respect for the difficulty of laying hands on a wild Indian. He did not forget this episode. We might liken the effect to what occurs in the mind of a man who has once stepped over a log onto a rattlesnake. He will think twice about every log for the rest of his life.[2]

Another problem chief who could not be tamed with words was the Tonto Apache known as Deltchay,[3] who promised peace in April 1873 but ran off to the mountains with his fighting men a month later. As this pattern was repeated over the next several years Crook developed an especially intense dislike for Deltchay. In frequent letters the general directed his young lieutenant, Walter Schuyler, in his efforts first to manage Deltchay, then to chase him down and capture him, and finally, when all patience had been exhausted, to kill him and prove it with the delivery of Deltchay's head. Little of this extended campaign is recorded in Crook's autobiography or preserved among his official papers. Crook sometimes instructed Schuyler to burn his letters after reading them, but for whatever reason (perhaps pride) Schuyler held on to the Deltchay letters. In these letters we may observe Crook's mind at work.[4]

Crook's care in planning is evident in the letter he wrote to Schuyler at Camp Verde, Arizona, in September 1873. Deltchay had come in promising peace yet again but made so much trouble that Schuyler sought permission to arrest him. Crook supported the lieutenant's plan and suggested he might begin with a raid on some of Deltchay's confederates still hiding in the nearby mountains. "Killing a few of them," Crook wrote, "will go to weaken Delche's influence and make his capture more easy, as doubtless this insubordination in the main originates with him." For the arrest itself he urged caution, careful planning, swift action, and the use of overwhelming force.

> Get sufficient men from the post so as to prevent a collision and do your utmost to prevent one, but should one unavoidably occur, have your men so posted that they can kill all the ring leaders who support Delche in his opposition. As soon as you make the arrest tell Delche that if his people make any attempt to rescue him that he will be the first one you will kill . . . Don't attempt to make the arrest unless you are sure of success as a failure will lead to bad consequences . . . make your disposition in such a

manner that you will have the Indians completely in your power . . . As soon as you make the arrest I wish you would advise me by messenger . . . I shall feel very anxious about you until I hear from you again. I have confidence in your doing the best under the circumstances.[5]

But things did not go as planned. Deltchay was one jump ahead of the young lieutenant. When Schuyler told the chief he was under arrest, Deltchay laughed. Schuyler then discovered that his Winchester rifle had been emptied of cartridges, and Deltchay's comrades all pulled rifles and pistols from beneath their clothes or blankets. Schuyler would have died where he stood if his Mojave scouts had not intervened. Deltchay and the other chiefs fled for the mountains. Soon some of the runaways came back, telling Crook they were sorry and begging the general to let them stay. At first he refused, saying he preferred to "drive them all back into the mountains, where I could kill them all." The Apache pleaded. "I finally compromised by letting them stay," Crook wrote, "provided they would bring in the heads of certain of the chiefs who were ringleaders."[6]

Deltchay's was among the heads Crook desired, and he was not speaking figuratively. He wanted the heads and he promised to pay for them. Schuyler meanwhile led a small group into the mountains after Deltchay. "I have only 15 men but they are picked shots and with two scouts we can make it lively for this chief if I can catch him," Schuyler wrote his father in December 1873. "His death will settle the business as he is the king thief of them all."

But Deltchay eluded Schuyler's small party. The following June, Schuyler went after him again, urged on by Crook, who wrote, "Start out your killers as soon as possible after the heads of Delche and Co. The more prompt these heads are brought in, the less liable other Indians, in the future, will be to jeopardize their heads." In mid-July 1874, Crook wrote yet again: "If you think you can make sure of Delchae you can make a scout against him." A week later some Tonto Apache brought Deltchay's head to Verde, and claimed the bounty. Soon thereafter another group delivered Deltchay's head to officers at the San Carlos Reservation. They also claimed the bounty.

In October, Crook wrote Schuyler to say he had solved the mystery. An Apache woman said the gossip on the San Carlos Reservation was that the first head belonged to Deltchay's son. But Crook was not put out by the deception, and he never complained about the request for double payment. "Being satisfied that both parties were earnest in their beliefs," he wrote, "and [since] the bringing in of an extra head was not amiss, I paid both bounties."[7]

Crook's approach was entirely practical. He did not share the attitude of western newspaper editors, who blamed every conflict on the Indians and called openly for their extermination. Crook believed that white avarice—"the almighty dollar"—caused most of the trouble. "The fact is there is too much money in this Indian business," he wrote to his friend Rutherford B. Hayes in November 1871. But in Crook's view there was no profit in arguing the justice of every clash till kingdom come. The fighting had to stop. Indians who resisted had to be got out of the way. By the time Crook's ambulance pulled up before Colonel Bradley's office at Camp Robinson on the morning of the second day of September, Crook had made up his mind that Crazy Horse had to be got out of the way. His plan was to place the chief under arrest and have him transported under military escort to a federal prison in Florida. Crook entrusted the job to his chief of scouts, Lieutenant William Philo Clark.

That something big was brewing at Camp Robinson was immediately apparent to Lucy Lee, the wife of Lieutenant Jesse Lee, when they drove into the military post sometime in the afternoon of September 2. Several companies of cavalry had just arrived from Fort Laramie and the place was alive with the coming and going of officers and men. General Crook had reached the post earlier in the day and was conferring with Colonel Bradley. "We found something unusual going on," Lucy Lee wrote a few weeks later to her hometown newspaper in Indiana, the *Greencastle Star.* "But of what nature," she added, "the mysterious manner of the knowing ones precluded all possibility of finding out."[8]

Lieutenant Lee, of course, had a pretty good idea what was hatching. As soon as he had safely deposited his wife and daughter at the home of a friend he set out to find Crook and Bradley. "I at once . . . told them there was some mistake," Lee wrote later. "All the Indians at Spotted Tail were quiet and had no intention of going north on the warpath."

Crook told Lee to make his case to Clark, who was busy with plans for the simultaneous arrest of Crazy Horse and Touch the Clouds. The discussion which followed, Lee said, "was by no means tame." Clark and Lee were friends, but Clark did not trust Lee's assurances about Touch the Clouds. Clark's mind was made up; nothing seemed to shake his faith in what he had been told by Frank Grouard. When Lee stated flatly that he could "guarantee no Indian from Spotted Tail would go north," Clark was incredulous and smiled in a dismissive, even jeering way.[9]

Lee countered by relating the whole story of the confrontation in Daniel Burke's house the previous day—what Touch the Clouds said, the argument between Grouard and Louis Bordeaux, how Grouard gradually backed down. Lee believed that it was his explanations, firm and patient, which eventually carried the day. "I finally succeeded in getting myself listened to," he wrote. Lee was assured that the roundup would be abandoned; the Indians "would not be disturbed." He felt the situation had been safely turned around. "Mister Lee," General Crook said to him soberly, "I don't want to make any mistake, for it would, to the Indians, be the basest treachery to make a mistake in this matter."

That was exactly how Lee saw it. Crook said he was glad Lee had come. With that, Lee felt "greatly relieved."

But soon Lee was worrying anew. Nothing was said about Frank Grouard's mistranslation, cause of the original alarm. Bradley called off the roundup with a very different explanation. He said news had arrived of the approach of a party of Miniconjou, the remnants of Lame Deer's band. Nothing should be done that might stampede this last group of hostiles. Waiting till the band came in meant delay of a day or two at most. Lee sensed a lingering reservation in Clark's mind, as well. "It still seemed to be the intention of Clark to have something done to Crazy Horse and his band—just what, I did not then know."

It was Bradley's custom to jot a few words in his diary about the events of the day. He recorded Crook's initial order to surround and disarm the chief, then added, "After consideration the movement was deferred."

Lieutenant Bourke wrote nothing in his diary about these unfolding events at the time, and when he came to it a year later he omitted all mention of the heated argument between Clark and Lee. Bourke described the delay in rounding up Crazy Horse's band as the result of Crook's innate caution and desire to be fair. "To give Crazy Horse one last chance for self-vindication," Bourke wrote, "General Crook sent him word that he wanted to hold a council with him . . . and hear what he had to say for himself." The time appointed was early the following morning, September 3. The place was the camp of Red Cloud and American Horse on Little White Clay Creek about two miles southeast of the agency. Not just Crazy Horse but all the chiefs were asked to be present.[10]

———

While Crook was meeting with Lee at Camp Robinson, Crazy Horse in his lodge on White Clay Creek was trying to read the minds of two Army officers who had ridden out for a visit. Later that day, Crazy Horse told He Dog that one of the officers was "the soldier chief from Fort Laramie," which may have meant Colonel Bradley, who had commanded at Laramie some years back. But it is more likely the officer was Colonel Julius Mason, commander of three companies of cavalry which had just arrived from Fort Laramie. In any event, the identity of the chief's visitors cannot be established with certainty. But they were Army officers, and they were but two more in the stream of men who came to tell Crazy Horse what to do. The chief was in a troubled frame of mind. Only a week earlier he had dreamed of death. He did not like these two visitors.

That afternoon, He Dog arrived in Crazy Horse's camp with a message from White Hat. He Dog's visit was serious and formal. He met in council with Crazy Horse and other leading men in the camp of the Hunkpatila. He said that White Hat had asked all the chiefs to move their lodges to a place near the foot of White Butte, a high wall of clay which dominated the skyline across the White River to the north of the agency. He Dog said that Three Stars—General Crook—was coming to the agency and the next morning wished to meet with the chiefs in council. He Dog knew that there was trouble, that feeling was bad, and he spoke plainly:

> All who love their wife and children, let them come across the creek with me. All who want their wife and children to be killed by the soldiers, let them stay where they are.

Crazy Horse did not share this view of the matter and did not want to meet with Three Stars, but he did not quarrel with He Dog. Instead he asked He Dog and Iron Hawk, a friend of both men, to come to his lodge to talk further. Here the historian is hungry for detail. Who else was in Crazy Horse's lodge when the three friends sat down to talk? The close followers of Crazy Horse were often at his side when he discussed important matters. Some had gone over to White Hat, like Iron Crow, Little Big Man, and He Dog himself. Others remained loyal to the chief, such as Looking Horse and Black Fox, a man He Dog did not trust. Both had been riding at Crazy Horse's side the day he surrendered at Camp Robinson. Were the chief's wives present? If Black Shawl was indeed consumptive, as the surgeon McGillycuddy reported, she may have been lying quietly in the gloom of the lodge, coughing up flecks of blood. The new wife, Ellen Larrabee, may have been sitting nearby, fastening on every word, looking for its hidden meaning. But of such matters He Dog says nothing, only tells his story.

Crazy Horse described for his friends the visit from the two officers earlier that afternoon. With them, he said, they brought gifts: a knife and two cigars. Tobacco was a sign of peaceful intent, but the gift of the knife disturbed the chief. He Dog later summed up Crazy Horse's uncomfortable thoughts:

> He did not like the way they shook hands with him, and he did not like their talk, and he did not like their gift. He thought the gift of the knife meant trouble was coming. He thought they shook hands with him as if they did not mean him any good. He was afraid there would be trouble at that council.

As for himself, He Dog said, he had made up his mind. He did not want trouble, he would do as White Hat requested, he would meet with Three Stars. He asked Crazy Horse, "Does this mean that you will be my enemy if I move across the creek?"

He Dog said the chief laughed in his face. Crazy Horse said:

> I am no white man! They are the only people that make rules for other people, that say, "If you stay on one side of this line it's peace, but if you go on the other side I will kill you all." I don't hold with deadlines. There is plenty of room; camp where you please.

Crazy Horse himself would not cross the creek or come to the council, on that he was adamant. But he did not speak harshly or angrily of this latest request from White Hat. He told He Dog,

> Tell my friend that I thank him and I am grateful, but some people over there have said too much. I don't want to talk to them anymore. No good would come of it.[11]

General Crook planned to meet with the chiefs the day after He Dog's talk with Crazy Horse. Billy Garnett and Baptiste Pourier were instructed to join Crook's party at the agency store in the morning to accompany the general to the Indian camp. The two men spent the night previous in the house where Garnett lived near the agency compound with his new wife, Emma Mills, then in the first months of pregnancy.[12]

Early on the morning of September 3, as Pourier and Garnett were heading to meet the general at Frank Yates's store, they were approached by Pourier's relative Woman Dress, then in his early thirties. In tribal politics, Woman Dress was close to his relative Red Cloud and "always stayed with him," according to Red Feather, brother-in-law of Crazy Horse. He meant that in political affairs Woman Dress sided with the chief. About this time he was photographed in the outfit given to him when he enlisted as a scout—military tunic with a yellow neckerchief. The expression on his face was watchful and grim. As so often, Garnett gives the fullest account of what happened next.

"Where are you going?" asked Woman Dress, who had been enlisted by Lieutenant Clark as a scout in Company B.

"We told him that we were going to White Clay," Garnett remembered, "to an Indian Council with General Crook and Lieutenant Clark."

"Don't you go there," said Woman Dress. "When you hold this council at White Clay, Crazy Horse is going to come in with sixty Indians, and catch General Crook by the hand, like he is going to shake hands, and he is going to hold on to him, and those sixty Indians are going to kill Crook and whoever he has with him."[13]

Woman Dress said he had been told of the plot by Lone Bear, one of Clark's informants, who had in turn learned of it from his brother Little Wolf. Woman Dress said Little Wolf had been spying on Crazy Horse over a period of time by pretending to court a girl in a nearby lodge. Enfolding the girl in his blanket in the customary way he would linger by the chief's lodge, close enough to hear what was going on within. He heard Crazy Horse say he was going to the council with Crook and there he would kill the general.

Garnett knew Woman Dress well. He had helped him to enlist as a scout in Company B, Garnett's own outfit at the time of the fight on the Red Fork of the Powder River. He considered Woman Dress a friend. But something about the man's story struck Garnett as wrong. For many years, Little Wolf had been in the north with Crazy Horse, he had been in the Custer fight, and he had come in to surrender at the agency only a few weeks before Crazy Horse himself, whom he called a friend. Little Wolf did not seem a candidate for spying on Crazy Horse. Whatever the cause, some doubt was forming in Garnett's mind.

"Just about then," Garnett remembered, "General Crook came up with an ambulance which would hold nine men." With the general were Lieutenants Clark and Bourke and some others, all heading for the council at White Clay Creek. As the ambulance approached, Baptiste Pourier ran up to catch the lead horses and brought them to a halt, then turned to Garnett, saying, "Now tell Crook what this Indian said."

"This Woman Dress, he was right there," Garnett recalled. "So the team was stopped, and I told General Crook just what this man, Woman Dress, said"—that Crazy Horse planned to kill Crook at the council— "if," Bourke recalled later, "Crook's words did not suit him." Bourke added that Woman Dress said he had been sent to warn Crook "by Spotted Tail and the other Indians."[14]

"Then General Crook studied a little bit," Garnett continues, "and he asked me, 'What do you know about this man, Woman Dress? Is he reliable? Does he tell the truth?'"

Garnett was not ready to pronounce. "General," he said, "this is a big undertaking and I could not say—I am going to leave it up to Baptiste Pourier, a man who is with me and he will tell you." Garnett explained that Pourier and Woman Dress were married to women who were first cousins.

Garnett recalled the exchange that followed.

> Bat says, "General, I want to tell you this man is a truthful man and whatever he tells you is the truth."
> So Crook studied again and said, "I never start anyplace but what I like to get there."
> Lieutenant Clark said, "General, it is no use to go."

He built an argument for turning back on the example of General Custer, killed at the Little Bighorn. Like Custer, Crook was irreplaceable; they could not afford to lose another such man, and Crook was traveling with too weak a party for protection.

> "There is no use for you to start in there."
> General Crook says, "What excuse I can make I do not know."
> Lieutenant Clark says, "You leave that to me."
> And General Crook said, "All right."[15]

It was probably the interpreter in Billy Garnett that backed away when Crook asked if Woman Dress told the truth. Over the course of his life

Garnett rarely explained how it felt to be so often in the middle, as much white as red, an employee of the government but still an Indian. His job as an interpreter was not to decide which loyalty came first. He occupied a middle ground. He did not choose sides, or decide who was to be trusted. It was an interpreter's job to render one man's meaning as accurately as he did another's. But something changed when Crook said all right. The inquiry into the motives of Crazy Horse had ended. What to do about him was the question now, and Garnett found himself willy-nilly one of those dragooned for the job. It was Clark who gave him his instructions.

First was to tell the chiefs gathered in the camp on the White Clay there would be no council. Crook worried the Indians might think he lacked grit, but Clark ignored that. He chose a simple explanation. "Billy," he said, "you go to the council and tell them a message has come for General Crook and he had to go back."

That was for all to hear. But Clark wanted to see a smaller group back at the military post as soon as they could come without causing remark. He gave Billy a list of names. First was American Horse, trusted completely ever since he had killed Sioux Jim for the Army. The others were all reliable men—no northern chiefs who had come in with Crazy Horse. It was only a couple of miles to the big Indian camp at the base of White Butte, an easy twenty-minute ride. American Horse was the chief Garnett approached when he arrived. "There was a lot of Indians there when I got to this place," he remembered. He took note of one man's absence but failed to see immediately what it meant: "Crazy Horse was not there and none of his followers were there either. I did not see any of them in this council."

American Horse listened to Garnett's message and the list of names, then told the interpreter, "I will attend to that." He went into the big council tent and loudly called out the news that Crook would not be coming, an important letter had pulled him away on other business, there would be no meeting. In the hubbub as the leading men gathered themselves to leave American Horse circulated quietly, whispering to those on Clark's list. "You go home," he told Garnett; "I will bring these men up." Garnett remembered that two or three hours passed in all between Clark's instructions outside Frank Yates's store and the arrival of the chiefs at Camp Robinson, where they gathered in the quarters of Colonel Bradley at the eastern end of officers' row.

Each of the buildings providing officers with quarters faced the parade ground and was surrounded by a covered porch. From the porch one looked out across the hard-packed parade ground. In the center at the far end, 160 yards distant, were two log buildings, the adjutant's office on the left where the business of the military post was conducted, and the guardhouse on the right where prisoners were confined. To the west of the parade ground were the cavalry barracks, to the east the infantry barracks. The road from the Red Cloud Agency and Little White Clay Creek approached the rear of officers' row, where entrance might be gained past a woodshed and through the kitchen. The Indians might have tied their horses out front, in plain sight, and climbed the porch for the meeting with Crook, or entered less conspicuously from the rear. Either way, it was quite a crowd that gathered in Bradley's big room in the afternoon of September 3, but not the colonel himself. Bradley was in his office on the far side of the parade ground; it seems likely that Crook wished to exclude him from the deliberations to follow.

Running the meeting in Bradley's big room were Crook and Clark, the general and his lieutenant. The deliberants included nearly twenty scouts and Indians. Garnett in his various accounts listed them by name: after the general and Clark came Garnett, Baptiste Pourier, and Frank Grouard as interpreters, followed by the chiefs and their leading men: Red Cloud, American Horse, Young Man Afraid of His Horses, Little Wound, No Water, and nine others.[16] No Water was the man who shot Crazy Horse in the face with a borrowed revolver when the chief ran off with No Water's wife. Every Indian in the room was Oglala; none had been at the Custer fight on the Little Bighorn. All had long histories of siding with Red Cloud and favoring peace with the whites. Garnett called them "friendly Indians." He reported that all were "surprised" when told the reason the morning's council had been called off—that Crazy Horse had plotted to murder the general by seizing his hand and stabbing him to death at the outset of the meeting. "They didn't know anything about it," Garnett related.

On the agenda was a single item: getting Crazy Horse out of the way. The discussion seems to have lasted an hour or more but the plan adopted was simple in the extreme. No argument over substance or details is recalled by Garnett, who summarized the talk in his customarily direct and unadorned way:

So it was planned that every one of those Indian chiefs was going to pick out four brave men of their respective bands, and that night, those picked men were going to the Crazy Horse village and kill Crazy Horse. The man who killed this man was going to get $300. There was a horse Lieutenant Clark had, and he was going to get that horse . . . So they said they were going to draw some ammunition, and they did and took it with them, which was late in the afternoon then. I was there and was told to stay around the post close.[17]

At the end of the meeting the Indians separated to make their arrangements for the move against Crazy Horse and his camp. Billy Garnett recalled that Crook and Bourke left the post more or less immediately, resuming their interrupted journey to the Wind River country in pursuit of the Nez Percé. No record survives of what Crook told Colonel Bradley before riding off, but the unfolding of events suggests the general said little—only that Crazy Horse was to be rounded up by Clark, the scouts, and the friendly Indians. Garnett says the meeting ended in late afternoon. Straight west of Camp Robinson was a range of high forested hills separating the various forks of Soldier's Creek as they dropped down into the White River. Dusk came abruptly when the sun fell behind those hills. Billy Garnett retired to the sutler's store run by J. W. Dear on the military post. There, he kept himself available as the lamps were lit with the approach of night.

Crook and Clark had planned to move quickly, before word got out, but it was no use. When Clark helped the Indians draw ammunition after the meeting ended, there was either commotion or talk. Very quickly first one friend of Crazy Horse, then another, brought word to him in his camp at the mouth of Little White Clay that cartridges were being secretly distributed. They told the chief that the whites were preparing to kill him. Crazy Horse's brother-in-law Red Feather learned of the bounty promised by White Hat to the man who killed Crazy Horse—money and the lieutenant's much-envied running horse, sorrel in color. Red Feather rode to Crazy Horse's camp to tell the chief what he knew, and other reports followed as night came on. From several people Crazy Horse learned about the story Woman Dress told—that he planned to kill Crook at the council. It disgusted Crazy Horse that people might think him capable of such an act. "Only cowards are murderers," he is said to have remarked.

But Crazy Horse did not ignore these many reports. He told his friends that he would take his sick wife to her parents for safety. "She was sick with a swollen arm," said Red Feather. Black Shawl Women's parents were camped on the creek that ran through the Spotted Tail Agency, forty miles to the east. Two friends planned to go with the chief: Kicking Bear and Shell Boy.[18]

It was probably close to the bugling of taps when Billy Garnett was approached in the sutler's store by an orderly from the commander's staff. It was night. The post was settling down. "Garnett, you are wanted at General Bradley's quarters," said the orderly, using Bradley's brevet rank from his service in the Civil War. "You are to take the back way and go into the house."

Garnett made his way to Bradley's house at the eastern end of officers' row, entered through the kitchen, and went into the big front room where Crook and the Oglala chiefs had planned out the killing of Crazy Horse a few hours earlier. In the big room, Garnett found Bradley and three others—the new agent for the Oglala, James Irwin; his interpreter, Leon Palladay; and a northern Indian. It was the last that aroused Garnett's caution. With Irwin was He Dog, the longtime friend of Crazy Horse. Clark may have convinced himself that He Dog was on the side of the whites now, but Garnett was not so sure.

Bradley went to the point. "What is that council that is held here today in my room?" he asked Garnett.

Garnett did not want to answer in the presence of He Dog. "General," he said, "isn't there some other room where you and I can go?"

Bradley took the point. He led Garnett through one room, then another, where Garnett then asked the general why he was asking such a question in front of a northern Indian. "Was it not planned out in my room there," Bradley answered, "for these Indians to kill Crazy Horse? The man who kills Crazy Horse to get three hundred dollars and Lieutenant Clark's running horse?"

The true answer was not complicated but Garnett still hesitated. "Is there any catch about this?" he said. "Where did you get it?"

"These men came up here with this story," Bradley answered.

"General," said Garnett, "that is supposed to be a private council and not to be given out, and I see you have a Northern Indian in there and I did not want to talk to you in his presence." Then he confirmed all Bradley had been told: the plan made, the bounty offered, the ammunition drawn, the chiefs sent off to ready themselves for killing Crazy Horse. Bradley's reaction was direct and simple, Garnett said later:

Bradley said it was too bad to get after a man of the standing of Crazy Horse
in this manner in the nighttime without his knowing anything about it.
"They ought to do this in broad daylight . . . The life of Crazy Horse is just
as sweet to him as my life is to me."[19]

Bradley's mind was made up quickly. He told Garnett, "You go back
where the orderly found you, and stay there."

Again Garnett crossed the darkened parade ground to the sutler's
store. Thirty minutes passed before another soldier approached, this time
the orderly for Clark. "Garnett," he said, "Clark wants you."

Now Garnett made his way to the last dwelling on the western end of
officers' row. Inside he found Clark pacing up and down, disgusted and
out of sorts. "These Indians can hold nothing," he said.

"Bradley has got hold of that council we had with the Indians today,"
he explained. What Bradley thought of the plan was obvious in what
Clark said next. The nighttime operation to kill Crazy Horse was off. In
its place was the previous daylight plan to arrest the chief and send him
out of the country. A direct order from Bradley must have left the lieutenant with no choice. "You go down to the Indian village right away,"
Clark told Garnett, "and stop those Indians approaching Crazy Horse.
When you go down, tell those Indians not to disturb Crazy Horse, but
tell all to report to Camp Robinson before sun-up in the morning."

Garnett made his way to the big camp on White Clay and sought out
the lodge of American Horse. A large group of Indians had gathered
behind the lodge, "plotting up something," Garnett said later. "I told
them not to bother themselves, not to kill Crazy Horse that night."

Garnett's last translation at the end of this long day was to put Clark's
new instruction into Lakota—to tell American Horse and the men gathered at his lodge to come instead to the military post before sun-up to
draw guns and ammunition for a different and larger operation with the
same ultimate purpose as the first, which was to get Crazy Horse out of
the way.

While these events were unfolding Lieutenant Jesse Lee's wife and
daughter were settling in with their old friends, Major Thomas B. Burrowes and his wife Ellen, who had been given a house on officers' row
after Burrowes's return from sick leave in June. Burrowes was a man broken by the hardships of frontier duty and Civil War wounds from which

he never fully recovered. He had already been waiting for years for an opening on the Army's retired list. Over time the two couples had often exchanged long visits.

During the evening, Jesse Lee learned that the following morning "the Crazy Horse band would be surrounded and their ponies and arms taken away and Crazy Horse taken prisoner." In a final meeting, Lee pressed his case with Clark and Bradley but found Clark, in particular, "fussy and headstrong and . . . determined in carrying out their plan." Concluding that further argument was useless, Lee told Clark and Bradley that he wanted to return at once with Spotted Tail himself to the agency to let Captain Burke know what was impending, and to give Spotted Tail time to organize his followers to talk the Indians through any excitement. "They wanted to keep Spotted Tail there but I insisted that if they were going to stir up excitement I would prefer to have Spot with me," Lee said later. On this point he prevailed.

Before departing Camp Robinson with Spotted Tail at about four in the morning, Lee left Clark with a final caution: to hold on tight once he got his hands on Crazy Horse. "Don't let Crazy Horse get away; he might come to Spotted Tail Agency," Lee cautioned.

"Lee," Clark replied in a sarcastic tone, "don't you worry about that. Crazy Horse can't make a move without my knowing it, and I can have him whenever I want him."[20]

29

"I am Crazy Horse! Don't touch me!"

IT WAS THE ARREST not the killing of Crazy Horse that Colonel Bradley had in mind when he dispatched his men to seize the chief on the morning of Tuesday, the 4th of September, 1877. But arrest only did not mean half measures; Bradley sent two groups strong enough for war—eight troops of cavalry and infantry under Colonel Julius Mason and four hundred friendly Indian scouts under Lieutenant Clark. The entire force numbered seven or eight hundred men. In Clark's view the roster of chiefs supporting the soldiers proved the increasing isolation of Crazy Horse, whose village had dwindled in the first few days of September to about seventy lodges. More than twice that number had surrendered with him in May. Red Cloud, Little Wound, American Horse, and Young Man Afraid of His Horses all rode under Clark's command. But that was not all. Clark had been working the Indians all summer, and among the scouts setting out to arrest the chief were some of Crazy Horse's oldest friends, not only Little Big Man but others who had been by his side in the north for years like Jumping Shield, Big Road, and He Dog. Even one of Crazy Horse's uncles, Bull Head, was among the scouts riding toward the chief's village near the mouth of Little White Clay Creek.[1]

The two groups had been slow to assemble and it was nine o'clock before they departed, the cavalry and two companies of infantry following down one bank of the White River in the direction of Crazy Horse's village, while the Indians with fresh issue of guns and ammunition rode down the other. The whole post was on hand to watch them set out. Luke Voorhees, a manager of the stage company that connected the military posts along the White River to Fort Laramie and Cheyenne, reported in the *Cheyenne Leader* that the soldiers brought with them heavy weapons. Included were two Gatling guns. It was widely known that Custer had refused to take a Gatling gun with him on the way to the Little Bighorn, protesting that it would slow him down. The Army did not intend to allow that mistake again. Further firepower was promised by a field gun, "an old brass affair drawn by six mules," according to Sergeant Kelly of the 14th Infantry. Voorhees recognized the figure of Little Big Man, stripped to his breechcloth after his custom, riding at the head of "the red cavalry."

The Indians on their ponies were all painted and dressed for war. Their rapid progress down the creek alarmed the Indians camped in small clusters along the way. Many simply grabbed their children and horses and stampeded back to the Red Cloud Agency for protection. Others chanced the few minutes it took Indian women to strike a lodge and pack a travois for flight. Voorhees calculated that within an hour as many as five thousand Indians were milling about the agency stockade. He did not notice the many others who fled into the hills and surrounding prairie.[2]

Lucy Lee planted herself on the wide wraparound porch of her friends Thomas and Ellen Burrowes. Others joined them to wait for the inevitable couriers bringing news. Men came and went across the parade ground, and at the far side the guard at Post Number 1 marched back and forth between the line of field guns and the guardhouse. For a time after the departure of the arresting party all was quiet. Then came the first hint of the course of events: the sound of shooting from several miles down Little White Clay, ten or fifteen shots in a sudden, rapid volley. The rattle of gunfire convinced many at the post, Lieutenant Lemly wrote later, that "the ball had opened in earnest." After awhile a courier arrived and the news quickly spread that Crazy Horse had been killed. "This was considered good news," Lucy Lee wrote in one of her regular letters to the *Greencastle Star* back home in Indiana a few days later.

"Presently a second report came that Crazy Horse had not been killed, but the village was entirely surrounded and captured. This was not quite so good news as the first," she wrote.

"Then came word that Crazy Horse had gotten away."[3]

In his village on the south bank of the White River near the mouth of Little White Clay Creek, Crazy Horse had been keeping track of events. He had come for peace, but the soldiers had been treating him as an enemy. For several days, he seems to have done nothing but listen. He brooded about the words of the Army officers who visited him on the afternoon of September 2. He did not go out to attend the council with Crook on the morning of the 3rd but soon learned that it had been canceled. Later, he was told about the claim that he had planned to kill the general. As events progressed through Monday night and early Tuesday morning, Indians hurried with news from the agency and the military post to Crazy Horse's village and back again. Crazy Horse was told when ammunition was issued to the men who had been charged with killing him. He was told that the plans were changed during the hours of darkness, that an arrest was planned, that the arresting party was assembling at Camp Robinson, that the party had started on its way.

Bearing one of the first reports on Monday night had been Red Feather, the brother of the chief's wife. Before riding back to the agency, Red Feather said later, the chief gave him his gun and gun case, keeping only a knife. Early Tuesday morning, Red Feather and a friend left the military post to inform Crazy Horse that the soldiers were coming. The unarmed chief was still in his lodge. "He was waiting like that for the soldiers," Red Feather said. When word came of the soldiers' approach Red Feather went out to meet them.[4]

As the "friendly" Indians and scouts neared the site of Crazy Horse's village, Billy Garnett rode first with one group, then with another, carrying messages from Lieutenant Clark to the different tribes and bands and returning with reports. Clark believed he had worked the bigger part of the Indians over to the white side, but Garnett did not share his confidence. He thought many of the "friendlies" in the arresting party were actually loyal to Crazy Horse and would rally to his side if it came to fighting. Crazy Horse's onetime friend Little Big Man was much in evidence, now dashing out in front of the scouts, now hurrying back with news or instructions. Feelings were running high and nerves were tense. When a coyote suddenly appeared running alongside the stream half a dozen Indians impulsively fired at the animal; this was the volley of shots heard back at the post and nervously interpreted as the opening clash in a fight. Shortly afterward, as the scouts began to near the site of Crazy Horse's village, they encountered Indians coming out to meet them. One of the first told Billy Garnett that Crazy Horse was catching his horse. "Crazy Horse is either going to fight or he is going to run away," said the man from the village. Garnett immediately spurred up his horse to take this news to Clark.

Moments later as he crossed Little White Clay, Garnett was hailed by another Indian, the Miniconjou Looking Horse, who had surrendered with Crazy Horse in May. Garnett had been there when Looking Horse rode in beside the other close followers and war comrades of Crazy Horse. Garnett had been the interpreter on May 12 when Crazy Horse and twenty others, including Looking Horse, touched the pen and enlisted as scouts for Clark. But Looking Horse was angry with Clark on this day. He called out sharply to Garnett, "Where are you going? I have just scolded Clark and I am going to scold the crowd you are with"— meaning the Indian scouts Garnett had just left on the far side of the creek.

Moments later Garnett delivered his message to Clark, who agreed with Garnett that a fight looked probable, but told him, "Don't shoot unless they start in on you." Garnett reported that he had seen Looking Horse. "He was sassy when I met him," said Garnett. It was Garnett who was worked up and spoiling for a fight at this point, not Clark.[5]

While Garnett was off talking with Clark, Looking Horse rode up to the band of Oglala scouts Garnett had left on the east bank of Little White Clay. Two of the party rode forward to meet him, Woman Dress and Bull Head. Looking Horse shouted at the scouts, abusing them for siding with the white men. "You people are all Indians," he cried. "Why don't you have pity on one another?"[6]

"I don't allow anyone to come in front of me when I am going anywhere," responded Bull Head. At the same moment, Bull Head or Woman Dress—accounts differ—shot Looking Horse's pony from under him. Bull Head, using the butt of his gun, and several others then "pounded up" Looking Horse and took his gun and pistol. They left him unconscious beside his dead horse in the trail. He Dog watched it all; he said a brother of Looking Horse known as White Cow Killer dragged the man's body out of the way and left it in the shade of a tree before catching up with the others.[7]

Feelings were now approaching a dangerous level. Only five or six hundred yards short of Crazy Horse's village, Garnett's group of scouts came in sight of an organized band of Crazy Horse's fighters collected on a knoll. The seventy men were outnumbered but defiant. At that moment, Little Big Man returned from one of his dashes out in front. "It looks like Crazy Horse is going to show a fight," he reported.

A boy of fifteen or sixteen armed with a revolver dashed down the hill toward the scouts, who opened a way for him. Garnett worried that it was the friends of Crazy Horse who let him pass, but it is possible they only took pity on him. Everybody seemed to recognize this boy and knew he had taken part in the Custer fight. Right behind the boy came another defiant figure mounted on a paint horse and wearing a double-trail, eagle-feather warbonnet. Billy Garnett had never seen this man before, but others knew him. His name was Black Fox, one of the last two Shirt Wearers of the Oyuhpe band. Black Fox was a half brother of Kicking Bear and Flying Hawk, both war comrades of Crazy Horse, and he was married to a sister of Touch the Clouds.[8]

Black Fox charged up to the approaching body of scouts and called out a threat or a challenge, the ritual words of a man preparing to fight no matter the odds. He was armed and ready, carrying a Springfield carbine and a revolver. Behind him about thirty of the warriors from the village were running their ponies back and forth, ready for anything but for the moment holding their fire. Billy Garnett remembered the words of Black Fox:

> I have been looking all my life to die. Ever since I have been big enough to fight I have been looking for one. I never was killed up to this time. I have seen nothing but the clouds and the ground.[9]

After Black Fox had said his piece, Garnett remembered, he took out his knife and clenched it between his teeth. "The biting of the knife" was a Sioux way of asserting veracity; Black Fox intended to be understood as ready to throw himself away in battle.

American Horse was there in the front rank of the scouts. "Brother-in-law," he called out, "hold on, let up." He stepped forward with a pipe, holding it out. "Think of the women and children behind you. Hold on, we have not come down for anything like that. We came down to save you." With these soothing words, appropriate for a Shirt Wearer trying to avoid bloodshed within the tribe, American Horse stepped out closer to Black Fox, offering him the stem of the pipe. Black Fox had now removed the knife from his teeth to say, "*Hau!*"—a word signifying attention and assent, almost as if to say, "Oh yes! I am listening!"

Black Fox called out He Dog's name also, and asked him to come forward. All three men now prepared to smoke sitting on the ground, perhaps fifteen or twenty feet in front of the line of scouts. He Dog had his eye on Black Fox's knife; he worried that Black Fox might try to kill him or American Horse and he noted that American Horse was apparently worrying about the same thing. But everything had changed when American Horse offered the pipe. The three men passed the pipe and Black Fox said the people were his now; when Crazy Horse was gone he was the chief. "I come to die but you saved me," he said. "Crazy Horse has gone with his wife," he said, adding that he "thought he had to die today" and "I am glad to hear you are peaceable." Then Black Fox called out to the men on their horses racing about behind him. They were giving their horses a second wind, getting ready for war.

"All over," said Black Fox. "Stop this running—Go back." The mounted men all turned away and headed back for the village.

Garnett was impressed by the level of control wielded by Black Fox, who explained further.

> Crazy Horse is gone. He listened to too many bad talks. I told him we came in for peace, but he would listen to them. Now he is gone and the people belong to me.[10]

What Black Fox said was puzzling. Crazy Horse was a warrior. There were plenty of men still willing to fight by his side. What was the weakness that made him run away with only his sick wife and two friends?

At just about this moment, Lieutenant Clark joined the big body of scouts on the east bank of the creek. Little Big Man and others had told Clark that Crazy Horse had set out on horseback for the Spotted Tail Agency, some forty miles to the east, together with Black Shawl Woman and Shell Boy and Kicking Bear, a brother of Black Fox. One of the scouts had seen Crazy Horse and the others passing over a rise in the prairie to the east.

Clark was determined to capture the chief and redeem the morning's failure. He quickly organized and dispatched three groups of scouts to chase Crazy Horse down, sending about twenty-five or thirty men in all. A first group took a northern track under Clark's most trusted man, Three Bears, and a second followed a little to the south under He Dog and American Horse. But it was on No Water that Clark depended for success. At the council with Crook in May, No Water had sided decisively with the whites. "There is no more laughing at our great father," No Water had said in the council. "We can't take our great father's word up in our hands and go off and laugh at it any more."

No Water had personal reasons for chasing down Crazy Horse. After he had shot the chief in the face in 1870, No Water had become a chief in his own right, taking over the Tacnaitca or Badger band of the Oglala following the death of his father Black Twin, also known as Holy Bald Eagle. Now Clark promised No Water the addition of lodges from Crazy

Horse's dismembered band, along with two or three hundred dollars in cash, if he brought Crazy Horse as a captive to the lieutenant's quarters. It was forty miles to the Spotted Tail Agency. Crazy Horse had a head start, but No Water spared no effort in the chase. He told Clark later that he rode two ponies so hard they died under him, trying to catch up.[11]

Some of the scouts in pursuit later complained to Billy Garnett that it was impossible to catch the chief, who had a fast horse and a trick for preserving the strength of his mount. On approaching a hill, Crazy Horse always eased to a walk and made his way to the summit slowly, but downhill and on level ground he ran his horses all the way. Thus his mounts got a chance to blow and remained fresh while the scouts, quirt as they might, managed only to come in sight of Crazy Horse and his party far ahead. They told Garnett they could make out the woman riding in the lead, with the three men behind. But they never closed within shooting distance, they said.

What Jesse Lee learned from some of the pursuing scouts at Camp Sheridan that evening was different. The scouts said that Crazy Horse was not running but "riding along quite leisurely with his sick wife." Lee reported that the scouts drew close, called to Crazy Horse, and "asked him to go back with them" to Camp Robinson. Red Feather said the chief had given away his gun. Perhaps that is why he did not threaten but only scolded the scouts with stinging words: "I am Crazy Horse! Don't touch me! I'm not running away."

It was enough. The scouts dropped back. When they came in sight of Sheridan's gates, the twin buttes which marked the final stretch of road into the military post and the Spotted Tail Agency, the scouts veered off. Crazy Horse with his wife and friends rode down to the Indian camps along the creek, where he sought out the lodge of his friend and teacher, Horn Chips. The scouts on their lathered horses went the other way, to the military post three miles up the creek, to report that the chief was coming to the agency.[12]

30

"He feels too weak to die today."

AS CRAZY HORSE WAS setting off with his wife and friends at about ten o'clock on that Tuesday morning, Lieutenant Jesse Lee and Spotted Tail arrived at the chief's agency forty miles east where they found the post commander, Captain Daniel Burke, counting the horses and recording the names of some seventy members of Lame Deer's band of Miniconjou, just arrived from the north. Lee and Burke called a meeting of the leading men of Spotted Tail's Brulé and told them what was happening that day at Red Cloud. All expected trouble to follow. To meet it there were two companies of soldiers under Burke's command, not more than ninety men, supported by several hundred warriors who answered to Spotted Tail. None of the soldiers or Brulé chiefs knew how the northern Indians would respond if fighting broke out.

The military post at Camp Sheridan was built at the same time as Camp Robinson and looked much the same—a collection of wood-frame buildings surrounding a dusty parade ground, with corrals, hayricks, piles of cordwood, and a sutler's store. Rising beyond the post to the north like a palisade was an escarpment of white clay buttes known as the Beaver Wall. In front of the post was a winding creek, dry in places much of the year, never more than a few feet wide, which had its source in the pine-covered ridges to the south. From the post the creek made its way along the curving arc of the Beaver Wall toward its juncture with the White River a few miles to the north. The course of the stream, one of the many throughout the West known as Beaver Creek, was marked by grassy bottomlands, brushy thickets, and groves of cottonwood trees. Some of the bigger, older trees were traditional sites for scaffold burials of the dead. This was not the Beaver Creek where Crazy Horse hoped to have his agency—that was hundreds of miles north in the Tongue River country—but it had long been a favored camping ground of the Oglala and Brulé Sioux.

The Spotted Tail Agency buildings were a half mile up Beaver Creek, south of the military post. About two and a half miles north along the creek bed, roughly three miles from the military post, was the center of the big camp of the northern Indians who had come in to surrender with Touch the Clouds. The campsites of other bands and family groups continued along the creek bed a good many miles in both directions, both north and south of the agency.

Somewhere along this stream the parents of Black Shawl Woman had raised their lodge, where Crazy Horse hoped his wife might be treated and cured by a medicine man. Since he stopped first at the lodge of Horn Chips it is probable he hoped Chips would cure his wife. Also along the creek were the lodges of Standing Bear, who had remained with Touch the Clouds after coming in, and of Fast Thunder, who called Crazy Horse cousin. Fast Thunder, an Oglala, picked Beaver Creek for his home and lived with Spotted Tail's Brulé because he knew the site well and had often camped or wintered there before the agency was established in 1873.[1]

Expecting trouble, Lieutenant Lee and Captain Burke sent some of "the reliable chiefs" in the company of the interpreters Charles Tackett and Joe Merrivale down the creek to the village of Touch the Clouds in the hope they might keep things calm and provide early warning if trouble broke out. At about four o'clock in the afternoon a runner from the Crazy Horse camp arrived in the Miniconjou village with news that there was fighting at Red Cloud. This man "at once set about to stir up excitement," according to Lee. The Brulé chief Roman Nose tried to calm the people. "There will be no trouble here," he said.

But almost immediately the excitement flared again with the arrival of Crazy Horse himself. "This came like a thunder clap from a clear sky," Lee reported later. No other Indian equaled Crazy Horse in his ability to arouse intense excitement. The often-feared stampede was under way in moments. Three hundred lodges in the Miniconjou village came down with "magic swiftness," said Lee—a sure sign the Indians were all ready to bolt. Black Crow, one of "the reliable chiefs," raced back down the creek to the post with the news: "Crazy Horse is in the northern camp." Touch the Clouds soon arrived at the agency as well. He too had heard of Crazy Horse's approach. Burke and Lee sent him back to his village with a request to bring Crazy Horse in to the military post.

It was at about this moment that a courier reached Camp Sheridan bearing a written message from Clark, who had promised to keep Lee informed. As Lee remembered it, Clark's note was all calm reassurance:

There has been no fight. Crazy Horse's band is just going into camp and will give up their guns without trouble in all probability. Crazy Horse has skipped out for your place. Have sent after him. Should he reach your agency, have Spotted Tail arrest him, and I will give any Indian who does this $200.[2]

Hard on the heels of the courier with Clark's note came fifteen or twenty scouts on lathered horses to tell Lee and Burke what the officers already knew—that Crazy Horse was heading their way. These scouts were evidently the men the chief told not to touch him. The soldiers instructed them to turn their horses loose in the post corral and to conceal themselves in the soldiers' barracks. Lee and Burke now climbed into a military ambulance with the interpreter Louis Bordeaux and the post doctor Egon Koerper to head down Beaver Creek in the direction of the northern camp. About ten or fifteen minutes later, not more than a mile down the creek, the ambulance came in sight of a mass of mounted Indians, at least three hundred in all, dressed for war, carrying weapons, shouting and singing. What they intended, Lieutenant Lee did not know. In the front rank was a knot of four men: Touch the Clouds and White Thunder on either side of a man Lee did not recognize, and just behind them Black Crow. Charging First, the son of Touch the Clouds, said that Crazy Horse had agreed to abide by the advice of his friend, and was coming with him to the post voluntarily. In that moment as they approached the post Lee saw for the first time the man who had been the object of so much white anger and fear: the light-haired, unarmed, silent, "rather sad-faced" figure of Crazy Horse.[3]

Lee and Burke got a good look at the chief as they shook hands with him. He was surprisingly slight—not over five feet six inches in height, was Lee's guess. But it was the sorrow of Crazy Horse's expression that struck Lee most. After that, Lee noted the chief's inner agitation—fear, doubt, hope, confusion; he couldn't settle later on a single word to describe it. The excited mass of Indians now accompanied Lee back toward the military post with Crazy Horse and his companions following closely behind the ambulance, where Lee and Burke were exchanging their first impressions of the chief.

To Lee, Crazy Horse seemed "very much distressed." Black Crow and White Thunder, riding within arm's reach of Crazy Horse, had agreed to shoot and kill the chief at the first sign of any effort to escape. That the chief knew he was trapped seemed evident. "He had been under a severe nervous strain all day, and it plainly showed," Lee said. Burke and Lee were both impressed by the chief. Listening from his seat in the ambulance, Louis Bordeaux was surprised to hear the high opinion Lee and Burke held of Crazy Horse, who had not yet spoken.

> They agreed that he was an able young man, destined, if no ill fortune prevented, to become great among his people; that he was not trained like the old chiefs in speaking and in diplomacy; he was not spoiled by any acts to gain advantage, but was straightforward and meant what he declared and could be depended on to perform what he promised.[4]

It did not occur to Lee and Burke that it was Crazy Horse's promises that best explained his agitation. The record of unfolding events speaks clearly. He had promised peace but was met repeatedly by anger, demands, and threats. His friends all gave him conflicting advice. The Army seemed to understand nothing he said. That morning the man whose name was a byword for courage had run away from a fight, leaving Black Fox to confront the whites with a knife in his teeth, and now Crazy Horse was being hurried along by a chaotic mass of angry Indians, some his friends, others eager to kill him. But still he did not resist. He merely rode along with the others to the military post because the white officers had asked him to.

As the large group made its way toward the parade ground in front of the adjutant's office at Camp Sheridan everybody feared a big fight. This was the second time in a single day that a major bloodletting seemed to hang in the balance as rival bands of armed men struggled for possession of Crazy Horse. Spotted Tail now joined the group in front of the adjutant's office, bringing more armed men and swelling the crowd to six hundred or more, all constantly in motion, calling out, tense, carrying loaded weapons. They halted in front of the adjutant's office, where Captain Burke and Lieutenant Lee tried to talk to Crazy Horse, who remained on his horse. The officers told Crazy Horse he must go back to Camp Robinson. They tried to reassure him, Bordeaux remembered, "that he would not be hurt; that he should be protected, etc., but he refused to speak."[5] The chief had uttered not a word during the ride up to the military post, not a word as the crowd swelled in front of the adjutant's office, not a word as Burke and Lee told him what he must do.

Now Spotted Tail took center stage and made a speech to Crazy Horse, saying plainly how things were. Lee had heard many Indian

In May 1877 Crazy Horse gave a small ledger book containing ten drawings to a visiting newspaper reporter, George Wallihan of the *Cheyenne Leader*, but refused to say whether any of the drawings represented his own exploits. In this winter scene, a man wearing a blanket coat "counts coup" by striking a Crow enemy with the butt of his rifle.

After the battle of Wounded Knee in 1890 an Army officer acquired a book of
116 drawings, now called the Red Hawk Ledger after the man most often portrayed.
Six of the drawings depict the war exploits of Tasunka Witko (translated here as
His Crazy Horse); in this one he spears a Crow warrior, dismounted after his horse
was wounded with an arrow.

Little Big Man on horseback counts coup on a Crow warrior by striking him with his bow. On foot in the same fight he kills a Crow carrying a feathered lance, and a third Crow is apparently also killed or wounded. The artist's name is signed in both English and by use of a name glyph—a drawing of a running bear to indicate his alternate name, Pursuing Bear.

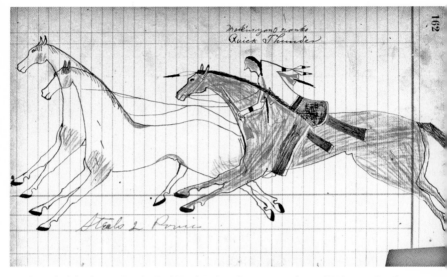

Several of the drawings in the Red Hawk Ledger depict war exploits of Wakinyan Oranko (Quick Thunder), whose name does not appear on agency rolls. The Oglala chief Fast Thunder, who called Crazy Horse cousin, was probably the man shown here stealing two ponies.

Crazy Horse distinguished himself in both phases of the battle of the Little Bighorn, killing soldiers during Major Reno's retreat back across the river, and later when he led the charge that split General Custer's force in two. In this drawing by Amos Bad Heart Bull, Crazy Horse is painted all over with hail spots, and rides a paint horse said by friends to be a favorite.

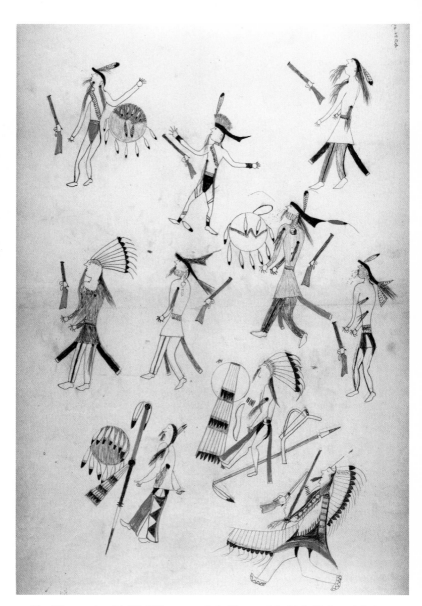

The Minneconjou chief Red Horse recorded a history of the Little Bighorn fight in forty-one large, colored drawings. In this one he depicts the bodies of ten warriors as they lay on the field at the end of the battle. The location of their wounds is shown, and all appear to be vomiting blood, a sign the wounds were fatal. Each man is dressed distinctively and it is likely that the artist could have named them.

Red Horse recorded a fact that many warriors at the Little Bighorn preferred to forget—the mutilation of soldiers' bodies. The practice derived from a Plains Indian belief that an enemy mutilated in this world would bear his wounds into the next. Many of the bodies have also been stripped of their clothes, which the Sioux valued.

No photograph was ever taken of Crazy Horse, but his last moments were recorded by several Oglala artists who knew him, including Standing Bear, who was at the scene, and Amos Bad Heart Bull, a nephew of He Dog. One fact was remembered with special clarity by almost every witness—Little Big Man's effort to hold Crazy Horse as he struggled to escape, shown here in Bad Heart Bull's drawing.

speeches but few struck him with the force of this one, with "its telling points and pauses, emphasized and punctuated by the click of loaded rifles." Spotted Tail was wearing a blanket in the Indian fashion; no feathers or staff or weapon signaled his status. He was standing close enough to Crazy Horse almost to touch him. His words were few but clear and ringing.

> We never have trouble here. The sky is clear, the air is still and free from dust. You have come here and you must listen to me and my people. I am chief here. We keep the peace. We, the Brules, do this. They obey me, and every Indian who comes here must listen to me. You say you want to come to this agency and live peaceably. If you stay here you must listen to me. That is all.[6]

At the conclusion of Spotted Tail's speech, his followers, three hundred or more in number, all shouted assent and approval—"*Hau! Hau!*" Still Crazy Horse said nothing. While this standoff persisted there suddenly appeared on horseback a well-known figure from the band of Brulé known as the Wajajes. Louis Bordeaux immediately recognized the medicine man Horn Chips. Bordeaux noted that his hair hung down the middle of his back in a single braid. Horn Chips jumped down from his horse and approached the two chiefs in front of the adjutant's office. Excited and passionate, Horn Chips spoke directly to Crazy Horse, Bordeaux remembered, "saying that he was afraid to die, that he was a coward." Then he turned to Spotted Tail and denounced him with the same spirit: "You are a coward!" Horn Chips took firm hold of the arm of Captain Burke and spoke to him with force and passion: "Crazy Horse is brave, but he feels too weak to die today. Kill me! Kill me!"

Horn Chips commanded the soldiers to hang him and let Crazy Horse live a hundred years—to hang him and let Spotted Tail live a hundred years. They were cowards!

Burke laughed. "We don't want to hang you," he said to Horn Chips. "We don't want to hang anybody."[7]

Crazy Horse feels too weak to die today. This extraordinary statement came from a man who had talked with him earlier that afternoon, and who had shared an intimate history with him all their adult lives. Few men knew Crazy Horse better than Horn Chips. Why did he call the bravest man of the Oglala a coward? What did he mean when he said that Crazy Horse feels too weak to die today?

The answer appears to lie in the word "weak." It will be recalled that one of the earliest reports of the Custer fight came from the Oglala Horned Horse, whose son White Eagle had been killed early in the fight. Horned Horse immediately left the fight and went up onto a hill overlooking the field to mourn his dead son "as he was too weak to fight." Whites might say that the fight had been knocked out of him. He did not have the moral energy or clarity of mind to fight. Horn Chips had spoken to Crazy Horse earlier that afternoon, and he understood his mood. Something internal blocked Crazy Horse from readiness to fight. He was not looking to die.[8]

With the approach of darkness Horn Chips fell quiet. The big crowd of Indians began to break up at the edges and drift away. Spotted Tail told Crazy Horse that he did not want any disturbance at his agency. He asked Crazy Horse if he would go into the adjutant's office and have a talk with Captain Burke and Lieutenant Lee. Crazy Horse then uttered his first words since meeting the officers up along Beaver Creek. He said, "I will."[9]

It was a small group that entered the adjutant's office along with Crazy Horse: Spotted Tail, Touch the Clouds, the two officers, Louis Bordeaux and Joe Merrivale, and Egon Koerper. To Lee, Crazy Horse as he entered the adjutant's office seemed to be trembling with inner tension. Away from the excitement of the standoff on the parade ground, Crazy Horse was asked why he had come to the Spotted Tail Agency. "He said he had come away from Red Cloud with his sick wife," Lee wrote the commissioner of Indian affairs three weeks later, "and to get away from trouble there." At Red Cloud, Crazy Horse added, "there were bad winds blowing. He did not understand why but it was so."[10]

This simple and direct reply marked a new tone. As Bordeaux interpreted Crazy Horse's words, he was struck by the chief's intelligence and calm good sense. "He was evidently not a talkative man," Bordeaux recalled later, "but on the occasion he made quite a long speech and his remarks showed him to be a silent man of careful thought and good judgement, and accustomed to councils on important affairs, a man of more than ordinary mental ability."

It seemed to Bordeaux that Lee and Burke were equally impressed. Crazy Horse explained himself at length and with care. He disputed in detail much that had been said about him, and especially the threatening interpretation of his words by Frank Grouard. He told the officers what he had told He Dog and others: he had come to the agency for peace.

He said that when he came in from the north and met the officers and others on Hat Creek, he presented the pipe of peace to the Great Spirit there and said he wanted peace and wanted no more war and promised that he would not fight against any nation anymore, and that he wants to be at peace now.[11]

But what the whites desired was not clear. At first they wanted him to go to Washington and then they wanted him to turn the other way and go out to fight the Nez Percé. He did not want to fight the Nez Percé, although he had been willing to do it. "He did not want trouble." But trouble seemed to be looking for him. That morning when he saw a great force of soldiers and Indian scouts approaching his camp he rode away with his sick wife "to avoid disturbance." According to Lucy Lee Crazy Horse told Spotted Tail he had been pulled in so many directions that "for twenty-seven nights he had neither rest nor sleep." Lieutenant Lee summarized the warring impressions in the chief's mind that made him seem "like a frightened, trembling, wild animal brought to bay":

I want no trouble. I came here because it is peace here. I want to get away from the trouble at Red Cloud. They have misunderstood and misinterpreted me there. I brought my sick wife up here to an Indian doctor. I would like to be transferred to this agency. They gave me no rest at Red Cloud. I was talked to night and day and my brain is in a whirl. I want to do what is right.[12]

In the course of this serious talk, Lee and Burke both reassured the chief they meant him no harm, that he would be welcome at the Spotted Tail Agency if he meant what he said, but that he had to return to Camp Robinson first and explain himself to the commander there, Colonel Bradley. Crazy Horse agreed to do this. The officers told him to return with Touch the Clouds to the latter's camp and in the morning they would go together to Camp Robinson. Lee felt safe in promising the chief he would get a fair hearing and not be harmed.

But behind this apparent understanding suspicions lingered. The whites had orders. They were expected to return Crazy Horse to Camp Robinson. As the Indians were preparing to depart for the night, Burke quietly took Touch the Clouds aside to say that Crazy Horse was now in

his charge—"he must not let him escape in the night." Touch the Clouds
promised that "he would not let him get away." Burke took one additional
precaution. With the Indians he sent two trusted scouts from Spotted
Tail's camp, Good Voice and Horned Antelope, to keep watch through
the night. Of these two Good Voice was the leader, recently promoted to
sergeant of scouts, and a man close to High Bear and Fast Thunder. Louis
Bordeaux reports the instructions given to Good Voice and Horned
Antelope; since he had translated everything else that afternoon and
evening it is likely he translated these instructions as well. If Crazy Horse
tried to escape, the two scouts were told, they were to shoot his horse; and
if he resisted they were to kill him.[13]

From Camp Robinson Clark and Bradley both sent off telegrams to
Crook expressing more confidence than they probably felt. In midafternoon, Clark reported that Crazy Horse's village had "scattered like a
frightened covey of quail" but that the chief himself left only with his own
lodge—a gentle way of confessing that he got away. Clark assured Crook
that No Water and others had been sent after Crazy Horse with a
promise of two hundred dollars for success. "I have great hopes that they
will get him." A little later Clark sent a second telegram. "Not more than
20 lodges got away."

At about two o'clock in the morning, Bradley cabled Crook to say that
a courier from Camp Sheridan reported that Crazy Horse had been "captured." Clark dispatched a third telegram reporting Burke's plan to bring
Crazy Horse back to Camp Robinson later in the day. Clark's recommen-
dation: put the chief in the guardhouse on arrival, send him on to Fort
Laramie immediately, and keep him moving to Omaha with two or three
of his own people "so that they can assure people on return that he has
not been killed." Clark was beginning to feel genuine confidence. "Everything quiet and working first rate."

From Cheyenne, where he was about to board the Western Express,
Crook cabled General Sheridan in Chicago, in effect treating Clark's plan
as already accomplished. "The successful breaking up of Crazy Horse's
band has removed a heavy weight off my mind," Crook added, "and I
leave here feeling perfectly easy."

But this confidence was writ on water. Crazy Horse was not really captured, and despite Clark's claim his people had not been rounded up.
Lucy Lee said it was a case of herding cats. The soldiers and scouts sent

out to capture Crazy Horse in the morning started his people back toward the agency, and some got there, but the greater part evaporated in the rough country, disappearing a few at a time among rocks and cotton-wood thickets. One of the officers told Lucy, "They brought in only the tail-end of the village." By morning, almost all had disappeared again, heading east for the Spotted Tail Agency, hurrying after Crazy Horse.[14]

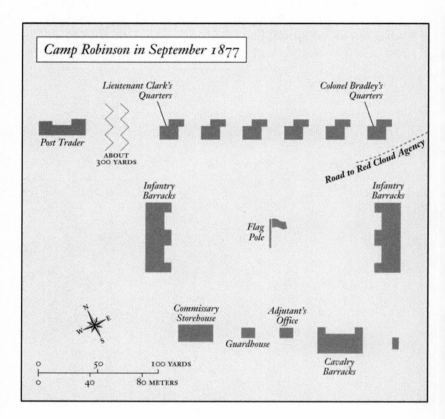

Camp Robinson in September 1877

Lieutenant Clark's Quarters

Colonel Bradley's Quarters

Post Trader

ABOUT 300 YARDS

Road to Red Cloud Agency

Infantry Barracks

Infantry Barracks

Flag Pole

Commissary Storehouse

Adjutant's Office

Guardhouse

Cavalry Barracks

N W E S

0   50   100 YARDS
0   40   80 METERS

31

"I heard him using the brave word."

IT WAS IN THE village of Touch the Clouds on Beaver Creek that Crazy Horse spent his last night, but where he slept is unknown. From the Red Cloud Agency he had brought no lodge, just a packhorse with a few necessaries and personal possessions, including, by one report, his *sicun*, or medicine bundle. On his last night, therefore, Crazy Horse was someone's guest. Many years later, members of the Standing Bear and Fast Thunder families both said the chief had visited, stayed, or shared a meal with them before returning to Camp Robinson. There is no substantial account of his thoughts or conversation on that last night, but it is clear that he grew apprehensive, and that he did not know what to do. If he had expected fighting he would have known exactly what to do. He would have arisen early, performed his medicine, and prepared himself for battle.

Crazy Horse had been meticulous about his medicine on the day of the Custer fight, preparing and painting himself at length. He prayed. He gathered up the soft earth that collects at the entrance to a gopher hole. He sprinkled the earth over his horse's shoulders and flanks, standing first at his horse's head, then by his tail, and finally making marks with his fingers in the sprinkled earth.

Horn Chips said that in preparing for battle Crazy Horse painted his face with red earth, making a zigzag streak from the top of his forehead down one side of his nose to his chin. White Bull said Crazy Horse painted his face with "hail spots," dipping his fingers into white paint and lightly touching himself here and there. Amos Bad Heart Bull, the nephew of He Dog and Short Bull, depicted Crazy Horse in the Custer fight painted all over yellow with white dots. On that day, Crazy Horse took some of the powder from the small medicine bundle he wore about his neck and sprinkled it onto a small hot fire made of buffalo droppings.

In battle he sometimes wore the dried body of a red hawk attached to his hair at the side of his head and one or two eagle feathers taken from the center of the tail of what the Oglala called the spotted eagle. From his shoulders he sometimes hung the hide of a colt. The Crow said they recognized Crazy Horse in battle by this horsehide cape. Crazy Horse was aggressive in battle, charging in front, and he was always closer to the Crow, they said, than to his own people. It is evident he was not expecting to fight on his last day, because he made none of his customary preparations—no paint, no earth markings on his horse. The father of Crazy Horse went further, saying that everything might have been different if his son had done the sacred things properly on the morning of his last day. Waglula said this often before his own death, according to Ota Kte (Kills Plenty), son of Standing Bear, who was with the chief on this last day and was close enough to touch him at the moment he received his fatal wound.[1]

When Crazy Horse rose on September 5, 1877, he dressed himself in the plain clothes of everyday life: a white cotton shirt with blue stripes, deer-hide leggings, and beaded moccasins. Around his waist or over his shoulder was a red wool trade blanket. On his belt was a leather case holding a whetstone. Somewhere on him he carried a trade knife much worn with use, sharpened down to a slender blade six inches in length, used by Crazy Horse for cutting tobacco.

In addition to these items, certain sacred objects were always about his person. From a deer-hide thong over his left shoulder hung a small stone with a hole in it that he wore under his left arm. Crazy Horse also wore another, smaller stone secured behind his ear. In his hair were one or two strands of slough grass, reddish in color, and the feather of a spotted eagle. From his neck hung a small deer-hide bag, dyed red, containing various powders prepared for him by Horn Chips. Two of the ingredients were the dried heart of an eagle and the dried seed of the wild aster, it was said. With Touch the Clouds and High Bear he left the village sometime after eight thirty in the morning, probably riding a buckskin horse.[2]

In this manner Crazy Horse presented himself at the Spotted Tail Agency at nine o'clock in the morning, as promised, but he now regretted his too-quick agreement of the night before to ride back to Camp Robinson with Lieutenant Lee. He told Lee he was "afraid something would happen." He did not spell out his fear but simply said, "If I go to Red Cloud there will be trouble." He wanted Lee to go on without him, to explain everything to Colonel Bradley, and to arrange for Crazy Horse and his people to live henceforth with the Brulé people on Beaver Creek. Lee patiently repeated all his counterarguments of the night before— Crazy Horse needed to go back to smooth things over with his "good words" and "set himself right." Crazy Horse resisted.

"I had hard work to persuade him that he should go," recalled Lee. Gradually an agreement was hammered out. If Crazy Horse would go and explain himself, Lee promised that he would give a full report of all their talk at Camp Sheridan, and to say he was willing for the band of Crazy Horse to join the people at the Spotted Tail Agency. Both sides agreed as well that they would leave their arms behind, a concession, Lee wrote, "which, under the circumstances, Major Burke and I felt we could make." The lieutenant reassured the chief again that no one wanted to harm him, and insisted that Crazy Horse ought to make this effort not for his own sake, but for the sake of his people. "I finally told him that he was no coward and could face the music over there," Lee said. "This remark seemed to appeal to him and he said he would go."[3]

But not quite yet. Escorting Crazy Horse on the six- or eight-hour ride across country would be Lee and Bordeaux, riding in an Army ambulance drawn by four mules. Touch the Clouds got into the ambulance for the journey but Crazy Horse refused to do so. He said it made him sick to ride in a wagon, but something deeper was at work.

"He seemed very suspicious about starting, fearing that something was going to happen to him," Lee's wife wrote soon after these events. It seems that heated words were exchanged. It happened that this moment was witnessed by Little Bull, an Indian scout returning from a hunt for stolen horses. On riding into the Spotted Tail Agency, Little Bull saw a large gathering of Indians and soldiers surrounding a horse-drawn wagon. In the center of the group, Little Bull said later, was Crazy Horse, who "was asked to get down from his horse and he would not do so." The whites "wanted Crazy Horse to ride in the wagon," Little Bull said, "but Crazy Horse would not ride in the wagon." Now it was Lee's turn to concede a point. "Crazy Horse asked to ride horseback," he reported, "which request was granted."[4]

But still Crazy Horse was not ready to depart. He had arrived at the agency that morning riding bareback. Now he wanted to return to the village of Touch the Clouds for his saddle. "He insisted," Louis Bordeaux recalled. Again his request was granted, but this time a large group went along with him, including Lee and Bordeaux in the ambulance with Touch the Clouds, accompanied by Burke, Charles Tackett, and "a few of the friendly Indians," according to Bordeaux. One of the friendly Indians was Charging First, the sixteen-year-old son of Touch the Clouds, a scout in his father's company. Good Voice and Horned Antelope were again instructed to stick close to the chief as they had the night before. While Crazy Horse was saddling his horse at Touch the Clouds's village on Beaver Creek, Burke was quietly conferring with Lee, telling him how to handle matters.

Lee was eager to start out, but just as Bordeaux was about to summon the chief he disappeared into Touch the Clouds's lodge to share a breakfast with his friend of coffee, bread, and meat. Bordeaux joined them. Even after his breakfast, out of excuses at last, Crazy Horse still shrank from setting out. He told Bordeaux, "You go on and I will come after you."

Lee did not protest. He climbed into the ambulance with Bordeaux, crossed Beaver Creek, and started out over the flat expanse of grass heading west. Lee and Bordeaux were soon relieved to see Crazy Horse coming after them as he had promised, followed closely by Good Voice and Horned Antelope and more distantly by a group of northern Indians from Touch the Clouds's camp.[5]

From the many hesitations of Crazy Horse in the course of the morning it is clear that he was deeply apprehensive. What he wanted, he said, was to avoid trouble. The trouble he feared at Camp Robinson was not anything he planned to start himself. He had made no preparations for a fight, and was agreeing to put himself into a situation where a fight would be suicidal. What made him hesitate was distrust of the whites, who had planned to kill him Monday night, sent eight hundred men to arrest him Tuesday morning, and put a price of two hundred dollars on his head when he tried to flee the "bad winds blowing" at the Red Cloud Agency. Arguing against the plain meaning of these bald facts were only the promises of Lieutenant Jesse Lee. In the end, Crazy Horse set aside his doubts and chose to trust Lee's repeated assurances that he would not be harmed, that he might move his people to Beaver Creek, that all might still be well.

It was not a large party that headed west from the village of Touch the Clouds at midmorning or a bit later on September 5. Captain Burke, Charley Tackett, and some of the friendly Indians had turned back for the military post. Setting out with Lee in the ambulance were Louis Bordeaux and four Indians, Touch the Clouds and High Bear, northern Indians who were considered to be friends of Crazy Horse, and the Brulé Swift Bear and Black Crow, both trusted by the whites. Near the ambulance rode Crazy Horse with a number of friends and allies—seven in all, according to Lee. One of them was Horn Chips. Another was Standing Bear, married to a cousin of Crazy Horse, who "advised him not to fear and not make any break but submit and return to Fort Robinson peacefully and explain himself." But before leaving, Standing Bear told his wife to keep the horses close to the lodge.[6]

Other friends who traveled with Crazy Horse were the Brulé Turning Bear, who had argued in favor of going back to Camp Robinson and vowed never to abandon him, and the Oglala Yellow Horse.[7] Mingled with the Crazy Horse Indians were the ever-present scouts Good Voice and Horned Antelope and "a few other reliables." The whole party numbered about twenty, most on horseback while a few drove wagons. Lee estimated that about half of the group were reliables. Among them, Lee recalled, was Fast Thunder, who traveled in a light spring wagon with his wife of a dozen years seated beside him, the woman known originally as Sagyewin (Cane Woman) and then as Tsunka Opi (Wounded Horse). Later in the 1880s she took the name Jennie, and in her application for a pension in the 1920s she identified herself simply as Jennie Fast Thunder. Lee was confident of Fast Thunder's loyalty to the whites, but at the same time he was an Oglala and called Crazy Horse cousin. The chief probably thought of Fast Thunder as not an enemy, and perhaps a friend.[8]

The willingness of Lee to travel so far across open country without arms or military escort suggests more trust than he actually felt. Burke and Lee did not want to lose their captive and had arranged a scheme to tighten their grip. Lee called it "a risky experiment." An hour or two after the group left Touch the Clouds's village, as it crossed Bordeaux Creek "about fifteen miles out," according to Lee, several friendlies from the Spotted Tail Agency rode into sight and joined the travelers. No fuss was made of their arrival, but inevitably it shifted the balance between friends and enemies of Crazy Horse. After a bit other riders appeared, followed by still more, a few at a time. These men were all armed. All were loyal to Spotted Tail. Following further back, but drawing steadily closer over the course of the afternoon, were the twenty or thirty Oglala scouts sent after the chief by Lieutenant Clark the previous day. Included in this latter group were No Water, who had said he would shoot Crazy Horse, Clark's protégé Three Bears, Whirlwind, and Red Cloud's brother Spider. By the time Lee's ambulance was halfway to Camp Robinson the immediate party had more than doubled in size, from twenty to fifty or more. At least forty scouts loyal to Spotted Tail now rode close herd on Crazy Horse, who "realized," Lee said, "that he was practically a prisoner."[9]

September is a hot month in western Nebraska. The journey was long. Lee seems to have relaxed as the group was joined by the friendlies. Sometime in midafternoon, Bordeaux reports, he and the lieutenant both drifted off to sleep as the ambulance bounced along. When they woke Crazy Horse had disappeared. A few hurried questions established that the chief had spurred up his horse, ridden on ahead, and disappeared over the brow of a hill. When the friendlies caught up with Crazy Horse he explained that he wanted only to water his horse.

Things had changed between Lee and Crazy Horse by this time; now the lieutenant did not hesitate to tell the chief what he must do: ride directly behind the ambulance and stay close. "He saw at once that he was closely guarded," Lee recalled. The chief's trust had run thin. "He seemed nervous and bewildered, and his serious expression seemed to show that he was doubtful of the outcome." Lee addressed these doubts as he had all the others, promising Crazy Horse for the fifth time "that no harm would happen to him if he would keep quiet and act all right."[10]

Many years later, Fast Thunder's wife told one of Standing Bear's sons that during part of the journey Crazy Horse rode in the wagon, seated beside Fast Thunder, while she sat behind. To Jennie Fast Thunder, Crazy Horse seemed troubled. Ota Kte (Kills Plenty) translated Jennie's word as "sad" in one account of what she told him, but changed the word to "low-spirited" in a second version published a little later. Fast Thunder tried to reassure the man he called cousin.

> Be brave, they have promised to make you a great chief. No matter if they try to kill you, be brave. You and I have fought together and we are not afraid to die together. But they have promised not to harm you, so be brave![11]

"But Crazy Horse remained sad and talked very little," Jennie Fast Thunder remembered.

By half past three o'clock, Lee with Crazy Horse now riding close to hand had crossed Chadron Creek and was within fifteen miles of Camp Robinson. On the road they met a number of Indians with lodges in tow hurrying in the opposite direction. These people said they were running away from trouble at the Red Cloud Agency and wanted to join the Spotted Tail Agency. Lee worried that the fleeing Oglala might suddenly rally to Crazy Horse and help him to escape. He scribbled a quick message and sent it ahead by fast courier, urging the agent at Red Cloud to keep his Indians "off the road, so that we could go in quietly."

To Clark at the same time, Lee sent a note asking if he should deliver Crazy Horse to the agency or to the military post. Lee was hoping the answer would be the agency, a sign that the Army was still willing to talk things through. Lee made his own view clear enough in his note; he said that Crazy Horse was being delivered not by force but by persuasion, and that the chief had been promised that he could state his case. But Lee did not say what he was now beginning to understand—that his repeated assurances had given Crazy Horse something Lee did not have the power to deliver, a promise of safe conduct.

An hour later Lee received Clark's terse answer. "Dear Lee: Gen. Bradley wishes you to drive direct to his office with Crazy Horse. Yours, Clark."[12]

Three years earlier Lee had been in charge of building the military post at Camp Robinson. He knew that the commander's office was in a log building just beside the guardhouse. From Clark's answer, Lee concluded that Crazy Horse was to be arrested and confined. "But I still hoped," Lee wrote later, "that he would be allowed to say a few words in his own behalf."

Lee received Clark's answer when he was still about four miles short of the Red Cloud Agency. As they passed along the southern shore of the White River, the crier in each of the Oglala camps was calling out instructions from the leading men: the people were to stand back and keep away from the procession of ambulance and Indians when they passed by the agency. No crowds gathered but all were on edge; Charging First remembered that "our arrival caused great excitement." His father, Touch the Clouds, ordered the men he trusted to close in around Crazy Horse and the ambulance and to keep an eye out for the first man among the Oglala to draw a gun. As they approached and passed the agency buildings a scout was sent racing ahead to the military post to say Crazy Horse was coming. The agent, James Irwin, sent a telegram to the commissioner of Indian affairs: "A large body of Indian soldiers have just passed the Agency on way to the Post having him in custody. All quiet."

A little beyond the agency on the road to the military post was a bridge. Here Horn Chips noted that the Red Cloud Indians all had their guns cocked, ready for fighting, but Crazy Horse was surrounded too closely—"he was guarded by good boys."[13]

He Dog saw the approach of the procession from the spot where he had camped at the foot of the White Buttes. He wanted to give Crazy Horse "a good talking-to"—to say "I knew this was coming" and to urge him a final time "to listen to me, and go back with me to Washington." He sent a man out to tell the scouts to bring Crazy Horse to his lodge. But of course he did not have authority for that, and the procession did not alter course.

Seeing this, He Dog stripped for war. He took off his leggings and his shirt and put on his warbonnet. He mounted his horse bareback and pursued the ambulance and the procession of Indians, catching up with them as they approached the military post by the road from Red Cloud, which curved past the row of officers' quarters to the parade ground with the adjutant's office and the guardhouse at the far end. Crazy Horse was in the lead, ahead of the ambulance. He Dog noticed that he was wearing a red blanket. By this time, the Oglala scouts loyal to Red Cloud had pulled up with the rest so Crazy Horse and his few friends were surrounded and hemmed in by hostile scouts. The whole party now numbered about eighty.

One of the scouts shouted to He Dog to keep back, but He Dog ignored the warning and rode up to Crazy Horse and shook his hand. "I saw that he did not look right," He Dog remembered. "I said, 'Look out—watch your step—you are going into a dangerous place.' "

He was nervous, bewildered, doubtful of the outcome. He was sad, low spirited, and spoke little. He did not look right. Every description suggests eroding trust and reluctance to go forward.

Crazy Horse spoke to his friend He Dog. "He asked him if he had any weapons, and of course He Dog had a scout gun with him."[14]

The hour of their arrival was not recorded. Charging First said "the sun was low." He noted soldiers drilling on the parade ground, so it may have been the moment of evening parade. Billy Garnett remembered that it was "fully two hours before sunset." A correspondent for the *Chicago Times* said it was "about six o'clock." The office of the commissioner of Indian affairs logged receipt of Irwin's telegram at 9:42 p.m., Washington time.

It was late in the day, the sinking sun was probably blocked by the hills to the west of the military post, dusk was coming, and the parade ground was rapidly filling. Lee in the ambulance and Crazy Horse with his few friends were surrounded by eighty scouts loyal to Spotted Tail or Red Cloud, and they in turn were pressed by other Indians hurrying in from the camps. Soldiers on the parade ground were apparently falling into formation. It seems someone was expecting trouble. The post surgeon, Valentine McGillycuddy, and a handful of soldiers were standing about the guardhouse and adjutant's office as Lee approached.[15]

Lee was expecting to meet Clark, but he was nowhere to be seen. In his absence, taking charge, was the officer of the day, Captain James Kennington, a man in continuous pain since he had been thrown forward onto the pommel of his saddle at Slim Buttes almost exactly a year earlier. Scar tissue constricted his urinary tract. Several times a day Kennington was required to pass a catheter up through his penis to draw off urine, a procedure he would continue for the remainder of his life.

In front of the adjutant's office, Lee was met by Lieutenant Frederic Calhoun, brother of one of the officers killed at the Little Bighorn. It was Calhoun who had vented his fury at Crazy Horse in a letter to a friend that spring, expressing the wish that the Indians be exterminated, and who traveled to Leavenworth in July to participate in the reburial of his brother's remains. Lee remembered that Calhoun informed him "at once" of Colonel Bradley's wishes.

"Turn him over to the officer of the day," Calhoun directed.

"The truth flashed across my mind, that he was to be put in the guardhouse, a prisoner," Lee remembered.

"No, not yet," he told Calhoun. Lee asked "if Crazy Horse could say a few words" to Bradley before he was placed in Kennington's charge.

Only Bradley could answer that, Calhoun responded.

Lee led Crazy Horse to a chair inside the adjutant's office. Keeping the chief company in the office while Lee set out across the parade ground to Bradley's quarters were Swift Bear, Touch the Clouds, High Bear, Black Crow, and Good Voice. It was two hundred yards to Bradley's quarters. There was quite a crowd of Indians to watch Lee cross the parade ground.

Lee found Bradley in a bully mood. "Well, Mister Lee, you got him!" he said—"rather exultantly," Lee remembered.

"Yes, and I want to ask if he can be heard."

"Have you got your orders?" Bradley responded.

"Yes," Lee answered.

"Obey them," said Bradley.

But Lee was not yet ready to surrender the point. His assurances to Crazy Horse were now paper thin—the right to "say a few words." Lee felt that his honor and self-respect hung on those few words. He did what officers seldom dared and no superiors welcomed: he argued.

"General Bradley," he began, using the commander's brevet rank, "do you know under what circumstances we got this man? Your soldiers did not succeed in getting him yesterday. He came to me voluntarily, and now I have him here on a promise that he can have an opportunity to be heard. General Bradley, can he be heard?"

Two days later, when all was over, Bradley reported, "My orders from General Crook were to capture the chief, confine him, and send him under guard to Omaha." There was no latitude in Bradley's orders, and he gave Lee none.

"He informed me, in no doubtful terms," Lee related, "that it was no use. The orders were peremptory; he could not change them; General Crook himself could not change them, and nothing further need be said, and the sooner I turned over Crazy Horse the better."

Bradley added, "It's too late to have any talk."

Lee grasped at this straw. "Can he be heard in the morning?"

Several moments of silence followed. Bradley finally said, "Have him put in the guard house and not a hair of his head will be injured."

Lee's wife, suggesting what Lee hesitated to say outright, wrote later, "My husband returned with feelings that cannot be described."

At this moment, crossing the parade ground to the adjutant's office, Lee's courage failed him. He could not bring himself to tell Crazy Horse the plain truth, that he was to be made a prisoner and taken away. Lee based one final assurance on "the glimmering hope that on the morrow Crazy Horse might be heard." He returned to the Indians waiting in the adjutant's office and said,

> I am only a little chief and cannot get you a hearing now, but the commanding officer says that if you will go with this man (pointing to Captain Kennington, officer of the day) not a hair of your head will be injured.

This was the sixth time that Lee had assured Crazy Horse he would not be harmed. What he told the chief was true and it was not true. No hearing now implied chance of a hearing later, and Lee knew that, absent a miracle, there was to be no hearing ever. But he said no hearing now,

and Crazy Horse chose to accept this frail suggestion of a promise. He
said "*Hau! Hau!*" in acceptance and assent, and took Kennington by the
hand in greeting. As Kennington, holding Crazy Horse by the hand, led
him out of the adjutant's office to cross the twenty yards separating it
from the guardhouse, Lee quietly approached Touch the Clouds and
High Bear to explain to them "as best I could" the limits of his authority and the actual "situation of affairs." Louis Bordeaux interpreted for
him. Charging First was standing near his father, Touch the Clouds, and
several other chiefs, including Big Road and Standing Bear.

"The matter is in the hands of my superior officers and I can do nothing," Lee said. Bordeaux remembered that Lee told the chiefs "the officers would take care of Crazy Horse to which they all replied, 'All
right.' "[16] Charging First remembered that Lee directed his father to take
Crazy Horse "over to the house where the door stands ajar" and to
remain there overnight with the chief. Lee further instructed Touch the
Clouds, as Charging First recalled, that he would be given the job of taking Crazy Horse east "to see the president" and to stay with him and perhaps return with him. To Crazy Horse, Touch the Clouds said, "We will
go to the house where the door stands ajar and there we will spend the
night."

"It was getting dusk," Charging First remembered. "Crazy Horse said,
'All right.' "[17]

Lee estimated that his arrival in the ambulance, his conversations with
Calhoun outside the adjutant's office, and with Bradley in his quarters, the
walk back across the parade ground and his brief report to Crazy Horse
that there could be no hearing now—all that, Lee guessed, occurred
"within about 15 minutes after my arrival." What happened next as he was
talking to the Indians outside, Lee thought, took "less than a minute."[18]

About sixty feet of open ground separated the adjutant's office from the
guardhouse. Lined up nearby were several field howitzers like the ones
Crazy Horse saw in his dream. Captain Kennington held one of Crazy
Horse's hands. Little Big Man, wearing a red shirt, took the other as
Crazy Horse stepped outside the door. "As they walked toward the
guardhouse," Garnett said later, "Little Big Man kept talking to Crazy
Horse and assuring him that wherever he was taken he would go with him
and stand by him."

Turning Bear walked in front of the little group. Behind them were

Wooden Knife, a Miniconjou from Touch the Clouds's camp, and another man named Leaper. Two soldiers of the guard followed in the rear, gesturing to the crowd to keep back. Crazy Horse was wearing his red blanket over his shoulders.

Red Cloud and his followers were standing just outside the door to the adjutant's office. He Dog was near them. Kennington and Little Big Man turned left toward the guardhouse, leading Crazy Horse away from the group around Red Cloud. They continued past a second big group gathered beside American Horse, who was on horseback. It was twenty paces to the guardhouse, a short walk requiring no more than a few moments. On several occasions He Dog had been sent to the jail by White Hat to get Indians locked up there by the soldiers. He knew they were taking Crazy Horse to the post jail. "But Crazy Horse did not know it," He Dog said.[19]

There were eight hundred soldiers at Camp Robinson on this day, and many of them were now forming up in line around the parade ground, infantry in front, cavalry behind. Hundreds of Indians had now joined the eighty who rode in with Crazy Horse and more were arriving every moment. Many were in war dress and were carrying guns.

Lieutenant Clark was watching from the far side of the parade ground, near the officers' quarters. He had just sent Billy Garnett to tell the officers to put Crazy Horse in the guardhouse. Frank Grouard was nearby but keeping out of sight. Near the entrance to the guardhouse was an uncle of Crazy Horse, probably Little Hawk. Horn Chips, Thunder Hawk, Black Crow, Fast Thunder, and Swift Bear were close to the door. Fast Thunder's wife was standing nearby. Woman Dress was in the crowd, as were Crazy Horse's new wife, Ellen Larrabee, and one of her sisters, probably Zoe.

As Crazy Horse neared the guardhouse, some people in the crowd said, "It's the jail!" Touch the Clouds and some others in the group right around Crazy Horse stopped where they were. Captain Charles King said later that the friends of Crazy Horse were "persuaded to halt where they did." If his friends had gone on in with him, King believed, nothing would have happened.

Red Feather and his friend White Calf had been peering in a back window of the adjutant's office. They came back out front to watch the group approach the guardhouse. They heard Little Big Man say, "We'll do whatever White Hat says." Near him were Iron Hawk, friend of Crazy Horse, and Long Bear, friend of Little Big Man.[20]

"I could see a guard marching back and forth," Charging First remembered.

"A soldier was walking back and forth with a bayonet over his shoulder," Red Feather said.

The soldier stepped back and lowered his weapon to let Kennington and the others go in through the door that was ajar. The weapon was the infantry version of the Springfield trapdoor rifle. Locked onto the end of the rifle was a standard issue bayonet with an eighteen-inch blade. Standing Bear remembered that this guard wore a beard like Lincoln's—no mustache. Bordeaux remembered that the man's beard was red. Charging First remembered that the man was standing by the door on a low porch or deck in front of the house.

Outside, the scouts loyal to Red Cloud and Spotted Tail were to one side, the northern Indians friendly to Crazy Horse on the other. They dared not approach too close to one another. Many in both groups were on excited horses. The crowd was dense now. Those in front were pushed by those behind. Many people were pressed together. It was hard to see.

Billy Garnett was coming across the parade ground; he was heading for the adjutant's office when he saw the commotion at the guardhouse, perhaps sixty or seventy feet distant. Charging First was following his father and Crazy Horse. He saw them step up onto the little porch. Inside the guardhouse were two scouts, Plenty Wolves and Yellow Horse. Turning Bear was still in front as they entered the building. Billy Garnett stopped where he was in the middle of the parade ground. He heard a noise inside the building. He Dog also heard the noise.

The officer of the guard, Lieutenant Henry Lemly, was inside the building. There were two rooms. Turning Bear, leading the way, entered the first room through the door that had been ajar with the rest close on his heels. To the right was a door into a second room. In the door was a window with bars. The door opened. In the second room were several men. It was said later that these men were wearing chains. Their feet were attached to iron balls. The chains could be heard rattling.

Charging First heard a shout from inside the building. Turning Bear shouted out, "It's the jail!" He shouted, "Turn back!" He rushed back out through the door that had been ajar. Charging First heard the man rushing out say, "There are bodies hanging in that room!"[21]

In this instant Crazy Horse lost his weakness. "When the inner door was opened to pass Crazy Horse in," Billy Garnett said later, "it dawned on him that he was a prisoner."

With tremendous force Crazy Horse lunged back, pulling away from the door. Little Big Man grabbed him around the waist, trying to hold him, shouting, "Don't do that!" The two men swung about wildly as Crazy Horse struggled. Captain Kennington was trying to seize and hold him. Crazy Horse grabbed the ornaments in Little Big Man's hair and ripped them free. Little Big Man's red shirt was torn away. Crazy Horse shouted, "Let me go! Let me go!" From beneath his red blanket Crazy Horse pulled his tobacco knife with the six-inch blade. Little Big Man tried to grab his wrists, shouting, "Nephew, don't do that!" Crazy Horse slashed Little Big Man's wrist—"to the bone," said Lieutenant Lemly.

Crazy Horse's red blanket fell from his shoulders to the floor. In a holster at his waist was a revolver with white grips. As they swung about the door, half in and half out, Plenty Wolves plucked the revolver from its holster and said, "I have got the gun!" A man said to be the uncle of Crazy Horse, probably Little Hawk, grabbed this revolver from Plenty Wolves's hand.[22]

Still grappling, Crazy Horse and Little Big Man spun out of the guardhouse door into the crush gathered outside. Billy Garnett was about sixty feet away. He heard the shouting and a sound of chains from inside and saw the two men bursting out. "The two whirled into the space between the scouts and the surging Indians on the opposite side," he said.

Jennie Fast Thunder and Horn Chips were there when Crazy Horse burst out. Horn Chips said, "Crazy Horse made a grunt and struggled." Garnett heard Crazy Horse too. "It sounds like a growl as Crazy Horse repeats, 'Let me go! Let me go!' " Jennie Fast Thunder said, "I heard him using the brave word—*H'g un*, the word a warrior uses when he wishes to keep up his courage."[23]

Little Big Man was bleeding, his shirt torn. Captain Kennington had drawn his sword. Guns were being cocked in the crowd of Indians. Some of the soldiers of the guard were cocking their guns. Kennington shouted, "Don't shoot! Don't shoot!" Garnett saw the guard with the red beard; he was holding his rifle and bayonet at the ready. Kennington tried to get at Crazy Horse with his sword but Crazy Horse was lunging about too wildly, too many Indians were in the way. Louis Bordeaux heard Kennington shouting, "Stab the sonofabitch! Stab the sonofabitch!"

Lieutenant Lee at this instant was standing sixty feet away outside the adjutant's office. The commotion caught his attention. He saw Swift Bear, Black Crow, and Fast Thunder grappling with Crazy Horse as he tried to lunge free, throwing himself this way, that way. Lee heard a voice shouting, "Kill him! Kill him!"[24]

By Lee's estimate, less than a minute had passed since Crazy Horse walked out of the adjutant's office, holding Captain Kennington by the hand.

32

"He has looked for death, and it has come."

HE DOG SAID THAT nonsense was sometimes talked about Crazy Horse—that he treated war like a game, did not kill his enemies, but rode right up to strike them with a quirt for the honor of the thing. It was not so, said He Dog. In battle Crazy Horse was practical and single-minded.

> Crazy Horse always stuck close to his rifle. He always tried to kill as many as possible of the enemy without losing his own men . . . [he] would always jump off his horse to fire . . . He wanted to be sure that he hit what he aimed at . . . He didn't like to start a battle unless he had it all planned out in his head and knew he was going to win. He always used good judgement and played safe.[1]

But Crazy Horse was not afraid to risk death. Many Indians saw him make a brave run, riding past the enemy and giving them a target to shoot at. It had a practical purpose—to empty their guns. But it also had a moral purpose—to make the enemy weak. After that was the moment for all to attack. This risky tactic required boldness and a readiness to die, and the readiness could not be feigned. The Oglala did not expect always to win. They frankly admitted that death and sorrow were never distant. The four hard things in life, they said, were hunger in winter, defeat in battle, the death of a wife, and the death of a first-born child. To endure these sorrows, they said, four virtues were required: giving freely, showing bravery in battle, having fortitude in hardship, and keeping one's word. To break one's word drained away a man's "brave heart"; it made him weak and fearful. Better to die young and lie naked on the prairie than live to walk with a cane and be wrapped up on a scaffold. The brave word which Crazy Horse used—*H'g un* or *hengh*—was described by Billy Garnett as a growl sound, by Baptiste Pourier as closer to a grunt, the sound a bear makes "when he seizes and squeezes." To utter the sound of a bear called on the power of the bear, the courage a man needed when he was alone, surrounded by enemies.[2]

Outside the guardhouse, Garnett watched the struggling men emerge. He saw the soldier guard with his rifle lowered, bayonet pointed at Crazy Horse, "watching the scuffle." All was in confusion. He Dog heard Red Cloud and American Horse shout, "Shoot to kill!" At the same moment, Captain Kennington, sword pointed up in the air, said, "Don't shoot! Don't shoot!"

Garnett said the guard was "gazing" at the struggling men. He extended his arms holding the rifle "as if making a thrust," Garnett said. American Horse said that "he himself during the scuffle threw his gun down on Crazy Horse to shoot him," but the crush was too great, others got in the way. While American Horse was maneuvering for a shot at Crazy Horse, the chief swung his body with great force trying to pull free of the men holding him, Swift Bear, Black Crow, and Fast Thunder. The shirtless Little Big Man had let go now; the blood was flowing freely from his slashed arm. Yellow Horse said the point of the bayonet was actually touching Crazy Horse in the small of his back on the right side, "just enough to make him feel the bayonet." Then the butt of the guard's rifle touched the wall of the guardhouse, and the surging weight of the struggling men pushed Crazy Horse onto the bayonet. Garnett said Crazy Horse threw himself into the guard's extended bayonet. American Horse said, "[H]e surged against a bayonet."

"It was more of an accident than otherwise," said Garnett.

But He Dog said the guard "lunged—twice—with his bayonet." As Sergeant William F. Kelly watched the struggling Indians come forward in his direction, "I saw Wm. Gentles, an old soldier, and a veteran of the Mormon campaign of 1857, give Crazy Horse a thrust with his bayonet. The thrust was delivered with lightning-like rapidity, and the next instant he had his gun at carry, as though nothing had happened."

"The sentry came in behind them and ran Crazy Horse through once," Red Feather said.

Louis Bordeaux said the guard made two heavy lunges with his bayonet. The first was "a heavy thrust . . . going nearly through him." The second thrust missed and the bayonet stuck hard in the frame of the door that had stood ajar. When the guard pulled the bayonet free his rifle shot back and the butt hit Horn Chips in the shoulder, breaking his collarbone. Chips said his shoulder was dislocated by the guard's gun when the guard "jerked the bayonet from Crazy Horse's body."

"Let me go," said Crazy Horse, according to Billy Garnett. "You've got me hurt now!"

Swift Bear, Black Crow, and Fast Thunder all let go.

"Crazy Horse staggered backwards," said He Dog. Bordeaux said Crazy Horse "was still on his feet [but] backed up and finally fell." "Crazy Horse fell groaning," said Yellow Horse. "Crazy Horse gave a deep groan, staggered forward and dropped his knife and fell," said Sergeant Kelly. "I saw Crazy Horse fall down and groan," said Charging First. When Standing Bear saw Crazy Horse fall he leveled his gun to shoot the soldier who had stabbed him, but he was grabbed and held back by Swift Bear and Thunder Hawk, who took his gun. Now Standing Bear approached Crazy Horse and reached down to him to help him up. Crazy Horse looked up at him and said, "Brother-in-law, I am finished."

Ellen Larrabee appeared from the crowd and came up to the chief. One of her sisters—probably Zoe, wife of the post blacksmith—told a friend later that she saw the guard wipe his bayonet on Crazy Horse's blanket.

Someone shouted that a guard had stabbed Crazy Horse with his bayonet.[3]

"They have stabbed me," said Crazy Horse, according to He Dog. Jennie Fast Thunder heard Crazy Horse say, "They have killed me." The bayonet went in "low down and pretty well around toward his back," said Standing Soldier.

On the ground Crazy Horse was bent in on himself—"doubled-up," said Lemly—convulsing with pain, writhing this way and that. People were crowding in around him. Woman Dress was standing nearby. Several times he heard Crazy Horse say, "Father, I want to see you." Touch the Clouds had picked up Crazy Horse's red blanket, dropped just outside the door of the guardhouse. As he leaned down to spread the blanket over Crazy Horse, the chief "seized him by the hair and jerked him this way and that," said Red Feather, who watched it.

"You all coaxed me over here," Crazy Horse said to Touch the Clouds, "and then you ran away and left me!" The words must have bitten deep; within a few minutes Touch the Clouds accused Lieutenant Jesse Lee of the same thing. "You fooled me," Touch the Clouds said.

"I did not tell the guard to do that," Lee protested.[4]

Touch the Clouds was not the only man Crazy Horse accused of betrayal. Jennie Fast Thunder said that after Crazy Horse was stabbed and fell to the ground, her husband helped Standing Bear place the injured man on a blanket. Jennie later told a granddaughter that she heard Crazy Horse accuse her husband, "Cousin, you killed me. You are with the white people."[5]

In the first moments, Lieutenant Lemly thought Crazy Horse might be "possuming"—pretending to be hurt. Billy Garnett thought he had received "only a small stab." It is likely that Touch the Clouds was the first to look closely at the wound itself. He dropped down beside Crazy Horse on the ground, raised his shirt, and saw a cut about an inch long. Charging First, close to his father, said the chief had been "stabbed right above the hip bone." Blood was seeping from the hole in Crazy Horse's lower back.[6]

Dr. Valentine McGillycuddy said he had been watching the commotion from twenty-five feet away. Soon after Crazy Horse fell to the ground, McGillycuddy made his way through the crush around the chief's body and examined the wound closely enough to know that it was serious. "He was frothing at the mouth, pulse weak and intermittent, blood trickling from the upper edge of his hip."[7]

By this time the soldiers of the guard, a dozen in number, had closed in around the wounded man, and were now surrounded in turn by hundreds of Indians. Half wanted to avenge the stabbing of the chief and the rest wanted to make sure he did not escape alive. For several tense moments it seemed a general fight would break out and there would be a big killing. Charging First knocked a gun aside which one of the scouts had pointed at his father. Standing Bear moved to stop someone from getting close enough to shoot Crazy Horse. The man said to be the uncle of Crazy Horse hit Little Big Man hard in the stomach with the butt of his gun, knocking him to the ground. "You are always in the way," he said. Jennie Fast Thunder said, "By this time the excitement had increased and I was terribly frightened."[8]

The northern Indians insisted that Crazy Horse must not be moved, but Kennington was determined to carry out his original orders. "Pick up that Indian and carry him to the guardroom," he ordered, according to Lemly.

Four soldiers dropped their rifles and approached Crazy Horse. As they prepared to lift up the wounded man rifles and carbines immediately appeared from beneath Indian blankets. With shouts and vigorous signs they made it clear Crazy Horse must not be moved into the guardhouse.

Lemly heard the hammers pulled back on many guns, but before a shot could be fired Baptiste Pourier stepped forward from the crush and said what Lemly could not. "For God's sake, Captain, stop," Pourier shouted, "or we are all dead men."[9]

Things were quickly slipping out of control. At this moment General Crook's favorite scout, Frank Grouard, rode up to Bordeaux on horseback. "Get on behind me, Louis," said Grouard. "Let's get out of here and go where there are more soldiers. There is going to be trouble."[10]

When they rode off, McGillycuddy, Lemly, and Kennington were left without an interpreter. None knew a word of Lakota. None knew which were the friendly Indians and which were hostile.

While the standoff persisted at the spot where Crazy Horse lay, excitement swept through the Indians swarming about the military post. "Some of the friendly Indians stripped off their blankets and leggings like a flash, ready for war," wrote Angie Johnson, the wife of Lieutenant Charles A. Johnson, in a letter to her sister two days later. "The crowds of Indians," wrote Lucy Lee, "began yelling and running in the greatest confusion." In the excitement, Red Cloud's Oglala and Billy Garnett at first retreated across the parade ground to Clark's quarters, where Garnett told the lieutenant that Crazy Horse had been stabbed.

The northern Indians meanwhile went to Bradley's quarters at the opposite end of officers' row. There Lucy Lee, Angie Johnson, and others had gathered to watch the confused struggle. "For a few minutes it looked like serious trouble," Angie Johnson wrote. "The Indians were whooping and yelling and very much excited. The Indian soldiers [scouts] were very anxious to pitch into the northern Indians." Among the northerners were many who wanted revenge for the stabbing of Crazy Horse. Lieutenant Lee in front of Bradley's quarters tried to reassure the northern Indians, who feared that the soldiers forming a cordon around the parade ground would attack them next. While Lee was speaking the man said to be an uncle of Crazy Horse rode up, revolver in hand, apparently intending to kill either Lee or Bordeaux. "Two friendly Indians," wrote Lucy Lee, "took hold of his horse and led it away."[11]

For a short period the small group around Crazy Horse was half forgotten but trapped in place by just enough northern Indians to make a fight of it if the chief was moved. McGillycuddy says that during this interval he crossed the parade ground to warn Bradley that "the Indians are ugly"—and moving Crazy Horse into the guardhouse would mean killing. Bradley was unmoved. His orders were to put the chief in the guardhouse. Heading back across the parade ground McGillycuddy spotted Grouard peering out "from around the corner of the commissary." McGillycuddy called to him for help interpreting, but Grouard ducked back out of sight. A few moments later McGillycuddy caught sight of his regular interpreter in front of his quarters across the parade ground, John Provost. McGillycuddy waved him over and Provost joined the group around Crazy Horse.

Nothing had changed. The chief still writhed on the ground, and the northern Indians refused to let him be moved. McGillycuddy reports that he went to Bradley a second time. "The old chap hated to give in," he wrote later, "but finally agreed."[12]

Billy Garnett said Lieutenant Clark, standing in front of his quarters at the western end of officers' row, gave him Bradley's new instructions: "Take him and put him in the adjutant's office." Now, as suddenly as the two groups of Indians had rushed away, they changed their minds and charged back, recrossing the parade ground at a run. It was Red Cloud's friendly Oglala who reached the guardhouse first, in effect seizing control of the spot where Crazy Horse lay in pain on the ground. On the parade ground swarmed the northern Indians who were angry and frightened. "The study now was to avoid a conflict over possession of the dying man's body," said Garnett. American Horse managed to quiet passions with a short, reasonable speech.

> Maybe the man is badly hurt and maybe he is not. We will take him into the same place where they had the talk, and see how much he is hurt, and probably the Indians' doctors can save him. It will not do to let him lie here.[13]

The place where they had the talk was the adjutant's office, not the guardhouse. The change of place seemed to calm the passions of the northern Indians. Few of the Indians had seen the scuffle close up. They were in doubt how the chief had been injured, or how badly he was hurt. They favored letting the doctor look at him. The tension eased. "Presently the carbines were lowered and the dangerous hammers released," said Lemly.[14]

As the scouts prepared to move Crazy Horse on a blanket into the adjutant's office, the crowds of Indians began to disperse. At about this moment Lieutenant Clark for the first time approached the spot where Crazy Horse lay. He told He Dog that he might go up to the chief. It seems He Dog was the third person to look closely at the chief's wound.

Lying near Crazy Horse on the ground he noticed the bayonet used to stab him; close by was the chief's knife with the six-inch blade. Both were red with blood. "He was gasping hard for breath," said He Dog.

"See where I am hurt," Crazy Horse asked his friend. "I can feel the blood flowing."[15]

He Dog lifted away the shirt and saw two deep wounds. One had pierced the small of the back. A second stab had entered between Crazy Horse's lower ribs. This thrust went deep too, said He Dog. The point of the bayonet almost came through on the other side, just under the chief's heart. There, He Dog said, "a lump was rising under the skin where the thrust ended." The swollen place was turning blue. He Dog saw blood leaking from Crazy Horse's nostrils, suggesting that a lung had been pierced as well. "He was in agony," said He Dog. "Blood flowed from his mouth," said Charging Girl, a daughter of Red Cloud.[16]

When the crowds in front of the guardhouse had thinned and the danger of a clash had receded, several Indians picked up Crazy Horse on his red blanket and carried him into the adjutant's office. There was a cot in the room but Crazy Horse insisted that he be placed on the floor. "He was restless and turning in great pain," said Louis Bordeaux, who spent several hours that night watching over the chief in the adjutant's office. McGillycuddy concluded there was nothing he could do to treat the chief's injury; the bayonet had punctured one or both kidneys and he was bleeding to death internally. "His case was hopeless," said McGillycuddy.

The only relief he could offer was morphine, part of every surgeon's pharmaceutical kit since the Civil War. It was sometimes sprinkled directly into a wound but McGillycuddy used a hypodermic syringe. The dose recommended at the time was a quarter grain of morphine mixed in three or four drops of water. Relief was prompt. Crazy Horse relaxed; the twisting and turning ceased and his groans eased. Soon he was drifting in and out of sleep while the men in the room talked and waited for him to die. "McGillycuddy said he could not last till midnight," remembered Bordeaux.[17]

Clark sent General Crook three telegrams in rapid succession after Crazy Horse was stabbed. The first reported the seizure and wounding of the chief. In the second he told the general, "I am trying to persuade all Indians" that Crazy Horse had stabbed himself with his own knife, and added, "The doctor reports he has no pulse in either arm." The third requested

Crook's approval to discharge Crazy Horse from his position as an enlisted scout for the U.S. Army, backdating the official paperwork to August 31.[18]

Soon after Crazy Horse was moved into the adjutant's office the parade ground emptied. Most of the Indians had gone back to their villages around the Red Cloud Agency, a mile or two east, while the northern Indians set up camp inside the agency stockade. For the moment it was quiet, but Bradley prepared for trouble. "They feared an attempt would be made to rescue him in the night," Angie Johnson wrote to her sister, "so the soldiers were kept ready for instant action all night, pickets out in every direction and everything warlike." Clark sent Billy Garnett to the agency to fetch Red Shirt, Tall Man, and some other scouts to help guard the military post through the night. Coming back along the road in the dark Garnett was suddenly fired at by a sentry who "thought we were hostile Indians." Before he could call out his identity other nervous soldiers began shooting too, but none of the group was injured. Later, standing outside Clark's quarters, Garnett told He Dog that it was dangerous to be out as the sentries were nervous. "You better stay there with Crazy Horse," he said. But He Dog refused and made his way safely past the sentries heading back to his camp. When he reached the bridge on the road to the agency he encountered Waglula coming toward the military post with his wife. The old man asked about his son and He Dog told him, "They stabbed him but he is not dead yet . . . you must hurry to him."[19]

McGillycuddy settled down for a death watch. "No one came to the adjutant's office that night," McGillycuddy said later, "and it was dismal and lonesome." His only companions at the outset were Captain Kennington, the officer of the day; Lieutenant Lemly, the officer of the guard; and Louis Bordeaux, serving as interpreter. The senior surgeon on the post, Dr. Charles E. Munn, may have looked in from time to time. The little group was soon joined by Touch the Clouds, who had been stopped at first outside the building. Lee said he told Touch the Clouds he could not go in with his gun. "I have trusted thousands of you white people, and now all of you mistrust me—but one man," Touch the Clouds told Lee. "You may not trust me, but I will trust you. You can take my gun." Touch the Clouds entered the adjutant's office with his son, Charging First, who said they were told that Crazy Horse had been "stabbed up through his kidneys."[20]

Shortly after the arrival of Touch the Clouds, Billy Garnett, standing outside Clark's quarters, was approached by Crazy Horse's father. "He wanted to go in," Garnett remembered, but he was armed. "Old Man," Garnett said, "you cannot get in there unless you give up your knife." Waglula surrendered all his weapons: knife, bow, and quiver of arrows.

"Son, I am here," he said as he approached the wounded man on the floor of the adjutant's office. "How is it with you?"

"I am hurt bad," said Crazy Horse. "I am going to die. Tell the people they cannot depend on me any more."[21]

When she heard this, Crazy Horse's stepmother began to cry. Waglula and Touch the Clouds also cried.

The watchers later agreed that the wounded chief was for the most part silent over the next few hours, drifting between drugged sleep and bouts of pain. When Crazy Horse spoke at all it was sometimes hard to hear or to understand. Lemly recorded shortly after the event that Crazy Horse at one point "spoke indistinctly about bayonets." The correspondent writing as "Philander" said more plainly that Crazy Horse "asserted that he had been struck with a bayonet, as he felt it penetrate his side." At that hour the Army's official version of events insisted the chief had stabbed himself. Lemly recorded that McGillycuddy did what he could to convince Waglula and Touch the Clouds it was a knife, not a bayonet, which had pierced Crazy Horse.

> Dr. McGillycuddy showed them the cross section of a bayonet by thrusting it through a sheet of paper, and also that of the knife, endeavoring to explain the different wounds the two would cause, but, I fear, with little success.[22]

But during those hours of quiet, several witnesses report hearing some remark from Crazy Horse absolving them of blame. Late in the evening, Angie Johnson reported, he summoned the strength to shake hands with McGillycuddy "and said '*Wash-ta.*' That is their word for 'good,' meaning it is all right." Soon after Waglula's arrival, Bordeaux reports, Crazy Horse told the interpreter, "I don't know why they stabbed me." He added, "No white man is to blame for this . . . I blame the Indians." His anger was all focused on one man—Little Big Man. "But he got away."[23]

Bordeaux knew Crazy Horse was dying. "He was growing cold," he said. At about ten o'clock, Touch the Clouds said Crazy Horse wanted to see Lieutenant Lee, and Louis Bordeaux was sent to deliver the request. He found Lee and his wife in the quarters of Captain Burrowes, who warned it could be dangerous. "He may never come back," Burrowes said to Lucy. But Lee went, and recorded later that Crazy Horse did not blame him for what happened. "If I had listened to you," the wounded man said, according to Lee, "I would not now be in this fix."

"Things looked suspicious to me," Crazy Horse explained to Lee. "I did not know what might happen, and I did not know whom I could trust."[24]

But during most of the vigil nothing was heard from Crazy Horse but the sound of his breathing and the occasional moan or gasp. After Waglula and his wife had cried themselves out the first time, the old man began to talk about his life and family. He said he was sixty-six years old, that a previous son was already dead, killed by the Shoshones. Crazy Horse did not want to fight the whites, he said, but the whites hunted him in his own country, they attacked the villages—"they had to defend themselves." Crazy Horse did not want to live on an agency or eat beef, but hunt buffalo, of which there were still plenty.

> He said that his son had been his only protection, and that, as he was now gone, he was poor and friendless; that while they were north, his son had taken good care of him, and they always had plenty of game to eat.

"But he was not left alone," said Waglula. Every courier that came out from the agencies said, "Come in! Come in!" The whites promised to hunt him until he came in or was driven north into Canada to join Sitting Bull. "At last he came." But that was not the end of the trouble. "Spotted Tail and Red Cloud . . . had to stand aside and give him the principal place in council." They became jealous.

"They were the cause of his poor boy lying there," said Waglula. "He was killed by too much talk."[25]

To speak of ultimate things like dying, death, and the spirit realm beyond this world, the Sioux used a kind of poetry of indeterminacy. They explained what they could and consigned the rest to a category of things humans cannot know, or had perhaps forgotten. There was no single correct way to explain these matters, and the hardest of all was to explain the *wakan*. Anything *wakan* was said to be sacred or powerful. The Oglala shaman Napsu (Finger) told a white doctor, "Anything that has a birth must have a death. The *Wakan* has no birth and it has no death." Toyanke

Waste Win (Good Seat Woman), born in the mid-1820s and speaking in her eighties, carried the explanation further:

> *Wakan* was anything that was hard to understand. A rock was sometimes *wakan*. Anything might be *wakan*. When anyone did something that no one understood, this was *wakan*. If the thing done was what no one could understand, it was *Wakan Tanka*. How the world was made is *Wakan Tanka*. How the sun was made is *Wakan Tanka*. Where the spirits and ghosts are is *Wakan Tanka*.

The *ni* of a man is the breath of his life. When a man dies his *ni*—his spirit—leaves his body and makes its way to the spirit world. Some said the spirit world was in the south; others said it was in the west. Some called the spirit world the region beyond the pines that grow on the westernmost edge of the world. "That is where the shadows of the dead dance," it was said. Conica Wanica (No Flesh) agreed that people in olden times said the spirit world "was beyond the pines," but he also said, "No man knows where the spirit world is. It is at the other end of the spirit way."

A man's *ni* did not begin its journey to the spirit world right away. It lingered for a time near the place where the man had died. During this period his spirit had the power to harm the living, therefore people tried to please it, to help it prepare for the journey, to provide it with the things whose spirit would help it on its way—a horse, perhaps, or a gun, a shield, a book of drawings or anything else that had been precious to a person in life. To commend the spirit of the dead man his friends and relatives would blacken their faces and cut themselves with knives or drive wooden pegs through the skin of their legs to show the god that their grief was sincere.

The journey was not easy. "He must cross a river on a very narrow tree," said Good Seat Woman. Not all succeed in making the journey. If a man had a companion on the journey it would go more easily. The *ni* of a man he had killed, or a man killed for him by a friend or relative, would help him on his way. That *ni* would be his captive and servant in the spirit world. A man who died fighting would try to kill an enemy so he would not have to travel alone.

To make the journey a man needed to pray for help. In his youth, sometime prior to 1850, the Hunkpapa Red Weasel was told by Sun Dreamer "that I may pray with my mouth, but if I *sing* the prayer it will be heard *sooner* by *Wakan Tanka*." A dying man, therefore, knowing the mysteries that lie ahead, will sing a prayer to help him on his way. Every man should prepare such a song, said No Flesh.[26]

Accounts of Crazy Horse's final moments are difficult to sort out. At about ten o'clock, McGillycuddy remembered, he noted that Crazy Horse's "heart was giving out . . . I started to give him a glass of brandy, but the old man objected, making signs that his son's 'brain whirled.' " Now, after Waglula's talk about his son, the old man seemed so undone to McGillycuddy that he gave him a drink of whiskey. This, Lemly noted, "he seemed to relish amazingly. He rose and shook hands all around, exclaiming, '*Hau, Kola!*' "[27]

The hour was late. Baptiste Pourier had replaced Louis Bordeaux as interpreter about the time Lee paid his visit. Crazy Horse uttered some final words but the immediate witnesses left confusing and garbled accounts of what he said.

Looking back over his life, McGillycuddy sometimes waxed poetic. In several of his accounts of the death of Crazy Horse he remembered that near the end the sound of a bugle came from the parade ground. He remembered that it was "the lonesome call for taps." In one letter he said it was at about nine o'clock, the traditional hour for lights out; in another about eleven. He thought Crazy Horse had uttered a cry he used to sing out on going into battle—"A good day to fight, a good day to die! Brave hearts."

There, McGillycuddy wrote, the chief's voice faded off. But the doctor spoke no Lakota; he had no idea what the words were.[28]

Lemly said the words came "in a weak and tremulous voice." But it was not a war cry he uttered. Crazy Horse was not speaking but singing, Lemly reported—"the weird and now-famous death song of the Sioux."

Baptiste Pourier was there. He remembered no last words and no singing. The hour was closing on midnight—some say eleven o'clock, others eleven thirty, or eleven forty.

Bat was the first to discover that Crazy Horse was dead. He remarked to the doctor that he was dead. The doctor said he guessed not, but on feeling of him found it was so. Then they feared to announce it to Crazy Horse Sr. on account of his grief. So Bat suggested giving him a drink of grog which was done, Bat getting his portion also. The old man expressed his satisfaction, saying it was good. Calling Bat his son, which he usually did, he said, "It was good, that will open my heart."[29]

Because he spoke Lakota, it was Bat's job to convey the news to Waglula. The old man had called him Cinksi (Son); perhaps Pourier addressed the old man as Ate (Father).

"Don't take it hard," Bat said. "Your son is dead."

It landed like a blow. The brave word burst out of Waglula: *"Hengh!"*—like the grunt of a bear.

Then Waglula said, *"Micinci watoye sni te lo."*

It seems no one translated these words for Lee, Lemly, McGillycuddy, Bradley, Clark, or the correspondent writing as Philander. What Waglula said was, "My son is dead without revenging himself." He would enter the spirit world alone. Then the old man and his wife began to sing and to cry, at first in a torrent which "seemed uncontrollable."

> Finally they became quieter, and settled in a crooning manner on their knees, bending over and caressing the prostrate and lifeless form, both chanting in an indescribably weird manner the now-famous Sioux death song. The deep guttural of the one blended with the shrill treble of the other, and both were cracked by age. No one who witnessed or heard the old couple can forget the sad scene, or their strangely impressive, and mournful dirge.[30]

Various things were said after Crazy Horse was pronounced dead. Philander quoted Touch the Clouds as saying Crazy Horse "had courted death ever since his arrival here, and that at last he had met it, and that he had got what he deserved." Philander was unfamiliar with the warrior culture of the Oglala and he missed the point. What Touch the Clouds said was:

"It is good. He has looked for death, and it has come."[31]

33

"He still mourns the loss of his son."

LOUIS BORDEAUX AND BAPTISTE Pourier were the first to tell William Philo Clark that Crazy Horse was dead. It was not yet daylight; the lieutenant had been out somewhere. On entering his quarters, where Bordeaux and Pourier had been sleeping, Clark asked, "How is my friend, Crazy Horse, getting along?"

"He is dead," said Pourier.

Bordeaux remembered that Clark was slow to believe what he had been told. He seemed confused, almost stunned. He started to leave the room, then abruptly turned back. "Is it true that he is dead?" he asked.

Bordeaux told him it was true. He said Crazy Horse had been dying when Pourier had come to relieve him a little after eleven. About midnight Pourier came back with the news that the chief was dead.

"It is a shame! It is a shame!" said Clark. Bordeaux remembered the lieutenant as "a man of great humanity." He was overcome; he sat down, covered his face with his hands, and wept. "That man ought not have been killed," he said. "It's a shame the way he was treated."[1]

But within an hour or two, when Clark reported the news to General Crook in a short telegram, he had worked his way to a broader view. He assured the general, "The death of this man will save trouble." A day later General Sheridan in Chicago told reporters much the same: "Crazy Horse was a mischievous and dangerous malcontent, and it is a good thing that he is dead."[2]

An oppressive consciousness of guilt visited Lieutenant Jesse Lee the day after Crazy Horse was killed. "No one can imagine my feelings this morning," he wrote in his diary. "Was it treachery or not? . . . My part in this transaction is to me a source of torture." It was Lee who had persuaded Crazy Horse to return to Camp Robinson, Lee who told him he could explain himself to Colonel Bradley, Lee who assured him repeatedly that he would not be harmed. "I had a long talk with General Bradley," Lee wrote. "He did most of the talking. I felt so miserable that I could scarcely say anything."[3]

In a letter to Bradley six months later Lee said that the day after the killing of Crazy Horse was one of the few times when he felt overwhelmed, unable to go on. "You saw me once in that condition, and the good word from the good friend came from you," Lee wrote. "You may have forgotten the occasion but I never shall."[4]

Lee lived another fifty years, distinguished himself in China and in the Philippines, and retired as a general, but he never shook his sense of guilt. In the small standing army of the day it was well known among officers that Lee counted the killing as "the saddest reminiscence" of his career.[5]

But "sad" did not explain his torment. Lee believed it was treachery that killed Crazy Horse. His part had been to mask the treachery with promises. Crook's name was on the orders, and Bradley said there was nothing he could do to change them. No one blamed Lee, but he blamed himself. He remembered too clearly the many hesitations of Crazy Horse, and the six times Lee promised he would not be harmed. Over the years, Lee discussed the killing often with his friend Captain Charles King, and King made his own inquiries about the orders to confine Crazy Horse in the guardhouse. He concluded the orders came from department headquarters in Omaha, or division headquarters in Chicago. Who told Crook or Sheridan that Crazy Horse had to be jailed and sent into exile? On this point, King wrote to a friend in 1921, "John Bourke was always mysterious and non-committal, and Philo Clark impressively silent."

But it made little matter who insisted that Crazy Horse be jailed. It was Lee who led him to his fate. "Lee grieved long over the incident," King wrote.[6]

Jesse Lee died in Washington in April 1926.

News of the chief's death was widely reported in the press. Follow-up stories insisted that most of the Indians were glad to be rid of him. The chiefs said that Crazy Horse had brought it on himself. It was reported that by his own count he had killed thirty-eight whites—four of them women. Crook meanwhile abandoned the Nez Percé campaign in Wyoming. On September 9 he returned to Omaha, then left for Washington on the 13th—lucky to be alive, the *Omaha Bee* reported. According to "a friend of General Crook," Crazy Horse had planned to kill Crook in council—"he intended to talk pretty saucy to the general, and in case the general should say anything about it, he would kill him." Only then, the *Bee* said, had the chief's arrest been ordered.[7]

The usual source of anonymous stories from the Omaha headquarters of the Department of the Platte was the adjutant general, General Robert Williams. It seems likely he had this story from Lieutenant Clark, who passed through Omaha on his way to Washington for the long-planned meeting of the chiefs with President Hayes. There Red Cloud again protested the government's plan to move the Indians east. "The Missouri River is the road to whiskey and ruin," Red Cloud said at a meeting with Hayes in the White House.[8]

But Hayes was adamant. Rations for the winter had already been shipped to the Missouri. "It is too late to remove your supplies," said Hayes. "The winter will soon come on, the streams be frozen up. Next spring places can be selected near White River that will suit you."[9]

With this promise the Indians had to be content. Preparations for the move were already far along when the chiefs returned to Nebraska. The undertaking was immense. About ten thousand Indians of all ages and conditions of health would be required to ride or walk two hundred miles across open prairie at a season of the year notorious for sudden snowstorms and plunging temperatures. Driven along with the Indians would be fifteen thousand ponies and two thousand beef cattle for rations. Lieutenant Jesse Lee hired thirty wagons and teams to move goods and people, many of whom had no horses and were too old or sick to walk. To complicate matters a thousand northern Indians who had surrendered in the spring, Miniconjou under Touch the Clouds and the Sans Arcs under Red Bear, now refused to travel east to the Missouri with the Brulé. They were joined by the thousand or more Indians who had stampeded to the Spotted Tail Agency after the killing of Crazy Horse. In a meeting with the chiefs on October 15, General Crook gave them permission to travel instead with Red Cloud's Oglala. He had little choice. In a cable to Sheridan in Chicago, Crook reported that the Indians had "expressed a desire to comply with the wish of the President that they should go near the Missouri." This meant only that they had agreed to start out. Much ambiguity lingered around the word "near."[10]

In the last days of October the Indians from both agencies set out. On

November 2, Lieutenant Clark and Red Cloud's Oglala joined up with the Miniconjou and the remnants of Crazy Horse's band where Beaver Creek emptied into the White River. The weather was foul—"snow, rains, wretched roads," Clark reported to Crook. Clark did not want to add the northern Indians to his own. He spent an entire day arguing, but the chiefs refused to rejoin the Spotted Tail Indians traveling with Jesse Lee.

"It was useless to try and get them to go on and overtake Lee," Clark told Crook. "If forced, they would, I think, have gone north."

It began to snow heavily on November 3 and the weather continued foul for three days. When the combined camps finally resumed their march the northern Indians "moved slowly and reluctantly towards the Missouri," reported a cavalry officer. Gradually the northern Indians, covering only seven or eight miles a day, fell behind the larger party of Red Cloud's Oglala. To Billy Garnett they blamed the condition of their horses, saying they were "jaded and could not stand to travel faster." At the end of each day's march there was drumming and singing in the huge camp, spread out along three miles of riverbank. The talk went on deep into the night. Some of the northern chiefs had traveled to Washington to see the president but Clark sensed the fragility of the consent that kept them moving east. Five or six days into the march, Clark reported to Secretary of the Interior Carl Schurz that "these people are wild, stubborn, restless and still smarting under the bitter feelings engendered by the killing of Crazy Horse."

Even Clark's most trusted scout, Three Bears, was full of anger. The Indians were going east through their own land, he said. If the commissioners said they had given the land up when they signed away the Black Hills, they were lying. "I was then a soldier on the Indian side and at that very Council I had one hundred young men there to see and know that nothing of the kind was done," Three Bears told Clark. "We had ears and heard what was said." Three Bears was one of the men Clark had trusted to take over the remnants of Crazy Horse's band. To lose the trust of Three Bears, in Clark's view, was to risk losing all. Sitting among the Indians at night, fascinated and repelled by "their painted faces looking particularly savage and wild by the light of their campfires," Clark said, "civilization and gentleness and kindness look very faint and far off."[11]

The handful of Army officers and enlisted men were too few to keep the big assemblage together and moving by force. The Indians must come of their own will or not at all. The Oglala agent James Irwin did not trust the "northern fire eaters . . . It is an even question with me," he wrote early in the march, "whether the northern Indians will go with us or break off . . . and go north."

The answer came about three weeks into the journey when Clark and the Oglala approached the present site of Interior, South Dakota. Here the White River bent away from its northerly course to point east toward the Missouri. Beyond the White River to the north, stretching away over a sea of grass, was a ladder of rivers—the Bad River, the Cheyenne River, the Moreau, the Grand—climbing up through traditional Sioux hunting grounds all the way to "grandmother's land," the Sioux name for Canada, then ruled by Queen Victoria. First one group of northern Indians wheeled away and left the line of march, then a second. The Indians had been "possuming," said Billy Garnett, "saving their horses for a hard march after they should break away."

There was little to be done. Clark sent a small group after the first defectors, hoping to coax them back, but none returned. Finally, in late November, the larger part of the northern Indians—Clark said a hundred of 250 lodges; Garnett said half; Irwin said all but thirty—headed off into the prairie with ponies, baggage, women, and children. Among them were at least six chiefs who had just returned from the trip to Washington: Big Road, Red Bear, He Dog, Little Hawk, Jumping Shield, and Touch the Clouds. The last, keeping a promise to Jesse Lee, only led his people back to their old agency at the mouth of the Cheyenne. But the rest of the northern Indians intended to leave the white world behind for good, and go back to the old life of hunting and raiding. All Clark's patient working of the Indians was undone in a moment. Only two northern chiefs stayed behind: No Water and Little Big Man. Both had made enemies by helping the whites to capture and kill Crazy Horse. "They dared not trust themselves up north," said Garnett.[12]

Not long after the northern Indians broke away, Red Cloud and his people stopped about eighty miles short of the new agency. The next year, with Crook's help, the Oglala moved back west to the rolling prairie and pine-studded hills around Big White Clay and Wounded Knee creeks just across the Nebraska line in South Dakota. The new agency, the Oglala's fourth and last, where they still live today, was named after the tree-covered hills which traversed the countryside: Pine Ridge.

For the rest of his life, which was not long, Clark pondered his failure with Crazy Horse. He told himself nothing could be done with the chief. "He attributed every concession and kind act to fear," he wrote. On the march to the Missouri, Clark learned that Crazy Horse, dead for two months, was traveling with the people. Clark records this discomfiting fact in a letter of November 7 to Secretary Schurz written "In camp on White River." Likely the fact was told him one night as he sat conversing by sign language with the Indians in their blankets around campfires. Or it may have been Billy Garnett who translated a remark from the Lakota. Somewhere among the baggage piled on wagons and horse-drawn travois, Clark was told, the Indians were "hauling along" the body of Crazy Horse, wrapped in his red blanket. Clark did not know—perhaps he never asked—why the family of Crazy Horse would bring his body on such a journey. Normally a curious man, he let this question lie. The presence of the body made him uneasy. "Even as a dead chief," he wrote, "he exercises an influence for evil."

"In camp on White River"—with these words Clark recorded the last known location of the body of Crazy Horse.

As the news spread of the killing of Crazy Horse on the night of September 6, the Indians in their camps were "thrown into the greatest fever of excitement," according to the Episcopal priest at the Spotted Tail Agency, the Reverend William J. Cleveland. Louis Bordeaux cited "intense excitement" at both agencies, and Lieutenant Jesse Lee said a general stampede was threatened by "wild rumors" of Spotted Tail's arrest and of impending attack by Pawnee scouts or the Army. Angry and afraid, more than a thousand Oglala fled the Red Cloud Agency. Most went east to the Spotted Tail Agency to be near the northern Indians, but some went out into the open country north of the agencies, just beyond the easy reach of the Army or the friendly scouts. Most of the chiefs had urged Crazy Horse to make the trip to Washington, but his killing brought many of them up short. Some thought he had been killed in cold blood—lied to, tricked into entering the guardhouse, stabbed by prearrangement while three men held him. "Fast Thunder . . . was shocked," said his grandson Matthew King, who often heard the old man talk about the fatal moment. "He got mad . . . he left the fort and camped someplace in the hills between what is now Hay Springs and Chadron, to cool down." With friends, Fast Thunder "discussed the tragedy of their leader. They didn't know what to do . . . [or] who could be trusted."

"Turning Bear tried to rally the hostiles to action," said a mixed-blood woman who wrote histories of many of the leading Sioux of the period.

"Half the Indians were for fighting and half were against it. All the chiefs had to talk a good deal to keep their men from breaking out."

"The chiefs by good counsel kept them quiet," Lieutenant Lee said.

He Dog said Red Cloud and Bad Wound held a big feast so they could talk to the Indians who wanted to fight and take revenge. "Start nothing," said Red Cloud, according to He Dog. "Bad Wound cautioned them to behave themselves, and not to start anything." Horses and blankets were given out to pay for the killing of Crazy Horse. "Indians have been making presents to his kin," said Clark. The danger flared up and then faded over a period of four days. "Now everything is again as quiet as though nothing had ever occurred," wrote Lucy Lee when it was over. Four days was the traditional time for an initial outburst of grief at the death of a leading man. Much of the excitement which alarmed the whites was only natural lamentation and tears.[13]

In the small hours of September 6, Waglula and his wife left the adjutant's office, where the body of Crazy Horse lay on his red blanket. He crossed the parade ground to the quarters of Lieutenant Clark, looked in through an open window, and saw Billy Garnett sharing a bed with Louis Bordeaux. He reached in, took Garnett by the shoulder, and shook him awake. "Nephew," he said, "get up, my son is dead." He wanted the return of his knife and bow and arrows but Garnett said no, they could not be returned till daylight.

The old couple waited nearby through the night. From the camps could be heard the crying and singing and drumming which began when the people learned that Crazy Horse was killed. At first light, Angie Johnson heard Waglula wailing his grief and asked her husband to offer him something to eat. "But he couldn't eat much," she remarked in a letter to her sister. "Then the mother of Crazy Horse came and both of them went across the parade ground and down to the office where his body was, both crying and singing their mournful death song."

At the adjutant's office the parents were given an Army wagon with a team of mules to move their son's body. Jesse Lee remembered that the parents were crying loudly as they walked beside the wagon carrying their son. As the little group made its way along the road to the Red Cloud Agency two miles distant the white teamster driving the mule team was suddenly approached and threatened by a man on horseback carrying a gun. Garnett was told that this was the uncle of Crazy Horse who had been so active the day before. Now, rushing up to the wagon, the uncle pointed his gun at the teamster but was halted by a shout from Touch the Clouds, who was riding in the wagon. Once again the uncle allowed himself to be talked away. Reaching the agency without further incident, the party sought out the lodge of relatives, where they prepared the body of Crazy Horse for burial.[14]

Among those in the lodge were the father and stepmother of Crazy Horse, his brother-in-law Red Feather, and several others, including a woman named White Woman One Butte. It would have been customary to ask a *wicasa wakan* to be present. Horn Chips, although injured in the struggle the day before, would have been a natural choice. He would have shared a pipe with Waglula before doing anything further. If those preparing Crazy Horse's body had followed custom they would have painted his face red and cut a lock of hair from above his forehead, because one of the souls, or *ni*, of a person was believed to reside in the hair. This lock of hair would have been presented to his stepmother. She would have wrapped it in a piece of cloth and put it aside, not to be disturbed for four days. All the while, many prayers and songs would have been recited or sung. But those who were present recorded only a few details. Red Feather said he helped to remove the chief's clothes, stained with his blood. Low on one side of Crazy Horse's back, Red Feather saw the inch-long cut where the bayonet had gone in. White Woman One Butte cleaned the chief's body. When she was done Red Feather helped to dress him in a fresh buckskin shirt. Finally his body was wrapped in his red blanket.[15]

About the middle of the day, when Crazy Horse's body had been properly prepared, his parents tied it to a travois drawn by a buckskin horse. According to the correspondent Philander, this was "just before noon." The parents refused an offer to keep the Army ambulance they had used in the morning. They preferred to take their son's body back to the Spotted Tail Agency on a travois in the customary way. Jesse Lee remembered that a small boy led the buckskin horse pulling the travois. Black Elk saw the parents leaving and remembered "that Crazy Horse's father rode a white-faced bay with white hind legs . . . The mother was riding a brown mare with a bay colt." He Dog said Crazy Horse's body had been placed in a coffin lashed to the travois. He said the chief's wife, Tasina Sapawin, was one of the group, and that a party of twenty-three mourners, stripped to their skin, followed the travois. Such a group would have been singing and crying out in noisy grief. Many members would have cut their hair or gashed their arms and legs or driven wooden pegs through their skin. He Dog said that Waglula sang out as they traveled that his son "died in victory. That's the way brave men die—in victory."[16]

For seven or eight hours the travois carrying Crazy Horse's body made its way across the prairie toward the twin buttes known as Sheridan's Gates. Earlier that day, Standing Bear had arrived in his camp on Beaver Creek with news of the chief's death. "They were preparing a travois when I left," he said, according to his son, Kills Plenty, "and they are going to bring his body here." Standing Bear's wives along with other members of the band gathered on the bluff just west of Beaver Creek to wait for the arrival of the chief's body. "My stepmothers and their mother were all in mourning, and were crying most of the time," remembered Kills Plenty. "Soon we saw them coming in the distance. They had his body on a travois and were moving slowly." The family of the dead man were all singing and walking apart from the others, "because they had a dead body with them." It was nearly dark—seven or eight o'clock in the evening—when the group mounted the last ridge of hills overlooking Camp Sheridan. Many of the whites at the post down on the plain below were frightened by the sound of the singing of the Indians. As dark fell, big fires were lit on the hill where the travois stopped and in the camps along Beaver Creek. Singing, drumming, and chanting continued throughout the night.[17]

Jesse Lee and his family returned to the agency the following day. Fearing an attack by angry Indians during the long ride across open country, the anxious lieutenant gave his wife a revolver so she might kill herself to avoid capture. He promised that he would kill their daughter Maude and then himself. But the journey was quiet, and the Indians at the agency, far from blaming Lee, posted a guard to watch over his quarters the night of their return. In the morning, on going to his office, Lee could see on the hill above the camp the body of Crazy Horse wrapped in a red blanket. It had been placed in the branches of a tree on the bluff above Camp Sheridan, "not half a mile away." Some days later, perhaps fearing that his son's body would be disturbed by wolves, the father asked Lee to surround the site with a fence to protect it. "So Jack Atkinson and I loaded a spring wagon with a few posts and some rough planks and went up there," Lee remembered, "and in an hour made a fence." Lucy packed a basket of food for the old man and his wife, who were grateful.

"Old Crazy Horse said, in sobbing tones," Lee remembered, " '*Ottah*

(Father) you and the other white men are my friends in this great sorrow.' "[18]

Soon after the death of Crazy Horse, his father took back the name he had given his son and ceased to be known as Waglula. The fact that Lee called him "old Crazy Horse" may mean he had already taken back the name by the time Lee built the fence.

A few days later Lieutenant Henry Lemly paid a visit to Lee at the Spotted Tail Agency, where the singing and drumming still continued at night in the camps. Like most other whites, Lemly found the loud, prolonged grief of the Indians disturbing. He described what he saw in the *New York Sun:*

> The grave was left in charge of the chief mourners . . . without food or drink, naked, and hideously blackened, eight figures lie around the corpse and howl. Night and day they do nothing but howl, and every Sioux, be it a buck or a squaw, who passes near, howls, too.

Lemly somehow felt safer using the word "howl" to describe the cries of grief. But he did not feel safe enough to visit the burial site of the chief himself. A civilian photographer who had been staying at the Spotted Tail Agency, James Hamilton, was braver; he mounted the hill above the agency and took two stereoviews of the burial site.[19]

Gradually, as Army officers and agency officials kept assuring their bosses, things quieted down. For about five weeks the body of Crazy Horse remained on the hill overlooking the agency. During this period, Red Feather remembered, "a war-eagle came to walk about on the coffin every night. It did nothing, only just walked about."[20] It seems likely that during this period Crazy Horse the father began the extended ceremony known as ghost keeping. The anthropologist Alice Fletcher, who made a seven-week journey across the plains with a party of Oglala a few years later, described in a paper for Harvard's Peabody Museum the difficult duties of a father keeping the ghost of a child:

> During this interval [of six months to a year] he cannot eat dog meat or any flesh scraped from the skin or hide of an animal. He cannot cut open the head of any animal to get the brains, strike or break any ribs or do any butchering. He cannot take a gun, pistol, arrows or any weapon in his hand. He cannot run, go in swimming, make any violent movement, shake a blanket, his clothing, or in any way disturb the air. No one must pass before him or touch him, and to prevent this disaster a coal of fire is always kept about

two feet in front of him as he sits in his tent. Although he remains with his family he must live apart from his wife, and on no account take a child in his arms, for if he should so forget himself the child would surely die.

The ceremony of ghost keeping had several purposes. One was to soften the shock and pain of separation for the soul of the dead person as well as for those who survived. It was thought that the soul of the deceased would linger about a lock of hair kept in the proper way. At the end of the ceremony in six months or a year a grand feast and giveaway would be held and the lock of hair would be taken from its special wrapping and buried or preserved by the mother. In either case, the soul of the dead child would then be free to depart. Another goal of the ceremony was to calm anger and reconcile enemies.

If at any time during the period of keeping the lodge the father should by any accident hear of any violent words or deeds, he must at once perform certain rites which will avert the evil consequences to him or his family. He must take a few coals of fire, and lay on them a bunch of sweet grass, or sprays of cedar. As the smoke rises he must crouch over the coals bringing his blanket close about his body, drawing it over his head and face so as completely to shut him in with the smoke . . . while the aromatic fumes circle his entire person . . . The keeping of a ghost lodge is a signal of peace and cancels all grudges between parties. The father may not smoke with any one lest he should consort with a man who was at enmity with some other person. The Indians in explanation pointed out that it was for the purpose of enforcing peace in a man's actions and thoughts that he was forbidden to take weapons in his hand; and the coal of fire placed before him while sitting in his tent was indicative of his setting himself apart for this religious duty, "the coal being like a partition between the father and all the world."

During the period of ghost keeping, the lock of hair in its wrapping would be added to other objects in a special bundle prepared by the mother and sisters or other close female relatives of the dead child. In addition to the lock of hair the bundle would contain the pipe smoked at the outset by the *wicasa wakan* and the father of the dead child. The parents might enclose other items as well—things sacred to the deceased, or merely small items of comfort, anything they thought appropriate. All were rolled into a bundle about six inches thick and two feet long. A male relative would cut three crotched sticks and the ghost bundle would be hung from this tripod in the ghost lodge, a small, separate dwelling used for this purpose alone. The lodge and the bundle on its tripod would travel with the family wherever it might go for the next six months or a year. Setting up the tripod would be a first order of business on arriving at a new camping place.

To travel with the tripod was customary, but to bring the actual body of the dead child was unusual. It is likely that Crazy Horse the father decided to do so because the whole tribe was making a permanent move and no one could be sure of his ability to return. In the last week of October 1877, Crazy Horse the father started out with the northern Indians, Miniconjou under Touch the Clouds and the remnants of Crazy Horse's Hunkpatila band. They were camped at the confluence of Beaver Creek and the White River in the first days of November when Clark and Red Cloud's Oglala joined them. It was there Clark learned that Crazy Horse's body was being "hauled along," a fact commonly known by the Indians. When the journey east was resumed Crazy Horse the father brought along the travois bearing the body of his son, now apparently placed in its wrapping inside a raised, cage-like wicker frame attached to the drag poles of the travois. In the family group were the wife of Crazy Horse the father; his full sister, Rattling Stone Woman (Tunkanawin), and Tasina Sapawin, widow of the dead Crazy Horse. A granddaughter of Rattling Stone Woman, eleven years old at the time of the removal, said the group traveled in the rear of the procession, which meant that they would be the last to leave camp in the morning and the last to arrive in the evening. In late November, they ended their journey with Red Cloud's Oglala at the forks of the White River, where they spent the winter and following spring. All returned at the end of the summer of 1878 when both agencies moved back away from the Missouri to new sites just across the line in South Dakota. Crazy Horse the father and his wife settled on the Rosebud Reservation with a band known as the Salt Users. With them on arrival, according to Kills Plenty, was the travois with its wicker cage which the people believed to contain the body of Crazy Horse. But something was now different. "They did not build up a tripod at this time," remembered Kills Plenty, referring to an important part of the ceremony of ghost keeping.

> One day we heard that the parents had opened this bundle which was supposed to contain the body of their son, and there was nothing but rags inside! What had they done with the body and where was it buried? Nobody could tell. It was a secret of Crazy Horse's family.[21]

Over the following years, stories gradually emerged about the secret burial of Crazy Horse. It seems that his father when he fell behind one day early in the journey took the body and hid it in a crevice among the white clay buttes lining the route to the White River. The granddaughter of Rattling Stone Woman, a first cousin of Crazy Horse once removed, told several people that the body was initially hidden on the way north at a site between the later reservation communities of Wounded Knee and Porcupine. In the following year, the father secretly moved the body to a new location, telling no one, not even Tasina Sapawin. "They were afraid [she] would marry again and reveal the burial place," said the cousin. But Tasina Sapawin never married again. Her brother Red Feather confirmed this story. "His father hid his body so not even my sister knew where it was buried," he said.

But Jennie Fast Thunder said that was not so. She knew Tasina Sapawin before she died in the 1920s in the Porcupine district of the Pine Ridge Reservation. In the summer of 1932 she told Kills Plenty, now known as Luther Standing Bear, "Whenever anyone asked her about the grave of her husband she always replied, 'I shall never tell anyone where he is. It was your jealousy that killed him.'"

Horn Chips in the early 1900s claimed that he had been present at every burial and reburial of Crazy Horse and knew where the body was. He told Walter Camp the chief's bones were buried for the last time in 1883 in a rawhide sack. According to Billy Garnett, Horn Chips offered to sell the secret but found no takers. Woman Dress told his friend James Cook in 1911 that "just one man know where the place he was buried. But I don't see that man." The sister of Crazy Horse who was married to Red Sack told Cook that "she helped bury him at a secret place in the Pine Ridge hills," but she refused to name the place. As recently as 1999 Woodrow Respects Nothing, then in his seventies, grandson of Jacob Respects Nothing and Sophie White Cow Tribe, told a white friend that his grandparents had helped move the body to a site along the clay buttes between Wounded Knee and Manderson. "But it was never told where his body was buried," Respects Nothing added.[22]

Crazy Horse the father often talked about his son in the years after his death. He said things might have turned out differently if his son had prayed and prepared his medicine properly on the fatal day. He told Red Feather that he thought Doctor McGillycuddy might have poisoned his son. He saw the doctor fill his syringe and inject some stuff into his son's body. "He died awful quick after that," said Crazy Horse the father.

The chief of the Sans Arcs who went north to Canada, Red Bear, explained to his son why the old man kept Crazy Horse's burial site a secret. "He did not want any white or any one of the jealous Indian chiefs who had helped the white soldiers by betraying Crazy Horse to touch Crazy Horse's body."[23]

But Crazy Horse the father managed to put aside bitter feelings, and in August 1879 he found an opportunity to extend the hand of friendship to Secretary of the Interior Carl Schurz. It is not likely that Crazy Horse the father had been told of Schurz's role in the cascading events which resulted in the death of his son. But Schurz was the highest government official Crazy Horse the father ever met, and it was to Schurz he made his gesture. In the last days of August, the secretary came west with a party of friends to visit the Spotted Tail Agency before continuing on to Wyoming where General Crook planned to take him hunting. Traveling with Schurz were a *New York Times* reporter, John M. Carson; Count Donhoff, the secretary of the German legation in Washington; and Webb Hayes, son of the president and godson of Crook. The previous year, when it had become safe at last for whites to travel in the old Sioux hunting grounds, Hayes, Crook, and the Fort Laramie trader John S. Collins made the first of twelve annual fall hunts in the mountains around Laramie.

Schurz's party arrived at the agency on August 28, after a fourteen-hour, eighty-seven-mile wagon journey from the Rosebud landing on the Missouri. On Saturday, about twelve hundred Indians gathered to meet Schurz, who was sitting with his companions on a raised platform built for the occasion by the agent, Major Cicero Newell. In a grand circle on the ground in front of the platform were the chiefs and leading men of the new agency, and between the chiefs and the platform, sitting in a chair, was Spotted Tail. "He was dressed in plain blue, without ornament of any kind," Carson wrote the following day. The gathering formed a scene of "barbaric splendor" which both impressed and disgusted Carson. The Indians were all dressed in their finery and mounted on "their best ponies," but Carson was evidently a fastidious man. "Some of the warriors were dressed and painted with taste," he wrote, as if a critic at the opera, "but the large portion of them were hideous with paint and repulsive in dirty garments."[24]

Schurz made some general opening remarks, followed by Spotted Tail, who spoke of Indian aspirations to become civilized. Then other chiefs rose to speak in the customary way. The turn arrived of Crazy Horse the father. In his hands he held a gift for Secretary Schurz: a war club which Crazy Horse the father, having completed the ceremony of ghost keeping, was now permitted to hold. John Carson, the *Times* reporter, made inquiry about the father. "He still mourns the loss of his son," he wrote, "and moves about in an aimless way, descanting upon the qualities of the dead Crazy Horse." A member of Schurz's party summarized the father's remarks:

> Old chief Crazy Horse made a speech to him [Secretary Schurz], presenting the tomahawk he had carried all his life and which he had received from his father. He said that as he had no son who could inherit it, and he was at peace with the White Father and had no further use for the weapon, he presented it in token of friendship.[25]

Crazy Horse the father died about 1880. His wife had died the previous year.[26]

34

"When I tell these things
I have a pain in my heart."

DURING A STAY AT the new Red Cloud Agency a few days later, Secretary Schurz and his party one afternoon rode a dozen miles out into the country to visit the camps of Young Man Afraid of His Horses and Little Big Man. From the latter, John M. Carson wrote, "a few trinkets and curiosities were purchased." Webb Hayes was the buyer of a large painting on muslin ten feet long and six feet wide on which Little Big Man had depicted some episodes from his life. The price was four dollars. Drawn in India ink and painted in red and yellow were several images of horses and men, some of them fighting. One of the men had two lines rising from his head to separate images: one of a man, the other of a bear. These were probably intended as name glyphs for the artist's two names, Wicasa Tanka Ciqala (Little Big Man) and Matowakuwa (Chasing Bear). Later, after young Hayes brought the painting back to his father's house in Fremont, Ohio, an explanatory note was attached saying, "Sketch of the life of Little Big Man, who killed Crazy Horse in 1877 and thus became a renegade Indian."[1]

The word "renegade" suggests that Little Big Man found some lingering difficulty in explaining himself to the Oglala. With the help of Alfred Riggs, a missionary fluent in Lakota, he wrote to President Hayes in August 1878 seeking permission to travel to Canada to bring back his friend Big Road, who had gone north with the rest of the Hunkpatila band the year before. "In what I did in obedience to the President in regard to Crazy Horse," Little Big Man said, "I did what was difficult."[2]

But he was not ashamed of what he did. A white schoolteacher at Pine Ridge, Edith Sickels, opened "quite a friendship" with Little Big Man during the 1880s while teaching his daughter, Oohoola (Bones), also known by the Christian name of Maud. "He always took great satisfaction," Sickels said, "in displaying his silver medal, on which was inscribed,

'Given to Little Big Man for valiant services at the death of Crazy Horse.' " The medal had been given to Little Big Man in Washington by President Hayes.[3]

In a letter to Walter Camp in 1919, General Hugh Scott mentioned Little Big Man's silver medal "received for service in the death of Crazy Horse . . . He was a nervy, earnest little devil that would take hold of your hand and would squeeze the blood out of it when he shook hands with you."[4]

Little Big Man is thought to have died about 1887.

The great northern herd of buffalo did not last long after the Indians were confined to reservations. In the spring of 1881, Luther North, commander of the Pawnee scouts in 1876 with his brother Frank, came across a small herd of thirty-three buffalo while trailing a cow in the Sand Hills of Nebraska. That country had been criss-crossed for years by cowboys and hunters. "No one dreamed of seeing any buffalo there," North wrote. But suddenly in the distance ahead of him he saw a herd lying down, including five new calves. "I almost fell off my horse with astonishment." North quickly fetched his brother and a niece and nephew, staying at a friend's ranch. "Ed had never seen a wild buffalo before," he wrote of the nephew, "and of course wanted to kill one." This he managed, but the rest of the herd escaped. North learned later that all had been killed by some Indians from the Spotted Tail Agency. "I think they were the last buffalo ever seen on the north side of the Platte River in Nebraska," he wrote.[5]

At that time there were still plenty of buffalo in the north, but the hunting pressure was relentless. Seeking meat and robes over the winter of 1881–82, Baptiste Pourier rode up into the Black Hills "and hunted, just hunted," he said many years later while giving a deposition to a lawyer.

> And at that time every hill and every little place where you could put up a tent, there was two or three hunters there and just as soon as it would be light enough [the witness here clapped his hands several times] that is all you would hear all day until sundown. If the moon would shine, they would shoot all night. And they kept that up.[6]

What Lieutenant Hugh Scott found astonishing was the speed with which the great northern herds vanished.[7] Lieutenant Richard Irving

Dodge had seen the destruction of the herds south of the Platte. Passing through a favorite hunting ground one fall he found only the carcasses of dead animals. "The air was foul with sickening stench," he wrote, "and the vast plain, which only a short twelvemonth before teemed with animal life, was a dead, solitary, putrid desert."[8]

Now the smell of rotting buffalo carcasses moved to the northern plains. "There were about three thousand men on the range killing buffalo for their hides," Scott wrote of the summer of 1883. That September, with a fellow officer, Scott rode five hundred miles looking for buffalo without finding so much as a fresh track. On the journey they met "an old Sioux Indian" who had been doing the same thing with better luck. He had killed one old scabby bull.

Scott was an accomplished sign talker and discussed the disappearance of the buffalo with the old man, who offered two theories. One was that the buffalo had gone up into Canada. His second theory was that the buffalo had gone back into the ground to rest, and would surely come again. But they did not come again. A year later, in August 1884, Scott killed a final buffalo. He never saw another.[9]

Twenty years after Scott's last kill some Oglala came to visit the anthropologist Clark Wissler in his quarters at Pine Ridge. They had been told that Wissler owned an old-time buffalo robe. "A venerable man," Wissler remembered, "asked to see and feel the skin." Others followed. They touched the deep fur, knelt before the robe, prayed, and sang. Sometimes the sick were brought to see and touch Wissler's robe. The depth of their feeling made Wissler ashamed. He had never seen a wild buffalo and had never tasted their meat. "The suddenness of the loss was the appalling part of it," Wissler wrote.[10]

After rejoining his old outfit, the 2nd Cavalry, Lieutenant William Philo Clark caught the attention of General Sheridan. In November 1880, he joined Sheridan's staff in Chicago, and followed him to Washington three years later when Sheridan was appointed general of the Army, replacing Sherman. In the fall of 1884 Clark was completing a dictionary of the Indian sign language which Sheridan had requested for military use on the frontier. In writing the book Clark made such heavy use of his diaries that the dictionary amounts almost to a memoir. Under the entry for "courtship" he mentioned the scout who feigned the wooing of an Indian woman "just outside of Crazy Horse's lodge . . . while his quick ears took in every word that was uttered in the lodge." What the spy learned, Clark wrote, "eventually led to the necessary killing of the chief himself."[11]

Clark was loath to marry. He was irritated by the manners of the women of his day. He preferred the healthy, easy ways of Indian women, who did not, for example, "treat their sisters . . . who may have yielded their virtue . . . with that fine scorn, contempt, hatred and loathing which civilized women so cheerfully accord." He thought that the corsets and stays of Victorian women's dress distorted and weakened the female body, while Indian women "are strong and usually healthy." He told several Indian friends, including Red Cloud, that he had taken no wife so he might be free to rise in his career.[12]

But in Chicago while stationed at Sheridan's headquarters Clark was much in circulation, like any young bachelor officer. By the time he followed Sheridan to Washington he was engaged to a woman named Cornelia McAvoy. A wedding date had not yet been set when Clark fell ill on September 19, 1884. Three days later he died in his rooms. His hometown newspaper, the *Carthage Republican* of New York State, reported "inflammation of the bowels." Peritonitis has been suggested as the probable cause. On his office desk at the War Department when Clark died were the final pages of his dictionary, wrapped and addressed for the post. *The Indian Sign Language* was published the following year in Philadelphia and has never been out of print. Clark's diaries have been lost.[13]

Frank Grouard did not prosper after his eighteen months as General Crook's favorite scout. He did odd jobs, worked as a meat hunter, lived off and on in Sheridan, Wyoming, and was sometimes attached to Fort McKinney. There in 1890 he was in charge of a detachment that recovered the bodies of some whites killed by Oglala at the outset of the Bozeman War twenty-five years earlier. At the end of the year he took a job at $10.50 a day to help count the dead at Wounded Knee, where he was photographed looking heavy and seedy. In 1893, he was reunited with his father, the Mormon missionary, for the first time in thirty-five years. The father had tracked him down to Sheridan after reading a newspaper notice of his son's book of memoirs, written with Joe DeBarthe, which did not sell well. In 1902, trying to drum up a permanent job at the Pine Ridge Agency, he ran into trouble with the tribal police for getting Standing Soldier drunk.

Frank Grouard died on August 15, 1905, of alcoholism, according to a doctor who knew him in St. Joseph, Missouri. Friends raised money to pay for his funeral.[14]

Twice by the time he was thirty years old Billy Garnett made a conscious choice to live with the Oglala and to be an Oglala. Once was in the late summer of 1878 when the Oglala turned back from the Missouri and moved without permission to a new site on Big White Clay Creek in South Dakota. It fell to Garnett to tell the Oglala agent, James Irwin, that the Indians were going. "What are you going to do?" Irwin asked him.

"I'm going with them," Garnett said.

"If you go with those Indians," Irwin said, "I will have to dismiss you as interpreter."

Garnett said he was going anyway. Young Man Afraid of His Horses, American Horse, Little Big Man, and others welcomed Garnett's decision to join them in the move. In time, the Indian Department accepted the new site, and about a year later the new agent, Doctor Valentine McGillycuddy, gave Billy his old job back as interpreter. He held the job for the rest of his life.[15]

On at least one other occasion Garnett was also asked to choose between the white and Indian worlds. The moment may have come on the trip to Washington in 1877, or on a subsequent trip in 1885, the year Garnett turned thirty. Accounts agree that the moment came during a trip east. From time to time over the years members of his father's family in Virginia had contacted Billy in a friendly way, and once, according to an often-repeated family story, asked him in a serious and formal way if he would like to move east, go to school, and make his home in the white world. These people were rich, his grandson, James Garnett, said; they held out the promise of a comfortable life and a position of respect as his father's only child. The young Garnett asked for a night to think it over. The following day, according to James Garnett, Billy thanked these people for their kindness but said he guessed not.

"I've lived all of my life as an Indian so far," he said, "and I guess I'll die as an Indian."[16]

Garnett spent nearly fifty years working with the Oglala. He was paid to interpret but he was involved somehow in almost every facet of reservation life, beginning in the 1880s with carrying out the government's decision to require every Indian to adopt a Christian and a family name, and to stick with it in the manner of whites. To a clerk who recorded the names on the agency roll, Garnett spelled out first the Lakota version and then translated it into English. But he fell into difficulty, he once told a reservation storekeeper, with the name of Taku Oholasni. This he said was untranslatable. The clerk asked for an approximation. Garnett said it couldn't be done. The clerk insisted.

"In Indian," Garnett said, "it means 'Don't Give a Damn for Anything.' "

The clerk wrote down, "Respects Nothing."[17]

Garnett worked closely with McGillycuddy when the agent organized a body of Indian police and he was often about the guardhouse where offenders were locked up for minor offenses or kept until they could be transported to Hot Springs or Deadwood for trial on serious charges. The fate of Crazy Horse came up in conversation one night in the late 1880s while Garnett was passing time in the guardhouse with Little Wolf, brother of Lone Bear, who had been out with Crazy Horse's band until the last. Both of the brothers were employed as Indian police. Little Wolf was wondering why things had gone as they did. "Now we come in from the north with Crazy Horse," he said, as Garnett remembered. "We intended to be peaceable with the white people, the same as the other Indians. I wonder why Crazy Horse was treated the way he was and finally died."

Garnett was caught by surprise. He thought back ten years. It was all quite clear in his mind. "You killed him," Garnett said to Little Wolf.

It was Little Wolf's turn to be amazed. "I killed him?"

"Yes, you killed him."

"I killed Crazy Horse?" Little Wolf said. "How can that be? I who fought with him all through the north—have always been with him—was his friend—How did I kill him?"[18]

"I told him that his talk killed him," Garnett remembered. " 'You told your own brother, Lone Bear, that Crazy Horse was going to kill General Crook.' "

"I never told my brother any such stuff," said Little Wolf. "I never knew that I had anything to do with this. I am going to see my brother."

Little Wolf did not let the matter drop, and soon afterward he returned to see Garnett with Lone Bear in tow. Lone Bear said, "Billy, my brother scold me about Crazy Horse's death. He says . . . that I told Woman Dress that General Crook was going to be killed. I never told Woman Dress any such thing."

Some months later Lone Bear and Little Wolf confronted Woman

Dress with Garnett's story. Woman Dress called it a lie, and, taking his nephew Louis Shangreau along, made his way in an angry mood to find Garnett.

"You can tell as good a lie as any one I ever saw," Woman Dress said to Garnett.

"Woman Dress, what am I lying about?"

"Me," said Woman Dress. "I had a gray blanket on in this council and I heard Crazy Horse say 'Tomorrow there is going to be a council on over at White Clay, the Indian village, and Crook is going to be there. I will catch Crook by the hand and pretend like I was going to shake hands with him and make quick work of him and whoever he will have with him.'

"Now that is what I heard Crazy Horse say. You said in the guardhouse that Little Wolf was the one who told Lone Bear, and Lone Bear told me. It was me, myself, that heard Crazy Horse, and now you tell lies about me and say that I got it from Lone Bear."

While Woman Dress and Louis Shangreau were raking Garnett up one side and down the other he felt a tap from behind. Turning around, he found Baptiste Pourier. "You come here just in time," Garnett said. He explained what the argument was about and Pourier said, "I will tell—I know exactly how it happened."

Louis Shangreau was the audience. Pourier related the encounter on the morning of September 3, 1877, with Woman Dress outside the agency trader's store at the Red Cloud Agency, how Woman Dress warned Pourier and Garnett the general's life would be in danger if he went to the council with Crazy Horse. Pourier heard Woman Dress say that it was Lone Bear who heard Crazy Horse threaten to kill Crook, and Lone Bear told his brother Little Wolf, and Little Wolf told Woman Dress—that's how Woman Dress knew. When Crook asked if Woman Dress could be trusted, Pourier vouched for him. While Pourier told the story, Woman Dress said not a word.

Shangreau was convinced. "You are a big liar," he said to his uncle, "and you are the cause of a good man's death and you are jealous of him."

Pourier repeated the verdict, pointing his finger at Woman Dress. "You are a liar," he said, "and you are the cause of a good man's death."

Woman Dress said nothing.

Lieutenant Clark died without being told of Woman Dress's lie, but Crook lived to hear it. Garnett and Pourier told him the whole story when he visited the Pine Ridge Reservation in 1889 to persuade the Oglala to sign yet another piece of paper giving up land.

———

By the late 1880s, Crook's fighting days were over. He was promoted to major general in 1888 and succeeded to command of the Military Division of the Missouri, the post once held by Sheridan. In Chicago, Crook took up residence in the city's Grand Pacific Hotel, where Sheridan paid him a courtesy visit. An afternoon playing cards in Chicago's Calumet Club was their last meeting. Their relationship, long strained, had ended in bitter disagreement when Sheridan more or less forced Crook to resign after a frustrating campaign against the Apache in Arizona.

But the break between the two men went back much further, to Sheridan's hogging of credit, as Crook saw it, for Union victories in the Shenandoah Valley during the Civil War. Crook long brooded on the injustice. During a stagecoach ride through a spring blizzard in 1887 Crook complained bitterly to an aide of his treatment by Sheridan.

Twenty years after the battles at Cedar Creek and Fisher's Hill, Crook spent a day riding over the ground. He remembered Sheridan's promise to give him credit and his failure to do so, first in his official report of the battle, then in the memoirs published shortly after Sheridan's death in August 1888. By that time Crook detested Sheridan, who had grown chubby in his last years. A news correspondent noted the buttons were ready to fly off Sheridan's coat, and his trousers "fitted very snugly to the general's fat legs." Sheridan's doctors blamed a heart condition but Crook thought the fault lay with Sheridan himself, puffed up by the celebrated poem about his twenty-mile ride to save the day at Winchester.

"The adulations heaped on him . . . turned his head," Crook wrote, "which, added to his natural disposition, caused him to bloat his little carcass with debauchery and dissipation, which carried him off prematurely."[19]

It was in the summer of 1889, a year after Sheridan's death, that Crook as one of a three-man commission progressed from one Sioux reservation to another arguing that the Sioux should vote to accept the terms of the Dawes Act. This scheme, passed by Congress, would divide the Great Sioux Reservation into six separate units and would allot each head of family a quarter section of land—160 acres. "Surplus" lands after the division would be sold. Everyone understood that the land would be taken whether the Sioux voted for the act or not, but feeling against it ran stubbornly high and Crook spent many days pushing the case for acceptance. At Pine Ridge in June 1889 he heard from Woman Dress that Little Hawk, uncle of Crazy Horse, "was talking very sassy" and was making trouble about signing the treaty. Crook sent for Little Hawk and asked him, "Why are you making trouble about this treaty?"

Little Hawk answered at length. When Crazy Horse came in to surrender, he said, the Indians had dressed up Lieutenant Clark with a warbonnet and war shirt in token of friendship. When they came back from Canada to stay for good they did the same thing with McGillycuddy—dressed him up in token of friendship.

"I have been faithful to you people," Little Hawk said to General Crook. "Your Indians are telling lies about me like they told about Crazy Horse, and now are you going to kill me?"

Crook, brought up short by this question, sought explanation from Garnett and Pourier, who told him about the confrontation with Woman Dress. The news put the general into a thoughtful mood, Garnett recalled.

"Bat," he said, "Billy knew more than you did, he did not recommend Woman Dress that time." To Garnett it seemed that Crook was going over the meaning of this, making up his mind in a careful way.

"I ought to have gone to that council and I should not have listened to Clark," Crook said. "I never started any place but I got there."

Later, Crook assured Little Hawk that bad talk would not lead to his killing. "I found out about what made the trouble about Crazy Horse," he said. "You Indians made the trouble. I felt sorry for that."

He urged Little Hawk to sign the treaty.

"I am afraid of it," Little Hawk said. "We sign for certain things, and after you people go away you get other things down in the treaty that were not there . . . In all of these treaties it is the same way . . . I am afraid to touch that pen."

"All right, it is up to you," Crook said. "It is better for you to sign, but you can sign or not, just as you wish."

In the end, Little Hawk signed the treaty. Crook went away. Very soon afterward the Indian Department cut food rations in half, hunger soon reached a dangerous level, the reservations were swept by an Indian religious movement, and frightened whites called for the military to put down the ghost dancers who prayed for the return of the buffalo. It all ended with a big killing of several hundred Indians, mostly Miniconjou, mostly women and children, beside the creek called Wounded Knee in

December 1890. Crook saw none of it. He had died before breakfast on March 21, 1890, in his rooms at the Grand Pacific Hotel in Chicago, exercising with the big wooden pins called Indian clubs. Crook was a leaner, hardier man than Sheridan, but he died the same way, of a heart attack.

After passage of a pension act in March 1917, Garnett helped scores of Indians to obtain a monthly stipend. This was a time-consuming task requiring depositions, hearings, and the submission of numerous documents, but Garnett made a point of helping every eligible scout or widow get a pension. He even helped many he had learned to dislike. Woman Dress was one of these. Like Little Big Man, Woman Dress was angrily shunned by many Indians who blamed him for the death of Crazy Horse. "He was like a two-edged sword against his own people," said one of them in 1930. But Garnett had personally helped Woman Dress to enlist, translating his name for Lieutenant Clark. He knew for a fact that Woman Dress had been a scout and was eligible, so he helped him get a pension.

Woman Dress died on January 9, 1921.

William Garnett, after many refusals, was himself granted a pension of twenty dollars a month by special act of Congress in 1924. He died after a short illness on October 12, 1928, and was buried in the Catholic cemetery north of Kyle on the Pine Ridge Reservation.

The rancher James Cook, who had befriended Red Cloud in the early 1870s, was often visited in later years on his ranch in western Nebraska by Indians from the Pine Ridge Reservation. Red Cloud came frequently until his death in 1909, while others continued up until the 1940s. Among the visitors were Red Cloud's daughter, Charging Girl, born about 1860, and her husband, John Kills Above. The agency rolls carried Charging Girl as Susie Kills Above. On their visits they sometimes sang old songs, which were translated by Joe Sierro. These songs were all short, no more than twenty or thirty words. They are notable for their directness and simplicity. Some were traditional songs, some were about well-known people or events, and some had belonged to noted figures, including Charging Girl's father, Red Cloud. A tintype photograph of Red Cloud, taken on one of his trips to Washington, was one of Charging Girl's prized possessions.

"These songs are sung without the words first," Cook wrote in a memorandum transcribing a dozen of them, "then with words, then without the words again. This is repeated two or three times."[20]

One night at Cook's ranch in June 1937, Kills Above and his brother, Kills Chief, sang a very old warrior's song which they said was from "the time before the white man came."

> I lie anywhere.
> I fight and die anywhere.
> On the ground or in the water I am ready to die, anytime.
> No matter whether I am young or old.

Several songs were of the kind called "honor songs," sung to commemorate a noted figure, and one was a death song. The words in this song, according to Kills Above and Knife Chief, were the words sung by Crazy Horse "after he was killed," meaning after he had received a fatal wound.

> My friends, have courage.
> Me, I cannot do anything any more.
> Me, I can no more go to war.
> I am dead. I help no more.
> Crazy Horse said so and died.

Charging Girl talked about her life at length that night, only a few months before dying on October 7, 1937. "I always can remember everything very good up until now," she said, according to Cook's typed notes. "I am very weak now," she added. "Wherever I go I always take my picture of my father along."

Charging Girl talked about the hanging of two Indians at Fort Laramie in 1865, when she was four or five years old. She told of her father's trips to Washington, and about the hunger suffered during the tribe's first year at the agency on the White River, when men had to bring food from Fort Laramie, a two-day ride each way. She spoke about the killing of Crazy Horse when she was sixteen or seventeen years old. "When he was stabbed," Charging Girl said, "the Indians were holding him, and he said, 'Leave me alone. I want to get revenge.'"

A few years earlier, when Crazy Horse's wife was still alive, Charging Girl asked her where he was buried. "No, I'll never tell," answered Tasina Sapawin. "I have raised my hand and his relatives have raised their hands, that we will never tell."

One night during the march to the Missouri, Charging Girl said, the tribe was camped near a hill when the family of Crazy Horse rejoined the people. They had gone off with the travois carrying his body, no one knew where. "All the camp cried and mourned," she said. "In the night time they returned. The whole tribe sang and cried . . .

"When I tell these things I have a pain in my heart."[21]

35

"I'm not telling anyone what I know about the killing of Crazy Horse."

THE MAN WHO TOOK the name Sword was in New York City on the day Crazy Horse was killed. Sword had been one of the Oglala scouts who led Generals Crook and Sheridan to the Little Bighorn battle site in the summer of 1877. It was during that trip that Hunts the Enemy discarded his old name and took his brother's—Man That Owns a Sword (Miwakan Yuha). Back at the Red Cloud Agency in late August, Sword was hired to appear in a new play starring William F. Cody, a scout and guide for the Army who was already nationally famous as Buffalo Bill, hero of many dime novels. Sword and the Hunkpapa Sioux Two Bears traveled east with Buffalo Bill and his wife and daughter to the Cody home in Rochester, New York, arriving about the 1st of September. In a saloon on Front Street during their stay "two beakers of foaming lager [were] placed before them," courtesy of Buffalo Bill. "The chiefs took their glasses with as much grace and ease as if natives of Berlin," wrote a correspondent for the *Rochester Union*. "[They] quaffed the amber-colored fluid without flinching and when another pot was placed before them were nothing loth."[1]

Sword and Two Bears played roles as friendly Indians who helped Buffalo Bill in *May Cody, or Lost and Won*, a play written by one of Cody's Army friends, Captain Andrew S. Burt. It opened at the Bowery Theater in New York on September 3, the day Crook had planned to meet with Crazy Horse in council. On succeeding days, when Crazy Horse fled the agency, when he was killed, and when his body was taken away by his parents, Sword appeared nightly on the stage of the Bowery Theater. By this time he had decisively cast his lot with the whites. In an account of his life written in Lakota, Sword said that the power of the white Army convinced him that Wakan Tanka was inferior to the white man's god. He put aside his identity as a traditional war leader or *blota hunka*, a bear dreamer, a *pejuta wicasa*, and a leader of sun dances and joined the Episcopal Church, eventually becoming a deacon. He took the Christian name George. He cut his hair. He built a house. He accepted appointment as captain of police on the new Pine Ridge Agency and once defied Red Cloud, saying, "I wear the uniform of the Great Father, and the army of the Great Father is back of me."[2]

But respect for Lakota religion did not die in George Sword. "The scars on my body show that I have danced the sun dance," he told the new agency doctor in 1896, James R. Walker. "No Lakota will dispute my word." When Walker wanted to study Lakota religion, Sword came to his aid. One of Walker's interpreters was Bruce Means, a son-in-law of Fast Thunder. The most serious health problem at Pine Ridge in 1896 was tuberculosis; as many as half the Oglala were infected. Walker concluded that his work would be easier if he had the help of traditional medicine men, of whom five remained active at Pine Ridge. Three were very old. None would speak freely to Walker until Sword convinced them that Wakan Tanka did not want them to carry their knowledge to the grave.

The traditional knowledge of the Sioux was in jeopardy on all the Sioux reservations, where the medicine men and women were growing old while younger people were not interested in the old songs and ceremonies. Officials encouraged this pattern, saying they wanted to kill the Indian to save the man. Sun dances, giveaways, and coming-of-age ceremonies for young women were all prohibited, and the rules were enforced by a Court of Indian Offenses. In school, Sioux children were forbidden to speak Lakota. Traditionals said the circle had been broken, and the life of the Lakota was coming to an end. "We come to you as from the dead," Old Buffalo (Tatanka Ehanni), born in 1845, told the anthropologist Frances Densmore on the Standing Rock Reservation. "The things about which you ask us have been dead to us for many years. In bringing them to our minds we are calling them from the dead, and when we have told you about them they will go back to the dead, to remain forever."[3]

Before they died the medicine men passed on some of what they knew to self-selected students like Densmore and Walker. In effect, Walker became an Oglala. Once ordained, or formally accepted into the ranks of medicine men, Walker was free to ask any question and eligible to learn any secret, with only a few exceptions. The final steps required him to have a vision and to receive a *sicun*, or sacred bundle. Both were provided by Short Bull. A *sicun* was a collection of objects of power, consecrated in sacred ways. Any man could have a *sicun* but no man could safely treat it with disrespect. George Sword told Walker that he might be a Christian but he still feared the power of his medicine bundle. "I will write of the old customs and ceremonies for you," he said. "But the secrets of the shamans I am afraid to write, for I have my old outfit as a shaman, and I am afraid to offend it. If a shaman offends his ceremonial outfit, it will bring disaster on him."

Into Walker's ceremonial outfit, or medicine bundle, Short Bull placed the following objects of power: "the tusk of a bear, the claw of an eagle, the rattle of a rattlesnake, a wisp of human hair, and a wisp of sweetgrass." These objects were wrapped inside the skin of a fawn, tanned to the softness of butter.[4]

George Sword died in 1910.

Matthew King, a grandson of Fast Thunder, learned to smoke cigarettes from his great-grandmother Cane Woman (Sagyewin) about 1906, when Matthew was four years old. The family lived on Fast Thunder's allotment a few miles north of the community of Wounded Knee and a few miles south of the community of Manderson on the Pine Ridge Reservation. Fast Thunder had chosen good bottomland along the creek where he planted crops and pastured cattle and horses. By the time Matthew was born, Fast Thunder's family had moved from a canvas lodge to a log cabin on a rise overlooking what was called the Manderson Road. Cane Woman, mother of Fast Thunder's wife, Jennie Wounded Horse, was in her nineties and blind. It was Matthew's job at four to keep Cane Woman company and lead her around by the elbow. The two of them spent the day together.[5]

Cane Woman loved to smoke, Matthew King remembered, but her hands shook too much to roll a cigarette. She had to ask others to hold the paper and shake out the Bull Durham tobacco when she wanted a smoke. "Nobody wanted to roll all those cigarettes for Cane Woman," King said, "so she had me do it for her." This was not easy for the boy, but in time he learned to make a tolerable cigarette. "Matthew," Cane Woman would say when the mood struck, "roll one and light me!" It was natural to get it going with a few puffs himself. Soon he liked a smoke as much as Cane Woman. She didn't mind. One day she said, "Roll one for yourself." After that he generally made two cigarettes and they smoked together.

Fast Thunder was counted among the "progressives" on Pine Ridge, the men who had one wife, sent their children to school, drove wagons, attended church, earned money by freighting or farming, and made no show when performing traditional ceremonies. He raised ducks and chickens. Baptiste Pourier and Fast Thunder were the first on the reservation to raise oats, and after that, remembered his grandson, Paul Red Star, "he was the first Indian to own a horse-powered threshing machine." During the ghost dance trouble he sided with the government. Black Elk remembered that Fast Thunder and American Horse came to urge him "to put this ghost dance aside quietly." At a huge meeting of seven thousand Oglala a week before the killing at Wounded Knee, Fast Thunder was elected to ride out with Big Road and Little Wound to talk peace with the ghost dancers, who had taken refuge in a protected valley in the Badlands known as the Stronghold. There was no game in the Badlands, so the ghost dancers and their families lived on beef stolen from white ranchers and the progressives. After the trouble was over, Fast Thunder submitted a claim to the government for the loss of fifty-six cattle. He was luckier than American Horse, whose house was burned.[6]

But in other ways, Fast Thunder remained a traditional. It was said that moccasins were the first thing whites adopted from Indians, and the last thing Indians gave up. But it was not just the wearing of moccasins that connected Fast Thunder to traditional life. He had two wives until 1895, when he separated from the second, a cousin of Jennie Wounded Horse named Locator. He did not cut his hair, he counted a man rich who had many horses, on important occasions he smoked a traditional pipe with a red catlinite bowl and a wooden stem decorated with porcupine quills, and when he did not feel well, or wanted to pray, he prepared a sweat bath. The rocks found along Wounded Knee Creek were no good for a sweat, in Fast Thunder's view; they cracked and broke when water was poured on them. The right kind of rocks, heavy and dense, could be found sixty miles southwest near the new town of Chadron, across the line in Nebraska. One of his granddaughters, Stella Swift Bird, remembered that Fast Thunder always returned home with some of these rocks when he went to Chadron.

But most importantly, Fast Thunder talked to his grandchildren of the old days. His reputation as a fighter was well known. George Sword, who became a captain of the Indian police at Pine Ridge, said Fast Thunder had been the bravest fighter at the Wagon Box Fight in 1867—he was the one who rode closest to the enemy. William Garnett said it was Fast Thunder and Scraper, both wearing eagle-feather warbonnets, who had charged first into the Cheyenne camp on the Red Fork of the Powder River in November 1876.

It was natural that Fast Thunder's grandchildren, growing up in the quiet poverty of the reservation, should sit breathless listening to the old man's stories. When he took off his shirt they saw the sun dance scars on his back and on his chest. He told them he once stood for four days on a high spot overlooking Beaver Creek until a snake came to him in a vision and spoke to him. He was afraid of water because a bear came to him in a dream and bears are afraid of water. As a bear dreamer, Fast Thunder had the power to heal; he was a *pejuta wicasa*. At a naming ceremony when he was little, Matthew King was given names by his grandparents. His grandmother Jennie Wounded Horse said her husband helped everybody so she named Matthew "Helper" in honor of Fast Thunder.

Matthew's grandfather also gave him a name. In his youth, he explained, he was once in a big fight with Pawnee who killed some of his friends and wounded Fast Thunder badly with arrows. One arrow he pulled right out, but the other went all the way through his body. Fast Thunder said he reached around and broke off the point where it emerged from his back and then pulled the shaft of the arrow out the front. "I hid in a gully in some tall grass and used my medicine herbs to treat my wounds," he told Matthew. "I'm hard to kill."

That was the name Fast Thunder gave his grandson: "Hard to Kill."

The boy Matthew often went out walking with his grandfather in the country along Wounded Knee Creek, sometimes up in the hills, sometimes down by the water. Fast Thunder would bring his old scout gun with him, a Springfield trapdoor carbine. He told many stories of the old warring and hunting days but sometimes he talked about the time Crazy Horse was killed. He told Matthew he was one of those who persuaded Crazy Horse to go back to Camp Robinson. The white soldiers told him Crazy Horse would not be harmed. They only wanted to talk to him. Crazy Horse feared a trick but felt he had no choice. All his life Crazy Horse had gone out alone, but he did not want to leave the people and go out alone now. "How can I be free all by myself?" he said to Fast Thunder.[7]

When he urged Crazy Horse to go back and explain himself to the white soldiers, Fast Thunder thought he was doing the right thing. When the soldiers tried to put Crazy Horse in the guardhouse many people had seen Fast Thunder holding Crazy Horse as he struggled to break free. As the years passed Fast Thunder and his wife remembered that moment differently, as if he only caught hold of Crazy Horse when he was stabbed, and helped lower him to the ground. Jennie Wounded Horse told her grandchildren that she began to sing a brave song as soon as Crazy Horse was stabbed, and covered him with her blanket.

But one memory nothing could soften. Jennie told her grandchildren that when Crazy Horse was lying mortally wounded on the ground, he accused Fast Thunder of betrayal. "Cousin, you killed me," Jennie remembered him saying. "You are with the white people."[8]

Fast Thunder suffered with these memories. "I never saw anyone so sad," said his grandson Matthew. The old man, then in his seventies, would sit down by the creek and shake his head and say, "They tricked me! They tricked me!" Sometimes it was sorrow he expressed, sometimes anger. When he was angry he would ride into town and shoot his gun.

To Matthew, the old man was a kind of hero, a brave warrior in the old days, and then a farmer who made himself rich raising cattle and horses. His brand was "707," Matthew remembered, because that was how many horses he had. His cousin Paul Red Star also remembered hearing about that big herd of horses. Fast Thunder spoke for the people in council, defended the people against agency officials, went to Washington, helped others. But there was a shadow on him. "All most people remembered about him," Matthew King said in the mid-1980s, when he was eighty himself, "was that he helped do in Crazy Horse. They never let him forget it. People had no mercy on him. Even today they haven't forgiven him."[9]

Fast Thunder died on March 4, 1914, in the town of Manderson. To his widow Jennie Wounded Horse he left $215 cash, ten horses valued at $300, and the log house he had built along the Manderson Road. Jennie Wounded Horse lived in the house until her own death on January 2, 1934.[10]

When He Dog, Big Road, and Little Hawk returned from Canada in 1881 they settled near the community of Kyle on the Pine Ridge Reservation, far from Red Cloud's people and from Red Cloud himself, who slept on a metal frame bed and lived in a two-story clapboard house built for him by the government in the village of Pine Ridge, near the agency offices. Bitter feelings between the followers of Red Cloud and Crazy Horse were never dispelled. When Eleanor Hinman and her friend Mari Sandoz visited Pine Ridge in 1930 to research the life of Crazy Horse

they took care not to side openly with one faction or the other, but some
of the old-timers still refused to say anything. When the interpreter John
Colhoff sought out Crazy Horse's uncle Little Hawk, he refused to meet
with the two women. "No questions had been asked about Crazy Horse
at the time of his death," Colhoff explained, "and he did not care to
answer any now."[11] Another interpreter helping Hinman and Sandoz was
Samuel Stands. Sensing that some of the Indians were telling less than
they knew, Stands went out on his own one night to meet privately with a
man he would identify only as an "old timer."

"The old man's reply as quoted by Stands was, 'I'm not telling anyone—white or Indian—what I know about the killing of Crazy Horse,' "
Hinman wrote. " 'That affair was a disgrace, and a dirty shame. We killed
our own man.' "[12]

If He Dog blamed anyone for the death of Crazy Horse, it was Red
Cloud. He had confronted the chief angrily in the first moments after
Crazy Horse was stabbed, while he still lay writhing on the parade
ground. "You said nothing like this would ever happen again," He Dog
said. "You promised there would be no more blood shed. Now look . . . !"
He told his son that he accused Lieutenant Clark of the same thing at the
same time, and even slapped the officer in the face.[13]

But He Dog never flatly blamed Red Cloud, Clark, or anyone else by
name for engineering his friend's death. "I am an old man now and shall
not live many years longer," he told Hinman in the first of their three
interviews. "It is time for me to tell these things."[14]

When He Dog had enlisted as a scout, Clark put the name He Wolf
down on his enlistment papers. In the 1920s, when He Dog applied for a
pension the Army could not find his records and denied his application.
Hunger and even outright starvation, especially of the elderly in isolated
cabins in remote corners of the reservation, was common at Pine Ridge
until the 1940s. He Dog in his eighties could not walk, could not see, and
had no source of income. "It used to be a disgrace to the Sioux to eat
horse meat," He Dog told General Hugh Scott. "Now we can hardly help
ourselves from it."

To live, He Dog depended on a niece, on his younger brother Short
Bull (who did get a pension), and on the provisions his friend John Colhoff brought him from time to time. He told Colhoff he could not repay
his kindness in this world, "but when he got 'there' he would have it
announced in the camp just what J. had done for him on earth."[15] Black
Elk asked Eleanor Hinman for two cents a word to talk about Crazy

Horse, and estimated the story would take two weeks to tell. But He Dog asked for nothing.

Much of what is known about the life of Crazy Horse comes from He Dog. He told General Scott in 1920 that he still mourned Crazy Horse fifty years after his death. Of his friend, He Dog implied only one criticism: he should have bent more, he should have said yes more. But his weakness was small compared to the thing that made him the greatest fighter of the Sioux. "When he came on the field of battle," He Dog told Scott, "he made everybody brave."[16]

He Dog died in 1936.

AFTERWORD

"No man is held in more veneration here than Crazy Horse."

STRANGE COMBINATIONS OF FORGETTING and remembrance followed the death of Crazy Horse and, in time, of those who knew him. Now even those who knew those who knew him are disappearing. Among the general public the memory of Crazy Horse at first faded. In 1927 one of General Crook's favorite mule packers, Henry W. Daly, wrote a brief memoir of the 1876 summer campaign, conceding that Crook did not win at the Rosebud. The explanation was not far to seek, in Daly's view: "Crazy Horse was the greatest strategist among the western Indians." But by the 1920s, Daly found, all the talk was about Sitting Bull. "One scarcely ever hears of Crazy Horse," Daly wrote. "He has, I mean, left no impression on the popular mind."[1]

This did not remain true for long. In the 1940s, the Polish-American sculptor Korczak Ziółkowski was seized by an ambition to carve a mountain in the Black Hills that would dwarf even Mount Rushmore. Henry Standing Bear, who had been in the Custer fight, suggested that Crazy Horse would be a proper subject for the sculptor, and in 1948 Ziółkowski began his herculean project to blast a mountain into a likeness of the chief. When Ziółkowski began, few survived who still remembered Crazy Horse, and despite much searching no one had found a photograph of him. One of the first to look was John Gregory Bourke, who wrote Crook's widow shortly after the general's death to ask if a Crazy Horse photograph was among his papers. Mary Crook said there was not, and suggested that Bourke contact the old Fort Laramie sutler, John Collins, the general's hunting friend. Collins did not have one, either, and told Bourke to ask Ben Paddock, a trader at Fort Robinson. So it went for fifty years. Many photographs were touted for a time but all proved to be of someone else. Ziółkowski admitted he could get no closer than a likeness of the "spirit" of Crazy Horse, which in his sketches, and later as carved into the mountain itself, gave the chief a noticeably Slavic cast.

In 1949, on his way home from Rapid City where he had taken a job in the Sioux Museum, John Colhoff happened by the sculptor's project in the Black Hills. From the window of his bus, he saw a sign pointing to the Crazy Horse mountain. There a collection box had been set up beside the road, with a sign asking for money. "Poor old Crazy Horse," Colhoff wrote a friend, "the one thing he fought against the whites for—[they] are now using his name to make money."[2]

The face on the mountain belonged to a figure of defiance and resistance, but among the Oglala the chief was remembered in a different way, for the power given him by the Wakan Tanka. Fast Thunder's grandson, Matthew King, did not seek the spirit of Crazy Horse among the granite crags in the Black Hills but nearby on the gently rounded Bear Butte, where Lakota and Cheyenne still go to pray. King was born in 1902 and was active in the revival of traditional Lakota language, religion, and culture until his death in 1989. What he knew about Crazy Horse came mainly from his grandparents. "Crazy Horse used to say, 'When I die I'll come back as thunder and lightning.'" King did not think of this as poetry or metaphor. "Sometimes when I go up on Bear Butte," King told a friend, "he speaks to me from the sky. His voice is thunder, his tongue is lightning."[3]

Matthew King's were not the only stories about Crazy Horse to pass down through the Fast Thunder family. Several of his grandchildren lived with their families along the Manderson road on the flats and hills west of Wounded Knee Creek. When Theodore Means, son of Fast Thunder's daughter Fannie, came back from the war in Europe he quit drinking, established the first chapter of Alcoholics Anonymous at Pine Ridge, and began to take sweat baths and study traditional religion with Ben Black Elk, son of the well-known *wicasa wakan* who lived in Manderson. Beginning in the 1930s, Black Elk, although a practicing Catholic, set out to preserve the rituals associated with the sacred pipe, teaching them to the white scholars and writers John Neihardt and Joseph Epes Brown, who was living in Black Elk's home when he met Ted Means in the 1940s.[4] Brown was impressed by Means, and developed a strong feeling for his eighty-year-old mother, Fannie, who gave Brown a bow that had belonged to her father, Fast Thunder. It was not only Black Elk who told Brown about the last of the buffalo-hunting days and the greatest of the warrior chiefs who fought the whites. "No man is held in more veneration here than Crazy Horse," Brown wrote in a letter home. "He is always being talked about when any group gathers. His place of burial is still a mystery, and probably always shall be, which is good; but it is believed that he is not over a mile from here."[5]

Not only the memory of Crazy Horse but certain items belonging to the chief had been preserved as well by the people living on the Manderson road, including one that had been entrusted to Ted Means some time in the late 1930s. It seems unlikely that Ted ever told Joe Brown what it was, where it was, or how it was obtained. The story was told to me by Ted's granddaughter, Barbara Means Adams, who had learned it from her grandmother Theresa, Ted's wife, in the late 1960s. Ted had been dead four or five years by then. Barbara was in her early twenties and already the mother of four children, the youngest still toddlers. One day without warning or preamble of any kind Theresa asked Barbara to drive her down to Minatare, Nebraska, a small town near Scott's Bluff on the North Platte River. It's a three-hour drive down to Minatare; Barbara protested that she had no one to leave the kids with, but Theresa was agitated and adamant—she had to go, there was something she had to get, Barbara had a car and there was no one else to take her. So Barbara piled all four boys into the back seat and headed down the Manderson road to Wounded Knee and Pine Ridge, following the old route to Minatare. On the way, Theresa told Barbara what they were going to get, and forty years later Barbara told me.

For many years before the Second World War, Theresa said, Pine Ridge Indians went south in the fall to pick potatoes on the big farms along the Platte River down in Nebraska. Every September hundreds of them would gather in tent camps on the farms where they worked, often setting up in the same place, under the same big old cottonwood tree or in the same grassy spot along an irrigation ditch, year after year. Among those taking their families south for a month or six weeks every year were Ted Means and his first cousin Stella Swift Bird, daughter of Fast Thunder's oldest boy, carried as Mark Red Star on the agency rolls, but called Old Man Flesh by his family. Until the war got in the way, Ted Means and Stella Swift Bird pitched their tents side by side every year along a windrow of cottonwoods on a place owned by a Japanese farmer just outside of Minatare. The last trip down, Theresa said, was in the fall of 1942, just before Ted joined the Army and everything changed.[6]

Barbara's cousin, Pete Swift Bird, remembers Theresa well. She was a daughter of Edward Two Two, an Oglala who often toured with Wild

West shows and died in Germany at the beginning of the First World War. After Ted died in the mid-1960s, when Pete Swift Bird was still a toddler, Theresa remained in the house on the Manderson road. The old log house built by Fast Thunder had been replaced by a newer, one-story, stucco structure, but there was an outhouse and a water pump out back. Theresa was a round, grandmotherly type who loved to feed people, and she "did magic with that old ledge-back, wood-burning kitchen stove," according to Pete. In the 1960s, when Pete was a small child and his parents were working, he lived with his grandmother, Stella, out in the country in a house with no electricity. They often visited Theresa Means on the Manderson road, and there Pete would see his cousin Barb, who was in her twenties.

"My grandma was a slim, frail figure," Pete Swift Bird remembered of Stella. "Living with her was like being in a mother's womb." She was in her late sixties, born in 1897, old enough to start a family the year Fast Thunder died in 1914. She loved to tell stories of the old days and she told them in Lakota. Pete's teacher in third grade was Mabell Kadlecek, the wife of a Nebraska rancher with a place on Beaver Creek a few miles south of the old Spotted Tail Agency. Mabell and her husband, Edward, were friendly with a number of elderly Pine Ridge Indians, including Pete's grandmother, Stella Swift Bird. The Kadleceks had come to believe that a big old cottonwood tree down along the creek on their place had been the first burial site of Crazy Horse. When the body of Crazy Horse was moved, the Kadleceks believed, its final resting place was in a crevice between some big rocks on a pine-covered hillside overlooking their ranch. Every year, Mabell Kadlecek would take her third-grade class in a bus down to the ranch and show them the grassy flat along Beaver Creek where Fast Thunder had conducted a sun dance in 1877, so the old Indians said. And she pointed out to her students the big old cottonwood tree, then still standing (but now gone), where the body of Crazy Horse was first buried.

Pete saw the tree like all the other kids, but when he was in the sixth grade his grandmother, Stella Swift Bird, told him it wasn't so. She said the body of Crazy Horse had been hidden in the white clay buttes along the Manderson road. She said her father, Old Man Flesh, remembered all his life something Crazy Horse told him when he was only twelve or thirteen years old. "He told Flesh never to trust those people, the *wasicus*," Stella Swift Bird told her grandson. She said Crazy Horse left everybody and went out into the country alone. She said Old Man Flesh kept Crazy Horse's *chekpa*, which Pete Swift Bird called a medicine bundle. "It was a black, beaded ball with his belly button in it and Old Man Flesh buried it with him," Pete remembered. "That's the story I heard from Stella and from my Dad. It was in the sweat lodge when you heard that kind of thing."

When Barbara Adams told me Theresa's story she also used the words "medicine bundle," but she clearly meant something different—the much larger object containing a man's *sicun*. Theresa told Barbara she knew exactly where she was going. It was the place where they used to camp. They set up the tent every year in the same place, on the farm owned by the Japanese man, under a great big old cottonwood tree. When they got to Minatare, Theresa would tell Barbara exactly where to go.

But when they got to Minatare, everything seemed strange and misplaced. Theresa grew agitated. She couldn't understand what had happened. Barbara drove her four boys and her grandmother all around Minatare for an hour, turning up every road, looking for that cottonwood tree. But they never found the tree, and nothing in the town itself looked familiar. The fields were bigger, the old windrows of Chinese elms had been taken out, the road into town was wider and followed a different route, buildings were boarded up or missing. Theresa discovered in an hour everything that had changed in twenty years—the potato and sugar beet farms had moved to the center of the state, retail business had all migrated eight miles up the road to Scott's Bluff, the big cottonwood dooryard trees had been mostly cut down. By the end of that hour Theresa admitted she could no longer find the spot where they had pitched their tent in 1942.

They did not get back home till after dark. On the long drive home Theresa told Barbara what she had gone to retrieve. It would be a very interesting thing to have. On the last day of his life, Theresa said, Crazy Horse gave Fast Thunder his medicine bundle for safekeeping. After Crazy Horse was killed, Fast Thunder took this medicine bundle to the Pine Ridge reservation and kept it in his log house on the Manderson road. After Fast Thunder died in 1914 his wife, Jennie Wounded Horse, preserved the medicine bundle, telling no one about it outside the family. Before Jennie died in 1934 she entrusted the medicine bundle to a relative who lived on the Manderson road, Nellie Ghost Dog, who passed it on in turn to Ted Means, Fast Thunder's grandson. In 1942, fearing the dislocations of war, Barbara's grandparents decided to bury the medicine bundle in Minatare. They pitched their tent right beside the big cotton-wood tree so they would always be able to find the place again. Inside the tent at night the family dug a hole six feet deep.

But before they buried the medicine bundle, Theresa told Barbara, they decided to open the bundle. When I asked Barbara how big it was, she said her grandmother described it as about the size of a baby. On the outside of the bundle was a blanket. Inside the blanket were several layers of cloth. Inside the cloth was a bag made of tanned deerskin. It was this bag which would hold a man's *sicun*—special stones that had power, or certain herbs and sweet-smelling grasses, or parts of animals that had vis-ited the owner in visions and dreams.

What Crazy Horse had placed in his medicine bundle Theresa did not know. When the family started to open the deerskin bag, she said, they suddenly heard a great roar of flapping wings against the walls of the tent; scores of owls were beating their wings outside, loud as thunder. Tradi-tional Lakotas believe that owls warn of death. The sound frightened all of them. They wrapped up Crazy Horse's bundle and buried it right away.

On the way home from Minatare, Theresa was in despair; she felt they had all failed somehow—lost the precious thing entrusted to them. This was not Barbara's conclusion. She thought a powerful message of assur-ance could be read in the beating of the owls' wings. My own view shifts back and forth. In one mood it seems to me that Crazy Horse did not want the *wasicu*s to get his medicine bundle and they didn't. Thus he died in victory, as his father said. But at other moments it seems that Theresa's story is plainer in meaning, and marks a divide between the things that have been lost and the things that survive.[7]

METHODS, SOURCES, AND
ACKNOWLEDGMENTS

This book attempts many things, but first among them is the attempt to explain why Crazy Horse was killed. What the various characters in the story wanted, in addition to things that angered, alarmed, and frightened them, further confused by bad luck and misunderstanding, and driven by circumstances beyond anyone's control, all contributed to the unfolding of events that ended with the killing. General Crook and the officers under his command were ready at one point to ask rival chiefs to murder Crazy Horse, but in the end did not. What I think happened emerges in the course of the narrative and in my view requires no explicit enumeration of causes and circumstances at the end—no summation of the case before it goes to jury. My effort here has been to tell the story in a way that helps readers to experience its weight and quality—the feel of it.

The sources employed in telling this story come mainly from documents, such as diaries, letters, official reports, books, newspaper articles, notes jotted down by participants, and the like. In a few cases the sources are objects or drawings. The reader may feel confident that every factual claim in the telling of the story, unless openly identified as speculation, has some identifiable source. If the weather is described as hot, or a character is said to have thought this or feared that, or a scene is described as dusty, or it is claimed that an Indian drawing on a pipe made an audible puffing sound, then there is some reason for believing so, and in almost all cases the source is cited in an endnote. Some readers may find the number of notes irritating, but others would hardly feel able to go on if left to wonder in frustration what (if anything) stood behind a new and unfamiliar fact. The challenge in writing true narrative is to offer two pleasures to the reader more or less simultaneously—the urgency of the story (which is why we tell or read it), and the richness of the evidentiary record (there when you need it).

There is much new material in this book, but it rests on a foundation of primary sources previously collected, published, or located in archives by several generations of scholars, including a productive fraternity of historians of the Plains Indian Wars at work since the 1960s. Many of these writers worked for the National Park Service, where their research focused on the primal question of history—what happened? Their books and articles recount, mainly without judging, the military seizure of the Great Plains from Native Americans in the half century after Francis Parkman traveled west on the Oregon Trail to visit in the lodges of the Oglala. My encounter with these writers began in the fall of 1999 when I spent a week in northwest Nebraska, where Tom Buecker, curator of the Fort Robinson Museum, turned me loose in his office with a copying machine and a week's free rein in his matchless Crazy Horse file. Buecker had just published *Fort Robinson and the American West*, his magisterial history of the fort's first twenty-five years.* His chapter on the killing of Crazy Horse is lucid and frank, but struck me as several hundred pages too short. Buecker's wife, Kay, welcomed me on many trips to Nebraska, and Tom's generosity with his materials freed me to spend my own years of research in new territory.

Two other scholars and writers also gave me extraordinary help with their deep knowledge of Native Americans, the Lakota in particular, and of the history of the Plains Indian Wars. Mike Cowdrey, an independent scholar living in California, is the author of two books (one on horse masks, another on a collection of Cheyenne ledger drawings),† frequently provides curatorial notes for museum and auction catalogs, and has long studied Plains Indian religion and culture. We have exchanged hundreds of e-mails but never met. For years my day was often brightened by unexpected photos or documents from Cowdrey, and my accounts of Lakota religion and political organization in particular were enriched by his readiness to identify error and answer questions.

The world of the frontier military was opened to me principally by Jack McDermott, who grew up in South Dakota and was altered forever at the age of six when he saw Errol Flynn in *They Died with Their Boots On*, not the truest but still the greatest of movies about George Armstrong Custer. McDermott joined the National Park Service in 1960 and is the author of many books on the frontier military and the northern plains, most recently *Red Cloud's War*, forthcoming in two volumes from the University of Oklahoma Press. I met McDermott at a Fort Robinson history conference and have corresponded and traveled frequently with him since. On many occasions Jack and his wife, Sharon, offered me a place to stay in Rapid City, and on the road Jack generally knew where to get a piece of red meat and a martini. He also walked me over the ground at Powder River, the Rosebud, and the Little Big Horn, where he listened politely to my analysis of the battle. Like Buecker and Cowdrey, McDermott was generous with the fruit of his years of research, letting me carry away anything I found useful from his forty file drawers of old news clips, pamphlets, notes, and photocopies. Much of the pleasure in working on this book came from conversations with Buecker, Cowdrey, and McDermott, who all answered numerous questions over a period of years, read the long version of the book in manuscript, made suggestions I was glad to follow, and corrected many errors. Those that remain are no fault of theirs.

Many other scholars and writers offered friendly help as well, including Peter Bolz, Christina Burke, Nan Card, Ephraim Dickson, John A. Doerrer, Candace Greene, Jerome Greene, Jim Hanson, Paul Hedren, Paul Andrew Hutton, Mabell Kadlecek, Hans Kharkheck, Sandra Lowry, Eli Paul, Gail and Jim Potter, and William K. and Marla Powers. Many of their books are cited in the endnotes. For locating pension files at the National Archives I am grateful to Michael Murphy. On trips to Nebraska I often stayed in Chadron's Old Main Street Inn, run by Jeanne Goetzinger, who introduced me to Matthew Red Shirt. I am especially grateful to Margaret Black Weasel,

---

*Thomas R. Buecker, *Fort Robinson and the American West, 1874–1899* (Nebraska State Historical Society, 1999), since followed by *Fort Robinson and the American Century, 1900–1948* (Nebraska State Historical Society, 2002).

†Mike Cowdrey, et al., *American Indian Horse Masks* (Hawk Hill Press, 2007), and Cowdrey, *Arrow's Elk Society Ledger* (Morning Star Gallery, 1999). Cowdrey has long been at work on a biography of the Crow chief Plenty Corps.

her daughter Barbara Means Adams, and Barbara's cousin Pete Swift Bird for their stories of life among the descendants of Fast Thunder.

First among those who helped me to understand the Lakota was Harry Thompson of Tamworth, New Hampshire, a most remarkable man. A few months after he turned ninety, with the cautiously granted permission of his daughter, Jane, I drove Harry out to Fort Hale, South Dakota, where he had grown up on the Lower Brulé reservation. He was hoping to shoot an antelope with a new rifle sighted in for three hundred yards. While Harry was hunting I spent a week a couple of hundred miles farther west at Fort Robinson walking the ground where Crazy Horse spent his last months. During the long days on the road out and back Harry told me many stories that opened my mind to a different way of looking at the world. Ten years later at Harry's hundredth birthday he asked how the book was coming, and added, "I hope to live long enough to read it." He did.

Readers of the first draft of this book were my wife, Candace, Susan Braudy, Nicky Dawidoff, Priscilla McMillan, and Nicola Smith. All made valuable suggestions that I tried to follow. A not-quite-final draft, shorter by a hundred pages, was read by Crystal Gromer, after which I cut another twenty. Reading a manuscript is work; with a red pencil in hand, hard work. My gratitude is deep. Finally, I would like to thank my brother, Bushrod, who alone remembers my fascination with the Plains Indians when I was twelve years old, and in recent years listened on morning walks when I went back at it again; and my longtime champion at Knopf, Ashbel Green. I have been privileged to work with two great editors; Ash is one of them and I am braced by his friendship.

NOTES

Introduction

1. Robert A. Clark, ed., *The Killing of Chief Crazy Horse*, 75–100.
2. The name of Woman Dress is usually given in a possessive form as Woman's Dress, but I have elected to use the shorter version for the following reasons: he is referred to as Woman Dress in verbatim transcripts of interviews with Billy Garnett, his numerous letters to his friend James H. Cook of Nebraska are all signed Woman Dress, and his name appears as Woman Dress in pension records and on his grave marker in St. Paul's Cemetery on the Pine Ridge Reservation in South Dakota.
3. Raymond J. DeMallie, ed., *The Sixth Grandfather*, 178, 184.
4. Dewey Beard described his experience at Wounded Knee in a meeting with the commissioner of Indian affairs in Washington, 11 February 1891, *Report of the Commissioner of Indian Affairs*, 1891, vol. 1, pp. 179–81.
5. The numerous names, words, and remarks presented in the Lakota language in this book are almost all reproduced as found in various printed sources and documents without benefit of diacritical marks or scholarly correction. For syntax and pronunciation, interested readers should consult the two authoritative books by Eugene Buechel, S.J.; *A Grammar of Lakota* (Rosebud Education Society, 1939) and *Lakota Dictionary* (Red Cloud Indian School, 1983). S and C followed by a vowel are usually soft, as in *akicita* (ah-*kee*-chee-ta—soldier), *Tunkasila* (Tunk-*ah*-shee-la—grandfather) or *Unci* (*Oon*-chee—grandmother).

1. *"When we were young, all we thought about was going to war."*

1. "Sioux" is a term derived by early French trappers from a Chippewa word. President Thomas Jefferson used the term in his instructions to Lewis and Clark, and it has been standard ever since. "Teton Lakota" was the term used by the western Sioux for themselves. They were comprised of seven bands, or "council fires": the Oglala, Hunkpapas, Miniconjou, Sans Arcs (No Bows), Brulé or Sicanju ("Burnt Thighs"), Miniconjou Sihasapa or Blackfeet, and Two Kettles. A standard work on the Teton Lakota is Royal B. Hassrick, *The Sioux*.
2. "There is a treaty": Dee Brown, *Fort Phil Kearny*, 34. The officer was Colonel Henry B. Carrington, soon to be commander of Fort Phil Kearny.
3. Crazy Horse was identified as the leader of the decoys by the Cheyenne Two Moons (George E. Hyde, *Red Cloud's Folk*, 146), and by Charles A. Eastman, *Indian Heroes and Great Chieftains*, 43. Sword's presence is reported by George Colhoff, a trader who married an Oglala woman in the 1860s; Eli Ricker inter-

view with George Colhoff, Richard E. Jensen, ed., *The Soldier and Settler Interviews*, 215. American Horse told Eli Ricker he was one of the decoys, Richard E. Jensen, ed., *The Indian Interviews*, 280.

4. Several boyhood exploits are described by Eastman, ibid., 38ff. Eastman was a Santee Sioux who graduated from Dartmouth College and earned a medical degree, later serving as a doctor on the Pine Ridge Reservation in South Dakota in the 1890s. Eli Ricker interview with Horn Chips, 14 February 1907, Jensen, ed., *The Indian Interviews*, 273. The suicide of Rattle Blanket Woman is recorded by Victoria Conroy in a letter to James McGregor, 18 December 1934, reprinted in Richard G. Hardorff, ed., *The Surrender and Death of Crazy Horse*, 265ff. Crazy Horse's friend White Rabbit reported that the elder man's second wife was a sister of Rattle Blanket Woman; Luther Standing Bear, *Land of the Spotted Eagle*, 181. See also He Dog interview with Eleanor Hinman, 7 July 1930, *Oglala Sources*. The war expedition led by the elder Crazy Horse is recorded in the Cloud Shield winter count for 1844–45, and he is cited again in reference to the burial of his brother, who was probably He Crow; Garrick Mallery, "Picture Writing of the American Indians," 463.

5. He Dog interview with Eleanor Hinman, 7 July 1930. Eagle Elk interview with John Neihardt, 27 November 1944, John Neihardt Papers, no. 3716. Eli Ricker interview with Horn Chips, Jensen, ed., *The Indian Interviews*. See also Thunder Tail's narrative in Eugene Buechel, *Lakota Tales and Texts*, 628.

6. He Dog interview with Eleanor Hinman, 7 July 1930.

7. The year spent with the Brulé may have included the Battle of Blue Water Creek in September 1855, and this may be why some writers—especially Mari Sandoz—have suggested that Crazy Horse witnessed or took part in the battle.

8. fight with Arapahos: He Dog is explicit in identifying the enemy as Arapahos. He Dog interview with Eleanor Hinman, 7 July 1930, 9. Red Cloud in R. Eli Paul, ed., *Autobiography of Red Cloud*, 138, describes the annihilation of a village of fifty Arapaho lodges, encountered on their way to visit the Gros Ventres. Red Cloud was angry over a defeat at the hands of the Gros Ventres the previous summer. Flying Hawk, the brother of Kicking Bear, describes a fight with the Gros Ventres in which Crazy Horse at sixteen rescued Hump; it is possible all three accounts refer to the same fight. M. I. McCreight, *Firewater and Forked Tongues*, 133.

9. He Dog interview with Eleanor Hinman, 7 July 1930. See also Helen H. Blish, *A Pictographic History of the Oglala Sioux*, 112.

10. Mallery, "Picture Writing of the American Indians," 722.

11. Paul, ed., *Autobiography of Red Cloud*, 36ff. Other sources for the early life of Red Cloud include the Colhoff winter count, which reports the return of Cloud Shield with news of Red Cloud's death; Hyde, *Red Cloud's Folk;* and a William Garnett letter to Doane Robinson, 5 December 1923, Don Russell Papers. A standard biography is James C. Olson, *Red Cloud and the Sioux Problem*.

12. Charles P. Jordan Papers, quoted in Paul, ed., *Autobiography of Red Cloud*, 11. Jordan was married to Julia Walks First, who was a niece of Red Cloud and a cousin of Spotted Tail; information inscribed on the back of a cabinet photo of Julia Walks First, author's possession.

13. Paul, ed., *Autobiography of Red Cloud*, 75; undated note by James Cook, James C. Cook Papers, Box 92.

14. One of eleven songs performed by Red Cloud's grandson Jim and two of his sons-in-law, Kills Above and Kills Chief. Translated by Joe Sierro for James

Cook at his ranch in Agate Springs, Nebraska, in 1931. Three-page typescript in the James C. Cook Papers.

15. having a large family: Francis Parkman noted in 1846, "A Sioux of mean family can seldom become a chief—a chief generally arises out of large families, where the number of relatives who can back him in a quarrel and support him by their influence, gives him weight and authority." Francis Parkman, *The Journals of Francis Parkman*, 441.

16. Ibid., 446. Miller's remark about Bull Bear's "imperious will" may be found in Marvin C. Ross, *The West of Alfred Jacob Miller* (University of Oklahoma Press, 1951), 45. The German doctor was Frederik A. Wislizenus (1810–1889); he recorded his impression in *A Journey to the Rocky Mountains in 1839* (Missouri Historical Society, 1912), 58, 138. Sources for the story of Bull Bear include the Cloud Shield winter count; Mallery, "Picture Writing of the American Indians," 603; Rufus Sage, *Rocky Mountain Life* (Wentworth, 1846), 121; William Garnett letter to V. T. McGillycuddy, 6 March 1922, Elmo Scott Watson Papers, Box 30, Colhoff winter count for the year 1910; Lawrence Bull Bear and Charles Turning Hawk, interviews with Scudder Mekeel, 10 September 1931, Silas Afraid-of-Enemy, Peter Bull Bear, interpreters, Scudder Mekeel, Field Notes; Scudder Mekeel letter to George Hyde, 11 September 1931, author's possession; and Parkman, *The Journals of Francis Parkman*, vol. 2, passim.

17. Charles W. Allen, *From Fort Laramie to Wounded Knee*, 55. See Sage, *Rocky Mountain Life*, passim, for numerous examples of Indians under the influence of whiskey.

18. Paul, ed., *Autobiography of Red Cloud*, 67ff. Other sources not already cited are the Cloud Shield winter count, and the Charles Turning Hawk interview with Scudder Mekeel, 10 September 1931. Among others killed were Blue Bird, Blue Horse, White Hawk, and Red Cloud's brother (or brother-in-law) Yellow Lodge.

19. He was referring to the society of chiefs. At varying times the Short Hairs (Naca Omniciye) were also known as the Pehin Pteptecela (because they braided short, curly buffalo hair into their own), or Hanskaska—the Tall Ones. In very early times the chiefs were known as Tatanka Wapahun—Wearers of the Buffalo Headdress. It was said that long ago a medicine man had a dream that showed him how to make the headdress *wakan* by attaching to it a small bag containing sacred things. Over time the buffalo headdress was slowly replaced by the eagle-feather headdress, and the name for the chiefs' society changed as well.

20. Clark Wissler, *Societies and Ceremonial Associations*, 8, 36ff.

21. Helen Blish interview notes, 23 July 1929, quoted in Hinman, introduction to *Oglala Sources*, p. 47.

22. The Sioux were as conflicted about *winkte*s as whites. A good account can be found in Hassrick, *The Sioux*, 133–35. An extensive treatment can also be found in the unpublished manuscript account of sign language prepared by General Hugh B. Scott, preserved in his papers at the Library of Congress.

23. This version of the story of the *winkte* was told to George Bird Grinnell in 1914 by the Cheyenne White Elk, who took part in the Fetterman fight when he was about seventeen years old. It can be found in George Bird Grinnell, *The Fighting Cheyennes*, 237–38.

24. Stanley Vestal, *Warpath*, 65.

25. Jensen, ed., *The Indian Interviews*, 281.

26. Colonel Carrington's official report implied that Fetterman and a fellow officer

shot each other to avoid capture. His wife Margaret Carrington, in a memoir, said the temples of both men were "so scorched with powder as to leave no doubt" they had shot each other. But it appears that American Horse with his knife did the job. The Army surgeon who examined the bodies after the battle wrote, "Colonel Fetterman's body showed his thorax to have been cut crosswise with a knife, deep into the viscera; his throat and entire neck were cut to the cervical spine, all around. I believe that mutilation caused his death." Margaret Carrington, *Absaraka: Home of the Crow* (Lakeside Press, 1950), 237. Report of Dr. Samuel D. Horton, Fort Phil Kearny files.

27. Grinnell, *The Fighting Cheyennes*, 243.

28. This rare circumstance would not be repeated for another 133 years, in 1999. Because the earth is closer to the sun by several million miles on the shortest day of the year, and because the full moon on December 21, 1866, coincided with perigee (the point at which the moon in its orbit passes closest to the earth), the amount of reflected light from the moon striking the earth was dramatically greater than usual. Information courtesy of Brad Mehlinger.

29. Colhoff winter count.

2. "I have always kept the oaths I made then, but Crazy Horse did not."

1. Allyne (Jane) Garnett Pearce, *You Must Give Something Back* (H. V. Chapman and Sons, 2000), 37ff.

2. In *The Great Platte River Road*, 480–521, Merrill J. Mattes devotes two chapters to Fort Laramie, where the ascent began toward the continental divide. These journal excerpts are quoted on 225 and 516.

3. Walter Camp interview with William Garnett, 1907, Walter Camp Papers, Box 2. Garnett translated his mother's name, Akitapiwin, as Looks at Him; other sources give the English as Looking Woman. The fullest treatment of the Boye, Boyer, or Bouyer family is to be found in John S. Gray, *Custer's Last Campaign*. See also V. T. McGillycuddy letter to Elmo Scott Watson, 10 February 1922, Elmo Scott Watson Papers.

4. The woman with the frank gaze has been identified as the wife of an Oglala named Grey Eyes. See Allen Chronister, "1868 Sioux at Fort Laramie," *Whispering Wind* (2008) 38, no. 1. A nearly complete set of the Gardner photos is in the National Anthropological Archives at the Smithsonian Institution.

5. John S. Collins, *My Experiences in the West* (Lakeside Press, 1970), 21ff.

6. For the Sand Creek massacre see Robert Utley, *The Indian Frontier* (New Mexico, 1984), 86ff. John D. McDermott, *Circle of Fire*, passim and 60ff. There is substantial doubt whether any of the executed were guilty as charged. See also Susan Bordeaux Bettelyoun and Josephine Waggoner, *With My Own Eyes*, 84, 164; Walter Camp interview with William Garnett, 1907, Walker Camp Papers; and *Rocky Mountain News*, 27 June 1865. Big Crow's accuser is described in the *Daily Times* of Leavenworth, Kansas, 14 March 1865.

7. Bettelyoun and Waggoner, *With My Own Eyes*, 91.

8. Eli Ricker interview with William Garnett, 15 January 1907, Jensen, ed., *The Indian Interviews*, 102

9. Gli Naziwin: Garnett translates his grandmother's name as Comes and Stands. Walter Camp interview with William Garnett, 1907. It might also be translated as Woman Who Returns and Stands.

10. "Billy was then": John Bratt, *Trails of Yesterday*, 121. Memory had corrupted the name to "Garner," but it is clear Bratt means Garnett; he refers both to his father and his later employment as interpreter on the Pine Ridge Reservation.

11. Eli Ricker interview with W. R. Jones, 23 January 1907, Richard E. Jensen, ed., *The Soldier and Settler Interviews*, 174ff.

12. Bratt, *Trails of Yesterday*, 128.

13. "John was cross-eyed": Ibid., 119.

14. "Mean to his mother": Ibid., 121.

15. Charles M. Robinson III, ed., *The Diaries*, vol. 4.

16. Thompson killed Hunter: Thompson was himself later killed in a quarrel over horses by John Portuguese Phillips and some soldiers. Eli Ricker interview with W. R. Jones, 23 January 1907. See also John Hunter, Fort Laramie name files.

17. Eli Ricker interview with William Garnett, Jensen, ed., *The Indian Interviews*, 40.

18. James Walker, notes, c. 1900, American Museum of Natural History; Clark Wissler, *Societies and Ceremonial Associations*, 7.

19. This account of the making of the Shirt Wearers is based on Eli Ricker interview with William Garnett, 10 January 1907. Eleanor Hinman interview with He Dog, 7 July 1930, *Oglala Sources*, 11–12; Wissler, *Societies and Ceremonial Associations*, 7, 36, 39–40; and "History of Crazy Horse," eleven-page typescript narrative based on testimony of He Dog, Josephine Waggoner Papers. This last document can also be found in Richard G. Hardorff, ed., *The Surrender and Death of Crazy Horse*, 132ff. It was prepared by Joseph Eagle Hawk, a son of He Dog, and was apparently intended to accompany a collection of twenty-one ledger drawings, now lost.

20. Calico was an informant about 1907 of the photographer Edward S. Curtis, who recorded details of his life in *The North American Indian* (University Press, 1908), vol. 3, pp. 16, 183.

3. *"It is better to die young."*

1. the Light Haired Boy: Eli Ricker interview with Horn Chips, 14 February 1907, Richard E. Jensen, ed., *The Indian Interviews*, 273ff.; "When we first": James C. Olson, *Red Cloud and the Sioux Problem*, 105; others spoke for him: Eli Ricker interview with William Garnett, 15 January 1877, Jensen, ed., *The Indian Interviews*, 1ff. Red Cloud was a tireless and effective talker, and his collected words would fill a stout tome. "He was a very quiet man": He Dog interview, 7 July 1930, Eleanor H. Hinman, *Oglala Sources*, 12–13.

2. "A man on horseback": Eli Ricker interview with William Garnett, Jensen, ed., *The Indian Interviews*, 117. The lake in question was probably Lake DeSmet. White Buffalo Shaking Off the Dust, the father of Wooden Leg, also had a mysterious encounter at Lake DeSmet, where he killed a deer that had been grazing underwater, only to have it pull itself back together and run off after he had cut the animal up and packed it into camp. Thomas B. Marquis, trans., *Wooden Leg*, 145–46.

3. shell necklace: Short Bull interview, 13 July 1930, Hinman, *Oglala Sources*, 39; "thirty-seven people": Angeline Johnson letter, 7 September 1877, *Nebraska History* (summer 1996); slough grass: Iron Horse to Luther Standing Bear, summer 1932, reported in the *Los Angeles Times Sunday Magazine*, 22 January 1933.

4. W. P. Clark, *The Indian Sign Language*, 183.

5. M. I. McCreight, *Chief Flying Hawk's Tales* and *Firewater and Forked Tongues*, 139. A sister-in-law of Crazy Horse also reported that Crazy Horse wore only a blade of grass in his hair and "offered to go right down in the White River valley and find some of the type of red blade of grass that he wore." Will G. Robinson letter to Elmo Scott Watson, 29 November 1948, *Wi-iyohi*, monthly bulletin of the South Dakota Historical Society, vol. 1, no. 6, 1 September 1947, Elmo Scott Watson Papers.

6. Joseph No Water, interview with Scudder Mekeel, September 1931, Scudder Mekeel, Field Notes.

7. Francis Parkman, *The Oregon Trail Journal*, 450.

8. He Dog interview, 13 July 1930, Hinman, *Oglala Sources*, 15–16. Bad Heart Bull was the father of the famous Oglala ledger artist Amos Bad Heart Bull.

9. He Dog says left nostril, Horn Chips says right nostril. But all other accounts report a scar on the left side of his face. He Dog interview, 13 July 1930; Eli Ricker interview with Horn Chips, 14 February 1907, Jensen, ed., *The Indian Interviews;* "It took some months": Eagle Elk interview, 27 November 1944, John Neihardt Papers.

10. Scudder Mekeel, *The Economy of a Modern Teton Dakota Community*, 5.

11. Dee Brown, *Fort Phil Kearny*, 76. Of course, the Cheyenne and their Sioux allies would not have been content with half.

12. Clark Wissler, Field Notes.

13. There were two classes of powerful or sacred persons called "medicine men" by whites: *wicasa wakan* (mysterious or sacred men), who were spiritual advisers, makers of powerful charms for love or war, interveners with Wakan Tanka; and *wicasa pejuta* ("medicine men"), who healed with the use of herbs and other natural remedies—doctors in the American sense.

14. Benson Lanford note in Christie's sale catalog, 12 January 2006. See also J. Owen Dorsey, *Tenth Annual Report of the Bureau of American Ethnology*, 436.

15. Wissler, Field Notes, 96.

16. The Lakota name for Scott's Bluff (Ma E-ya Paha) comes from an undated note by James Cook, James C. Cook Papers, Box 92. Frank Kicking Bear (1889–1965), son of the Kicking Bear who was a war comrade of Crazy Horse and later a leader of the ghost dance movement, identified Scott's Bluff as the site for Crazy Horse's vision. Edward Kadlecek and Mabell Kadlecek, *To Kill an Eagle*, 116.

17. "the odor of their flow": Wissler, Field Notes. Headdresses, shields, and lances were never brought inside the lodge, Wissler notes, "for fear they would be contaminated by the presence of women," 37.

18. Royal B. Hassrick, *The Sioux*, 335. See also Clark, *The Indian Sign Language*, 273.

19. Information from John Blunt Horn in Clark Wissler, *Societies and Ceremonial Associations*, 44.

20. "that species of desperation": Francis Parkman, *The Journals of Francis Parkman*, vol. 2, p. 444.

21. "looking for death": Colhoff winter count, 1870.

22. Brief accounts of this event are given by Flying Hawk and He Dog's brother Short Bull. McCreight, *Chief Flying Hawk's Tales* and *Firewater and Forked Tongues*, 138–39. Short Bull interview, 13 July 1930, Hinman *Oglala Sources*, 32.

23. McCreight quotes Flying Hawk as saying the killing occurred when "his younger brother was on a campaign in the country about which is Utah." To me

this sounds like a garbled translation of a report that he was fighting Utes or in the Ute country. McCreight, *Chief Flying Hawk's Tales*. Eagle Elk interview, 27 November 1944, John Neihardt Papers, no. 3716.

24. George Catlin, *Letters and Notes on the . . . North American Indians* (Dover, 1973), vol. 1, p. 221. Catlin spells the chief's name as Ha-wan-je-tah; Red Horse Owner's winter count dates the event to 1835: "He Wanji Ca tatanka wankici kicizaca"—"He Wanji Ca fought with a buffalo." The independent scholar Mike Cowdrey thinks Lone Horn's fight with a buffalo never occurred.

25. Letter from Post Chaplain Alpha Wright, Fort Laramie, 19 April 1870, to the editor, "Our Wyoming Letter" (Plattsmouth) *Nebraska Herald*, 5 May 1870, 2.

26. He Dog interview with Eleanor Hinman, 13 July 1930, *Oglala Sources*.

27. Accounts of the battle in which High Backbone was killed can be found in Eleanor Hinman's interviews with He Dog and Red Feather, *Oglala Sources*, and the Colhoff winter count for the years 1870, 1927, and 1940.

28. "a smooth rock face": The best known of these picture-covered rock faces was called Painted Cliffs, also known as Deer Medicine Rocks. Black Elk said there were four ways a man might predict the future: in a trance during the sun dance; in a dream or vision; by correctly reading the petroglyphs at Deer Medicine Rocks; and in the final moments before dying. Raymond J. DeMallie, ed., *The Sixth Grandfather*, 181.

29. Wissler, Field Notes, 128.

30. W. C. Brown letter to Hugh Scott, 14 April 1919, Hugh Scott Papers.

31. Joe DeBarthe, *Life and Adventures of Frank Grouard*, 181.

4. *"Crazy Horse was as fine an Indian as he ever knew."*

1. John Colhoff letter to George Hyde, 30 May 1949, author's possession.

2. Richard E. Jensen, ed., *The Soldier and Settler Interviews*, 271.

3. Brian Jones, "Those Wild Reshaw Boys," *English Westerners' Society: Sidelights of the Sioux Wars* (1867), 45, n. 126. The fullest account of this episode is to be found in Eli Ricker's interview with Billy Garnett, Richard E. Jensen, ed., *The Indian Interviews*, 104ff. Much information on the Richard family may also be found, in John D. McDermott, *Frontier Crossroads: the History of Fort Caspar and the Upper Platte Crossing* (City of Caspar, Wyoming, 1997).

4. Captain Henry W. Patterson letter to General George D. Ruggles, 14 September 1869, NA/RG 393, Fort Fetterman, Letters Sent, quoted in Brian Jones, "John Richard Jr. and the Killing at Fetterman," *Annals of Wyoming* (fall 1971), 243.

5. Chase in Winter pension file, National Archives. Chase in Winter had many wives before marrying Her Many Horses in 1876; she had previously been married for five years (1867–1872) to Yellow Bear, the chief murdered by John Richard while Billy Garnett watched in 1872.

In his affidavit, Chase in Winter remarked, "The interpreter [when he enlisted as a scout at Camp Robinson in October 1876] would not put down my correct name and gave me the name of Red Man. I also have a name, an Indian name that is not permitted to be used." Included in his pension file was a sealed envelope marked, "To be Opened by the Chief of the S.E.D. [Special Examination Division], providing said reviewer is *not* a woman." In the envelope was a note from the examiner explaining that Chase in Winter's Indian name was

White Inside of a Cunt. Such names were not uncommon among the Oglala. Thomas R. Buecker and R. Eli Paul, eds., *The Crazy Horse Surrender Ledger*, 158ff., includes many, such as Pisses in the Horn, Shits in His Hand, Tanned Nuts, Snatch Stealer, and Soft Prick. I have wondered if the last-named might have been the Oglala warrior alluded to by Francis Parkman in his journal thirty years earlier (June 1846): "A young Indian with an extraordinary name, importing that his propensities were the reverse of amorous, came with his squaw and child to camp, on his way to the fort, where he means to leave his squaw in charge of [Joseph] Bissonnette, while he goes to war." Francis Parkman, *The Oregon Trail Journal*, 448–49.

Such names reflected a natural frankness and directness in language. Parkman in July 1846 described a typical evening of conversation in an Oglala lodge in which their host, "an old man . . . kept up a constant stream of raillery—especially about the women, declaring in their presence that he had lain with them, at which they laughed, without the slightest inclination to blush. [Antoine] Reynal says, and indeed it is very observable, that *anything* may be said without making a girl blush; but that liberties cannot be taken with a young girl's person without exciting her shame." Ibid., 451.

6. Fast Thunder and Tall Man pension files, National Archives. In the 1890s Cane Woman changed her name to Wounded Horse and was called Jennie; she died in the 1930s. Short Bull's marriage to Good Enemy Woman took place in 1880 in Canada, where they had fled following the killing of Crazy Horse. After leaving Short Bull she married Tall Man and remained with him until his death on the Pine Ridge reservation in 1912. In 1881 all three returned to the United States and surrendered to military authorities.

7. Relatives of Baptiste Pourier later suggested that bad blood between John Richard Jr. and Yellow Bear had existed for some time, and that the chief's people said there was a price on Richard's head: "Whoever kills *Wasicun Tamaheca* will have tongue to eat"—tongue being one of the choice parts of the buffalo. Hila Gilbert, *Big Bat Pourier* (The Mills Company, 1968), 17–18.

8. Jensen, ed., *The Indian Interviews*, 108.

9. Leander P. Richardson, "A Trip to the Black Hills," *Scribner's* (April 1877).

10. Eli Ricker interview with William Garnett, Jensen, ed., *The Indian Interviews*.

11. Notes by Colonel C. G. Coutant, c. 1886, *Annals of Wyoming* (winter 1942), quoted in John C. Thompson, "In Old Wyoming," *Wyoming State Tribune*, 12 December 1941. See also the *Wyoming Tribune*, 23 March 1872, copy in the Fort Laramie NHS library.

   A few days after the killing of Powell a single-trail, antelope-horn headdress of eagle feathers was left on the battlefield after a brief skirmish. Powell's nephew was given the headdress and it descended through the family to my friend Jim Schley, who has been working on a book about the headdress, trying to establish who owned it originally, and who ought to have it now. Family legend says that Indians tried to negotiate the return of the headdress in 1872, and that the man who sought it was Little Big Man. Experts say the headdress is of Cheyenne origin and belonged to a member of a warrior society.

12. Eli Ricker interview with William Garnett. Harry Young, *Hard Knocks*, 117. Charging Girl narrative, James C. Cook Papers.

13. Thomas R. Buecker, *Fort Robinson and the American West*, 4.

14. Young, *Hard Knocks*, 149ff. Other accounts can be found in Eli Ricker's interview

with William Garnett, and in the Charging Girl narrative, which quotes the messenger. A good overall account is in Buecker, *Fort Robinson and the American West.* Harry Young gets the date and several other details wrong but is otherwise amply supported by Garnett. Kicking Bear was identified as the actual or probable shooter by Garnett, by Black Elk in Raymond J. DeMallie, ed., *The Sixth Grandfather,* 154, and in the Colhoff winter count for the year 1873.

15. J. W. Dear letter of 12 February 1874 to O. N. Unthank, Western Union telegrapher at Fort Laramie, *Nebraska History* (January–March 1924).

5. *"A Sandwich Islander appears to exercise great control in the Indian councils."*

1. Donald F. Danker, ed., *Man of the Plains: Recollections of Luther North, 1856–1882* (University of Nebraska Press, 1961), 321. Frank Grouard is often mentioned in diaries, letters, memoirs, and official documents of the Indian wars period, but the principal sources for his life are Joe DeBarthe, *Life and Adventures of Frank Grouard;* John S. Gray, "Frank Grouard: Kanacka Scout or Mulatto Renegade?" *Westerners Brand Book* (October 1959); and the Eli Ricker interviews published in two volumes by the University of Nebraska Press in 2005.

2. A full issue of the *Museum of the Fur Trade Quarterly* (fall/winter 2009) is devoted to the fight at Crow Butte. When Frank Grouard arrived at the Red Cloud Agency in northwest Nebraska he entered the orbit of the military post at Camp (after 1878 Fort) Robinson. An authoritave account of the post's role in the Indian wars may be found in Thomas R. Buecker, *Fort Robinson and the American West* (Nebraska State Historical Society, 1999).

3. DeBarthe, *Life and Adventures of Frank Grouard,* 20.

4. John S. Gray depends heavily on a lengthy article by George Boyd in the *Bismarck Tribune,* 8 November 1876.

5. *Frank Leslie's Illustrated Newspaper,* October 13, 1877.

6. John Colhoff letter to Helen Blish, 7 April 1929, Mari Sandoz Papers; DeBarthe, *Life and Adventures of Frank Grouard,* 30ff.

7. D. S. Stanley to CIA, 7 April 1872, M234/R127, quoted in David Eckroth and Harold Hagen, *Baker's Battle on the Yellowstone* (Frontier Heritage Alliance, 2004), 27. Edward S. Curtis says Spotted Eagle was born in 1842; the White Bull winter count gives his birth year as 1834.

8. Transcript of He Dog interview, 24 July 1931, Hugh Scott Papers.

9. Major Eugene Baker, well known on the frontier as the commander of the troops who had massacred a band of Blackfeet on the Marias River in 1870, led one of the two surveying parties along the Yellowstone that summer—a detachment of five hundred men making its way east from Fort Ellis. A second group was proceeding west under General Stanley. Stanley Vestal, *Sitting Bull,* 131. The hands-off policy was described to Vestal, pen name of Walter S. Campbell, by elderly Hunkpapas in the 1930s.

10. U.S. Special Agent Simmons letter of 8 December 1872 from Fort Peck, Montana Territory, Office of Indian Affairs, Letters Received, NA/RG 75, quoted in Eckroth and Hagen, *Baker's Battle on the Yellowstone,* 67.

11. Vestal, *Sitting Bull,* 128.

12. "one young warrior": E. S. Topping, *Chronicles of the Yellowstone* (1883; Ross and Haines, 1968), 92. The most succinct overall account of the Baker expedition

and the fight at Arrow Creek can be found in M. John Lubetkin, "No Fighting to Be Apprehended," *Montana* (summer 2006), in which Lubetkin argues that from the acorn of this small encounter a mighty oak did grow. The fight halted the surveying effort, Lubetkin shows, creating a delay which weakened Jay Cooke's Northern Pacific Railroad Company and indirectly led to its bankruptcy a year later. That, in turn, helped precipitate the Panic of 1873, followed by six years of nationwide depression, which provided a major incentive for the Sioux War of 1876 in order to open up the goldfields in the Black Hills. Of this chain of events the Sioux of course had no clear idea. An extremely thorough account of the fight can also be found in Eckroth and Hagen, *Baker's Battle on the Yellowstone*.

The Indian version of events may be found in Vestal's two books, *Warpath*, 137ff., and *Sitting Bull*, 125ff.; and in Robert M. Utley, *The Lance and the Shield*, 106ff.

13. Captain Carlile Boyd letter of 6 September 1872, Letters Received, Military Division of the Missouri, NA/RG 393, quoted in Eckroth and Hagen, *Baker's Battle on the Yellowstone*, 67.

14. "That was the first fight": DeBarthe, *Life and Adventures of Frank Grouard*, 52.

15. Ibid.

16. Gray, "Frank Grouard: Kanacka Scout or Mulatto Renegade?"

17. DeBarthe, *Life and Adventures of Frank Grouard*, 54.

18. He Dog's family is variously identified in the pension files of Little Shield and Grant Short Bull, two of his brothers; in Scudder Mekeel's interviews with He Dog's son Joseph Eagle Hawk and his brother Grant Short Bull; and in the Colhoff winter count.

19. The splitting and resplitting of the northern Oglala is described in Eleanor Hinman's interview with He Dog, 7 July 1930, *Oglala Sources*, and in the Colhoff winter count.

20. DeBarthe, *Life and Adventures of Frank Grouard*, 181–82. Other references to Crazy Horse's daughter may be found in Richard G. Hardorff, *The Oglala Lakota Crazy Horse;* and the remarks of John Colhoff and Red Feather; Hinman, *Oglala Sources*, 9, 29, 32.

21. Raymond J. DeMallie, ed., *The Sixth Grandfather*, 207.

22. The correspondent, John F. Finerty, accompanied General Crook for the *Chicago Times*. The boy was killed in the fight at the Rosebud. John F. Finerty, *War-Path and Bivouac*, 95. There are numerous accounts of Sioux grieving for the dead. Full descriptions may be found in Clark Wissler, Field Notes; Alice Fletcher, "Ghost-Keeping"; and Edward S. Curtis, *The North American Indian* (University Press, 1908), vol. 3, pp. 99ff. For a serious modern treatment see Stephen Huffstetter, *Lakota Grieving* (St. Joseph's Indian School, 1998).

23. DeBarthe, *Life and Adventures of Frank Grouard*, 181–82. Many stories told of Crazy Horse by Grouard are confirmed by other sources, suggesting that one way or another he had learned a lot about the chief, who was the constant subject of gossip and rumor in the Indian camps. It is likely that Grouard passed these stories on to DeBarthe, who then placed Grouard himself at the scene of action as a way of lending drama to the story of the scout's life.

24. *Cheyenne Daily Leader*, 3 April 1875.

25. DeCost Smith, *Red Indian Experiences*, 42.

26. Richard E. Jensen, ed., *The Indian Interviews*, 118ff.

27. *New York Herald*, 29 May 1875, quoted in James C. Olson, *Red Cloud and the Sioux Problem*, 178.

28. Billy Garnett to Eli Ricker, Jensen, ed., *The Indian Interviews*, 2. Garnett was married seriatim to two of Nick Janis's daughters—Zuzella and Fillie—and he often came to the aid of his father-in-law.

29. Garnett ran away from his first school after a day or two, and his early enlistment papers in the 1870s were all signed with an X by his name. Exactly when he learned to read is unknown, but a number of letters survive from the 1910s and '20s in which Garnett writes fluently of the Indian wars period.

30. Eli Ricker interview with W. R. Jones, 23 January 1907, Richard E. Jensen, ed., *The Settler and Soldier Interviews*, 178.

6. *"Gold from the grass roots down."*

1. "so many inevitable causes": Lieutenant G. K. Warren, *Preliminary Report of Explorations in Nebraska and Dakota in the Years 1855–56–57* (U.S. Government Printing Office, 1875), 19ff, 52–53.

2. the first Lakota: American Horse winter count, Garrick Mallery, "Picture Writing of the American Indians," 383.

3. "a short little man": Testimony of Stella Swift Bird, granddaughter of Fast Thunder, speaking on 5 May 1969, Edward Kadlecek and Mabell Kadlecek, *To Kill an Eagle*, 145ff.

4. Army officers who stayed on after the Civil War generally reverted to previous ranks; Custer in 1874 was a lieutenant colonel, but as a courtesy he, like other officers, was addressed by his highest Civil War rank. In Custer's case that was major general.

5. "a Yanktonai known as Goose": William E. Curtis, *Chicago Inter-Ocean*, 15 August 1874, Herbert Krause and Gary D. Olson, *Prelude to Glory*.

6. The story of Goose and the wind cave can be found in Aris B. Donaldson, *St. Paul Daily Pioneer*, 29 July 1874, and William E. Curtis, *Chicago Inter-Ocean*, 30 July 1874; William E. Curtis writing as "C" in the *New York World*, 2 August 1874, all reprinted in Krause and Olson, *Prelude to Glory*, 51–52, 110, 160, 162.

7. Newspaper correspondents with Custer spelled it "wassum" or "washsum." Buechel's standard Lakota-English dictionary defines *wasun* as, "The den or hole of small animals, of snakes and bugs; any hole in the ground."

8. The surgeons: are identified in Lawrence A. Frost, ed., *With Custer in 74: James Calhoun's Diary of the Black Hill Expedition* (Brigham Young University Press, 1979). A full account can also be found in John M. Carroll and Lawrence A. Frost, eds., *Private Theodore Ewert's Diary of the Black Hills Expedition of 1874* (Consultant Resources, Inc., 1976).

9. Bloody Knife and Bear's Ears: Ben Innis, *Bloody Knife: Custer's Favorite Scout* (Smoky Water Press, 1994), passim. Bear's Ears' story can be found in Samuel Barrows, *New York Tribune*, 24 June 1874, and in William E. Curtis, *Chicago Inter-Ocean*, 29 July 1874, both included in Krause and Olson, *Prelude to Glory*.

10. Innis, *Bloody Knife*, p. 115, and William E. Curtis, *Chicago Inter-Ocean*, 18 August 1874.

11. "Do not dare to fire": James Power, *St. Paul Daily Press*, 16 August 1874.

12. Slow Bull: Curtis, *Chicago Inter-Ocean*, 18 August 1874, says One Stab was married to a daughter of Red Cloud, but Samuel Barrows, writing in the *New York Tribune*, 18 August 1874, says Slow Bull was Red Cloud's son-in-law. Krause and Olson, *Prelude to Glory*, 122, 214. James Power in the *St. Paul Daily Press*, 16 August 1874, agrees with Barrows that it was Slow Bull who had married a

daughter of Red Cloud; Aris B. Donaldson in the *St. Paul Daily Pioneer* adds that they had four children, "one at the breast." Adding to the confusion are other references to a certain Slow Bear, also married to a daughter of Red Cloud; Carrie Slow Bear was interviewed by Eleanor Hinman in 1930. Despite these similarities it does not seem likely that Slow Bull and Slow Bear were the same person.

13. "A not uncomely squaw": Barrows, *New York Tribune*, 18 August 1874, Krause and Olson, *Prelude to Glory*, 214.

14. Stabber's father: American Horse winter count; Garrick Mallery, "Picture Writing of the American Indians," 605.

   Cloud Shield winter count dates his death to 1783–1784. Lewis and Clark identified him as chief of the Shiyo (Sharp-Tailed Grouse) band of the Oglala, and records his name as War-char-par (On His Guard); the historian George Hyde believes this was probably a corruption of Wachape (Stabber). George E. Hyde, *Red Cloud's Folk*, 30. Buechel gives the spelling as *wacape* — "to stab." Were these two men named Stabber the father and grandfather of the chief met by Custer? There is no definitive evidence, but the inheritance of names was common among the Sioux, chiefs commonly inherited their status, and no Oglala would be surprised to learn that an Oglala chief named Stabber in 1874 had descended from an Oglala chief named Stabber in 1804.

15. Francis Parkman, *The Oregon Trail Journal*, 470.

16. "Send word to the Great Father": Report of a meeting with Dr. H. W. Mathews, reprinted in George P. Belden, *The White Chief* (C. F. Yent, 1872), 390ff.

17. "afraid of the whites": Barrows, *New York Tribune*, 18 August 1874, Krause and Olson, *Prelude to Glory*, 214.

18. Custer announced: Ibid.

19. Long Bear: This man is variously identified by newspaper correspondents on the expedition as Slim Bear or Long Bear. The Lakota is not given; I am guessing that it is *hanska*, a word meaning tall, long, or slim often used in Lakota names, where it is usually translated as "long." In my index of several thousand Oglala names eighteen are prefaced by the word "Long," none by the word "Slim." There are several other references to Long Bear as an active figure among the Oglala in the 1870s and after.

20. "I may as well": Ibid. The names of the respective Indians are given by Curtis.

21. Barrows, *New York Tribune*, 18 August 1874, Krause and Olson, *Prelude to Glory*, 212ff.

22. Colonel Thaddeus Stanton brought the news from the agencies to Colonel John E. Smith, commanding at Fort Laramie. On 4 August 1874 he passed on the news to the headquarters of General Sheridan and the Division of the Missouri in St. Paul. Krause and Olson, *Prelude to Glory*, 124.

23. "I could whip": Luther Heddon North, *Man of the Plains*, 187–88.

24. "their own bad faith": Custer report to the Assistant Adjutant General, Department of Dakota, 2 August 1874, reprinted in the *New York World*, 16 August 1874.

25. "the heart of the hills": "Life of Goose," Josephine Waggoner Papers.

26. Ibid.

27. William E. Curtis, *Chicago Inter-Ocean*, 27 August 1874, Krause and Olson, *Prelude to Glory*, 126–27.

28. Forsyth's report, reprinted in the *Chicago Tribune*, 27 August 1874.

29. "accept the president's terms": *Cheyenne Daily Leader*, 28 May 1875.

30. "I do not like General Custer": *New York Herald*, 27 August 1874. The Fort Laramie commander was Lieutenant Colonel Luther P. Bradley, who would be commander at Camp Robinson when Crazy Horse was killed three years later. See also James C. Olson, *Red Cloud and the Sioux Problem*, 173ff.; and Eli Ricker interview with William Garnett, Richard E. Jensen, *The Indian Interviews*, 82ff.

31. "I want you to think": Associated Press dispatch, reprinted in the *Chicago Tribune*, 27 May 1875. Grant's use of the direct form has been restored to the text.

32. The origins of the Allison commission are described in Olson, *Red Cloud and the Sioux Problem*, 177ff.

7. *"We don't want any white men here."*

1. "Northern Indians": More recently scholars have begun to call them "non-treaty Indians."

2. nineteen hundred lodges: James C. Olson, *Red Cloud and the Sioux Problem*, 203. Grouard's biographer, Joe DeBarthe, later quoted Grouard as saying that about a thousand northern Indians attended a council with Young Man Afraid. The site of the village was near the present Dayton, Wyoming, about a dozen miles west of Sheridan.

3. "I don't want to go": Joe DeBarthe, *Life and Adventures of Frank Grouard*, 84ff., also 97; Stanley Vestal, *Sitting Bull*, 133.

4. George E. Hyde, *Red Cloud's Folk*, 82; G. K. Warren, "Explorations in Nebraska," *Report of the Secretary of War*, 1858.

5. "They didn't seem to take": Caroline Frey Winne in a letter to her brother from the Sidney Barracks, 27 February 1875, Frey Family Papers. Other accounts of pipe etiquette can be found in W. P. Clark, *The Indian Sign Language*, 295, 302; Walter S. Schuyler, "Notes on Indians," quoting Frank Grouard, 20 December 1876, Walter S. Schuyler Papers; and Royal B. Hassrick, *The Sioux*, passim. An excellent account of pipe etiquette and custom can be found in the August 1931 Field Notes of Scudder Mekeel. There are scores of accounts of Indians smoking in council, and Indians formally posing for photographs were often depicted holding a long pipe or pipe bag, with its distinctive panel of beadwork and long, quill-wrapped fringes. But so far as I know there is only a single photograph of an Indian in council actually smoking—one taken by Alexander Gardner at Fort Laramie in 1868, showing Old Man Afraid of His Horses surrounded by Indians and soldiers, drawing a puff on a pipe.

6. "Don't do things hastily": Hila Gilbert, *Big Bat Pourier* (The Mills Company, 1968), 43; DeBarthe, *Life and Adventures of Frank Grouard*, 86.

7. According to Short Bull: Short Bull interview, 13 July 1930, Eleanor H. Hinman, *Oglala Sources*, 34. The following March an Oglala named Crawler was sent out from the Red Cloud Agency to remind the northern Indians of their promise, saying, "It is spring, we are waiting for you."

8. "fight me, too": DeBarthe, *Life and Adventures of Frank Grouard*, 86.

9. "We don't want": John G. Bourke, *On the Border with Crook*, 245. For their hardships and dangers run—"their lives were constantly in danger"—Louis Richard and Young Man Afraid and the men they led north were promised one hundred American horses. *Chicago Tribune*, 17 September 1875.

10. "When the tribe first": Clark Wissler, *Societies and Ceremonial Associations;* Wissler's text is a slight rewording of Richard Nines, Notes on the Dakota Indians, Pine Ridge, South Dakota, American Museum of Natural History.

11. "so dreadfully dirty": Carolyn Frey Winne is typical of white women on the frontier in two ways: initial dislike of Indians, followed by a slow deepening of understanding, tolerance, curiosity, and eventually even respect. Winne's letters, rich and numerous, are found in the Frey Family Papers. A fine general treatment is in Glenda Riley, *Women and Indians on the Frontier* (University of New Mexico Press, 1984). White male attitudes are the subject of Sherry Smith, *The View from Officers' Row* (University of Arizona Press, 1990).

12. "no better than the others": Caroline Frey Winne letters, Frey Family Papers. For Red Fly's trip to Washington see Edward B. Tuttle, *Three Years on the Plains*, 102; for Two Lance's feat see Alfred T. Andreas's *History of the State of Nebraska* (The Western Historical Company, 1882), part 4: Lincoln County; Luther Heddon North, *Man of the Plains*, 125.

13. gophers were dangerous animals: James R. Walker, *Lakota Belief and Ritual*, 169.

14. Arapaho women: Lieutenant Henry R. Lemly, "Among the Arapahoes," *Harper's Magazine* (March 1880), 500. "A peculiar and disagreeable odor pervades everything that belongs to them," Lemly wrote. The origins of the smell included "the tanning and drying of beef or buffalo, cooking, etc." Lemly was the officer who accompanied the Arapaho from the Red Cloud Agency to the Wind River Reservation in western Wyoming in October 1877.

15. "nauseous-smelling savages": Francis M. A. Roe, *Army Letters from an Officer's Wife* (D. Appleton and Co., 1909), 10.

16. "muskrat and polecat": St. George Stanley, "Recollections of the Bozeman Trail," *Colorado Miner*, 1 June 1878, reprinted in Marc H. Abrams, ed., *Crying for Scalps* (Abrams Publications, 2007), 31.

17. "I can describe it": William Hooker, *The Bullwhacker: Adventures of a Frontier Freighter* (World Book, 1924), 26.

18. "smoke and grease": Clark, *The Indian Sign Language*, 183.

19. "at a long distance": J. Lee Humfreville, *Twenty Years Among Our Savage Indians*, 80.

20. "It still carries": The Crazy Horse gift ledger was donated to the Denver Art Museum in 1987. The museum's acquisition notes include several letters by the grandson and other descendants of Wallihan, who died in 1922. During the Great Sioux War Wallihan was writing for the *Cheyenne Ledger* under the pen name of "Rapherty." We shall encounter him again in the latter chapters of this book.

21. "live on such stuff": Luther Standing Bear, *My People the Sioux*, 59. When he went to the Carlisle Indian school, Ota Kte was assigned "Luther" as his Christian name, and took his father's name for his last.

22. "Her face was swollen": John Bratt, *Trails of Yesterday*, 117ff. Bratt reports that the girl was "a trading squaw"—that is, one of the Indian women regularly sold to passing whites.

23. "yield to the seducer": John F. Finerty, *War-Path and Bivouac*, 70.

24. "a pup to a blanket": *Chicago Tribune*, 21 September 1875.

25. "was a pander": Lemly, "Among the Arapahoes," p. 494. According to Edward B. Tuttle, it was Father Pierre DeSmet who found Friday as a boy and sent him to be schooled in St. Louis. *Three Years on the Plains*, 45. Other references to the life of Friday, named for the day of the week on which he was found, are Hyde, *Red Cloud's Folk*, 122, and Henry W. Daly, *American Legion Monthly* (April 1927), reprinted in Peter Cozzens, *The Long War for the Northern Plains*, 250ff.

26. Even General Sheridan: Paul Andrew Hutton, *Phil Sheridan and His Army*, 10.

27. "The best-looking women": Josephine Waggoner, "Life of Spotted Tail," Josephine Waggoner Papers. "Statement of Carl Iron Shell, 13 May 1969," quoted in Edward Kadlecek and Mabell Kadlecek, *To Kill an Eagle*, 79.

28. "to destroy their villages": Hutton, *Phil Sheridan and His Army*, 63.

29. Mo-nah-se-tah: Custer and his wife both described this girl at length in memoirs published twenty years apart. See General George Armstrong Custer, *My Life on the Plains*, 415ff.; and Elizabeth Custer, *Following the Guidon* (University of Oklahoma, 1966), 90ff.

30. "I will never harm": Peter J. Powell, *Sweet Medicine*, vol. 1, p. 120, citing testimony of John Stands in Timber and other Cheyenne.

31. George Bent letter to George Hyde, September 1905, Colorado Historical Society. See also George Bird Grinnell, *The Fighting Cheyennes*, 62. The Oglala George Sword notes, "A man may smoke alone but if he is doing so as a ceremony he should smoke the pipe until its contents are all consumed and then he should empty the ashes into the fire so that all may be consumed. This is because if the contents of a pipe that is smoked as a ceremony are emptied on the ground someone may step on them, or spit on them, and this would make *Wakan Tanka* angry." Medicine Arrow was missing no bets. Walker, *Lakota Belief and Ritual*, 76.

32. "From another buckskin": Custer, *My Life on the Plains*, 554ff.

33. "If you are acting": George Bent to George Hyde, September 1905.

34. Other accounts can be found in the testimony of Kate Bighead, *She Watched Custer's Last Battle* (Published by the author, 1927), Thomas B. Marquis; "made the peace pipe": Charles J. Brill, *Custer, Black Kettle and the Fight on the Washita* (University of Oklahoma, 2001), especially 225ff.; and Vestal, *Warpath and Council Fire*. George Bird Grinnell says that the Cheyenne knew Medicine Arrow as Rock Forehead (Ho ho ne vi uhk tan uh), *The Fighting Cheyennes*, 307. Father Powell translates the name as Stone Forehead. In the 1920s Magpie was active in the effort to regain the Black Hills. He was interviewed by Charles J. Brill in 1930.

35. Custer, *My Life on the Plains*, 600.

36. "the beauty of youth": Elizabeth Custer, *Following the Guidon*, 95.

37. "an exceedingly comely": Custer, *My Life on the Plains*, 415.

38. "We have knocked": Myles Keogh letter to Tom Keogh, 9 May 1869, MS 3885, National Library, Dublin, Ireland, quoted in Hutton, *Phil Sheridan and His Army*, 389.

39. "They were accused": "Life of Turning Bear," Josephine Waggoner Papers.

40. Letter to President Grant of 8 March 1876, signed by seventeen Brulé chiefs, Spotted Tail Agency files, M234/R841.

41. Commissioner of Indian Affairs, Annual Report to the Secretary of the Interior, 1863.

42. "Sitting Bull said": Nelson A. Miles, "Rounding Up the Red Men," *Cosmopolitan* (June 1911), quoted in Cozzens, *The Long War for the Northern Plains*, 434.

43. "Look at me": Charles Larpenteur, *Forty Years a Fur Trader on the Upper Missouri* (University of Nebraska, 1989), 360.

8. *"The wild devils of the north."*

1. Dispatch dated 29 September 1875, *Chicago Tribune*, 9 October 1875.

2. Edgar Beecher Bronson, *Reminiscences of a Ranchman* (University of Nebraska, 1962), 239.

3. "Digest of Indian Commissioner Reports," *South Dakota Historical Collections* 29 (1958), 328. Daniels misleadingly identifies the culprits as the "Bad Face band of the Oglalas."

4. Little Big Man's parents and sister are identified in Scissons family genealogy, and in Adeline S. Gnirk, *The Saga of Ponca Land* (Gregory Times Advocate, 1979). See also undated news clip and handwritten letter by Black Horse, son of Sioux Jim and nephew of Little Big Man, 26 June 1935, both mistakenly placed in the pension file of Navajo Black Horse, C. 2307680. Black Horse was well known during the early reservation period and at various times met General Hugh Scott, Captain Charles King, and Walter Camp. The Colhoff winter count for 1908 gives Sioux Jim's name as Fishgut. "The younger son [Black Horse] became one of the famous Indian scouts, that went north in the autumn [of 1876] . . . and took part in the battle against the Cheyennes November 25, where . . . he fought against his two older brothers." Eli Ricker interview with William Garnett, 15 January 1907, Richard E. Jensen, ed., *The Indian Interviews.*

5. Eli Ricker interviews with Charles Turning Hawk, a son of Bad Wound, 19 February 1907, and with William Garnett, 15 January 1907, Jensen, ed., *The Indian Interviews.* For Red Dog's personal history and the names of his warrior sons see John Colhoff letter to George Hyde, 2 May 1949, author's possession; and agents' letters, Elmo Scott Watson Papers, Box 39.

6. Eli Ricker interview with Charles Turning Hawk.

7. *Chicago Tribune*, 3 September 1875.

8. Ibid.

9. Paul Andrew Hutton, *Phil Sheridan and His Army*, 9, 39.

10. Ulysses Grant, *Personal Memoirs* (Library of America, 1990), 27. Anson Mills, *My Story*, 32.

11. Some close associates: Red Cloud chose Red Dog and Young Man Afraid; Spotted Tail picked Two Strike and Swift Bear. The understanding of Sioux tribal politics begins with lists of names like this one; in almost every major controversy confronted by Red Cloud we find Red Dog and Young Man Afraid playing a part; the same is true of Spotted Tail, Two Strike, and Swift Bear. Over the decades of the protracted Sioux war between 1854 and 1891 the lists of chiefs and their associates for the most part change only with death; once allied, always allied. The only exception occurs in the last few months of the life of Crazy Horse, who, almost unique among Sioux chiefs, was deserted by many of his friends.

12. *Chicago Tribune*, 21 September 1875.

13. Ibid., 20 September 1875.

14. In his memoirs the freighter Harry Young remarked, "Another prominent and very bad Indian [at the Red Cloud Agency in 1873] was Red Dog. He always wore a hunting jacket made entirely of scalps that he himself had taken . . . In the back of this jacket was a woman's scalp. She in life was a white woman and a blonde. I suppose he killed and scalped her in the Minnesota massacre . . . as he took a very active part in that affair. I could have purchased that jacket at one time for about five dollars' worth of powder and lead, and wished in later days that I had done so, as today [1915] it would be worth a large sum of money." It is possible that this was the jacket which disgusted James Howard of the *Chicago Tribune;* at the same time it is unlikely Red Dog took any blond scalps in the Minnesota massacre of 1862, in which the Hunkpapas played no part. Harry Young, *Hard Knocks*, 116.

15. *Chicago Tribune*, 25 September 1875.
16. James C. Olson, *Red Cloud and the Sioux Problem*, 207.
17. Dispatch of 27 September, *Chicago Tribune*, 29 September 1875.
18. Red Cloud's son was known among whites as Jack Red Cloud; his sister Charging Girl provides his Sioux name. Charging Girl narrative, James H. Cook Papers.
19. Raymond J. Demallie, ed., *The Sixth Grandfather*, 172.
20. Olson, *Red Cloud and the Sioux Problem*, 209.
21. *Chicago Tribune*, 9 October 1875.
22. *Cheyenne Daily Leader*, 9 October 1875, reprinted from the *New York Herald*, 2 October 1875.
23. Bull Eagle was dragged from the battlefield to safety by White Bull, a fellow Miniconjou. Stanley Vestal, *Warpath*, 62.
24. William Welsh letter to Columbus Delano, Secretary of the Interior, 8 July 1872. Copy in author's possession.
25. *Chicago Tribune*, 1 October 1875.
26. Although unannounced, President Grant's policy is clear. It is best described by John S. Gray in *Centennial Campaign*, 23ff.

9. *"This whole business was exceedingly distasteful to me."*

1. "a misunderstanding with": The words are from John F. Finerty of the *Chicago Times*, who got to know Grouard well on General Crook's Big Horn and Yellowstone Expedition in the summer of 1876. His account of Grouard's life is correct in the main, doubtful in some details, but generally in an interesting way. *War-Path and Bivouac*, 64.
2. Joe DeBarthe, *Life and Adventures of Frank Grouard*, 86–87. Grouard's marriage to Sally is reported in a John Colhoff letter to Helen Blish, 7 April 1929, "From Eleanor's notebook," Mari Sandoz Papers. Details of the killing by Rowland may be found in a voucher issued by the agent, J. J. Saville, to Billy Garnett, for feeding eighty-five Sioux hired to protect the agency, M234/R720; and in a memorandum of 27 November 1875, signed by Cheyenne chiefs who agreed to settle it, Rowland, Saville, and two others; Office of Indian Affairs, Letters Received, Red Cloud Agency, M234/R720. See also Frank Goings letter to James Cook, 18 August 1934, James C. Cook Papers; and George E. Hyde, *Red Cloud's Folk*, 214. For the month of December 1875 Grouard was paid $75.25 as a "laborer," Office of Indian Affairs, Letters Received, Red Cloud Agency, M234/R720.
3. Charles M. Robinson III, ed., *The Diaries*, vol. 1, p. 209.
4. DeBarthe, *Life and Adventures of Frank Grouard*, 88.
5. George Colhoff told Eli Ricker in 1906 that both scouts told him the same thing. Richard E. Jensen, ed., *The Soldier and Settler Interviews*, 215.
6. Martin F. Schmitt, *General George Crook*, 87. Crook died before he finished telling the story of his life; the surviving manuscript, discovered by its editor in 1942, stops on 18 June 1876, the day after Crook's fight against Crazy Horse at the Rosebud in Montana.
7. Ibid., 84ff.
8. James Greer to Lieutenant L. W. V. Kennon, Crook's aide-de-camp in the 1880s. Kennon kept a diary in which he recorded many of Crook's anecdotes and opinions; if Crook had been a better-known figure Kennon's lively diary would

have long since gone into print. The letter is quoted by Martin Schmitt in his introduction to Crook's autobiography, ibid., xxii. The diary can be found among Crook's papers at the Carlisle Barracks.

9. Schenk was interviewed by a reporter for the *Washington Chronicle* in 1883 and is quoted in ibid.

10. Azor Nickerson, "Major General George Crook and the Indians," 32, copy in the Walter S. Schuyler Papers.

11. Schmitt, ed., *General George Crook*, 5.

12. Ibid., 23–24.

13. The diagnosis was erysipelas, a bacterial infection of the skin and subcutaneous fat. Crook became addicted to the morphine he took for pain. "It was some time before I could sleep well without it." Ibid., 32.

14. Ibid., 70–71.

15. Alfred Kroeber, *Handbook of the Indians of California* (Dover, 1976), 73–74. Kroeber spells the God's name as Wohpekumeu. Crook's account of Indian beliefs and stories is found in Schmitt, ed., *General George Crook*, 68ff.

16. Ibid., 40–41. Rattlesnake venom attacks the blood or the brain, and sometimes both. What Crook suffered was an infection, not the equivalent of a rattlesnake bite.

17. Ibid., 47.

18. Ibid., 52.

19. Ibid., 68. An account of the military careers of the Garnett cousins can be found in Matthew W. Burton, *The River of Blood*. While Crook was pursuing the Yakima Indians Garnett's wife and child both died suddenly of a fever at Fort Simcoe; Garnett took their bodies east for burial in Brooklyn, New York's Greenwood Cemetery, and never returned to California. He resigned his commission at the outset of the Civil War, joined the Confederate Army, and was killed at Corrick's Ford in 1861.

20. Schmitt, ed., *General George Crook*, 62.

21. Ibid., 64.

22. Ibid., 87.

23. Robinson, ed., *The Diaries*, vol. 1, p. 207.

24. These quotes may be found in ibid., 213, 177, 176.

25. Diary entry for 13 March 1876, ibid., 243.

26. Ibid., 248.

10. *"I knew this village by the horses."*

1. Raymond J. DeMallie, ed., *The Sixth Grandfather*, 155ff.

2. These events, sadly typical of the violent life of the plains, are unusual only in being fully recorded. The account given here comes from ibid., 164ff.; Helen H. Blish, *A Pictographic History of the Oglala Sioux*, 396–98; and the Colhoff winter count entry for the year 1875. Colhoff says the dead Loafers included Last Elk, Owl Hoop, and Kills in Timber. Amos Bad Heart Bull recorded their names as Not Afraid of the Enemy (Tóka Kapi Pesni), Black Moccasin (Tahanpe Sapa), Takes the Gun Away (Maza Wakan Wicaki; note the word for gun—maza wakan, mysterious or powerful iron); Bear Hoop (Mato Cankleska); Kills in Timber (Canowica Kte); High Eagle (Wanbli Wakatinya); and Last Dog (Sunka Chakela). Colhoff reports that Young Iron lived into old age on the Pine Ridge Reservation. The Crow version of this story has been recorded in great detail by

Mike Cowdrey, who included a copy in a letter to the author, 2 October 2009. Cowdrey identifies the dismembered Crow as Plain Magpie.

3. Crook's Powder River expedition of March 1876 is recorded in several places, including Charles M. Robinson III, ed., *The Diaries*, vol. 1; John G. Bourke, *On the Border with Crook*, 256ff.; Joe DeBarthe, *Life and Adventures of Frank Grouard*, 88ff.; J. W. Vaughn, *The Reynolds Campaign on Powder River* (University of Oklahoma, 1961); and Robert Strahorn, dispatches for the *Denver Rocky Mountain News* and other newspapers, reprinted in Peter Cozzens, *The Long War for the Northern Plains*, 200ff. A standard account of the 1876 campaigns may also be found in Paul Hedren, *Fort Laramie and the Great Sioux War* (University of Oklahoma, 1998).

4. Robinson, ed., *The Diaries*, vol. 1, pp. 231–32; DeBarthe, *Life and Adventures of Frank Grouard*, 89–90.

5. The Bourke and Grouard accounts are in frequent conflict about the names of creeks and the camping spots of Crook's column. A close study of both with frequent reference to DeLorme's *Montana Atlas and Gazetteer*, which maps the terrain at four miles to the inch, suggests that Grouard was right when he remembered that he followed Hanging Woman Creek up to the headwaters of Otter, not Pumpkin Creek, as claimed by Bourke, which joins the Tongue much further down and runs north-south, not east-west.

6. Strahorn, *Rocky Mountain News*, 7 April 1876, dispatch datelined 18 March in camp on the Powder River, reprinted in Cozzens, *The Long War for the Northern Plains*, 216.

7. Colonel J. J. Reynolds, 3rd Cavalry, to Headquarters, Department of the Platte, 24 February 1877. After the battle Reynolds was formally charged by General Crook for numerous failures, leading to a full-scale court-martial. Copy provided to the author by Jack McDermott. Reynolds was convicted but soon pardoned and allowed to resign by President Grant, who had been his classmate at West Point. DeBarthe, *Life and Adventures of Frank Grouard*, 95ff.

8. DeBarthe, *Life and Adventures of Frank Grouard*, 97.

11. *"He is no good and should be killed."*

1. "The soldiers are right here!": Thomas B. Marquis, trans., *Wooden Leg*, 164.

2. According to He Dog: Helen H. Blish, *A Pictographic History of the Oglala Sioux*, 391–92.

3. "It is spring": Red Feather interview, 8 July 1930, Eleanor H. Hinman, *Oglala Sources*, 25. Bourke in his diary confirms that two lodges of Indians "from Red Cloud Agency . . . had come in that morning to trade." Charles M. Robinson III, ed., *The Diaries*, vol. 1, p. 255.

4. "Two Moons had": Thomas B. Marquis, trans., *Wooden Leg*, 164ff.

5. only one Indian: The dead Cheyenne was identified by George Bent in a letter to George Hyde, 18 April 1914, Beinecke Library, Yale University, cited in J. J. Vaughn, *The Reynolds Campaign on Powder River* (University of Oklahoma, 1961), 129. The Cheyenne Black Eagle told George Bird Grinnell that during the fight he was told two Indians had been killed—a Cheyenne and a Sioux. Amos Bad Heart Bull, a nephew of He Dog, drew a large picture of the battle in which he located the body of only one dead Indian—the one whose body was found on the shoulder overlooking the camp. Wooden Leg reports that two Indians were wounded in the fighting as well. Grinnell, Notebook 347, Braun Research

Library, Southwest Museum, Los Angeles, cited in Jerome A. Greene, *Lakota and Cheyenne*, 10. Lieutenant William Philo Clark recorded that "one Sioux and one squaw" were killed in the fight; it is possible that she had died by the time he began to question Indians at the Red Cloud Agency in the summer of 1877; Clark, "Sioux War Report," 14 September 1877, Department of the Platte, Letters Received.

6. "I can never": Marquis, trans., *Wooden Leg*, 172.
7. White Bull, Box 105, Notebooks 5 and 8, Walter S. Campbell Collection, University of Oklahoma, quoted in Robert M. Utley, *The Lance and the Shield*, 130. Grouard's presence at the fight was the news of the plains, and several Indians reported his shouting at the outset of a fight. For the belief of some whites that Grouard was warning, not challenging or taunting, the Indians, see George Boyd, *Bismarck Tribune*, 8 November 1876, quoted in John S. Gray, "Frank Grouard: Kanaka Scout or Mulatto Renegade?" *Westerners Brand Book* (October 1959).
8. Robinson, ed., *The Diaries*, vol. 1, p. 254.
9. Ibid.; in transferring his diary entry into his book, *On the Border with Crook*, John G. Bourke says the victim was "cut limb from limb," 279.
10. Joe DeBarthe, *Life and Adventures of Frank Grouard*, 104.
11. Bourke, *On the Border with Crook*, 278.
12. Strahorn, *Rocky Mountain News*, 7 April 1876, reprinted in Peter Cozzens, *The Long War for the Northern Plains*, 217ff.
13. Caroline Frey Winne to Samuel Ludlow Frey, 16 April 1876, Frey Family Papers.
14. Robinson, ed., *The Diaries*, vol. 1, p. 257.
15. P. H. Sheridan, *Personal Memoirs*, vol. 1, p. 166.
16. Ibid., 177, 180.
17. Paul Andrew Hutton, *Phil Sheridan and His Army*, 2.
18. Shelby Foote, *The Civil War* (Random House, 1974), vol. 3, p. 244.
19. Rutherford B. Hayes, *Diary and Letters* Web site of the Rutherford B. Hayes Presidential Center, vol. 5, pp. 463–64, posted on the Internet by the Hayes Presidential Center in Fremont, Ohio.
20. Martin F. Schmitt, ed., *General George Crook*, 82.
21. Foote, *The Civil War*, vol. 3, p. 554.
22. Sheridan, *Personal Memoirs*, vol. 2, pp. 28–29. Something of Sheridan's character is revealed here too; in his memoirs he reports writing to Grant "the dispatch announcing we had sent Early's army whirling up the valley." In fact he was borrowing the phrase from his chief of staff, who got into all the newspapers at the time with his report, "We have just sent them whirling through Winchester." Sheridan's words at the time were more prosaic, saying that "after a most stubborn and sanguinary engagement . . . [we] completely defeated him." Civil War generals were mainly proud as peacocks, Sheridan as openly as any, Crook silently within. See Foote, *The Civil War*, vol. 3, p. 554.
23. Schmitt, ed., *General George Crook*, 127.
24. Ibid., 131.
25. Foote, *The Civil War*, vol. 3, p. 557.
26. Ibid., 540.
27. Schmitt, ed., *General George Crook*, 133.
28. Foote, *The Civil War*, vol. 3, p. 570.
29. Schmitt, ed., *General George Crook*, 134.

30. An account of the origin of Read's poem can be found in John Fleischman, "The Object at Hand," *Smithsonian* (November 1996). The poem itself has been often reprinted, and can be found on the Internet.

31. Sheridan, *Personal Memoirs*, vol. 2, p. 35. "In consequence of the enemy's being so well protected from a direct assault, I resolved . . . to use again a turning column against his left, as had been done on the 19th at Opequon [Winchester]." Well, yes, maybe; Sheridan was in command; it was his decision that determined what was done. But all the men who had been present on the night in question understood that putting things this way was Sheridan's way of grabbing the credit for himself—for both battles. The memoirs were not published until 1888, so the full flower of Crook's anger waited until then. But from the beginning he knew he was being pushed into the background.

12. *"Crook was bristling for a fight."*

1. John F. Finerty, *War-Path and Bivouac*, 6. Finerty was the only correspondent to write a book about the campaign.

2. Ibid., 69–70.

3. John G. Bourke, *On the Border with Crook*, 288.

4. Charles M. Robinson III, ed., *The Diaries*, 272ff.

5. Martin F. Schmitt, ed., *General George Crook*, 189ff.

6. Bourke, *On the Border with Crook*, 296.

7. Hastings letter to Commissioner of Indian Affairs John Q. Smith, 24 January 1876, Office of Indian Affairs, Letters Received, Red Cloud Agency, M234/R720.

8. Eli Ricker interview with William Garnett, Richard E. Jensen, ed., *The Indian Interviews*.

9. Jordan letter to General Luther Bradley at Fort Laramie, 24 April 1876, Secretary of the Interior, Indian Division, Letters Received, M825/R10.

10. Cutting of rations and the hunger that followed was a principal cause of the so-called ghost dance outbreak of 1890–91. Once the buffalo were gone, hunger on the reservations sometimes ended in outright starvation; deaths especially among the elderly in remote cabins at Pine Ridge were reported regularly through the 1930s.

11. Hastings letter to CIA, 5 June 1876, Office of Indian Affairs, Letters Received, Red Cloud Agency, M234/R720.

12. Raymond J. DeMallie, ed., *The Sixth Grandfather*, 171; Eli Ricker interview with William Garnett, 15 January 1907, Jensen, ed., *The Indian Interviews*. Jack Red Cloud's Sioux name is found in the Charging Girl narrative, James H. Cook Papers.

13. Robinson, ed., *The Diaries*, vol. 1, p. 290. See also Paul L. Hedren, *Fort Laramie and the Great Sioux War*, 100, and DeMallie, ed., *The Sixth Grandfather*, 170.

14. "Expedition Excerpts," Robert Strahorn writing as Alter Ego, *Cheyenne Daily Leader*, 9 April 1876. This passage ended a paragraph on Grouard lifted verbatim by John F. Finerty for use in *War-Path and Bivouac*, 64.

15. Joe DeBarthe, *Life and Adventures of Frank Grouard*, 109.

16. Finerty, *War-Path and Bivouac*, 68. Bourke in his diary suggests that the speech maker was Good Heart.

17. "Major General George Crook and the Indians," Azor Nickerson, copy in the Walter S. Schuyler Papers, 24. Robinson, ed., *The Diaries*, vol. 1, p. 315.

18. Robinson, ed., *The Diaries*, vol. 1, pp. 274, 365. Some observers thought a

rawhide shield held at the right angle could even deflect a lead musket ball, especially if some thrifty opponent had reduced the charge to save powder.

19. Ibid., 294–95. Bourke gives a compressed version of the visit in *On the Border with Crook*, 292.

20. Richard Nines interview with Woman Dress, 16 February 1912, American Museum of Natural History, quoted in slightly different form in Clark Wissler, *Societies and Ceremonial Associations*, 95. See also Robinson, ed., *The Diaries*, vol. 2, pp. 52–53.

21. Robinson, ed., *The Diaries*, vol. 2, p. 53. Later Yellow Grass changed his name to Long Hair, claiming to be in spiritual communion with the spirit of Custer. Several reports of this man were received by the officer commanding at the Cheyenne River Agency on the Missouri. Fool Bear and Important Man to Colonel W. H. Wood, 11th Infantry, at the Cheyenne River Agency, Intelligence Report, 24 January 1877; Eagle Shield to Colonel W. H. Wood, 11th Infantry, at the Cheyenne River Agency, Intelligence Report, 16 February 1877, both Sioux War files.

22. Beginning in the early 1870s the noted Yale paleontologist O. C. Marsh enlisted the help of Red Cloud on bone-hunting expeditions in Nebraska. See Mark Jaffe, *The Gilded Dinosaur* (Crown, 2000).

23. Walter S. Schuyler, "Notes on Indians," 20 December 1876, Walter S. Schuyler Papers.

13. *"I give you these because they have no ears."*

1. John G. Bourke, *On the Border with Crook*, 296; Charles M. Robinson III, ed., *The Diaries*, vol. 1, p. 305. Little Hawk (born c. 1848) gave an account to George Bird Grinnell in 1908; it is found among the Grinnell Papers and also in Jerome A. Greene, *Lakota and Cheyenne*, 21ff.

2. One Bull, a nephew of Sitting Bull, described the meeting of the chiefs and Sitting Bull's dream to Walter Campbell (Stanley Vestal) about 1930; the latter's notes can be found in the Walter S. Campbell Papers and are summarized in Stanley Vestal, *Sitting Bull*, 148, and Robert M. Utley, *The Lance and the Shield*, 136.

3. Information from White Bull and One Bull to Walter Campbell, Walter S. Campbell Papers, summarized in Vestal, *Sitting Bull*, 149–51, and in Utley, *The Lance and the Shield*, 137–38.

4. Little Hawk account, Greene, *Lakota and Cheyenne*, 21ff.

5. Thomas B. Marquis, trans., *Wooden Leg*, 198. See also Utley, *The Lance and the Shield*, 140, and Raymond J. DeMallie, ed., *The Sixth Grandfather*, 172ff.

6. The numbers of fighting men given here can be found in John S. Gray, *Centennial Campaign*, 120, Charles A. Eastman, *Indian Heroes and Great Chieftains*, 43, and Stanley Vestal, *Warpath*, 187.

7. Helen H. Blish, *A Pictographic History of the Oglala Sioux*, 39. Discussion of the dances can be found in Clark Wissler, *Societies and Ceremonial Associations*, 82ff.

8. The first translation is from G. H. Pond, the second from Alice Fletcher. Frances Densmore, *Teton Sioux Music*, 205–06.

9. The literature on the subject of Sioux religious thinking is truly large, but a good place to begin is the work of James Walker, a medical doctor who spent two decades on the Pine Ridge Reservation beginning in the 1890s. The major work

published in his lifetime is *The Sun Dance and Other Ceremonies of the Oglala Division of the Teton Dakota*, Anthropological Papers of the American Museum of Natural History, published in 1917. Also important are Walker's posthumous collection of materials edited by Raymond J. DeMallie and Elaine Jahner, *Lakota Belief and Ritual; Sioux Indian Religion* (University of Nebraska, 1980), edited by DeMallie and Douglas R. Parks; two books by Joseph Epes Brown, *The Sacred Pipe: Black Elk's Account of the Seven Rites of the Oglala Sioux* (University of Oklahoma Press, 1953), and *Animals of the Soul: Sacred Animals of the Oglala Sioux* (Element, 1992), and Frances Densmore's *Teton Sioux Music*.

10. A detailed drawing of White Bull in battle on the Rosebud, complete with *wotawe*, can be found in Joseph White Bull, *Lakota Warrior* (University of Nebraska, 1968), translated and edited by James H. Howard, plate 13 and pp. 48–49. In the drawing he shows himself carrying a carbine; further details are recorded in Vestal, *Warpath*, 186. In this account White Bull says he was armed with a seventeen-shot repeating rifle, probably a Henry, but his own drawing clearly depicts a carbine.

11. William K. Powers reports that another name for Chips was Tahunska (His Leggins), *Yuwipi*, 90. Chips told Eli Ricker that he was also known as Encouraging Bear.

12. Robert H. Ruby, *The Oglala Sioux: Warriors in Transition* (Vantage Press, 1955), 52. Ruby was the agency doctor at Pine Ridge in the early 1950s, when the name and influence of Horn Chips were still strong. Medicine men of that period considered him to have been the founder of *yuwipi* medicine, and they told Ruby that it was Horn Chips who had first used the procedure for a vision quest—*hanbleceya*—which became standard. William Powers, who was often at Pine Ridge and knew many of the old-time medicine men during the same period, thinks Ruby's informant was George Plenty Wolf.

    A full account of a vision quest supervised by Horn Chips may be found in Royal B. Hassrick, *The Sioux*, 272ff. The event is undated but presumably occurred during the reservation period (after 1878) as Horn Chips directed the supplicant, Black Horse, to the top of Eagle Nest Butte, a frequent fasting site a few miles south of Wanblee on the Pine Ridge Reservation.

13. He Dog describes the whistle, the feather, and the rock worn under Crazy Horse's left arm. Red Feather confirms the stone, adding the detail that it was white. Eleanor H. Hinman, *Oglala Sources*, 12–13. There is an extensive discussion of sacred stones and the songs associated with them in Densmore, *Teton Sioux Music*, 205ff.

14. Luther Standing Bear, *Land of the Spotted Eagle*, 208.

15. Not to be confused with He Dog's brother of the same name. The Brulé Short Bull was a leading figure in the ghost dance episode which ended with the fight at Wounded Knee in 1890. Walker arrived at Pine Ridge in 1896. Walker, *Lakota Belief and Ritual*, xiii, 47–48.

16. Peter Bordeaux was a nephew of Susan Bordeaux Bettelyoun and of Louis Bordeaux, one of the interpreters who were deeply involved in events leading up to the death of Crazy Horse and were present the night he was killed. Charles Fire Thunder (1890–1974) was the son of a leading Oglala who had taken part in the Horse Creek fight and the Bozeman War and was later an important figure in the early reservation period. The elder Fire Thunder (1849–1937) was a member of Big Road's Oyukhpe band, and was a friend of Crazy Horse. Much of what

these and other informants of their generation had to say about Crazy Horse is confirmed by contemporary accounts, which argues that their other claims also should be considered seriously. Edward Kadlecek and Mabell Kadlecek, *To Kill An Eagle*, 79, 89.

17. Walter Camp interview with Horn Chips, c. 11 July 1910, quoted in Richard G. Hardorff, ed., *The Surrender and Death of Crazy Horse*, 89. Eli Ricker interview with Horn Chips, 14 February 1907, Richard E. Jensen, ed., *The Indian Interviews*, 273ff.

18. Eagle Elk interview, 27 November 1944, John Neihardt Papers, no. 3716.

19. Clark Wissler, Field Notes, 197. The same summer Thunder Bear told Wissler he also had the power to split storms. In 1974 the writer and artist Thomas E. Mails said he was a witness when the medicine man and thunder dreamer Fools Crow split a storm threatening the success of a fair on the Rosebud reservation. Mails, *Fools Crow*, 2–3. See also Walker, *Lakota Belief and Ritual* (University of Nebraska, 1980), 153–54.

14. *"I found it a more serious engagement than I thought."*

1. John F. Finerty, *War-Path and Bivouac*, 55. The best modern account of the battle of the Rosebud was for many years J. W. Vaughn, *With Crook at the Rosebud* (Stackpole Books, 1956). Much additional information may be found in John D. McDermott, *General George Crook's 1876 Campaigns: A Report Prepared for the American Battlefield Protection Program* (Frontier Heritage Alliance, 2000).

2. Lieutenant James E. H. Foster, 3rd Cavalry, *Chicago Tribune*, 5 July 1876, reprinted in Peter Cozzens, *The Long War for the Northern Plains*, 265ff. According to Bourke, Foster was also an artist and hoped to sell his sketches to *Harper's Weekly*. Charles M. Robinson III, ed., *The Diaries*, vol. 1, p. 308.

3. Wayne R. Kime, ed., *The Powder River Expedition Journals of Colonel Richard Irving Dodge* (University of Oklahoma Press, 1997).

4. Luther Heddon North, *Man of the Plains*, 207.

5. Finerty, *War-Path and Bivouac*, 80. See also John G. Bourke, *On the Border with Crook*, 310.

6. Anson Mills relates that Crook was playing cards; Bourke reports that he was with him near the spring when the first shots were heard. Anson Mills, *My Story*, 405. Bourke, *On the Border with Crook*, 314.

7. Joe DeBarthe, *Life and Adventures of Frank Grouard*, 117.

8. Official Report of Captain A. S. Burt, 9th Infantry, 20 June 1876, reprinted in Vaughn, *With Crook at the Rosebud*, 225.

9. Henry thought he owed his life to the seventeen-year-old son of Washakie, who was taking part in his first battle. *Harper's Weekly*, 7 July 1895.

10. Thomas B. Marquis, trans., *Wooden Leg*, 200.

11. Finerty, *War-Path and Bivouac*, 85.

12. Robinson, ed., *The Diaries*, vol. 1, p. 326.

13. Finerty, *War-Path and Bivouac*, 86–87; Robinson, ed., *The Diaries*, vol. 1, pp. 326–27.

14. Vaughn, *With Crook at the Rosebud*, 63.

15. Finerty, *War-Path and Bivouac*, 90–91.

16. He meant, of course, that he was sure he was near the village—he *almost* had it, he was *about* to have it. But there was no village there. Anson Mills, *My Story*, 408.

17. Ibid., 409.
18. Richard E. Jensen, ed., *The Soldier and Settler Interviews*, 267. Crook confirms Pourier's story with two brief remarks in his official report of 20 June 1876, saying he had been convinced the hostiles had the canyon "well covered. Our Indians refusing to go into it saying it would be certain death . . . to go down the canyon to the supposed location of the village." Quoted in Vaughn, *With Crook at the Rosebud*, 216. Pourier told Ricker that Crook was also persuaded to drop his plan because his men had run short of ammunition, a claim supported by Grouard. The latter's account of Mills's venture down the canyon is confusing; it seems evident that DeBarthe did not grasp the sequence of events. DeBarthe, *Life and Adventures of Frank Grouard*, 116–22.
19. Mills, *My Story*, 408.
20. Robinson, ed., *The Diaries*, vol. 1, p. 328.
21. Mills, *My Story*, 409.
22. Daniel Pearson, "Military Notes, 1876," *U.S. Cavalry Journal* (September 1899), quoted in Vaughn, *With Crook at the Rosebud*, 81–82.
23. Finerty, *War-Path and Bivouac*, 96. Bourke quotation from Robinson, ed., *The Diaries*, vol. 1, p. 330.
24. Arnold's story of the campaign can be found in Josephine Waggoner, "Rekindling Campfires," an account in pencil of the life of Ben Arnold, South Dakota Historical Society, Pierre, South Dakota. Waggoner's manuscript was the basis, inadequately acknowledged, for Lewis Crawford's book of the same name, first published in 1926. It has been reissued with a foreword by Paul Hedren as *The Exploits of Ben Arnold* (University of Oklahoma Press, 1999).
25. Crook to Sheridan, 19 June 1876, quoted in Robinson, ed., *The Diaries*, vol. 1, p. 335.

15. *"I am in constant dread of an attack."*

1. Charles M. Robinson III, ed., *The Diaries*, vol. 1, 339ff.
2. John F. Finerty, *War-Path and Bivouac*, 107–11.
3. Crook's reaction is found in ibid., 129. Finerty misdates the arrival of Sheridan's message as having come with news of the Custer fight on 10 July. Bourke's diary makes clear that it was awaiting Crook in camp on 4 July. The text of Sheridan's message comes from Robinson, ed., *The Diaries*, vol. 1, p. 354.
4. Robinson, ed., *The Diaries*, vol. 1, p. 356.
5. Josephine Waggoner, "Rekindling Campfires," South Dakota Historical Society, Pierre, South Dakota.
6. Thomas Tobey, handwritten diary, Box 3, Folder 98, WAMSS S-1354, Beinecke Library, Yale University; Calhoun's Appointment, Commissions, and Personal File, 569 ACP 1875, National Archives.
7. Tobey diary. Bourke's diary positively identifies Arnold as one of those who brought the news.
8. Robinson, ed., *The Diaries*, vol. 1, pp. 360ff.
9. Ibid., 361. The numbers cited by Bourke are wrong but the account of the fight—Custer wiped out, Reno battered but alive—is roughly correct.
10. John G. Bourke, *On the Border with Crook*, 334.
11. Robinson, ed., *The Diaries*, vol. 1, p. 368.
12. Davenport's dispatch in the *New York Herald* of 6 July 1876 has been reprinted in

Jerome A. Greene, *Battles and Skirmishes of the Great Sioux War*, 26ff. See also Robinson, ed., *The Diaries*, vol. 1, pp. 381–82.

13. Josephine Waggoner, "Rekindling Campfires." Crook was explaining to Arnold why he didn't send out a detachment to find the Indians who had killed a teamster near Laramie that spring.

14. Robinson, ed., *The Diaries*, vol. 1, pp. 381–82.

15. Charles King, *Campaigning with Crook* (Harper and Brothers, 1890), 158.

16. Ibid., 58.

17. Robinson, ed., *The Diaries*, vol. 2, pp. 46, 75.

18. Ibid., 52.

19. Ibid., 83. Bourke does not include this remark in his later book, *On the Border with Crook*.

20. King, *Campaigning with Crook*, 87.

21. Robinson, ed., vol. 2, p. 72; King, *Campaigning with Crook*, 121. I am indebted to Mark Nelson for copies of contemporary newspaper articles and other materials he has collected for a projected biography of Clark.

22. Robinson, ed., vol. 2, p. 84; Thomas Burrowes, Appointments, Commissions, and Personal File, 681 ACP 1872, National Archives.

23. Robinson, ed., *The Diaries*, vol. 2, p. 89.

24. Ibid., 57.

25. Finerty, *War-Path and Bivouac*, 182–83.

16. *"General Crook ought to be hung."*

1. Raymond J. DeMallie, ed., *The Sixth Grandfather*, 184.

2. The Lakota name for the Moreau River in South Dakota. Lakota names for natural features can be found in Eugene Buechel's Lakota-English dictionary and in Virginia Driving Hawk Sneve, *The Dakota's Heritage* (Brevet Press, 1973), an invaluable compendium of place-names.

3. Stanley Vestal, *Warpath*, 206ff. It is possible that Dog Goes is an alternate name or a variant translation for some better-known Oglala.

4. Charles M. Robinson, ed., *The Diaries*, vol. 2, p. 93.

5. Interviews with Eagle Shield, Swollen Face (Ite Po), and Red Horse, Colonel W. H. Wood letters to AAG, Department of Dakota, 19, 21, and 27 February 1877, Sioux War files. Colonel Wood, in command of the Cheyenne River Agency on the Missouri, filed a number of detailed intelligence reports based on conversations with surrendered hostiles during the months following the Custer fight. Together these dispatches offer one of the best accounts of Indian thinking in the last phase of the Sioux War.

6. Oliver C. C. Pollock, "With the Third Cavalry in 1876," reprinted in Jerome A. Greene, *Indian War Veterans: Memories of Army Life and Campaigns in the West, 1864–1898* (Savas Beatie, 2007), 103ff.

7. Walter S. Schuyler letter to his father, 1 November 1876, Walter S. Schuyler Papers.

8. David Mears, "Campaigning Against Crazy Horse," NSHS Proceedings No. 15 (1907), reprinted in Peter Cozzens, *The Long War for the Northern Plains*, 465.

9. Robinson, ed., *The Diaries*, vol. 2, pp. 86ff. See also John G. Bourke, *On the Border with Crook*, 362ff., and John F. Finerty, *War-Path and Bivouac*, 182ff. The best overall account of this episode is Jerome Greene, *Slim Buttes, An Episode of the Great Sioux War* (University of Oklahoma, 1982).

10. Letter of Samuel Sumner to King, 4 September 1918, James H. Cook Papers.

11. John S. Gray, *Centennial Campaign*, 245; Charles M. Robinson III, *General Crook and the Western Frontier*, 194.

12. "Mills on Slim Buttes," Walter Camp, 24 January 1914, in the Robert Willison Collection, Denver Public Library. Quoted in Greene, *Slim Buttes*, 54.

13. Ibid., 54. See also Joe DeBarthe, *Life and Adventures of Frank Grouard*, 153.

14. James H. Cook, undated note in James H. Cook papers, Box 92.

15. "Proceedings of an Army Retiring Board . . . 25 April 1887," James Kennington personal file, 242 ACP 1871, National Archives.

16. James H. Cook, undated note in James C. Cook Papers.

17. DeBarthe, *Life and Adventures of Frank Grouard*, 157. All accounts of the fight at Slim Buttes make mention of this incident. See also Greene, *Slim Buttes*, 75; Robinson, ed., *The Diaries*, vol. 2, pp. 109ff.; Charles King, *Campaigning with Crook* (Harper and Brothers, 1890), 111ff.

18. In 1927, the year before he died, Pourier was asked by a newspaper reporter at his home near Manderson, South Dakota, if he had ever killed and scalped an Indian in combat: " 'Only once,' he said, 'and I do thank god for it. I killed that red devil and I skelped him, too, right on the spot.' Turning to his son he added: 'Pete, that Injun was some kin to your ma, second cousin or something.' " L. A. Lincoln, "Pourier Tells," *Rocky Mountain News*, 13 November 1927, copy in John Hunton Collection, American Heritage Center, University of Wyoming, Laramie. According to William Garnett, the Indian killed by Pourier was Iron Shield. William Garnett letter to Valentine McGillycuddy, 21 April 1926.

19. Robinson, ed., *The Diaries*, vol. 2, p. 110.

20. Jesse Brown and A. M. Willard, *The Black Hills Trails* (Rapid City Journal Company, 1924), 234, cited in Greene, *Slim Buttes*, 168.

21. It seems likely that this man was the American Horse who was a son of old Smoke, brother of Charging Bear, who was captured at Slim Buttes and soon enlisted as a scout with Crook's command. Wallace Amiotte, letter to George Hyde, 1 March 1951, author's collection.

22. King, *Campaigning with Crook*, 131.

23. Captain Andrew S. Burt, *Cincinnati Commercial*, 17 September 1876, quoted in Greene, *Slim Buttes*, 72.

24. Greene, *Slim Buttes*, 70ff. and footnotes.

25. The text of both passes was printed in the *New York Tribune*, 18 September 1876, and is quoted in ibid., 73.

26. King, *Campaigning with Crook*, 126.

27. General Hugh Scott letter, National Archives, quoted by J. W. Vaughn, *With Crook at the Rosebud* (Stackpole Books, 1956), p. 40.

28. Edward S. Curtis, *North American Indian* (University Press, 1908), vol. 3, p. 21.

29. King, *Campaigning with Crook*, 104; Walter S. Schuyler letter to his father, 1 November 1876, Walter S. Schuyler Papers.

30. Finerty, *War-Path and Bivouac*, 191.

31. King, *Campaigning with Crook*, 108.

32. Captain Andrew Burt, *Cincinnati Commercial*, 17 September 1876, quoted in Greene, *Slim Buttes*, 172.

33. Private Alfred McMackin, *Ellis County Star*, 12 October 1876, quoted in Robinson, *General Crook and the Western Frontier*, 195.

34. Daniel C. Pearson, "Military Notes," *U.S. Cavalry Association Journal* (September 1899), reprinted in Cozzens, *The Long War for the Northern Plains*, 236ff.

35. King, *Campaigning with Crook*, 159. A fuller version of the song can be found in Robinson, *General Crook and the Western Frontier*, 195.
36. Sheridan to Crook, 11 September 1876, Office of the Adjutant General, Letters Received, M666/R271.
37. *New York Times*, 11 October 1876.
38. Dispatch from Custer City in the Black Hills, dated 22 September and published in the *New York Times*, 12 October 1876, quoted in Greene, *Slim Buttes*, 112.
39. Caroline Frey Winne letter, 29 October 1876, Frey Family Papers.

17. *"You won't get anything to eat! You won't get anything to eat!"*

1. Leander P. Richardson, "A Trip to the Black Hills," *Scribner's Monthly* (April 1877).
2. Garnett was married twice again: to Emma Mills in 1877 and to Filla (known as Fillie), a second daughter of Nick Janis and his Oglala wife, Martha He Bear, in 1884. William Garnett pension file, NA.
3. Jeffrey Ostler, *The Plains Sioux and U.S. Colonialism*, 67.
4. Henry Benjamin Whipple, *Lights and Shadows of a Long Episcopate* (Macmillan, 1899), chap. 25.
5. *Daily State Journal* (Nebraska), dispatch datelined Red Cloud Agency, Nebraska, 20 September; issue of 23 September 1876.
6. Charles A. Eastman, *Indian Heroes and Great Chieftains*. For Sioux Jim's Lakota name see Helen Blish notes of interview with Short Bull, 23 July 1929, Mari Sandoz Papers; Colhoff winter count for 1908; and John Colhoff interview with Scudder Mekeel, September 1931, AMNH. Short Man pension file, National Archives. Sioux Jim's son Black Horse, who said he was a nephew of Little Big Man, signed on as a scout that fall and remained a well-known figure among the Pine Ridge Oglala into the 1920s. Several sources identify Sioux Jim as in fact half Cheyenne, as was Little Big Man. Undated news clip and handwritten letter by Black Horse, son of Sioux Jim, 26 June 1935, both mistakenly placed in pension file of Navajo Black Horse, C. 2307680, National Archives. See also Eli Ricker interview with William Garnett, 15 January 1907, Richard E. Jensen, ed., *The Indian Interviews*, 96–97.
7. Eli Ricker interview with William Garnett, 15 January 1907, 88.
8. Others were American Horse, Afraid of Bear, Red Dog, Little Wound, Fire Thunder, Swift Bear, Red Leaf, and Three Bears. *Daily State Journal* (Nebraska), dispatch from Red Cloud Agency.
9. Eli Ricker interview with William Garnett, 1907, 87–89.
10. Whipple, *Lights and Shadows*, chap. 25.
11. Statement of Mrs. James Redwing, granddaughter of Big Bat Pourier, Don Russell Papers.
12. George H. Holliday, *On the Plains in '65* (n.p. 1883), 90–91, quoted in John D. McDermott, *Circle of Fire*, 154; George E. Hyde, *Red Cloud's Folk*, 282.
13. George Crook letter to General O. O. Howard, 20 February 1883, George Crook letter book 1, no. 30, Rutherford B. Hayes Memorial Library, Fremont, Ohio.
14. Eli Ricker interview with William Garnett, 1907, Jensen, ed., *The Indian Interviews*, 9ff.
15. Luther North, *Man of the Plains*, 202ff.

16. Unsigned report, *Sydney Telegraph*, 27 October 1876, Elmo Scott Watson Papers, Box 42.

17. Lieutenant H. R. Lemly calls Swift Bear "a very eloquent Indian, who was chiefly responsible in having Spotted Tail declared chief." Lemly, writing in the *New York Sun*, 14 September 1877, quoted in Richard G. Hardorff, ed., *The Surrender and Death of Crazy Horse*, 238ff.

18. Paper prepared by George Sword and Clarence Three Stars, James R. Walker, *Lakota Society*, 87. Sword took his brother's name in 1877; before that he was known as Hunts the Enemy. Eli Ricker interview with William Garnett, 1907, Jensen, ed., *The Indian Interviews*, 45.

19. Red Cloud testimony in depredation claim of John Richard Jr., 17 July 1896, RG 123, Claim 3373. See also R. Eli Paul, ed., *Autobiography of Red Cloud*, 34ff.; Hyde, *Red Cloud's Folk*, 36; and Edward S. Curtis, *North American Indian* (University Press, 1908), vol. 3, p. 187. Edward B. Tuttle, *Three Years on the Plains*, 199. On a passenger train the chief was asked how many white men he had killed. To the interpreter traveling with him, Charles P. Jordan, who had married his niece, Red Cloud said, "Tell your friend I have been in 80 battles." Charles P. Jordan Papers, quoted in *Autobiography of Red Cloud*, 11.

20. Clark Wissler, *Societies and Ceremonial Associations*, 61.

21. A large glass plate negative of Morrow's photo, broken cleanly in two, can be found in the Elmo Scott Watson Papers. See generally Eli Ricker interview with William Garnett, 1907, Jensen, ed., *The Indian Interviews*.

18. *"When spring comes, we are going to kill them like dogs."*

1. Colonel Mackenzie was so angry at Howard that he asked Lieutenant Frank L. Shoemaker to take a formal affidavit from Garnett; Letters Received, Secretary of the Interior, Indian Division, M825/R10. Bourke lists fifty-four names of Sioux scouts who served on the Powder River expedition. See John G. Bourke, *On the Border with Crook*, 391. See also Eli Ricker interview with William Garnett, Richard E. Jensen, ed., *The Indian Interviews*, and Joe DeBarthe, *Life and Adventures of Frank Grouard*, 166.

2. Affidavit of Lieutenant Henry W. Lawton, Camp Robinson. Document included in Garnett's pension file, National Archives.

3. Eli Ricker interview with William Garnett, *The Indian Interviews*, 25. See also Richard Irving Dodge, *Powder River Journals*, 81; and Short Man pension file, National Archives.

4. W. P. Clark, *The Indian Sign Language*, published in 1885. This is one of the two or three best accounts of Plains Indian life and culture, and its numerous anecdotes are the closest Clark ever came to writing a memoir. It should be read as a book, from start to finish, and not simply consulted. It is evident that Clark kept a diary, but it seems to have been lost at the time of his death; only one brief section, describing his trip down the Yellowstone to join Crook in August 1876, can be found in the Montana Historical Society. Garnett identifies Rowland as Clark's tutor in sign talk.

5. In September 1878, only two years out of West Point, Lieutenant Hugh Scott lived for three days with Red Cloud in his lodge. Like Clark, Scott was an enthusiastic student of plains sign language and remarked that he had never known another man to sign in such a tight circle. An extensive dictionary of signs may

be found in Scott's papers at the Library of Congress. Hugh L. Scott, *Some Memories of a Soldier,* 96–97.

6. Eli Ricker interview with William Garnett, *The Indian Interviews,* 45ff.

7. Clark, *The Indian Sign Language,* 405.

8. DeBarthe, *Life and Adventures of Frank Grouard,* 164ff. Grouard said he had lost his voice, but does not identify his illness further. Baptiste Pourier said the Sandwich Islander was often laid low during the summer campaign by a case of syphilis.

9. Luther North, *Man of the Plains,* 207.

10. "Garnett says Clark had the most gratifying reputation all around, among white men and Indians, of any officer he ever knew. He was a brave, generous and noble man and officer." Eli Ricker interview with William Garnett, *The Indian Interviews,* 38. Garnett's view was confirmed by Lieutenant Jesse Lee, later the acting agent at the Spotted Tail Agency, who wrote, "Lieutenant Clark possessed in high degree a personal magnetism and pleasing manner that charmed everyone . . . He was successful in almost every move." Jesse M. Lee, "The Capture and Death of an Indian Chieftain," *Journal of the Military Service Institution of the United States* (May–June 1914), quoted in Peter Cozzens, *The Long War for the Northern Plains,* 530. Bourke provides the full text of Special Order No. 1; Charles M. Robinson III, ed., *The Diaries,* 152–53.

11. Historians have long assumed that the Plains Indians acquired horses about 1730–1750; the independent scholar Mike Cowdrey argues that the Brulé obtained horses in the 1690s, and that Pawnee on horses attacked the Oto in Iowa in the same decade. I accept Cowdrey's date.

12. North, *Man of the Plains,* 209.

13. Robinson, ed., *The Diaries,* 167.

14. Ibid., 170–71.

15. Jensen, ed., *The Indian Interviews,* 15–16. It is instructive to read Bourke's diary entry for 19 November 1876 beside Garnett's memory of what was said in 1907; the interpreter included every point recorded by Bourke at the time, as well as a number of others.

16. Robinson, ed., *The Diaries,* 173. On the way north to join Crook's expedition Li-heris-oo-la-shar, also known under his American name, Frank White, had been serving as sergeant of scouts. One day the detachment of Pawnee scouts passed Shell Creek, site of a long-ago Pawnee victory over the Ponca which was the subject of a song that Luther North particularly liked. North called on the scouts to sing this famous song and was baffled when all talking ceased and no one sang. North was about to repeat his call when Li-heris-oo-la-shar quietly explained: "*Ah-ti-us* [Father], we have a Ponca with us. It would make him feel badly if we sang that song." Robert Bruce, *The Fighting Norths and Pawnee Scouts* (Nebraska State Historical Society, 1932), 42; North, *Man of the Plains,* 200.

17. Wayne R. Kime, ed., *The Powder River Expedition Journals of Colonel Richard Irving Dodge,* 74–75. See also Colonel Richard Irving Dodge, *33 Years Among Our Wild Indians* (Archer House, 1959), 200, 368ff.

18. There are several books about Pickett's charge, but no account captures it more dramatically than Shelby Foote's in *The Civil War* (Random House, 1963), vol. 2, pp. 531ff. The life of Richard B. Garnett and of his cousin Robert, also a Confederate general and also killed in the war, are the subject of Matthew W. Burton, *The River of Blood.*

19. He later changed his name to Red Horse after the death of his father of that name. Eli Ricker interview with William Garnett, *The Indian Interviews,* 26.

20. Ibid., 24. See also Robinson, ed., *The Diaries*, 176; Kime, ed., *The Powder River Journals*, 78.

21. Kime, ed., *The Powder River Journals*, 82.

22. Eli Ricker interview with William Garnett, 26. Bourke does not mention the Sioux role in planning the fight. In his report later to Sheridan, Crook said Sitting Bear "gave information which determined me to carry out my original plan (operating against the Cheyennes first)." It is hard not to conclude that Crook shaded his report to conceal his debt to an Indian strategist. See also Robinson, ed., *The Diaries*, 194.

23. Eli Ricker interview with William Garnett, 28. A full treatment of this fight may be found in Jerome Greene, *Morning Star Dawn* (University of Oklahoma), 2003).

24. Ibid., 29.

25. Ibid., 31.

26. Clark, *The Indian Sign Language*, 82. "Thenceforward the two were very much together," Clark wrote, "and became brothers by adoption." This ceremony was known as *hunka*.

27. It is probable that these two men were the keeper of the sacred buffalo hat and a helper carrying a banner fringed with buffalo tails called nimhoyoh (the turner), which had the power to ward off danger. Mike Cowdrey identified these two figures for me. Coal Bear was the keeper of the hat; George Bird Grinnell, *The Fighting Cheyennes*, 370. For a general discussion of the sacred arrows and buffalo hat of the Cheyenne see Peter J. Powell, *Sweet Medicine*.

28. Eli Ricker interview with William Garnett, 14ff.; DeBarthe, *Life and Adventures of Frank Grouard*, 168; Jerry Roche, *New York Herald*, 11 December 1876, quoted in Cozzens, *The Long War for the Northern Plains*, 385.

29. Bourke says three of Dull Knife's sons were killed in the fight; Garnett says two, and since he knew both I trust his number. J. G. Bourke, "Mackenzie's Last Fight with the Cheyennes," *Journal of the Military Service Institution* 11 (1890).

30. Bourke later gave the necklace, previously owned by High Wolf, to the Smithsonian. These discoveries are recorded in Robinson, ed., *The Diaries*, vol. 2, p. 196; Bourke, *On the Border with Crook*, 403; Eli Ricker interview with William Garnett; and Jerry Roche, *New York Herald*, 11 December 1876, 428.

31. Eli Ricker interview with William Garnett, 35–36. See also Eddie Herman letter to George Hyde, 1 March 1951, and John Colhoff letter to George Hyde, 30 May 1949, author's collection.

32. Eli Ricker interview with William Garnett, 38.

33. Ibid., 43.

34. Garnett says it was the Indians who proposed to talk in the hostiles; Bourke credits General Crook, but Crook's dispatches to Sheridan tell the story: before the meeting with the scouts on 20 or 21 December he was planning to press on after the hostiles. Afterward he planned to give talk a chance. Robinson, ed., *The Diaries*, vol. 2, p. 222.

35. Crook's handwritten text was preserved by Bourke in his diary, ibid., 224–26.

19. *"All the people here are in rags."*

1. A good summary of the Cheyenne's condition can be found in Jerome A. Greene, *Morning Star Dawn* (University of Oklahoma, 2003), 16off. Luther North later wrote: "Those poor Cheyennes were out in that weather with noth-

ing to eat, and no shelter (we had burned their village) and hardly any clothing. It was said that many children died. It makes me sort of sick to think of it." Luther Heddon North, *Man of the Plains*, 217. A few days after the fight Lieutenant Bourke was visited in his tent "one dismally cold night" by Three Bears. The scout's "eyes were moist, and he shook his head mournfully as he said, 'Cheyenne papoose heap hung'y.' " John G. Bourke, *On the Border with Crook*, 407. Other details may be found in Eli Ricker interview with William Garnett, 15 January 1877, Richard E. Jensen, ed., *The Indian Interviews*; Charles M. Robinson III, ed., *The Diaries*, vol. 3; George Bird Grinnell, *The Fighting Cheyennes*, 381–82; John Stands in Timber and Margot Liberty, *Cheyenne Memories*, 218. Short Bull interview, 13 July 1930, Eleanor H. Hinman, *Oglala Sources*, 37. The Cheyenne Wooden Leg was fulsome in his praise of the Oglala's generosity; Thomas B. Marquis, trans., *Wooden Leg*, 287.

2. Robinson, ed., *The Diaries*, vol. 3.

3. Colonel W. H. Wood letter from Cheyenne Agency, 24 January 1877, to AAG, Department of Dakota, Sioux War files. See also Harry Anderson, "Sioux Pictorial Account," *North Dakota History* (July 1955); and William Garnett letter to V. T. McGillycuddy, 21 April 1926, copy in Fort Robinson Museum.

4. Colonel W. H. Wood report to the Assistant Adjutant General, Department of the Missouri, 28 December 1876, from the Cheyenne River Agency. A son of the Miniconjou chief White Robe, recently arrived at the Cheyenne River Agency, told Wood that some of the chiefs "want to quit fighting and come in."

5. Spotted Elk interview, Colonel W. H. Wood letter to the AAG, Department of Dakota, 1 March 1877, Sioux War files. Further accounts of this episode can be found in Raymond J. DeMallie, ed., *The Sixth Grandfather*, 199–200; Short Bull interview, 13 July 1930, Hinman, *Oglala Sources*, 37; and John F. Finerty, *War-Path and Bivouac*, 262.

6. Gets Fat with Beef, Red Skirt, Hollow Horn, and Bull Eagle are the names provided by Black Elk; DeMallie, ed., *The Sixth Grandfather*, 199–200. Colonel W. H. Wood, quoting the Miniconjou Fool Bear and Important Man, gives the names of the peace talkers as Sitting Bull the Good from the Red Cloud Agency, and the Yearling, Fat Hide, and Bad Leg, all from the Cheyenne River Agency of the Miniconjou.

7. The core of the story is related by Black Elk, DeMallie, ed., *The Sixth Grandfather*, 199–200. A good summary of the sources for this episode can be found in Jerome A. Greene, *Yellowstone Command* (University of Nebraska, 1991), 277–78; and Kingsley Bray, *Crazy Horse*, 447–48. See also Thomas B. Marquis, *Memoirs of a White Crow Indian* (University of Nebraska, 1974), 270; and Mari Sandoz, *Hostiles and Friendlies* (University of Nebraska, 1959), 87ff.

8. Colonel W. H. Wood report from Cheyenne River Agency to the AAG, Department of the Missouri, 24 January 1877, Sioux War files.

9. Ibid. See also the account of this man given by Frank Grouard to Lieutenant Bourke, 8 August 1876, Robinson, ed., *The Diaries*, vol. 2, pp. 52ff.; and Eagle Shield to Colonel W. H. Wood, Cheyenne River Agency, Intelligence Report, 16 February 1877, Sioux War files.

10. Colonel W. H. Wood report to the AAG, Department of the Missouri, 24 January 1877, from Cheyenne River Agency, Sioux War files.

11. Red Horse and White Eagle interviews, Colonel W. H. Wood letter to the AAG, Department of Dakota, 27 February 1877, Sioux War files.

12. The capture of the women is described in Grinnell, *The Fighting Cheyennes*, 384; Luther S. Kelly, *Yellowstone Kelly* (University of Nebraska, 1973), 169; and Marquis, trans., *Wooden Leg*, 290. The whole episode, culminating in the fight at Wolf Mountain on 7 January 1877, is related in Greene, *Yellowstone Command*, 160ff.

13. Report of Colonel W. H. Wood, 26 February 1877, Sioux War files; Short Bull interview, 13 July 1930, 3.

14. DeMallie, ed., *The Sixth Grandfather*, 202.

15. *Rocky Mountain News*, 15 February 1877.

16. Sheridan to Crook, 5 February 1877, telegrams from the field, Department of the Platte, Letters Received, Box 48.

17. George Crook letter on behalf of Lieutenant Jesse Lee, 27 July 1888, 2141 ACP 1878, National Archives.

18. Sword's autobiography names himself, Crow Fire, Running Hawk, Black Mountain Goat, Iron Shell, High Bear, Long Whirlwind, Inside the Curtain, He Touches Thick Blood, Tail Less [Few Tails], Good Rump, Bear's Nostrils, Hopa, Two Faces, and Tall Man, with one or two others whose names Sword had forgotten. "Sword's Acts Related," translated by Ella Deloria, Colorado Historical Society. Short Bull named two of the Indians with Sword as Crow Hawk and Running Fire, but Running Hawk and Crow Fire seem to be correct. Short Bull interview, 13 July 1930, 37.

   Ella Deloria, who never met Sword, translates his penultimate name as "Enemy Bait," but Billy Garnett remembered it as Hunts the Enemy. I have elected to trust Garnett because Garnett was the interpreter who helped Lieutenant Clark reenlist Hunts the Enemy as a scout in March 1877; because Army enlistment records carry his name as Hunts the Enemy; because Garnett is our source for dating a change of name from Hunts the Enemy to Sword in 1877; because Garnett knew Sword from the 1860s until his death in 1910; and because Garnett in effect gave hundreds of Oglala their permanent white names by translating them into English for white officials. In quoting from Ella Deloria's translation of Sword's autobiography I have therefore silently replaced "Enemy Bait" with "Hunts the Enemy," for reasons of clarity and consistency.

19. Major Horace Neide letter to J. G. Bourke, 10 February 1877, Sioux War files, M1495/R4.

20. "Sword's Acts Related."

21. Eli Ricker interview with George Sword, 29 April 1907, Jensen, ed., *The Indian Interviews*, 327ff. Statement of George Sword, 5 September 1896, Bruce Means, interpreter, James R. Walker, *Lakota Belief and Ritual*, 74.

22. Ella Deloria translates the words of Sword as "The Indians' president" but it is clear that he meant the customary "Great Father." "Sword's Acts Related."

23. Eli Ricker interview with William Garnett, 15 January 1877, 59.

24. At the Little Bighorn Iron Hawk suffered a wound typical for a man on horseback shot by an enemy on the ground—the bullet had entered under his ribs and ripped up through his body before it lodged somewhere in his trunk. Eli Ricker interview with William Garnett, 45.

25. Eli Ricker interview with Iron Hawk, 12 May 1907, Jensen, ed., *The Indian Interviews*, 314ff. DeMallie, ed., *The Sixth Grandfather*, 175, 192. Red Feather interview, 8 July 1930, Hinman, *Oglala Sources* 25. "Sword's Acts Related."

26. "Sword's Acts Related."

27. Red Feather interview, 8 July 1930, 25.

28. Walter Camp interview with William Garnett, 1907, Walter Camp Papers, Box 2.

29. W. P. Clark to John G. Bourke, 24 February 1877, Department of the Platte, Letters Received, Box 48.

30. Ibid.

31. Lieutenant Jesse Lee to Lieutenant Bourke, 10 March 1877, Sioux War files, M1495/R4.

32. Lieutenant F. Schwatka autograph letter to his father, 5 February 1877, Gilder Lehrman Document No. GLC06913. World Wide Web

33. F. C. Boucher letter, 25 March 1877, forwarded to Department of the Platte by Captain Anson Mills, Letters Received, Box 49, Sioux War files, M1495/R4.

34. Lieutenant Jesse Lee letter to Captain Anson Mills, 5 April 1877, quoted in Richard G. Hardorff, ed., *The Surrender and Death of Crazy Horse*, 102.

35. The word *hou*—not "how," as depicted in so many western novels and movies—was an expostulation of acceptance and agreement, and it was a common response to things said in any large gathering. Jesse Lee, "The Capture and Death of an Indian Chieftain," *Journal of the Military Service Institution of the United States* (May–June 1914), quoted in Peter Cozzens, *The Long War for the Northern Plains*, 529.

36. Fanny McGillycuddy diary, copy in the Fort Robinson Museum.

37. He Dog interview, 13 July 1930, Hinman, *Oglala Sources*, 19.

38. Red Feather interview, 8 July 1930, 25; W. P. Clark to J. G. Bourke, 3 March 1877, quoted in Hardorff, *The Surrender and Death of Crazy Horse*, 160.

39. Eli Ricker interview with Horn Chips, 14 February 1907, Jensen, ed., *The Indian Interviews*. George Wallihan, writing as "Rapherty," reports the planting of the stake. *Cheyenne Daily Leader*, 28 May 1877.

40. DeMallie, ed., *The Sixth Grandfather*, 202.

20. *"I want this peace to last forever."*

1. Caroline Frey Winne to her brother Lud, 25 February 1877, New-York Historical Society.

2. Robert H. Steinbach, *A Long March: The Lives of Frank and Alice Baldwin* (University of Texas, 1989), 119–20. Long quote: Alice Baldwin to her husband Frank from Sioux City, 31 March 1877, Baldwin Papers, Huntington Library. See also Alice Blackwood Baldwin, *An Army Wife on the Frontier, 1867–1877* (University of Utah Library, 1975).

3. Tom Buecker, "Frederic S. Calhoun," *Greasy Grass* 10 (May 1994).

4. Frederic S. Calhoun letter to Charles Turner, 27 April 1877, 569 ACP 1875, National Archives. Turner forwarded the letter with a note to the president's son, Webb Hayes, but nothing came of it.

5. Sherman's remark was technically an "endorsement"—an officer's comment on a document being passed forward. Copies of the relevant documents can be found in Department of the Platte, Letters Received, Box 50; and Secretary of the Interior, Indian Division, Letters Received, M825/R10. See also Thomas R. Buecker, *Fort Robinson and the American West*, 104.

6. Mackenzie's report is summarized in a covering document dated 18 April 1877, Department of the Platte, Letters Received, Box 49. *Chicago Times*, 26 May 1877.

7. Walter Camp interview with Jesse Lee, 27 October 1912, Walter Camp papers.

8. Department of the Platte, Letters Received, Box 49.

9. *Rocky Mountain News*, 6 May 1877.

10. Rosenquest joined the Army in 1871 as an enlisted man at the age of sixteen, was commissioned a second lieutenant in 1876, and was second in command of Company F, 4th Cavalry, during the attack on the Cheyenne that November. A year later he deserted from the Army, an act he blamed on the influence of a "fast set" in St. Louis who had introduced him to liquor. Later in New York City he was manager of the Fourteenth Street Theater. He recounts much of this personal history in a letter to President McKinley in 1898, asking permission to rejoin the Army to fight in the Spanish-American War. Rosenquest ACP file 4527–1876, National Archives.

11. Eli Ricker interview with William Garnett, 15 January 1877, Richard E. Jensen, ed., *The Indian Interviews*. He Dog said the leading men with Crazy Horse in May 1877 included his own brother Little Shield, now recovered from a gunshot wound in the arm he had received at the Little Bighorn, and Kicking Bear (brother of Little Shield's wife), Black Fox, Looking Horse, Charging (another name of Little Big Man), Two Lance, Good Weasel, Hard to Hit, Iron White Man, Magpie, Thunder Iron, and Kills Alone. Iron Hawk, Big Road, and Little Hawk, the uncle of Crazy Horse, were also part of the inner group. See He Dog account, eleven-page typescript, Museum of the Fur Trade, Chadron, Nebraska; Little Shield pension file, National Archives; and Charles M. Robinson III, ed., *The Diaries*, vol. 2, p. 63.

12. Little Killer was the brother of Club Man, who was married to Crazy Horse's older sister. Little Killer interview, 12 July 1930, Eleanor H. Hinman, *Oglala Sources*, 6, 39.

13. James Cook, undated memo quoting a statement to him by Lieutenant Clark at the old Red Cloud Agency, James H. Cook Papers. For names and numbers of those who surrendered see Thomas R. Buecker and R. Eli Paul, eds., *The Crazy Horse Surrender Ledger*.

14. These accounts include He Dog account in the Colhoff winter count for the year 1936, Elmo Scott Watson Papers, 1936. He Dog account, eleven-page typescript. He Dog, Red Feather, and Whirling interview with Hugh Scott, 19 August 1920, reprinted in Richard G. Hardorff, ed., *Lakota Recollections of the Custer Fight*, 73ff. Undated Walter Camp interview with Thomas Disputed (A Kinichaki), Bruce R. Liddic and Paul Harbaugh, *Custer & Company*, 121ff. Eli Ricker interview with William Garnett, 15 January 1907; William Garnett interview with General Hugh Scott, 19 August 1920, SDSHS; Robinson, ed., *The Diaries*, vol. 2, pp. 63ff. Little Killer interview, 12 July 1930, and Short Bull interview, 13 July 1930, Hinman, *Oglala Sources*, 38. W. P. Clark, *The Indian Sign Language*, 296. Walter Camp interview with Horn Chips, c. 11 July 1910, quoted in Richard G. Hardorff, ed., *The Surrender and Death of Crazy Horse*, 89. *New York Herald*, 7 May 1877.

15. He Dog account, eleven-page typescript.

16. He Dog, Red Feather, and Whirling interview with Hugh Scott, 19 August 1920.

17. He Dog account, eleven-page typescript.

18. Walter Camp interview with Horn Chips, c. 11 July 1910, 89.

19. Interviews with Little Killer and Short Bull, 12–13 July 1930, Hinman, *Oglala Sources*, 38.

20. Robinson, ed., *The Diaries*, vol. 2, p. 66.

21. "From a Military Correspondent at Red Cloud," *Cheyenne Daily Leader*, 9 May 1877.
22. John G. Bourke, *On the Border with Crook*, 413.
23. The names of these men, and the numbers of women and children who accompanied them, can be found in Buecker and Paul, eds., *The Crazy Horse Surrender Ledger*, 157–64. Bourke says 117 guns were found. Lieutenant C. A. Johnson, in a letter to the commissioner of Indian affairs written the same day, says the number of guns and pistols was 109. Red Cloud Agency files, M234/R721.
24. Eli Ricker interview with William Garnett, 15 January 1877, 49.

21. *"I cannot decide these things for myself."*

1. William Philo Clark shared the Indian view of dog: "The meat combines the flavors of bear and pork, and is wonderfully nutritious; one can undergo a great deal of hard work, especially hard riding, after a hearty meal of dog." W. P. Clark, *The Indian Sign Language*, 154. Strahorn's stories appeared in the *Denver Daily Tribune*, 18 May 1877, and in the *Rocky Mountain News*, 18 and 20 May 1877. John W. Ford's presence for the *Chicago Times* is reported by George Wallihan, *Cheyenne Daily Leader*, 27 May 1877; he is identified in Paul L. Hedren, *Fort Laramie and the Great Sioux War*, 44, 58, 124, 200.
2. There is no readily available account of the career of Wallihan. This one has been assembled from the columns of the *Cheyenne Leader*; an 1880 miner's diary kept by his brother Allen, who later became a noted wildlife photographer (ms. no. 654, Colorado Historical Society); a letter of 25 June 1877 from Samuel Wallihan, MD, to Secretary of the Interior Carl Schurz (Carl Schurz Papers); and articles in the *Rocky Mountain News* in April 1873. The acquisition notes of the Denver Art Museum for a ledger book attributed to Crazy Horse include a brief memoir written by Wallihan in 1915. It appears that George Wallihan was also the author in 1917 of a John Philip Sousa piece called "The Love That Lives Forever." Wallihan worked for the *Denver Post* for many years and died in 1922.
3. Accounts of Wallihan's trip to the Black Hills can be found in *Cheyenne Leader*, 23 April 1876, 7 July 1876, and 28 April 1877. On 4 April 1877 the *Leader* reported, "Died, in Footville, Wis., 29 March 1877, of hemorrhage of the lungs, Mrs. Lucy L. Wallihan, mother of the city editor of *The Leader*." Wallihan's parents had returned to Wisconsin the previous year. A full account of the rush may be found in John D. McDermott, *Gold Rush: The Black Hills Story* (South Dakota State Historical Society, 2001).
4. *Cheyenne Daily Leader*, 8 and 10 May 1877. The Black Hills were in the Dakota Territory.
5. The dime's worth of gold is reported in Watson Parker, *Gold in the Black Hills* (University of Oklahoma, 1966), 25. "Life of Goose," Josephine Waggoner Papers.
6. *New York Sun*, 23 May 1877; probably written by Lieutenant H. R. Lemly.
7. Red Feather interview, 8 July 1930, Eleanor H. Hinman, *Oglala Sources*, 29. *Denver Daily Tribune*, 18 May 1877, writer unknown, quoted in Richard G. Hardorff, ed., *The Surrender and Death of Crazy Horse*, 209ff.
8. *Cheyenne Daily Leader*, 16 May 1877.
9. Ibid., 23 and 27 May 1877.
10. Ibid., 23 May 1877.

11. The story of the pipe was published in the *Rocky Mountain News*, 12 January 1879. Ella is not named in the story, but the dating and details of the occasion closely match Wallihan's visit of 18 May 1877. For further details see Nancy and Edwin Bathke, "A. G. Wallihan: Colorado's Pioneer Nature Photographer," *Denver Brand Book*, 1995, 345ff, and Allen Wallihan's diary in the Colorado Historical Society.

12. George Wallihan, two-page manuscript typed in Pomona, California, in 1915, Denver Art Museum acquisition notes. Two of the drawings are reproduced in Janet Catherine Berlo, *Plains Indian Drawing* (Harry N. Abrams, 1996). One of these drawings from the Crazy Horse gift ledger depicts the same event, drawn by the same artist, as a drawing in the Louis Bordeaux/Deadwood ledger book ("Shooting Cat Killing Two Pawnee Squaws") sold by the Skinner Auction Gallery in September 2009. The independent scholar Mike Cowdrey believes the killings depicted in the Bordeaux/Deadwood ledger book drawings, many of "Pawnee squaws," represent incidents from the 1873 massacre.

13. Wallihan writing as "Rapherty," *Cheyenne Daily Leader*, 30 May 1877.

14. Among the chiefs were Little Wound, Red Dog, No Water, Young Man Afraid of His Horses, Little Hawk, Touch the Clouds, Red Bear, Spotted Tail, Two Bears, Hunts the Enemy, High Bear, Iron Hawk, Little Crow, He Dog, and many others.

15. *Cheyenne Daily Leader*, 28 May and 6 September 1877. Bradley did not witness the kneel personally; he probably heard about it after arriving to assume command of the post the following day. Bradley letter to his mother, 8 September 1877, Lot no. 576, HCA Auction site, February 2004. See also John W. Ford, *Chicago Times*, 26 May 1877. The writer Ian Frazier, who has written more passionately about Crazy Horse than anyone else, found the whole idea of Crazy Horse kneeling in front of Crook insupportable. Frazier refused to record it as a fact. I don't much like writing it down myself. See Ian Frazier, *The Great Plains* (Farrar, Straus and Giroux, 1989).

16. Walter S. Schuyler to General Robert Williams, Adjutant General, Department of the Platte, 26 May 1877; Letters Received, Box 50. *Chicago Times*, 26 May 1877. Wallihan reported very similar language in the *Cheyenne Daily Leader*, 28 May 1877.

17. The first part of this quotation was remembered later by Garnett; the second part was reported at the time by John W. Ford. See Richard E. Jensen, ed., *The Indian Interviews*, 51ff., and *Chicago Times*, 26 May 1877.

18. Eli Ricker interview with William Garnett, 15 January 1907, Jensen, ed., *The Indian Interviews*, 54. Schuyler to General Robert Williams, Adjutant General, 26 May 1877, Department of the Platte, Letters Received, Box 50.

19. Charles M. Robinson III, ed., *The Diaries*, vol. 2, pp. 298–300.

20. Story datelined Camp Sheridan, 15 July, from the *New York Daily Tribune*, 7 September 1877. Eli Ricker interview with William Garnett, 1907, Jensen, ed., *The Indian Interviews*, 59.

21. Story datelined Camp Sheridan, 15 July, from the *New York Daily Tribune*, 7 September 1877.

22. Bradley to Ione, 26 May 1877, Luther Bradley Papers.

23. Lieutenant Clark telegram to Lieutenant Walter S. Schuyler, 13 June 1877, reports that "the application to go out hunting was renewed" by Crazy Horse at a meeting with the chief in his camp. For reports that Crazy Horse was to be

made head chief see Eli Ricker interview with William Garnett, Jensen, ed., *The Indian Interviews*, 117, and Luther Standing Bear, *Land of the Spotted Eagle*, 179.

24. He Dog and Short Bull interviews, 13 July 1930, Hinman, *Oglala Sources*, 24.

25. Planting trees: Colonel Bradley letter to Ione, 11 July 1877. Susan Bordeaux Bettelyoun and Josephine Waggoner, *With My Own Eyes*, 108–09.

26. Report of Lieutenant Schwatka, 9 July 1877, Department of the Platte, Letters Received, Box 51. Lieutenant Jesse Lee letter to CIA, 30 June 1877, Spotted Tail Agency, M234/R841. Further details of the killing can be found in Mardi Anderson, "Gilbert C. Fosdick II, Stagecoach Driver," Buffalo County Historical Society 25, no. 3 (May–June, 2002).

22. *"It made his heart heavy and sad to think of these things."*

1. James R. Walker, *The Sun Dance and Other Ceremonies of the Oglala*, 61. Walker's account is the most complete, and is based on his conversations with Little Wound, American Horse, Bad Wound, Short Bull, No Flesh, Ringing Shield, Thomas Tyon, and George Sword. Other sources used here include Left Heron (aka Breast, *Makula*), born 1850, interview with Scudder Mekeel, 18 September 1931, John Colhoff, interpreter, AMNH; Frances Densmore, *Teton Sioux Music*; Martha Beckwith, "Mythology of the Oglala," *Journal of American Folklore* (October–December 1930); W. P. Clark, *The Indian Sign Language*, 361ff.; and Eli Ricker interview with Billy Garnett, Richard E. Jensen, ed., *The Indian Interviews*, 54ff.

2. Kill Eagle was named in the *Cheyenne Daily Leader*, 20 July 1877. Fool or Foolish Heart was identified as sun dance chief by Dana Long Wolf, letter of W. O. Roberts, superintendant of the Pine Ridge Agency, to Professor E. P. Wilson at Chadron State College, 13 June 1940, cited in Kingsley Bray, *Crazy Horse*, 310, 456. Bray identifies Fool Heart as a Sans Arc. The only two Fool Hearts of whom I know are a Yanktonai signer of the 1868 treaty and a son of the Miniconjou Lame Deer who surrendered at Camp Sheridan on 10 September 1877. They must be ruled out. See letters of J. M. Lee to Colonel L. P. Bradley, 10 and 12 September 1877, Luther Bradley Papers. The five dancers are identified by James Chase in Morning and Alfred Ribman in Edward Kadlecek and Mabell Kadlecek, *To Kill an Eagle*, 41. Walking Eagle is identified in Thomas R. Buecker and R. Eli Paul, eds., *The Crazy Horse Surrender Ledger*. The brother of the elder Chase in Morning who died of wounds received at the Little Bighorn was Black Whiteman; Raymond J. DeMallie, ed., *The Sixth Grandfather*, 194, 198.

Also present on 29 June was Colonel Bradley, the new commander of Camp Robinson, who described the dance at unaccustomed length in his diary. Luther Bradley Papers. Accounts of the Crazy Horse sun dance are further confused by Garnett's recollection that there were two sun dances on the White River that summer: the Crazy Horse dance that climaxed on 29 June, and a second dance that climaxed about 8 or 9 July 1877 held by Spotted Tail and Red Cloud. According to Lieutenant Frederick Schwatka, who described his experience in "The Sun Dance of the Sioux," *Century Magazine* (December 1890), the dance he attended "was in June." Lieutenant Jesse Lee at the Spotted Tail Agency wrote the commissioner of Indian affairs on 30 June to report, "The barbaric Sun Dance is now in full operation and all the Indians, almost without exception are enthusiastic on it." Lee to CIA, 30 June 1877, Spotted Tail Agency, M234/R841.

Clark, Bradley, and Garnett all state explicitly that they witnessed the dance of Crazy Horse's people, and that is the one described here, so far as the evidence permits.

3. Left Heron (aka Breast, *Makula*), born 1850, interview with Scudder Mekeel. It is worth noting that this remark by Left Heron posits important elements of Sioux tribal chronology. Using Left Heron's numbers suggests that White Buffalo Woman instructed the Sioux in the use of the sacred pipe about 1695, and the first sun dance was performed about 1765. The third significant date in Sioux history marks the tribe's first acquisition of horses; this date was recently adjusted back a generation to c. 1700 by Mike Cowdrey in *Plains Indian Horse Masks*.

4. Eli Ricker interview with William Garnett, Jensen, ed., *The Indian Interviews*, 55; and Clark, *The Indian Sign Language*, 362.

5. One who stayed home was Dr. Valentine McGillycuddy, contract surgeon at the post. Fanny McGillycuddy diary, 29 June 1877, SDSHS.

6. The conversation with White Bull can be found in Clark, *The Indian Sign Language*, 104. The second remark, which I believe was also made by White Bull, is on 116. Most of the Cheyenne were led south to the Indian Territory by Lieutenant Henry W. Lawton at the end of May.

23. *"They were killed like wolves."*

1. As noted previously, in time his name would be shortened to Sword, and preceded by the Christian name George. George Sword would become chief of police and a leading figure on the Pine Ridge Agency until his death in 1910. Other scouts on the excursion were Red Shirt, Little Battle, No Neck, Horned Horse (also known as Little Bull), Sorrel Horse, and Joe Bush, also known as Big Belly Sorrel Horse and as Fast Bull. Eli Ricker interview with William Garnett, Richard E. Jensen, ed., *The Indian Interviews*, 54.

2. Charles M. Robinson III, ed., *The Diaries*, vol. 2, p. 323ff. See also the Colhoff winter count.

3. Robinson, ed., *The Diaries*, vol. 2, p. 329.

4. Celia was an Ohio girl; she married Ford in 1870 in Nebraska. A daughter, Edith, was born the following year, and a son, Hugh, in 1876. Ford himself had been born in New York City in 1842. For an account of his time at Fort Laramie see Ford's handwritten notes, dated Christmas 1917, on the endpapers of a copy of Elizabeth Custer's memoir, *Boots and Saddles*, sold by Heritage Auction Galleries in Texas on 8 June 2008. The book was purchased with a single bid for $3,500.

5. Ford's story appeared in the *Chicago Times*, 26 May 1877. Ford is identified as the *Times*'s correspondent by Bourke in *The Diaries*, vol. 2, p. 255; and his return as a *Times* correspondent to the Red Cloud Agency on 23 May 1877 with General Crook is reported by George Wallihan writing as "Rapherty," *Cheyenne Daily Leader*, 27 May 1877. Bourke praises Ford's appearance on the Fort Laramie stage in *The Diaries*, vol. 1, p. 208. There are also passing references to Ford in Paul L. Hedren, *Fort Laramie and the Great Sioux War*, 44, 58, 124, 200.

6. *Chicago Times*, 26 May 1877.

7. Ford lists the camps with their chiefs from south to north as follows: Hunkpapas (Sitting Bull), Oglala (Crazy Horse), Miniconjou (Fast Bull), Sans Arcs (Red

Bear), Cheyenne (Ice Bear), Santee and Yanktonai (Red Point, also known as Inkpaduta), and Blackfeet (Scabby Head). This order of the camps has been tweaked and adjusted numerous times over the years, but the most important revision is the placement of the Cheyenne, which all authorities now agree was the northernmost camp on the morning of 25 June. Getting the order right is important because Indian accounts of the battle often orient descriptions of the fight by reference to the different camps; things get badly confused, for example, if you don't think the Cheyenne were northernmost, and were camped directly opposite the wide ford at the mouth of Muskrat Creek and Medicine Tail Coulee. *Chicago Times,* 26 May 1877.

8. This simple description of the action established an Indian version of what happened which never altered thereafter, but was supported and elaborated upon by dozens of other Indian accounts collected over the next three decades. The literature on the Custer fight dwarfs the record of almost every other battle in American history, not excepting Gettysburg and Normandy, and the writers are often contentious. A good introduction to the argument can be found in Robert Utley, *Custer and the Great Controversy: The Origin and Development of a Legend* (1962; University of Nebraska Press, 1998). Those determined to devote a decade to following up the story may work their way through Utley's bibliography. A compendium of basic documents is in W. A. Graham, *The Custer Myth.*

In 2003 I toured the battlefield with my friend T. D. Hobart, our godson Robert A. Wells, now a lieutenant in the Marines, and Jack McDermott, a retired National Park Service historian who has written numerous books on the Plains Indian wars and knows the Custer fight well.

The problem for the historian of the battle may be summed up as follows: Custer's men were found dead in clumps, clusters, and lonely spots, spread widely over the field. Bodies and relics of the fighting were found along a ridge leading to the rise known as Custer Hill. Some of the officers were found dead with their commands, some not. The colonel himself and a big group were found just below the brow of the hill. Indian accounts and the evidence of the field showed that many men had gone down—or possibly up; maybe both—the ravine known as Medicine Tail Coulee, which ran from the bluffs on the east bank down to the river across from the Indian camp. A second ravine known as Deep Coulee runs up away from the Medicine Tail ford toward Custer Hill at an angle that might have been made by a bank shot in billiards. More bodies were found in a line running down and away from Custer Hill back toward the river. The battle was fluid over the whole field. The fighting seems to have unfolded in a whirlpool action, but in which direction? How did experienced officers, Custer chief among them, lose command cohesion and end up with their men dead all over the place?

The Indians, for their part, were often puzzled by what the soldiers did, but their account of the unfolding action is straightforward enough, and it suggests that Crazy Horse played a central role in breaking the organized resistance of Custer's command. Their version of what happened, picked up by Lieutenant Clark and others in conversation with the Indians, helps to explain the growing respect of the military for the chief and his ability as a war leader.

9. John F. Finerty, *War-Path and Bivouac,* 93.

10. Robinson, ed., *The Diaries,* vol. 2, pp. 336ff.

11. Wheeler lost his hooves while chasing the Nez Percé Indians later that fall;

Bourke had his pair manufactured into inkstands and later gave one to a Philadelphia museum. Colonel Homer W. Wheeler, *Buffalo Days* (Bobbs Merrill, 1923), 184. There was much talk in later years of the sorrel with three white forelegs, reported to be in the possession of one Indian or another.

12. Bourke thought these were the graves of Boston and Tom Custer, brothers of the general. One was actually his nephew, "Autie" Reed.

13. The indispensable Richard Hardorff has devoted a book to identifying them. After collating all Indian casualty counts he concluded that about forty Indians were killed at the Little Bighorn. *Hokahey!*, 130.

14. Robinson, ed., *The Diaries*, vol. 2, p. 341. Spotted Horn Bull, Red Hawk, Foolish Elk, Turtle Rib, Iron Hawk, Flying Hawk, Red Feather, and He Dog all tell closely similar versions of this story.

15. Sheridan letter to Sherman, 23 August 1876, Sheridan Papers, LOC, quoted in Paul Andrew Hutton, *Phil Sheridan and His Army*, 329.

16. Clark to Crook, 18 August 1877, recorded by Bourke in vol. 26 of his diaries, transcribed by the author. This document was dropped from the published version of the diaries.

17. William Philo Clark, Report to Adjutant General, Department of the Platte, 14 September 1877, edited by Thomas Buecker, reprinted in *Greasy Grass* (May 1991). This report is also reprinted at the end of vol. 2 of Bourke's diaries. See also Thomas R. Buecker, *Fort Robinson and the American West*, 90.

24. *"The soldiers could not go any further, and they knew that they had to die."*

1. Black Elk's account of the Little Bighorn can be found in Raymond J. DeMallie, ed., *The Sixth Grandfather*, 180ff. The history of Black Elk's father is discussed in Eli Ricker's interview with William Garnett, 15 January 1877, Richard E. Jensen, ed., *The Indian Interviews*, 59. Good White Buffalo Woman's story can be found in James McLaughlin, *My Friend the Indian* (Houghton Mifflin, 1910), 162ff. McLaughlin translates her name as Beautiful White Cow. Gregory Michno translates it as Pretty White Buffalo. I choose "good" because the Lakota word *waste* describes seven kinds of virtue, only one of which is conveyed by "pretty."

One source of the enduring fascination of the Custer fight is watching the slow success of the relentless effort by historians to establish what happened; with the exception of the assassination of John F. Kennedy no other event in human history, I believe, has been the object of such focused curiosity, or of such intent to establish a comprehensive knowledge of the battle. To cite only one among numerous examples I direct readers to archaeological studies, which have mapped successive firing positions of both Indians and whites over the field through recovery of bullets and cartridge casings. The use of at least fifteen surviving firearms by Indians or whites has been positively confirmed through matching the distinctive firing pin signature of gun and cartridge. In some cases the gun can be tracked through the battle from one cartridge to the next. How far down this road can researchers hope to go? Trust me when I say that the Custer fight fraternity wants to go *all* the way. See Douglas D. Scott, "Archeological Perspectives on the Battle of the Little Big Horn," in Charles E. Rankin, ed., *Legacy: New Perspectives on the Battle of the Little Big Horn* (Montana Historical Society, 1996); and Richard Allen Fox, *Archaeology, History and Custer's Last Battle: The Little Big Horn Reexamined* (University of Oklahoma, 1993).

A recent subject of intense scrutiny has been Indian accounts, the first of which were collected within a week or two of the fight. Among the last survivors, voluble until the end, were Eagle Elk, interviewed by John Neihardt in 1944, and Iron Hail, also known as Dewey Beard, who died ten years later. But not even that marked the end. Sitting around kitchens and telling stories over coffee is a communal pastime of the Lakota, and relatives of battle survivors continue to tell stories down to the present day. In the first forty or fifty years after the battle these Indian accounts were avidly sought by a handful of passionate amateurs, but for more than a century historians of the battle have for the most part dismissed the Indian accounts as too erratic, confusing, and, above all, personal to be useful. Colonel W. A. Graham, who published the first substantial collection of Indian accounts, said that he nevertheless gave up any attempt to fit them into white versions of the battle. "The Indian accounts contradicted each other to such an extent that I found them irreconcilable," he wrote. He advised a reader "to do with them as all who have studied them have done, and reconcile them if and as he can." *The Custer Myth*, 3–4.

No serious student would argue that now. The best summation of Indian accounts of the day of battle is Gregory F. Michno, *Lakota Noon: The Indian Narrative of Custer's Defeat* (Mountain Press Publishing, 1993), which quotes from fifty-eight separate Indian interviews to retell the unfolding of the battle in fifteen-minute segments. This is a belated but brave start to telling the Indian side of the story. Who says something is often as important as what is said. The necessary next step, in my view, is to integrate the recorded accounts with substantial biographies of the tellers. The ultimate goal of the exercise is to establish the deep texture of the event as it was experienced at the moment when the Indians of the plains were forced to give up their life as roaming hunters of buffalo.

2. White Bull's estimate was three hundred Hunkpapa lodges, four to five hundred for the Oglala, 2,300 lodges in all. Richard G. Hardorff, ed., *Indian Views of the Custer Fight*, 152.

3. He Dog interview, 24 July 1931, Hugh Scott Papers. The size of the village, immense in early white accountings, tended to diminish with later, more careful estimates. In four separate articles and books published over thirty-five years the respected western historian Robert Utley at first thought Custer had confronted three thousand warriors; by the time he published his biography of Sitting Bull, *The Lance and the Shield*, in 1993, he had settled on a number of eighteen hundred as more likely. Gregory Michno, who parses this question with characteristic rigor in *Lakota Noon* (4–20), hazards no firm number of his own, but seems open to the sober guess of Charles Eastman, the Santee Sioux medical doctor who practiced on the Pine Ridge Reservation at the time of the Battle of Wounded Knee (1890). Eastman was, of course, fluent in Lakota, knew many of the leading men of the Sioux, and thought Custer was defeated by as few as a thousand warriors. Eastman, "The Sioux Narrative," *Chatauquan* (1900), partially reprinted in Graham, *The Custer Myth*, 96–97.

In the confusion there are several firm numbers, beginning with the size of the band which surrendered with Crazy Horse—899 people in all, of whom 217 were men with families, and another 186 were boys. Between 24 February and 10 May 1877 there arrived at the Red Cloud Agency in separate groups 558

Cheyenne with 113 men and 132 boys; and an additional 154 Lakota men, all from the north and most of them Oglala. Thomas R. Buecker and R. Eli Paul, ed., *The Crazy Horse Surrender Ledger*, 101–20. Similar groups of Miniconjous and a few Brulé came in to surrender at the Spotted Tail Agency in April 1877, 917 persons in all, according to Lieutenant Jesse Lee, including 208 men and 211 boys. Spotted Tail Agency, M234/R841. Hostiles surrendering at both White River agencies therefore total at least 692 men. We may assume that all or almost all had been in the fight at the Little Bighorn. In addition to these, about three hundred northern Indians surrendered to General Miles on the Tongue River, and a band estimated at about 165 lodges (seven to eight hundred people) crossed into Canada with Sitting Bull. Robert M. Utley, *The Lance and the Shield*, 181–82. Throughout this period still other groups were surrendering at the Standing Rock and Cheyenne River agencies on the Missouri, and at all agencies uncounted Sioux slipped into camp whose absence had never been noticed or recorded. But counting carefully, it's still hard to push the total of Sioux fighting men at the Little Bighorn past two thousand.

4. White Bull interview with Walter S. Campbell in 1932, Western History Collection, University of Oklahoma, reprinted in Hardorff, ed., *Indian Views of the Custer Fight*, 149ff.

5. Among them were Owl Bull, Medicine Bird, Kills Enemy in Winter, Dirt Kettle, and Knife, the only one of the group to bring his wife.

6. For the purpose of this account I am relying on the careful chronology established by John S. Gray in *Custer's Last Campaign*. Gray argues convincingly that Custer's men were traveling on St. Paul time, the location of General Terry's headquarters; that they synchronized their watches; and that they noted the time often enough during the day to allow a tight and accurate chronology of events. Some Indian accounts agree roughly with Gray's chronology; others differ wildly. But Gray says the shooting started with the beginning of Reno's charge on the Hunkpapa camp at three minutes past three o'clock on the afternoon of 25 June; Sitting Bull, whose lodge was in the Hunkpapa camp, said the attack came "some two hours past the time when the sun is in the center of the sky." I interpret that as rough agreement. Interview with Sitting Bull dated 17 October 1877 from Fort Walsh, Northwest Territory, *New York Herald*, 16 November 1877, reprinted in Graham, *The Custer Myth*, 65.

7. Black Bear interview with Walter Camp, 18 July 1911, with Philip Wells as interpreter, reprinted in Kenneth Hammer, ed., *Custer in '76*, 203ff. He Dog also discussed this episode with Walter Camp, 13 July 1910, with William Berger as interpreter, reprinted in Hammer, ed., *Custer in '76* (University of Oklahoma, 1976), 205ff. Black Bear told Camp his group had gone on to the agency "as we were not hostiles." It was He Dog's understanding, probably from Black Bear himself, that the problem was Custer's rapid travel—Black Bear could never hope to overtake him. In fact, Custer halted about a half hour later on Davis Creek. I do not intend to reconstruct the whole of the battle with this level of detail, only to show how I have gone about it and to suggest the extent of the materials available.

8. Interview with Kill Eagle, 18 September 1876, *New York Herald*, 6 October 1876; reprinted in Graham, *The Custer Myth*, 48.

9. Interview in 1909 with Runs the Enemy by Joseph K. Dixon, *The Vanishing Race* (Bonanza, n.d.), 171. Runs the Enemy was listed in the Red Cloud census of the

Oglala in the early 1880s, Garrick Mallery, "Picture Writing of the American Indians," 579.

10. Ash Creek is now called Reno Creek.

11. Walter S. Campbell interview with White Bull, 1932, Western History Collection, University of Oklahoma, reprinted in Hardorff, ed., *Indian Views of the Custer Fight*, 149ff. See also Richard G. Hardorff, *Hokahey!*, 134.

12. "Thunder Bear's Version of Custer's Fight," given to Edward Curtis, 1907, Collection 1143, Box 3, Folder 3.8, Natural History Museum of Los Angeles County, reprinted in Hardorff, ed., *Indian Views of the Custer Fight*, 87ff. Report of the woman killed comes from White Bull, Brave Wolf, and Hump, collected by Lieutenant Oscar F. Long during a tour of the Custer battlefield with General Miles, June 1878; Report of 27 June 1878, reprinted in Hardorff, ed., *Indian Views of the Custer Fight*, 43ff.

13. He Dog interview with Walter Camp, 13 July 1910, with William Berger as interpreter, reprinted in Hammer, ed., *Custer in '76* (University of Oklahoma, 1976), pp. 205ff.

14. For readers encountering the battle for the first time it should be clarified here that the battle included two separate fights: an attack by Custer's second in command, Major Marcus Reno, on the Hunkpapa village at the southern end of the big Indian camp; and a separate, slightly later fight which developed downriver between the Indians and Custer's immediate command, of whom there were no survivors. Some Indian accounts distinguish between these two fights by reference to the first group of soldiers (Reno) and the second group of soldiers (Custer). I have adopted this approach in the hope that it will help to portray the whole of the battle in the way that the Indians experienced and remembered it.

15. Mary Crawler interview with Frank Zahn, 1931, Little Soldier interview by Joseph G. Masters, Box 2, Folder 15, Kansas State Historical Society, both reprinted in Hardorff, ed., *Indian Views of the Custer Fight*, 173ff., 92ff.

16. He Dog interview with General Hugh Scott, 24 July 1931, Hugh Scott Papers.

17. Red Feather interview with Hugh Scott, 19 August 1920, copy in the Hugh Scott Papers, reprinted in Richard G. Hardorff, ed., *Lakota Recollections of the Custer Fight*, 81ff.

18. Brave Bear account in George Bent letter to George Hyde, 8 March 1906, MSS SC 860, Brigham Young University, reprinted in Hardorff, ed., *Indian Views of the Custer Fight*, 80ff.

19. Accounts given to Tim McCoy and first published in Graham, *The Custer Myth*, 109.

20. Walter Camp interview with Henry Standing Bear, 12 July 1910, reprinted in Hammer, ed., *Custer in '76*, 214ff. The elder Standing Bear (1837–1898) later added the Christian name George; his daughter, identified by her brother Luther as Wanbli Koyaki Win, later took the name Emily, and it was her son, Robert Dillon, who recorded her memories of the Custer fight, which are included in Pute Tiyospaye (*Lip's Camp*, Crazy Horse School, 1978), 43. For the Standing Bear family generally see Luther Standing Bear, *My People the Sioux*.

21. Joseph G. Masters, quoting Mark Spider from an interview in 1936, *Shadows Fall on the Little Horn* (University of Wyoming Library, 1951), 41–42. Peter Bordeaux, born in 1879, later reported that the items in Crazy Horse's medicine bag consisted "of dried heart and brain of an eagle, mixed with dry, wild aster seed compound to make a bullet proof medicine." Bordeaux statement of 11 June 1969, Edward Kadlecek and Mabell Kadlecek, *To Kill an Eagle*, 89. White Bull

reported Crazy Horse's method of painting himself, cited in a Walter S. Campbell letter of 16 July 1948, Walter S. Campbell Papers, quoted in Richard G. Hardorff, ed., *The Surrender and Death of Crazy Horse*, 26off.

22. Shoots Walking statement to Walter S. Campbell, c. 1935, Box 111, Western History Collections, University of Oklahoma, reprinted in Hardorff, ed., *Indian Views of the Custer Fight*, 166ff.

23. DeMallie, ed., *The Sixth Grandfather*, 183, 190.

24. Red Feather interview with Hugh Scott, 19 August 1920, reprinted in Hardorff, ed., *Lakota Recollections of the Custer Fight*, 81ff. Nick Rouleau interview with Eli Ricker, 20 November 1906, conveying information from Austin Red Hawk, Hardorff, ed., *Lakota Recollections of the Custer Fight*, 37ff. "Thunder Bear's Version of Custer's Fight."

25. Information from Flying Hawk, M. I. McCreight, *Firewater and Forked Tongues*, 49–55.

26. Hamlin Garland, "General Custer's Last Fight as Seen by Two Moon," *McClure's Magazine* (September 1908), reprinted in Graham, *The Custer Myth*, 101. Report by Red Horse, Colonel W. H. Wood, Commanding Post, Cheyenne Agency, 27 February 1877, reprinted in Graham, *The Custer Myth*, 56.

27. Brave Bear account in George Bent letter to George Hyde.

28. Walter S. Campbell interview with White Cow Walking, White Eagle's brother, who recovered the body that night, 2 September 1929, reprinted in Hardorff, ed., *Indian Views of the Custer Fight*, 133ff.

29. Nick Rouleau interview with Eli Ricker, conveying information from Austin Red Hawk, Shot in the Face, Big Road, and Iron Bull, 20 November 1906, Richard E. Jensen, ed., *The Indian Interviews*.

30. DeMallie, ed., *The Sixth Grandfather*, 183.

31. Public remarks by Gall, 25 June 1886, *D. F. Barry's Notes on the Custer Battle*. See also Gall's account as reported in the St. Paul *Daily Globe*, 27 June 1886, and the St. Paul *Pioneer Press*, 18 July 1886, reprinted in Richard Upton, ed., *The Battle of the Little Big Horn and Custer's Last Fight* (Upton and Sons, 2006).

32. The Indians almost certainly did not know during the battle, and probably did not generally learn until it was well over, that the commander of the soldiers was Custer, or that the first attack on the Hunkpapa village had been led by Major Reno. Most accounts of the battle use the common historians' shorthand of referring to groups by their leaders—Custer did this, Reno did that, etc. I have tried to avoid this, identifying Reno's force as the first group of soldiers, and Custer's immediate command as the second group.

33. Thomas L. Riggs, "Sunset to Sunset," *South Dakota Historical Collections* 29 (1958), 187.

34. He Dog interview with Walter Camp, 13 July 1910.

35. The chronology given here comes from Gray, *Custer's Last Campaign*. The sightings of Custer on the bluffs were all recorded by men in Reno's detachment, but anything they saw from the flat south of the Hunkpapa camp was of course visible to the Indians as well. The three cheers were described by White Bull, Brave Wolf, and Hump to Lieutenant Oscar F. Long during a tour of the Custer battlefield with General Miles, June 1878, Report of 27 June 1878, reprinted in Hardorff, ed., *Indian Views of the Custer Fight*, 43ff.

36. Undated Walter Camp interview with Thomas Disputed (A Kinichaki), Bruce R. Liddic and Paul Harbaugh, *Custer & Company*, 121ff.

37. Garland, "General Custer's Last Fight as Seen by Two Moon." Gall walked over

the battlefield and described its course at a commemoration of its tenth anniversary; St. Paul *Pioneer Press*, 18 July 1886, reprinted in Graham, *The Custer Myth*, 89. Feather Earring interview with Hugh Scott, 9 September 1919, reprinted in Graham, *The Custer Myth*, 97.

38. Iron Hawk interview with Eli Ricker, 13 May 1907, Jensen, ed., *The Indian Interviews*, 314. Also reprinted in Hardorff, ed., *Lakota Recollections of the Custer Fight*, 49ff. Feather Earring interview with Hugh Scott, 9 September 1919. He Dog interview with Walter Camp, 13 July 1910.

39. There is much controversy about Custer's route after he diverged from Reno's command at about 2:45 on the afternoon of 25 June. Lieutenant Godfrey thought he swung far to the right and never approached the river at all. Other writers suggest he raced far downstream, then doubled back. And so on. What follows here is what the Indians themselves appear to say. In my view it has the twin virtues of simplicity and of representing the testimony of witnesses.

40. He Dog interview with Walter Camp, 13 July 1910.

41. Flying Hawk interview with Eli Ricker, 8 March 1907, near Big Bat's on Pine Ridge, Hardorff, ed., *Lakota Recollections of the Custer Fight*, 49ff.

42. Red Horse account, Mallery, "Picture Writing of the American Indians."

43. The chronology here is Gray's in *Custer's Last Campaign*.

44. *Leavenworth Weekly Times*, 18 August 1881, reprinted in Hardorff, ed., *Indian Views of the Custer Fight*, 63; and in Graham, *The Custer Myth*, 74.

45. See generally Richard Allan Fox, Jr., *Archaeology, History and Custer's Last Battle* (University of Oklahoma, 1993) for a careful reading of artifact finds as evidence how the battle went. One of Fox's principal arguments is that an orderly defense was managed only at the very outset on Calhoun Ridge, where the pattern of shells and Indian bullets suggests a regulation skirmish line. Elsewhere the men were piled all close in one on another in a classic sign of panic on the battlefield, or were killed in chaotic dispersion hither and yon over the field. Interview with Yellow Nose, *Chicago Inter-Ocean*, 24 March 1912, reprinted in Hardorff, ed., *Indian Views of the Custer Fight*, 97ff.

46. Thomas L. Riggs, "Sunset to Sunset."

47. Interview with Low Dog [1847–1894] at Fort Yates, 30 July 1881, *Leavenworth Times*, 14 August 1881, reprinted in Hardorff, ed., *Indian Views of the Custer Fight*, 63ff.

48. Brave Bear account in George Bent letter to George Hyde, 8 March 1906. John Neihardt interview with Eagle Elk, 1944, partially reprinted in Hardorff, ed., *Lakota Recollections of the Custer Fight*, 104–05. DeMallie, ed., *The Sixth Grandfather*, 185. Thomas B. Marquis, trans., *Wooden Leg*, 234.

49. Account by the Arapaho Waterman given to Tim McCoy; first published in Graham, *The Custer Myth*, 109. See also Peter J. Powell, *Sweet Medicine*, 119; and Hardorff, *Hokahey!*, 65–67.

50. Nick Rouleau interview with Eli Ricker, conveying information from Austin Red Hawk, Shot in the Face, Big Road, and Iron Bull.

51. Information from Flying Hawk, McCreight, *Firewater and Forked Tongues*, 49–55. Public remarks by Gall, 25 June 1886, *D. F. Barry's Notes on the Custer Battle*.

52. Account by the Arapaho Waterman given to Tim McCoy.

53. He Dog interview with Walter Camp, 13 July 1910. He Dog, Red Feather, and Whirling interview with Hugh Scott, 19 August 1920, reprinted in Hardorff, ed., *Lakota Recollections of the Custer Fight*, 73ff.

54. Foolish Elk interview with Walter Camp, 22 September 1908, Louis Roubideaux and A. G. Shaw, interpreters, reprinted in Hammer, ed., *Custer in '76*, 197ff.

55. White Bull interview with Walter S. Campbell, 1932. Garland, "General Custer's Last Fight as Seen by Two Moon." Foolish Elk interview with Walter Camp.

   Where the bodies lay is marked by gravestones erected in 1890 on the sites of earlier markers; unfortunately the Army captain who performed the work had about 236 stones—too many for the 210 men who actually died with Custer. He seems to have doubled up the stones at some of the sites along the arc of the battle, preserving the pattern but confusing the precision of the actual lie. For that reason the number of dead cited here for each site is approximate.

56. Unidentified news clipping from Pine Ridge, dated 25 September 1936, reprinted in Hardorff, ed., *Indian Views of the Custer Fight*, 149ff. Brave Bear account in George Bent letter to George Hyde, 8 March 1906. Report of Captain R. E. Johnston, Standing Rock Agency, 18 September 1876, published in the *New York Herald*, 6 October 1876, reprinted in Graham, *The Custer Myth*, 48.

57. *Leavenworth Times*, 18 August 1881. Red Horse account, Garrick Mallery, "Picture Writing of the American Indians." DeMallie, ed., *The Sixth Grandfather*, 186.

58. Black Elk in DeMallie, ed., *The Sixth Grandfather*, 193.

59. Standing Bear interview with Eli Ricker, 12 March 1907, Hardorff, ed., *Lakota Recollections of the Custer Fight*, 57ff. Hamlin Garland, "General Custer's Last Fight as Seen by Two Moon." Eli Ricker interview with Respects Nothing, Jensen, ed., *The Indian Interviews*, reprinted in Hardorff, ed., *Lakota Recollections of the Custer Fight*, 25ff. The man in buckskins has been convincingly identified as the mixed-blood scout Mitch Bouyer.

60. Red Horse account, Garrick Mallery, "Picture Writing of the American Indians." All of these extraordinary drawings have been reproduced in Herman J. Viola, *The Little Big Horn Remembered* (Times Books, 1999). "Thunder Bear's Version of Custer's Fight."

61. Respects Nothing and Eagle Ring interview with Eli Ricker, Jensen, ed., *The Indian Interviews*, reprinted in Hardorff, ed., *Lakota Recollections of the Custer Fight*, 25ff. Unidentified news clipping from Pine Ridge, dated 25 September 1936. Account by the Arapaho Waterman given to Tim McCoy. Powell, *Sweet Medicine*, 117; John Stands in Timber and Margot Liberty, *Cheyenne Memories*, 121.

62. Interview with Little Killer by Chicago researcher Julia Abrahamson in 1937. Typewritten note by George Hyde with three photographs, papers in the author's possession.

63. W. P. Clark, *The Indian Sign Language*, 155.

64. Thomas Marquis interview with Kate Bighead, 1927, "She Watched Custer's Last Battle," reprinted in Marquis, *Custer on the Little Big Horn*. Peter Powell also heard this story from Little Face, Mary Little Bear Inkanish, and John Stands in Timber. His retelling can be found in Powell, *Sweet Medicine*, 119ff.

65. Short Bull interview, 13 July 1930, Eleanor H. Hinman, *Oglala Sources*, 36.

66. The words are those of John Stands in Timber, who heard this story from Charles Whistling Elk (b. 1876), who was repeating the words of his father, Braided Locks (1840–1936), who later adopted the Christian name of Arthur

Brady. See *Cheyenne Memories*, 105, and mentions of "Brady Locks"; Powell, *Sweet Medicine*, 366; and references to Braided Locks in George Bird Grinnell, *The Fighting Cheyennes*. For the identity of Braided Locks–Arthur Brady see "Notice to Repatriate Cultural Items in the Possession of the Buffalo Bill Historical Center, Cody, WY"; *Federal Register* 61, no. 74 (1996), 16644–16645. The cultural items were sun dance rattles previously owned by Braided Locks.

In 1963, at a Wyoming State Historical Convention, John Stands in Timber described the petroglyph to Glenn Sween of Sheridan, Wyoming, who made an acrylic cast in 1969. The drawing has since been removed or destroyed by looters or vandals. *The Sheridan Press*, 27 August 1993.

25. *"It is impossible to work him through reasoning or kindness."*

1. Walter Camp interview with Jesse Lee, Greencastle, Indiana, 27 October 1912, Walter Camp Papers.
2. ADG, Division of the Missouri to Crook, 18 April 1877, Department of the Platte, Letters Received, Box 49.
3. Bradley to Crook, 16 July 1877, Adjutant General's Office, Letters Received, Division of the Missouri, M666/R282.
4. Luther Bradley Papers. Included are diaries, numerous letters to Ione, occasional letters from fellow officers, and notebooks filled with odd jottings in which Bradley recorded his travels, what he learned about plainscraft, the names and fates of his horses, a detailed record of his military service, the warrior strength of various Sioux bands in 1867, and a great deal else.
5. V. T. McGillycuddy letter to Elmo Scott Watson, 7 September 1923, Elmo Scott Watson Papers. Much information on Provost's brief life is to be found in the pension file of Jennie Shot Close, Provost's wife, IWC 1,605,272, National Archives.
6. Bradley describes the old man and his stick in a letter to Ione of 30 May 1877. There is a substantial literature about Sioux winter counts, of which scores survive. An excellent introduction would be Candace S. Green and Russell Thornton, *The Year the Stars Fell* (Smithsonian, 2007), which reproduces a number of winter counts from the collections of the Smithsonian Institution. The best documented winter count was compiled by George Colhoff for the years 1759–1945, exceptional for the span of years covered and the identity of Colhoff's informants. About half of it was published by William K. Powers, who received it from Colhoff's son John in the mid-1940s, and the rest can be found in the Elmo Scott Watson Papers, Box 39, Folder 589. The names of the years match those of many other counts, but Colhoff added substantial information about the events from his eight elderly Sioux informants: Chasing Raven, Chase in Winter, He Dog, Little Shield, Kills a Hundred, Little Killer, Short Bull, and Whirlwind Man. It's a good bet that the old man's history stick had much in common with the Colhoff winter count.
7. Charles M. Robinson III, ed., *The Diaries*, vol. 2, p. 277; Fannie McGillycuddy diary, Nebraska State Historical Society; V. T. McGillycuddy letter to E. A. Brininstool, 21 April 1926, James C. Cook papers.
8. Some sources say her first name was Helen, but pension and agency records refer to her as Ellen, which is presumably what she told officials. Ellen's last name is spelled in almost as many different ways as there are sources, including Larvie,

Laravie, Laravere, Larrabie, Larrabbee and Larrabee. The last is perhaps the most common of all and is used here because that is the spelling used to record Joe Larrabee's presence among the Cheyenne in Thomas R. Buecker and R. Eli Paul, eds., *The Crazy Horse Surrender Ledger*, 58. The marriages of the Larrabee girls can be found in James M. Robinson, *West from Fort Pierre: The Wild World of James (Scotty) Philip* (Westernlore Press, 1974), 51. Pourier's version of events was given to Eli Ricker, in an interview with Baptiste Pourier, 6 March 1907, Richard E. Jensen, ed., *The Soldier and Settler Interviews*, 271. Many of the relatives of Crazy Horse have been established by Richard G. Hardorff in his *The Oglala Lakota Crazy Horse*. Indians seeking pensions frequently referred to Lieutenant Clark as White Hat, and the Lakota for his name comes from the Blue Horse pension file. Details of Ellen Larrabee's family were provided by Tom Larvie and Mrs. Clown to William J. Bordeaux, son of Louis Bordeaux and grandson of James Bordeaux, who records them in *The Man Who Conquered Custer* (Privately published, 1944), 70–71, 94–95.

9. Tom's version was told to William J. Bordeaux in Norris, South Dakota, in 1944; *The Man Who Conquered Custer*, 94–95. Victoria Conroy, eleven years old at the time of Crazy Horse's death, was a relative by marriage on his mother's side. In a letter to James MacGregor, superintendent at Pine Ridge, 18 December 1934, she remarked, "He only had Miss Laravere a month or so when he was killed." Conroy letter, Burnside Papers, Iowa Historical Department, reprinted in Richard G. Hardorff, ed., *The Surrender and Death of Crazy Horse*, 265. A correspondent for the *New York Tribune* visited the agencies in the first week of June and remarked that "[Spotted Tail] does not, like Crazy Horse, limit himself to one wife." Story datelined Camp Sheridan, 15 July, from the *New York Daily Tribune*, 7 September 1877.

10. Ghost Bear affidavit, 5 June 1928; Sioux Bob/Zuzella Little Bear pension file, IWO 15177. The Sioux Bob/Ellen Larrabee connection is found in Kingsley M. Bray, *Crazy Horse*, 318. For Ellen's marriage to Kills a Hundred see Susie Kills One Hundred pension file, XC-2,624,082. Eli Ricker interview with William Garnett, 15 January 1907, Richard E. Jensen, ed., *The Indian Interviews*, 58–59.

11. Clark to Crook, 1 August 1877, Letters Received, War AGO, Division of the Missouri, M666/R282. Clark to Crook, 18 August 1877, Robinson, ed., *The Diaries*, vol. 3, p. 513. Clark's horse is identified by Red Feather, Eleanor H. Hinman, *Oglala Sources*, 27.

12. Garnett identifies Lone Bear and Little Wolf as brothers, and Eleanor Hinman says that Lone Bear was also a brother of Woman Dress. See Hinman, *Oglala Sources*, 48, n. 34.

13. Richard Nines interview with Woman Dress, 16 February 1912, AMNH; quoted in slightly different form in Clark Wissler, *Societies and Ceremonial Associations*, 95.

14. It goes like this: Walks As She Thinks, the mother of Red Cloud, was a sister of both Smoke and White Thunder Woman, two of whose daughters became the mothers in their turn of Josephine Richard and Gray Cow, who respectively married Baptiste Pourier and Woman Dress. Brushing aside the fine detail Red Feather simply said, "Woman Dress was Red Cloud's first cousin and always stayed with him." Red Feather interview, 8 July 1930, Hinman, *Oglala Sources*, 29. See also Hila Gilbert, *Big Bat Pourier* (The Mills Company, 1968); Wallace Amiotte letter to George Hyde, 10 November 1959, author's possession; and

Pourier's pension file. In a letter of 7 November 1939 [author's possession] to George Hyde, Philip F. Wells writes, "[A]bout Black Twin or Bad Face. I know nothing about the man himself, but his son Woman Dress, I was very well acquainted with." The society memberships of Woman Dress are cited in Wissler, *Societies and Ceremonial Associations*, 95–99.

15. Robinson, ed., *The Diaries*, vol. 2, pp. 483ff. John G. Bourke, *On the Border with Crook*, 418.

16. Mrs. Carrie Slow Bear interview, 12 July 1930, Hinman, *Oglala Sources*, 40. Lieutenant Jesse Lee letter to Walter Camp, 6 November 1912, reports on the favoritism, Walter Camp Papers. Little Killer interview, 12 July 1930, Hinman, *Oglala Sources*, 42; Luther Standing Bear, *Land of the Spotted Eagle*, 181.

17. Crazy Horse family connections are difficult to pin down. The chief's sister is variously reported as the wife of Club Man (by Little Killer) and Clown (by William J. Bordeaux). Further complicating matters is the report of James H. Cook that he had been given a whetstone once owned by Crazy Horse by the chief's sister, the wife of Red Sack. If Crazy Horse had but one sister, as He Dog claimed, then Club Man and Clown may have been alternate names for the same person, or Crazy Horse's sister may have been married to different men at different times.

18. Susan Bordeaux Bettelyoun and Josephine Waggoner, *With My Own Eyes*, 108–09; Eli Ricker interview with William Garnett, 15 January 1907. Mrs. Carrie Slow Bear interview, 12 July 1930.

19. The chief's reluctance to believe the worst is found in Eli Ricker interview with Charles Eastman, 20 August 1907, Jensen, ed., *The Indian Interviews*, 286.

20. Report of Commissioner of Indian Affairs, 1859, abstracted in *South Dakota Historical Collections* 27 (1954), 193. Hugh L. Scott, *Some Memories of a Soldier*, 49ff.

21. Scott, *Some Memories of a Soldier*, 52. At just about the same moment—July 1877—the North brothers went to Ogallala, Nebraska, to buy cattle for a new ranching enterprise. Looking out over the vast pens of cattle driven up from Texas, Luther asked his brother Frank how the numbers of cattle compared with the buffalo herds they'd seen on a hunting trip in 1870 with Buffalo Bill Cody. "He replied, 'I think there were ten times as many buffalo in sight then as there are cattle.' " On inquiry they were told the Ogallala corrals held forty thousand cattle. The buffalo were gone from Nebraska, Kansas, and Texas, but they remained in Montana. Luther Heddon North, *Man of the Plains*, 238.

22. Lieutenant W. P. Clark to Lieutenant W. S. Schuyler, 13 June 1877, Sioux War files, M1495/R4.

23. For the record, the Red Cloud Agency census in early 1877 reports sixty-four lodges and 441 people in the band of Young Man Afraid of His Horses, fifty-six lodges and 356 people in Yellow Bear's Melt Band, 135 lodges and 964 people in Little Wound's Cut-off band, 145 lodges and 899 people in Crazy Horse's Hunkpatila band, sixty-four lodges and 446 people in American Horse's Loafer band, seventy-three lodges and 468 people in Red Cloud's Bad Face band, seventy-six lodges and 474 people in Red Leaf's Wahjahjah band, and fifty-seven lodges and 339 people of northern Cheyenne. Buecker and Paul, eds., *The Crazy Horse Surrender Ledger*, passim.

24. The council at the Red Cloud Agency is described by Benjamin Shopp, letter to CIA, 15 August 1877, Red Cloud Agency files, M234/R721, reprinted in Richard G. Hardorff, ed., *The Surrender and Death of Crazy Horse*, 168ff. Clark to Crook, 1 August 1877, Letters Received, War AGO, Division of the Missouri,

M666/R282. Crook to AAG, Military Division of the Missouri, 1 August 1877, cited in Charles M. Robinson III, *General Crook and the Western Frontier*, 215. *Cheyenne Daily Leader*, 7 August 1877.

25. Bradley to Crook, 16 July 1877, AGO, Letters Received, Division of the Missouri.

26. Jesse M. Lee, "The Capture and Death of an Indian Chieftain," *Journal of the Military Service Institution of the United States* (May–June 1941), reprinted in Peter Cozzens, *The Long War for the Northern Plains*, 531. Bradley to ADG, 15 August 1877, Robinson, ed., *The Diaries*, vol. 3. Clark letter to Crook, 18 August 1877, Robinson, ed., *The Diaries*, vol. 3, reprinted in Hardorff, *The Surrender and Death of Crazy Horse*, 171ff.

26. *"If you go to Washington they are going to kill you."*

1. Little Killer interview, 12 July 1930, and He Dog interview, 13 July 1930, Eleanor H. Hinman, *Oglala Sources*, 23, 42.

2. John G. Bourke, *On the Border with Crook*, 415.

3. H. R. Lemly letter to E. A. Brininstool, 17 June 1925, *Hunter-Trapper-Trader* (May 1933), quoted in Peter Cozzens, *The Long War for the Northern Plains*, 542–48. Walter Camp interview with Horn Chips, c. 11 July 1910, quoted in Richard G. Hardorff, ed., *The Surrender and Death of Crazy Horse*, 85. William F. Kelly, Grant Shumway, ed., *History of Western Nebraska* (The Western Publishing Company, 1921), vol. 2, pp. 544ff.

4. William Philo Clark letters to W. S. Schuyler, 10 and 11 June 1877, Sioux War files, M1495/R4. *Cheyenne Daily Leader*, 25 July 1877. James Irwin letter to CIA, 13 July 1877, Red Cloud Agency files, M234/R721.

5. W. R. Felton, writing as "California Bill," in the *Cheyenne Ledger*, 10 July 1877. For a thorough account of Calhoun see Tom Buecker, *Greasy Grass* (May 1994); also *Cheyenne Ledger*, 13 July 1877, for Indians going north, and 4 August 1877, which describes the officers' burial at Fort Leavenworth. Benjamin Shopp reports four horses as the price of a rifle, letter to CIA, 15 August 1877, reprinted in Hardorff, ed., *The Surrender and Death of Crazy Horse*, 168ff.

6. Shopp to CIA, 15 August 1877.

7. Ibid.

8. He Dog interview, 13 July 1930, 24. He Dog account, eleven-page typescript, Museum of the Fur Trade, Chadron, Nebraska.

9. Colhoff winter count for the year 1877.

10. The winter count on deerskin: Joe DeBarthe, *Life and Adventures of Frank Grouard*, 80. Charles M. Robinson III, ed., *The Diaries*, vol. 2, p. 298, and vol. 3, p. 68.

11. DeBarthe, *Life and Adventures of Frank Grouard*, 100, 182. See Bordeaux interviews with Eli Ricker, 31 August 1907, Richard E. Jensen, ed., *The Indian Interviews*, 280, and Walter Camp, 6 and 7 July 1910, Bruce R. Liddic and Paul Harbaugh, *Custer & Company*, 137ff.

12. See Bordeaux interviews with Eli Ricker, 31 August 1907, and Walter Camp, 6 and 7 July 1910.

13. Jesse M. Lee, "The Capture and Death of an Indian Chieftain," *Journal of the Military Service Institution of the United States* (May–June 1941), quoted in Peter Cozzens, *The Long War for the Northern Plains*, 531.

14. Reference to Black Fox and the movement of northern Indians to join Crazy

Horse can be found in the affidavit of Charging First, son of Touch the Clouds, 3 October 1921, SDHS, Clark's letter to Crook, 18 August 1877, Lieutenant Jesse Lee letter to CIA, 2 August 1877, M234/R841, and Daniel Burke letter to General Luther P. Bradley, 16 August 1877, USMHI, Carlisle Barracks.

15. Lieutenant G. A. Dodd interview with Billy Hunter, requested by J. G. Bourke; Robinson, ed., *The Diaries*, vol. 3, pp. 65ff. Bradley letter to his mother, 8 September 1877, text and facsimile published as Lot no. 576, HCA Auction site, 17 February 2004. The image of the letter confirms the hand as unmistakably Bradley's. Lee, "The Capture and Death of an Indian Chieftain."

16. Clark letter to Crook, 18 August 1877.

17. W. P. Clark, *The Indian Sign Language*, 155. DeBarthe, *Life and Adventures of Frank Grouard*, 182.

27. *"We washed the blood from our faces."*

1. Bradley's letter to Colonel Robert Williams, Adjutant General of the Department of the Platte, 31 August 1877, is reprinted in Charles M. Robinson III, ed., *The Diaries*, vol. 3, p. 12. The original can be found in the National Archives, Department of the Platte, Letters Received, Box 52. Colonel Williams's cable to Crook on the westbound train, Crook's reply to Bradley on 1 September, and Sheridan's cable to Crook on the same day, are all found in *The Diaries*, vol. 3, p. 504. Sheridan's cable to Washington explaining the change in orders is in the Red Cloud Agency files, M234/R721.

2. Sheridan's order approving additional scouts is included in Office of the Adjutant General, Letters Received, M266/R259. See also Jesse M. Lee, "The Capture and Death of an Indian Chieftain," *Journal of the Military Service Institution of the United States* (May–June 1914).

3. Eli Ricker interview with William Garnett, 15 January 1907, Richard E. Jensen, ed., *The Indian Interviews*, 60.

4. Clark's letter to Burke is quoted in Lee, "The Capture and Death of an Indian Chieftain," reprinted in Peter Cozzens, *The Long War for the Northern Plains*, 532.

5. Jesse Lee, Report to the Commissioner of Indian Affairs, 30 September 1877, Spotted Tail Agency, Letters Sent. Walter Camp interview with Jesse Lee, 27 October 1912, Walter Camp Papers.

6. V. T. McGillycuddy letter to William Garnett, 24 June 1927, Robert A. Clark, ed., *The Killing of Chief Crazy Horse*, 123. McGillycuddy's account of these events in this letter is garbled in a complex way, but he seems to have identified correctly the most important of the misinterpretations of Touch the Clouds's speech at the meeting on 31 August 1877.

7. For details of Bordeaux's life see his sister's memoir, Susan Bordeaux Bettelyoun and Josephine Waggoner, *With My Own Eyes;* Eli Ricker interview with Louis Bordeaux, 31 August 1907, Jensen, ed., *The Indian Interviews*, 290; and the roster of employees at the Spotted Tail Agency, 30 September 1877, M234/R841.

8. Walter Camp interview with Jesse Lee, 27 October 1912.

9. Louis Bordeaux interviews with Walter Camp in July 1912 (Bruce R. Liddic and Paul Harbaugh, *Custer & Company*, 121ff.) and with Eli Ricker, 31 August 1907. See also Walter Camp interview with Jesse Lee, 27 October 1912.

10. Lee, "The Capture and Death of an Indian Chieftain," 533.

11. In the enlistment records He Dog is recorded as He Wolf, an error which pre-

vented him from receiving a pension in later life. Details of He Dog's life can be found in the pension files of his brothers Short Bull and Little Shield, and in his interviews with Hugh Scott, 19 August 1920, and 24 July 1931, Hugh Scott Papers; Eleanor H. Hinman, *Oglala Sources*, and Helen H. Blish, *A Pictographic History of the Oglala Sioux*, nos. 346, 348, pp. 315–80. See also the interviews with Joseph Eagle Hawk, He Dog, and others conducted in the summers of 1930 and 1931 by Scudder Mekeel, American Museum of Natural History.

12. He Dog reported the killing of his brother in the Wagon Box fight to Hugh Scott, 24 July 1931, Hugh Scott Papers. Clark letter to Crook, 18 August 1877. He Dog interview, 7 July 1930, Hinman, *Oglala Sources*, 19.

13. The Sorebacks and the origin of the name are found in Scudder Mekeel's interview with Joseph Eagle Hawk, American Museum of Natural History, where the word is spelled Tcankauhan; and in the Colhoff winter count for the year of He Dog's death, 1936, where the word is spelled Cankahuhan.

14. Irwin described the situation in back-to-back letters to the commissioner of Indian affairs, 31 August and 1 September 1877, Red Cloud Agency files, M234/R721.

15. L. P. Bradley to R. Williams, 31 August 1877, Department of the Platte, Letters Received, Box 52.

28. *"I can have him whenever I want him."*

1. Martin F. Schmitt, ed., *General George Crook*, 170–71, 184.

2. John G. Bourke, *On the Border with Crook*, 169; Charles M. Robinson III, *General Crook and the Western Frontier*, 125–26.

3. In his autobiography, and in letters to Lieutenant Walter S. Schuyler in the 1870s, Crook variously spells the chief's name as Deltchay, Delche, Deltche, Delchay, DelChay, and Delchae.

4. The Deltchay letters are preserved among a substantial collection of the lieutenant's papers which were later donated by his family to the Huntington Library, in San Marino, California.

5. Crook to Walter S. Schuyler, 15 September 1873, Walter S. Schuyler Papers.

6. Schmitt, ed., *General George Crook*, 182. See also "Major General George Crook and the Indians," Azor Nickerson, copy in the Walter S. Schuyler Papers.

7. Crook letters to Schuyler of 13 July, 8 August, and 30 October 1874, Schuyler papers.

8. Lucy Lee report to the *Greencastle* [Indiana] *Star*, n.d., datelined Camp Sheridan, Nebraska, 18 September 1877, reprinted in E. A. Brininstool, *Crazy Horse*, 62ff.

9. Lee is our only source for this argument. His version of events can be found in three letters to Walter Camp, of 13 and 24 May 1910, and 6 November 1912; in his official report of 30 September 1877, and in his long account in the *Journal of the Military Service Institution of the United States* (May–June 1914), reprinted in Peter Cozzens, *The Long War for the Northern Plains*, 528ff. Other relevant documents by and about Lee can be found in the papers of Luther Bradley and in Lee's ACP file in the National Archives.

10. Bradley diary, 2 September 1877, Luther Bradley Papers, Charles M. Robinson III, ed., *The Diaries*, vol. 3, p. 73.

11. He Dog's accounts of these conversations were made on 7 and 13 July 1930 with Eleanor Hinman; they are found in *Oglala Sources*, 18–24.

12. The child died at birth. For details of Garnett's wives and children see William Garnett pension file, NA, XC 2–643–650.

13. Garnett provided three accounts of the events surrounding the killing of Crazy Horse: one to Lieutenant George Dodd for the use of Lieutenant Bourke in 1878, now published in *The Diaries*, vol. 3, pp. 513ff.; one to Eli Ricker in 1907, now published in Richard E. Jensen, ed., *The Indian Interviews*, 60ff.; and one to General Hugh Scott in August 1920, a copy of which can be found in the South Dakota State Historical Society. The first departs from the other versions on several sensitive points and must be treated with care; the second is full and rich without apparent bias but is in effect retold by Ricker; the third is essentially a six-thousand-word transcript of Garnett's testimony as he delivered it. Numerous other documents provide ancillary detail about the meeting of Crook and Woman Dress.

14. Bourke, *On the Border with Crook*, 420.

15. Garnett's long account was given to General Hugh Scott, 19 August 1920.

16. The nine others were Yellow Bear (son of the chief Garnett had seen killed), Red Dog, No Flesh, High Wolf, Black Bear, Dog (a member of Yellow Bear's Melt band), Slow Bull, Blue Horse, and Three Bears, the man closest to Lieutenant Clark.

17. William Garnett account to General Hugh Scott, 19 August 1920.

18. Eli Ricker interview with Charles Eastman, 20 August 1907, Jensen, ed., *The Indian Interviews*, 286–87. See also Charles A. Eastman, *Indian Heroes and Great Chieftains*, 46–47, and the Eleanor Hinman interview with Red Feather, 8 July 1930, *Oglala Sources*, 26–27. Crazy Horse's companions in flight are identified in Eli Ricker interview with William Garnett, 15 January 1907, Jensen, ed., *The Indian Interviews*.

19. Eli Ricker interview with William Garnett, Jensen, ed., *The Indian Interviews*, 62. The rest of Garnett's account quoted here comes from his later interview with General Scott in August 1920.

20. Walter Camp interview with Jesse Lee, 27 October 1912, Walter Camp Papers. Jesse Lee, Report to the Commissioner of Indian Affairs, 30 September 1877. Jesse M. Lee, "The Capture and Death of an Indian Chieftain."

29. *"I am Crazy Horse! Don't touch me!"*

1. According to Lemly there were one hundred lodges in Crazy Horse's village at the end of August. Bourke in his diary reports that on the night of 3 September the number had fallen to seventy-three. Lieutenant H. R. Lemly, writing in the *New York Sun*, 14 September 1877, reprinted in Richard G. Hardorff, ed., *The Surrender and Death of Crazy Horse*, 238ff. Charles M. Robinson III, ed., *The Diaries*, vol. 3. He Dog identifies Bull Head as an uncle of Crazy Horse, and reports his presence with the scouts. He Dog interview with Eleanor Hinman, 13 July 1930, *Oglala Sources;* and He Dog account, eleven-page typescript, Museum of the Fur Trade, Chadron, Nebraska.

2. Luke Voorhees letter in the *Cheyenne Daily Leader,* 7 September 1877.

3. Lemly, *New York Sun,* 14 September 1877. Lucy Lee letter dated 18 September 1877 in the *Greencastle* (Indiana) *Star,* n.d., reprinted in E. A. Brininstool, *Crazy Horse,* 62ff. The files of the *Greencastle Star* have largely been lost.

4. Red Feather interview, 8 July 1930, Hinman, *Oglala Sources,* 27.

5. The meeting with Looking Horse is described by Garnett in his interview with Hugh Scott and to Judge Eli Ricker, and by He Dog to his nephew Eagle Hawk. The *Chicago Times*, 5 September 1877, reported that Looking Horse was shot. Colonel Bradley in a letter to his mother said two people died in the Crazy Horse affair: the chief, and another man, unnamed—but not Looking Horse, who survived into the early 1900s.

6. Bull Head and Buffalo Head are cited in the Battiste Good and High Hawk winter counts under both variant names as having commemorated the dead in the Custer fight.

7. The encounter with Looking Horse is described by Garnett in his interview with Hugh Scott, and by He Dog in his account given to his nephew, Joseph Eagle Hawk.

8. Black Fox's status as a Shirt Wearer was reported by Black Moccasin, interview on 11 September 1931 with Scudder Mekeel, Silas Afraid of Enemy, interpreter; American Museum of Natural History. Robert Strahorn reported that Black Fox was a "brother-in-law of Crazy Horse." *Cheyenne Daily Leader*, 18 September 1877.

9. Black Fox's words are recorded by Garnett in slightly differing form in his interviews with Hugh Scott and Eli Ricker.

10. Eli Ricker interview with William Garnett, Jensen, ed., *The Indian Interviews*, 64. "The biting of the knife": Royal B. Hassrick, *The Sioux*, 39.

11. *Chicago Times*, 26 May 1877.

12. Jesse M. Lee, "The Capture and Death of an Indian Chieftain," *Journal of the Military Service Institution of the United States* (May–June 1941), quoted in Peter Cozzens, *The Long War for the Northern Plains*, 536. Horn Chips told Eli Ricker that Crazy Horse came to his lodge on Beaver Creek, Jensen, ed., *The Indian Interviews*, 276.

30. *"He feels too weak to die today."*

1. Statements of Mary Pacer and Jessie Romero Eagle Heart, both granddaughters of Fast Thunder; Edward Kadlecek and Mabell Kadlecek, *To Kill an Eagle*, 2, 21.

2. Jesse M. Lee, "The Capture and Death of an Indian Chieftain," *Journal of the Military Service Institution of the United States* (May–June 1941), quoted in Peter Cozzens, *The Long War for the Northern Plains*, 535–36.

3. Lee often described these events, most notably in his Report to the Commissioner of Indian Affairs, 30 September 1877; in an interview with Walter Camp, 27 October 1912, Walter Camp Papers; Lee, "The Capture and Death of an Indian Chieftain." In a letter to Walter Camp of 13 May 1910 Lee wrote, "I never saw Crazy Horse till he came with his wife to Spotted Tail Agency." Walter Camp Papers. See also Charging First affidavit, 3 October 1921, South Dakota Historical Society.

4. Eli Ricker interview with Louis Bordeaux, 30 August 1907, Richard E. Jensen, ed., *The Indian Interviews*, 290ff. Lee's impressions come from the sources already cited.

5. Ibid.

6. Lee, "The Capture and Death of an Indian Chieftain," 535–36.

7. This episode is described by two witnesses: Louis Bordeaux and Jesse Lee, and by Lee's wife, Lucy. See Eli Ricker interview with Louis Bordeaux, 30 August

1907; Lee, "The Capture and Death of an Indian Chieftain," 536; and Lucy Lee letter dated 18 September 1877 in the *Greencastle* (Indiana) *Star*, n.d., reprinted in E. A. Brininstool, *Crazy Horse*, 62ff.

8. The early life of Horn Chips is described by Robert H. Ruby, *The Oglala Sioux: Warriors in Transition* (Vantage, 1955), 52. William K. Powers, *Yuwipi* (University of Nebraska, 1982), 94, thinks Ruby heard this story from George Plenty Wolf in the early 1950s. Reference to Horn Chips's stone medicine is found in Luther Standing Bear, *Land of the Spotted Eagle*, 208. See also He Dog and Red Feather interviews with Eleanor Hinman, *Oglala Sources*, and Mari Sandoz, 30 June 1931, quoted in Richard G. Hardorff, ed., *The Surrender and Death of Crazy Horse*, 120. The experience of Horned Horse is related by John W. Ford in the *Chicago Times*, 26 May 1877, and by John F. Finerty, *War-Path and Bivouac*, 137.

9. Eli Ricker interview with Louis Bordeaux, 294.

10. Lieutenant Jesse Lee, Report to the Commissioner of Indian Affairs, 30 September 1877. Louis Bordeaux interview with Walter Camp, 6 and 7 July 1910, Bruce R. Liddic and Paul Harbaugh, *Custer & Company*, 137ff.

11. Eli Ricker interview with Louis Bordeaux.

12. Lucy Lee letter dated 18 September 1877. Lee, Report to the Commissioner of Indian Affairs, 30 September 1877.

13. Good Voice was promoted for his investigation of the murder of a mail courier in June 1877. Fast Thunder and High Bear also took part. See reports of Lieutenant Frederick Schwatka, 8 and 9 July 1877, Department of the Platte, Letters Received, Box 51.

14. Lucy Lee letter dated 18 September 1877.

31. *"I heard him using the brave word."*

1. For Crazy Horse's medicine see the drawings of Amos Bad Heart Bull, in Helen H. Blish, *A Pictographic History of the Oglala Sioux*, nos. 219 and 272, pp. 315–80; Luther Standing Bear, *Land of the Spotted Eagle*, 209, and "One Indian the White Man Never Conquered," *Los Angeles Times*, 22 January 1933; statements of Joseph Black Elk, Peter Bordeaux, and James Chase in Morning, Edward Kadlecek and Mabell Kadlecek, *To Kill an Eagle*; Eli Ricker interview with Horn Chips, 14 February 1907; and Mark Spider interview in 1936, Joseph G. Masters, *Shadows Fall on the Little Horn*, 41–42.

2. Crazy Horse's dress on the fatal day was reported by White Calf in an interview with Eleanor Hinman, 11 July 1930, *Oglala Sources*, 41. His clothes are depicted by Standing Bear in a painting on muslin sold by Sotheby's; the red medicine bag is clearly shown; see note 24. The knife is described by Jesse Lee in a letter to Walter Camp, 24 May 1910, Walter Camp Papers; and by H. R. Lemly, *Military Service Institution of the United States*, reprinted in Peter Cozzens, *The Long War for the Northern Plains*, 542–48. The whetstone and case were given by Crazy Horse's sister to James H. Cook; identification card handwritten by Harold J. Cook, son of James Cook, James H. Cook Papers.

3. Lee's version of the day's events are mainly recorded in his Report to the Commissioner of Indian Affairs, 30 September 1877; his interview with Walter Camp, 27 October 1910; and his article, "The Capture and Death of an Indian Chieftain," *Journal of the Military Service Institution of the United States* (May–June 1914), reprinted in Cozzens, *The Long War for the Northern Plains*, 537.

4. Little Bull was a son of Horned Horse, and after the latter's death took his

father's name. Crazy Horse's refusal to dismount is recorded in Little Bull's pension file, National Archives, Pension Certificate 2615707. See also Lee, "The Capture and Death of an Indian Chieftain," and Lucy Lee letter dated 18 September 1877 in the *Greencastle* (Indiana) *Star.*

5. Eli Ricker interview with Louis Bordeaux, 30 August 1907, Richard E. Jensen, *The Indian Interviews,* 290ff.

6. Waglula was a brother of the wife's mother. Luther Standing Bear, *My People the Sioux,* 84; "advised him not to fear": Remarks of Henry Standing Bear prepared for unveiling of the Crazy Horse Monument at Fort Robinson, 5 September 1934, copy in Fort Robinson Museum files. Henry was the elder brother of Luther.

7. Henry Standing Bear interview with Walter Camp, July 1910, Indiana University, reprinted in Richard G. Hardorff, ed., *The Surrender and Death of Crazy Horse,* 114. A brief biography of Turning Bear is found in the Josephine Waggoner Papers. He Dog reports that Yellow Horse was in the group, He Dog account, eleven-page typescript, Museum of the Fur Trade, Chadron, Nebraska.

8. Much information about the Fast Thunder family can be found in Kadlecek and Kadlecek, *To Kill an Eagle;* Mathew King and Harvey Arden, ed., *Noble Red Man* (Beyond Words, 1994); the interview of Jennie Fast Thunder by Luther Standing Bear, included in *Land of the Spotted Eagle;* and in the pension file for Jennie Fast Thunder, National Archives.

9. Lee, "The Capture and Death of an Indian Chieftain." The Oglala following in the wake of the friendly Brulé are identified by William Garnett and Lieutenant H. R. Lemly, writing in the *New York Sun,* 14 September 1877.

10. Lucy Lee letter dated 18 September 1877; Lee, "The Capture and Death of an Indian Chieftain."

11. Standing Bear, *Land of the Spotted Eagle,* 182. The first version, differing only in punctuation and the choice of a few words, appeared in the *Los Angeles Times,* 22 January 1933. Standing Bear said Jennie was "a distant relative," and that he spoke to her outside her log house near Wounded Knee Creek in the summer of 1932. She died two years later, on 2 January 1934.

12. E. A. Brininstool, *Crazy Horse,* 30. The message loses the greeting and salutation in the text printed in Cozzens, *The Long War for the Northern Plains,* 538.

13. The camp criers are described in the *Chicago Tribune,* 11 September 1877, reprinted in Hardorff, ed., *The Surrender and Death of Crazy Horse,* 248. James Irwin to J. Q. Smith, Red Cloud Agency files, M234/R721. Eli Ricker interview with Horn Chips, 14 February 1907, Jensen, ed., *The Indian Interviews,* 273–77. Affidavit of Charging First, 3 October 1921; copy at South Dakota Historical Society, Pierre, South Dakota.

14. He Dog's fullest account of this day is found in interviews with Eleanor Hinman, 7 July 1930, *Oglala Sources;* and with Joseph Eagle Hawk, He Dog account, eleven-page typescript.

15. McGillycuddy quoted by Elmo Scott Watson, *Crawford Tribune,* 7 September 1934.

16. Louis Bordeaux interview with Walter Camp, 6 and 7 July 1910, Bruce R. Liddic and Paul Harbaugh, *Custer & Company,* 137ff.

17. Lee's version of this event is recorded in three places, as cited earlier. The memory of Charging First is recorded in his affidavit of 3 October 1921 and his pension file.

18. "Within about fifteen minutes": Jesse Lee letter to Walter Camp, 13 May 1910,

copy in the Swan Library, Little Bighorn National Historic Site; "less than a minute": Lee, Report to the Commissioner of Indian Affairs, 30 September 1877.

19. Eli Ricker interview with William Garnett, Jensen, ed., *The Indian Interviews*, 70; He Dog interview, 7 July 1930.

20. "persuaded to halt": Captain Charles King to retired General William Carey Brown, 17 October 1921, William Carey Brown Papers, University of Colorado, Boulder. Red Feather interview, 8 July 1930, Hinman, *Oglala Sources*. White Calf mentions the presence of Iron Hawk and Long Bear. Little Big Man asked Long Bear to take charge of his band during a proposed trip to Canada; James O'Beirne to CIA E. A. Hayt, 27 August 1878, Red Cloud Agency, Letters Received, M234.

21. Red Feather and Charging First describe this moment. Turning Bear is identified by many sources, including the Colhoff winter count, Susan Bordeaux Bettelyoun, and He Dog.

22. "When the inner door was opened": Eli Ricker interview with William Garnett, 15 January 1907, Jensen, ed., *The Indian Interviews*; "Don't do that": Yellow Horse, quoted in Colhoff winter count; Eli Ricker interview with Standing Soldier, 20 November 1906, Jensen, ed., *The Indian Interviews*; "the uncle of Crazy Horse": this may have been Little Hawk, but it is Garnett who identified him as reported to be an uncle, and Garnett ought to have recognized Little Hawk without difficulty.

23. "The two whirled": Eli Ricker interview with William Garnett, 15 January 1907; "Crazy Horse made a grunt": Eli Ricker interview with Horn Chips, 273ff; "It sounds like a growl": Eli Ricker interview with William Garnett, 15 January 1907; "the brave word": Standing Bear, *Land of the Spotted Eagle*, 182.

24. "Don't shoot": William Garnett interview with Hugh Scott, 19 August 1920, SDHS; Standing Bear held by Thunder Hawk, Little Big Man shirtless: Painting on muslin by George Standing Bear, Sotheby's catalog, sale 2 December 1998, with notes by Mike Cowdrey; Christie's catalog, sale 29 June 2006; "Stab the sonofabitch!": Eli Ricker interview with Louis Bordeaux, 30 August 1907.

32. *"He has looked for death, and it has come."*

1. He Dog interviews with Eleanor Hinman, 7 and 13 July 1930, *Oglala Sources*.

2. The four hardships and the four virtues: Black Elk, Raymond J. DeMallie, ed., *The Sixth Grandfather*, 362, and Luther Standing Bear, *Land of the Spotted Eagle*, 113; H. Scudder Mckeel, *The Economy of a Modern Teton Dakota Community*, 3; Clark Wissler, Field Notes, 101; "Better to die young": Clark Wissler, *Societies and Ceremonial Associations*, 40, and W. P. Clark, *The Indian Sign Language*, 1273; "*hengh*": Eli Ricker interview with Baptiste Pourier, 6 March 1907, Richard E. Jensen, ed., *The Soldier and Settler Interviews*, 264.

3. a guard had stabbed him: Affidavit of Charging First, 3 October 1921; copy in South Dakota Historical Society, Pierre, South Dakota; "Brother-in-law, I am finished": Remarks of Henry Standing Bear prepared for unveiling of the Crazy Horse Monument at Fort Robinson, 5 September 1934, copy in Fort Robinson Museum files.

4. "doubled-up": Lieutenant Henry R. Lemly writing anonymously in the *New York Sun*, 14 September 1877, reprinted in Richard G. Hardorff, ed., *The Surrender and Death of Crazy Horse*, 238ff; "Father, I want to see you": James H. Cook let-

ter to John Neihardt, 3 March 1920, John Neihardt Papers; "You fooled me": Affidavit of Charging First, 3 October 1921.

5. "Cousin, you killed me": Jesse Means Romero Eagle Heart, statement in Edward Kadlecek and Mabell Kadlecek, *To Kill an Eagle*, 100.

6. "Might be possuming": Lemly, writing in the *New York Sun*, 14 September 1877; "only a small stab": William Garnett affidavit for Hugh Scott, 19 August 1920, South Dakota Historical Society; "right above the hip bone": Affidavit of Charging First, 3 October 1921.

7. V. T. McGillycuddy letter to Elmo Scott Watson, 13 April 1922, Elmo Scott Watson Papers. McGillycuddy has left a number of accounts of the killing, of which the most complete is a letter to William Garnett of 24 June 1927, reprinted in Robert A. Clark, ed., *The Killing of Chief Crazy Horse*, 121ff. Lemly and Garnett both say that McGillycuddy did not appear on the scene until after Crazy Horse had been removed to the adjutant's office, but the correspondent writing as "Philander" in the *Chicago Tribune*, 11 September 1877, confirms that McGillycuddy was with Captain Kennington during the standoff in front of the guardhouse. It was McGillycuddy's nature to place himself at the center of every story; in this instance he credits himself with preventing a bloodbath by persuading Colonel Bradley to reverse his order to place the wounded chief in the guardhouse. No one else makes mention of the doctor's role in this regard, but it may have happened as he tells it.

8. "You are always in the way": Eli Ricker interview with William Garnett, Richard E. Jensen, ed., *The Indian Interviews*, 71; "I was terribly frightened": Luther Standing Bear interview with Jennie Fast Thunder, *Land of the Spotted Eagle*, 182–83.

9. "For God's sake, Captain": H. R. Lemly, *Military Service Institution of the United States*, quoted in Peter Cozzens, *The Long War for the Northern Plains*, 542–48.

10. "Let's get out of here": Louis Bordeaux interview with Walter Camp, July 1912, Bruce R. Liddic and Paul Harbaugh, *Custer & Company*, 121ff.

11. "For a few minutes": Angeline Johnson letter to her sister, 7 September 1877, reprinted in *Nebraska History* (summer 1996); "Two friendly Indians": Lucy Lee letter dated 18 September 1877 in the *Greencastle* (Indiana) *Star*, n.d., reprinted in E. A. Brininstool, *Crazy Horse*, 62ff.

12. "from around the corner," "The old chap hated": V. McGillycuddy letter to William Garnett, 24 June 1927, Clark, ed., *The Killing of Chief Crazy Horse*, 125–26.

13. "Maybe the man is badly hurt": Eli Ricker interview with William Garnett, Jensen, ed., *The Indian Interviews*, 72.

14. Lemly, *Military Service Institution of the United States*.

15. "See where I am hurt": He Dog interview, 7 July 1930, 20–21.

16. "Blood flowed": Charging Girl narrative, notes taken by James Cook, 8 June 1937, James C. Cook Papers.

17. "He was restless": Eli Ricker interview with Louis Bordeaux, 30 August 1907, Jensen, ed., *The Indian Interviews*, 300; "His case was hopeless": McGillycuddy quoted by Elmo Scott Watson, *Crawford Tribune*, 7 September 1934. Standard dose from John Biddle, *Materia Medica* (1865), courtesy of Ian Isherwood, an authority on medicine in the Civil War.

18. "I am trying to persuade": The text of the telegrams was transcribed by John Gregory Bourke and can be found in Charles M. Robinson III, ed., *The Diaries*, vol. 3, p. 509.

19. "They feared an attempt": Angie Johnson letter to her sister, 7 September 1877. Tall Man pension file, IWO 16355 Ctf 11113, National Archives; "You better stay there": He Dog account, eleven-page typescript, Museum of the Fur Trade, Chadron, Nebraska. He Dog's meeting with Waglula is from the Joseph Eagle Hawk document, Grace Raymond Hebard Papers, University of Wyoming, Laramie.

20. "No one came": V. T. McGillycuddy letter to William Garnett, 24 June 1927; "I have trusted thousands": Walter Camp interview with Jesse Lee, 27 October 1912, Walter Camp Papers; see also Jesse M. Lee, "The Capture and Death of an Indian Chieftain," *Journal of the Military Service Institution of the United States* (May–June 1941), quoted in Peter Cozzens, *The Long War for the Northern Plains*, 539; "stabbed up through": Charging First affidavit.

21. "He wanted to go in": William Garnett affidavit for Hugh Scott; "Son, I am here": Eli Ricker interview with Louis Bordeaux, 300; "How is it with you": Louis Bordeaux interview with Walter Camp, 6 and 7 July 1910, Liddic and Harbaugh, *Custer & Company*, 137ff.; "I am hurt bad": Statement of Connie Utterback, *South Dakota Historical Review* (October 1935), cited in James M. Robinson, *West from Fort Pierre: The Wild World of James (Scotty) Philip* (Westernlore Press, 1974), 51; "I am going to die": Louis Bordeaux interview with Walter Camp; "Tell the people": Statement of Connie Utterback.

22. "asserted that he had": "Philander," *Chicago Tribune*, 11 September 1877; "Doctor McGillycuddy showed": Lemly, writing in the *New York Sun*.

23. "And said '*Wash-ta*' ": Angeline Johnson letter, 7 September 1877; "No white man is to blame": Eli Ricker interview with Louis Bordeaux, 30 August 1907; "But he got away": Louis Bordeaux interview with Walter Camp, 6 and 7 July 1910.

24. "He may never come back": Lucy Lee letters of 1928–1929 to E. A. Brininstool, *Crazy Horse*, 71ff.; "If I had listened to you": Walter Camp interview with Jesse Lee, 27 October 1912.

25. Waglula's talk was recorded by Lieutenant Lemly, writing in the *New York Sun*; "Philander," *Chicago Tribune*, 11 September 1877; and V. T. McGillycuddy letter to Elmo Scott Watson, 13 April 1922.

26. The two main sources on Lakota religious practice and belief, from which the quotes used here were taken, are Frances Densmore, *Teton Sioux Music*, and James R. Walker, *Lakota Belief and Ritual*.

27. "heart was giving out": V. T. McGillycuddy letter to William Garnett, 10 May 1926; "He seemed to relish": Lemly, writing in the *New York Sun*.

28. McGillycuddy letters to James H. Cook, 25 July 1934, and Eleanor Hinman, 6 May 1930, Hinman, *Oglala Sources*.

29. "Bat was the first": Eli Ricker interview with Baptiste Pourier, 6 March 1907, 264.

30. "My son is dead": Ibid.; "Finally they became quieter": Lemly, writing in the *New York Sun*.

31. "it has come": L. P. Bradley, Report to the Adjutant General, Department of the Platte, 7 September 1877, Sioux War files, M1495/R4, reprinted in Richard G. Hardorff, ed., *The Surrender and Death of Crazy Horse*, 183.

33. *"He still mourns the loss of his son."*

1. Bordeaux described this moment on three occasions: to Eli Ricker on 30 August 1907; and to Walter Camp in July 1910 and July 1912. See Richard E. Jensen,

ed., *The Indian Interviews*, 300–01; Bruce R. Liddic and Paul Harbaugh, *Custer & Company*, 121ff., 137ff.

2. Clark telegram to Crook, 6 September 1877, Charles M. Robinson III, ed., *The Diaries*, vol. 3, p. 510. *Chicago Times*, 7 September 1877.

3. E. A. Brininstool, *Crazy Horse*, 38–39. Brininstool obtained a few pages from Lee's diary from his widow in the 1920s or from his daughter about 1949. The diary has now been lost.

4. Lee to Bradley, 21 April 1878, Luther Bradley Papers.

5. Captain Fred R. Brown, *History of the Ninth U.S. Infantry* (R. R. Donnelley, 1909), 119.

6. Charles King to retired General William Carey Brown, 17 October 1921, William Carey Brown Papers, University of Colorado, Boulder.

7. killed thirty-eight whites: Clark letter to CIA, 10 September 1877, Department of the Platte, Letters Received, Box 53; also M234/R841; reprinted in Richard G. Hardorff, ed., *The Surrender and Death of Crazy Horse*, 186; "intended to talk": *Omaha Bee*, 13 September 1877, reprinted in Hardorff, ed., *The Surrender and Death of Crazy Horse*, 260.

8. "The Missouri River": *Chicago Tribune*, 28 September 1877.

9. "It is too late": Ibid., 2 October 1877.

10. Crook to Sheridan, 15 October 1877, Red Cloud Agency files, M234/R721.

11. "moved slowly": Lawson to AG Platte, 4 December 1877, Secretary of the Interior, Indian Division, Letters Received, M825/R10; they blamed the condition: Eli Ricker interview with William Garnett, Jensen, ed., *The Indian Interviews*, 76; "these people are wild": Clark to Schurz, 7 November 1877, Spotted Tail Agency, M234/R841.

12. "northern fire eaters": Irwin letter to E. A. Hayt, CIA, 5 November 1877, Red Cloud Agency files, M234/R721; "possuming," "They dared not": Eli Ricker interview with William Garnett, Jensen, ed., *The Indian Interviews*, 74. See also Clark to Carl Schurz, 7 November 1877, Letters Received, Spotted Tail Agency, M234/R841.

13. "thrown into the greatest fever of excitement": W. J. Cleveland letter to Bishop William Hobart Hare, 7 September 1877, Center for Western Studies, Augustana College; "intense excitement": Louis Bordeaux affidavit, 9 October 1914, South Dakota State Historical Society; "wild rumors": Lieutenant Jesse Lee, Report to the Commissioner of Indian Affairs, 30 September 1877; "Fast Thunder . . . was shocked": Statement of Mathew King, 14 April 1970, Edward Kadlecek and Mabell Kadlecek, *To Kill an Eagle*, 125–26. Also see Mathew King and Harvey Arden, eds., *Noble Red Man* (Beyond Words, 1994), 38–39; "Turning Bear tried": Note on Turning Bear, Josephine Waggoner Papers; "Start nothing": He Dog account, eleven-page typescript, Museum of the Fur Trade, Chadron, Nebraska; "Indians have been making presents": W. P. Clark to J. G. Bourke, 9 September 1877, Robinson, ed., *The Diaries*, vol. 3, p. 512; "Now everything is again": Lucy Lee letter dated 18 September 1877 in the *Greencastle* (Indiana) *Star*, n.d., reprinted in Brininstool, *Crazy Horse*, 62ff.

14. "Nephew, get up": William Garnett interview with Hugh Scott, 19 August 1920. See also Lieutenant H. R. Lemly, writing in the *New York Sun*, 14 September 1877; H. R. Lemly letter to E. A. Brininstool, 17 June 1925, *Hunter-Trapper-Trader* (May 1933), quoted in Peter Cozzens, *The Long War for the Northern Plains*, 542–48; Eli Ricker interview with William Garnett, 73; "Then the mother": Angeline Johnson letter, 7 September 1877; this was the uncle of Crazy

Horse: Eli Ricker interview with William Garnett, 15 January 1907, 73; Daniel Burke letter to General Luther P. Bradley, 7 September 1877, Luther Bradley Papers.

15. Red Feather's presence: Red Feather interview, 8 July 1930, Eleanor H. Hinman, *Oglala Sources*, 29; White Woman One Butte's presence: Statement of Julia Hollow Horn Bear, 4 January 1963, Kadlecek and Kadlecek, *To Kill an Eagle*, 109. The customary rites or preparation of a favored child for burial were recorded in 1882 by Alice Fletcher, "The Shadow or Ghost Lodge: A ceremony of the Oglala Sioux," *Peabody Museum Papers* 3, 296–307.

16. "just before noon": "Philander," *Chicago Tribune*, 11 September 1877; "Crazy Horse's father rode": Raymond J. DeMallie, ed., *The Sixth Grandfather*, 204; "Died in victory": He Dog account, eleven-page typescript.

17. "They were preparing": Luther Standing Bear, *My People the Sioux*, 87. See also Address of Charles C. Hamilton, Sioux City, Iowa, 27 November 1928, *Annals of Iowa*, 3rd ser., vol. 42, no. 3 (1972), 809–34, and the various accounts of Jesse Lee. Hamilton was the son of a photographer who was operating a studio at the agency at the time Crazy Horse was killed; he describes the alarm of the soldiers and of his father at the news that Crazy Horse's body was on its way. If a photograph of Crazy Horse was ever taken it is likely that James Hamilton was the man who did it.

18. Sources for the manner of the burial of Crazy Horse include Lucy Lee letters to Brininstool dated November 1928 and February 1929; Walter Camp interview with Jesse Lee, 27 October 1912, Walter Camp Papers; Jesse Lee, diary entry, 8 September 1877, reprinted in Brininstool, *Crazy Horse*, 39; Jesse Lee, "The Capture and Death of an Indian Chieftain," *Journal of the Military Service Institution of the United States* (May–June 1914), reprinted in Peter Cozzens, *The Long War for the Northern Plains*, 528ff., and address of Charles C. Hamilton. Louis Bordeaux interview with Walter Camp, 6 and 7 July 1910, Liddic and Harbaugh, *Custer & Company*, 137ff.

19. Lemly, writing in the *New York Sun*.

20. Red Feather interview, 8 July 1930, Hinman, *Oglala Sources*, 29.

21. Letter from the granddaughter of Rattling Stone Woman, Mrs. Victoria Conroy of Hot Springs, South Dakota, to James H. McGregor, Pine Ridge Superintendent, dictated to Josephine Waggoner, 18 December 1934, Raymond A. Burnside Papers, Iowa State Historical Department, quoted in Hardorff, ed., *The Surrender and Death of Crazy Horse*, 265ff. Standing Bear, *My People the Sioux*, 100.

22. "They were afraid": Victoria Conroy letter; "His father hid his body": Red Feather interview, 8 July 1930; "Whenever anyone asked her": Remark of Jennie Fast Thunder, quoted in Standing Bear, *Land of the Spotted Eagle*, 183; Buffalo Chips and William Garnett: Jensen, ed., *The Indian Interviews*; told Walter Camp: Walter Camp interview with Horn Chips, c. July 1910, quoted in Hardorff, ed., *The Surrender and Death of Crazy Horse*, 88; "just one man know": Woman Dress letter to James Cook, 7 January 1911, James H. Cook Papers; "She helped bury him": Acquisition note on whetstone given to James Cook by the wife of Red Sack, identified as Crazy Horse's sister, James H. Cook Papers; "But it was never told": Woodrow Respects Nothing to Cleve Walstrom, author, *Search for the Lost Trail of Crazy Horse* (Dageforde Publishing, n.d.), 117–19.

23. "He died awful quick": Red Feather interview, 8 July 1930; "He did not want any

white": Statement of Howard Red Bear (1871–1968), son of Philip Red Bear, 13 August 1966, quoted in Kadlecek and Kadlecek, *To Kill an Eagle*, 133. By the late 1870s, the Sioux understood that whites were in the habit of routinely looting burial sites.

24. *New York Times*, 15 September 1879. Carson is identified in the diary of Webb Hayes found at the Rutherford B. Hayes Presidential Center, Fremont, Ohio. See also John Collins, *My Experiences in the West* (Lakeside Press, 1970), 167–78, which relates Schurz's visit in September 1879.

25. "He still mourns": *New York Times*, 22 September 1877. Typed notes deposited with Schurz's papers in the Library of Congress.

26. Susan Bordeaux Bettelyoun and Josephine Waggoner, *With My Own Eyes*, 110.

34. *"When I tell these things I have a pain in my heart."*

1. The painting was probably intended as a tipi liner. The acquisition notes and Webb Hayes's diary of the trip are found in the Rutherford B. Hayes Presidential Center, Fremont, Ohio.

2. "In what I did": Little Big Man to President Hayes, 1 August 1878, Letters Received, Office of Indian Affairs, M234/R234, copy in the Fort Robinson Museum files.

3. "He always took": Sickels to W. Fletcher Johnson, *Life of Sitting Bull and History of the Indian War of 1890–91* (Edgewood Publishing, 1891), 113. The actual text reads, "A Token of regard for gallant services rendered to the whites at the death of Crazy Horse." It is dated 29 September 1877, and is presented to *"Mahtia-Cowa,"* an eccentric rendering of the Lakota for Chasing Bear, an alternate name of Little Big Man. Riggs spelled the name "Matowakuwa." The medal was later acquired by the Union Pacific Railroad, which lent it to the Museum of Nebraska History in Lincoln, where it is on display. It was first identified by Paul L. Hedren, "The Crazy Horse Medal: An Enigma from the Great Sioux War," *Nebraska History*, summer 1994 and summer 1996.

4. Scott to Walter Camp, 19 April 1919, Walter Camp Papers, Box 2, Folder 4.

5. Luther Heddon North, *Man of the Plains*, 278–79.

6. Testimony of Baptiste Pourier, 21 September 1923, Ralph H. Case, *Black Hills Depositions*, 621ff., copy provided by Ephraim Dickson. See Ralph Case papers, I. D. Weeks Library, University of South Dakota.

7. Hugh L. Scott, *Some Memories of a Soldier* (Century Company, 1928), 110, 123–24.

8. Richard Irving Dodge, *The Plains of the Great West* (Archer House, 1959), 133.

9. Scott, *Some Memories of a Soldier*, 123.

10. Clark Wissler, *Red Man Reservations* (Collier Books, 1971), 62.

11. W. P. Clark, *The Indian Sign Language*, 130.

12. "Their sisters," "are strong and usually healthy,": Clark, *The Indian Sign Language*, 208, 279.

13. Obituaries appeared in the *Army and Navy Journal*, 27 September 1884, the *Carthage Republican*, 14 October 1884, and by A. E. Bates in the proceedings of *The Sixteenth Annual Reunion of the Association of the Graduates of the United States Military Academy*, 12 June 1885, 43–48.

14. counting the dead: Eli Ricker interview with W. A. Birdsall, 22 December 1906, Richard E. Jensen, ed., *The Settler and Soldier Interviews*, 45; reunited with

his father: *Sheridan Post*, 20 April 1893; died of alcoholism: Typed note dated 1953, Charles D. Humberd, MD, of Barnard, Missouri, tipped into a copy of DeBarthe's book listed for sale on the Internet, March 2006.

15. "What are you going to do": Eli Ricker interview with William Garnett, Jensen, ed., *The Indian Interviews*, 77. The interpreter's job fell open when the incumbent, John Provost, killed a man because his heart was bad. He later died in prison. See Julia B. McGillycuddy, *Blood on the Moon* (University of Nebraska, 1990), 114ff.

16. "I've lived all of my life": Interviews with James Garnett and his sister Joanne Cuny, Sturgis, South Dakota, 3 September 2001. The 1885 meeting with members of the Garnett family is recounted by the widow of General Pickett, southern commander on the occasion when General Richard Garnett was killed at Gettysburg, *Cosmopolitan*, March and April 1914.

17. Raleigh Barker, *Tales from a Reservation Storekeeper* (American Studies Press, 1979), 22–23. See also Robert H. Ruby, *The Oglala Sioux* (Vantage, 1955), 33.

18. "I killed Crazy Horse?": Eli Ricker interview with William Garnett, Jensen, ed., *The Indian Interviews*, 66ff. All other quotes in this section come from Garnett's affidavit for Hugh Scott, 19 August 1920, South Dakota Historical Society.

19. Lieutenant Lyman V. Kennon, 21 March 1887, *Diary 1886–1890*, George Crook Papers; "fitted very snugly": *New York World*, quoted in Phil Andrew Hutton, *Phil Sheridan and His Army*, 370; "The adulations heaped": quoted in Martin F. Schmitt, ed., *General George Crook*, 134.

20. James H. Cook papers.

21. Charging Girl narrative, James C. Cook Papers.

35. *"I'm not telling anyone what I know about the killing of Crazy Horse."*

1. *Rochester Union*, quoted in *Cheyenne Daily Leader*, 2 September 1877. See also Louis S. Warren, *Buffalo Bill's America* (Knopf, 2005), 192ff.; Sandra K. Sagala, *Buffalo Bill on Stage* (University of New Mexico, 2008), 101ff.

2. "I wear the uniform": V. T. McGillycuddy letter to Elmo Scott Watson, 19 July 1927, Elmo Scott Watson Papers.

3. Frances Densmore, *Teton Sioux Music*, 412.

4. Walker's introduction to Lakota religion can be found in James R. Walker, *Lakota Belief and Ritual*, passim. See especially Walker's autobiographical statement, 45–50, and the statement of George Sword, 5 September 1896, Bruce Means, translator, 74–75.

5. Principal sources for the history of the Fast Thunder family include Mathew King and Harvey Arden, ed., *Noble Red Man* (Beyond Words, 1994); Edward and Mabell Kadlecek, *To Kill an Eagle* (1981); Barbara Means Adams, *Prayers of Smoke* (Celestial Arts, 1990); Fast Thunder's pension file in the National Archives; and interviews with Barbara Adams and Pete Swift Bird.

6. "he was the first Indian": Statement of Paul Red Star, 7 February 1964, Kadlecek and Kadlecek, *To Kill an Eagle*, 142; "to put this ghost dance aside": Raymond J. DeMallie, ed., *The Sixth Grandfather*, 269; fifty-six cattle: Jeffrey Ostler, *The Plains Sioux and U.S. Colonialism*, 139, n. 38.

7. "How can I be free": King and Arden, eds., *Noble Red Man*, 38–39.

8. "Cousin, you killed me": Statement of Jesse Romero Eagle Heart, 5 November 1962, Kadlecek and Kadlecek, *To Kill an Eagle*, 100.

9. King and Arden, eds., *Noble Red Man*, 40.

10. Fast Thunder's date of death and estate are from his pension file, National Archives. Jennie Wounded Horse's date of death is from statement of Jessie Romero Eagle Heart, born 1906, speaking on 5 November 1962, Kadlecek and Kadlecek, *To Kill an Eagle*, 2.

11. Eleanor Hinman, introduction to *Oglala Sources*, 7.

12. Ibid., 3.

13. "You said nothing": "History of Chief Crazy Horse," by Rev. Joseph Eagle Hawk, Grace Raymond Hebard Papers, University of Wyoming, Laramie. This document is a variant of the eleven-page typescript in the Museum of the Fur Trade, Chadron, Nebraska, and of the He Dog statement concerning the death of Crazy Horse, Box 4, Folder 3, Don Russell Papers, Buffalo Bill Historical Center.

14. "I am an old man": Hinman, *Oglala Sources*, 9.

15. "It used to be a disgrace": Hugh Scott interview with He Dog and Red Feather, 24 July 1931, Hugh Scott Papers; "but when he got 'there' ": Scudder Mekeel, Field Notes, summer 1931, 2 August 1931.

16. General Hugh Scott letter, National Archives, quoted by J. W. Vaughn, *With Crook at the Rosebud* (Stackpole Books, 1956), 40.

Afterword

1. Henry W. Daly, *American Legion Monthly* (April 1927), reprinted in Peter Cozzens, *The Long War for the Northern Plains*, 250ff.

2. Bourke correspondence about Crazy Horse photo, October 1890, John Gregory Bourke Papers; likeness to the "spirit": Ziółkowski statement of purpose, 29 May 1949, *Story Telling in Stone* (pamphlet, 1983); "Poor old Crazy Horse": John Colhoff letter to George Hyde, 2 May 1949, author's possession.

3. Mathew King and Harvey Arden, eds., *Noble Red Man* (Beyond Words, 1994), 39–40.

4. Black Elk's teachings can be found in John Neihardt, *Black Elk Speaks*, Ray DeMallie, ed., *The Sixth Grandfather*; and Joseph Epes Brown, *The Sacred Pipe* (University of Oklahoma, 1953).

5. Joseph Epes Brown, *The Spiritual Legacy of the American Indian* (World Wisdom, 2007), 108, 115. See also Brown, *The Sacred Pipe*.

6. The story of the Fast Thunder family comes from the Fast Thunder pension file; Edward Kadlecek and Mabell Kadlecek, *To Kill an Eagle*; Barbara Adams, *Prayers of Smoke* (Celestial Arts, 1990); and interviews with Barbara Adams, 7 September 2001 and 26 April 2004; with Barbara's mother, Margaret Black Weasel, 24 May 2004; and with Pete Swift Bird by telephone, 13 January and 8 February 2006; in Porcupine, South Dakota, 23 and 24 September 2007, and in Pine Ridge, 26 April 2009. Barney Wickard told me of life in Minatare since the 1930s in interviews on 28 April 2004 and 28 April 2009.

7. Barbara Adams died on 10 August 2005 in the Rapid City, South Dakota, Regional Hospital. Her mother, Margaret Black Weasel, died there a few months later.

BIBLIOGRAPHY

Books and Periodicals

The literature on the Plains Indians, the Battle of the Little Bighorn, and related subjects is vast, and fine bibliographies abound. A good choice for those with a vigorous interest in the Sioux would be Jack W. Marken and Herbert T. Hoover, *Bibliography of the Sioux* (Scarecrow Press, 1980). The list that follows is for the convenience of readers. It includes only those works frequently cited in this book. Many additional sources are identified in the notes. Much other material, including previously unpublished documents and letters, may be found at www.thekillingofcrazyhorse.com.

Allen, Charles W. *From Fort Laramie to Wounded Knee: In the West That Was.* University of Nebraska Press, 1997.

Bettelyoun, Susan Bordeaux, and Josephine Waggoner. *With My Own Eyes: A Lakota Woman Tells Her People's Story.* University of Nebraska Press, 1988.

Blish, Helen H. *A Pictographic History of the Oglala Sioux.* University of Nebraska Press, 1968.

Bourke, John G. *On the Border with Crook.* 1891. University of Nebraska Press, 1971.

Bratt, John. *Trails of Yesterday.* University of Nebraska Press, 1921.

Bray, Kingsley M. *Crazy Horse: A Lakota Life.* University of Oklahoma Press, 2006.

Brininstool, E. A. *Crazy Horse: The Invincible Oglala Sioux Chief.* Wetzel Publishing Co., 1949.

Brown, Dee. *Fort Phil Kearny: An American Saga.* G. P. Putnam, 1962.

Buechel, Eugene. *Lakota Tales and Texts: In Translation.* Tipi Press, 1998.

Buechel, Eugene, and Paul Manhart, eds. *Lakota Dictionary.* University of Nebraska Press, 2002.

Buecker, Thomas R. *Fort Robinson and the American West, 1879–1899.* Nebraska State Historical Society, 1999.

Buecker, Thomas R., and R. Eli Paul, eds. *The Crazy Horse Surrender Ledger.* Nebraska State Historical Society, 1994.

Burton, Matthew W. *The River of Blood and the Valley of Death.* The General's Books, 1998.

Clark, Robert A., ed. *The Killing of Chief Crazy Horse.* 1976. University of Nebraska Press, 1988.

Clark, W. P. *The Indian Sign Language.* 1885. University of Nebraska Press, 1982.

Cozzens, Peter. *The Long War for the Northern Plains: Eyewitnesses to the Indian Wars, 1865–1890.* Stackpole Books, 2004.

Custer, General George Armstrong. *My Life on the Plains: Or, Personal Experiences with Indians.* Citadel Press, 1962.

DeBarthe, Joe. *Life and Adventures of Frank Grouard.* 1894. University of Oklahoma Press, 1958.

DeMallie, Raymond J., ed. *The Sixth Grandfather: Black Elk's Teachings Given to John G. Neihardt.* University of Nebraska Press, 1984.

Densmore, Frances. *Teton Sioux Music.* Bulletin of American Ethnology, No. 61. Government Printing Office, 1918.

Eastman, Charles A. *Indian Heroes and Great Chieftains.* Dover, 1997.

Finerty, John F. *War-Path and Bivouac: Or, the Conquest of the Sioux.* 1890. University of Oklahoma Press, 1961.

Graham, W. A. *The Custer Myth.* Stackpole Books, 1953.

Gray, John S. *Centennial Campaign: The Sioux War of 1876.* Old Army Press, 1976.

———. *Custer's Last Campaign: Mitch Boyer and the Little Bighorn Reconstructed.* University of Nebraska Press, 1991.

Greene, Jerome A. *Battles and Skirmishes of the Great Sioux War, 1876–1877: The Military View.* University of Oklahoma Press, 1993.

———. *Lakota and Cheyenne: Indian Views of the Great Sioux War, 1876–1877.* University of Oklahoma Press, 1994.

Grinnell, George Bird. *The Fighting Cheyennes.* 1915. University of Oklahoma Press, 1956.

Hardorff, Richard G., *Hokahey! A Good Day to Die: The Indian Casualties of the Custer Fight.* Arthur H. Clark, 1993.

———. *The Oglala Lakota Crazy Horse: A Preliminary Genealogical Study.* J. M. Carroll & Co., 1985.

Hardorff, Richard G., ed. *Cheyenne Memories of the Custer Fight.* 1995. University of Nebraska Press, 1998.

———. *Indian Views of the Custer Fight: A Source Book.* Arthur H. Clark, 2004.

———. *Lakota Recollections of the Custer Fight: New Memories of Indian-Military History.* 1991. University of Nebraska Press, 1997.

———. *The Surrender and Death of Crazy Horse: A Source Book About a Tragic Episode in Lakota History.* Arthur H. Clark, 1998.

Hassrick, Royal B. *The Sioux.* University of Oklahoma Press, 1964.

Hedren, Paul L. *Fort Laramie and the Great Sioux War.* 1988. University of Oklahoma Press, 1998.

Hinman, Eleanor H. *Oglala Sources on the Life of Crazy Horse.* Nebraska State Historical Society, 1976. Reprint from *Nebraska History* 57, no. 1 (spring 1976).

Humfreville, J. Lee. *Twenty Years Among Our Savage Indians.* Hartford Publishing Co., 1897.

Hutton, Paul Andrew. *Phil Sheridan and His Army.* 1985. University of Oklahoma Press, 1999.

Hyde, George E. *Red Cloud's Folk: A History of the Oglala Sioux Indians.* University of Oklahoma Press, 1937.

———. *Spotted Tail's Folk: A History of the Brulé Sioux.* 1961. University of Oklahoma Press, 1976.

Jensen, Richard E., ed. *Voices of the American West.* Vol. 1: *The Indian Interviews of Eli S. Ricker, 1903–1919.* University of Nebraska Press, 2005.

———. *Voices of the American West.* Vol. 2: *The Soldier and Settler Interviews of Eli S. Ricker, 1903–1919.* University of Nebraska Press, 2005.

Kadlecek, Edward, and Mabell Kadlecek. *To Kill an Eagle: Indian Views on the Last Days of Crazy Horse.* Johnson Books, 1982.

Krause, Herbert, and Gary D. Olson. *Prelude to Glory: A Newspaper Accounting of Custer's 1874 Expedition to the Black Hills.* Brevet Books, 1974.

Liddic, Bruce R., and Paul Harbaugh. *Custer & Company: Walter Camp's Notes on the Custer Fight.* University of Nebraska Press, 1998.

Mallery, Garrick. "Picture Writing of the American Indians." *Tenth Annual Report of the Bureau of American Ethnology, 1888–1889.*

Marquis, Thomas B., trans. *Wooden Leg: A Warrior Who Fought Custer.* University of Nebraska Press, n.d.; repr.

Mattes, Merrill J. *The Great Platte River Road: The Covered Wagon Mainline via Fort Kearny to Fort Laramie.* Nebraska State Historical Society, 1969.

McCreight, M. I. *Chief Flying Hawk's Tales: The True Story of Custer's Last Fight.* Alliance Press, 1936.

———. *Firewater and Forked Tongues: A Sioux Chief Interprets U.S. History.* Trail's End Publishing Co., 1947.

McDermott, John D. *Circle of Fire: The Indian War of 1865.* Stackpole Books, 2003.

Mekeel, Scudder. *The Economy of a Modern Teton Dakota Community.* Yale University Publications in Anthropology, 1936.

Mills, Anson. *My Story.* Privately published, 1918.

North, Luther Heddon. *Man of the Plains.* Edited by Donald F. Danker. University of Nebraska Press, 1961.

Olson, James C. *Red Cloud and the Sioux Problem.* University of Nebraska Press, 1965.

Ostler, Jeffrey. *The Plains Sioux and U.S. Colonialism from Lewis and Clark to Wounded Knee.* Cambridge University Press, 2004.

Parkman, Francis. *The Journals of Francis Parkman.* Edited by Mason Wade. Harper & Brothers, 1947.

———. *The Oregon Trail Journal.* Edited by Mason Wade. Harper & Brothers, 1947.

Paul, R. Eli, ed. *Autobiography of Red Cloud: War Leader of the Oglalas.* Montana Historical Society Press, 1997.

Powell, Peter J. *Sweet Medicine: The Continuing Role of the Sacred Arrows, the Sun Dance, and the Sacred Buffalo Hat in Northern Cheyenne History.* University of Oklahoma Press, 1969.

Powers, William K., ed. "Colhoff Winter Count: 1759–1896," *American Indian Tradition* 52, vol. 9, no. 1 (1963). A second text of the winter count is found in the Elmo Scott Watson Papers. This text runs from 1759 to 1945; it is missing entries for the years 1842–1893, but includes much important additional material in entries for the later years.

Robinson, Charles M. III. *General Crook and the Western Frontier.* University of Oklahoma Press, 2001.

Robinson, Charles M. III, ed. *The Diaries of John Gregory Bourke.* 4 vols. University of North Texas Press, 2003–2010.

Sandoz, Mari. *Crazy Horse: The Strange Man of the Oglalas.* Alfred A. Knopf, 1942.

Schmitt, Martin F., ed. *General George Crook: His Autobiography.* University of Oklahoma Press, 1946.

Scott, Hugh L. *Some Memories of a Soldier.* Century Co., 1928.

Sheridan, P. H. *Personal Memoirs of P. H. Sheridan.* Charles L. Webster & Co., 1888.

Smith, DeCost. *Red Indian Experiences.* George Allen & Unwin Ltd., 1949.

Standing Bear, Luther. *Land of the Spotted Eagle.* Houghton Mifflin, 1933.

———. *My People the Sioux.* 1928. University of Nebraska Press, 1975.

Stands in Timber, John, and Margot Liberty. *Cheyenne Memories.* Yale University Press, 1967.

Tuttle, Edward B. *Three Years on the Plains: Observations of Indians, 1867–1870.* University of Oklahoma, 2002.

Utley, Robert M. *The Lance and the Shield: The Life and Times of Sitting Bull.* Henry Holt & Co., 1993.

Vestal, Stanley. *Sitting Bull, Champion of the Sioux.* 1932. University of Oklahoma Press, 1957.

———. *Warpath: The True Story of the Fighting Sioux Told in a Biography of Chief White Bull.* 1934. University of Nebraska Press, 1984.

———. *Warpath and Council Fire.* Random House, 1948.

Walker, James R. *Lakota Belief and Ritual.* University of Nebraska Press, 1980.

———. *Lakota Myth.* University of Nebraska Press, 1983.

———. *Lakota Society.* University of Nebraska Press, 1982.

———. *The Sun Dance and Other Ceremonies of the Oglala Division of the Teton Dakota.* Anthropological Papers of the American Museum of Natural History, vol. 16, pt. 2, 1917.

Wissler, Clark. *Societies and Ceremonial Associations in the Oglala Division of the Teton-Lakota.* Anthropological Papers of the American Museum of Natural History, vol. 11, pt. 1, 1912.

Young, Harry. *Hard Knocks.* Laird & Lee, 1915.

Manuscripts

John Gregory Bourke Papers. Nebraska State Historical Society, Lincoln, NE.

Luther Bradley Papers. U.S. Army War College, Carlisle Barracks, PA.

Walter Camp Papers. Brigham Young University, Provo, UT.

Walter S. Campbell (Stanley Vestal) Papers. University of Oklahoma, Norman, Oklahoma.

George Colhoff winter count. Elmo Scott Watson Papers, Newberry Library, Chicago, IL. Part of this winter count was published by William K. Powers in *American Indian Tradition,* vol. 9, no. 1 (1963).

James C. Cook Papers. Agate Springs Fossil Beds National Monument, Harrison, NE.

George Crook Papers. U.S. Army War College, Carlisle Barracks, PA.

Denver Library, Denver, CO.

Frey Family Papers. New-York Historical Society, New York, NY.

George Bird Grinnell Papers. Braun Research Library, Southwest Museum, Los Angeles, CA.

Rutherford B. Hayes Presidential Center, Fremont, OH.

Houghton Library, Harvard University, Cambridge, MA.

Vertical files, Fort Phil Kearny Library, Story, Wyoming.

Scudder Mekeel, Field Notes, 1931–1932. American Museum of Natural History, New York, NY.

National Archives, Washington, DC.

John Neihardt Papers. University of Missouri, Columbus, MO.

New York Public Library, New York, NY.

Don Russell Papers. Buffalo Bill Historical Center, Cody, WY.

Mari Sandoz Papers. Love Library, University of Nebraska, Lincoln, NE.

Carl Schurz Papers. Library of Congress, Washington, DC.

Hugh Scott Papers. Library of Congress, Washington, DC.

Walter S. Schuyler Papers. Huntington Library, San Marino, CA.

South Dakota State Historical Society, Pierre, SD.

Josephine Waggoner Papers. Museum of the Fur Trade, Chadron, NE.

James Walker Papers. Colorado Historical Society, Denver, CO.

Elmo Scott Watson Papers. Newberry Library, Chicago, IL.

Clark Wissler, Field Notes, 1902, AMNH Expedition to Pine Ridge. American Museum of Natural History, New York, NY.

Western Americana Collection. Beinecke Library, Yale University, New Haven, CT.

INDEX

Photographic Credits

American Horse. *Photo by D. S. Mitchell, National Anthropological Archives 0210300.*

George Sword with Buffalo Bill Cody and members of Cody's theatrical troupe. *Buffalo Bill Historical Center P.69.22.*

Camp Sheridan. *Photo by Charles Howard, October 1877, National Anthropological Archives 0236900.*

Board fence surrounding traditional scaffold, Spotted Tail Agency. *Photo courtesy of Larry Ness.*

Little Big Man. *National Anthropological Archives 03215a.*